13

OCEAN SHIPS

OCEAN SHIPS

ALLAN RYSZKA-ONIONS

Ian Allan
PUBLISHING

Contents

Front cover: *Stock library image.*
Half title: **Carnival Corporation (Cunard Line Ltd.)** : QUEEN MARY 2 : *ARO*
Title page: **Mano Maritime** : ROYAL IRIS : *Douglas Cromby*
Back cover, top: **A. P. Møller** : LEDA MAERSK : *ARO*
Back cover, bottom: **Mediterranean Shipping Co. S.A.** : MSC ELENI : *ARO*

First published 1964
This 16th edition 2013

ISBN 978 0 7110 3744 1

Published by Ian Allan Publishing

an imprint of Ian Allan Publishing Ltd

Printed in Estonia

Visit the Ian Allan Publishing website at
www.ianallanpublishing.com

Distributed in the United States of America and Canada
by BookMasters Distribution Services.

Preface

I would like to welcome you to *Ocean Ships 2013*. As with earlier editions, the book provides details of the major cruise ships operating world-wide and the fleets of many shipping companies operating deep-sea routes to British and northern European ports. As in the previous edition, all illustrations are in colour and in addition to information provided previously, this new edition contains further, more detailed information on the listed ships.

The IMO number is an identifier allocated to a ships hull prior to building; it remains with the ship regardless of name changes or modifications and by adding this information to *Ocean Ships* it will hopefully aid the reader in keeping track of vessels through any name changes they may undergo between now and any future edition of *Ocean Ships*. Additionally, I have attempted to provide information on the cargo carrying capacity of many vessels; for container ships, I have included a teu (20ft equivalent units) figure and for car carriers a ceu (car equivalent units) figure. The figures are intended as a guide, as for any vessel there is often significant variance between figures quoted by the builder, the operator and the registration society! I have also given cubic metre figures for the capacity of gas carriers and an indication of lift capacity for heavy lift vessels. Additionally, I have also tried to give more detailed descriptions of vessels, based on the three letter system used by Lloyds in their now defunct Blue Lists.

The four years since the previous edition, have seen some remarkable changes in the world of international shipping. Visually perhaps the most apparent change has been in the size and shape of container ships. The need to reduce the shipping cost/box has resulted in slower running, more efficient diesel engines and larger vessels now capable of carrying up to 18,000teu. With boxes stacked up to 8 high on deck and vessel lengths approaching 400 metres, it became necessary to site the navigation bridge amidships in order to give acceptable forward visibility. The casualties of this need to reduce shipping costs are smaller boxboats, some of which are meeting the breaker's torch on the beaches of the sub-continent at the tender age of 15 or 16 years.

The poor freight rates in the bulker market have seen the demise, for the second time, of Sanko Steamship Company, but it has not slowed down the rate of production of these vessels from the many shipyards in China. On the otherhand, we have seen the introduction of the World's largest ore carriers, of 400,000dwt, built specifically to service the ever growing needs of the Chinese market for Brazilian iron ore, although it now appears the vessels are not allowed to enter Chinese ports and the ore has to be trans-shipped prior to delivery. The rapid growth of the Brazilian economy has also brought about an increase in the number of shuttle tankers required to service their growing offshore oil industry. The increasing demand for natural gas has also seen burgeoning order books for the specialist builders of these sophisticated vessels. Historically using steam turbine power units fuelled by burn-off gas, the new generation are powered by more efficient dual fuel diesel elcctric units.

Vehicle carriers have also increased in size to over 70,000gt and are often fitted with movable decks which also permit the carriage of large loads. Some recently delivered vessels have also been fitted with an array of solar cells on the top deck, producing sufficient electricity to supply the ship's energy requirements whilst alongside. The popularity of cruising seems to be showing no slow-down and most of the major operators have new tonnage on order, generally for mega-carriers catering for upwards of 3,000 passengers, although there has also been an increase in the number of small companies offering 'expedition' cruises particularly to the North and South Poles.

I would like to express my thanks to all who have provided their excellent photographs and to my many friends, acquaintances and correspondents for their interest, comments and information.

It has been a great challenge to follow David Hornsby who has produced previous nine editions of *Ocean Ships* and I hope this new edition is as well received as previous editions.

Allan Ryszka-Onions
Havant, England
January 2013

Disclaimer

Glossary

The companies in each section are listed in alphabetical order under the main company name, followed by the country of origin. Individual 'one-ship' owning companies are not given, but in some cases subsidiary fleets are separately listed. Other variations in ownership, joint ownership, management or charter are generally covered by footnotes. Funnel and hull colours are those normally used by the companies, although these may vary when a vessel is operating on a particular service, or on charter to another operator.

Name   registered name
Eng   all vessels are single screw motorships unless indicated after the name as having more than one screw or other types of main propulsive machinery as follows
       as   sail with auxiliary engines
       df   dual fuel diesel electric
       tf   trifuel diesel electric
       me   diesel with electric drive
       gm   combined gas turbine and diesel with electric drive
       gt   gas turbine with electric drive
       st   steam turbine
       p   directional pod propulsion system

Flag

Ant	Netherlands Antilles	Chl	Chile	Isr	Israel	Pmd	Madeira
Are	United Arab Emirates	Chn	China	Ita	Italy	Prt	Portugal
		Cni	Canary Islands	Jpn	Japan	Qat	Qatar
Arg	Argentina	Cym	Cayman Islands	Kor	South Korea	Rif	French International
Atf	Kerguelen Islands	Cyp	Cyprus	Kwt	Kuwait	Rus	Russia
Atg	Antigua and Barbuda	Deu	Germany	Lbr	Liberia	Sau	Saudi Arabia
		Dis	Danish International	Lux	Luxembourg	Sgp	Singapore
Aus	Australia	Dnk	Denmark	Lva	Latvia	Swe	Sweden
Bel	Belgium	Egy	Egypt	Mex	Mexico	Tha	Thailand
Bgr	Bulgaria	Eth	Ethiopia	Mhl	Marshall Islands	Twn	Taiwan
Bhr	Bahrain	Fin	Finland	Mlt	Malta	Usa	United States of America
Bhs	Bahamas	Fra	France	Mys	Malaysia		
Bmu	Bermuda	Gbr	United Kingdom	Nis	Norwegian International	Vct	St. Vincent and Grenadines
Bra	Brazil	Gib	Gibraltar				
Brb	Barbados	Grc	Greece	Nld	Netherlands	Ven	Venezuela
Brn	Brunei Darussalam	Hkg	Hong Kong (China)	Nor	Norway	Zaf	South Africa
Can	Canada	Hrv	Croatia	Pan	Panama		
Che	Switzerland	Iom	Isle of Man (British)	Phl	Philippines		

Year   year of completion - not necessarily of launching or commissioning.
GT   gross tonnage - not weight, but volume of hull and enclosed space measured under 1969 International Tonnage Convention
DWT   deadweight tonnes - maximum weight of cargo, stores, fuel etc — one tonne (1000 kg) equals 0.984 ton (British)
LOA   overall length (metres); (- -) length between perpendiculars
bm   overall breadth of hull (metres) - some vessels have greater width to superstructure/bridge etc.
kts   service speed in normal weather and at normal service draught — one knot equals 6,050ft per hour or 1.146 mph.
type   general description of type of vessel

bbu	bulk carrier	gpc	cargo/part container	tci	tanker - icebreaker
bbp	bulk - pitch carrier	gmp	cargo/multipurpose	tco	tanker- chemicals and oil products
bcb	bulk/container	grf	refrigerated cargo		
bce	cement carrier	fff	fish factory ship	tcr	tanker - crude oil
boh	cargo - open hatch	lng	liquefied natural gas	tcs	tanker - shuttle
bor	ore carrier	lpg	liquefied petroleum gas	tfj	tanker - fruit juice
bsd	bulk - self discharging	mlv	livestock carrier	mve	vehicle carrier
bwc	bulk woodchip carrier	ocl	cable layer	ucc	cellular container
cbo	ore/bulk/oil carrier	ohl	heavy-lift / semi-submersible	urc	ro-ro / container
ggc	general cargo	tch	tanker – molten sulphur	urh	ro-ro / heavy lift
ghl	heavy-lift vessel			urr	roll-on, roll-off

pass   maximum number of passengers in lower and upper berths or (———) in lower berths only
remarks:
       conv   converted from other ship type (with date where known)
       ex: previous names followed by year of change to subsequent name
       c/a   name as completed
       l/a   name at launch or 'float-out' prior to completion
       l/dn   name allocated when laid-down at commencement of construction
       pt: part of ship
       len   date hull lengthened
       rbt   rebuilt
       sht   date hull shortened
       wid   date hull widened
       NE   date re-engined
       teu   twenty-foot equivalent unit (one teu equals about 14 tonnes deadweight)
       ceu   car equivalent units (based on typical family car of 1,500kg)
       cr   number of cranes on heavy lift and multipurpose vessels and their maximum safe working load (swl), only those over 100t lift included – NB, in may cases the cranes can be used in tandem
       m³   cargo capacity of gas carriers in cubic metres

PART ONE
Passenger Liners and Cruise Ships

Transocean Tours : ASTOR : *ARO*

All Leisure Holidays Ltd.   **U.K.**

Voyages of Discovery, U.K.

Funnel: *White with narrow turquoise band below blue top or with pale/dark blue wave symbol.* **Hull:** *White with blue or red boot-topping.* **History:** *Commenced cruises in 1984 with chartered ships until acquiring vessel in 2004.* **Web:** *www.voyagesofdiscovery.com*

7108514	Discovery		(2)	Bmu	1972	20,216	169	25	18	689	ex Platinium-02, Hyundai Pungak-01, Island Princess-99, Island Venture-72
8709573	Voyager		(2)	Bhs	1990	15,271	153	20	18	556	ex Alexander von Humboldt-12, Alexander von Humboldt II-08, Jules Verne-08, Walrus-07, Nautican-96, Crown Monarch-94

Swan Hellenic, U.K.

Funnel: *Dark blue with gold swan symbol.* **Hull:** *Dark blue with red boot-topping.* **History:** *Commenced operations in 1954 as Swan's Hellenic Cruises by Swan travel agency using chartered ships. Acquired 1983 by P&O, but closed by Carnival acquisition in 2007, when brand acquired by Lord Sterling and 2008 recommenced operations after acquisition by All Leisure.* **Web:** *www.swanhellenic.com*

All Leisure Holidays Ltd (Voyages of Discovery) : DISCOVERY : *M. Lennon*

All Leisure Holidays Ltd (Voyages of Discovery) : VOYAGER : *M. Lennon*

IMO#	name	screws	flag	year	gt	loa	bm	kts	pass	former names
9144196	Minerva	(2)	Bhs	1996	12,449	133	20	14	350	ex Explorer II-08, Alexander von Humboldt-05, Explorer II-05, Saga Pearl-05, Minerva-03, l/a Okean

Hebridean International Cruises Ltd., U.K.

Funnel: *Red with narrow black top.* **Hull:** *Black with narrow white line above red boot-topping.* **History:** *Founded 1988 as Hebridean Island Cruises to 2006.* **Web:** *www.hebridean.co.uk*

6409351	Hebridean Princess	(2)	Gbr	1964	2,112	72	14	14	49	ex Columba-89

Ambassadors International   U.S.A.
Windstar Cruises Ltd.

Funnel: *White with turquoise symbol.* **Hull:** *White with turquoise band and blue boot-topping.* **History:** *Founded 1984 as Windstar Sail Cruises Ltd. Holland America acquired a 50% share in 1987 and the balance in 1988, before being taken over by Carnival Corp. Sold to Ambassadors International Inc in 2007.* **Web:** *www.windstarcruises.com*

8603509	Wind Spirit	(as/me)	Bhs	1988	5,736	134	16	11	150	
8420878	Wind Star	(as/me)	Bhs	1986	5,307	134	16	11	150	
8700785	Wind Surf	(as/me2)	Bhs	1989	14,745	187	20	15	453	ex Club Med 1-97, l/a La Fayette

Carnival Corporation   U.S.A.

Funnel: *Red forward, blue aft, separated by vertical curved white arc.* **Hull:** *White with narrow red band, blue boot-topping.* **History:** *Founded 1972 as Carnival Cruise Lines Inc until 1993. Betweem 1989 and 2001 acquired numerous other operators to become the largest cruising company with many brands aimed at different markets. The expansion continued with joint venture with TUI in 2006 and a joint venture with Iberojet in 2007, the same year as Swan Hellenic was closed down and Windstar Cruises was sold.* **Web:** *www.carnivalplc.com or www.carnivalcorp.com*

9555723	Carnival Breeze	(me2p)	Pan	2012	128,500	304	37	22	3,652	
9198355	Carnival Conquest	(me2)	Pan	2002	110,239	290	36	19	3,700	
9070058	Carnival Destiny	(me2)	Bhs	1996	101,353	272	36	18	3,336	
9378474	Carnival Dream	(me2p)	Pan	2009	128,251	304	37	22	3,646	
8711344	Carnival Ecstasy	(me2)	Pan	1991	70,526	262	32	18	2,634	ex Ecstasy-07
9118721	Carnival Elation	(me2p)	Pan	1998	70,390	262	32	20	2,634	ex Elation-07
8700773	Carnival Fantasy	(me2)	Pan	1990	70,367	261	32	18	2,634	ex Fantasy-07
9041253	Carnival Fascination	(me2)	Bhs	1994	70,538	262	32	18	2,624	ex Fascination-07
9333149	Carnival Freedom	(me2)	Pan	2007	110,320	290	36	21	3,783	
9198367	Carnival Glory	(me2)	Pan	2003	110,239	290	36	22	3,700	
9053878	Carnival Imagination	(me2)	Bhs	1995	70,367	262	32	18	2,624	ex Imagination-07

Ambassadors International (Windstar Cruises) : WIND SURF : *M. Lennon*

IMO#	name	screws	flag	year	gt	loa	bm	kts	pass	former names
9187489	Carnival Inspiration	(me2)	Bhs	1996	70,367	262	32	18	2,634	ex Inspiration-07
9224726	Carnival Legend	(me2p)	Pan	2002	85,942	293	32	22	2,680	
9278181	Carnival Liberty	(me2)	Pan	2005	110,320	285	32	22	3,700	
9378486	Carnival Magic	(me2p)	Pan	2011	128,048	304	37	22	3,652	
9237357	Carnival Miracle	(me2p)	Pan	2004	85,942	293	32	22	2,680	
9120877	Carnival Paradise	(me2p)	Pan	1998	70,390	262	32	21	2,634	ex Paradise-07
9223954	Carnival Pride	(me2p)	Pan	2001	85,920	293	32	22	2,680	
8711356	Carnival Sensation	(me2)	Bhs	1993	70,538	262	32	20	2,634	ex Sensation-07
9188647	Carnival Spirit	(me2p)	Pan	2001	85,920	293	32	22	2,680	
9333163	Carnival Splendor	(me2)	Pan	2008	113,323	290	36	22	3,540	
9138850	Carnival Triumph	(me2)	Bhs	1999	101,509	272	36	21	3,470	
9236389	Carnival Valor	(me2)	Pan	2004	110,239	290	36	22	3,710	
9172648	Carnival Victory	(me2)	Pan	2000	101,509	272	36	22	3,470	

newbuildings: un-named cruise liner, 135,000gt, 4,000px (Fincantieri (2016)]

Aida Cruises, Germany

Funnel: *White with 'AIDA' (letters in blue, red, yellow and green respectively).* **Hull:** *White with red 'lips' and 'eye' and blue wave symbols on bows.* **History:** *Originally founded 1999 as joint venture between by P&O and Arkona Touristik which merged with Seetours International in 2000.* **Web:** *www.aida.de*

9221566	AIDAaura *	(me2)	Ita	2003	42,289	203	28	19	1,582	
9362542	AIDAbella	(me2)	Ita	2008	69,203	249	32	21	2,030	
9398888	AIDAblu	(me2)	Ita	2010	71,304	252	32	21	2,174	
9112789	AIDAcara	(2)	Ita	1996	38,557	193	28	18	1,186	ex Aida-01
9334856	AIDAdiva	(me2)	Ita	2007	69,203	252	32	21	2,030	
9334868	AIDAluna	(me2)	Ita	2010	69,203	252	32	21	2,030	
9490052	AIDAmar *	(me2)	Ita	2012	71,304	249	32	21	2,174	
9490040	AIDAsol *	(me2)	Ita	2011	71,304	252	32	21	2,174	
9601132	AIDAstella	(me2)	Ita	2013	71,300	253	32	21	2,050	
9221554	AIDAvita *	(me2)	Ita	2002	42,289	203	28	19	1,582	

newbuildings: 2 x un-named cruise ship (2015.2016)
 * owned by Costa Crociere SpA

Costa Crociere SpA, Italy

Funnel: *Yellow with blue 'C' and black top.* **Hull:** *White with blue boot-topping.* **History:** *Founded 1924 and entered passenger shipping 1947. Acquired by Airtours and Carnival joint venture in 1997, Carnival acquiring complete control in 2001.* **Web:** *www.costacruise.com or www.costacruises.co.uk*

6910544	Club Harmony *		Mhl	1969	25,558	176	26	20	1,000	ex Harmony Princess-11, Costa Marina-11, Italia-90, Regent Sun-86, Axel Johnson-86 (conv: ucc 1986-90)
9187796	Costa Atlantica	(me2p)	Ita	2000	85,619	293	32	22	2,680	
8716502	Costa Classica	(2)	Ita	1991	52,926	221	31	19	1,766	

Carnival Corporation (Aida Cruises) : AIDASOL : *Nico. Kemps*

Carnival Corporation (Costa Crociere) : COSTA LUMINOSA : *Hans Kraijenbosch*

Carnival Corporation (Costa Crociere) : COSTA neoROMANTICA : *C. Lous*

Carnival Corporation (Costa Crociere) : COSTA SERENA : *M. Lennon*

IMO#	name	screws	flag	year	gt	loa	bm	kts	pass	former names
9398917	Costa Deliziosa	(me2p)	Ita	2010	92,720	294	32		2,828	
9479864	Costa Fascinosa	(me2)	Ita	2012	113,216	290	36	21	3,780	
9479852	Costa Favolosa	(me2?)	Ita	2011	113,216	290	36	21	3,780	
9239783	Costa Fortuna	(me2)	Ita	2003	102,587	272	36	20	3,470	
9239795	Costa Magica	(me2)	Ita	2004	102,587	272	36	20	3,470	
9398905	Costa Luminosa	(me2p)	Ita	2009	92,720	294	32		2,828	
9237345	Costa Mediterranea	(me2p)	Ita	2003	85,619	293	32	22	2,680	
8821046	Costa neoRomantica	(2)	Ita	1993	57,150	230	40	19	1,782	ex Costa Romantica-12 (rbt 2011)
9378498	Costa Pacifica	(me2)	Ita	2009	114,288	290	36	21	3,780	
9343132	Costa Serena	(me2)	Ita	2007	114,147	290	36	21	3,780	
9109031	Costa Victoria	(me2)	Ita	1996	75,166	253	32	23	2,200	
9183506	Costa Voyager	(2)	Ita	2000	24,391	180	26	28	927	ex Grand Voyager-11, Voyager-05, Olympia Voyager-04, Olympic Voyager-01

newbuildings: one 132,500gt 4,947 px cruise ship [Fincantieri : Costa Diadeema (2014)]
*managed by Polaris Shipping Co.

Cunard Line Ltd., U.K.

Funnel: *Red with two narrow black rings and black top.* **Hull:** *Charcoal grey with red boot-topping.* **History:** *Founded 1840 as British and North American RMSP Co by Samuel Cunard, becoming Cunard Steam-Ship Co Ltd in 1878. Merged with White Star Line in 1930's. Company acquired by Trafalgar House Investments in 1971 and acquired Norwegian America Cruises in 1983. Trafalgar acquired by Kvaerner in 1996 and Cunard sold to Carnival in 1998.* **Web:** *www.cunard.com or www.cunard.co.uk*

IMO#	name	screws	flag	year	gt	loa	bm	kts	pass	former names
9477438	Queen Elizabeth	(me2p)	Bmu	2010	90,901	294	32	23	2,092	
9421061	Queen Mary 2	(gme4p)	Bmu	2003	148,528	345	41	29	2,620	
9320556	Queen Victoria	(me2p)	Bmu	2007	90,049	294	32	23	2,014	

Holland-America Line, Netherlands

Funnel: *White with black/white ship symbol within double black ring, narrow black top or vents.* **Hull:** *Black with red boot-topping.* **History:** *Founded 1873 as Nederlandsch Amerikaansche Stoomvaart Maatschappij. Later Holland America Cruises Inc until 1983 merger with Westours Inc to form Holland America Westours Inc to 2002. Acquired 50% share in Windstar Cruises in 1987 and acquired Home Lines in 1988. Acquired by Carnival in 1989.* **Web:** *www.hollandamerica.com*

IMO#	name	screws	flag	year	gt	loa	bm	kts	pass	former names
9188037	Amsterdam	(me2p)	Nld	2000	62,735	238	32	21	1,738	
9378448	Eurodam	(me2p)	Nld	2008	86,273	285	32	22	2,104	
8919257	Maasdam	(me2)	Nld	1993	55,575	219	31	20	1,629	
9378450	Nieuw Amsterdam	(me2p)	Nld	2010	86,273	290	32	24	2,106	
9230115	Noordam	(gme2p)	Nld	2006	82,318	290	32	24	1,800	
9221281	Oosterdam	(gme2p)	Nld	2003	82,305	285	32	22	2,388	
8700280	Prinsendam	(2)	Nld	1988	38,848	204	29	21	837	ex Seabourn Sun-02, Royal Viking Sun-99
9122552	Rotterdam	(me2)	Nld	1997	61,849	238	32	22	1,620	
8919269	Ryndam	(me2)	Nld	1994	55,819	219	31	20	1,629	
8919245	Statendam	(me2)	Nld	1993	55,819	219	31	20	1,629	
9102992	Veendam	(me2)	Nld	1996	57,092	219	31	20	1,629	
9156515	Volendam	(me2)	Nld	1999	61,214	237	32	22	1,824	
9226891	Westerdam	(gme2p)	Nld	2004	82,348	285	32	22	1,800	
9156527	Zaandam	(me2)	Nld	2000	61,396	237	32	22	2,272	
9221279	Zuiderdam	(gme2p)	Nld	2002	82,305	285	32	22	1,848	

newbuilding:un-named cruise ship, 99,000gt, 2,660 px [Fincantieri Q3, 2015]

Carnival Corporation (Cunard Line) : QUEEN ELIZABETH : *Hans Kraijenbosch*

IMO#	name	screws	flag	year	gt	loa	bm	kts	pass	former names

Iberojet Cruceros SL, Spain

Funnel: *Dark blue with yellow 5-pointed starfish.* **Hull:** *White.* **History:** *Subsidiary formed jointly with Spanish tour operator Orizonia Corp (25%).* **Web:** *www.cruceros.iberojet.es*

IMO#	name	screws	flag	year	gt	loa	bm	kts	pass	former names
8314134	Grand Celebration	(2)	Pmd	1987	47,263	223	28	19	1,896	ex Celebration-08
8217881	Grand Holiday	(2)	Prt	1985	46,052	222	28	22	1,794	ex Holiday-09
9172777	Grand Mistral	(me2)	Pmd	1999	48,200	216	29	19	1,667	ex Mistral-05

P&O Cruises Ltd., U.K.

Funnel: *Yellow.* **Hull:** *White with red boot-topping.* **History:** *Founded 1837 as Peninsulat Steam Navigation Co, becoming Peninsular & Oriental Steam Navigation Co in 1840. P&P-Orient Lines formed 1961 when remaining Orient Lines shares acquired. Princess Cruises acquired 1974. P&O Princess Cruises remerged from P&O in 2000. Acquired by Carnival in 2003.* **Web:** *www.pocruises.co.uk*

IMO#	name	screws	flag	year	gt	loa	bm	kts	pass	former names
9210220	Adonia	(me2)	Bmu	2001	30,277	181	25	18	777	ex Royal Princess-11, Minerva II-07, R Eight-03
9226906	Arcadia	(me2p)	Bmu	2005	83,781	285	32	22	2,556	l/dn Queen Victoria
9169524	Aurora	(me2)	Bmu	2000	76,152	270	32	24	1,878	
9424883	Azura	(me2)	Bmu	2010	115,055	290	36	22	3,076	
9169550	Oceana	(me2)	Bmu	1999	77,499	261	32	21	2,272	ex Ocean Princess-02
9050137	Oriana	(2)	Bmu	1995	69,840	260	32	24	2,108	
9333175	Ventura	(me2)	Bmu	2008	116,017	290	36	22	3,100	

newbuilding: un-named cruise ship 141,000gt, 3,611px [Fincantieri Monfalcone (2015)]

Carnival Corporation (Holland America Line) : MAASDAM : *Nico Kemps*

Carnival Corporation (Holland America Line) : NIEUW AMSTERDAM : *M. Lennon*

Carnival Corporation (P&O Cruises) : ORIANA : *Douglas Cromby* [note redesigned stern]

Carnival Corporation (Princess Cruises USA) : PACIFIC PRINCESS : *M. Lennon*

Carnival Corporation (Princess Cruises) : RUBY PRINCESS : *M. Lennon*

P&O Cruises Australia Ltd., Australia

Funnel: *Blue with small white 'Pacific' and large yellow 'Star or Sun'.* **Hull:.** *White with broad blue above narrow yellow bands.*
History: *Formed 1987 as P&O Resorts Pty Ltd to 1998, then as P&O Australian Resorts Pty Ltd to 2004.* **Web:** *www.pocruises.com.au*

IMO#	name	screws	flag	year	gt	loa	bm	kts	pass	former names
8521232	Pacific Dawn	(me2)	Gbr	1991	70,285	245	32	19	1,900	ex Regal Princess-07
8521220	Pacific Jewel	(me2)	Gbr	1990	70,310	245	32	19	1,900	ex Ocean Village Two-09, AIDAblu-07, A'Rosa Blu-04, Crown Princess-02
8611398	Pacific Pearl	(me2)	Gbr	1989	63,786	246	32	19	1,692	ex Ocean Village-10, Arcadia-03, Star Princess-97, Sitmar Fairmajesty-89

Princess Cruises Inc., U.S.A.

Funnel: *White funnel with blue/white 'Princess' flowing hair insignia.* **Hull:** *White with green boot-topping.* **History:** *Founded 1965 and acquired by P&O in 1974. Acquired Sitmar in 1988. Demerged as P&O-Princess Cruises in 2000 and acquired by Carnival in 2003.* **Web:** *www.princesscruises.com*

IMO#	name	screws	flag	year	gt	loa	bm	kts	pass	former names
9215490	Caribbean Princess *	(me2)	Bmu	2004	112,894	290	36	22	3,798	l/dn Crown Princess
9229659	Coral Princess	(gme2)	Bmu	2002	91,627	294	32	21	2,581	
9293399	Crown Princess	(me2)	Bmu	2006	113,561	290	36	22	3,599	
9103996	Dawn Princess	(me2)	Bmu	1997	77,441	261	32	21	1,950	
9228198	Diamond Princess *	(me2)	Bmu	2004	115,875	290	38	23	2,600	l/dn Sapphire Princess
9333151	Emerald Princess	(me2)	Bmu	2007	116,000	290	36	22	3,599	
9192351	Golden Princess	(me2)	Bmu	2001	108,865	290	36	22	3,300	
9104005	Grand Princess	(me2)	Bmu	1998	108,806	290	36	22	3,300	
9230402	Island Princess	(gme2)	Bmu	2003	91,627	294	32	24	2,581	
9187899	Ocean Princess	(me2)	Bmu	1999	30,277	181	25	18	688	ex Tahitian Princess-09, R Four-02
9187887	Pacific Princess	(me2)	Bmu	1999	30,277	181	25	18	688	ex R Three-02
9378462	Ruby Princess	(me2)	Bmu	2008	113,561	290	36	22	3,599	
9228186	Sapphire Princess *	(me2)	Bmu	2004	115,875	290	38	23	3,078	l/dn Diamond Princess
9150913	Sea Princess	(me2)	Bmu	1998	77,499	261	32	19	2,342	ex Adonia-05, Sea Princess-03
9192363	Star Princess	(me2)	Bmu	2002	108,977	290	36	22	3,211	
9000259	Sun Princess	(me2)	Bmu	1995	77,441	261	32	21	2,342	
newbuildings:										
9584712	Royal Princess		Bmu	2013	141,000				3,600	L - 27:08:2012
9584624	Regal Princess		Bmu	2014	141,000				3,600	

* owned by Princess Cruise Lines, Bermuda.

Seabourn Cruises Inc., U.S.A.

Funnel: *White with three narrow white lines forming 'S' on blue shield and blue top.* **Hull:** *White with pale blue band and blue boot-topping.* **History:** *Founded 1987 by Norwegian industrialist. Carnival acquired 25% in 1991, a further 25% in 1996 and the balance in 1998.* **Web:** *www.seabourn.com*

IMO#	name	screws	flag	year	gt	loa	bm	kts	pass	former names
9008598	Seabourn Legend	(2)	Bhs	1992	9,961	135	19	16	212	ex Queen Odyssey-96, Royal Viking Queen-94, l/dn Seabourn Legend
9417086	Seabourn Odyssey	(me2)	Bhs	2009	32,346	198	26	19	450	
8707343	Seabourn Pride	(2)	Bhs	1988	9,975	134	19	16	212	
9483126	Seabourn Quest	(me2)	Bhs	2011	32,346	198	26	19	450	
9417098	Seabourn Sojourn	(me2)	Bhs	2010	32,346	198	26	19	450	
8807997	Seabourn Spirit	(2)	Bhs	1989	9,975	134	19	16	212	

Carnival Corporation (Seabourn Cruises) : SEABOURN PRIDE : *David Walker*

Carnival Corporation (Seabourn Cruises) : SEABOURN SOJOURN : *C. Lous*

Classic International Cruises : ATHENA : *ARO*

Cruise & Maritime Voyages : MARCO POLO : *C. Lous*

Classic International Cruises   Portugal

Funnel: *White with white sailing ship symbol on dark blue disc, narrow black top.* **Hull:** *White with blue band, blue boot-topping.*
History: *Founded 1991 as subsidiary of Arcalia Shipping Co. Ltd., Portugal.* **Web:** *www.cic-cruises.cm*

IMO#	name	screws	flag	year	gt	loa	bm	kts	pass	former names
6419057	Arion	(2)	Pmd	1965	5,888	117	17	18	312	ex Nautilus 2000-99, Astra I-99, Astra-96, Istra-91
5383304	Athena *	(2)	Ita	1948	16,144	160	21	18	566	ex Caribe-05, Valtur Prima-03, Italia Prima-00, Italia I-93, Fridtjof Nansen-93, Volker-86, Volkerfreundschaft-85, Stockholm-60
5124162	Funchal	(2)	Pmd	1961	9,563	153	19	14	442	
5282483	Princess Danae	(2)	Pmd	1955	16,531	162	21	17	497	ex Baltica-96, Starlight Princess-94, Anar-92, Danae-92, Therisos Express-74, Port Melbourne-72 (conv : ggc 1974)
5282627	Princess Daphne **	(2)	Prt	1955	15,833	162	21	17	500	ex Ocean Monarch-08, Ocean Odyssey-02, Switzerland-02, Daphne-96, Akrotiri Express-74, Port Sydney-72 (conv. ggc 1974)

* chartered until 2014 and managed for World Cruises Agency, Portugal, ** chartered to Ambiente Kreuzfahrten for 3 years from April 2012
Vessels often chartered out to other operators.
NB: Classic International Cruises in administration late 2012, vessels under arrest in various ports as of December 2012. .

Cruise & Maritime Voyages   U.K.

Funnel: *White with dark blue 'CMV' below sail symbol or dark blue with symbols on white disc.* **Hull:** *Dark blue with red boot-topping.*
History: *Founded 2010.* **Web:** *www.cruiseandmaritime.com*

IMO#	name	screws	flag	year	gt	loa	bm	kts	pass	former names
6417097	Marco Polo *		Bhs	1965	22,080	176	24	16	850	ex Aleksandr-91, Aleksandr Pushkin-91
7358561	Ocean Countess **	(2)	Pmd	1976	17,593	164	23	17	950	ex Ruby-08, Ocean Countess-07, Lili Marleen-06, Ocean Countess-05, Olympia Countess-04, Olympic Countess-01, Awani Dream 2-98, Cunard Countess-96

chartered from: * Global Maritime, Greece, ** Majestic International Cruises Inc

Peter Deilmann Cruises   Germany

Funnel: *White with red 'D' outline containing insignia.* **Hull:** *White with red band.* **History:** *Founded 1973.* **Web:** *www.deilmann.co.uk*

IMO#	name	screws	flag	year	gt	loa	bm	kts	pass	former names
9141807	Deutschland	(2)	Deu	1998	22,496	175	23	20	600	

Passat Kreuzfahrt GmbH   Germany

Funnel: *White with light blue dolphin on dark blue disc interrupting three narrow dark blue bands.* **Hull:** *White with red or blue boot-topping.* **Web:** *www.hansakreuzfahrten.de*

IMO#	name	screws	flag	year	gt	loa	bm	kts	pass	former names
7347536	Delphin	(2)	Bhs	1975	16,214	156	22	21	554	ex Kazakhstan II-96, Byelorussiya-93

operated by subsidiary Hansa Kreuzfahrten.

Disney Cruise Line : DISNEY FANTASY : *Jörn Prestien*

IMO#	name	screws	flag	year	gt	loa	bm	kts	pass	former names

Disney Cruise Line   U.S.A.

Funnel: *Red with white 'Mickey Mouse' symbol over three black waves, black top.* **Hull:** *Black with white band above red boot-topping.*
History: *Founded 1995 as a subsidiary of Walt Disney World Corp.* **Web:** *www-disneycruise.com*

IMO#	name	screws	flag	year	gt	loa	bm	kts	pass	former names
8434254	Disney Dream	(me2p)	Bhs	2010	129,690	340	38		4,000	
9445590	Disney Fantasy	(me2p)	Bhs	2012	129,750	340	38		4,000	
9126807	Disney Magic	(me2)	Bhs	1998	83,338	294	32	21	2,500	
9126819	Disney Wonder	(me2)	Bhs	1999	83,308	294	32	21	2,500	

Hurtigruten Group   Norway

Funnel: *Black with white 'H' symbol above white wave on red disc or black with broad white band edged with narrow red bands.*
Hull: *Black with broad red band.* **History:** *Service commenced 1893 by Vesteraalens Dampskibs, alter being joined by Bergenske Dampskibs and Nordenfjeldske Dampskibs in 1894 and by Ofotens Dampskibs in 1936.* **Web:** *www.hurtigruten.co.uk*

IMO#	name	screws	flag	year	gt	loa	bm	kts	pass	former names
9231951	Finnmarken	(2)	Nor	2002	15,000	139	22	15	638	
9370018	Fram	(me2p)	Nor	2007	12,700	110	20	16	382	
9039119	Kong Harald	(2)	Nor	1993	11,200	122	19	15	490	
5424562	Lofoten		Nor	1964	2,621	87	13	16	147	
9247728	Midnatsol	(2)	Nor	2003	16,151	136	22	15	652	
9107772	Nordkapp	(2)	Nor	1996	11,386	123	20	15	464	
9048914	Nordlys	(2)	Nor	1994	11,200	122	19	15	482	
9107784	Nordnorge	(2)	Nor	1997	11,384	123	20	18	455	
5255777	Nordstjernen †		Nor	1956	2,191	81	13	15	114	
6905745	Polar Star *	(me2)	Brb	1969	3,963	87	21	18	105	
9107796	Polarlys	(2)	Nor	1996	12,000	123	20	15	479	
9040429	Richard With	(2)	Nor	1993	11,205	122	19	15	483	
9233258	Trollfjord	(2)	Nor	2002	15,000	136	22	15	648	
8019368	Vesteralen	(2)	Nor	1983	6,261	109	17	15	316	

operating Norwegian Coastal voyages and seasonal voyages to Alaska, Antarctica and Central America.
* owned by Karlson Shipping, Norway. † Nordstjeran sold to Vestland Rederi, 12:2012

Louis Cruise Lines   Cyprus

Funnel: *White with red sun/wave symbol above dark blue 'L', black top.* **Hull:** *White with red or dark blue boot-topping.*
History: *Founded 1935 and commenced shipping owning in 1987.* **Web:** *www.louisgroup.com or www.louiscruises.com*

IMO#	name	screws	flag	year	gt	loa	bm	kts	pass	former names
7046936	Coral * †	(2)	Mlt	1971	14,194	148	22	24	912	ex Triton-05, Sunward II-91, Cunard Adventurer-77
7827213	Louis Cristal	(2)	Mlt	1980	25,611	159	25	21	1,452	ex Cristal-11, Opera-07, Silja Opera-06, Superstar Taurus-02, Leeward-00, Sally Albatross-95, Viking Saga-86
7927984	Louis Olympia	(2)	Cyp	1982	37,773	215	28	20	1,595	ex Thomson Destiny-12, Sunbird-05, Song of America-99
6821080	Orient Queen	(2)	Mlt	1968	15,781	160	23	20	928	ex Bolero-04, Starward-95

managed by subsidiary Core Marine and * owned by Louis Hellenic Cruises subsidiary
See also Thomson Cruises (under TUI), Transocean Tours, Holland America (under Carnival Corp.) and Norwegian Cruise (under Star Cruise)
† laid up Elefsis since 08:12:2011

Louis Cruise Line : ORIENT QUEEN : *M. Lennon*

Majestic International Cruises Inc.   **Greece**

Mediterranean Classic Cruises (formerly Monarch Classic Cruises)
Funnel: *White with blue swan symbol on yellow disc or* charterers colours. **Hull:** *White or dark blue with red boot-topping.*
History: *Founded 2002.* **Web:** *www.mccruises.gr*

| 6602898 Ocean Majesty | (2) | Prt | 1966 | 10,417 | 131 | 19 | 20 | 613 | ex Homeric-95, Ocean Majesty-95, Olympic-95, Ocean Majesty-94, Kypros Star-89, Sol Christiana-86, Juan March-85 |

Also see Cruise & Maritime Voyages, UK

Mitsui-OSK Lines K.K.   **Japan**
Funnel: *Light red.* **Hull:** *White.* **History:** *See cargo section.* **Web:** *www,mopas.co.jp*

| 8700474 Fuji Maru | (2) | Jpn | 1989 | 23,235 | 167 | 27 | 20 | 603 |
| 8817631 Nippon Maru | (2) | Jpn | 1990 | 22,472 | 167 | 24 | 18 | 607 |

MSC Crociere S.A.   **Italy**
Funnel: *White with 'M' over 'SC'.* **Hull:** *White with narrow blue band, blue boot-topping.* **History:** *Formed 1986 as Mediterranean Shipping Cruises, a subsidiary of Mediterranean Shipping Co. (formed 1970) and renamed in 2002.* **Web:** *www.msccruises.com*

| 7902295 Melody | (2) | Pan | 1982 | 35,143 | 205 | 27 | 20 | 1,492 | ex Starship Atlantic-97, Atlantic-88 |

MSC Crociere S.A. : MELODY : *Hans Kraijenbosch*

MSC Crociere S.A. : MSC LIRICA : *F. de Vries*

IMO#	name	screws	flag	year	gt	loa	bm	kts	pass	former names
9210141	MSC Armonia	(me2p)	Pan	2001	58,714	251	29	21	2,087	ex European Vision-04
9585285	MSC Divina	(me2)	Pan	2012	137,936	333	38	22	3,887	
9359791	MSC Fantasia	(me2)	Pan	2008	137,936	333	38	22	3,887	
9246102	MSC Lirica	(me2p)	Pan	2003	59,058	251	29	20	2,069	
9387085	MSC Magnifica	(me2p)	Pan	2010	95,128	294	32	22	3,013	
9320087	MSC Musica	(me2p)	Pan	2006	92,409	294	32	22	3,013	
9250464	MSC Opera	(me2p)	Pan	2004	59,058	251	29	20	2,055	
9320099	MSC Orchestra	(me2p)	Pan	2007	92,409	294	32	22	3,013	
9387073	MSC Poesia	(me2p)	Pan	2008	92,627	294	32	22	3,013	
9595321	MSC Preziosa	(me2)	Pan	2013	137,936	333	38	22	3,887	
9210153	MSC Sinfonia	(me2p)	Pan	2002	58,625	251	29	21	2,087	ex European Stars-04, l/a European Drea
9359806	MSC Splendida	(me2)	Pan	2009	137,936	333	38	22	3,887	l/dn as MSC Seranata

NB, MSC Preziosa, MSC take over of vessel originally ordered by Libyan Govt.

Nippon Yusen Kaisha   Japan

Crystal Cruises Inc., U.S.A.
Funnel: Black, large white side panels with blue symbol. **Hull**: White with narrow blue band. **History**: Formed 1989 by NYK (founded 1885 – see cargo section). **Web**: www.crystalcruises.com

9243667	Crystal Serenity	(me2p)	Bhs	2003	68,870	250	32	23	1,080	
9066667	Crystal Symphony	(me2)	Bhs	1995	51,044	238	31	21	975	

MSC Crociere S.A. : MSC MAGNIFICA : *ARO*

Phoenix Reisen : ARTANIA : *Hans Kraijenbosch*

IMO#	name	screws	flag	year	gt	loa	bm	kts	pass	former names

Yusen Cruise, Japan

Funnel: White with two red bands and black top. **Hull:** *White with blue boot-topping.* **Web:** *www.asukacruise.co.jp*

8806204	Asuka II	(me2)	Bhs	1990	50,142	241	30	22	960	ex Crystal Harmony-06

Jointly owned by Asuka Ship Co., Japan

Oceania Cruises   U.S.A.

Funnel: White with blue 'O' symbol. **Hull:** White. **History:** *Founded 2002, the three original ships being chartered until purchased in 2006. Private equity firm acquired majority stake in 2007.* **Web:** *www.oceaniacruiseline.com*

9438066	Marina	(me2)	Mhl	2011	66,084	252	32	20	1,260	
9200938	Nautica	(me2)	Mhl	2000	30,277	181	25	18	684	ex Blue Star-05, R Five-04
9156474	Regatta	(me2)	Mhl	1998	30,277	181	25	18	684	ex Insignia-03, R Two-03
9438078	Riviera	(me2)	Mhl	2012	66,172	252	32	20	1,260	

Managed by V. Ships Leisure SAM, Monaco

Fred Olsen Cruise Lines Ltd.   U.K.

Funnel: White with red oval and white/blue houseflag. **Hull:** White with green boot-topping. **History:** Shipping company originally founded 1848 in Norway and UK cruise subsidiary formed in 1997. **Web:** *www.fredolsencruises.com*

8506294	Balmoral	(2)	Bhs	1988	43,537	218	32	22	1,240	ex Norwegian Crown-07, Crown Odyssey-03, Norwegian Crown-00, Crown Odyssey-96 (len-07)
7108930	Black Watch	(2)	Bhs	1972	28,670	205	25	18	902	ex Star Odyssey-96, Westward-94, Royal Viking Star-91 (NE-05)(len-81)
7217395	Boudicca	(2)	Pan	1973	28,388	205	25	18	1,022	ex Grand Latino-05, SuperStar Capricorn-04, Hyundai Kumgang-01, SuperStar Capricorn-98, Golden Princess-96, Sunward-93, Birka Queen-92, Sunward-92, Royal Viking Sky-91 (NE)(leng-83)
9000699	Braemar	(2)	Pan	1993	24,344	196	23	18	1,116	ex Crown Dynasty-01, Norwegian Dynasty-99, Crown Majesty-97, Crown Dynasty-97, Cunard Dynasty-97, Crown Dynasty-95 (len-08)

Paul Gauguin Cruises   U.S.A.

Funnel: White. **Hull:** White boot topping. **History:** *formerly owned by Grand Circle Line, company sold in 2010 to Pacific Beachcomber Crocieres, Washington* **Web:** *www.pgcruises.com*

9111319	Paul Gauguin	(me2)	Bhs	1997	19,170	154	22	18	320	
9159830	Tera Moana *	(2)	Wlf	1990	3,504	100	14	16	90	ex Le Levant-12

* company web-site variously refers to the vessel as The Moana and Tere Moana.

Phoenix Reisen   Germany

Funnel: Turquoise with white seagull in flight over yellow sun. **Hull:** White with turquoise band, blue boot-topping. **History:** *German tour operator entered cruise business in 1988 by chartering the Maksim Gorkiy.* **Web:** *www.phoenixreisen.com*

7304314	Albatros	(2)	Bhs	1973	29,518	205	25	18	812	ex Crown-04, Norwegian Star I-02, Norwegian Star-01, Royal Odyssey-97, Royal Viking Sea-91 (len-83)
8913162	Amadea	(2)	Bhs	1991	29,008	190	25	21	604	ex Asuka-06
8201480	Artania	(2)	Bmu	1984	44,588	231	29	21	1,260	ex Artemis-11, Royal Princess-05

Managed by V. Ships Leisure SAM.

Ponant Cruises   France

Funnel: Black louvers with three white sail symbol. **Hull:** dark grey with red boot-topping. **History:** *Founded in 1988, formerly Cie. des Isles du Ponant until 2009.* **Web:** *www.ponant.com*

9502518	L'Austral		Wlf	2010	10,944	142	18	16	264	
9502506	Le Boreal		Wlf	2010	10,944	142	18	16	264	
	newbuildings									
9641675	Le Soleal		Wlf	2013	10,950	142	18	16	264	

* co-owned by Tapis Rouge Cruises, Spain. also operates small sail-cruise vessel **Le Ponant**.

Regent Seven Seas Cruises Inc.   U.S.A.

Funnel: White with purple 'Regent'. **Hull:** White with blue band and blue waterline above red boot-topping. **History:** *Originally founded 1992 as Diamond Cruise Line, later becoming Radisson Seven Seas Cruises to 2006. Acquired by Apollo Management equity group in 2008.* **Web:** *www.rssc.com*

9210139	Seven Seas Mariner	(me2p)	Wlf	2001	48,075	216	29	19	769	

IMO#	name	screws	flag	year	gt	loa	bm	kts	pass	former names
9064126	Seven Seas Navigator	(2)	Bhs	1999	28,550	171	24	17	542	l/dn Akademik Nikolay Pilyugin (1991)
9247144	Seven Seas Voyager	(me2p)	Bhs	2003	41,500	207	29	20	769	

Royal Caribbean International   Norway

Funnel: *White with blue crown and anchor symbol.* **Hull:** *White with blue band and blue boot-topping.* **History:** *Founded 1969 as Royal Caribbean Cruises Ltd by Norwegian shipowners Anders Wilhelmsen, I M Skaugen & Co and Gotaas-Larsen being renamed in 1997, when Celebrity Cruises was acquired.* **Web:** *www.royalcaribbean.com*

IMO#	name	screws	flag	year	gt	loa	bm	kts	pass	notes
9167227	Adventure of the Seas	(me3p)	Bhs	2001	137,276	311	39	23	3,840	
9383948	Allure of the Seas	(me3p)	Bhs	2010	225,282	362	47	22	6,318	66m max width
9195200	Brilliance of the Seas	(gt2p)	Bhs	2002	90,090	294	32	24	2,500	
9111802	Enchantment of the Seas	(me2)	Bhs	1997	82,910	301	32	22	2,730	(len-05)
9228368	Xpedition *		Ecu	2001	2,842	89	14	13	96	ex Sun Bay-04
9161728	Explorer of the Seas	(me3p)	Bhs	2000	137,308	311	39	23	3,840	
9304033	Freedom of the Seas	(me3p)	Bhs	2006	154,407	339	39	22	4,375	56m max width
9102978	Grandeur of the Seas	(me2)	Bhs	1996	73,817	279	32	22	2,440	

Ponant Cruises : LE BOREAL : *C. Lous*

Royal Caribbean International (Pullmantur Cruises) : ZENITH : *J. Kakebeeke*

IMO#	name	screws	flag	year	gt	loa	bm	kts	pass	former names
9349681	Independence of the Seas	(me3p)	Bhs	2008	154,407	339	39	21	4,375	56m max width
9228356	Jewel of the Seas	(gt2p)	Bhs	2004	90,090	293	32	24	2,500	
9070620	Legend of the Seas	(me2)	Bhs	1995	69,490	264	32	24	2,060	
9330032	Liberty of the Seas	(me3p)	Bhs	2007	154,407	339	39	21	4,375	56m max width
8819512	Majesty of the Seas	(2)	Bhs	1992	73,937	268	32	20	2,744	
9227510	Mariner of the Seas	(me3p)	Bhs	2004	138,279	311	39	22	3,807	
8819500	Monarch of the Seas	(2)	Bhs	1991	73,937	268	32	20	2,744	
9227508	Navigator of the Seas	(me3p)	Bhs	2003	138,279	311	39	22	3,807	
9383936	Oasis of the Seas	(me3p)	Bhs	2009	225,282	362	47	22	6,360	65m max width
9195195	Radiance of the Seas	(gt2p)	Bhs	2001	90,090	293	32	24	2,500	
9116864	Rhapsody of the Seas	(me2)	Nis	1997	78,491	279	32	22	2,416	
9228344	Serenade of the Seas	(gt2p)	Bhs	2003	90,090	293	32	24	2,501	
9070632	Splendour of the Seas	(me2)	Bhs	1996	69,130	264	32	24	2,066	
9116876	Vision of the Seas	(me2)	Bhs	1998	78,340	279	32	22	2,416	
9161716	Voyager of the Seas	(me3p)	Bhs	1999	137,276	311	39	22	3,840	

* managed for Islas Galapagos Tourismo
newbuildings.2 x 158,000gt, 4,100px cruise ships [Meyer Werft : Quantum of the Seas (2014), Anthem of the Seas (2015)]
1 x 225,282grt, 5,400px [STX France (2016)] = 1 option

Regent Seven Seas Cruises : SEVEN SEAS VOYAGER : *C. Lous*

Royal Caribbean International (Celebrity Cruises) : CELEBRITY ECLIPSE : *ARO*

IMO#	name	screws	flag	year	gt	loa	bm	kts	pass	former names

Azamara Cruises, U.S.A.

Funnel: *White with brown diamond symbol.* **Hull:** *White with brown diamond symbol and 'AZAMARA' towards stern.*
History: *Subsidiary formed 2007.* **Web:** *www.azamaracruises.com*

IMO#	name	screws	flag	year	gt	loa	bm	kts	pass	former names
9200940	Azamara Journey	(me2)	Mlt	2000	30,277	181	25	18	777	ex Blue Dream-07, R Six-05
9210218	Azamara Quest	(me2)	Mhl	2000	30,277	181	25	18	702	ex Blue Moon-07, Delphin Renaissance-06, R Seven-03

NB, ships to be refurbished and finished with dark blue hulls

Celebrity Cruises, U.S.A.

Funnel: *Black or black/white horizontal striped with large white diagonal cross (edged yellow on later vessels).* **Hull:** *White with broad black bands at lifeboat level and waterline.* **History:** *Founded 1989 by Chandris and acquired 1997. Formed Celebrity Expeditions in 2004.* **Web:** *www.celebritycruises.com*

IMO#	name	screws	flag	year	gt	loa	bm	kts	pass	former names
9072446	Celebrity Century	(2)	Mlt	1995	71,545	247	32	21	1,778	ex Century-08
9192399	Celebrity Constellation	(gt2p)	Mlt	2002	90,280	294	32	24	2,449	ex Constellation-07
9404314	Celebrity Eclipse	(me2p)	Mlt	2010	121,878	317	37	24	2,850	
9372456	Celebrity Equinox	(me2p)	Mlt	2009	121,878	317	37	24	2,850	
9189421	Celebrity Infinity	(gt2p)	Mlt	2001	90,228	294	32	24	2,449	ex Infinity-07
9189419	Celebrity Millennium	(gt2p)	Mlt	2000	90,963	294	32	24	2,449	ex Millennium-09
9506459	Celebrity Reflection	(me2p)	Mlt	2012	125,366	315	37	24	3,030	
9451094	Celebrity Silhouette	(me2p)	Mlt	2011	122,210	317	37	24	2,850	
9362530	Celebrity Solstice	(me2p)	Mlt	2008	121,878	317	37	24	2,850	l/a Solstice
9192387	Celebrity Summit	(gt2p)	Mlt	2001	90,280	294	32	24	2,449	ex Summit-08

newbuildings :
also see TUI Cruises joint venture.

Pullmantur Cruises, Spain

Funnel: *Dark blue with red striped globe symbol on pale blue edged white disc.* **Hull:** *White with red 'pullmantur cruises'.*
History: *Formed 2000 by established Spanish travel company. Acquired by Royal Caribbean in 2006.*
web: www.pullmanturcruises.com

IMO#	name	screws	flag	year	gt	loa	bm	kts	pass	former names
8024026	Atlantic Star	(st2)	Mlt	1984	46,087	240	28	21	1,600	ex Sky Wonder-09, Pacific Sky-06, Sky Princess-00, Fairsky-88
8716899	Empress	(2)	Mlt	1990	48,563	211	31	19	2,020	ex Empress of the Seas-08, Nordic Empress-04
8807088	Horizon	(2)	Mlt	1990	47,427	208	29	19	1,798	ex Pacific Dream-10, Island Star-09 Horizon-05
8512281	Sovereign	(2)	Mlt	1987	73,529	268	32	21	2,524	ex Sovereign of the Seas-08
8918136	Zenith	(2)	Mlt	1992	47,413	208	29	21	1,774	

Saga Group   U.K.

Funnel: *Yellow with narrow white band below narrow dark blue top.* **Hull:** *Dark blue with red boot-topping or white with black boot-topping (Spirit).* **History:** *Parent company founded in 1950's and entered shipping owning in 1997. Spirit of Adventure subsidiary formed 2005.* **Web:** *www.saga.co.uk/cruising*

IMO#	name	screws	flag	year	gt	loa	bm	kts	pass	former names
8000214	Quest for Adventure	(2)	Mlt	1981	18,591	164	23	18	540	ex Saga Pearl II-12, Astoria-09, Arkona-02, Astor-85

Royal Caribbean International (Celebrity Cruises) : CELEBRITY CONSTELLATION : *Nico Kemps*

IMO#	name	screws	flag	year	gt	loa	bm	kts	pass	former names
7214715	Saga Ruby	(2)	Gbr	1973	24,492	191	25	21	670	ex Caronia-05, Vistafjord-99
7822457	Saga Sapphire	(2)	Bhs	1981	37,301	200	29	21	706	ex Bleu de France-12, Holiday Dream-08, SuperStar Aries-04, SuperStar Europe-99, Europa-99

NB, Saga Ruby is scheduled to be retired 2014, Quest for Adventure scheduled to be renamed Saga Pearl II

Sea Cloud Cruises   Germany

Hull: *White.* **History:** *Founded about 1994 by subsidiary of Hansa Treuhand Group.* **Web:** *www.seacloud.com*

Saga Group : SAGA SAPPHIRE : *Douglas Cromby*

Sea Cloud Cruises : SEA CLOUD : *M. Lennon*

IMO#	name	screws	flag	year	gt	loa	bm	kts	pass	former names
8843446	Sea Cloud	(as2)	Mlt	1931	2,532	110	15	12	68	ex Sea Cloud of Grand Cayman-87, Sea Cloud-80, Antarna-79, Patria-64, Angelita-61, Sea Cloud-52, Hussar-35
9171292	Sea Cloud II	(as2)	Mlt	2000	3,849	117	16	14	96	
9483712	Sea Cloud Hussar †		Mlt		4,228					

owned by Hansa Shipmanagement GmbH,   † Spanish builders bankrupt in 2010, unlikely to be completed

Silversea Cruises   U.S.A.

Funnel: *White with blue 'SS' symbol.* **Hull:** *White.* **History:** *Founded by former owners of Sitmar after 1988 sale to P&O.*
Web: *www.silversea.com*

IMO#	name	screws	flag	year	gt	loa	bm	kts	pass	former names
8903923	Silver Cloud	(2)	Bhs	1994	16,927	156	21	17	314	
8806747	Silver Explorer	(2)	Gbr	1969	6,072	108	16	15	140	ex Prince Albert II-11, World Discoverer-08, Dream 21-01, Delfin Star-97, Baltic Clipper-92, Sally Clipper-92, Delfin Clipper-90
9192167	Silver Shadow	(2)	Bhs	2000	28,258	182	25	21	388	
9437866	Silver Spirit	(2)	Bhs	2009	36,009	199	26	19	540	
9192179	Silver Whisper	(2)	Bhs	2001	28,258	182	25	21	388	l/dn Silver Mirage
8903935	Silver Wind	(2)	Bhs	1995	16,927	156	21	17	296	

Silversea Cruises : SILVER CLOUD : *ARO*

Star Cruise AS Send. Berh. (Norwegian Cruise Line) : NORWEGIAN EPIC : *ARO*

Star Clippers Ltd.   Monaco

Funnel: *None.* **Hull:** *White.* **History:** *Founded 1991 as Star Clippers Inc. to 2000.* **Web:** *www.starclippers.com*

IMO#	name	screws	flag	year	gt	loa	bm	kts	pass	former names
8712178	Royal Clipper	(as)	Lux	2000	4,425	133	16	13	224	l/a Gwarek (1991), (len-91)
8915445	Star Clipper	(as)	Lux	1992	2,298	112	15	12	194	
8915433	Star Flyer	(as)	Lux	1991	2,298	112	15	12	194	l/a Star Clipper

Star Cruise AS Sendirian Berhad   Malaysia

Funnel: *Dark blue with yellow eight-pointed star on broad red band.* **Hull:** *White with red band and blue boot-topping.*
History: *Formed 1993 and acquired Norwegian Cruise Line in 2000.* **Web:** *www.starcruises.com*

IMO#	name	screws	flag	year	gt	loa	bm	kts	pass	former names
8314122	Henna *	(2)	Mlt	1986	47,262	225	28	19	1,800	ex Pacific Sun-12, Jubilee-04
8705278	MegaStar Aries	(2)	Pan	1991	3,264	82	14	16	82	ex Aurora II-94, l/a Lady Sarah
8705266	MegaStar Taurus	(2)	Pan	1991	3,341	82	14	16	82	ex Aurora I-94, Lady D-91, l/a Lady Diana
8710857	Star Pisces	(2)	Pan	1990	40,053	177	30	22	2,165	ex Kalypso-93
9008421	SuperStar Aquarius	(2)	Bhs	1993	51,309	230	32	18	2,100	ex Norwegian Wind-07, Windward-98 (len-98)
9008419	SuperStar Gemini	(2)	Bhs	1992	50,764	230	32	18	2,100	ex Norwegian Dream-12, Dreamward-98 (len-98)
8612134	SuperStar Libra	(2)	Bhs	1988	42,276	216	32	20	1,798	ex Norwegian Sea-05, Seaward-97
9141077	SuperStar Virgo	(me2)	Pan	1999	75,338	269	32	24	2,975	

* managed for HNA Tourism

Norwegian Cruise Line, U.S.A.

Funnel: *Dark blue with gold 'NCL' within gold square outline.* **Hull:** *White with red stripe (Norwegian Dawn with multi-coloured artwork), or dark blue, blue boot-topping.* **History:** *Founded in 1967 as Norwegian Caribbean Lines by Klosters Rederi, becoming Kloster Cruise AS in 1987 and Norwegian Cruise Line in 1996. Acquired Royal Viking Line in 1984 and Royal Cruise Line in 1989.* **Web:** *www.ncl.com*

IMO#	name	screws	flag	year	gt	loa	bm	kts	pass	former names
9606912	Norwegian Breakaway	(me2p)	Bhs	2013	144,017	354	43	21	4,000	
9195169	Norwegian Dawn	(me2)	Bhs	2002	92,250	292	32	25	2,500	l/dn SuperStar Sagittarius
9410569	Norwegian Epic	(me2p)	Bhs	2010	166,000	325	40	21	4,200	
9355733	Norwegian Gem	(me2p)	Bhs	2007	93,000	294	32	24	2,384	
9606924	Norwegian Getaway	(me2p)	Bhs	2014	144,017	354	43	21	4,000	
9304057	Norwegian Jade	(me2p)	Bhs	2006	92,250	294	32	24	2,400	ex Pride of Hawaii-08
9304045	Norwegian Jewel	(me2p)	Bhs	2005	91,740	294	32	24	2,400	
9342281	Norwegian Pearl	(me2)	Bhs	2006	93,500	294	32	24	2,400	
9128532	Norwegian Sky	(me2p)	Bhs	1999	77,104	260	32	20	2,450	ex Pride of Aloha-08, Norwegian Sky-04, l/dn Costa Olympia
9141065	Norwegian Spirit	(me2)	Bhs	1998	75,338	269	32	24	2,975	ex SuperStar Leo-04
9195157	Norwegian Star	(me2p)	Bhs	2001	91,740	294	32	24	2,500	l/dn SuperStar Libra
9218131	Norwegian Sun	(me2)	Bhs	2001	78,309	258	32	20	2,359	
9209221	Pride of America	(me2p)	Usa	2005	80,439	276	32	22	2,146	

newbuildings
1 new cruise ship 163,000gt, 4,200px [Meyer Werft (2015)] + 1 option

Transocean Tours   Germany

Funnel: *White with blue 't' symbol inside blue ring interrupting pale blue over blue narrow bands.* **Hull:** *White with pale blue over blue bands.* **History:** *Tour operator formed in 1954.* **Web:** *www.transocean.de or www.transoceancruises.co.uk*

IMO#	name	screws	flag	year	gt	loa	bm	kts	pass	former names
8506373	Astor	(2)	Bhs	1987	20,606	176	23	18	650	ex Fedor Dostoevskiy-95, Astor-88

TUI Cruises GmbH   Germany

Funnel: *White with red 'tui' logo.* **Hull:** *Dark blue with large white 'Mein Schiff' and light blue german phrases, red boot-topping.* **History:** *TUI dates back to 1968 and has undergone many changes since. TUI Cruises was formed 2009, as a joint venture bwtween TUI and Royal Caribbean.* **Web:** *www.tuicruises.com*

IMO#	name	screws	flag	year	gt	loa	bm	kts	pass	former names
9106297	Mein Schiff 1	(2)	Mlt	1996	76,998	264	32	21	1,896	ex Mein Schiff-10, Celebrity Galaxy-09, Galaxy-08
9106302	Mein Schiff 2	(2)	Mlt	1997	77,302	264	32	21	1,896	ex Celebrity Mercury-11, Mercury-08
	newbuildings									
	Mein Schiff 3			2014	99,300	295	36		(2,500)	*reported ordered from STX Turku*
	Mein Schiff 4			2014	99,300				(2,500)	*reported ordered from STX Turku*

Hapag-Lloyd Cruises, Germany

Funnel: *Orange with blue 'HL'.* **Hull:** *White with orange/blue band, red boot-topping.* **History:** *Formed by 1970 merger of the long-established Hamburg America and Norddeutscher Lloyd lines. Control acquired by Preussag group in 1997 and Hapag-Lloyd acquired control of travel group TUI in 1998.* **Web:** *www.hl-cruises.com*

IMO#	name	screws	flag	year	gt	loa	bm	kts	pass	former names
8907424	Bremen	(2)	Bhs	1990	6,752	112	17	16	184	ex Frontier Spirit-93
9156462	Columbus 2	(me2)	Mhl	1998	30,277	181	25	18	684	ex Insignia-12, R One-03
9183855	Europa	(me2p)	Bhs	1999	28,437	199	24	21	408	

IMO#	name	screws	flag	year	gt	loa	bm	kts	pass	former names
9138329	Hamburg **	(2)	Bhs	1997	15,067	145	22	18	423	ex C. Columbus-12
9000168	Hanseatic *	(2)	Bhs	1991	8,378	123	18	14	188	ex Society Adventurer-92
	newbuilding									
9616230	Europa 2	(me2p)	Mlt	2013	39,500	225	27	21	516	L - 06:07:2012 (STX France)

* chartered from Hanseatic Cruises GmbH until 2008 and ** operated by Plantours.

Quark Expeditions, U.S.A.

Funnel: *Chartered ships with various owners colours..* **Hull:** *Owners colours.* **History:** *TUI merged its expedition cruising subsidiaries in 2008, including Clipper Cruise Line (founded 1982, sold to Kuoni in 1999 and acquired by First Choice in 2006), Peregrine Adventures (formed 1977 as part of First Choice), Quark Expeditions (formed 1991) and First Choice Expeditions.* **Web:** *www.quarkexpeditions.com*

IMO#	name	screws	flag	year	gt	loa	bm	kts	pass	former names
7325629	Ocean Diamond	(2)	Wlf	1974	8,282	124	16	16	265	ex Le Diamant-12, Song of Flower-04, Explorer Starship-89, Begonia-87, Fernhill-74
7391422	Sea Adventurer	(2)	Bhs	1975	4,376	100	16	17	116	ex Clipper Adventurer-12, Alla Tarasova-97
8802068	Sea Spirit		Bhs	1991	4,200	91	15	15	112	ex Spirit of Oceanus-10, Megastar Sagittarius-01

TUI Cruises GmbH (Hapag-Lloyd Cruises) : EUROPA : *Nico Kemps*

TUI Cruises GmbH (Hapag-Lloyd Cruises) : HAMBURG : *M. Lennon*

IMO#	name	screws	flag	year	gt	loa	bm	kts	pass	former names
9152959	50 Let Pobedy *	(2)	Rus	2007	23,439	160	30	21	128	

* chartered from 'Atomflot' Federal State Unitary Enterprise, Russia. Also operates a number of smaller expedition ships including Akademik Ioffe, Akademik Sergey Vavilov, Akademik Shokalskiy, Kapitan Khlebnikov, Ocean Nova and Quest chartered from various owners and research organisations.

Thomson Cruises, U.K.

Funnel: *Pale blue with red 'tui' logo.* **Hull:** *White with blue over yellow over red bands, blue or red boot-topping.* **History:** *Long established holiday operator acquired by TUI in 2000. Island Cruises subsidiary formed 2002 as joint venture between Royal Caribbean and First Choice (control acquired by TUI in 2007) was closed early in 2009.* **Web:** *www.thomson-cruises.co.uk*

IMO#	name	screws	flag	year	gt	loa	bm	kts	pass	former names
8002597	Island Escape	(2)	Bhs	1982	40,132	185	27	18	1,863	ex Viking Serenade-02, Stardancer-90, Scandinavia-85
8027298	Thomson Celebration	(2)	Mlt	1984	33,933	215	27	21	1,340	ex Noordam-05
8407735	Thomson Dream	(2)	Mlt	1986	54,763	243	29	19	1,773	ex Costa Europa-10, Westerdam-02, Homeric-88 (len-90)
8814744	Thomson Majesty	(2)	Mlt	1992	40,876	207	33	31	1,460	ex Louis Majesty-12, Norwegian Majesty-09, Royal Majesty-97
8024014	Thomson Spirit	(2)	Mlt	1983	33,930	215	27	21	1,374	ex Spirit-03, Nieuw Amsterdam-02, Patriot-02, Nieuw Amsterdam-00

Other Cruise Ships

Aegean Experience Maritime, Greece

IMO#	name	screws	flag	year	gt	loa	bm	kts	pass	former names
7225910	Aegean Odyssey	(2)	Mlt	1973	11,906	141	21	17	350	ex Aegean 1-10, Aegean Dolphin-96, Dolphin-90, Aegean Dolphin-89, Alkyon-86, Narcis-85 (conv.urr/rbt-85-88)

chartered to Voyages to Antiquity, U.K.

Clipper Group, Denmark

IMO#	name	screws	flag	year	gt	loa	bm	kts	pass	former names
8802882	Corinthian II *	(2)	Mhl	1991	4,200	91	15	15	114	ex Island Sun-05, Sun-04, Renai I-03, Renaissance Seven-01, Regina Renaissance-98, Renaissance Seven-92
8802894	Island Sky **	(2)	Bhs	1992	4,200	90	15	15	114	ex Sky-04, Renai II-03, Renaissance Eight-01

* managed by International Shipping Partners, Miami and chartered out to Travel Dynamics
** managed by Salen Ship Management, Sweden, chartered to Noble Caledonia

East Mediterranean Cruises Ltd., Cyprus

IMO#	name	screws	flag	year	gt	loa	bm	kts	pass	former names
7111078	Venus	(2)	Bhs	1971	16,710	163	23	21	750	ex Rio-12, The Aegean Pearl -10, Perla-08, Seawing-05, Southward-95

G Adventures., Canada

IMO#	name	screws	flag	year	gt	loa	bm	kts	pass	former names
7211074	Expedition		Lbr	1972	6,334	105	18	14	124	ex Alandsfarjan-08, Tiger-86, N.F.Tiger-85, Kattegat-78, (rbt-08)

Aegean Experience Maritime (Voyages to Antiquity) : AEGEAN ODYSSEY : *David Hornsby*

IMO#	name	screws	flag	year	gt	loa	bm	kts	pass	former names

Institute for Shipboard Education, U.S.A.

IMO#	name	screws	flag	year	gt	loa	bm	kts	pass	former names
9183517	Explorer	(2)	Bhs	2001	24,318	178	26	27	836	ex Olympia Explorer-04, l/a Olympic Explorer

Japan Cruise Line, Japan

| 9160011 | Pacific Venus | (2) | Jpn | 1998 | 26,518 | 183 | 25 | 20 | 720 | |

Kristina Cruises Oy, Finland

| 7625811 | Kristina Katarina | | Fin | 1982 | 12,907 | 137 | 21 | 17 | 500 | ex The Iris-10, Francesca-00, Konstantin Simonov-96 |

Lindblad Expeditions, U.S.A.

| 8019356 | National Geographic Explorer | (2) | Bhs | 1982 | 6,100 | 109 | 17 | 17 | 148 | ex Lyngen-08, Midnatsil II-05, Midnatsol-03 |
| 6611863 | National Geographic Endeavour | | Ecu | 1966 | 3,132 | 89 | 14 | 15 | 110 | ex Endeavour-05, Caledonian Star-01, North Star-89, Lindmar-83, Marburg-82 (conv fff-83) |

Mano Maritime, Israel

| 7358573 | Golden Iris | (2) | Ita | 1977 | 16,852 | 164 | 23 | 19 | 812 | ex Rhapsody-09, Cunard Princess-95, l/a Cunard Conquest |
| 7032997 | Royal Iris | | Pan | 1971 | 9,159 | 142 | 22 | 21 | 1,000 | ex Eloise-04, The Azur-87, Azur-87, Eagle-75 (conv: ofy-82) |

Oceanwide Expeditions, Netherlands

| 8509181 | Ortelius | (2) | Cyp | 1989 | 4,575 | 91 | 17 | 12 | 106 | ex Marina Tsvetayeva-11 |

Orion Expedition Cruises, Australia

| 9273076 | Orion | | Bhs | 2003 | 3,984 | 103 | 14 | 16 | 130 | ex Sun Explorer-03 |
| 8708672 | Orion II | (2) | Mlt | 1990 | 4,077 | 88 | 15 | 15 | 100 | ex Clelia II-11, Renaissance Four-96 |

ResidenSea Ltd., Norway

| 9219331 | The World | (2) | Bhs | 2002 | 43,188 | 196 | 29 | 18 | 656 | |

operated by Silversea Cruises Ltd. with accommodation comprising 110 privately owned apartments and 88 guest suites

SeaDream Yacht Club, Norway

| 8203438 | SeaDream I | (2) | Bhs | 1984 | 4,333 | 105 | 15 | 17 | 116 | ex Seabourn Goddess I-01, Sea Goddess I-00 |
| 8203440 | SeaDream II | (2) | Bhs | 1985 | 4,333 | 105 | 15 | 17 | 116 | ex Seabourn Goddess II-01, Sea Goddess II-00 |

chartered from Stella Maritime, Bahamas for use as a floating University

Clipper Group : ISLAND SKY : *M. Lennon*

IMO#	name	screws	flag	year	gt	loa	bm	kts	pass	former names

Sete Yacht Management, Greece

8907216	Turama	(2)	Mlt	1990	8,343	116	17	18	229	ex Columbus Caravelle-04, Sally Caravelle-91, Delfin Caravelle-91

Société Services et Transports, Monaco

9007491	Club Med 2	(as/me2)	Fra	1992	14,983	187	20	15	392	

operated by Club Méditerranée and managed by V. Ships Leisure

The Peace Boat, Japan

5260679	The Oceanic	(st2)	Vut	1965	38,772	238	29	20	1,562	ex Oceanic-09 Starship Oceanic-98, Royale Oceanic-85, Oceanic-85

operating world cruises on charter to non-governmental organisation as 'The Peace Boat'. GP Cruise Inc.

Tropicana Cruises, Belize

7118404	Adriana	(2)	Skn	1972	4,490	104	14	16	312	ex Adriana-08, Aquarius-87

G Adventures : EXPEDITION : *M. Lennon*

Kristina Cruises Oy : KRISTINA KATARINA : *C. Lous*

Lindblad Expeditions : NATIONAL GEOGRAPHIC EXPLORER : *Nico Kemps*

Oceanwide Expeditions : ORTELIUS : *ARO*

PART TWO
Cargo Vessels and Tankers

Mediterranean Shipping Co. : MSC KATRINA : *J. Kakebeeke*

Agelef Shipping Co. (London) Ltd.   U.K.

Agelef Shipping Co (London) Ltd. founded 1968 to act as shipbrokers and agents for Alpha Tankers and Freighters Intl,
Amethyst Management Ltd., Anangel Maritime Services and Maran Tankers Management Ltd.

Alpha Tankers & Freighters International Ltd., Greece

Funnel: *White with black 'A' between narrow red bands below black top.* **Hull:** *Blue with red boot-topping.* **History:** *Related family company founded 1991.* **Web:** *www.alphatankers.com*

IMO#	name	flag	year	grt	dwt	loa	bm	kts	type	former names
9084494	Alpha Action	Grc	1994	77,211	150,790	274	45	14	bbu	ex Action-02, World Action-02
9221853	Alpha Afovos	Grc	2001	39,941	74,428	225	32	15	bbu	ex Anangel Afovos-01
9226530	Alpha Century	Grc	2000	87,407	170,415	289	45	14	bbu	ex Anangel Century-02
9455040	Alpha Confidence	Mlt	2011	89,991	177,830	292	45	15	bbu	
9221009	Alpha Cosmos	Grc	2001	87,378	169,770	289	45	15	bbu	ex Mineral York-02, Mineral Trader-01
9462811	Alpha Dignity	Mlt	2011	89,991	176,296	292	45	15	bbu	
9189081	Alpha Effort	Grc	1999	38,564	72,844	225	32	15	bbu	
9220990	Alpha Era	Grc	2000	87,407	170,387	289	45	14	bbu	ex Mineral Sakura-02
9423774	Alpha Faith	Grc	2008	91,373	178.104	292	45	14	bbu	
9185774	Alpha Flame	Grc	1999	38,852	74,545	225	32	14	bbu	ex United Support-04
9123374	Alpha Friendship *	Grc	1996	81,140	161,524	280	45	14	bbu	ex Anangel Friendship-02
9205811	Alpha Glory	Grc	1999	37,715	72,270	225	32	14	bbu	ex Hebei Glory-06, Sea Lotus-04
9189108	Alpha Happiness	Grc	1999	38,564	72,800	225	32	15	bbu	
9221865	Alpha Harmony	Grc	2001	39,941	74,492	225	32	14	bbu	ex Alpha Harmony I-02, Alpha Harmony-01
9221889	Alpha Melody	Grc	2002	39,941	74,374	225	32	15	bbu	l/a Anangel Melody
9212058	Alpha Millennium	Grc	2000	87,407	170,415	280	45	15	bbu	ex Anangel Millennium-02
9423762	Alpha Prudence	Grc	2008	91,373	178,002	292	45	14	bbu	
9146015	Annoula	Grc	1997	36,559	70,281	225	32	14	bbu	
9423918	Antonis Angelicoussis	Grc	2007	91,373	177,855	292	45	14	bbu	
9457012	Brave Sailor	Mlt	2011	89,991	176,283	292	45	15	bbu	
9189093	Future *	Grc	1999	38,564	72,893	225	32	15	bbu	ex Alpha Future-10
9233703	Maria A. Angelicoussi	Grc	2001	86,201	169,163	289	45	15	bbu	l/a Fabulous
9213375	Marvellous *	Grc	2000	86,201	169,150	289	45	15	bbu	ex Mineral Marvel-04, Marvel-04
9423920	Skythia	Mlt	2010	89,990	177,830	292	45	15	bbu	

* managed by associated company Amethyst Management Ltd,, Athens

Anangel Maritime Services Inc., Greece

Funnel: *White with green 'trefilli' between two narrow red bands beneath narrow black top.* **Hull**: *Light grey, dark grey or blue with red boot-topping.* **History**: *Anangel Shipping Company founded 1971, formerly trading since 1947 as A Angelicoussis and D Efthimiou, who had been shipowners since 1947, Anangel Maritime Services formed as management company in 1991.* **Web**: *www.agelef.co.uk*

IMO#	name	flag	year	grt	dwt	loa	bm	kts	type	former names
9074119	Anangel Ambition	Grc	1994	81,120	161,587	280	44	13	bbu	
9428463	Anangel Argonaut	Grc	2009	89,990	177,835	292	45	14	bbu	
9581681	Anangel Aspiration	Grc	2012	61,504	114,500	250	43	15	bbu	
9581239	Anangel Astronomer	Grc	2012	89,891	179,719	292	45	15	bbu	
9581241	Anangel Conqueror	Grc	2012	89,891	179,700	292	45	15	bbu	
9455533	Anangel Dawn	Grc	2011	61,504	114,091	250	43	15	bbu	
9179593	Anangel Destiny	Grc	1999	87,523	171,997	289	45	15	bbu	
9169603	Anangel Dynasty	Grc	1999	86,600	171,101	289	45	14	bbu	ex Yangtze Ore-02

Agelef Shipping Co. (Alpha Tankers & Freighters : ALPINE MELODY : *C. Lous*

IMO#	name	flag	year	grt	dwt	loa	bm	kts	type	former names
9176644	Anangel Eternity	Grc	1999	86,600	171,176	289	45	14	bbu	ex Virginie Venture-02
9295012	Anangel Explorer	Grc	2007	87,582	171,927	289	45	14	bbu	
9329459	Anangel Fortune	Grc	2005	88,844	175,000	289	45	14	bbu	
9434383	Anangel Glory	Grc	2012	91,656	180,391	292	45	14	bbu	
9440320	Anangel Grace	Grc	2011	91,656	180,391	292	45	14	bbu	
9434369	Anangel Guardian	Grc	2010	89,891	179,718	292	45	14	bbu	
9082350	Anangel Haili	Grc	1995	147,812	260,723	322	58	15	bor	ex Astro Luna-09, Tango-02, Diamond Iris-01 (conv tcr-09)
9470923	Anangel Happiness	Grc	2008	89,565	177,720	292	45	14	bbu	
9434412	Anangel Harmony	Grc	2010	91,656	180,055	292	45	14	bbu	
9286798	Anangel Innovation	Grc	2004	87,050	171,681	289	45	15	bbu	
9110652	Anangel Legend	Grc	1996	81,151	161,059	280	45	14	bbu	ex Bavang-03
9439072	Anangel Mariner	Grc	2011	89,891	179,700	292	45	14	bbu	
9458590	Anangel Merchant	Grc	2010	89,891	179,718	292	45	14	bbu	
9455569	Anangel Ocean	Grc	2011	61,504	114,007	250	43	15	bbu	
9332523	Anangel Odyssey	Grc	2006	87,485	171,660	289	45	14	bbu	
9111955	Anangel Omonia	Grc	1996	38,859	73,519	225	32	14	bbu	
9039640	Anangel Pride	Grc	1993	81,569	161,643	280	45	13	bbu	
9347176	Anangel Prosperity	Grc	2006	88,853	174,240	289	45	14	bbu	

Agelef Shipping Co. (Anangel Maritime Services) : ANANGEL ARGONAUT : *ARO*

Agelef Shipping Co. (Anangel Maritime Services) : ANANGEL SEAFARER : *ARO*

IMO#	name	flag	year	grt	dwt	loa	bm	kts	type	former names
9345764	Anangel Sailor	Grc	2006	87,050	171,681	289	45	14	bbu	
9434371	Anangel Seafarer	Mlt	2011	94,082	179,754	292	45	14	bbu	
9004786	Anangel Shagang	Grc	1992	154,532	277,218	328	57	15	bor	ex Astro Leon-09, Ambon-00; (conv tcr-09)
9455545	Anangel Sky	Grc	2011	61,504	114,078	250	43	15	bbu	
9039652	Anangel Solidarity	Grc	1993	81,569	161,545	280	44	13	bbu	
9045560	Anangel Splendour	Grc	1993	81,120	161,643	280	45	13	bbu	
9455557	Anangel Sun	Grc	2011	61,504	114,078	250	43	15	bbu	
9439060	Anangel Transporter	Grc	2010	89,891	179,718	292	45	14	bbu	
9434395	Anangel Vigour	Grc	2012	91,566	180,391	292	45	14	bbu	
9440332	Anangel Virtue	Grc	2012	91,566	180,391	292	45	14	bbu	
9332951	Anangel Vision	Grc	2007	87,485	171,810	289	45	14	bbu	
9458688	Anangel Voyager	Grc	2010	89,891	179,718	292	45	14	bbu	
9581708	Anangel Zenith	Grc	2013	63,898	114,500				bbu	
8812667	Anangel Zhongte	Grc	1989	138,648	246,732	321	57	15	bor	ex Astro Lupus-09, Navix Seibu-00; (conv tcr-09)
9000986	Ore Sudbury	Grc	1992	154,552	276,599	328	57	15	bor	ex Astro Libra-10, Irian-00; (conv tcr-10)
9286803	Pioneer	Grc	2004	87,050	171,681	289	45	15	bbu	

newbuildings:

Maran Tankers Management Inc., Greece

Funnel: *Light blue with yellow sun symbol on dark blue disc on broad light blue band.* **Hull:** *Black with red boot-topping.*
History: *Founded 1992 as Kristen Navigation Inc being renamed in 2009.* **Web:** *www.agelef.co.uk*

IMO#	name	flag	year	grt	dwt	loa	bm	kts	type	former names
9120944	Astro Antares	Grc	1996	53,074	98,875	248	43	15	tcr	
9122916	Astro Arcturus	Grc	1997	53,074	98,805	248	43	15	tcr	
9237072	Astro Challenge	Grc	2002	157,878	299,222	332	58	15	tcr	ex Maia-04, I/a Uvas
9389253	Astro Chloe	Grc	2009	158,327	320,000	333	60	15	tcr	
9235244	Astro Chorus	Grc	2001	159,016	305,704	332	58	16	tcr	ex Zeeland-03
9280873	Astro Perseus	Grc	2004	80,620	159,116	274	48	15	tcr	
9280885	Astro Phoenix	Grc	2004	80,620	159,055	274	48	15	tcr	
9281151	Astro Polaris	Grc	2004	80,620	159,074	274	48	15	tcr	
9235725	Astro Saturn	Grc	2003	57,022	105,166	248	43	-	tcr	
9235713	Astro Sculptor	Grc	2003	57,022	105,109	248	43	-	tco	
9120932	Astro Sirius	Grc	1996	53,074	98,805	248	43	15	tco	
9389265	Caesar	Mlt	2009	158,327	318,441	333	60	15	tcr	ex Astro Caesar-09
9257149	Elizabeth I. A.	Grc	2004	153,911	306,229	332	58		tcr	ex Elizabeth I. Angelicoussi-09
9147435	Maran Altair	Grc	1997	53,074	98,879	248	43	15	tco	ex Astro Altair-09
9414022	Maran Atlas	Grc	2009	56,957	105,096	244	42	15	tco	
9171448	Maran Callisto	Grc	1999	157,833	299,167	332	58	15	tcr	ex Astro Callisto-09, Picardie-03
9330563	Maran Canopus	Grc	2007	158,970	320,472	333	60	15	tcr	ex Astro Canopus-09
9174660	Maran Capella	Mlt	1998	79,714	159,713	274	48	15	tcr	ex Astro Capella-09
9389019	Maran Capricorn	Grc	2008	158,970	320,513	333	60	15	tcr	ex Astro Capricorn-09
9240512	Maran Carina	Grc	2003	153,911	306,314	332	58	15	tcr	ex Astro Carina-09
9257137	Maran Cassiopeia	Grc	2003	82,982	158,553	274	48	15	tcr	ex Astro Cassiopeia-09
9194127	Maran Castor	Grc	2001	153,911	306,344	332	58	16	tcr	ex Astro Castor-09
9073050	Maran Centaurus	Grc	1995	156,565	300,294	332	58	15	tcr	ex Astro Centaurus-09, Mindoro-00
9252333	Maran Corona	Grc	2003	153,911	306,092	332	58	16	tcr	ex Astro Corona-09

Agelef Shipping Co. (Maran Gas Maritime Inc.) : MARAN GAS CORONIS : *ARO*

IMO#	name	flag	year	grt	dwt	loa	bm	kts	type	former names
9227479	Maran Cygnus	Grc	2001	153,911	306,344	332	58	16	tcr	ex Astro Cygnus-09
9042063	Maran Lyra	Grc	1995	153,429	286,120	328	57	15	tcr	ex Astro Lyra-09, Flores-00
9402914	Maran Penelope	Grc	2009	79,890	158,267	274	48	16	tcr	
9399507	Maran Plato	Grc	2009	79,890	158,267	274	48	16	tcr	l/a Astro Plato
9402926	Maran Poseidon	Grc	2009	79,890	158,267	274	48	16	tcr	
9402902	Maran Pythia	Grc	2009	79,890	158,267	274	48	16	tcr	l/a Astro Pythia
9414034	Maran Sagitta	Grc	2009	56,957	105,071	244	38	16	tco	
9012905	Maran Taurus	Grc	1993	160,347	301,686	332	58	16	tcr	ex Astro Taurus-09, Eagle-07
9216705	Maria A. Angelicoussis	Grc	2000	153,911	306,283	332	58	15	tcr	
9413834	Patroclus	Grc	2009	79,890	158,267	274	48	16	tcr	ex Astro Patroclus-09
9412103	Pegasus	Grc	2009	79,890	158,267	274	48	16	tcr	ex Astro Pegasus-09
9412098	Phaethon	Grc	2009	79,890	158,267	274	48	16	tcr	ex Astro Phaethon-09

newbuildings: 3 x 319,000dwt tankers (2013/14)

Maran Gas Maritime Inc., Greece

Funnel: *Blue with blue 'M', 'G' and flame symbol on broad white band.* **Hull**: *Brown with red boot-topping.* **History**: *Founded 2003.*
Web: *www.marangas.com*

IMO#	name	flag	year	grt	dwt	loa	bm	kts	type	former names
9324435	Al Jassasiya (st)	Grc	2007	97,496	84,554	285	43	19	lng	145,800 m³
9302499	Rasgas Asclepius	Grc	2005	97,496	84,659	285	43	19	lng	145,800 m³ ex Maran Gas Asclepius-10
9331048	Maran Gas Coronis	Grc	2007	97,491	84,823	285	43	19	lng	145,800 m³
8320386	Simaisma (st)	Grc	2006	97,496	84,500	285	43	19	lng	145,800 m³
9308431	Umm Bab	Grc	2005	97,496	84,659	285	43	19	lng	145,800 m³

newbuildings: options taken up for 2 x 160,000m³ lng tankers with Hyundai for 2014/2015 delivery. 7 x 155,000m³ (Daewoo) 2013/15, 4 x lng tankers (Hyundai Samho) 2013/14
lng tankers up to 30% owned by Qatar Gas Transport Co and on 20-year charter to Ras Laffan Qatar-Mobil QM Gas project formed by subsidiaries of Qatar Petroleum and ExxonMobil.

Aggregate Industries U.K. Ltd.   U.K.

Funnel: *Blue with white Aggregate Industries logo above white 'YEOMAN' and 'GLENSANDA'.* **Hull**: *Red or black with red boot-topping.* **History**: *Founded 1923 as Foster Yeoman Ltd and acquired by Aggregate Industries UK Ltd in 2006.*
Web: *www.aggregate-uk.com*

IMO#	name	flag	year	grt	dwt	loa	bm	kts	type	former names
7422881	Yeoman Bank	Lbr	1982	24,870	38,997	205	27	15	bsd	ex Salmonpool-90
8912297	Yeoman Bontrup	Bhs	1991	55,695	96,725	250	38	15	bsd	ex Western Bridge-02
8912302	Yeoman Bridge	Bhs	1991	55,695	96,772	250	38	15	bsd	ex Eastern Bridge-00

Christian F. Ahrenkiel GmbH & Co.   Germany

Funnel: *Buff or buff with houseflag on blue band, or charterers colours.* **Hull**: *Black, dark blue, green or grey with red boot-topping.*
History: *Formed 1950 having previously being on the board of Hapag and his father having owned ships since 1910. Tankreederei Ahrenkiel founded in 1971, now United Chemical Transport (UCT) joint venture. Ahrenkiel Liner Services (ALS) formed 1982. In September 2012 entered into a joint marketing agreement with MPC for containership operations.*
Web: *www.ahrenkiel.net*

IMO#	name	flag	year	grt	dwt	loa	bm	kts	type	former names
9178276	Anglia *	Lbr	1999	26,047	30,703	196	30	20	ucc	2,262 teu; ex Columbus Australia-05, Cherokee-03, Panthermax-02, CanMar Supreme-02, Panther Max-01

Christian F. Ahrenkiel GmbH & Co. : AS ANDALUCIA : *ARO*

IMO#	name	flag	year	grt	dwt	loa	bm	kts	type	former names
9178288	Aquitania *	Lbr	2000	26,044	31,000	196	30	21	ucc	2,262 teu; ex Maersk Aquitania-03, Corrado-03, Lion Max-02
9204972	AS Alicantia *	Lbr	2000	26,047	30,554	196	30	20	ucc	2,262 teu; ex Safmarine Illovo-10, Alicantia-05, Commander-03, Jaguar Max-02
9204984	AS Andalusia *	Lbr	2001	26,047	30,703	196	30	20	ucc	2262 teu; ex Marfret Provence-10, AS Andalusia-08, Safmarine Mono-08, Andalusia-04, Centurion-03, Puma Max-02
9178290	AS Asturia *	Lbr	2000	26,047	31,000	196	30	20	ucc	2262 teu; ex CSAV Rio Rapel-09, Asturia-04, Comanche-03, Ocelot Max-02
9309409	AS Carelia *	Lbr	2006	28,592	39,374	222	30	22	ucc	2,824 teu: ex CMA CGM Tulip-11
9309411	AS Caria *	Lbr	2006	28,592	39,418	222	30	22	ucc	2,824 teu: ex Maersk Jakarta-11, Caria-06
9241205	AS Carinthia *	Lbr	2003	28.596	39,421	222	30	22	ucc	2,824 teu: ex CMA CGM Galilee-09, Norasia Rigel-07, Carinthia-04
9315824	AS Catalania	Lbr	2006	28,592	39,418	222	30	22	ucc	2,824 teu: ex Maersk Jeddah-11, Catalania-06
9315812	AS Cypria	Lbr	2006	28,592	39,426	222	30	22	ucc	2,824 teu: ex CMA CGM Orchid-11
9485887	AS Elbia	Lbr	2011	23,443	34,394	180	30	14	bbu	
9485899	AS Elenia	Lbr	2011	23,443	34,421	180	30	14	bbu	
9485930	AS Elysia	Lbr	2012	23,443	34,467	180	30	14	bbu	
9358436	AS Jutlandia *	Lbr	2006	35,564	44,174	223	32	22	ucc	3,398 teu; ex Johannesburg-10, MOL Will-08, Johannesburg-06
9164536	AS Oceania *	Lbr	1999	25,202	43,760	182	30	14	tco	ex St. Katharinen-12
9340477	AS Octavia **	Phl	2007	11,570	19,983	145	24	16	tco	ex Bow Octavia-11
9340489	AS Olivia **	Phl	2007	11,570	19,881	145	24	16	tco	ex Bow Omaria-11
9363819	AS Omaria **	Phl	2007	11,570	19,974	145	24	16	tco	ex Bow Omaria-11
9340439	AS Ophelia **	Phl	2006	11,561	19,991	145	24	16	tco	ex Bow Ophelia-11
9363821	AS Orelia **	Phl	2008	11,570	19,971	145	24	16	tco	ex Bow Orelia-11
9216729	AS Savonia *	Mhl	2000	17,167	21,614	169	27	20	ucc	ex Bahamian Express-08
9182631	AS Saxonia ***	Lbr	1999	19,131	25,414	189	27	20	ucc	1,716 teu: ex Delmas Cameroun-11, Saxonia-06, P&O Nedlloyd San Francisco-05, Saxonia-99
9208638	AS Scandia	Lbr	2000	19,131	24,973	189	27	22	ucc	1,716 teu: ex CMA CGM Puma-08, Scandia-03, P&O Nedlloyd Scandia-02, Scandia-02
9208356	AS Scotia	Lbr	2000	19,131	25,414	189	27	20	ucc	1,716 teu: ex Turin Express-09, Scotia-06, P&O Nedlloyd Scotia-02, Scotia-01
9453250	AS Valdivia	Lbr	2011	32,929	56,779	190	32	14	bbu	
9453212	AS Valentia	Lbr	2009	32,929	56,785	190	32	14	bbu	
9453248	AS Valeria	Lbr	2011	32,929	56,808	190	32	14	bbu	
9453262	AS Varesia	Lbr	2011	32,929	56,738	190	32	14	bbu	
9497414	AS Venetia	Lbr	2010	32,929	56,755	190	32	14	bbu	
9442641	AS Victoria	Lbr	2009	32,929	56,785	190	32	14	bbu	
9453236	AS Vincentia	Lbr	2010	32,929	56,785	190	32	14	bbu	
9453224	AS Virginia	Lbr	2009	32,929	56,799	190	32	14	bbu	
9253026	Cardonia *	Lbr	2003	27,779	39,383	222	30	22	ucc	2,826 teu: ex CMA CGM Ukraine-06, Cardonia-03
9253038	Carpathia *	Lbr	2003	27,779	39,443	222	30	22	ucc	2,826 teu: ex CMA CGM Greece-06, Carpathia-04
9241190	Cimbria *	Lbr	2002	27,779	39,358	222	30	22	ucc	2,826 teu
9485899	Confiance	Lbr	2011	23,443	34,421	180	30	14	bbu	ex AS Elenia-11
9253014	Cordelia *	Lbr	2003	27,779	40,878	222	30	22	ucc	2,826 teu:
9258466	Danubia	Lbr	2004	38,975	68,524	229	32	15	tco	ex Ocean Principal-05, Tavropos-04
9485904	Etoile	Lbr	2011	23,443	34,420	180	30	14	bbu	ex AS Eldoria-11
9142980	Normannia	Lbr	1997	24,987	42,648	183	31	14	bbu	ex Batu-07
9294513	Nildutch Durban	Lbr	2006	27,100	34,496	210	30	22	ucc	2,600 teu: ex AS Palatia-11, CMA CGM Oceano-08, Palatia-08, MOL Supremacy-08, Palatia-06
9294525	Niledutch Guangzhou	Lbr	2006	27,100	34,495	210	30	22	ucc	2,600 teu: ex Patria I-10, MOL Sunrise-08, Patria-06
9182643	Samaria	Deu	2000	19,131	25,360	189	27	20	ucc	1,716 teu: ex Calapadria-08, Samaria-04, P&O Nedlloyd Samaria-03, Samaria-00
9362712	Sevillia	Lbr	2008	21,019	25,884	180	28	20	ucc	1,795 teu: l/dn Manchester Strait
9430935	Sicilia	Lbr	2008	21,018	25,927	180	28	20	ucc	1,795 teu: l/dn Montreal Strait

newbuildings: two further 35,000 dwt bulk carriers due 2013 (AS Escadia and AS Estancia).
managed by Ahrenkiel Shipmanagement GmbH & Co KG (founded 1991 as Constantia Schiffahrts GmbH to 1999) or * managed for FHH Fonds Haus Hamburg GmbH & Co KG, ** Victoria Ship Management or *** for HCI Capital AG.

Allseas Marine S.A.   Greece

Funnel: Blue with two narrow white bands surrounding broad red band containing two white intertwined diamonds. or charterers colours. **Hull:** Maroon or grey with red boot-topping. **History:** Founded 2000, as a development of Eurocarriers S.A (founded 1993).
Web: www.allseas.gr

IMO#	name	flag	year	grt	dwt	loa	bm	kts	type	former names
9423035	Box Trader	Lbr	2010	36,087	42,483	229	32	23	ucc	3,414 teu

IMO#	name	flag	year	grt	dwt	loa	bm	kts	type	former names
9418377	Box Voyager	Lbr	2010	36,087	42,454	229	32	23	ucc	3,414 teu: l/d Buxpower
9184835	Calm Seas	Mhl	1999	38,468	74,047	225	32	14	bbu	ex Alterego-06, Little Athena-05, World Romance-05
9330991	CMA CGM Kingfish	Lbr	2007	54,309	65,974	294	32	25	ucc	5,042 teu
9330989	CMA CGM Marlin	Lbr	2007	54,309	65,949	294	32	25	ucc	5,042 teu
9305099	Coral Seas	Lbr	2006	40,485	74,476	225	32	14	bbu	ex Anny Petrakis-07
9169380	Deep Seas	Cym	1999	38,560	72,891	225	32	14	bbu	ex Ince Istanbul-06, Angel-05
9244219	Diamond Seas	Lbr	2001	38,846	74,274	225	32	14	bbu	ex Sundance-07, Panaxia-07, Lake Harmony-05
9465796	Dream Seas	Lbr	2009	40,170	75,151	225	32	14	bbu	ex Iorana-10
9394832	Friendly Seas	Lbr	2008	32,415	58,779	190	32	14	bbu	ex Nikolas II-08
9305104	Golden Seas	Lbr	2006	40,485	74,475	225	32	14	bbu	ex Iolcos Destiny-07
9491252	Kavala Seas	Lbr	2011	33,044	57,000	190	32	14	bbu	ex Minero Tres-11
9205847	Kind Seas	Mhl	1999	37,689	72,493	225	32	14	bbu	ex Miltiadis II-06 , Ikan Bawal-04
9252096	Maersk Diadema	Lbr	2006	52,701	58,281	292	32	24	ucc	4,546 teu: ex MSC Siena-12, Maersk Diadema-08, Charlotte Wulff-06
9400069	Maule	Lbr	2010	75,752	81,002	306	40	25	ucc	6,589 teu
9275646	MSC Emma	Mhl	2003	54,881	68,120	294	32	24	ucc	5,048 teu
9108178	OOCL China	Hkg	1996	66,046	67,625	276	41	24	ucc	5,344 teu
9108166	OOCL Hong Kong	Hkg	1996	66,046	67,637	276	40	24	ucc	5,344 teu
9491238	Paros Seas	Lbr	2011	33,044	57,000	189	32	14	bbu	ex Chungo Tres-11
9368838	Pearl Seas	Mhl	2006	40,485	74,483	225	32	14	bbu	ex Cap Bona-07, F.D. Mariano-07
9589097	Precious Seas	Lbr	2012	24,196	37,205	190	28	14	bbu	
9589085	Prosperous Seas	Lbr	2012	24,196	37,294	190	28	14	bbu	
9301146	Sapphire Seas	Lbr	2005	31,144	53,702	190	31	14	bbu	ex Kandy-07, l/a Filia Gem
9221633	Voula Seas	Lbr	2002	17,431	28,495	170	27	14	bbu	ex Destino Dos-12

newbuildings: 2 x 4,800 teu container ships and 2 x 37,200dwt bulkers [Zhejiang Quhua, yd 656/7 (Q4 2013)] [612/625 (Q4 2012)]

Alpha Ship GmbH   Germany

Funnel: Green with wide light green and narrow light blue 'darts' on broad cream band or charterers colours. **Hull:** Green, brown or red with red boot-topping. **History:** Founded 1992 as Jan R. Freese, later Reederei J. Freese & Partner to 1994.
Web: www.alphaship.de

9225421	Aries	Mhl	2000	23,722	29,240	194	28	21	ucc	1,804 teu: ex Maersk Itajai-08, Aries-01
9127526	AS Castor	Mhl	1997	14,241	18,445	159	24	19	ucc	1,129 teu: ex Cap Matatula-08, Castor-05, TMM Guadalajara-99, Castor-97
9127502	AS Mars	Mhl	1996	14,241	18,449	159	24	19	ucc	1,129 teu: ex Mars-07, Safmarine Emonti-01, Mars-00, Sea Viking-99, CMBT Mars-97, CGM La Bourdonnais-97, Mars-96

Allseas Marine S.A. : BOX TRADER : *Chris Brooks*

IMO#	name	flag	year	grt	dwt	loa	bm	kts	type	former names
9134581	AS Pegasus	Mhl	1997	23,722	29,229	194	28	21	ucc	1,804 teu: ex Pegasus-07
9193719	AS Poseidon	Mhl	1999	23,722	29,240	194	28	21	ucc	1,804 teu: ex Safmarine Memling-09, SCL Memling-02, Poseidon-99
9127514	AS Venus	Mhl	1996	14,241	18,400	159	24	19	ucc	1,129 teu: ex Venus-07, DAL Karoo-02, Venus-00, CMBT Encounter-97, Venus-96
9127784	Nadir	Mhl	1997	21,199	25,039	178	28	21	ucc	1,606 teu: ex Maersk Hong Kong-10, Nadir-98
9163192	Neptun	Mhl	1998	23,722	29,233	194	28	21	ucc	1,804 teu: ex CMA CGM Cortes-12, Cap Vincent-06, Neptun-02, Kota Perdana-00, Neptun-99
9127796	Orion	Mlt	1997	21,199	25,107	178	28	21	ucc	1,606 teu: ex Maersk Lima-99, Orion-98, TNX Mercury-98, l/a Orion
9193680	Pluto	Mhl	1999	23,722	29,210	194	28	21	ucc	1,804 teu:
9127538	Pollux	Mhl	1997	14,241	18,400	159	24	18	ucc	1,129 teu: ex Lykes Pelican-01, Pollux-00
9127801	Sirius	Mhl	1998	21,199	25,107	183	28	21	ucc	1,606 teu:
9134593	Taurus	Mhl	1998	23,722	29,260	194	28	21	ucc	1,804 teu: ex CMA CGM Castilla-09, Cap Victor-06, Columbus Waikato-06, Taurus-02, Kota Perabu-01, Taurus-99
9163207	Uranus	Mhl	1999	23,722	29,210	194	28	21	ucc	1,804 teu: ex Cap van Diemen-09, Uranus-06, Alianca Antuerpia-03, Uranus-01
9225433	Vega	Mhl	2000	23,722	29,240	194	28	21	ucc	1,804 teu: ex Maersk Valparaiso-08, Maersk Wellington-01, Maersk Itajai-01, Vega-00
9127813	Zenit	Mhl	1998	21,199	24,049	178	28	21	ucc	1,606 teu: ex MOL Universe-12, Safmarine Amazon-08, Maersk Wellington-01, Zenit-98

managed by Alpha Shipmanagement GmbH & Co KG

Atlanship S.A. Switzerland

Funnel: *White with narrow red diagonal line aft of blue triagle.* **Hull:** *Stone or white with red boot-topping.* **History:** *Founded 1982.*
Web: *www.atlanship.nl*

8407931	Orange Blossom	Lbr	1985	9,984	15,108	145	22	-	tfj	
9228370	Orange Sky	Lbr	2000	22,063	26,863	172	27	14	tfj	l/a May Oldendorff-01 (conv. bbu-02)
9564384	Orange Star	Lbr	2011	34,432	35,750	190	32		tfj	
9342580	Orange Sun	Lbr	2007	33,070	43,420	205	32	17	tfj	
9057123	Orange Wave	Lbr	1993	13,444	16,700	157	26	18	tfj	

Seereederei Baco-Liner GmbH Germany

Funnel: *Black with yellow/black 'bl' symbol on broad white band.* **Hull:** *Blue with white 'BACO-LINER', red boot-topping.*
History: *Founded 1979 and took over RMS Afrika Schiffahrts GmbH in 1992.* **Web:** *www.baco-liner.de*

7812115	Baco-Liner 1	Lbr	1979	22,345	21,801	204	29	15	ubc	
7904621	Baco-Liner 2	Lbr	1980	22,345	21,801	201	29	14	ubc	

Alpha Ship GmbH : AS VENUS : *Chris Brooks*

IMO#	name	flag	year	grt	dwt	loa	bm	kts	type	former names

BBG-Bremer Bereederungs GmbH & Co. KG　　　Germany

Funnel: White with blue 'BBG' on white diamond on blue band or charterers colours. **Hull:** *Blue or black with red boot-topping.*
History: *Founded 1984 as Frigomaris Shipping GmbH, taking over Ganymed Schiffahrts in 1985, renamed Frigomaris Reefer Schiffahrt to 1990, then Ganymed Shipping GmbH to 2003.* **Web:** *www.bbg-shipmanagement.com*

IMO#	name	flag	year	grt	dwt	loa	bm	kts	type	former names
9057496	Conti Chiwan	Lbr	1994	42,323	44,510	242	32	22	ucc	3,500 teu: ex Maersk Itea-09, P&O Nedlloyd Shanghai-05, MSC Munich-04, Norasia Hong Kong-02, MSC Houston-99, Norasia Hong Kong-98
9503275	Conti Flint	Lbr	2012	33,044	57,000	190	32	14	bbu	
9503287	Conti Fuchsit	Lbr	2012	33,055	57,000	190	32	14	bbu	
9476525	Conti Jade	Lbr	2012	51,265	93,252	229	38	15	bbu	
9476537	Conti Japsis	Lbr	2012	51,265	93,266	229	38	15	bbu	
9452634	Conti Peridot	Lbr	2011	33,036	57,001	190	32	14	bbu	
9452646	Conti Pyrit	Lbr	2011	33,036	56,956	190	32	14	bbu	
9452660	Conti Larimar	Lbr	2011	33,036	57,000	190	32	14	bbu	
9452658	Conti Lapislazuli	Lbr	2011	33,036	57,001	190	32	14	bbu	
9487653	Conti Opal	Lbr	2010	33,044	57,000	190	32	14	bbu	
9473274	Conti Saphir *	Lbr	2010	41,074	75,200	225	32	14	bbu	
9473315	Conti Selenit *	Lbr	2010	41,074	75,200	225	32	14	bbu	
9473327	Conti Serpentin *	Lbr	2011	41,074	75,200	225	32	14	bbu	
9113642	Conti Singa *	Deu	1996	42,336	44,510	242	32	22	ucc	3,500 teu: ex MSC Switzerland-05, Norasia Singa-02
9473341	Conti Spinell	Lbr	2011	41,074	75,200	225	32	14	bbu	
9519286	Pos Achat *	Lbr	2010	32,987	56,969	190	32	14	bbu	
9519298	Pos Alexandrit *	Lbr	2010	32,987	57,015	190	32	14	bbu	
9519303	Pos Almandin	Lbr	2010	32,987	56,988	190	32	14	bbu	
9519315	Pos Amazonit	Lbr	2010	32,987	57,015	190	32	14	bbu	
9519339	Pos Amethyst	Lbr	2011	32,987	56,889	190	32	14	bbu	
9519341	Pos Ametrin	Lbr	2010	32,987	56,855	190	32	14	bbu	
9551674	Pos Aquamarin	Lbr	2011	32,987	56,969	190	32	14	bbu	
9551686	Pos Aragonit	Lbr	2012	32,987	56,757	190	32	14	bbu	
9551698	Pos Aventurin	Lbr	2012	32,987	56,778	190	32	14	bbu	
9551703	Pos Azurit	Lbr	2012	32,987	56,771	190	32	14	bbu	
9474620	Pos Tansanit	Lbr	2011	51,195	92,776	229	38	15	bbu	c/a Conti Tansanit
9474632	Pos Topas	Lbr	2011	51,195	92,655	229	38	15	bbu	ex Conti Topas
9474618	Pos Tuerkis	Lbr	2012	51,195	92,759	229	38	15	bbu	l/a Conti Tuerkis
9474644	Pos Turmalin	Lbr	2012	51,195	92,750	229	38	15	bbu	l/a Conti Turmalin

* managed for Conti Reederei (Conti Holding GmbH)

Belships ASA　　　Norway

Funnel: Blue with blue 'S' inside 'C' above blue anchor within narrow blue ring on white disc. **Hull:** *Blue, dark grey or red with red boot-topping.* **History:** *Founded 1918 as Christen Smith & Co and 1926 as Skibs A/S Belships.* **Web:** *www.belships.com*

IMO#	name	flag	year	grt	dwt	loa	bm	kts	type	former names
9254836	Bulk Avenir *	Nis	2002	27,989	50,399	190	32	14	bbu	ex Sun Master-07
9140530	Super Challenge *	Pan	1996	17,977	28,581	172	27	14	bbu	ex IVS Super Challenge-03, Super Challenge-02
9490648	Belstar	Sgp	2009	32,837	58,018	190	32	14	bbu	
9490703	Belnor	Sgp	2010	32,837	58,018	190	32	14	bbu	
9490818	Belocean	Sgp	2011	32,839	58,018	190	32	14	bbu	

*owned by Belships Supramax Singapore : * managed by Belships Tianjin Shipmanagement, time-chartered until 2012*
Jointly owns Elkem Chartering, operating 13 'handymax' bulkers on time charter

Bergshav Shipholding AS　　　Norway

Funnel: White with white 'B' symbol on broad red band, separated by narrow white band from black top. **Hull:** *Brown with black 'BERGSHAV', red or grey boot-topping.* **History:** *Formed 1988 as Bergshav A/S and company now over 60% owned by Frontline.*
Web: *www.bergshav.com*

IMO#	name	flag	year	grt	dwt	loa	bm	kts	type	former names
9035266	Bregen (2)	Nis	1994	10,012	13,941	150	21	13	tco	
9307346	Larvik	Bhs	2006	35,711	61,213	213	32	14	tco	
8709133	City of Antwerp *	Pan	1989	41,353	12,761	183	31	19	mve	ex Hyundai No. 203-12, Atlantic Beauty-92, Hyundai No.203-90
9306641	Ocean Dignity †	Iom	2006	22,184	34,663	171	27	14	tco	
9167162	Ocean Quest †	Iom	2000	22,181	34,999	171	27	14	tco	ex Maersk Rochester-05
9306665	Ocean Spirit †	Iom	2005	22,184	34,603	171	27	14	tco	
9336402	SPT Challenger	Bhs	2007	57,657	105,786	241	42	15	tcr	
9337397	SPT Champion	Bhs	2007	57,657	105,786	241	42	15	tcr	
9336414	SPT Conqueror	Bhs	2007	57,657	105,786	241	42	15	tcr	
9336426	SPT Crusader	Bhs	2007	57,657	105,850	241	42	15	tcr	

* owned by Berytus Maritime, Lebanon. managed by Bergshav Management AS or † bare-boat chartered to Roxana Shipping, Greece (to 2016)

Bidsted & Co. A/S   Norway

Funnel: *Buff with large blue 'B' or lack with broad red band with large black 'D'.* **Hull:** *Black or red wih red boot-toping.*
History: *Formed1940.* **Web:** www.bidsted.dk

IMO#	name	flag	year	grt	dwt	loa	bm	kts	type	former names
9044023	Adriatic ID	Hkg	1994	13,712	22,059	158	25	14	bbu	Dorthe Oldendorff-09
9125918	Arctic ID	Pan	1996	17,209	28,251	170	27	16	bbu	ex Lake Joy-07, Solar Oceania-05, Sun Dream-02
9180011	Baltic ID	Hkg	1997	16,764	28,545	169	27	15	bbu	ex Castle Peak-07, Atlantic Island-05
9146807	Bering ID	Hkg	1997	17,879	28,611	172	27	15	bbu	ex Pitt Island-08, Citrus Island-05
9228992	Bianco Bulker	Pan	2001	30,008	52,027	190	32	14	bbu	
9284489	Bianco Dan	Pan	2004	30,619	55,628	190	32	14	bbu	ex Pescadores Bulker-06
9170286	Bianco ID	Mlt	1998	36,356	70,521	225	32	14	bbu	ex Bandai-05
9278739	Bianco Venture *	Pan	2004	19,828	33,773	175	28	14	bbu	
9608702	Bianco Olivia Bulker *	Mlt	2013	20,920		180	28	13	bbu	
9608697	Bianco Victoria Bulker *	Mlt	2012	20,928	32,178	180	28	13	bbu	
9124146	Caribbean ID *	Hkg	1996	18,108	27,940	169	27	14	bbu	ex Mount Cook-07, Shinyo Challenge-06, Admire-03
9515682	Danship Bulker *	Mlt	2009	17,025	28,291	169	27	14	bbu	
9520998	ID Black Sea *	Pan	2009	17,018	28,367	169	27	14	bbu	
8812631	ID Bulker *	Pan	1989	17,126	26,970	174	28	14	bbu	ex Ever Forest-01, Pine Forest-95
9624328	ID Copenhagen	Pan	2012	17,027	28,206	169	27	14	bbu	
9114610	ID Harbour *	Pan	1995	17,879	28,760	173	27	14	bbu	ex Oak Harbour-07, Wold Express-04
9223825	ID Mermaid	Bhs	2001	17,944	27,105	178	26	14	bbu	ex Clipper Mermaid-10
9519195	ID North Sea *	Mlt	2009	17,018	28,367	169	27	14	bbu	
9052604	ID Red Sea	Hkg	1994	38,267	70,029	225	32	14	bbu	ex Cedar 2-09, Freja Divine-09, Endeavour II-08, Delray-07, Bulk Phoenix-06, SD Triumph-06, Fareast Triumph-99
9104603	ID Tide	Hkg	1995	25,968	45,406	186	30	14	bbu	ex Nordtide-09, Western Tide-04
9111369	Idas Bulker *	Pan	1995	16,418	27,321	166	27	14	bbu	ex Skaw Bulker-03
9085572	Ideal Bulker *	Hkg	1994	16,721	28,460	169	27	14	bbu	ex J. Lucky-07, Diamond Bulker-03
9464546	Idship Bulker *	Hkg	2008	17,018	28,361	169	27	14	bbu	
9139971	Marine Bulker *	Pan	1996	17,542	28,322	177	26	14	bbu	ex Marine Island-06
9104196	Mediterranean ID	Hkg	1994	17,429	28,475	170	27	14	bbu	ex Amazonia-08, Apollo Bay-05, Clio Pacific-03, Oregon Rainbow III-01
9079169	Nordic Barents	Hkg	1994	27,078	43,732	190	31	14	bbu	ex Cedar 4-09, Izara Princess-09, Ice Power II-08 , Baffin-08 , Federal Baffin-05
9079157	Nordic Bothnia	Hkg	1995	27,078	43,706	190	31	14	bbu	ex ID Bothnia-09, Cedar 5-09, Moon Dancer-09, Ice Trader II-08, Franklin-08, Federal Franklin-05
9170298	Obelix Bulker *	HKg	1998	36,356	70,529	225	32	14	bbu	ex Great Pescadores-09, Babitonga-05 Great Pescadores-99
9106704	Pacific ID *	Hkg	1995	17,075	27,860	177	26	14	bbu	ex Patagonia-07, Tauroa Point-04, Atlantic Bulker-03
9057458	Pioneer Atlantic	Pan	1998	37,978	69,146	225	32	14	bbu	Cedar-1-09, Ice Dreamer-09, Navigator II-08, Foremost-07
9055620	Pioneer Pacific	Hkg	1994	23,975	70,003	225	32	14	bbu	ex Cedar 3-09, Dawn Voyager-09 , Endurance II-08 , Estepona-07, Bulk Patriot-06, CIC Horizon-06, Fareast Victory-00
9105396	Scan Bulker *	Pan	1995	16,446	27,308	166	27	14	bbu	ex General Pescadores-97
9111357	Spring Bulker *	Pan	1995	16,418	27,321	166	27	14	bbu	ex Spring Wave-06

* on charter to Lauritzen Bulkers

Blue Star Holding   Germany

E. R. Schiffahrt GmbH & Cie. KG

Funnel: *Black with white 'ER' on broad blue band edged with narrow white bands or charterers colours.* **Hull:** *Dark blue with pink boot-topping or charterers colours.* **History:** *Both companies formed 1998.* **Web:** www.nordcapital.com or www.er-ship.com

IMO#	name	flag	year	grt	dwt	loa	bm	kts	type	former names
9231236	APL Canada	Lbr	2001	65,792	68,025	277	40	26	ucc	5,762 teu: ex E.R. Canada-01
9231248	APL India	Lbr	2002	65,792	68,025	277	40	26	ucc	5,762 teu: ex E.R. India-02
9318046	CMA CGM Carmen	Lbr	2006	91,649	100,680	334	43	25	ucc	8,204 teu: l/a E.R. Tokyo
9305491	CMA CGM Don Carlos	Lbr	2006	91,649	101,496	334	43	25	ucc	8,204 teu: l/a E.R. Toulouse
9305506	CMA CGM Don Giovanni	Lbr	2006	91,649	100,680	334	43	25	ucc	8,204 teu: ex E.R. Toronto-06
9314973	CMA CGM Lavender	Lbr	2006	27,779	39,418	222	30	23	ucc	2,824 teu: ex E.R. Montpellier-06
9465318	CMA CGM Margrit	Lbr	2012	141,635	140,700	366	48	24	ucc	13,100 teu; ex MSC Margrit-12, l/a E.R. Castor
9314961	CMA CGM Mimosa	Lbr	2006	27,779	39,200	222	30	23	ucc	2,824 teu: ex E.R. Monaco-06
9305465	Cosco China	Deu	2005	91,649	101,570	335	43	25	ucc	8,204 teu: l/a E.R. Tianan
9305477	Cosco Germany	Deu	2006	91,649	101,532	335	43	25	ucc	8,204 teu: l/a E.R. Tianshan

IMO#	name	flag	year	grt	dwt	loa	bm	kts	type	former names
9285677	Cosco Long Beach	Lbr	2004	83,133	93,572	300	43	25	ucc	7,488 teu: I/a E.R. Shenzhen
9305489	Cosco Napoli	Deu	2006	91,649	101,491	335	43	25	ucc	8,204 teu: I/a E.R. Tianping
9285689	Cosco Seattle	Lbr	2004	83,133	93,728	300	43	25	ucc	7,488 teu: I/a E.R. Seattle
9285653	Cosco Shenzen	Lbr	2004	83,133	93,643	300	43	25	ucc	7,488 teu: I/dn E.R. Long Beach
9285691	Cosco Vancouver	Lbr	2004	83,133	93,638	300	43	25	ucc	7,488 teu: I/a E.R. Vancouver
9285665	Cosco Yokohama	Lbr	2004	83,133	93,659	300	43	25	ucc	7,488 teu: I/a E.R. Yokohama
9208021	CSAV Houston	Deu	2000	66,289	66,298	277	40	26	ucc	5,762 teu: ex E.R. Seoul-11, OOCL Malaysia-09, E.R. Seoul-00
9318101	Don Pascuale	Lbr	2007	91,649	101,477	334	43	25	ucc	8,204 teu: ex CMA CGM Don Pascuale-12, MSC Xian-09, I/a E.R. Trieste
9116369	E.R. Albany	Lbr	1996	30,280	35,966	202	32	22	ucc	2,825 teu: ex MacAndrews America-07, CMA CGM Egypt-06, E.R. Albany-04, Rhein-02, Zim Sydney-00
9483217	E.R. Barcelona +	Lbr	2010	32,672	55,783	188	32	14	bbu	
9483243	E.R. Basel	Lbr	2011	32,672	55,800	188	32	14	bbu	
9519066	E.R. Bavaria	Lbr	2010	93,186	179,436	292	45	15	bbu	
9507893	E.R. Bayern	Lbr	2010	93,186	178,978	292	45	15	bbu	
9507520	E.R. Bayonne	Lbr	2010	93,186	178,978	292	45	15	bbu	
9507908	E.R. Beilun	Lbr	2010	93,186	178,979	292	45	15	bbu	
9483188	E.R. Bergamo	Lbr	2009	32,672	55,783	188	32	14	bbu	
9214214	E.R. Berlin	Lbr	2000	66,289	67,660	277	40	26	ucc	5,762 teu: ex OOCL Germany-10, E.R. Berlin-01
9483255	E.R. Bern	Lbr	2011	32,672	55,783	188	32	14	bbu	
9483205	E.R. Bilbao +	Lbr	2010	32,672	55,783	188	32	14	bbu	
9483279	E.R. Bogense	Lbr	2012	32,672	55,783	188	32	14	bbu	
9483190	E.R. Bologna +	Lbr	2009	32,672	55,561	188	32	14	bbu	
9483229	E.R. Bordeaux	Lbr	2010	32,672	55,800	188	32	14	bbu	
9507519	E.R. Borneo	Lbr	2010	93,186	178,978	292	45	15	bbu	
9483267	E.R. Bornholm +	Lbr	2011	32,672	55,800	188	32	14	bbu	
9507881	E.R. Boston	Lbr	2010	93,186	178,978	292	45	15	bbu	
9519078	E.R. Bourgogne	Lbr	2010	93,186	178,906	292	45	15	bbu	
9505833	E.R. Brandenburg	Lbr	2010	93,186	179,436	292	45	15	bbu	
9507532	E.R. Brazil	Lbr	2010	93,186	178,978	292	45	15	bbu	
9426322	E.R. Bremen	Lbr	2003	27,322	34,418	212	30	22	ucc	2,496 teu: ex CCNI Manzanillo-10, Maersk Norfolk-07, E.R. Bremen-03
9239886	E.R. Bremerhaven	Lbr	2002	27,332	33,800	212	30	22	ucc	2,496 teu: ex Safmarine Cunene-12, E.R. Bremerhaven-02
9483231	E.R. Brest +	Lbr	2010	32,672	55,618	188	32	14	bbu	
9507788	E.R. Brighton +	Lbr	2010	32,672	55,783	188	32	14	bbu	

Blue Star Holding (E.R. Schiffahrt) : E.R. BASEL : *Chris Brooks*

IMO#	name	flag	year	grt	dwt	loa	bm	kts	type	former names
9116357	E.R. Brisbane	Lbr	1996	30,280	35,966	202	32	22	ucc	2,825 teu: ex CMA CGM Aegean-11, E.R. Brisbane-03, Pan Crystal-02, Zim Trieste-99, Pan Crystal-98, Hyundai Emerald-98, Zim Trieste-96
9507790	E.R. Bristol +	Lbr	2011	32,672	55,800	188	32		bbu	
9507544	E.R. Buenos Aires	Lbr	2010	93,186	178,978	292	45	15	bbu	
9301433	E.R. Caen	Lbr	2004	26,836	34,289	210	30	21	ucc	2,556 teu: ex CMA CGM Jaguar-09, E.R. Caen-04
9301445	E.R. Calais	Lbr	2005	26,718	34,567	210	30	21	ucc	2,556 teu: ex CMA CGM l'Astrolabe-10
9124354	E.R. Canberra	Lbr	1996	30,280	35,962	202	32	22	ucc	2,825 teu: ex CMA CGM Power-09, CMA CGM Virginia-05, Indamex Mumbai-04, E.R. Canberra-03, Donau-02, Hanjin Dalian-00
9301457	E.R. Cannes	Lbr	2005	26,836	34,263	210	30	21	ucc	2,556 teu: ex CMA CGM La Boussole-10, E.R. Cannes-05
9194878	E.R. Copenhagen	Lbr	1999	25,630	33,855	207	30	21	ucc	2,474 teu: ex Maersk Valencia-09, E.R. Copenhagen-99
9239903	E.R. Cuxhaven	Lbr	2002	26,200	33,800	212	30	22	ucc	2,496 teu: ex Maersk Newark-09, E.R. Cuxhaven-02
9282950	E.R. Dallas	Lbr	2004	54,592	67,170	294	32	25	ucc	5,043 teu: ex Maersk Dallas-12, E.R. Dallas-04
9124366	E.R. Darwin	Lbr	1996	30,280	35,966	202	32	22	ucc	2,825 teu: ex Suzhou Dragon-11, E.R. Darwin-10, China Star-09, E.R. Darwin-02, Ganges-02, Hanjin Genoa-00
9231250	E.R. Denmark	Lbr	2002	65,792	67,935	277	40	26	ucc	5,762 teu: ex APL Denmark-12, E.R. Denmark-02
9246346	E.R. Elsfleth	Lbr	2003	26,200	33,800	212	30	22	ucc	2,496 teu: ex Andes Bridge-08, Maersk Newcastle-07, E.R. Elsfleth-03
9152856	E.R. Fremantle	Lbr	1998	30,280	35,848	202	32	22	ucc	2,825 teu: ex CMA CGM Turkey-08, CSCL Indus-03, Indus-02, Hyundai Infinity-01
9160425	E.R. Hamburg	Lbr	1998	26,125	30,721	196	30	19	ucc	2,226 teu: ex Safmarine Niger-12, E.R. Hamburg-09, CSAV Shanghai-07, Las Americas Bridge-03, CSAV Shanghai-01, Aconcagua-99, I/a E.R. Hamburg
9239898	E.R. Helgoland	Lbr	2002	27,322	34,608	212	30	22	ucc	2,496 teu: ex Safmarine Zambezi-12, E.R. Helgoland-02
9238806	E.R. Kingston	Lbr	2003	39,941	50,900	264	32	24	ucc	4,253 teu: ex CMA CGM Kingston-11, E.R. Kingston-04, CMA CGM Kingston-03, I/a E.R. Kingston
9222467	E.R. Lübeck	Lbr	2000	25,624	33,855	207	30	21	ucc	2,474 teu: ex CSCL Fuzhou-08, E.R. Lübeck-01
9315848	E.R. Malmo	Lbr	2005	28,927	39,338	222	30	23	ucc	2,824 teu: ex Kota Permai-11, E.R. Malmo-05
9314985	E.R. Martinique	Lbr	2007	27,927	39,200	222	30	23	ucc	2,824 teu: ex ANL Burilla-12, CMA CGM Anemone-11 Anemone-10, CMA CGM Anemone-09, E.R. Martinique-07
9169500	E.R. Melbourne	Lbr	1998	36,603	45,383	232	32	23	ucc	3,400 teu: ex Indamex Cauvery-11, CMA CGM Constellation-04, Safmarine Vinson-03, E.R. Melbourne-02, Congo-02, Choyang Honour-01
9238789	E.R. New York	Lbr	2003	39,941	50,900	264	32	24	ucc	4,253 teu: ex CMA CGM Nilgai-11, ANL Pacific-04, CMA CGM New York-04, I/a E.R. New York
9211169	E.R. Pusan	Deu	2000	66,289	67,737	277	40	26	ucc	5,762 teu: ex OOCL Los Angeles-10, I/a E.R. Pusan
9160437	E.R. Santiago	Lbr	1998	26,125	30,720	196	30	19	ucc	2,226 teu: ex Safmarine Nyanga-12, E.R. Santiago-09, CSAV Ningbo-07, Copiapo-04, I/a E.R. Santiago
9194866	E.R. Stralsund	Deu	1999	25,630	33,855	207	30	21	ucc	2,474 teu: ex Maersk Napier-09, E.R. Stralsund-05, Indamex Tuticorin-04, E.R. Stralsund-03, Maersk Mendoza-02, I/a E.R. Stralsund
9231262	E.R. Sweden	Lbr	2002	65,792	68,025	277	40	26	ucc	5,762 teu: ex APL Sweden-12, E.R. Sweden-02
9169495	E.R. Sydney	Deu	1998	36,603	45,400	232	32	23	ucc	3,359 teu: ex SCI Kolkata-12, E.R. Sydney-09, YM Napoli-04, Amazonas-02, Choyang Zenith-01, I/a Zenith Globe
9246310	E.R. Wilhelmshaven	Lbr	2002	27,322	33,800	212	30	22	ucc	2,496 teu: ex Maersk New Orleans-07, E.R. Wilhelmshaven-02
9238791	E.R. Yantian	Lbr	2003	39,941	53,000	264	32	24	ucc	4,253 teu: ex-CMA CGM Yantian-11, I/a E.R. Yantian
9318058	Faust	Lbr	2006	91,649	100,680	334	43	25	ucc	8,204 teu: ex CMA CGM Faust-12, MSC Bengal-09, I/a E.R. Texas
9282962	Maersk Denver	Lbr	2004	54,592	67,170	294	32	25	ucc	5,043 teu: ex E.R. Denver-04

IMO#	name	flag	year	grt	dwt	loa	bm	kts	type	former names
9222986	Montevideo Express	Lbr	2001	66,289	68,196	277	40	26	ucc	5,762 teu: ex E.R. Los Angeles-11, MSC Los Angeles-10, CSCL Los Angeles-08, l/a E.R. Los Angeles
9214226	MSC Adriatic	Deu	2001	66,289	67,591	277	40	26	ucc	5,762 teu; ex OOCL France-09, E.R. Paris-01
9465277	MSC Altair	Lbr	2012	141,635	141,051	366	48	24	ucc	13,092 teu
9213571	MSC Antares	Deu	2000	66,289	67,557	277	40	26	ucc	5,762 teu: ex E.R. Amsterdam-08, P&O Nedlloyd Magellan-05, l/a E.R. Amsterdam
9465253	MSC Benedetta	Deu	2011	141,635	140,991	366	48	24	ucc	13,100 teu: l/a E.R. Benedetta
9465241	MSC Cristina	Lbr	2011	141,635	141,184	366	48	24	ucc	13,100 teu: l/a E.R. Cristina, l/d E.R. Sartori
9214202	MSC Gemma	Deu	2000	66,289	67,566	277	40	26	ucc	5,762 teu: ex E.R. London-09, P&O Nedlloyd Vespucci-05, l/a E.R. London
9077288	MSC Hobart	Lbr	1994	22,736	33,523	188	28	18	ucc	2,021 teu: ex E.R. Hobart-04, Mosel-02, Zim Koper-98, Hyundai Longview-96
9213583	MSC Mira	Lbr	2000	66,289	67,564	277	40	26	ucc	5,762 teu; ex E.R. Felixstowe-08, P&O Nedlloyd Torres-06, l/a E.R. Felixstowe

Blue Star Holding (E.R. Schiffahrt) : E. R. BORNEO : *Hans Kraijenbosch*

Blue Star Holding (E.R. Schiffahrt) : E. R. COPENHAGEN : *Chris Brooks*

IMO#	name	flag	year	grt	dwt	loa	bm	kts	type	former names
9465306	MSC Renee	Lbr	2012	141,635	140,958	366	48	24	ucc	13,092 teu: l/a E.R. Pollux
9465265	MSC Vega	Lbr	2012	141,635	140,989	366	48	24	ucc	13,092 teu
9102514	Nanching	Lbr	1995	16,175	22,900	185	26	19	ucc	1,728 teu: ex Pacific Navigator-12, Pacific Mariner-09, E.R. Cape Town-08, Panatlantic-04, Quadrant Express-99
9318060	Parsifal	Lbr	2006	91,649	101,505	335	43	25	ucc	8,204 teu: CMA CGM Parsifal-12, l/a E.R. Toulon
9222974	Suape Express	Lbr	2001	66,289	68,196	277	40	26	ucc	5,762 teu: ex E.R. Kobe-11, CSCL Kobe-11, l/a E.R. Kobe
9289544	Zim Beijing	Lbr	2005	54,626	66,939	294	32	25	ucc	5,075 teu: l/a Zim Beijing
9282974	Zim Savannah	Lbr	2004	54,626	67,170	294	32	25	ucc	5,075 teu: l/a E.R. Savannah

newbuildings: eight 135,000 grt container ships
shipping subsidiary of Erck Rickmers' investment group Nordcapital Ges. fur Unternehmensbeteiligungen mbH & Cie.
* managed by subsidiary Katharinen Schiffahrts GmbH & Cie KG (formed 2007)
managed by: + Wallem Shipmanagement

Ernst Komrowski Reederei KG (GmbH & Co.), Germany
Funnel: *White with white diamond at centre of blue/red diagonally quartered flag or charterers colours.* **Hull:** *Black or grey with red boot-topping.* **History:** *Formed 1923 as Ernst Komrowski Reederei GmbH to 1938.* **Web:** *www.komrowski.net*

IMO#	name	flag	year	grt	dwt	loa	bm	kts	type	former names
9123221	Adrian	Lbr	1997	16,793	22,994	185	25	19	ucc	1,728 teu: ex TMM Hidalgo-06, Delmas Tourville-03, Adrian-03, Ivory Star-02, TMM Manzanillo-01, Adrian-01, CSAV Barcelona-01, Adrian-99, Santa Paula-98, Adrian-97, Jan Ritscher-97
9358890	Balkan **	Mlt	2007	15,633	17,005	161	25	19	ucc	1,304 teu: ex CSAV Caribe-08
9273210	Julian	Ant	2004	40,160	73,513	225	32	14	bbu	ex Lowlands Julian-11, Bonanza-09
9358905	Heluan	Lbr	2007	15,633	16,960	161	25	19	ucc	1,304 teu
9215543	Merian	Deu	2000	40,562	74,717	225	32	14	bbu	ex Cinzia d'Amato-08
9102502	Vulkan	Lbr	1996	16,800	22,982	185	25	19	ucc	1,730 teu: ex Emirates Mekong-12, Vulkan-11, MOL Springbok-08, Vulkan-06, Marfret Caraibes-05, CMA CGM Karukera-04, Vulkan-01, CMA CGM Karukera-01, Vulkan-01, Cap York-00, Vulkan-99, CSAV Rengo-99, Vulkan-06
9349174	Taipan	Deu	2007	10,965	12,612	141	23	19	ucc	925 teu
9371402	Tongan	Deu	2007	10,965	12,600	141	23	19	ucc	925 teu: ex WEC Vermeer-09, Tongan-08

Reederei Blue Star GmbH
Funnel: *red with blue star on white circle and narrow black top over narow white bandor charterers colours.* **Hull:** *Black or grey with red boot-topping.* **History:** *Blue Star Shipping Co. founded 1911 in London, taken over by P&O Nedlloyd in 1998 and in 2005 sold to A.P.Moller-Maersk. In 2009,management taken over by Komrowski*
Web: *www.*

IMO#	name	flag	year	grt	dwt	loa	bm	kts	type	former names
9005534	Jervis Bay	Gbr	1992	50,235	59,093	292	32	22	ucc	4,038 teu; ex MSC Almeria-09, Jervis Bay-08

Blue Star Holding (E.R. Schiffahrts) : MSC VEGA : *J. Kakebeeke*

IMO#	name	flag	year	grt	dwt	loa	bm	kts	type	former names
9005546	Maersk Dalton	Gbr	1992	50,350	59,093	292	32	22	ucc	4,038 teu: ex MSC Dalton-10, Maersk Dalton-08, Repulse Bay-06
9005558	Maersk Darlington	Gbr	1993	50,350	59,093	292	32	22	ucc	4,038 teu: ex MISC Darlington-09, Maersk Darlington-07, Newport Bay-06
9005560	Maersk Dartford	Gbr	1993	50,350	59,093	292	32	23	ucc	4,038 teu: ex MSC Dartford-10, Maersk Dartford-08, Singapore Bay-06
9080613	Maersk Dauphin	Gbr	1994	50,350	59,093	292	32	22	ucc	4,038 teu: ex MSC Malaysia-09, Maersk Dauphin-07, Providence Bay-06, Shenzen Bay-94
9079547	Maersk Delano	Gbr	1994	50,350	59,093	292	32	22	ucc	4,038 teu: ex MSC Salerno-09, Maersk Delano-08, Shenzen Bay-06
9103037	Maersk Delmont	Gbr	1995	50,350	59,093	292	32	22	ucc	4,038 teu: ex Colombo Bay-06
9001253	Maersk Miami	Lbr	1994	56,248	55,238	279	38	23	ucc	4,038 teu: ex Nedlloyd Hongkong-06
9275050	Maersk Nottingham	Lbr	2004	26,833	34,300	210	32	21	ucc	ex P&O Nedlloyd Regina-06, I/dn Regina Star
9303534	Maersk Saigon	Lbr	2006	94,483	108,251	332	43	24	ucc	8,452 teu: ex P&O Nedlloyd Maria-06
9289922	Maersk Sana	Lbr	2004	94,724	94,724	335	43	24	ucc	8,452 teu: ex P&O Nedlloyd Mondriaan-06, Mondriaan Star-04
9289934	Maersk Santana	Lbr	2005	94,724	94,724	335	43	24	ucc	8,452 teu: ex P&O Nedlloyd Manet-06, Manet Star-05
9289946	Maersk Sarnia	Lbr	2005	94,724	94,724	335	43	24	ucc	8,452 teu; ex P&O Nedlloyd Michelangelo-06, Michelangelo Star-05
9306550	Maersk Seoul	Lbr	2006	94,483	108,343	332	43	25	ucc	8,402 teu
9299927	Maersk Seville	Deu	2006	94,724	97,552	335	43	24	ucc	8,452 teu: ex Mahler Star-06, P&O Nedlloyd Mahler-05
9299939	Maersk Sheerness	Lbr	2006	94,724	97,536	335	43	24	ucc	8,452 teu: ex P&O Nedlloyd Mendelssohn-06
9308649	Maersk Singapore	Lbr	2007	94,724	97,552	335	43	24	ucc	8,452 teu: I/a P&O Nedlloyd Montevideo
9308637	Maersk Sofia	Lbr	2007	94,724	97,549	332	43	24	ucc	8,452 teu; I/a Menotti Star
9303522	Maersk Stralsund	Lbr	2005	94,493	108,212	332	43	25	ucc	8,402 teu: ex P&O Nedlloyd Marilyn-05
9289958	Maersk Sydney	Deu	2005	93,511	97,535	335	43	24	ucc	7,500 teu: ex P&O Nedlloyd Miro-06, I/a Miro Star
9275024	Nedlloyd Adriana	Lbr	2003	26,833	34,567	210	30	22	ucc	2,556 teu: ex P&O Nedlloyd Adriana-05, Adriana Star-03
8915796	Nedlloyd Africa	Lbr	1992	48,508	50,792	266	32	21	ucc	3,604 teu
8915677	Nedlloyd America	Lbr	1992	48,508	50,620	266	32	21	ucc	3,604 teu
8915665	Nedlloyd Asia	Lbr	1991	48,508	50,620	266	32	21	ucc	3,604 teu
8915691	Nedlloyd Europa	Lbr	1991	48,508	50,792	266	32	21	ucc	3,604 teu
9001318	Nedlloyd Honshu	Lbr	1995	56,248	55,238	279	38	24	ucc	4,181 teu
9275036	Nedlloyd Juliana	Lbr	2003	26,833	34,273	210	30	22	ucc	2,556 teu: ex P&O Nedlloyd Juliana-06, Juliana Star-03
9275048	Nedlloyd Marita	Lbr	2003	26,833	34,295	210	30	22	ucc	2,556 teu: ex P&O Nedlloyd Marita-06, Marita Star-03
8915689	Nedlloyd Oceania	Lbr	1992	48,508	50,620	266	32	21	ucc	3,604 teu
9275062	Nedlloyd Valentina	Lbr	2004	26,833	33,315	210	32	19	ucc	ex P&O Nedlloyd Valentina-06, I/dn Valentina Star
9286774	Rio Taku *	Lbr	2004	26,833	34,287	210	30	22	ucc	2,556 teu: ex Maersk Nolanville-12, P&O Nedlloyd Susana-05, I/a Rio Taku

Blue Star Holding (Ernst Komrowski Reederei) : HELUAN : *ARO*

IMO#	name	flag	year	grt	dwt	loa	bm	kts	type	former names
9283693	Rio Teslin *	Lbr	2004	26,833	34,567	210	30	22	ucc	2,556 teu: ex Nedlloyd Teslin-12, P&O Nedlloyd Teslin-05, l/dn Rio Teslin
9183708	Rio Thelon *	Lbr	2004	26,833	34,567	210	30	22	ucc	2,556 teu: ex Nedlloyd Maxima-12, P&O Nedlloyd Maxima-05, l/a RioThelon
9286786	Rio Thompson *	Lbr	2004	26,833	34,567	210	30	22	ucc	2,556 teu: ex Nedlloyd Evita-12, P&O Nedlloyd Evita-06

*vessels managed by E.R. Schiffahrts or * by MPC Münchmeyer Peterson Steamship*

Arne Blystad A/S   Norway

Funnel: *Yellow with red 'B' on broad white band edged with narrow blue bands, narrow black top.* **Hull:** *Black or red wih red boot-topping.* **History:** *Formed 1989 as Blystad Shipping (USA) Inc. to 2003. Saga Tankers inc. 2010 30% owned, owns 40% share of Offshore Heavy Lift, inc. 2008, and 40% of Gram Car Carriers with P. D. Gram & Co.* **Web:** *www.blystad.no*

IMO#	name	flag	year	grt	dwt	loa	bm	kts	type	former names
7931454	Eagle †	Nis	1981	31,021	31,809	200	42		ohl	ex Heavy Lift Eagle-09, Willift Eagle-08, Lucky Lady-06 [conv tcr-06]
7915278	Falcon †	Nis	1981	31,027	31,908	200	42		ohl	ex Heavy Lift Falcon-09, Willift Falcon-08, Nilos-03 [conv tcr-06]
8616556	Hawk †	Nis	1989	38,722	53,000	226	45		ohl	ex Heavylift Hawk-09, Hawk-08, Hawker-08, Front Transporter-07, Genmar Transporter-04, Crude Transporter-03, Nord-Jahre Transporter-00, Jahre Transporter-93 [conv tcr-08]

Blue Star Holding (Blue Star Reederei) : MAERSK NOTTINGHAM : *C. Brooks*

Blue Star Holding (Blue Star Reederei) : NEDLLOYD JULIANA : *Hans Kraijenbosch*

IMO#	name	flag	year	grt	dwt	loa	bm	kts	type	former names
7915278	Osprey †	Nis	1989	38,722	53,000	226	45		ohl	ex Heavylift Ancora-09, Ancora-08, Songa Ancora-08, Ancora-05, Leon Spirit-04, Borja Tapias-04, Jahre Trader-98, [conv tcr-08]
9378321	Songa Crystal **	Mhl	2006	8,485	12,926	127	20	14	tco	ex Samho Crystal-06
9460459	Songa Diamond **	Mhl	2009	11,259	17,543	144	23	14	tco	
9461794	Songa Eagle **	Mhl	2009	8,505	13,250	128	20	14	tco	
9473937	Songa Emerald **	Mhl	2009	11,259	17,567	144	23	14	tco	
9482653	Songa Falcon *	Mhl	2009	8,505	13,224	128	20	14	tco	
9482665	Songa Hawk **	Mhl	2009	8,505	13,265	128	20	14	tco	
9473925	Songa Jade **	Mhl	2009	11,259	17,604	144	23	14	tco	
9473913	Songa Opal **	Mhl	2009	11,259	17,588	144	23	14	tco	
9444455	Songa Pearl **	Mhl	2008	11,259	17,539	144	23	14	tco	
9444479	Songa Ruby **	Mhl	2008	11,259	17,604	144	23	14	tco	
9444467	Songa Sapphire **	Mhl	2008	11,259	17,539	144	23	14	tco	
9460461	Songa Topaz **	Mhl	2009	11,259	17,596	144	23	14	tco	
9416109	Songa Winds **	Pan	2009	11,662	19,954	144	24	14	tco	

managed by Songa Shipmanagement or by * *Lauritzens Skibs Management, or* ** *Navig8 Chemicals Inc*
† *vessels owned by Offshore Heavy Transport AS*

Gram Car Carriers AS, Norway
Funnel: *black with dark blue 'G' in a white diamond outlined with dark blue on a broad light blue band or charterers colours* **Hull:** *dark blue wih red boot-topping.* **History:** *P.D. Gram began car carrier operations in 1974, now 40% owned by Blystad*

9407677	City of Oslo	Sgp	2010	20,209	4,693	140	22	18	mve	2,000 ceu
8912663	Cypress Trail	Nis	1988	42,447	12,763	184	30	17	mve	5,000 ceu
9209934	Eishun	Pan	1999	33,854	8,531	173	27	20	mve	3,500 ceu
9407665	Hoegh Caribia	Sgp	2010	20,209	4,693	140	22	18	mve	2,000 ceu
9481049	Viking Amber	Sgp	2010	39,362	12,471	167	28	18	mve	4,200 ceu
9188790	Viking Chance	Lbr	1999	33,863	10,834	164	28	18	mve	4,300 ceu: ex Modern Chance-11
9407689	Viking Constanza	Sgp	2010	20,209	4,696	140	22	18	mve	2,000 ceu
9481051	Viking Coral	Sgp	2011	39,362	12,588	167	28	18	mve	4,200 ceu
9481075	Viking Diamond	Sgp	2011	39,362	12,572	167	28	18	mve	4,200 ceu
9188818	Viking Drive	Hkg	2000	33,831	10,817	164	28	18	mve	4,300 ceu: ex Modern Drive-10
9514987	Viking Emerald	Sgp	2012	39,362	12,500	167	28	18	mve	4,200 ceu
9514999	Viking Ocean	Sgp	2012	39,362	12,500	167	28	18	mve	4,200 ceu
9398876	Viking Odessa	Sgp	2009	20,216	4,693	140	22	18	mve	2,000 ceu
9515008	Viking Sea	Sgp	2012	39,362	12,500	167	28	18	mve	4,200 ceu

vessels managed by OSM Ship Management, Singapore

Aug. Bolten Wm. Miller's Nachfolger (GmbH & Co.)KG Germany
Funnel: *Black with black 'B' inside red rectangle outline and diagonal cross on white houseflag or (*) black 'L' on blue-edged white disc at centre of blue diagonal crossed and edged houseflag on broad white band.* **Hull:** *Black with red boot-topping.* **History:** *Parent originally founded 1801 and shipping company formed in 1906. Joint owners of Eurasia Shipping & Management with B Schulte to 1988.* **Web:** *www.aug-bolten.de*

9238313	Antonia	Lbr	2002	22,072	34,655	179	28	14	bbu	ex Aquila Voyager-12, Valiant-08, Austyn Oldendorff-06, IVS Valiant-03

Arne Blystad A/S : SONGA JADE : *Nico Kemps*

IMO#	name	flag	year	grt	dwt	loa	bm	kts	type	former names
9427392	Callisto	Lbr	2010	15,861	25,009	157	27	14	ggc	
9363168	Daniela Bolten	Lbr	2008	14,501	23,641	151	26	14	bbu	
9574042	Diana Bolten	Lbr	2011	23,264	38,273	180	30	14	bbu	
9483451	Franziska Bolten	Lbr	2008	18,493	29,234	170	27	14	bbu	ex Western Wave-09, Yahua No.1-08
9427380	Helen Bolten	Lbr	2009	15,861	24,979	157	27	14	ggc	
9406063	Lilly Bolten	Lbr	2009	19,972	30,760	179	28	14	bbu	
9406049	Louisa Bolten	Lbr	2009	19,972	30,522	179	28	14	bbu	
9331749	Lucia	Lbr	2009	32,578	53,000	190	32	14	bbu	ex Lucia Bolten-11, ASL Manila-11
9149653	Marielle Bolten	Lbr	1997	19,354	29,534	181	26	14	ggc	
9330678	Marietta	Lbr	2009	32,578	53,000	190	32	14	bbu	ex Marietta Bolten-12, City of Amman-09
9138458	Paros	Lbr	1997	14,397	23,984	154	26	14	bbu	ex Pacific Bridge-03
9149665	Sigrun Bolten	Lbr	1997	19,354	29,534	181	26	14	ggc	ex Cielo di Savona-01, Sigrun Bolten-97

Lydia Mar Shipping Co. S.A., Greece

Funnel: *Black with house flag.* **Hull:** *black with red boot-topping.* **History:** *Bolten subsidiary founded 1981.* **Web:** *www.lydiamar.gr*

IMO#	name	flag	year	grt	dwt	loa	bm	kts	type	former names
	Amorgos	Mhl	2013	24,210	35.000	180	30	14	bbu	
	Ithaki	Mhl	2014	23,250	38,270	180	30	14	bbu	
9449780	Kefalonia	Mhl	2009	18,096	28,742	170	27	14	bbu	
9117387	Naxos	Mhl	1995	15,164	23,825	153	26	14	bbu	ex Hirosaki Cherry-04, Hirosaki Rainbow-01
9449792	Paxi	Mhl	2010	18,096	28,734	170	27	14	bbu	
9177985	Skyros	Cyp	1998	14,781	24,128	154	26	14	bbu	ex Diamond Star-03
9100396	Stavros P	Mhl	1994	25,943	45,863	190	31	14	bbu	ex Matira-08, Minoan Pride-05, New Generation-04
9181493	Tala	Mhl	1998	15,349	24,175	159	26	14	ggc	ex Bright Sky-11

BP Shipping Ltd. U.K.

Funnel: *Red with green band on broad white band beneath black top.* **Hull:** *Black with red boot-topping.* **History:** *Subsidiary of BP plc. Shipping company formed 1915 as British Tanker Shipping to carry oil for Anglo-Persian Oil Co., the forerunner of BP. 1956 renamed BP Tanker Co. Ltd. and in 1981 BP Shipping Ltd.* **Web:** *www.bp.com/shipping*

IMO#	name	flag	year	grt	dwt	loa	bm	kts	type	former names
9266841	British Beech	Iom	2003	58,070	106,138	241	42	15	tcr	
9288760	British Chivalry	Iom	2005	29,335	46,803	183	32	15	tco	
9307750	British Commerce (st)	Iom	2006	48,772	54,478	230	37	17	lpg	83,270 m³
9282493	British Cormorant	Iom	2005	63,661	113,782	250	44	15	tcr	
9307762	British Councillor (st)	Gbr	2007	48,772	54,450	230	37	18	lpg	83,270 m³
9307748	British Courage (st)	Iom	2006	48,772	54,533	230	37	18	lpg	83,270 m³

Aug. Bolten Wm. Miiller's Nachfolger : MARIELLE BOLTEN : *Chris Brooks*

IMO#	name	flag	year	grt	dwt	loa	bm	kts	type	former names
9288825	British Courtesy	lom	2005	29,214	47,210	183	32	14	tco	
9258894	British Curlew	lom	2004	63,661	114,809	250	44	15	tcr	
9297345	British Cygnet	lom	2005	63,462	113,782	250	44	15	tcr	
9333620	British Diamond (df)	lom	2008	102,064	84,553	288	44	20	lng	151,945 m³
9297371	British Eagle	lom	2006	63,462	113,553	250	44	15	tcr	
9333591	British Emerald (df)	lom	2007	102,064	84,303	282	44	20	lng	151,945 m³
9315769	British Emissary	lom	2007	23,270	37,651	194	27	15	tco	ex Aiolos-07, l/dn Alkividias
9312913	British Ensign	lom	2006	23,270	36,713	184	27	15	tco	ex Atlantas-06
9312925	British Envoy	lom	2006	23,270	37,582	184	27	15	tco	l/a Aktoras
9251573	British Esteem	Gbr	2003	23,235	37,220	183	27	15	tco	
9251561	British Explorer	Gbr	2003	23,235	37,321	183	27	15	tco	
9297369	British Falcon	lom	2006	63,462	113,553	250	44	15	tcr	
9285744	British Fidelity	lom	2004	29,335	46,803	183	32	14	tco	
9282481	British Gannet	lom	2005	63,661	114,809	250	44	15	tcr	
9288813	British Harmony	lom	2005	29,335	46,803	183	32	14	tco	
9266853	British Hazel	lom	2004	58,070	106,085	241	42	15	tcr	
9266865	British Holly	lom	2004	58,070	106,085	241	42	15	tcr	
9238040	British Innovator (st)	lom	2002	93,498	75,074	279	43	19	lng	138,000 m³
9277858	British Integrity	lom	2004	29,335	46,803	183	32	15	tco	
9397357	British Kestrel	lom	2006	63,462	113,553	250	44	15	tcr	
9285756	British Liberty	lom	2004	29,335	46,803	183	32	14	tco	
9285720	British Loyalty	lom	2004	29,335	46,803	183	32	14	tco	
9282479	British Mallard	lom	2005	63,661	114,809	250	44	15	tcr	
9250191	British Merchant (st)	lom	2003	93,498	75,059	279	43	19	lng	138,000 m³
9258870	British Merlin	lom	2003	63,661	114,761	250	44	15	tcr	
9247792	British Oak	lom	2003	57,567	106,500	241	42	15	tcr	
9258882	British Osprey	lom	2003	63,661	114,809	250	44	15	tcr	
9108255	British Pride	lom	2000	160,216	305,994	334	58	16	tcr	
9180152	British Progress	lom	2000	160,216	306,397	334	58	16	tcr	
9180164	British Purpose	lom	2000	160,216	306,307	334	58	16	tcr	
9282508	British Robin	lom	2005	63,462	113,782	250	44	15	tcr	
9333606	British Ruby (df)	lom	2008	102,064	84,491	282	44	20	lng	151,945 m³
9333618	British Sapphire (df)	lom	2008	102,064	84,455	282	44	20	lng	151,945 m³
9285718	British Security	lom	2004	29,335	46,803	183	32	14	tco	
9288837	British Serenity	lom	2005	29,214	47,210	183	32	14	tco	
9258868	British Swift	lom	2003	63,661	114,809	250	44	15	tcr	
9285706	British Tenacity	lom	2004	29,335	46,080	183	32	14	tco	

BP Shipping Ltd. : BRITISH ESTEEM : *Nico Kemps*

IMO#	name	flag	year	grt	dwt	loa	bm	kts	type	former names
9238038	British Trader (st)	Iom	2003	93,498	75,109	279	43	19	lng	138,000 m³
9288849	British Tranquility	Iom	2005	29,214	47,210	183	32	14	tco	
9285732	British Unity	Iom	2004	29,335	46,080	183	32	14	tco	
9266877	British Vine	Iom	2004	58,070	106,021	241	42	15	tcr	
9251822	British Willow	Iom	2003	57,500	106,000	241	42	15	tcr	

also see Alaska Tanker Co LLC, USA (formed 1999 jointly with Overseas Shipholding Group Inc and Keystone Shipping Group) under OSG

Briese Schiffahrts GmbH & Co. KG Germany

Funnel: *White with company logo.* **Hull:** *Blue or grey with green boot-topping.* **History:** *Founded 1983.* **Web:** *www.briese.de*

IMO#	name	flag	year	grt	dwt	loa	bm	kts	type	former names
9303302	BBC Amazon *	Atg	2007	12,936	17,300	143	23	15	ggc	I/a Hatzum
9436331	BBC Congo	Atg	2010	12,974	16,936	143	23	15	ghl	cr: 2(250) 1(80): I/a Strong Breeze
9571399	BBC Danube	Atg	2012	12,936	17,300	143	23	15	ghl	cr: 2(250) 1(80)
9347059	BBC Elbe *	Atg	2006	12,936	17,349	143	23	15	ggc	ex Hornumersiel-06
9347035	BBC Ems *	Atg	2006	12,936	17,349	143	23	15	ggc	ex Suderdamm-06
9508304	BBC Ganges	Atg	2010	12,974	16,944	143	23	15	ghl	cr: 2(250) 1(80):
9435868	BBC Hudson	Atg	2010	12,874	16,944	143	23	15	ghl	cr: 2(250) 1(80): ex Dornumersiel-09
9161168	BBC Seattle *	Lbr	1998	13,066	20,567	153	24	17	ggc	ex BBC Leer-12, NileDutch Privilege-08, Mellum-06, Libra Peru-02, CSAV Valencia-00, Cathrin Oldendorff-99
9347061	BBC Mississippi *	Atg	2006	12,936	17,349	143	23	15	ggc	ex Greetsiel-07
9571375	BBC Nile	Atg	2011	12,980	16,991	143	23	15	ghl	cr: 2(250) 1(80): I/a Osterbur
9161182	BBC Ostfriesland *	Lbr	1998	13,066	20,567	153	24	17	ggc	ex Delmas Nigeria-07, BBC Ostfriesland-06, Germana-06, BBC Argentina-04, Cielo di Caracas-02, Lily Oldendorff-01, Libra Chile-00, CSAV Genoa-00, Lily Oldendorff-99, Barrister-99, Lily Oldendorff-98
9537264	BBC Neptune	Lbr	2010	24,050	37,506	190	28	14	bbu	
9508316	BBC Oder	Atg	2010	12,974	16,953	143	23	15	ghl	cr: 2(250) 1(80):
9571387	BBC Parana	Atg	2012	12,980	16,953	143	24	15	ghl	cr: 2(250) 1(80):
9537276	BBC Pluto	Lbr	2010	24,050	37,495	190	28	14	bbu	
9202041	BBC Rheiderland *	Lbr	2000	13,066	20,144	153	24	17	ggc	ex Delmas Ghana-07, BBC Rheiderland-06, Paul Oldendorff-02
9508380	BBC Seine	Atg	2010	12,974	16,967	143	23	15	ghl	cr: 2(250) 1(80): I/a Pilsum
9436329	BBC Volga	Gib	2009	12,936	17,302	143	23	15	ggc	cr: 2(250) 1(80): I/a Ocean Breeze
9347047	BBC Weser	Atg	2006	12,936	17,290	143	23	15	ggc	ex STX Bright-12, BBC Weser-10, Westerdamm-06
9301122	Hooge	Gib	2005	15,633	16,921	161	25	19	ucc	1,402 teu
9435856	Kurt Paul	Atg	2009	12,936	17,354	143	23	15	ggc	
9301134	Langenes	Gib	2006	15,633	16,921	161	25	19	ucc	1,402 teu
9256315	Norderoog	Gib	2004	15,633	16,921	161	25	19	ucc	1,402 teu: ex Syms Peonia-08, Norderoog-04
9386988	Petkum	Deu	2008	15,633	16,921	161	25	19	ucc	1,402 teu
9303314	Sjard	Atg	2007	12,936	17,305	143	23	15	ggc	
9256327	Süderoog	Gib	2005	15,633	16,921	161	25	19	ucc	1,402 teu: ex Syms Bohenia-06, I/a Suderoog
9386976	Wybelsum	Gib	2008	15,597	16,921	161	25	19	ucc	1,402 teu

* operated by Briese Bischoff Chartering: also operates numerous smaller vessels

BP Shipping Ltd: BRITISH PURPOSE : *J. Kakebeeke*

Broström AB Sweden

Funnel: Blue with houseflag (blue 'AB' on white disc over red/blue horizontal bands) overlapping green rectangle on broad white band.
Hull: Blue or grey with red boot-topping. **History:** Broström AB formed 1934, orginally founded 1865 as A/B Tirfing to 1978, renamed Bröstrom van Ommeren Shipping after merger in 1998. Bröstrom Tankers SAS formed 1934 as Phs van Ommeren (France) SA (founded 1839), merged 1987 with Société d'Armement Fluvial et Maritime (SOFLUMAR) as Soflumar van Ommeren France SA to 1992, then Van Ommeren Tankers SA to 2000. Bröstrom AB merged with Maersk Tankers in 2009 and manages vessels under 25,000dwt. **Web:** www.brostrom.se

IMO#	name	flag	year	grt	dwt	loa	bm	kts	type	former names
9348302	Bro Agnes	Nld	2008	12,162	16,791	144	23	-	tco	
9356610	Bro Alma	Nld	2008	12,162	17,000	144	23	-	tco	
9344435	Bro Anna	Nld	2008	12,164	16,979	144	23	-	tco	
9059688	Bro Axel *	Sgp	1998	11,324	16,389	144	23	13	tco	ex United Axel-00
9254422	Bro Sincero ‡	Swe	2002	11,855	16,008	146	22	14	tco	
9308546	Evinco (me) ‡	Swe	2005	13,769	19,999	156	24	14	tco	
9308558	Excello ‡	Swe	2008	13,798	19,925	155	24	14	tco	
9013426	Navigo ‡	Swe	1992	10,543	16,775	145	22	14	tco	
9212589	Prospero (me) ‡	Swe	2000	11.793	18,119	146	22	14	tco	

*managed by Brostrom AB.   * owned by Brostrom Tankers Singapore Pte.*
‡ owned by Rederi AB Donsotank,Sweden (founded 1952 – www.donsotank.se).
Also see Rigel Schifahrts GmbH & Co KG

Hermann Buss GmbH & Cie. KG Germany

Funnel: White with blue outlined 'H' interlinked with blue 'B' interupting narrow blue/red/blue band or charterers colours. **Hull:** Green with red or black boot-topping or charterers colours. **History:** Family commenced ship-owning in 1838 and as Reederei Hermann Buss from 1967 to 1988. Acuired 50% share in Schulte & Bruns in 2005. **Web:** www.buss-gruppe.de

IMO#	name	flag	year	grt	dwt	loa	bm	kts	type	former names
9395020	APL Managua **	Atg	2006	15,375	18,291	166	25	19	ucc	1,284 teu: ex EWL Caribbean-07, l/a Medocean
9138317	Baltrum Trader	Atg	1999	25,361	34,017	207	30	21	ucc	2,470 teu: ex Clan Challenger-09, Baltrum Trader-07, P&O Nedlloyd Fremantle-00, Baltrum Trader-99
9509683	Berlin Trader	Lbr	2010	22,863	33,248	180	28	15	ggc	ex Opal Brilliance-11
9138276	Borkum Trader	Atg	1998	25,361	33,976	207	30	21	ucc	2,470 teu: ex CSAV Hamburgo-10, Brasil Star-99, Borkum Trader-98
9437062	CSAV Brasilia	Lbr	2010	52,726	65,710	294	32	24	ucc	5,303 teu: ex Vargas Trader-10, l/a Med Superior
9437050	CSAV Recife	Lbr	2010	52,726	65,741	294	32	24	ucc	5,303 teu: l/a Mederie
9407885	CSAV Rio de Janeiro	Lbr	2009	52,726	65,549	294	32	24	ucc	5,303 teu: l/a Medondra-09
9437048	CSAV Suape	Lbr	2009	52,726	65,700	294	32	24	ucc	5,303 teu: l/a Medbaffin-09
9377559	Donau Trader	Atg	2008	28,048	37,950	215	30	21	ucc	2,700 teu: ex TS Xingang-09, Donau Trader-08
9213105	Ems Trader	Atg	2000	25,535	33,917	200	30	21	ucc	2,452 teu: ex Alemania Express-05, Sea Cheetah-02, l/a Ems Trader
9138290	Juist Trader	Atg	1998	25,361	34,041	207	30	20	ucc	2,470 teu: ex Maruba Orion-10, Juist Trader-07, CP Canada-06, Cielo del Canada-05, Juist Trader-99
9158496	Jümme Trader	Atg	1998	25,355	33,987	207	30	21	ucc	2,474 teu: ex Monteverde-10, l/a Jumme Trader

Briese Schiffahrts : NORDEROOG : *ARO*

IMO#	name	flag	year	grt	dwt	loa	bm	kts	type	former names
9213117	Leda Trader	Deu	2000	25,535	33,917	200	30	22	ucc	2,452 teu: ex MOL Sunshine-09, Leda Trader-07, Cap Castillo-05, l/a Leda Trader
9509607	Lisbon Trader	Lbr	2009	22,863	31,182	179	28	15	ggc	ex Medamur-09
9594470	Madrid Trader	Lbr	2011	22,863	33,217	179	28	15	ggc	
9377561	Main Trader	Lbr	2008	28,048	37,950	215	30	21	ucc	2,700 teu: ex TS Qingdao-09, l/dn Main Trader
9634669	MCC Benoa	Atg	2012	17,769	21,762	175	25	20	ucc	1,749 teu
9634672	MCC Maura	Atg	2013	17,769	21,789	175	25	20	ucc	1,749 teu
9449845	Medcoral	Cyp	2009	17,068	21,206	180	25	18	ucc	1,496 teu
9509774	Medfrisia	Cyp	2009	17,068	21,120	180	25	18	ucc	1,496 teu
9437115	Medontario *	Cyp	2008	15,334	18,445	166	25	19	ucc	1,284 teu
9449821	Medpearl	Cyp	2009	17,068	21,281	180	25	18	ucc	1,496 teu
9437139	Michigan Trader *	Cyp	2008	15,334	18,414	166	25	19	ucc	1,284 teu: ex Medmichigan-08
9377573	Mosel Trader	Atg	2009	28,048	37,968	215	30	21	ucc	2,700 teu
9138305	Niledutch Shenzhen	Atg	1998	25,361	33,919	207	30	21	ucc	2,470 teu : ex Helgoland Trader-10, CSAV New York-10, Lykes Osprey-03, ECL Rotterdam-02, Maersk Sao Paulo-99, Helgoland Trader-99
9129811	Ocean Trader I	Lbr	1996	16,165	22,250	168	27	19	ucc	1,618 teu: ex Ocean Trader-10, Calapadria-03, Zim Brasil I-01, Atlantico-98, Ocean Trader-96
9509700	Oslo Trader	Lbr	2011	22,863	33,210	179	28	15	ggc	
9594494	Paris Trader **	Atg	2011	22,863	33,217	179	28	15	ggc	
9509645	Rome Trader	Lbr	2010	22,863	33,175	179	28	15	ggc	
9509621	San Marino Trader	Lbr	2010	22,863	33,217	179	28	15	ggc	
9449869	Spaarne Trader **	Nld	2012	17,068	21,800	180	25	18	ucc	1,496 teu : l/a Medmonte
9130121	Szczecin Trader	Deu	1998	16,803	22,900	185	25	19	ucc	1,730 teu: ex MOL Honesty-09, CMA CGM Kiwi-08, Maruba Trader-04, l/a Szczecin Trader
9395068	Vecht Trader **	Nld	2007	15,375	18,350	166	25	19	ucc	1,284 teu: ex Medatlantic-08
9437127	Vento di Maestrale †	Atg	2008	15,334	18,444	166	25	19	ucc	1,284 teu: Warnow Beluga-11
9437189	Victoria Trader	Lbr	2008	15,334	18,471	166	25	19	ucc	1,284 teu
9395109	Vliet Trader **	Nld	2007	15,375	18,278	166	25	19	ucc	1,284 teu: ex Medpacific-08
9395070	Warnow Dolphin	Atg	2007	15,375	18,276	166	25	19	ucc	1,284 teu: ex TS Kaohsiung-08
9509671	Warnow Moon †	Lbr	2010	22,863	31,264	179	28	15	ggc	
9395111	Warnow Orca *	Atg	2007	15,375	18,270	166	25	19	ucc	1,284 teu: ex APL Colima-12
9437141	Warnow Porpoise †	Atg	2008	15,334	18,464	166	25	19	ucc	1,284 teu
9509633	Warnow Sun †	Lbr	2010	22,863	33,227	179	28	15	ggc	
9437191	Warnow Vaquita †	Atg	2008	15,334	18,343	166	25	19	ucc	1,284 teu
9395032	Warnow Whale †	Atg	2007	15,375	18,318	166	25	19	ucc	1,284 teu: ex CMA CGM Corfu-09, Warnow Whale-07

newbuildings:

* owned or managed by 100% subsidiaries Medstar Shipmanagement Ltd, Cyprus, ** Reider Shipping BV, Netherlands (founded 1999 – (www.reidershipping.com) † managed by Marlow Ship Management Deutschland GmbH & Co KG (www.marlow-shipmanagement.de).

Carl Büttner-Bremen GmbH & Co. KG Tankreederei   Germany

Funnel: *Yellow with white 'CB' and four corner stars on red houseflag, narrow black top.* **Hull:** *Black with red boot-topping.*
History: *Formed 1856 as Carl Büttner GmbH to 2003.* **Web:** *www.carlbuettner.de*

IMO#	name	flag	year	grt	dwt	loa	bm	kts	type
9234616	Admiral	Gib	2002	16,914	23,998	168	26	15	tco
9258624	Apatura	Gib	2004	16,901	24,064	168	26	15	tco
9234628	Apollo	Gib	2003	16,914	24,028	169	26	15	tco
9327102	Aurelia	Gib	2006	16,683	24,017	168	26	15	tco
9247388	Aurora	Gib	2004	16,901	24,086	168	26	15	tco
9327097	Avalon	Gib	2006	16,683	23,434	168	26	15	tco

managed by Carl Büttner Shipmanagement GmbH. also operated smaller chemical tankers

BW Shipping Group   Norway

History: *Founded 1887 by Berge Bergesen and shipping company formed 1918 as Sigval Bergesen, then A/S Sig. Bergesen d.y. & Co to 1986, which merged in 1996 with A/S Havtor Management the gas tanker subsidiary of Kvaerner Shipping AS (formerly P Meyer to 1981 and Rederiet Helge R Meyer A/S to 1992 when merged with Irgens-Larsen A/S) as Bergesen dy ASA. In 2003 acquired by Sohmen family controlled World-Wide Shipping Group, Hong Kong (formed 1951), company being renamed Bergesen Worldwide ASA from 2005.*

Berge Bulk Norway AS, Norway

Funnel: *Green base with white 'B' on dark blue rectangle above green hull section on broad white band, dark blue top.* **Hull:** *Red with dark blue 'BERGE BULK' and logo, black or red boot-topping.* **History:** *Subsidiary formed in 2007.* **Web:** *www.bwbulk.com*

IMO#	name	flag	year	grt	dwt	loa	bm	kts	type	former names
9447548	Berge Aconcagua **	Iom	2012	184,011	388,000	361	65	14	bor	
9223590	Berge Aoraki *	Iom	2000	87,322	172,502	289	45	14	bbu	ex Cape Camellia-12, Cape Daisy-04
9221906	Berge Arctic *	Pan	2001	91,563	174,285	292	48	15	bbu	ex BW Arctic-10, Berge Arctic-06

IMO#	name	flag	year	grt	dwt	loa	bm	kts	type	former names
9164184	Berge Atlantic *	Nis	1998	91,962	172,704	292	48	16	bbu	
9439113	Berge Atlas *	Pan	2008	90,092	180,180	289	45	15	bbu	ex BW Atlas-10
9531882	Berge Blanc *	Iom	2012	151,073	297,160	327	55	15	bor	
9346380	Berge Bonde §	Pan	2005	104,727	206,312	300	50	15	bbu	
9036454	Berge Bureya *	Pan	1993	153,506	293,239	332	57	15	bor	ex BW Bureya-10, BW Bandeira-07, Sebu-07, Seki-94 (conv tcr-07)
9000998	Berge Denali *	Pan	1992	155,656	286,006	328	57	14	bor	ex BW Denali-10, BW Noto-08, Noto-06, Argo Thetis-00 (conv tcr-09)
8902424	Berge Elbrus *	Pan	1991	155,626	285,739	328	57	15	bor	ex BW Nile-09, Nile-06, Argo Pallas-00 (conv tcr-10)
9112090	Berge Enterprise *	Iom	1997	108,083	211,485	312	51	14	bbu	ex SG Enterprise-12, Jedforest-00, SG Enterprise-98
9447536	Berge Everest **	Pan	2011	195,199	388,133	361	65	14	bor	
8314471	Berge Fjord *	Pan	1986	159,534	310,698	332	57	13	bor	ex BW Fjord-10, Berge Fjord-06, Docefjord-00 (conv. cbo-02)
9122590	Berge Fuji *	Iom	1996	145,963	275,644	324	57	14	bor	Navix Astral-12
9447550	Berge Jaya **	Iom	2012	184,011	388,000	361	65	14	bor	
9036442	Berge Kibo *	Iom	1993	155,823	279,989	328	58	15	bor	ex BW Kibo-10, Sala-08 (conv. tcr-09)
9083964	Berge Lhotse	Iom	1995	146,393	257,616	326	57	14	bor	Oriental Beauty-12, Shinyo Sawako-10, Golden Stream-06
9448011	Berge Lyngor §	Pan	2009	104,727	206,312	300	50	15	bbu	
9447562	Berge Neblina **	Gbr	2012	184,011	388,000	361	65	14	bor	L - 13.08.2012
9406544	Berge Odel	Pan	2007	104,721	206,330	300	50	15	bbu	ex BW Odel-12
8406406	Berge Phoenix *	Iom	1986	154,098	290,793	334	62	14	bor	ex BW Phoenix-09, Berge Phoenix-06, Grand Phoenix-00 (conv. cbo-04),
9115705	Berge Prosperity *	Bhs	1996	108,083	211,201	312	51	14	bbu	ex SG Prosperity-12, Lauderdale-00, SG Prosperity-98
8420804	Berge Stahl *	Iom	1986	175,720	364,767	343	64	13	bor	
9567063	Berge Townsend	Iom	2012	91,971	175,588	292	45	14	bbu	
8314483	Berge Vik *	Pan	1987	159,534	310,686	332	57	13	bor	ex BW Vik-10, Berge Vik-07, Tijuca-02 (conv. cbo-04)
8800286	Berge Vinson *	Pan	1990	155,708	290,160	327	57	15	bor	ex BW Vinson-09, Grand King-08, Ness-04, Argo Hebe-00 (conv. tcr-10)
9161508	Berge Yotei	Iom	1997	87,322	172,846	289	45	14	bbu	ex Cape Wisteria-12, Cape Rosa-04

* managed by Berge Bulk Singapore, § chartered from Shoei Kisen Kaisha
** chartered to Vale S.A.

BW Fleet Management Pte., Singapore

Funnel: Blue with white 'B' above white 'W'. **Hull:** Light green or red with white 'BW' on dark blue diagonal stripe, red boot-topping.
History: formed 2005 after reorganisation of BW business. **Web:** www.bwgas.com

IMO#	name	flag	year	grt	dwt	loa	bm	kts	type	former names
9269245	Avra *	Bmu	2004	42,011	73,400	229	32	15	tco	ex Newlead Avra-11, Altius-10, Michele Iuliani-04
9324289	BW Amazon *	Pan	2006	43,815	76,565	229	32	15	tco	ex Amazon-06
9315070	BW Bauhinia *	Hkg	2007	156,569	301,019	332	58	14	tcr	
9324291	BW Columbia	Pan	2007	43,797	76,604	229	32	15	tco	
9365001	BW Danube *	Pan	2007	43,797	76,543	229	32	15	tco	

BW Shipping Gp. (Berge Bulk) : BERGE ODEL : *Chris Brooks*

IMO#	name	flag	year	grt	dwt	loa	bm	kts	type	former names
9315082	BW Edelweiss *	Hkg	2008	158,569	301,021	332	58	14	tcr	
9324306	BW Hudson *	Pan	2007	43,797	76,574	229	32	15	tco	
9307786	BW Kronborg	Pan	2007	42,048	73,708	229	32	15	tco	ex Torm Ugland-12
9258521	BW Lake *	Hkg	2004	158,557	298,564	332	58	15	tcr	ex World Lake-09
9324318	BW Lena *	Pan	2007	43,797	76,578	229	32	15	tco	
9258519	BW Lion *	Hkg	2004	158,557	298,563	332	58	15	tcr	ex World Lion-09
9385037	BW Lotus *	Hkg	2011	166,414	320,142	332	60		tcr	
9253117	BW Luck *	Hkg	2003	158,993	298,717	332	58	15	tcr	ex World Luck-09
9243150	BW Luna *	Hkg	2003	158,993	298,555	332	58	15	tcr	ex World Luna-08
9179701	BW Nysa *	Sgp	2000	157,814	299,543	332	58	15	tcr	ex Nysa-09, Argo Artemis-00
9324320	BW Orinoco *	Pan	2008	43,797	76,580	229	32	15	tco	
9385843	BW Peony *	Hkg	2011	166,414	320,014	332	60		tcr	
9341940	BW Rhine *	Pan	2008	43,815	76,578	229	32	15	tco	
9342217	BW Seine *	Pan	2008	43,797	76,578	229	32	15	tco	
9506069	BW Shinano *	Sgp	2008	43,797	76,594	229	32	15	tco	
9393084	BW Thames	Sgp	2008	43,797	76,586	229	32		tco	
9180281	BW Ubud *	Pan	1999	149,383	299,990	330	60	16	tcr	ex Ubud-09
9181649	BW Ulan *	Rif	2000	157,814	299,325	332	58	15	tcr	ex Ulan-06
9221918	BW Utah **	Rif	2001	157,814	299,498	332	58	15	tcr	ex Utah-08
9227948	BW Utik *	Hkg	2001	157,814	299,450	332	58	15	tcr	ex Utik-06
9393096	BW Yangtze	Sgp	2009	43,797	76,579	229	32		tco	
9393101	BW Zambeze	Sgp	2010	43,797	76,578	229	32		tco	
9274094	Compass *	Bmu	2006	41,589	72,735	229	32	15	tco	ex Newlead Compass-12, Stena Compass-10
9295036	Compassion *	Bmu	2006	41,589	72,782	229	32	15	tco	ex Newlead Compassion-12, Stena Compassion-10
9269257	Fortune *	Bmu	2004	42,011	73,495	229	32	15	tco	ex Newlead Fortune-11, Fortius-10, I/a Altius

BW Gas ASA, Norway

Funnel: *Blue with white 'B' above white 'W'.* **Hull:** *Light green or red with white 'BW' on dark blue diagonal stripe, red boot-topping.*
History: *Formed 2005 after reorganisation of BW business.* **Web:** *www.bwgas.com*

9256597	Berge Arzew (st)	Bhs	2004	93,844	77,470	277	43	19	lng	138,089 m³
9317987	Berge Nantong **	Hkg	2006	47,012	58,757	225	37	16	lpg	82,244 m³
9308493	Berge Ningbo **	Hkg	2006	47,012	58,899	225	37	16	lpg	82,252 m³

BW Shipping Gp. (Berge Bulk) : BERGE STAHL : *Hans Kraijenbosch*

IMO#	name	flag	year	grt	dwt	loa	bm	kts	type	former names
8902371	Berge Summit	Bhs	1990	44,690	50,748	230	37	15	lpg	78,488 m³ ex Sunny Hope-04
9370537	BW Austria	Nor	2009	48,502	54,707	226	37		lpg	84,603 m³ ex BW Duke-09, I/a Apollonia Gas
9208227	BW Borg	Bhs	2001	47,156	54,826	230	36	16	lpg	84,333 m³ ex Formosagas Apollo-07
9208239	BW Boss	Bhs	2001	47,156	54,586	230	36	16	lpg	84,301 m³ ex Formosagas Bright-07
9377781	BW Broker	Lbr	2007	45,805	53,600	227	36	16	lpg	80,138 m³
9307736	BW Confidence	Iom	2006	48,772	54,492	230	36	16	lpg	81,604 m³ ex British Confidence-12
9193721	BW Danuta	Nis	2000	49,288	56,824	226	36	18	lpg	78,552 m³ ex Berge Danuta-11
9193733	BW Denise	Nis	2001	49,292	56,745	226	36	18	lpg	78,637 m³ ex Berge Denise-06
9232515	BW Energy	Iom	2002	46,506	53,556	227	36	17	lpg	82,488 m³ ex Dynamic Energy-12
8814768	BW Havfrost	Nis	1991	34,946	44,995	205	32	15	lpg	57,180 m³ ex Havfrost-07
9009023	BW Havis	Nis	1993	34,951	49,513	205	32	15	lpg	57,139 m³ ex Havis-08
8912182	BW Helios	Nis	1992	34,974	49,513	205	32	15	lpg	57,160 m³ ex Helios-07
8131104	BW Hermes	Nis	1983	18,152	26,920	155	27	16	lpg	24,977 m³ ex Oscar Viking-06, Oscar Gas-96, Tielrode-90, I/a Petrogas II
9350288	BW Liberty	Bel	2007	48,456	55,056	226	37	15	lpg	ex Flanders Liberty-11
9350604	BW Lord	Nis	2008	48,502	54,691	226	37	17	lpg	84,615 m³ ex Olympia Gas-08
9350290	BW Loyalty	Bel	2008	48,456	55,056	226	37	15	lpg	ex Flanders Loyalty-12,
9253818	BW Nantes	Bmu	2003	35,190	44,773	216	32	17	lpg	59,399 m³ ex Berge Nantes-07
9247819	BW Nice	Bmu	2003	35,346	44,639	216	32	17	lpg	59,375 m³ ex Berge Nice-07
9350422	BW Prince	Nis	2007	47,194	54,368	225	37	-	lpg	82,383 m³
9353242	BW Princess	Nis	2008	47,194	53,500	225	37	-	lpg	82,383 m³

BW Shipping Gp. (BW Gas) : BW ARZEW : *Chris Brooks*

BW Shipping Gp. (BW Gas) : BW HAVFROST : *Chris Brooks*

IMO#	name	flag	year	grt	dwt	loa	bm	kts	type	former names
9230062	BW Suez Boston (st)	Nis	2003	93,844	77,410	277	43	19	lng	138,059 m³ ex Berge Boston-07
9368314	BW GDF Suez									
	Brussels (df)	Bmu	2009	103,670	89,452	295	43	19	lng	162,514 m³ ex BW Suez Brussels-09
9243148	BW Suez Everett (st)	Nis	2003	93,844	77,410	277	43	19	lng	138,028 m³ ex Berge Everett-08
9368302	BW GDF Suez									
	Paris (df)	Bmu	2009	103,670	89,556	295	43	19	lng	162,524 m³ ex BW Suez Paris-09
9306548	BW Trader	Sgp	2006	46,632	53,151	225	36	17	lpg	78,631 m³ ex Berge Trader-07
9232503	BW Vision	Bhs	2001	46,506	53,503	227	36	17	lpg	82,488 m³ ex Dynamic Vision-11
9267015	LNG Benue (st)	Bmu	2005	97,561	82,971	285	43	20	lng	145,952 m³
9266994	LNG Enugu (st)	Bmu	2005	97,561	83,160	285	43	20	lng	145,926 m³
9311581	LNG Imo (st)	Bmu	2008	98,798	83,688	288	43	19	lng	148,452 m³
9311567	LNG Kano (st)	Bmu	2007	98,798	83,961	288	43	19	lng	148,565 m³
9269960	LNG Lokoja (st)	Bmu	2006	98,798	83,965	288	43	19	lng	148,471 m³
9311579	LNG Ondo (st)	Bmu	2007	98,798	83,688	288	43	19	lng	148,478 m³
9267003	LNG Oyo (st)	Bmu	2005	97,561	83,068	285	43	20	lng	145,842 m³
9266982	LNG River Orashi (st)	Bmu	2004	97,561	83,068	285	43	20	lng	145,914 m³
9292101	Odin +	Sgp	2005	25,994	29,216	180	29	16	lpg	38,500 m³ ex BW Odin-11, Berge Odin-07

newbuildings: 2 x 155,000m³. lng tankers [Hyundai Heavy Industries] 2014/2015
* managed by Reederei F Laeisz GmbH, ** Anglo Eastern Ship Management + managed by Veder Rederi

Neu Seeschiffahrt GmbH, Germany

Funnel: *Blue/grey with blue 'NEU' on blue/white/blue horizontally striped flag on white rectangle.* **Hull:** *Black, dark grey or brown with red boot-topping.* **History:** *Formed 1958 as Krupp Seeschiffahrt GmbH to 1965, then other Krupp names until 1988, then Krupp-Lonrho GmbH Seeschiffahrt partnership to 1993, then Krupp Seeschiffahrt GmbH (part of ThyssenKrupp AG after 1997 merger) to 2001, when Bergesen acquired 51% control.* **Web:** *none found.*

IMO#	name	flag	year	grt	dwt	loa	bm	kts	type	former names
9334882	Abigail N	Lbr	2009	151,448	297,430	327	55	15	bor	
9002776	Bing N	Lbr	1992	154,030	322,941	339	55	14	bor	ex Bergeland-08
9398175	Daniel N	Lbr	2011	151,448	297,359	327	55	15	bor	
9597185	Edward N	Lbr	2011	91,374	176,000	292	45	15	bbu	
9377236	Ernest N **	Lbr	2009	36,459	43,563	205	32		lpg	60,000 m³
9127150	Eva N	Lbr	1997	107,512	218,283	305	53	15	bor	ex Berge Nord-08
9407122	Fritzi N **	Lbr	2009	47,141	58,448	225	37		lpg	
9377224	George N. **	Lbr	2009	36,459	36,459	205	32		lpg	
9597197	Harriette N	Lbr	2011	91,374	176,000	292	45	15	bbu	
9479163	Helen N	Lbr	2011	151,448	297,000	327	55	15	bor	
9398096	Hugo N	Lbr	2011	151,448	297,000	327	55	15	bor	
9084190	Janice N	Lbr	1995	148,533	264,340	322	58	15	bor	ex Diamond Hope-08 (conv tcr-11)
9377248	Jenny N **	Lbr	2009	36,459	43,538	205	32		lpg	60,000 m³
9479369	Julia N	Lbr	2012	151,200	297,077	327	55	15	bor	
9386299	Karoline N **	Lbr	2009	42,897	54,004	227	32		lpg	60,000 m³
8707226	Margot N ***	Lbr	1989	142,488	255,028	322	56	14	bor	ex Eastern Fortune-07, Honam Sapphire-97, Niels Maersk-91
8800274	Phyllis N	Lbr	1990	153,347	285,768	328	57	14	bor	ex Grand Explorer-08, Neon-04, Argo Elektra-00, Alexita-97, Argo Elektra-93 (conv tcr-10)
8618190	Rebekka N	Lbr	1990	144,223	249,378	322	56	14	bor	ex Azuma Enterprise-07, C. Voyager-01, Yukong Voyager-97 (conv. tcr-08)
9374088	Regena N	Lbr	2006	90,091	180,277	289	45	15	bor	

BW Shipping Gp. (Neu Seeschiffahrts GmbH) : DANIEL N. *Hans Kraijenbosch*

IMO#	name	flag	year	grt	dwt	loa	bm	kts	type	former names
9006851	Renate N	Lbr	1992	154,644	278,380	328	58	15	bor	ex Renata N-08, New Frontier-07, Nuri-07, Argo Daphne-00 (conv. tcr-08)
9386304	Ronald N **	Lbr	2008	42,897	54,004	227	32		lpg	60,000 m³
9085340	Saar N *	Lbr	1995	63,152	122,331	266	41	14	bbu	ex Saar Ore-03
9377406	Steven N	Pan	2010	151,448	297,462	327	55	15	bor	

newbuildings:
* owned by Commerz Real Fonds Beteiligungsgellschaft and managed by Pronav Ship Management GmbH, Germany
** managed by Neu Gas Shipping International , *** Blue Ocean Ship Mgmt.

Cardiff Marine Inc.   Greece

Funnel: *Black with blue band edged with yellow bands or blue with black top.* **Hull:** *Black or grey with red boot-topping.*
History: *Formed 1986, 70% owned by Economou family, and now run as three operating divisions.* **Web:** *www.cardiff.gr*

Dryships Inc. TMS Dry

History: *Formed 2004 as management subsidiary of Cardiff Marine Inc.*

IMO#	name	flag	year	grt	dwt	loa	bm	kts	type	former names
9493016	Alona	Mlt	2009	91,373	177,944	292	45	14	bbu	
9353620	Fernandina	Mlt	2006	88,853	174,204	289	45	14	bbu	
9087283	Global Victory	Mlt	1996	76,068	149,155	270	43	14	bbu	
9355161	Madeira	Mlt	2007	91,373	178,198	292	45	-	bbu	
9363015	Malindi	Mlt	2008	91,373	177,987	292	45	14	bbu	
9465708	Milagro	Mlt	2009	40,170	75,205	225	32	14	bbu	
9409182	Miramarin	Mlt	2010	73,779	85,523	300	40	25	ucc	6,572 teu: ex APL Dubai-12, Miramarin-11, CMA CGM Kessel-10
9363041	Omaha	Grc	2008	91,407	177,805	292	45	-	bbu	
9135652	Pacific Champ	Mlt	1996	25,503	43,229	185	31	14	bbu	
9135664	Pacific Royal	Pan	1997	25,503	43,210	185	31	14	bbu	
9480538	Panormos	Mlt	2009	91,373	178,006	292	45	14	bbu	
9480526	Parramatta	Mlt	2010	91,373	178,064	292	45	14	bbu	
9363035	Petani	Mlt	2008	40,170	75,528	225	32	14	bbu	
9346768	Pompano	Mlt	2006	88,853	174,240	289	45	14	bbu	
9493028	Pounda	Mlt	2009	91,373	177,897	292	45		bbu	
9363053	Sidari	Mlt	2007	40,170	75,204	225	32	-	bbu	

BW Shipping Gp. (Neu Seeschiffahrts GmbH) : RENATE N. *Hans Kraijenbosch*

IMO#	name	flag	year	grt	dwt	loa	bm	kts	type	former names
9363039	Sivota	Mlt	2008	91,373	177,804	292	45	-	bbu	
9465710	Striggla	Mlt	2009	40,170	75,196	225	32		bbu	
9363027	Tampa	Mlt	2008	91,373	177,987	292	45	-	bbu	
9346756	Ventura	Mlt	2006	88,930	174,316	289	45	-	bbu	

TMS Bulkers Ltd.

IMO#	name	flag	year	grt	dwt	loa	bm	kts	type	former names
9228174	Alameda	Mlt	2001	86,743	170,726	290	45	14	bbu	ex Cape Araxos-05
9465801	Amalfi	Mlt	2009	40,170	75,206	225	32	14	bbu	
9261360	Bargara	Mlt	2001	40,437	74,500	225	32	14	bbu	ex Songa Hua-07, De Hua Hai-06
9257084	Byron	Mlt	2003	30,928	51,201	192	32	14	bbu	ex Paros I-11, Clipper Gemini-09, VOC Gemini-06, Clipper Gemini-03
9260122	Capitola	Mlt	2001	40,437	74,816	225	32	14	bbu	ex Songa Hui-07, De Hui Hai-06
9248526	Capri	Mlt	2001	87,390	172,529	289	45	15	bbu	ex Gran Trader-08
9299604	Catalina	Mlt	2005	40,485	74,432	225	32	14	bbu	
9308869	Cohiba	Mlt	2006	88,930	174,234	289	45	14	bbu	ex Mineral Hong Kong-09
9200562	Coronado	Mlt	2000	38,818	75,706	225	32	14	bbu	ex Seafarer II-05, Seafarer-04
9216391	Ecola	Mlt	2001	39,893	73,931	225	32	14	bbu	ex Zella Oldendorff-07, Trave River-01
9634701	Fakarava	Mlt	2012	106,847	206,160	300	50	15	bbu	
9284570	Flecha	Mlt	2004	87,440	170,012	289	45	14	bbu	ex Nightflight-08, Cape Kassos-07
9257060	Galveston	Mlt	2002	30,928	51,201	190	32	14	bbu	ex Pachino-11, VOC Galaxy-08, Clipper Galaxy-03
9216406	Levanto	Mlt	2001	39,893	73,926	225	32	16	bbu	ex Heinrich Oldendorff-09, I/a Elbe River
9279513	Ligari *	Mlt	2004	38,851	75,845	225	32	14	bbu	ex Star of Emirates-06, I/a Hamburg Harmony
9223497	Maganari	Mlt	2001	39,126	75,941	225	32	14	bbu	ex Atacama-06, Semeli-05, Lowlands Kamsar-04
9294109	Majorca	Mlt	2005	40,485	74,477	225	32	13	bbu	ex Maria G.O.-07
9275957	Manasota	Mlt	2004	88,129	171,061	289	45	14	bbu	ex Katerina V-05
9189782	Marbella	Mlt	2000	37,831	72,561	225	32	14	bbu	Restless-07, Ayrton II-06, Millenniu Venture-05
9231298	Mendocino	Mlt	2002	39,727	76,623	225	32	14	bbu	ex Conrad Oldendorff-06
9325025	Montecristo	Mlt	2005	90,091	180,263	289	45	15	bbu	ex Mineral Monaco-09
9421831	Mystic	Mlt	2008	89,510	170,102	291	45	-	bbu	ex Golden Nassim-08
9180786	Ocean Crystal	Mlt	1999	38,372	73,688	225	32	14	bbu	ex Samsara-05, Ocean Crystal-05
9214123	Oregon	Mlt	2002	38,727	74,204	225	32	14	bbu	ex Athina Zafirakis-07, Jin Tai-04, Jin Hui-02
9272345	Partagas	Mlt	2004	88,930	173,880	289	45	14	bbu	ex Jin Tai-09, Mineral Shanghai-07
9413690	Rapallo	Mlt	2009	40,170	75,123	225	32	15	bbu	
9584504	Raraka	Mlt	2012	41,254	76,064	225	32	15	bbu	
9211597	Redondo	Mlt	2000	40,562	74,500	225	32	14	bbu	ex Liberty One-06, Alessandra d'Amato-06
9386512	Robusto	Bel	2006	88,930	173,949	289	45	15	bbu	ex Mineral London-09
9268992	Saldanha	Mlt	2004	38,886	75,707	225	32	14	bbu	ex Shinyo Brilliance-07
9236171	Samatan	Mlt	2001	40,437	74,823	225	32	14	bbu	ex Trans Atlantic-07, Yong Ler-05
9236195	Sonoma	Mlt	2001	40,437	74,786	225	32	14	bbu	ex Yong Kang-05
9310408	Sorrento	Mlt	2004	39,736	76,633	225	32	15	bbu	ex Federal Maple-08, Maple Ridge-07
9584499	Woolloomooloo	Mlt	2011	41,254	76,064	225	32	14	bbu	

Cardiff Marine Inc. (TMS Tankers) : SCORPIO : *Chris Brooks*

IMO#	name	flag	year	grt	dwt	loa	bm	kts	type	former names

TMS Tankers Ltd.

IMO#	name	flag	year	grt	dwt	loa	bm	kts	type	former names
9389083	Agrari	Grc	2009	58,428	107,009	244	42		tcr	
9516959	Belmar	Mlt	2011	61,332	115,903	244	32		tcr	
9297541	Bonita	Grc	2006	57,711	108,386	247	42	-	tcr	
9529499	Bordeira	Mlt	2013	81,380	158,513	274	48	15	tcr	
9395329	Botafogo	Grc	2010	58,418	106,892	244	42		tcr	
9522128	Calida	Mlt	2012	61,332	115,812	249	44		tcr	
9308857	Carmel	Grc	2006	58,418	104,493	244	42	15	tcr	
9528043	Daytona	Mlt	2011	61,332	115,896	249	44		tcr	
9395305	Desimi	Mlt	2011	156,651	296,865	330	50	14	tcr	
9395331	Corossol	Grc	2010	58,418	106,897	244	42		tcr	
9399492	Kamari	Grc	2009	83,545	156,853	280	45		tcr	
9427641	Karekare	Grc	2010	83,545	156,831	280	45		tcr	
9529487	Lipari	Mlt	2012	81,380	158,425	274	48	15	tcr	
9208833	Lovina	Grc	2005	58,418	104,493	244	42	15	tcr	
9427639	Matala	Grc	2010	83,545	156,827	280	45		tcr	
9389095	Mindoro	Grc	2009	58,418	106,850	244	42		tcr	
9297553	Montego	Grc	2006	57,711	108,402	247	42	-	tcr	
9377779	Monterey	Grc	2007	58,418	105,009	244	42	15	tcr	
9389100	Myrtos	Grc	2009	58,418	106,750	244	42		tcr	
9178317	Oriental Green	Mlt	1998	56,955	99,991	244	42	14	tcr	
9529475	Petalidi	Mlt	2011	81,380	158,532	274	48		tcr	
9384069	Saetta	Grc	2009	58,418	107,023	245	42	15	tcr	
9528031	Saga	Mlt	2011	61,332	115,739	249	44		tcr	
9383869	Sarasota	Grc	2008	58,418	104,856	244	42	14	tcr	
9389071	Scorpio	Grc	2009	58,418	107,157	245	42		tcr	
9395317	Solana	Mlt	2010	156,651	296,790	330	60		tcr	
9399478	Taipan	Grc	2009	83,545	157,048	275	48		tcr	
9408073	Toska	Grc	2009	83,695	156,929	275	48		tcr	
9158874	Universal Brave	Mlt	1997	156,692	301,242	331	58	15	tcr	
9158886	Universal Prime	Mlt	1997	156,692	299,985	331	58	15	tcr	
9427627	Vadela	Grc	2009	83,545	157,048	275	48		tcr	
9283306	Venice	Grc	2004	61,764	109,637	245	42	15	tcr	ex Maersk Pristine-07
9529293	Vilamoura	Mlt	2011	81,380	158,621	275	48		tcr	
9308821	Zuma	Grc	2005	58,418	105,188	244	42	15	tcr	ex Corcovado-06

newbuildings:

Carisbrooke Shipping PLC   U.K.

Funnel: *Buff with buff 'CS' on blue rectangle.* **Hull:** *Light grey with green waterline over red boot-topping.* **History:** *Formed 1969, took over Soetermeer Fekkes B.V. in 1999 and Beck Scheepvaart B.V. in 2003.* **Web:** *www.carisbrookeshipping.com*

IMO#	name	flag	year	grt	dwt	loa	bm	kts	type	former names
9243825	Mark C	Iom	2003	14,357	19,460	160	24	14	ggc	ex Innogy Sprite-05, Dina-C-03

also operates smaller vessels

Champion Tankers AS   Norway

Funnel: *Dark blue with white 'CT'.* **Hull:** *Black with red boot-topping.* **History:** *Founded 1994.* **Web:** *www.champion-tankers.no*

IMO#	name	flag	year	grt	dwt	loa	bm	kts	type	former names
9113147	Champion Cornelia	Nis	1996	28,337	44,999	183	32	14	tco	ex-Cariad-11, Libertad-01
9143697	Champion Express	Lbr	1999	22,680	43,157	192	29	14	tco	ex Isola Gialla-08
8800511	Champion Pioneer *	Nis	1990	22,572	40,525	176	32	14	tco	ex Scottish Wizard-06, Stride-02, Osco Stripe-95
8812772	Champion Spirit *	Nis	1991	28,256	45,998	183	32	14	tco	ex Flamenco-06
8812784	Champion Star	Nis	1991	28,256	45,999	183	32	14	tco	ex Fandango-06
9112117	Champion Tide	Nis	1996	26,218	46,166	181	32	14	tco	ex-Tikhvin-10
9127667	Champion Trader	Gbr	1997	21,897	40,727	188	29	14	tco	ex Isola Rossa-08

*managed by Genoa Maritime S.A., Greece or by Thome Ship Management Pte Ltd, Singapore. * owned by Champion Shipping A/S, Norway.*

Chandris Group   Greece

Funnel: *Dark blue with large white 'X'.* **Hull:** *Dark blue with red boot-topping.* **History:** *Founded 1911 as John D Chandris to 1942.* **Web:** *www.chandris-hellas.gr*

IMO#	name	flag	year	grt	dwt	loa	bm	kts	type	former names
9379612	Aegea	Grc	2009	61,303	115,878	249	44	14	tco	
9291236	Aktea	Grc	2005	60,007	107,091	248	43	15	tcr	
8705618	Al Nabila 5 *	Egy	1993	18,106	29,027	175	26	13	tco	ex Nordpolen-09, Chem Lily-08, Sun-06, Andrea-00
8906822	Alexia 2 *	Egy	1990	53,724	94,603	232	42	15	tco	ex Meribel-08, Atalandi-04, Glory Central-97
9173733	Althea	Grc	1999	56,841	105,401	248	43	15	tco	
9216248	Amira *	Mhl	2001	39,818	74,401	225	32	14	bbu	
9379624	Amorea	Grc	2009	61,303	115,760	249	44	14	tco	
9173721	Astrea	Grc	1999	56,841	84,999	248	43	15	tco	

IMO#	name	flag	year	grt	dwt	loa	bm	kts	type	former names
9291248	Athinea	Grc	2006	60,007	107,160	248	43	14	tco	
9284926	Australis	Grc	2003	156,914	299,095	330	60	16	tcr	ex Saga-04, l/a Front Saga
9227481	Britanis	Grc	2002	157,581	304,732	332	58	16	tcr	
9381172	Chris *	Mhl	2006	39,736	76,629	225	32	14	bbu	
9322267	Ellinis	Grc	2007	157,844	306,507	332	58	-	tcr	
9316672	Maribella	Mlt	2004	39,736	76,629	225	32	15	bbu	
9218789	Marichristina	Mlt	2001	40,121	74,410	225	32	15	bbu	ex SA Warrior-03
9281437	Marietta	Mlt	2004	40,135	73,880	225	32	15	bbu	ex World Prosperity-04
9434565	Marijeannie	Pan	2009	94,232	179,759	292	45	-	bbu	
9434553	Mariloula	Pan	2008	94,232	179,759	292	45	-	bbu	
9325063	Marinicki	Mlt	2005	39,738	76,629	225	32	15	bbu	
9447017	Mariperla	Mlt	2009	94,232	179,759	292	45	-	bbu	
9484493	Marivictoria	Grc	2009	94,232	179,759	292	45	-	bbu	
9216224	Myrto	Grc	2001	39,831	74,470	225	32	14	bbu	
9532757	Oceanis	Grc	2011	161,273	320,780	330	60	14	tcr	
9180138	Patris	Grc	2000	157,496	298,543	332	58	15	tcr	
9405423	Serenea	Grc	2009	81,502	158,583	274	48		tcr	
9406659	Sestrea	Lbr	2009	81,502	158,518	274	48		tcr	
9083287	Sharifa 4 *	Egy	1995	52,875	95,416	244	42		tcr	ex Falster Spirit-10, Bona Rover-00, Vendonna-96
9053127	Zeinat 3 *	Egy	1995	37,033	68,232	243	32		tco	ex Skiropoula-10

newbuildings:
*operated by independent subsidiary Chandris (Hellas) Inc, Greece (founded 1988). * owned by Pyramid Navigation Co.*

Chemikalien Seetransport GmbH   Germany

Funnel: *Blue with white 'ST' inside large white outlined 'C' on blue square on broad white band.* **Hull:** *Black, blue or red with blue or red boot-topping.* **History:** *Formed 1989.* **Web:** *www.cst-hamburg.de*

7328243	Annabella (st)	Lbr	1984	26,951	26,800	198	26	15	lng	35,500 m³ l/a Montana
9298313	Athens Star	Lbr	2005	41,966	71,869	229	32	14	tcr	
9191395	Chemtrans Jacobi *	Lbr	1999	25,202	43,716	182	30	14	tco	ex St. Jacobi-09
9270488	Chemtrans Moon	Lbr	2004	40,763	72,296	229	32	14	tcr	l/a Silver Dolphin
9183257	Chemtrans Petri *	Lbr	2000	28,534	47,228	183	32	14	tco	ex St. Petri-07
9182667	Chemtrans Ray	Lbr	2000	40,516	71,637	227	32	15	tcr	ex Emerald Ray-03
9167136	Chemtrans Rhine	Lbr	1999	22,181	35,024	171	31	14	tco	ex Maersk Rhine-09. Ras Maersk-00
9214745	Chemtrans Riga	Lbr	2001	22,184	34,810	171	27	14	tco	ex Maersk Riga-11. Roy Maersk-03
9167174	Chemtrans Rouen	Lbr	2000	22,181	34,860	171	27	15	tco	ex Maersk Rouen-10, Maersk Rye-03
9167186	Chemtrans Rugen	Lbr	2001	22,181	34,861	171	27	14	tco	ex Maersk Rugen-10, Maersk Ramsey-03
9270490	Chemtrans Sea	Lbr	2004	40,764	72,365	229	32	14	tco	ex Red Dolphin-04
9185504	Chemtrans Sky	Lbr	2000	37,033	63,381	229	32	14	tco	ex Asopos-04
9185516	Chemtrans Star	Lbr	2000	37,033	63.331	229	32	15	tcr	ex Aliakmon-03
9182655	Chemtrans Sun	Lbr	1999	40,516	71,675	227	32	15	tcr	ex Emerald Sun-03
9323560	Gandhi *	Lbr	2008	25,400	40,165	176	31	-	tco	
9259886	Green Point	Lbr	2003	29,982	49,511	183	32	14	tco	
9298325	Hamburg Star	Lbr	2005	41,966	73,869	229	32	14	tcr	
9247508	Hans Scholl *	Lbr	2004	25,399	40,250	176	31	15	tco	

Chandris Group : AMOREA : *Nico Kemps*

IMO#	name	flag	year	grt	dwt	loa	bm	kts	type	former names
7229447	Isabella (st)	Lbr	1975	26,952	27,235	198	27	18	lng	35,500 m³ ex Kenai Multina-78, l/a Kentown
9330343	London Star	Lbr	2006	41,966	73,869	229	32	14	tcr	
9247493	MS Simon	Lbr	2004	25,399	37,247	176	31	15	tco	
9241798	MS Sophie	Lbr	2004	25,399	37,247	176	31	15	tco	l/a Chemtrans Sophie
9330355	New York Star	Lbr	2006	41,966	73,869	229	32	14	tcr	
9496678	RBD Shanghai	Lbr	2010	51,255	93,260	230	38	14	bbu	
9298818	Revel	Lbr	2004	22,184	35,187	171	27	14	tco	ex Maersk Radiant-11
9185487	Siteam Jupiter **	Nis	2000	27,185	48,309	182	32	14	tco	ex Team Jupiter-08
9185499	Siteam Neptun **	Nis	2000	27,185	48,309	182	32	14	tco	ex Team Neptun-08
9239977	Tapatio †	Lbr	2003	26,914	46,764	183	32	14	tco	
9588615	Trans Hangzhu	Lbr	2012	51,195	92,828	230	38	14	bbu	
9496680	Trans Nanjiang	Lbr	2011	51,255	93,226	230	38	14	bbu	
9283643	Trans Pacific *	Lbr	2004	40,485	74,403	225	32	14	bbu	ex CMB Eline-05

newbuildings: 1 x 92,500dwt bulk carriers (Cosco)
* owned by subsidiary Chemtrans Overseas (Cyprus) Ltd and managed by Belchem Singapore Pte. Ltd. (formed 2004 jointly with Belships).
† managed for Laurin Tankers America Inc. ** chartered to Eitzen
Partner in Star Tankers Pool with Heidmat Inc and in Baumarine Pool. Also see Team Tankers Pool under Blystad Shipmanagement Ltd.

Chemikalien Seetransport GmbH : HANS SCHOLL : Nico Kemps

Chemikalien Seetransport GmbH : LONDON STAR : ARO

Chevron Corp   U.S.A.

Chevron Shipping Co. LLC, U.S.A.

Funnel: *White with three narrow blue bands, narrow black top.* **Hull:** *Black with red boot-topping.* **History:** *Formed 2005 as successor to ChevronTexaco Corp formed by 2001 by merger of Chevron Corp (founded 1906 as Standard Oil Co of California, merged 1926 with Pacific Oil Co (founded 1879) and acquired Gulf Oil Corp in 1984) and Texaco Inc (founded 1901 as The Texas Co to 1926, The Texas Corp to 1941 and The Texas Co to 1959). Subsidiary formed 1957 as California Shipping Co to 1965, then Chevron Shipping Co to 2001 and ChevronTexaco Shipping Co LLC to 2006.* **Web:** *www.chevron.com or www.chevrontexaco.com*

IMO#	name	flag	year	grt	dwt	loa	bm	kts	type	former names
9125736	Aberdeen	Bhs	1996	47,274	87,055	222	37	14	tcs	
9035010	Altair Voyager	Bhs	1993	80,914	135,829	259	48	15	tcr	ex Condoleezza Rice-01
9288875	Andromeda Voyager	Bhs	2005	160,808	320,472	333	60	15	tcr	
9581203	Antares Voyager	Bhs	2012	161,535	317,052	333	60	15	tcr	
9216717	Antonis I. Angelicoussis	Bhs	2000	156,758	306,085	332	58	15	tcr	
9289491	Aquarius Voyager	Bhs	2006	161,331	320,821	333	60	-	tcr	
9588299	Arcturus Voyager	Bhs	2010	161,535	317,052	333	60	-	tcr	
9295000	Aries Voyager	Bhs	2006	160,808	320,870	332	58	15	tcr	
9330604	Capricorn Voyager ‡	Bhs	2007	58,442	104,610	244	42	-	tcr	
9330599	Castor Voyager	Bhs	2006	58,088	104,866	244	42	-	tcr	
9035060	Cygnus Voyager	Bhs	1993	88,919	156,835	275	50	15	tcr	ex Samuel Ginn-03
9174218	Gemini Voyager	Bhs	1999	160,036	301,139	333	58	16	tcr	ex Richard H. Matzke-03
9131876	Kometik * (2)	Can	1997	76,216	126,646	272	46	14	tcs	
9249178	Neptune Voyager	Bhs	2003	58,088	104,875	244	42	-	tcr	
9250725	Northwest Swan (st)	Bmu	2004	96,165	73,676	280	43	19	lng	137,000 m³
9051600	Orion Voyager	Bhs	1994	88,919	156,447	275	50	15	tcr	ex Chevron Employee Pride-02, Chevron Africa-94
9164847	Phoenix Voyager +	Bhs	1999	160,036	310,137	333	58	16	tcr	ex J. Bennet Johnston-03
9174220	Regulus Voyager	Bhs	2000	160,036	310,138	331	58	16	tcr	ex Chang-Lin Tien-03
9051612	Sirius Voyager	Bhs	1994	88,919	156,382	275	50	15	tcr	ex Chevron Mariner-02
9482304	Sonangol Benguela (st) **	Bhs	2011	104,537	89,806	291	43	19	lng	160,500 m³
9482299	Sonangol Etosha (st) **	Bhs	2011	104,537	89,932	291	43	19	lng	160,500 m³
9475600	Sonangol Sambizanga (st) **	Bhs	2011	104,537	89,742	291	43	19	lng	160,500 m³
9249180	Stellar Voyager	Bhs	2003	58,088	104,801	244	42	-	tcr	
9256468	Vega Voyager	Bhs	2003	58,088	104,864	244	42	-	tcr	

newbuildings:
* jointly owned with Mobil Oil Corp (Exxon Mobil) and Murphy Oil Corp. managed by Canship Ugland Ltd, Canada.
** managed for Sonangol Shipping, Angola, † managed for Cambridge Petroleum Transport Corp, USA or ‡ for Mitsui Soko Co Ltd, Japan.
+ managed for Golden State Petrol IoM
See also Angelicoussis Shipping Group Ltd.

Chevron Corp. (Chevron Shipping Co. LLC) : CASTOR VOYAGER : M. Lennon

China Ocean Shipping (Group) Co.   China

Cosco Container Lines Co. Ltd., China

Funnel: *Blue with white vertical line through white ring above white 'COSCO', broad yellow base and narrow black top.* **Hull:** *Grey or black with blue 'COSCO', green or red boot-topping.* **History:** *Parent founded 1961 as China Ocean Shipping Co to 1993. Container subsidiary formed 1997 by amalgamation with Shanghai Ocean Shipping Co.* **Web:** *www.coscon.com*

IMO#	name	flag	year	grt	dwt	loa	bm	kts	type	former names
8318051	Bing He	Chn	1985	23,542	33,389	201	28	15	ucc	1,696 teu:
9139000	Buyi He	Pan	1997	36,772	44,911	243	32	21	ucc	3,400 teu: ex Chesapeake Bridge-01
8321711	Chao He	Chn	1985	19,835	25,955	170	28	17	ucc	1,322 teu
9120798	Chuanhe	Pan	1997	65,140	69,285	280	40	24	ucc	5,440 teu
9484003	Cosco Aden	Hkg	2012	40,447	49,963	260	32	24	ucc	4,250 teu
9345439	Cosco Africa	Pan	2008	114,394	110,038	349	46	25	ucc	10,046 teu
9345427	Cosco America	Pan	2008	114,394	109,950	349	46	25	ucc	10,046 teu
9246396	Cosco Antwerp *	Hkg	2001	65,531	68,910	280	40	25	ucc	5,440 teu
9345403	Cosco Asia	Pan	2007	114,394	109,968	349	46	25	ucc	10,046 teu: ex Hanjin Fuzhou-11, Cosco Asia-09
9484261	Cosco Auckland	Hkg	2012	40,447	49,955	260	32	24	ucc	4,250 teu
9516404	Cosco Belgium	Hkg	2013	153,666	156,605	366	51	24	ucc	13,386 teu
9335173	Cosco Boston	Pan	2007	54,778	68,241	294	32	25	ucc	5,100 teu: ex CMA CGM Scala-09, Cosco Boston-07
9484285	Cosco Colombo	Hkg	2012	40,447	49,971	260	32	24	ucc	4,250 teu
9300312	Cosco Dalian	Pan	2005	66,380	67,209	279	40	25	ucc	5,570 teu
9516478	*Cosco Denmark*	Hkg	2013			366	51	24	ucc	13,500 teu
9484297	Cosco Durban	Hkg	2012	40,447	50,006	260	32	24	ucc	4,253 teu
9516428	*Cosco England*	Hkg	2013			366	51	24	ucc	13,500 teu
9345415	Cosco Europe	Pan	2008	114,394	109,968	349	46	25	ucc	10,046 teu
9246401	Cosco Felixstowe *	Gbr	2002	65,532	69,107	280	40	24	ucc	5,440 teu
9484302	Cosco Fos	Hkg	2012	40,447	49,954	260	32	24	ucc	4,253 teu
9516416	*Cosco France*	Hkg	2013			366	51	24	ucc	13,500 teu
9516442	Cosco Genoa	Hkg	2012	40,447	49,944	260	32	24	ucc	4,253 teu
9484388	Cosco Haifa	Hkg	2012	40,465	52,000	260	32	24	ucc	4,253 teu
9221085	Cosco Hamburg *	Gbr	2001	65,531	69,193	280	40	24	ucc	5,440 teu
9227778	Cosco Hong Kong *	Gbr	2002	65,531	68,895	280	40	24	ucc	5,440 teu
9484273	Cosco Houston	Hkg	2012	40,447	49,921	260	32	24	ucc	4,250 teu
9484340	Cosco Istanbul	Hkg	2012	40,465	52,000	260	32	24	ucc	4,253 teu
9516454	*Cosco Italy*	Hkg	2014			366	51	24	ucc	13,500 teu
9355563	Cosco Kaohsiung	Chn	2008	115,776	111,414	349	46	25	ucc	10,020 teu: ex Cosco Indian Ocean-10
9516430	*Cosco Netherlands*		2013			366	51	24	ucc	13,500 teu
9335185	Cosco New York	Pan	2007	54,778	68,235	294	32	24	ucc	5,100 teu : ex CMA CGM Capri-09, Cosco New York-07
9334923	Cosco Oceania	Hkg	2008	115,776	111,385	349	46	25	ucc	10,020 teu
9355551	Cosco Pacific	Hkg	2008	115,776	111,315	349	46	25	ucc	10,020 teu: ex Hanjin Bilbao-11, Cosco Pacific-09
9516466	*Cosco Portugal*	Hkg	2014			366	51	24	ucc	13.500 teu
9120762	Cosco Qingdao	Pan	1997	65,140	69,285	280	40	24	ucc	5,440 teu: ex Yun He-01
9221073	Cosco Rotterdam *	Gbr	2002	65,531	69,224	280	40	25	ucc	5,440 teu
9221097	Cosco Shanghai *	Gbr	2001	65,531	69,192	280	40	25	ucc	5,570 teu
9221102	Cosco Singapore *	Gbr	2001	65,531	69,196	280	40	25	ucc	5,570 teu
9516442	*Cosco Spain*	Hkg	2014		152,860	366	51	24	ucc	13,500 teu
9355575	Cosco Taicang	Hkg	2009	115,993	111,499	349	46	25	ucc	10,046 teu: l/a Cosco Atlantic
9300324	Cosco Tianjin	Pan	2005	66,380	67,209	279	40	24	ucc	5,570 teu
9300300	Cosco Xiamen	Pan	2005	66,380	67,209	279	40	24	ucc	5,570 teu
9043639	Da He	Chn	1994	49,375	51,950	275	32	25	ucc	3,800 teu
8806101	Dong He	Chn	1990	37,143	47,625	236	32	19	ucc	2,701 teu
9046112	Empress Dragon	Pan	1994	46,734	46,103	276	32	24	ucc	3,494 teu
9041227	Empress Heaven	Pan	1993	46,734	46,099	276	32	24	ucc	3,494 teu : ex Ming Heaven-01, Empress Heaven-98
9046124	Empress Phoenix	Pan	1994	46,734	46,125	276	32	24	ucc	3,494 teu
9041239	Empress Sea	Pan	1994	46,734	46,074	276	32	24	ucc	3,494 teu
9060182	Fei He	Chn	1994	48,311	51,280	275	32	24	ucc	3,768 teu
9223760	Fei Yun He	Chn	2000	20,569	25,723	180	28	20	ucc	1,702 teu
8818740	Gao He	Chn	1990	37,143	47,625	236	32	19	ucc	2,761 tei
9139012	Hani He	Pan	1997	36,772	44,911	243	32	21	ucc	3,400 teu
9120786	Jin He	Pan	1997	65,140	69,285	280	40	24	ucc	5,440 teu
9139036	Jingpo He	Pan	1997	36,772	44,911	243	32	21	ucc	34,00 teu
9123772	Ling Yun He	Chn	2000	20,569	25,723	180	28	20	ucc	1,702 teu
9120748	Lu He	Pan	1997	65,140	69,285	280	40	24	ucc	5,440 teu
9139062	Luo Ba He	Pan	1998	36,772	44,700	243	32	21	ucc	3,400 teu
8806096	Min He	Chn	1989	37,143	47,625	236	32	19	ucc	2,761 teu
9139024	Naxi He	Pan	1997	36,772	44,911	243	32	21	ucc	3,400 teu
9043005	Xiu He	Pan	1993	22,746	33,650	188	28	18	ucc	1,932 teu: ex Pretty River-08

IMO#	name	flag	year	grt	dwt	loa	bm	kts	type	former names
8705242	Pu He	Chn	1990	35,963	46,136	236	32	19	ucc	2,716 teu
9214513	Qing Yun He	Chn	2000	20,624	21,200	180	28	20	ucc	1,702 teu
9072147	River Elegance	Pan	1994	48,161	49,945	277	32	24	ucc	3,802 teu
9072135	River Wisdom	Pan	1994	48,161	49,955	277	32	24	ucc	3,802 teu
9043641	Shan He	Chn	1994	49,375	51,985	275	32	24	ucc	3,800 teu
8514590	Song He	Chn	1986	24,438	33,265	199	29	16	ucc	1,668 teu
8705230	Tai He	Chn	1989	35,963	45,987	236	32	19	ucc	2,716 teu
9067570	Teng He	Chn	1994	48,311	51,280	275	32	24	ucc	3,768 teu
9223758	Teng Yun He	Chn	2000	20,569	25,723	180	28	20	ucc	1,702 teu
9400564	Tian An He	Chn	2010	54,005	63,165	294	32	25	ucc	5,090 teu
9390616	Tian Bao He	Chn	2009	54,005	62,997	294	32	25	ucc	5,090 teu
9437567	Tian Fu He	Chn	2010	54,005	63,143	294	32	25	ucc	5,090 teu
9437531	Tian Jin He	Chn	2010	54,005	63,187	294	32	25	ucc	5,090 teu
9400576	Tian Kang He	Chn	2010	54,005	63,296	294	32	25	ucc	5,090 teu
9400552	Tian Li He	Chn	2010	54,005	63,253	294	32	25	ucc	5,090 teu
9400538	Tian Long He	Chn	2010	54,005	63,195	294	32	25	ucc	5,090 teu
9437555	Tian Qing He	Chn	2010	54,005	63,001	294	32	25	ucc	5,090 teu
9437543	Tian Sheng He	Chn	2010	54,005	63,292	294	32	25	ucc	5,090 teu
9400526	Tian Xing He	Chn	2009	54,005	63,259	294	32	25	ucc	5,090 teu
9400540	Tian Xiu He	Chn	2010	54,005	63,188	294	32	25	ucc	5,090 teu
9400514	Tian Yun He	Chn	2009	54,005	63,142	294	32	25	ucc	5,090 teu
9120774	Wanhe	Pan	1997	65,140	69,285	280	40	24	ucc	5,440 teu
8318083	Xiang He	Chn	1985	24,043	30,939	200	28	17	ucc	1,686 teu
9139048	Xibohe	Pan	1997	36,772	44,911	243	32	21	ucc	3,400 teu
9043017	Ya He	Pan	1993	22,746	33,650	188	28	18	ucc	1,932 teu: ex Dainty River-08
8318025	Yu He	Chn	1986	24,043	30,940	200	29	17	ucc	1,686 teu
9067568	Yuan He	Chn	1994	48,311	51,280	275	32	24	ucc	3,768 teu
9120750	Yue He	Pan	1997	65,140	69,285	280	40	24	ucc	5,440 teu
9139050	Yuguhe	Pan	1997	65,140	69,285	280	40	24	ucc	5,440 teu
9043627	Zhen He	Chn	1993	49,375	51,985	275	32	24	ucc	3,800 teu
9067556	Zhong He	Chn	1993	48,311	51,280	264	32	23	ucc	3,768 teu
8321723	Zhuang He	Chn	1985	24,438	33,240	199	29	17	ucc	1,668 teu

newbuildings:
*operated by Cosco Container Lines Co. Ltd. and Cosco Shanghai Ocean Shipping Co or * by subsidiary Cosco Maritime UK Ltd.*

COSCO Guangzhou, China

Funnel: *Blue with white vertical line through white ring above white 'COSCO', broad yellow base and narrow black top.* **Hull:** *Grey or black with blue 'COSCO', green or red boot-topping.*

IMO#	name	flag	year	grt	dwt	loa	bm	kts	type	former names
9454711	Cosco Shengshi	Pan	2011	51,671	14,868	183	32	20	mve	5,000 ceu
9454723	Cosco Tengfei	Pan	2011	51,671	14,759	183	32	20	mve	5,000 ceu

COSCO is one of the world's largest shipping groups with numerous subsidiaries owning around 700 vessels with many more on order. COSCO also operate bulkers, ore carriers, tankers. The fleet is too large to include in this book and it is impossible to guess which ones may visit European waters.

China Shipping (Group) Co.   China

China Shipping Container Lines Co. Ltd.

Funnel: *Blue with blue 'CIS' on broad white/yellow band.* **Hull:** *Green with white 'CHINA SHIPPING LINE', red boot-topping.*
History: *Government controlled company formed 1997 by merging of various government shipping Bureau and Administrations.*
Web: *www.cnshippingdev.com*

IMO#	name	flag	year	grt	dwt	loa	bm	kts	type	former names
9285796	CSCL Asia	Hkg	2004	90,645	101,612	334	43	25	ucc	8,468 teu
9467263	CSCL Jupiter	Hkg	2011	150,853	155,480	366	51	26	ucc	14,300 teu
9467287	CSCL Mars	Hkg	2011	150,853	155,467	366	51	26	ucc	14,300 teu
9467265	CSCL Mercury	Hkg	2011	150,853	155,374	366	51	26	ucc	14,300 teu
9467316	CSCL Neptune	Hkg	2011	150,853	155,264	366	51	26	ucc	14,300 teu
9224336	CSCL Qingdao †	Mlt	2001	39,941	50,953	260	32	24	ucc	4,051 teu
9224348	CSCL Rotterdam †	Mlt	2002	39,500	50,863	260	32	24	ucc	4,051 teu
9467299	CSCL Saturn	Hkg	2011	150,853	155,426	366	51	26	ucc	14,300 teu
9466867	CSCL Star	Hkg	2011	150,853	155,470	366	51	26	ucc	14,300 teu
9467304	CSCL Uranus	Hkg	2012	150,853	155,300	366	51	26	ucc	14,300 teu
9467251	CSCL Venus	Hkg	2011	150,853	155,470	366	51	26	ucc	14,300 teu
9224324	CSAV Lanco †	Mhl	2001	39,941	50,953	260	32	24	ucc	4,051 teu: ex CSCL Tianjin
9309966	Xin Bei Lun	Chn	2005	41,482	52,223	263	32	24	ucc	4,250 teu
9314246	Xin Beijing *	Hkg	2007	108,069	111,571	337	46	25	ucc	9,580 teu: I/d Xin Hamburg
9312559	Xin Chang Sha	Chn	2005	41,482	52,214	263	32	24	ucc	4,250 teu
9304813	Xin Chang Shu	Chn	2005	66,452	69,303	280	40	25	ucc	5,668 teu
9304772	Xin Chi Wan	Chn	2004	66,452	69,271	280	40	25	ucc	5,668 teu
9262118	Xin Chong Qing	Chn	2003	41,482	50,188	263	32	24	ucc	4,051 teu
9234331	Xin Da Lian	Chn	2003	66,433	69,023	280	40	26	ucc	5,668 teu
9337949	Xin Da Yang Zhou	Chn	2009	90,757	102,418	335	43	25	ucc	8,530 teu

IMO#	name	flag	year	grt	dwt	loa	bm	kts	type	former names
9312597	Xin Dan Dong	Chn	2006	41,482	52,210	263	32	24	ucc	4,253 teu
9309930	Xin Fang Cheng	Chn	2005	41,482	52,106	263	32	24	ucc	4,250 teu
9337937	Xin Fei Zhou	Chn	2008	90,757	102,379	335	43	25	ucc	8,530 teu
9304796	Xin Fu Zhou	Chn	2004	66,452	69,303	280	40	26	ucc	5,668 teu
9309954	Xin Hai Kou	Chn	2005	41,482	52,212	263	32	24	ucc	4,250 teu
9523017	Xin Hang Zhou	Chn	2012	47,815	67,040	255	37	24	ucc	4,700 teu
9314222	Xin Hong Kong *	Hkg	2007	108,069	111,746	337	46	25	ucc	9,580 teu
9310044	Xin Huang Pu	Chn	2005	41,482	52,216	263	32	24	ucc	4,250 teu
8026074	Xin Jin Zhou	Chn	1982	33,267	34,477	216	32	18	ucc	2,159 teu: ex Maple River-02, Tor Bay-93
9523031	Xin Lan Zhou	Chn	2012	47,917	67,000	255	37	24	ucc	4,700 teu
9234355	Xin Lian Yun Gang	Chn	2003	66,433	69,023	280	40	26	ucc	5,668 teu
9307217	Xin Los Angeles *	Hkg	2006	108,069	111,889	337	46	25	ucc	9,580 teu
9337925	Xin Mei Zhou	Chn	2008	90,757	102,453	335	43	25	ucc	8,530 teu
9310056	Xin Nan Sha	Chn	2005	41,482	52,191	263	32	24	ucc	4,250 teu
9262132	Xin Nan Tong	Chn	2003	41,482	50,151	263	32	24	ucc	4,051 teu
9270464	Xin Ning Bo	Chn	2003	66,433	69,303	280	40	26	ucc	5,668 teu
9337913	Xin Ou Zhou	Chn	2007	90,757	102,460	335	43	25	ucc	8,530 teu
9270440	Xin Pu Dong	Chn	2003	66,433	69,303	280	40	26	ucc	5,668 teu
9304784	Xin Qin Huang Dao	Chn	2004	66,452	69,303	280	40	26	ucc	5,668 teu
9523005	Xin Qin Zhou	Chn	2012	47,917	66,904	255	37	24	ucc	4,700 teu
9270452	Xin Qing Dao	Chn	2003	66,433	69,423	280	40	26	ucc	5,668 teu
9310032	Xin Quan Zhou	Chn	2005	41,482	52,216	263	32	24	ucc	4,250 teu
9312561	Xin Ri Zhao	Chn	2005	41,482	52,191	263	32	24	ucc	4,250 teu
9309942	Xin Shan Tou	Chn	2005	41,482	52,157	263	32	24	ucc	4,250 teu
9307231	Xin Shanghai *	Hkg	2006	108,089	111,889	337	46	25	ucc	9,580 teu
9262144	Xin Su Zhou	Chn	2004	41,482	50,137	263	32	24	ucc	4,250 teu
9320465	Xin Tai Cang	Chn	2008	41,482	52,245	263	32	24	ucc	4,250 teu
9234343	Xin Tian Jin	Chn	2003	66,433	68,000	280	40	26	ucc	5,668 teu
9312573	Xin Wei Hai	Chn	2006	41,482	52,219	263	32	24	ucc	4,250 teu
9328596	Xin Wu Han	Chn	2009	41,482	52,233	263	32	24	ucc	4,253 teu
9270476	Xin Xia Men	Chn	2004	66,433	69,259	280	40	25	ucc	5,668 teu
9334935	Xin Ya Zhou	Chn	2007	90,757	102,395	335	43	25	ucc	8,530 teu
9304801	Xin Yan Tai	Chn	2005	66,452	69,303	280	40	26	ucc	5,668 teu
9234367	Xin Yan Tian	Chn	2004	66,433	68,023	280	40	26	ucc	5,668 teu
9320477	Xin Yang Pu	Chn	2008	41,482	52,200	263	32	24	ucc	4,253 teu
9320477	Xin Yang Shan	Chn	2005	41,482	52,242	263	32	24	ucc	4,250 teu
9262120	Xin Yang Zhou	Chn	2004	41,482	50,137	263	32	24	ucc	4,250 teu
9312585	Xin Ying Kou	Chn	2006	41,482	52,186	263	32	24	ucc	4,253 teu
9378814	Xin Zhan Jiang	Chn	2006	41,482	52,279	263	32	24	ucc	4,250 teu
9328601	Xin Zhang Zhou	Chn	2009	41,482	52,186	263	32	24	ucc	4,250 teu
9523029	Xin Zheng Zhou	Chn	2012	47,917	67,041	255	37	24	ucc	4,700 teu

newbuildings:

* managed by subsidiary China International Ship Management.
† chartered from KG Allgemeine Leasing GmbH & Co, Germany (founded 2003) and managed by V Ships (Germany) GmbH & Co KG.
In addition to the above, the company owns many smaller container ships, while other subsidiaries of China Shipping operate about 250 bulk carriers and tankers between 10,000-158,000 grt. See other chartered vessels with 'CSCL' prefix in index.
NB : it is rumoured that CSCL are in merger talks with Cosco Container Lines.

China Shipping Gp. (China Shipping Container Line) : CSCL JUPITER : Hans Kraijenbosch

Chinese-Polish Joint Stock Shipping Co.   China/Poland

Funnel: *Cream with cream 'C' and white 'P' on broad red band, narrow black top.* **Hull:** *Light grey with blue 'CHIPOLBROK', green over black boot-topping.* **History:** *Formed jointly by the governments of China and Poland on 15th June 1951.*
Web: *www.chipolbrok.com.cn or www.chipolbrok.com.pl*

IMO#	name	flag	year	grt	dwt	loa	bm	kts	type	former names
9432115	Adam Asnyk	Cyp	2009	24,115	30,346	200	28	19	ggc	
9432165	Chipolbrok Cosmos	Hkg	2011	24,142	30,281	200	28	19	ggc	
9432141	Chipolbrok Galaxy	Hkg	2010	24,142	30,330	200	28	19	ggc	
9272216	Chipolbrok Moon	Hkg	2004	24,167	30,460	200	28	19	ggc	
9432147	Chipolbrok Star	Hkg	2010	24,142	30,346	200	28	19	ggc	
9272230	Chipolbrok Sun	Hkg	2004	24,167	30,396	200	28	19	ggc	
8821943	Chongming	Hkg	1993	18,177	22,109	170	28	16	ggc	
8513728	Chopin	Cyp	1988	13,930	18,144	159	23	15	ggc	
9133410	Hong Xing	Chn	1997	18,207	22,271	170	28	16	ggc	ex Taixing-12
8821925	Jia Xing	Hkg	1992	18,177	22,109	170	28	16	ggc	ex Bao Zheng-92
9432153	Kraszewski	Cyp	2011	24,221	30,435	200	28	19	ggc	
8513716	Lu Xun	Chn	1988	13,843	18,144	159	23	15	ggc	
9272228	Leopold Staff	Cyp	2004	24,167	30,469	200	28	19	ggc	
8513730	Moniuszko	Mlt	1989	13,938	18,144	159	23	15	ggc	
9133422	Norwid	Mlt	1998	18,202	22,258	170	28	16	ggc	
9432139	Parandowski	Cyp	2010	24,115	30,346	200	28	19	ggc	
8821929	Szymanowski	Cyp	1991	18,252	22,313	170	28	16	ggc	
8821931	Wieniawski	Mlt	1992	18,208	22,130	170	28	16	ggc	
9271925	Wladyslaw Orkan	Cyp	2003	24,167	30,435	200	28	19	ggc	
9150303	Yongxing	Hkg	1998	18,207	22,309	170	28	16	ggc	

Cido Shipping (H.K.) Co. Ltd.   Hong Kong (China)

Funnel: *Charterers colours.* **Hull:** *Black or blue or long-term charterers colours with red boot-topping.* **History:** *Founded 1993 as Cido Maritime Corp and Cido Shipping Co Ltd, which were merged in 2004.* **Web:** *www.cidoship.com*

IMO#	name	flag	year	grt	dwt	loa	bm	kts	type	former names
9360336	Atlantic Breeze	Hkg	2007	29,266	47,128	183	32	14	tco	
9332303	Atlantic Frontier	Hkg	2007	29,266	47,128	183	32	14	tco	
9332315	Atlantic Gemini	Hkg	2008	29,266	47,128	183	32	14	tco	
9337511	Atlantic Grace	Hkg	2008	29,266	47,128	183	32	14	tco	
9374372	Atlantic Hope	Hkg	2008	29,266	47,128	183	32	14	tco	
9455052	Atlantic Sirius	Hkg	2010	23,342	36,677	184	27	14	tco	
9337523	Atlantic Star	Hkg	2008	29,266	47,128	183	32	15	tco	
9464560	Atlantic Symphony	Hkg	2009	23,342	36,677	184	27	15	tco	
9309629	Bow Rio	Hkg	2005	11,986	19,998	146	24	14	tco	
9418930	Caribbean Emerald	Pan	1985	24,929	9,234	151	27	17	mve	2,551 ceu: ex Bellflower-92
9279331	CCNI Andino	Pan	2004	59,217	18,381	200	32	18	mve	6,500 ceu: ex Höegh Durban-12, Hual Durban-07
9335874	Charlotte Bulker **	Hkg	2007	19,831	32,132	176	29	14	bbu	

Chinese-Polish J/S Shipping Co. : CHIPOLBROK MOON : J. Kakebeeke

IMO#	name	flag	year	grt	dwt	loa	bm	kts	type	former names
9303156	Dream Angel	Pan	2006	41,662	15,089	186	28	19	mve	4,075 ceu
9303168	Dream Beauty	Pan	2006	41,662	15,119	186	28	19	mve	4,075 ceu
9325788	Dream Diamond	Pan	2007	41,662	15,069	186	28	20	mve	4,113 ceu
9325790	Dream Diva	Pan	2007	41,662	15,068	186	28	20	mve	4,113 ceu
9334246	Dream Jasmine	Pan	2008	41,662	15.068	186	28	20	mve	4.113 ceu
9360568	Dream Orchid	Pan	2009	41,662	15,097	186	28	20	mve	4,113 ceu
8319689	European Emerald	Pan	1984	37,996	13,208	175	29	18	mve	4,266 ceu: ex Nissan Maru-92
9335886	Fortune Amaryllis	Hkg	2008	19,831	32,114	176	29	14	bbu	ex Nord Singapore-10
9535864	Fortune Apricot	Hkg	2010	33,036	57,034	190	32	14	bbu	
9304125	Fortune Clover	Hkg	2006	40,080	77,430	225	32	14	bbu	
9340556	Fortune Iris	Hkg	2009	42,665	82,372	225	32	14	bbu	
9340544	Fortune Miracle	Hkg	2009	42,665	82,338	225	32	14	bbu	
9535876	Fortune Plum	Hkg	2010	33,036	57,053	190	32	14	bbu	
9317523	Fortune Sunny	Hkg	2008	42,665	82,338	225	32	14	bbu	
9614921	Fortune Violet	Hkg	2012	92,745	181,366	292	45	16	bbu	
9340570	Grand Champion	Pan	2008	59,217	18,262	200	32	19	mve	6,400 ceu
9169316	Grand Choice	Pan	1999	50,309	16,669	179	32	19	mve	4,373 ceu
9303182	Grand Cosmo	Pan	2006	59,217	17,750	200	32	20	mve	6,502 ceu
9355238	Grand Dahlia	Pan	2009	59,217	18,054	200	32	20	mve	6,502 ceu
9303223	Grand Diamond ++	Pan	2007	59,217	18,058	200	32	19	mve	6,502 ceu
9303170	Grand Duke	Pan	2005	59,217	18,315	200	32	20	mve	6,502 ceu
9339806	Grand Hero ++	Pan	2007	59,217	18,085	200	32	19	mve	6,502 ceu
9355240	Grand Legacy	Pan	2009	59,217	17,550	200	32	19	mve	6,502 ceu
9228306	Grand Mark	Pan	2000	50,310	16,681	179	32	19	mve	4,373 ceu
9247584	Grand Mercury ++	Pan	2002	58,947	19,121	200	32	20	mve	6,501 ceu
9303209	Grand Neptune	Pan	2006	59,217	17,550	200	32	20	mve	6,400 ceu
9303194	Grand Orion	Pan	2006	59,217	18,312	200	32	20	mve	6,400 ceu
9169328	Grand Pace	Pan	1999	50,309	16,714	179	32	19	mve	5,100 ceu
9284776	Grand Pavo	Pan	2005	59,217	18,376	200	32	20	mve	6,502 ceu
9339844	Grand Pearl ++	Pan	2008	59,217	18,090	200	32	19	mve	6,502 ceu
9284764	Grand Phoenix	Pan	2005	59,217	18,383	200	32	20	mve	6,400 ceu
9247572	Grand Pioneer	Pan	2002	58,947	19,120	200	32	20	mve	6,500 ceu
9181479	Grand Quest	Pan	2000	50,309	16,702	179	32	19	mve	5,100 ceu
9184940	Grand Race	Pan	2000	50,309	16,689	179	32	19	mve	4,373 ceu
9325221	Grand Ruby	Pan	2007	59,217	18,117	200	32	19	mve	6,400 ceu
9325233	Grand Sapphire ++	Pan	2007	59,217	18,099	200	32	19	mve	6,400 ceu
9355252	Grand Vega	Pan	2009	59,217	18,049	200	32	19	mve	6,400 ceu
9303211	Grand Venus	Pan	2006	59,217	13,500	200	32	20	mve	6,400 ceu
9334234	Grand Victory ++	Pan	2008	59,217	18,299	200	32	19	mve	6.400 ceu
9301067	Great Challenger	Hkg	2005	88,594	176,279	289	45	15	bbu	
9268916	Great Dream	Hkg	2004	19,829	33,745	169	28	14	bbu	
9282780	Great Morning	Hkg	2004	17,679	28,310	177	26	14	bbu	
9301079	Great Navigator	Hkg	2006	88,594	176,303	289	45	15	bbu	
9268930	Great River	Hkg	2004	19,829	33,700	175	28	14	bbu	
9268942	Great Summit	Hkg	2005	19,829	33,745	169	28	14	bbu	
9279329	Höegh Dubai †	Pan	2004	58,947	19,121	200	32	19	mve	6,501 ceu: ex Hual Dubai-06
9267663	Höegh Oceania †	Pan	2003	58,947	19,121	200	32	19	mve	6,500 ceu: ex Hual Oceania-05

Cido Shipping (H.K. Co.) : GRAND COSMO : *ARO*

IMO#	name	flag	year	grt	dwt	loa	bm	kts	type	former names
9276406	Hyundai Harmony	Pan	2002	13,267	17,800	162	26	19	ucc	1,032 teu
9378618	LR2 Pioneer ††	Pan	2008	59,172	115,273	244	42	-	tcr	
9378620	LR2 Polaris ††	Pan	2008	59,172	115,273	244	42	-	tcr	
9378632	LR2 Poseidon ††	Pan	2009	59,300	114,500	244	42	-	tcr	
9410301	Maersk Wolgast	Hkg	2010	18,123	22,314	173	27	19	ucc	1,805 teu
8600179	Marine Reliance	Mhl	1987	35,750	11,676	174	30	17	mve	3,000 ceu
9231688	Modern Express	Pan	2001	33,831	10,817	164	28	21	mve	3,060 ceu
9188829	Modern Link	Pan	2000	33,831	10,419	164	28	18	mve	3,000 ceu
9188805	Modern Peak	Pan	1999	33,831	10,817	164	28	18	mve	3,000 ceu
9494486	Oriental Angel	Hkg	2012	35,246	59,941	200	32	14	bbu	
9332810	Pacific Apollo	Hkg	2007	59,164	115,577	244	42	15	tcr	
8919984	Pacific Beauty ‡	Pan	1992	147,910	258,096	322	58	15	bor	ex Pacific Venus-02 (conv tcr-10)
9332822	Pacific Brave	Hkg	2007	59,164	115,677	244	42	15	tcr	
9333785	Pacific Condor	Hkg	2007	59,164	115,577	244	42	14	tcr	
9073438	Pacific Crystal ‡	Hkg	1994	148,159	264,158	322	58	15	bor	ex Diamond Falcon-03 (conv tcr-10)
9343340	Pacific Empire	Hkg	2008	59,164	115,577	244	42	15	tcr	
9075723	Pacific Garnet ‡	Pan	1995	156,280	277,047	329	57	15	bor	ex C.Navigator-07, Yukong Navigator-97 (conv tcr-10)
9413779	Pacific Jewel	Hkg	2009	28,754	48,012	180	32	14	tco	
9270749	Pacific Oasis	Pan	2004	28,799	47,999	180	32	14	tco	
9077410	Pacific Opal ‡	Pan	1995	156,280	278,157	329	57	15	bor	ex C.Planner-07, Yukong Planner-97 (conv tcr-10)
9270737	Pacific Polaris	Pan	2004	28,799	47,999	180	32	14	tco	
9514171	Pacific Poppy	Hkg	2011	56,326	104,621	228	42	14	tcr	
9288426	Pos Courage +	Hkg	2004	40,014	76,801	225	32	14	bbu	
9294484	Pos Dignity +	Hkg	2004	40,014	76,810	225	32	14	bbu	
9288461	Pos Eternity +	Hkg	2005	39,964	76,295	225	32	14	bbu	
9291389	Pos Freedom +	Hkg	2005	30,743	55,695	190	32	14	bbu	
9288473	Pos Glory +	Hkg	2004	39,964	76,508	225	32	14	bbu	
9291391	Pos Harmony +	Hkg	2005	30,743	55,695	190	32	14	bbu	
9303924	Pos Island +	Hkg	2006	30,743	55,710	190	32	14	bbu	
9427550	Spring Sky	Hkg	2010	25,745	9,301	165	26	20	mve	2,520 ceu
9427562	Spring Wind	Hkg	2010	25,745	9,274	165	26	20	mve	2,520 ceu
9077836	Topaz Ace *	Pan	1995	48,210	14,696	180	32	18	mve	5,317 ceu

newbuildings:

*chartered out to * Mitsui OSK, ** to Lauritzen, + to STX, ++ Eukor Car Carriers Inc. † to Leif Höegh & Co, †† to Torm LR2 Pool or to other owners. managed by *** Stena Weco ‡ Univan Ship Management Ltd or ‡‡ by The Schulte Group*
NB : late November 2011, it was reported 30 product tankers were to be sold to Diamond S Shipping, USA

Clipper Group (Management) Ltd   Bahamas

Clipper Marine Services A/S, Denmark

Funnel: *Black with white 'C' symbol.* **Hull:** *Black with white 'CLIPPER', red boot-topping   * green with red boot topping.*
History: *Formed 1972 and with subsidiaries currently operates some 240 vessels, 90 of which are owned or part-owned.*
Web: *www.clipper-group.com*

IMO#	name	flag	year	grt	dwt	loa	bm	kts	type	former names
9397236	Clipper Harmony	Bhs	2009	19,831	31,887	176	29	14	bbu	
9397248	Clipper Hope	Bhs	2010	19,831	31,883	176	29	14	bbu	
9283837	Clipper Lasco *	Bhs	2004	16,954	28,200	169	27	14	bbu	
9515723	Clipper Lis	Bhs	2009	17,018	28,321	169	27	14	bbu	
9368326	Clipper Macau †	Bhs	2008	11,864	17,110	143	22	15	ggc	ex Gabrielle Scan-12, BBC Rio Grande-11, Beluga Gravitation-08
9232462	Clipper Magdalena †	Bhs	2001	11,894	17,520	143	22	15	ggc	ex Magdalena Green-12
9187045	Clipper Makiri †	Nld	1999	11,894	17,539	143	22	16	ggc	ex Makiri Green-12
9208198	Clipper Marinus †	Bhs	2000	11,894	17,539	143	22	16	ggc	ex Marinus Green-12
9208203	Clipper Marissa †	Bhs	2000	11,894	17,539	143	22	16	ggc	ex Marissa Green-12
9247405	Clipper Marlene †	Bhs	2001	11,894	17,539	143	22	16	ggc	ex Marlene Green-12
9368338	Clipper Miami †	Bhs	2009	11,864	17,110	143	22	15	ggc	ex BBC Rhine-12, Beluga Gratification-08
9473224	Clipper Nassau †	Bhs	2011	12,795	17,257	144	23	16	ggc	
9473236	Clipper Newark †	Bhs	2011	12,795	17,273	144	23	16	ggc	
9473248	Clipper Newhaven †	Bhs	2011	12,795	17,299	144	23	16	ggc	
9473250	Clipper New York †	Bhs	2012	12,795	17,287	144	23	16	ggc	
9406075	Clipper Talent	Bhs	2009	19,972	30,475	179	28	14	bbu	
9320300	Clipper Target	Bhs	2006	19,918	30,587	179	29	14	bbu	
9406099	Clipper Tarpon	Bhs	2009	19,972	30,427	179	28	14	bbu	
9406116	Clipper Terminus	Bhs	2009	19,972	30,425	179	28	14	bbu	
9320348	Clipper Tenacious	Bhs	2007	19,918	30,634	179	29	14	bbu	ex Kent Tenacious-12, Clipper Tenacious-10
9406037	Clipper Titan	Bhs	2009	19,972	30,439	179	28	14	bbu	
9375953	Clipper Trader	Bhs	2008	19,972	30,487	179	28	14	bbu	ex Clipper Tsuji-09
9406051	Clipper Tradition	Bhs	2009	19,972	30,465	179	28	14	bbu	
9406024	Clipper Triumph	Bhs	2009	19,972	30,472	179	28	14	bbu	
9320312	Clipper Trust	Bhs	2007	19,918	30,611	179	29	14	bbu	

IMO#	name	flag	year	grt	dwt	loa	bm	kts	type	former names
9285407	Clipper Valour	Bhs	2003	22,072	34,790	179	28	14	bbu	

newbuildings:
*vessels managed by Clipper Bulk A/S, Denmark, or * by Clipper Bulk (Singapore) Pte Ltd (founded 2007 – www.clipper-bulk.com)*
† Clipper Projects Pool. A j/v set up 2012 between Clipper Gp., Enzian Ship Management, Switzerland and Freese Shipping, Germany

Campbell Shipping Co. Ltd., Bahamas

Funnel: *Buff with device and Campbell banner.* **Hull:** *green with white 'CAMPBELL' red boot topping* **History:** *Associate company founded 2009.* **Web:** *www.campbellshipping.com*

IMO#	name	flag	year	grt	dwt	loa	bm	kts	type	former names
9542520	CS Calla	Bhs	2011	24,065	37,479	189	28	14	bbu	
9542532	CS Calvina	Bhs	2011	24,065	37,456	189	28	14	bbu	
9542544	CS Candy	Bhs	2012	24,065	37,459	189	28	14	bbu	
9406104	CS Caprice	Bhs	2010	19,972	30,465	178	28	14	bbu	ex Clipper Anemone-10, l/d Clipper Taurus
9406087	CS Caroline	Bhs	2010	19,972	30,420	178	29	14	bbu	l/a Clipper Tango
9320295	CS Chara	Bhs	2006	19,918	30,634	179	28	14	bbu	ex Bossclip Trader-09
9406128	CS Crystal	Bhs	2010	19,972	30,478	179	28	14	bbu	l/a Clipper Terra
9255189	CS Manatee	Bhs	2002	17,944	27,128	178	26	14	bbu	ex DS Manatee-09
9237395	CS Sacha	Bhs	2001	16,963	28,379	169	27	14	bbu	ex Captain Corelli-09, Caprice Venture-01
9300192	CS Salina	Bhs	2004	20,225	32,355	177	28	14	bbu	ex Angel Rainbow-09
9221360	CS Savannah	Bhs	2000	18,050	26,865	170	27	14	bbu	ex Prince Rupert-09, Atlantic Venus-06, Virginia Rainbow II-01
9252058	CS Solaris	Bhs	2001	16,963	28,492	169	27	14	bbu	ex Willow Point-09, Ocean Bulker-06
9569944	CS Sonoma	Bhs	2010	32,987	56,704	190	32	14	bbu	
9569932	CS Soraya	Bhs	2010	32,984	56,700	190	32	14	bbu	
9285419	CS Vanguard	Bhs	2004	22,072	34,812	179	28	14	bbu	ex DS Vanguard-09

newbuildings: two further 32,000 dwt bulk carriers for 2012 delivery [Zhong Chuan Heavy Inds.]

Dockendale Shipping Co. Ltd., Bahamas

Funnel: *White with red 'D' and 'S' above points of black anchor.* **Hull:** *Black with white 'DOCKENDALE' or 'DOCKSHIP' red boot-topping.* **History:** *Associate company founded 1973, but became dormant in 1974 before re-entering shipping in 1985.* **Web:** *www.dockendale.com*

IMO#	name	flag	year	grt	dwt	loa	bm	kts	type	former names
9351737	African Blue Crane *	Bhs	2007	31,328	55,970	190	32	14	bbu	
9257046	African Eagle *	Bhs	2003	17,944	27,102	178	26	14	bbu	ex DS Mascot-03
9257058	African Falcon *	Bhs	2003	17,944	27,101	178	26	14	bbu	ex Clipper Majestic-03
9343613	African Halcyon *	Bhs	2007	20,346	32,245	177	28	14	bbu	
9284362	African Hawk *	Bhs	2004	17,944	27,101	178	26	14	bbu	
9599779	African Hornbill *	Bhs	2011	34,795	61,440	200	32	14	bbu	
9295579	African Ibis *	Bhs	2004	20,211	32,347	177	28	14	bbu	
9612143	African Osprey *	Bhs	2012	24,212	34,697	180	30	14	bbu	
9317767	African Robin *	Bhs	2005	19,783	31,982	176	29	14	bbu	
9403059	African Sanderling *	Bhs	2008	32,379	58,798	190	32	14	bbu	
9086966	African Sun *	Bhs	1994	26,040	45,208	188	31	13	bbu	ex Haoning Glory-10, Nord Viking-08 Claror-02, Libre II
9303364	African Swan *	Bhs	2005	19,887	32,776	177	28	14	bbu	

Clipper Group (Clipper Marine Services) : CLIPPER TENACIOUS : *Chris Brooks*

IMO#	name	flag	year	grt	dwt	loa	bm	kts	type	former names
9182710	Certoux **	Bmu	2000	86,192	169,159	289	45	13	bbu	ex Daphne-12, Yue Shan-07
9269063	Chambesy **	Bmu	2004	88,292	171,995	289	45	14	bbu	ex Pacific Fortune
9131840	Champel **	Bmu	1998	85,849	168,968	292	46	13	bbu	
9074511	Choulex **	Bmu	1996	77,211	150,961	274	45	13	bbu	ex Sanko Spark-10, World Spark-04
9143051	Confignon *	Bmu	1997	85,437	170,896	289	45	13	bbu	ex Orchid River-12
9589164	Pinchat **	Bmu	2012	44,326	81,290	229	32	14	bbu	

*operated by Metall und Rohstoff (MUR) Shipping ** operated by SwissMarine Services S.A.*

CMA CGM Holding S.A.   France

Funnel: *Red 'CMA and blue 'CGM' on white band between blue base and red top.* **Hull:** *Blue with white 'CMA CGM', red boot-topping.*
History: *Amalgamation in 1999 of Cie. Maritime d'Affretement (founded 1978) and Cie. Generale Transatlantique SA (founded 1854 and state-controlled from 1933), which itself was a 1977 merger of CGT and Cie. des Messageries Maritimes (founded 1948). ANL name acquired 1998 (formed 1956 as Australian Coastal Shipping Commission, becoming Australian Shipping Commission in 1974 and Australian National Line in 1989. Cheng Lie Navigation Co Ltd acquired 2007 (founded 1971).*
Web: *www.cma-cgm.com or www.anl.com.au*

IMO#	name	flag	year	grt	dwt	loa	bm	kts	type	teu / notes
9451965	CMA CGM Africa Four	Bhs	2010	40,827	51,619	228	37	21	ucc	3,718 teu
9451905	CMA CGM Africa One	Bhs	2010	40,827	51,634	228	37	21	ucc	3,718 teu
9451939	CMA CGM Africa Three	Bhs	2010	40,827	51,604	228	37	21	ucc	3.718 teu
9451927	CMA CGM Africa Two	Bhs	2010	40,827	51,608	228	37	21	ucc	3,718 teu
9335197	CMA CGM Alcazar *	Pan	2007	54,778	68,282	294	32	25	ucc	5,060 teu
9454448	CMA CGM Alexander von Humboldt	Gbr	2013	175,000	185,000	396	54	24	ucc	16,000 teu; l/d CMA CGM Vasco da Gama
9450648	CMA CGM Almaviva	Fra	2011	89,787	107,000	334	43	25	ucc	8,465 teu
9350381	CMA CGM Amber *	Gbr	2008	49,810	50,200	282	32	24	ucc	4,389 teu
9295971	CMA CGM America **	Cyp	2006	42,382	52,683	268	32	25	ucc	4,043 teu: ex Laja-06, l/dn Conti Nantes
9454395	CMA CGM Amerigo Vespucci	Fra	2010	152,991	156,887	366	51	24	ucc	13,344 teu
9410727	CMA CGM Andromeda	Gbr	2009	131,332	128,760	363	46	24	ucc	11,356 teu
9410741	CMA CGM Aquila	Gbr	2009	131,332	128,550	363	46	24	ucc	11,356 teu
9360154	CMA CGM Aristote	Gbr	2007	17,594	21,267	170	27	21	ucc	1,691 teu
9280598	CMA CGM Bellini *	Bhs	2004	65,247	72,500	277	40	24	ucc	5,770 teu
9222297	CMA CGM Berlioz *	Fra	2001	73,157	80,250	300	40	25	ucc	6,628 teu
9222302	CMA CGM Bizet §§	Lbr	2001	73,157	80,238	300	40	25	ucc	6,628 teu
9317963	CMA CGM Blue Whale *	Gbr	2007	54,309	65,892	294	32	25	ucc	5,040 teu
9410753	CMA CGM Callisto	Gbr	2010	131,332	128,550	363	46	24	ucc	11,356 teu
9314947	Camellia §	Hkg	2006	28,927	39,200	222	30	23	ucc	2,824 teu: ex CMA CGM Camellia-08
9410765	CMA CGM Cassiopeia	Gbr	2011	131,332	128,550	363	46	24	ucc	11,356 teu
9449819	CMA CGM Cendrillon	Gbr	2010	90,931	109,021	334	43	25	ucc	8,465 teu
9410777	CMA CGM Centaurus	Gbr	2011	131,332	128,550	363	46	24	ucc	11,356 teu
9335202	CMA CGM Chateau d'If	Cyp	2007	54,778	68,281	294	32	25	ucc	5,060 teu: l/a Cosco Norfolk

CMA CGM Holding S.A. : CMA CGM ANDROMEDA : *Chris Brooks*

IMO#	name	flag	year	grt	dwt	loa	bm	kts	type	former names
9280603	CMA CGM Chopin *	Fra	2004	69,022	73,235	277	40	24	ucc	5,770 teu
9453559	CMA CGM									
	Christophe Colomb	Fra	2009	153,022	157,092	366	51	24	ucc	13,344 teu
9410789	CMA CGM Columba	Gbr	2011	131,332	128,550	363	46	25	ucc	11,356 teu
9350393	CMA CGM Coral	Gbr	2008	49,810	50,200	282	32	24	ucc	4,389 teu
9454400	CMA CGM									
	Corte Real	Gbr	2010	150,269	156,898	366	51	24	ucc	13,344 teu
9450624	CMA CGM Dahlia	Fra	2011	90,931	109,021	334	43	25	ucc	8,465 teu
9235907	CMA CGM									
	Debussy §	Grc	2001	73,157	80,251	300	40	26	ucc	6,628 teu
9248112	CMA CGM Eiffel *	Bhs	2002	49,855	58,344	282	32	26	ucc	4,367 teu
9299642	CMA CGM Fidelio	Fra	2006	107,898	108,000	334	43	24	ucc	9,415 teu: l/a CMA CGM Othello
9450600	CMA CGM Figaro	Fra	2010	90,931	109,021	334	43	25	ucc	8,465 teu
9348704	CMA CGM Florida	Gbr	2008	54,309	65,800	294	32	25	ucc	5,042 teu
9261908	CMA CGM									
	Fort St. Georges	Fra	2003	26,342	30,450	198	30	21	ucc	2,226 teu
9261889	CMA CGM									
	Fort St. Louis	Fra	2003	26,342	30,804	198	30	21	ucc	2,226 teu
9261891	CMA CGM									
	Fort St. Pierre	Atf	2003	26,342	30,804	198	30	21	ucc	2,226 teu
9261906	CMA CGM									
	Fort Ste. Marie	Fra	2003	26,342	30,804	198	30	21	ucc	2,226 teu
9410791	CMA CGM Gemini	Gbr	2011	131,332	128,550	363	46	24	ucc	11,356 teu

CMA CGM Holding S.A. : CMA CGM CHRISTOPHE COLOMB : *ARO*

CMA CGM Holding S.A. : CMA CGM CORTE REAL : *Hans Kraijenbosch*

IMO#	name	flag	year	grt	dwt	loa	bm	kts	type	former names
9351127	CMA CGM Georgia	Gbr	2008	54,309	65,890	294	32	25	ucc	5,042 teu
9360142	CMA CGM Herodote	Gbr	2007	17,594	18,860	170	27	21	ucc	1,691 teu
9362322	CMA CGM Homere	Gbr	2007	17,594	21,264	170	27	21	ucc	1,691 teu
9356309	CMA CGM Hydra +	Gbr	2009	128,600	131,831	347	46	24	ucc	11,038 teu
9134646	CMA CGM Impala	Gbr	1996	16,803	22,990	185	25	19	ucc	1,728 teu: ex Semira-03, P&O Nedlloyd Amado-03, Semira-02, CGM Seville-02, Semira-97
9454450	CMA CGM Jacques Cartier	Gbr	2013	175,000	185,000	396	54	24	ucc	16,020 teu: l/d CMA CGM Zheng He
9326770	CMA CGM Jamaica +	Cyp	2006	41,899	53,663	264	32	23	ucc	4,298 teu
8912754	CMA CGM Junior S	Mlt	1994	9,600	12,310	150	22	18	ucc	1,012 teu: ex Active F-04, Perak-04, Sea Scandia-97, Maersk Miami-96, Fiona I-94
9339545	CMA CGM Kailas	Pan	2006	21,971	24,279	196	28	22	ucc	1,850 teu
9450612	CMA CGM La Scala	Gbr	2010	90,931	109,021	334	43	25	ucc	8,465 teu
9224946	CMA CGM La Tour *	Bhs	2001	26,050	30,442	196	30	22	ucc	2,226 teu
9199795	CMA CGM La Traviata *	Atf	2006	91,410	101,779	334	43	25	ucc	8,204 teu
9409194	CMA CGM Lamartine	Gbr	2010	73,779	85,446	300	40	25	ucc	6,572 teu
9454412	CMA CGM Laperouse	Gbr	2010	150,269	57,092	366	51	24	ucc	13,344 teu
9399208	CMA CGM Leo	Mlt	2010	131,332	131,236	366	46	25	ucc	11,312 teu
9399193	CMA CGM Libra	Mlt	2009	131,332	131,325	366	46	25	ucc	11,312 teu
9314923	CMA CGM Lilac	Hkg	2005	28,927	39,262	222	30	23	ucc	2,824 teu
9410806	CMA CGM Lyra	Gbr	2011	131,332	131,266	363	46	25	ucc	11,356 teu
9454424	CMA CGM Magellan	Gbr	2010	150,269	157,254	366	51	24	ucc	13,344 teu
9224958	CMA CGM Manet *	Cyp	2001	26,050	30,442	196	30	21	ucc	2,226 teu
9454436	CMA CGM Marco Polo	Gbr	2012	175,001	186,470	396	54	22	ucc	16,020 teu
9192428	CMA CGM Matisse *	Cyp	1999	25,777	32,274	196	30	21	ucc	2,226 teu
9409209	CMA CGM Maupassant	Gbr	2010	73,779	85,450	300	40	25	ucc	6,572 teu
9299800	CMA CGM Medea	Fra	2006	107,711	113,964	334	43	24	ucc	9,415 teu
9280615	CMA CGM Mozart	Fra	2004	69,247	72,500	277	40	24	ucc	5,770 teu
9356311	CMA CGM Musca +	Gbr	2009	128,600	131,830	347	46	24	ucc	11,038 teu
9299630	CMA CGM Nabucco	Fra	2006	91,410	101,810	334	43	24	ucc	8,204 teu
9351141	CMA CGM New Jersey	Bhs	2008	54,309	65,890	294	32	25	ucc	5,042 teu
9299812	CMA CGM Norma	Fra	2006	107,711	113,909	334	43	24	ucc	9,415 teu
9189160	CMA CGM Okapi	Gbr	2000	16,803	22,900	185	25	19	ucc	1,748 teu: ex Mina K-03, CMA CGM Seville-03, Mina K-02, Alianca Hamburgo-01, l/a Mina K
9299628	CMA CGM Otello	Bhs	2005	91,410	101,810	334	43	24	ucc	8,204 teu: l/a CMA CGM Fidelio

CMA CGM Holding S.A. : CMA CGM MARCO POLO : *ARO*

IMO#	name	flag	year	grt	dwt	loa	bm	kts	type	former names
9399210	CMA CGM Pegasus	Mlt	2010	131,332	131,268	366	46	24	ucc	11,312 teu
9362437	CMA CGM Platon	Gbr	2007	17,594	21,263	170	27	24	ucc	1,691 teu
9280627	CMA CGM Puccini	Fra	2004	69,022	73,234	277	40	24	ucc	5,770 teu
9248124	CMA CGM Puget *	Bhs	2002	49,855	58,548	282	32	24	ucc	4,367 teu
9221839	CMA CGM Ravel §§	Lbr	2001	73,059	79,465	300	40	25	ucc	6,628 teu
9299654	CMA CGM Rigoletto	Fra	2006	107,711	114,004	334	43	24	ucc	9,415 teu
9280637	CMA CGM Rossini	Fra	2004	65,730	73,235	277	40	24	ucc	5,770 teu
9295969	CMA CGM Sambhar **	Cyp	2006	42,382	51,870	268	32	25	ucc	4,043 teu: ex Lontue-06, Araya-04, I/dn Conti Nice
9072111	CMA CGM Simba	Gbr	1994	11,062	15,166	158	23	18	ucc	1,049 teu: ex TMM Durango-05, MSC Nigeria-04, P&O Nedlloyd San Pedro-01, Kent Merchant-99, Maersk Libreville-98, Antje-97, Lanka Amila-97, Antje-94
9280641	CMA CGM Strauss *	Bhs	2004	65,247	73,235	277	40	24	ucc	5,770 teu
9331000	CMA CGM Swordfish	Gbr	2007	54,309	65,987	294	32	25	ucc	5,052 teu
9331012	CMA CGM Tarpon	Gbr	2007	54,309	65,903	294	32	25	ucc	5,042 teu
9356294	CMA CGM Thalassa +	Cyp	2008	128,600	131,938	347	46	24	ucc	11,038 teu
9399222	CMA CGM Titan	Mlt	2011	131,332	128,550	366	46	24	ucc	11,312 teu
9450636	CMA CGM Titus	Gbr	2011	90,931	109,021	334	43	25	ucc	8,465 teu
9199783	CMA CGM Tosca	Bhs	2006	91,410	101,818	334	43	24	ucc	8,204 teu
9192430	CMA CGM Utrillo *	Cyp	1999	25,777	32,274	196	30	21	ucc	2,226 teu
9280653	CMA CGM Verdi *	Bhs	2004	65,247	73,235	277	40	24	ucc	5,770 teu
9314935	CMA CGM Violet	Hkg	2006	28,927	39,262	222	30	23	ucc	2,824 teu
9351139	CMA CGM Virginia	Gbr	2008	54.309	65,890	294	32	25	ucc	5,042 teu
9286267	CMA CGM Vivaldi *	Bhs	2004	90,745	101,661	334	43	24	ucc	8,238 teu
9317975	CMA CGM White Shark *	Gbr	2007	54,309	53,790	294	32	25	ucc	5,040 teu
9072094	Delmas Swala	Gbr	1994	11,062	15,166	158	23	18	ucc	1,049 teu: ex Macandrews Swala-08, CMA CGM Swala-06, Elbstrom-05, Cala Puebla-04, Elbstrom-02, P&O Nedlloyd Dakar-01, Urundi-99, Elbstrom-98, UB Lion-98, Lanka Ruwan-97, Elbstrom-95,
9125607	Ville d'Aquarius	Cyp	1996	40,465	49,229	259	32	24	ucc	3,940 teu: ex Lykes Tiger-03, Ville d'Aquarius-02
9125619	Ville d'Orion	Cyp	1997	40,465	49,208	259	32	23	ucc	3,940 yeu: ex ANL California-03, Ville d'Orion-03

newbuildings: *four 9,200teu vessels to be chartered from China International Marine Containers, [STX Dalian - 2014]*
* *owned by subsidiaries CMA Ships UK Ltd (formed 1990 as Donrich Ltd, later CMA UK Ltd to 1999, then CMA CGM UK Ltd to 2003 and CMA CGM (UK) Shipping Ltd to 2007) or ** by ANL Container Line Pty Ltd, Australia. owned by ‡ Target Marine, + various finance houses,*
§ Samartzis Maritime Enterprises Co. SA, Greece, §§ Aeolos Management S.A.
Subsidiary Cheng Lie Navigation Co Ltd, Taiwan owns six 15,000 grt container ships operating in Far East.
Also see other vessels with 'CMA CGM' prefixes in index

Delmas Armement, France

Funnel: Blue with white waterwheel device. **Hull:** Black with white 'DELMAS' or 'OTAL', red boot-topping. **History:** Formed 1864 as Société Navale Delmas-Vieljeux until 1971. Acquired Navale et Commerciale Havraise Peninsulaire from CNN-Worms Group (1986), Chargeurs Réunis (1988) and amalgamated with L Martin & Cie in 1991. Later 1991 taken over by SCAC (Bollore Group) as SCAC-Delmas-Vieljeux. Acquired by CMA-CGM in 2006. **Web:** www.delmas.com

IMO#	name	flag	year	grt	dwt	loa	bm	kts	type	former names
9225782	Delmas Keta *	Bhs	2003	26,047	30,450	196	30	21	ucc	2,226 teu: ex MOL Rainbow-08. Louis Delmas-03
9239850	Elisa Delmas **	Bhs	2002	16,916	20,979	169	27	20	ucc	1,641 teu
9239862	Flora Delmas **	Bhs	2002	16,916	21,420	169	27	20	ucc	1,641 teu
9225770	Julie Delmas	Bhs	2002	26,047	30,453	196	30	21	ucc	2,226 teu
9220859	Kumasi	Bhs	2001	26,061	30,450	196	30	21	ucc	2,226 teu: ex WAL Ubangi-04, Catherine Delmas-03
7704605	Laura Delmas **	Bhs	1979	35,748	22,564	197	32	20	urc	1,351 teu: ex Kintampo-02, Towada-98, Kintampo-97, Nedlloyd Rochester-96, Rochester-88, Nedlloyd Rochester-86
7704590	Lucie Delmas **	Bhs	1979	35,748	22,564	197	32	19	urc	1,351 teu: ex Kagoro-03, Nedlloyd Rotterdam-96, Rotterdam-88, Nedlloyd Rotterdam-86
9220847	Marie Delmas *	Bhs	2001	26,061	30,450	196	30	21	ucc	2,226 teu
9239874	Nala Delmas **	Bhs	2002	16,916	20,944	169	27	20	ucc	1,641 teu: ex Gaby Delmas-06
9220861	Nicolas Delmas **	Bhs	2002	26,061	30,450	196	30	21	ucc	2,226 teu
8315205	Rosa Delmas **	Gbr	1985	32,951	27,577	185	32	16	urc	1,446 teu: ex Rosa Tucano-98, Calapoggio-95, Rosa Tucano-93
7724306	Saint Roch **	Bhs	1980	16,744	24,260	187	32	18	urc	1,183 teu: ex Höegh Belle-81

newbuildings: *three urc vessels for 2014 delivery [Hyundai Mipo]*
* *managed by CMA Ships UK Ltd or ** by Midocean (IOM) Ltd, Isle of Man*

Cie. Maritime Belge S.A.   Belgium

Bocimar International N.V., Belgium

Funnel: *Blue with blue 'B' on broad yellow band.* **Hull:** *black, blue or orange with blue or red boot-topping, some with 'Bocimar' in white.* **History:** *Parent founded 1895 and formed from 1930 merger of Cie Belge Maritime du Congo SA and Lloyd Royal Belge SA. Armement Deppe (founded 1863) merged 1984. Acquired Merzario in 1989 and Woermann from Essberger (Deutsche Afrika-Linien) in 1990. Group taken over by Savery family in 1991. 43% share of Canmar (formed 1984) sold to CP Ships in 1993. Bocimar formed 1970.* **Web:** *www.cmb.be*

IMO#	name	flag	year	grt	dwt	loa	bm	kts	type	former names
9597991	CMB Adrien *	Hkg	2011	20,846	32,663	180	30	14	bbu	
9474254	CMB Ariane *	Hkg	2011	23,432	33,660	180	30	14	bbu	
9267417	CMB Biwa	Bel	2002	29,963	53,505	190	32	15	bbu	ex Lake Biwa-06
9474228	CMB Boris *	Hkg	2011	23,432	33,716	180	28	14	bbu	
9597977	CMB Catrine *	Hkg	2012	20,846	32,618	180	28	14	bbu	
9559705	CMB Charlotte *	Hkg	2010	20,846	32,646	180	28	14	bbu	
9649873	*CMB Diego*	Hkg	2013		36,000				bbu	
9559690	CMB Edouard *	Hkg	2010	20,846	32,648	180	28	14	bbu	
9588419	CMB Giulia *	Hkg	2012	22,137	23,500	180	28	14	bbu	
9405019	CMB Jialing **	Hkg	2010	30,962	55,090	190	32	14	bbu	
9474230	CMB Julliette *	Hkg	2011	23,432	33,683	180	30	14	bbu	
9474278	CMB Kristine *	Hkg	2011	23,432	33,684	180	30	14	bbu	
9649861	*CMB Laszlo*	Hkg	2013		36,000				bbu	
9492907	CMB Leon	Hkg	2012	32,400	58,000	190	32	14	bbu	Tsuneishi sc145 L - 09:07:2012
9474266	CMB Liliane *	Hkg	2011	23,432	33,674	180	30	14	bbu	
9425875	CMB Maxime **	Hkg	2010	32,296	57,982	190	32	14	bbu	
9498937	CMB Mistral *	Hkg	2009	18,499	29,130	170	27	14	bbu	ex JBU Mistral-10
9474280	CMB Paule *	Hkg	2011	23,432	33,717	180	30	14	bbu	
9597989	CMB Virginie *	Hkg	2011	20,846	32,519	180	28	14	bbu	
9474199	CMB Weihei *	Hkg	2010	23,432	33,716	180	30	14	bbu	
9474242	CMB Yasmine *	Hkg	2011	23,432	33,647	180	30	14	bbu	
9528196	FMG Grace	Hkg	2012	106,952	205,236	300	50	14	bbu	
9528201	FMG Matilda	Hkg	2012	106,952	205,203	300	50	14	bbu	
9224740	Mineral Antwerpen ‡	Pan	2003	87,495	172,424	289	45	15	bbu	
9272383	Mineral Beijing	Bel	2004	88,930	174,083	289	45	15	bbu	
9309021	Mineral Belgium	Bel	2005	88,930	173,806	289	45	14	bbu	
9264790	Mineral China	Bel	2003	88,292	171,128	289	45	14	bbu	l/a CIC Oslo
9474137	Mineral Dalian	Bel	2009	94,863	180,171	295	46	14	bbu	ex FMG Cloudbreak-12
9508392	Mineral Dragon	Bel	2008	91,373	178,062	292	45	14	bbu	
9575668	Mineral Faith	Hkg	2012	91,971	175,620	292	45	14	bbu	c/a Bulk Majesty
9489845	Mineral Haiku	Pan	2010	90,423	180,242	289	45	16	bbu	
9384954	Mineral Hokkaido	Pan	2008	90,423	180,159	289	45	15	bbu	
9614892	Mineral Honshu	Hkg	2012	92,727	181,408	292	45	15	bbu	
9567025	Mineral Hope	Hkg	2012	91,971	175,591	292	45	15	bbu	c/a Bulk Charity
9314064	Mineral Kyoto	Bel	2004	90,398	180,310	289	45	15	bbu	

Cie. Maritime Belge S.A. (Bocimar International) : CMB VIRGINIE : *Roy Fenton*

IMO#	name	flag	year	grt	dwt	loa	bm	kts	type	former names
9345366	Mineral Kyushu	Pan	2006	90,091	180,211	289	45	14	bbu	
9585106	Mineral Manila	Bel	2011	93,733	179,842	292	45	15	bbu	
9519767	Mineral New York	Bel	2010	91,971	175,841	292	45	15	bbu	
9336945	Mineral Nippon	Pan	2007	101,933	203,275	300	50	14	bbu	
9416848	Mineral Ningbo	Bel	2009	91,373	178,120	292	45	15	bbu	
9283681	Mineral Noble	Bel	2004	88,179	170,649	289	45	15	bbu	ex Mineral Kiwi-04
9413717	Mineral Oak	Hkg	2010	91,373	177,921	292	45	15	bbu	
9374040	Mineral Shikoku +	Pan	2006	104,727	206,312	300	50	14	bbu	
9224738	Mineral Sines ‡	Pan	2002	87,495	172,319	289	45	15	bbu	
9519779	Mineral Stonehenge	Bel	2010	91,971	175,713	292	45	15	bbu	
9456678	Mineral Subic	Hkg	2011	93,695	179,397	292	45	15	bbu	
9292565	Mineral Tianjin	Bel	2004	88,930	174,096	289	45	15	bbu	
9175066	Mineral Water	Bel	1999	85,695	170,201	289	45	14	bbu	ex Ingenious-07

newbuildings: 4 further x 36,000dwt bulkers [Samjin yd 1054-57 (2013/14)], 1 x 58,000dwt bulker
Partner in Cape International Pool formed jointly with Ofer (Zodiac), Belships, Moller, Torvald Klaveness and Overseas Shipholding Corp.
* owned by Bohandymar Ltd. ** Bocimar Hong Kong Ltd., + on charter from Cypress Maritime
managed by Anglo-Eastern (Antwerp) NV or Anglo-Eastern Ship Management Ltd, Hong Kong.
† managed by 28% owned Wah Kwong Ship Management, Hong Kong or ‡ by Oak Maritime (Canada) Ltd., Canada.

Euronav N.V., Belgium

Funnel: Black, white flag with narrow red horizontal cross on broad white cross on blue disc or ** blue with gold overlapping 'GO'.
Hull: Black with white 'EURONAV', with red boot-topping. **History:** Formed 1989 by Compagnie Nationale de Navigation (acquired 1986 by Worms Group from Elf Oil), France and Mercurius Group, Sweden. By 1995 jointly owned by CMB and CNN as Euronav Luxembourg SA. In 1998 CMB acquired 90% share of CNN, which was sold in 1999 and later demerged from CMB. **Web:** www.euronav.com

IMO#	name	flag	year	grt	dwt	loa	bm	kts	type	former names
9530905	Alsace *	Grc	2012	161,177	320,350	333	60	16	tcr	
9387554	Antarctica	Grc	2009	160,991	291,180	333	60	16	tcr	
9290347	Ardennes Venture	Hkg	2004	161,045	318,000	333	60	16	tcr	
9230969	Artois	Atf	2001	159,456	298,330	334	60	16	tcr	
9321706	Cap Charles *	Grc	2006	81,324	158,880	274	48	-	tcr	
9229295	Cap Diamant *	Grc	2001	94,729	160,044	277	53	14	tcr	
9380738	Cap Felix	Bel	2008	81,324	158,765	274	48	-	tcr	
9128283	Cap Georges *	Grc	1998	81,148	147,443	274	48	14	tcr	
9321691	Cap Guillaume *	Grc	2006	81,324	158,889	274	48	-	tcr	
9158147	Cap Jean *	Grc	1998	81,148	146,439	274	48	14	tcr	
9330874	Cap Lara *	Grc	2007	81,324	158,826	274	48	-	tcr	
9137648	Cap Laurent *	Grc	1998	81,148	147,436	274	48	14	tcr	
9274434	Cap Leon *	Grc	2003	81,328	159,048	274	48	-	tcr	
9321718	Cap Philippe *	Grc	2006	81,324	158,880	274	48	-	tcr	
9274446	Cap Pierre *	Grc	2004	81,328	159,048	274	48	-	tcr	
9160229	Cap Romuald *	Grc	1998	81,148	146,639	274	48	14	tcr	
9380740	Cap Theodora	Grc	2008	81,324	158,819	274	48	14	tcr	
9321720	Cap Victor *	Grc	2007	81,324	158,880	274	48	-	tcr	
9541380	Captain Michael *	Grc	2012	81,427	157,648	275	48		tcr	
9516117	Devon *	Grc	2011	81,427	157,642	275	48		tcr	
9516105	Eugenie *	Grc	2011	81,427	157,672	275	48		tcr	
9233272	Famenne	Atf	2001	159,456	298,412	333	60	15	tcr	
9416692	Felicity	Bel	2009	81,247	157,667	275	48		tcr	
9236004	Filikon *	Grc	2002	78,845	149,989	274	48	15	tcr	ex Paros-04

Cie. Maritime Belge S.A. (Euronav N.V.) : CAP ROMUALD : *Chris Brooks*

IMO#	name	flag	year	grt	dwt	loa	bm	kts	type	former names
9236016	Finesse *	Grc	2003	78,845	150,709	274	48	15	tcr	ex Anafi-04
9235256	Flandre	Atf	2004	159,016	305,704	332	58	15	tcr	
9416733	Fraternity	Bel	2009	81,427	157,667	275	48		tcr	
9171436	Luxembourg	Atf	1999	157,833	298,997	332	58	15	tcr	
9530890	Maria	Grc	2012	81,427	157,523	275	48	15	tcr	
9387542	Olympia	Atf	2008	160,991	315,981	333	60	16	tcr	
9224272	FSO Asia	Mhl	2001	234,006	441,893	380	68	16	tcr	ex TI Asia-09, Hellespont Alhanbra-04
9235268	TI Europe	Bel	2002	234,006	442,000	380	68	16	tcr	ex Hellespont Tara-04
9290086	TI Hellas	Bel	2005	161,127	319,254	333	60	16	tcr	ex Chrysanthemium-05
9230907	TI Topaz	Bel	2002	161,135	319,430	333	60	16	tcr	ex Crude Topaz-05, Oriental Topaz-05

newbuildings: Samsung # 1904 150,000 dwt (2013) 9530917

*managed by Euronav Ship Management SAS, France or * by Euronav Ship Management (Hellas) Ltd, Greece and operating mainly in Tankers International Pool formed jointly with Klaus Oldendorff, Sanko, Overseas Shipholding Group, Shinyo, Petronas, Oak Maritime, Wah Kwong and Essar Shipping.*

Cobelfret N.V.   Belgium

Funnel: *Yellow with red 'C' on white diamond on blue band.* **Hull:** *Black, grey or red with green or red boot-topping.* **History:** *Formed 1928.* **Web:** *www.cobelfret.com*

IMO#	name	flag	year	grt	dwt	loa	bm	kts	type
9172208	Lowlands Beilun *	Mlt	1999	85,906	170,162	289	45	14	bbu
9227003	Lowlands Brilliance *	Mlt	2002	85,906	169,631	289	45	14	bbu
9304289	Lowlands Camellia *	Pan	2006	40,042	76,807	225	32	14	bbu
9345611	Lowlands Erica *	Pan	2007	89,603	176,862	289	45	16	bbu
9294472	Lowlands Ghent *	Mlt	2004	40,014	76,801	225	32	14	bbu
9218777	Lowlands Longevity	Bel	2001	86,848	173,018	289	45	15	bbu
9304239	Lowlands Maine *	Pan	2005	40,039	76,784	225	32	14	bbu
9304186	Lowlands Nello *	Sgp	2004	40,040	76,830	225	32	14	bbu
9317559	Lowlands Opal *	Pan	2007	30,678	55,381	190	32	14	bbu
9271614	Lowlands Orchid *	Pan	2005	88,594	176,193	289	45	15	bbu
9303845	Lowlands Phoenix *	Pan	2004	89,543	177,036	289	45	14	bbu
9464417	Lowlands Queen *	Pan	2008	39,737	76,585	225	32	14	bbu
9590826	Lowlands Sunrise *	Pan	2011	92,752	181,458	292	45	15	bbu

operated by Cobelfret Bulk Carriers NV, Belgium.   * *on time-charter from various Philippine, Singapore and Japanese owners.*

Compania Sud-Americana de Vapores S.A.   Chile

Funnel: *Red with deep black top.* **Hull:** *Grey or white with red or green boot-topping.* **History:** *Founded 1872, acquired Norasia Services SA, Switzerlandand in 2008 and has a minority 27% interest in Navieros Group controlled Compania Chilena de Navegacion Interoceanica SA, Chile (CCNI).* **Web:** *www.csav.com*

IMO#	name	flag	year	grt	dwt	loa	bm	kts	type	former names
7433610	Braztrans I *	Bra	1980	22,011	38,186	194	28	15	bbu	ex Docemarte-99
9224324	CSAV Lanco	Mhl	2001	39,941	50,953	260	32	24	ucc	4,051 teu; ex CSCL Tianjin-10
9197351	Mapocho	Chl	1999	16,986	21,182	168	27	20	ucc	1,587 teu; ex Kribi-02, ANL Okapi-02, Fesco Endeavor-01, Kribi-00

Cobelfret N.V. : LOWLANDS SUNRISE : *Nico Kemps*

IMO#	name	flag	year	grt	dwt	loa	bm	kts	type	former names
9447897	Tempanos	Lbr	2011	88,586	94,649	300	46	23	ucc	8,005 teu
9612882	Tirua	Lbr	2012	88,586	94,375	300	46	23	ucc	8,005 teu
9612870	Tolten	Lbr	2012	88,586	94,600	300	46	23	ucc	8,005 teu
9447914	Torrente	Lbr	2011	88,586	94,661	300	46	23	ucc	8,005 teu
9447873	Tubul	Lbr	2011	88,586	94,666	300	46	23	ucc	8,005 teu
9569970	Tucapel	Lbr	2012	88,586	94,650	300	46	23	ucc	8,005 teu

newbuildings:
managed by Southern Shipmanagement (Chile) Ltd (www.ssm.cl)
owned * by subsidiary Cia. Libra de Navegacao (formed 1977 as Cia Maritima Nacional Ltda to 1999 – www.libra.com.br)
also see chartered vessels with 'CSAC', 'Norasia' and 'CCNI' prefixes in index.

ConocoPhillips Inc. U.S.A.

Funnel: *Red with white 'globe' device.* **Hull:** *Black with red boot-topping.* **History:** *Founded as Continental Oil Co in 1875 on merger of Marland Oil Co and Continental Oil and Transportation Co until renamed Conoco Inc in 1979 and amalgamated with Phillips Petroleum Co in 2002.* **Web:** *www.conocophillips.com*

IMO#	name	flag	year	grt	dwt	loa	bm	kts	type	former names
9244063	Polar Adventure * (2)	Usa	2004	85,387	141,739	273	46	16	tcr	
9206614	Polar Discovery (2)	Usa	2003	85,387	140,320	273	46	16	tcr	
9193551	Polar Endeavour (2)	Usa	2001	85,387	141,740	273	46	16	tcr	l/a Arco Endeavour
9250660	Polar Enterprise * (2)	Usa	2005	85,387	141,739	273	46	16	tcr	
9193563	Polar Resolution (2)	Usa	2002	85,387	141,737	273	46	16	tcr	
9075345	Randgrid (me2) **	Bhs	1995	75,273	122,535	266	46	15	tcs	ex Heidrun-96

managed by Conoco Shipping Co., USA * owned by subsidiary Polar Tankers Inc. (formed 1980 as ARCO Marine Inc until 2000 when acquired by Phillips Petroleum (both USA), ** owned by Teekay Shipping Partners, Norway

Costamare Shipping Co. S.A. Greece

Funnel: *Blue with black top or charterers colours.* **Hull:** *Grey or black with red boot-topping.* **History:** *Formed 1975. Subsidiary, Ciel Shipmanagement S.A. founded 2001.* **Web:** *www.costamare.com*

IMO#	name	flag	year	grt	dwt	loa	bm	kts	type	former names
8703397	Akritas **	Hkg	1987	42,304	39,579	250	32	22	ucc	3,152 teu: ex Cap Akritas-10, Safmarine Igoli-07, APL Costa Rica-03, APL Pacific-01, MSC Pacific-01, Houston Express-99, Saturn-98, California Saturn-97
9308508	Cosco Beijing	Grc	2006	109,149	107,504	351	43	25	ucc	9,383 teu
9305570	Cosco Guangzhou	Grc	2006	109,149	107,526	351	43	25	ucc	9,383 teu
9308510	Cosco Hellas	Grc	2006	109,149	107,483	351	43	25	ucc	9,383 teu
9305582	Cosco Ningbo	Grc	2006	109,149	107,492	351	43	25	ucc	9,383 teu
9305594	Cosco Yantian	Grc	2006	109,149	107,498	351	43	25	ucc	9,383 teu
9200823	Halifax Express	Grc	2000	54,437	66,818	294	32	24	ucc	4,843 teu; ex New York Express-12
8906731	Karmen *	Lbr	1991	37,209	47,230	236	32	21	ucc	3,029 teu: ex Japan Sea-10, Zim Japan-07, Japan Sea-04, Zim Japan-04
8906755	Konstantina *	Mlt	1992	37,209	47,230	236	32	22	ucc	3,029 teu: ex Zim Israel-11
9157703	Koroni	Lbr	1998	39,582	48,244	258	32	24	ucc	3,842 teu: ex Bunga Raya Dua-12
9157698	Kyparissia	Mys	1998	39,582	48,304	258	32	24	ucc	3,842 teu: ex Bunga Raya Satu-12
9244946	Maersk Kalamata	Grc	2003	74,656	81,094	304	40	25	ucc	6,246 teu
9107887	Maersk Kawasaki	Grc	1997	81,488	90,456	318	43	25	ucc	7,908 teu: ex Kirsten Maersk-07

Costamare Shipping Co. : COSCO YANTIAN : *Hans Kraijenbosch*

IMO#	name	flag	year	grt	dwt	loa	bm	kts	type	former names
9244934	Maersk Kingston	Grc	2003	74,661	81,183	304	40	25	ucc	6,252 teu: ex Safmarine Antwerp-08, I/a Maersk Kobe
9196840	Maersk Kobe	Grc	2000	74,661	81,584	304	40	25	ucc	6,252 teu: ex Safmarine Himalaya-07, Sealand Virginia-03
9085560	Maersk Kokura	Grc	1997	81,488	84,900	318	43	25	ucc	7,908 teu: ex Katrine Maersk-08
9244022	Maersk Kolkata	Grc	2003	74,656	81,577	304	40	25	ucc	6,246 teu
9085522	Maersk Kure	Grc	1996	81,488	82,135	318	43	25	ucc	7,908 teu: ex Regina Maersk-07
8906743	Marina *	Mlt	1992	37,209	47,230	236	32	21	ucc	2,402 teu: ex Zim Hong Kong-11
9142942	Messini	Lbr	1997	25,499	34,167	200	30	21	ucc	2,392 teu: ex Pembroke-12, Kota Pahlawan-09, CMA CGM Emerald-04, Pembroke Senator-03, P&O Nedlloyd Fos-01, ECL Europa-99, Pembroke Senator-99
9030723	MSC Antwerp **	Hkg	1993	50,501	59,567	292	32	23	ucc	3,808 teu: ex Sophia Britannia-09, Kirishima-99
9618305	MSC Athens	Grc	2013	92,500	110,875	300	48	22	ucc	8,800 teu
9618317	MSC Athos	Grc	2013	92,500	110,875	300	48	22	ucc	8,800 teu
8417948	MSC Challenger **	Hkg	1986	39,678	37,915	233	32	21	ucc	2,050 teu: ex Navarino-04, Zim Shenzhen-02, California Zeus-98, Hidaka Maru-88
7825411	MSC Kyoto	Grc	1981	43,325	53,540	270	32	23	ucc	3,876 teu: ex Maersk Tokyo-07, Lexa Maersk-97
8613310	MSC Mandraki	Grc	1988	52,191	60,639	294	32	23	ucc	4,437 teu: ex Maersk Mandraki-08, Marit Maersk-04
9256755	MSC Methoni *	Lbr	2003	73,819	85,824	303	40	24	ucc	6,408 teu: ex MSC Viviana-11
8613308	MSC Mykonos	Grc	1988	52,191	60,639	294	32	23	ucc	4,437 teu: ex Maersk Mykonos-09, Marchen Maersk-05
9007817	MSC Namibia II *	Lbr	1991	23,953	31,829	181	31	18	ucc	1,928 teu: ex Maersk Vermont-11, Endeavour-06, Ibn Khaldoun-97, China Sea-94, CMB Drive-91
8907931	MSC Pylos *	Lbr	1991	27,103	29,651	178	32	18	ucc	1,848 teu: ex Oranje-11, Safmarine Oranje-11, Oranje-05, Safmarine Oranje-04, S.A. Oranje-00, Oranje-96, Afrika-91
9007831	MSC Reunion *	Lbr	1992	23,953	31,829	181	31	18	ucc	1,928 teu: ex MSC Sudan II-11, Maersk Maine-11, Enterprise-06, Ibn Zuhr-97, CMB Dawn-92
9275634	MSC Romanos **	Hkg	2003	54,881	68,209	294	32	23	ucc	5,048 teu: ex MSC Linzie-11
9007829	MSC Sierra II *	Lbr	1991	23,953	21,829	181	31	18	ucc	1,928 teu: ex Maersk Maryland-11, Endurance-06, Ibn Jubayr-97, CMB Dolphin-91
9243306	MSC Ulsan **	Hkg	2002	40,108	51,020	258	32	24	ucc	4,132 teu
9400289	Navarino	Grc	2010	91,354	102,303	335	43	26	ucc	8,530 teu: ex Hyundai Navarino-12, MSC Navarino-11, I/a Carmen
9200811	Oakland Express	Grc	2000	54,437	66,781	294	32	24	ucc	4,843 teu: ex Kuala Lumpur Express-08
9117181	Prosper **	Lbr	1996	17,287	22,183	175	27	20	ucc	1,684 teu: ex Forever Prosperity-11, Montania-09, YM Jakarta-06, Montania-06
9197545	Sealand Illinois	Grc	2000	74,661	81,584	304	40	25	ucc	6,252 teu
9196864	Sealand Michigan	Grc	2000	74,583	81,584	304	40	25	ucc	6,252 teu
9196838	Sealand New York	Grc	2000	74,661	81,584	304	40	25	ucc	6,252 teu
9196852	Sealand Washington	Grc	2000	74,661	81,584	304	40	25	ucc	6,252 teu
9200809	Singapore Express	Grc	2000	54,415	66,793	294	32	24	ucc	4,890 teu
9216092	Stadt Lübeck	Pan	2001	13,764	16,764	155	25	19	ucc	1,040 teu: ex New Confidence-10, I/a Stadt Lübeck
9111486	Zagora *	Mlt	1995	10,795	14,100	163	23	17	ucc	1,162 teu: ex CMA CGM Belem-04, Hasselwerder-02, CMBT Oceania-00, Hasselwerder-96
9231810	Zim New York **	Hkg	2002	53,453	62,740	294	32	24	ucc	4,839 teu: ex China Sea-06, Zim New York-04
9280847	Zim Piraeus **	Hkg	2004	53,453	62,740	294	32	24	ucc	5,042 teu: ex Yangtze Star-06, Zim Piraeus-05
9231822	Zim Shanghai **	Hkg	2002	53,453	66,597	294	32	24	ucc	4,839 teu

newbuildings: 3 x 9,000teu containerships [SungdongS4010/11 (2013)],[Jiangnan Changxing H1068-70 (2013/14)] for MSC charter
5 x 8,800teu containerships [Sungdong S4020-4014 (2013)] for Evergreen charter,
** owned or managed by associated Ciel Shipmanagement SA, Greece (formed 2001) or ** by Shanghai Costamare Ship Management Co Ltd, China (founded 2005)*

d'Amico Societa di Navigazione SpA   Italy

Funnel: Yellow with blue 8-pointed star. **Hull:** Grey or black with white or yellow 'd'AMICO', red boot-topping. **History:** Formed 1951.
Web: www.damicoship.com

IMO#	name	flag	year	grt	dwt	loa	bm	kts	type	former names
9122045	Cielo di Agadir †	Mar	1996	16,800	22,984	184	25	20	ucc	1,728 teu: ex CCNI Magallanes-11, Mercosul Pescada-07, Sofia Russ-01, CSAV Vancouver-00, Sofia Russ-00, Cielo del Venezuela-99, Sofia Russ-99, CSAV Rungue-98, Sofia Russ-96

IMO#	name	flag	year	grt	dwt	loa	bm	kts	type	former names
9143879	Cielo di Casablanca †	Mar	1998	9,146	9,950	121	23	18	ucc	951 teu; ex Dartmoor-10, CMA CGM Estrella-08, Maersk Felixstowe-06, Ridvan Ozeler-03
9585651	Cielo di Dublino †	Lbr	2011	23,758	37,064	183	28	14	bbu	
9277486	Cielo di Genova †	Pan	2005	20,211	32,354	177	28	14	bbu	
9341512	Cielo di Guangzhou	Lbr	2006	25,507	38,875	168	29	14	tco	
9380829	Cielo di Livorno †	Pan	2008	22,718	37,277	178	29	14	bbu	
9225330	Cielo di Londra +	Lbr	2001	23,680	36,032	183	27	14	tco	
9241815	Cielo di Milano	Ita	2003	25,400	40,081	176	31	15	tco	
9225251	Cielo di Monfalcone	Ita	2002	27,839	37,450	186	29	14	ggc	
9235696	Cielo di Napoli	Ita	2003	25,400	40,081	176	31	15	tco	
9225328	Cielo di Parigi +	Lbr	2001	23,680	36,032	183	27	15	tco	
9241802	Cielo di Roma	Ita	2003	25,382	40,096	176	31	15	tco	
9231614	Cielo di Salerno +	Lbr	2002	23,680	36,031	183	27	15	tco	
9585663	Cielo di San Francisco †	Lbr	2011	23,758	37,056	183	28	15	bbu	
9370408	Cieli di Savona ‡	Pan	2008	21,192	33,225	180	28	14	bbu	
9595149	Cielo di Vaiano †	Lbr	2012	23,790	37,064	183	28	15	bbu	
9225249	Cielo di Vancouver	Ita	2002	27,828	37,420	186	29	14	ggc	
9174608	High Challenge +	Lbr	1999	28,238	46,475	183	32	14	tco	
9289740	High Courage +	Lbr	2005	30,048	46,991	183	32	14	tco	
9424649	High Efficiency ††	Pan	2009	28,231	46,547	183	32	15	tco	
9272391	High Endeavour +	Lbr	2004	30,028	46,991	183	32	14	tco	ex High Star-04

d'Amico Soc. di Nav. SpA : CIELO DI ROMA : *ARO*

d'Amico Soc. di Nav. SpA : CIELO DI SAVONA : *Chris Brooks*

IMO#	name	flag	year	grt	dwt	loa	bm	kts	type	former names
9272929	High Endurance +	Lbr	2004	30,028	46,991	183	32	14	tco	ex High Pearl-04
9282510	High Energy ‡	Pan	2004	28,245	46,874	180	32	15	tco	
9308223	High Light ‡	Pan	2005	28,245	46,843	180	32	15	tco	
9512747	High Pearl ‡	Sgp	2009	28,813	48,023	180	32	15	tco	
9301005	High Performance +	Lbr	2005	30,081	51,303	183	32	15	tco	
9282522	High Power	Pan	2004	28,245	46,866	180	32	15	tco	
9325324	High Presence +	Sgp	2005	28,245	48,400	180	32	15	tco	
9282558	High Priority +	Sgp	2005	28,245	46,847	180	32	15	tco	
9300996	High Progress +	Lbr	2005	30,081	51,303	183	32	15	tco	
9292357	High Prosperity +	Sgp	2006	28,794	48,711	183	32	15	tco	
9455703	High Seas +	Lbr	2012	29,841	51,768	183	32	15	tco	
9174610	High Spirit +	Lbr	1999	28,238	46,473	183	32	14	tco	
9424651	High Strength ††	Pan	2009	28,231	46,592	183	32	15	tco	
9455820	High Tide +	Lbr	2012	29,841	51,768	183	32	15	tco	
9289738	High Valor +	Lbr	2005	30,048	46,991	183	32	15	tco	
9365817	High Venture +	Lbr	2006	29,942	51,088	183	32	15	tco	
9287168	Medi Baltimore	Ita	2005	39,976	76,469	225	32	14	bbu	
9377688	Medi Bangkok †	Pan	2006	29,986	53,466	189	32	14	bbu	
9279549	Medi Cagliari	Ita	2004	38,877	75,772	225	32	14	bbu	ex Medi Vancouver-07
9300221	Medi Chennai †	Pan	2005	30,822	55,862	190	32	14	bbu	
9301043	Medi Hong Kong	Ita	2006	42,887	82,790	229	32	14	bbu	
9310642	Medi Lausanne †	Pan	2006	42,887	83,002	229	32	14	bbu	
9340491	Medi Lisbon †	Pan	2006	32,379	58,710	190	32	14	bbu	
9249271	Medi Nagasaki †	Lbr	2003	29,295	53,098	189	32	14	bbu	
9403164	Medi Segesta †	Pan	2009	32,379	58,730	190	32	14	bbu	
9350343	Medi Sentosa §	Pan	2008	44,147	83,690	229	32	14	bbu	
9284269	Medi Shanghai †	Pan	2005	31,232	56,094	190	32	14	bbu	
9189768	Medi Tokyo	Ita	1999	38,835	74,356	225	32	14	bbu	
9339480	Medi Valencia	Ita	2008	31,236	56,014	190	32	14	bbu	
9302774	Medi Venezia	Ita	2005	39,727	76,602	225	32	14	bbu	
9273818	Medi Vitoria †	Lbr	2004	39,729	76,616	225	32	14	bbu	

newbuildings: two + 2 options 40,000dwt tco [Hyundai Mipo (2014)] for d'Amico Tankers Dublin
† owned by d'Amico Dry Ltd, Ireland (founded 2002) and + owned by d'Amico Tankers, Dublin, †† owned by DM Shipping, Dublin (51% owned by d'Amico Shipping) and managed by Ishima Pte Ltd., Singapore.
§ jointly owned by Mitsui & Co Ltd and managed by Orient Marine Co Ltd, Japan. ‡ chartered from Far Eastern owners
Smaller tankers operate in 'Handytankers' Pool and other bulk carriers (52-76,000 dwt) with 'Medi' prefix chartered from various owners.

A/S Thor Dahl Shipping   Norway

Funnel: *Various operating company or charterers colours.* **Hull:** *Various, including black with red boot-topping.* **History:** *Founded 1990.* **Web:** *www.thordahl.no or www.jdb.no*

IMO#	name	flag	year	grt	dwt	loa	bm	kts	type	former names
9401673	Mell Selarang	Bhs	2009	18,326	23,332	175	27	19	ucc	1,740 teu: ex Thorstar-12, Cape North-12
9148025	Thorscape	Cyp	1997	29,022	34,907	196	32	21	ucc	2,908 teu: ex Amasis-11, ANL Empress-03, Ibex Empress-02, Amasis-97
9401661	Thorsriver	Bhs	2008	18,326	23,329	175	27	19	ucc	1,740 teu: ex Cape Nelson-12
9149873	Thorstream	Cyp	1998	16,803	23,007	185	25	20	ucc	1,730 teu: Nordstar-11, P&O Nedlloyd Pampas-02, Nordstar-01, Niver Austral-00, Nordstar-99, CSAV Rio Uruguay-99
9135638	Thorswave	Cyp	1996	29,022	35,021	196	32	21	ucc	2,959 teu: ex Eos I-08, Zim Mumbai-07, Eos I-06, Ming Dynasty-02, Hyundai Dynasty-98, Eos I-96

operated by Thor Dahl Management AS (formed 1996 as Jahre Dahl Bergesen to 2005 and now owned by AS Thor Dahl Shipping (52.5%), Bulls Tankrederi AS (22.5%) and management) and managed by Jahre-Wallem AS (formed by JDB 50%, Wallem 40% and B. Skaugen 10%)

Danaos Shipping Co. Ltd.   Greece

Funnel: *Blue or charterers colours.* **Hull:** *Black with red boot-topping or charterers colours.* **History:** *Founded 1976 as successor to Roumeli Shipping formed in early 1970's when Dimitris Coustas bought out partners in joint venture (formed 1963).* **Web:** *www.danaosshipping.gr*

IMO#	name	flag	year	grt	dwt	loa	bm	kts	type	former names
9433793	CMA CGM Attila	Mlt	2011	91,498	101,474	335	43	25	ucc	8,533 teu
9436367	CMA CGM Bianca	Mlt	2011	91,498	101,433	335	43	25	ucc	8,533 teu
9473028	CMA CGM Melisande	Mlt	2012	91,498	101,376	335	43	25	ucc	8,530 teu
9401099	CMA CGM Moliere	Mlt	2009	72,884	83,293	300	40	25	ucc	6,540 teu
9406611	CMA CGM Musset	Mlt	2010	72,884	83,264	300	40	25	ucc	6,540 teu
9406623	CMA CGM Nerval	Mlt	2010	72,884	83,319	300	40	25	ucc	6,540 teu
9406635	CMA CGM Rabelais	Mlt	2010	72,884	83,318	300	40	25	ucc	6,540 teu
9406647	CMA CGM Racine	Mlt	2010	72,884	83,217	300	40	25	ucc	6,540 teu
9436379	CMA CGM Samson	Mlt	2011	91,498	100,383	335	43	25	ucc	8,533 teu
9436355	CMA CGM Tancredi	Mlt	2011	91,498	101,386	335	43	25	ucc	8,530 teu
9285990	CSCL America	Cyp	2004	90,645	101,612	334	43	25	ucc	8,468 teu; ex MSC Baltic-09, CSCL America-07

IMO#	name	flag	year	grt	dwt	loa	bm	kts	type	former names
9285988	CSCL Europe	Cyp	2004	90,645	101,612	334	43	25	ucc	8,468 teu
9307243	CSCL Le Havre	Cyp	2006	108,069	111,790	337	46	26	ucc	9,580 teu
9307229	CSCL Pusan	Cyp	2006	108,069	111,889	337	46	26	ucc	9,580 teu
9278117	Derby D.	Cyp	2004	39,941	50,814	260	32	23	ucc	4,253 teu: ex Bunga Raya Tiga-11, Maersk Derby-09, P&O Nedlloyd Caracas-05
9278105	Deva	Cyp	2004	39,941	50,828	260	32	23	ucc	4,253 teu; ex Bunga Raya Tujah-10, Maersk Deva-09, Vancouver Express-08, Maersk Deva-06, P&O Nedlloyd Caribbean-06
9035993	Duka	Cyp	1992	51,836	61,152	275	37	26	ucc	4,651 teu: ex Hyundai Duke-12, APL Duke-12, Hyundai Duke-11
9001045	Elbe	Grc	1991	37,134	44,008	243	32	22	ucc	2,932 teu: ex Jiangsu Dragon-11, CMA CGM Elbe-10 Hanjin Bremen-03
9443047	Hanjin Algeciras	Mlt	2011	35,595	44,144	223	32	23	ucc	3,459 teu
9443011	Hanjin Buenos Aires	Mlt	2010	35,595	44,060	223	32	23	ucc	3,459 teu
9443059	Hanjin Constantza	Mlt	2011	35,595	44,012	223	32	23	ucc	3,459 teu
9484924	Hanjin Germany	Lbr	2011	114,144	122,962	349	46	25	ucc	10,070 teu
9484948	Hanjin Greece	Lbr	2011	114,144	122,959	349	46	25	ucc	10,070 teu
9484936	Hanjin Italy	Lbr	2011	114,144	122,961	349	46	25	ucc	10,070 teu
9443023	Hanjin Santos	Mlt	2010	35,595	44,164	223	32	23	ucc	3,459 teu
9443035	Hanjin Versailles	Mlt	2010	35,595	44,080	223	32	23	ucc	3,459 teu
8718110	Hope	Cyp	1989	46,697	45,570	276	32	22	ucc	3,918 teu; ex YM Yantian-11, Hope-03, OOCL Hope-00
9149859	Hyundai Advance	Pan	1997	21,611	24,766	182	30	21	ucc	2,181 teu: ex Wan Hai 251-00, Hyundai Advance-98
9475703	Hyundai Ambition	Lbr	2012	140,979	140,565	367	48	24	ucc	12,562 teu
9158587	Hyundai Bridge	Pan	1998	21,611	24,766	182	30	21	ucc	2,181 teu
9035981	Hyundai Commodore	Cyp	1992	51,836	61,152	275	37	25	ucc	4,651 teu: APL Commodore-12, ex Hyundai Commodore-11, MOL Affinity-09, Hyundai Commodore-08
9065625	Hyundai Federal	Cyp	1994	51,841	61,152	275	37	24	ucc	4,411 teu : ex APL Federal-12, Hyundai Federal-11, APL Confidence-09, MOL Confidence-08, Federal-04, Hyundai Federal-03
9149847	Hyundai Future	Pan	1997	21,611	24,799	182	30	21	ucc	2,181 teu
9158575	Hyundai Highway	Pan	1998	21,611	24,799	182	30	21	ucc	2,181 teu
9158563	Hyundai Progress	Pan	1997	21,611	24,766	182	30	22	ucc	2,181 teu: ex Wan Hai 252-00, Hyundai Progress-98
9475686	Hyundai Smart	Lbr	2012	141,770	141,458	367	48	24	ucc	12,562 teu
9475698	Hyundai Speed	Lbr	2012	140,979	141,356	367	48	24	ucc	12,562 teu
9149861	Hyundai Sprinter	Pan	1997	21,611	24,600	182	30	21	ucc	2,181 teu
9149835	Hyundai Stride	Pan	1997	21,611	24,777	182	30	21	ucc	2,181 teu
9475674	Hyundai Tenacity	Lbr	2012	141,770	140,565	366	48	24	ucc	12,562 teu
9473731	Hyundai Together	Lbr	2012	141,770	141,565	366	48	24	ucc	12,562 teu
9149823	Hyundai Vladivostok	Pan	1997	21,611	24,766	182	30	21	ucc	2,181 teu: ex CMA Oakland-01, Hyundai Vladivostok-99
8608585	Independence	Cyp	1986	41,413	38,624	248	32	22	ucc	2,571 teu: ex CMA CGM Vanille-10, Independence-07, MOL Independence-03, Alligator Independence-01

Danaos Shipping Co. : HYUNDAI AMBITION : *Chris Brooks*

IMO#	name	flag	year	grt	dwt	loa	bm	kts	type	former names
8913679	Kalamata	Grc	1991	37,134	43,967	243	32	22	ucc	2,932 teu; ex California Dragon-11, CMA CGM Kalamata-10, Hanjin Singapore-03
9001033	Komodo	Grc	1991	37,134	43,966	243	32	22	ucc	2,932 teu: ex Shenzhen Dragon-11, CMA CGM Komodo-10, Hanjin Elizabeth-03
8705486	Lotus	Grc	1988	42,809	40,638	253	32	22	ucc	2,914 teu: ex CMA CGM Lotus-10, Victory I-07, MOL Victory-03, Alligator Victory-01
8819940	Marathonas	Pan	1991	52,181	60,350	294	32	23	ucc	4,814 teu: ex MSC Marathon-10, Maersk Marathon-08, Mc-Kinney Maersk-06
8819964	Messologi	Pan	1991	52,181	60,350	294	32	23	ucc	4,814 teu: ex Maersk Messologi-11, Mayview Maersk-06
8718122	MV Honour	Cyp	1989	46,697	44,851	275	32	22	ucc	3,918 teu: ex Al Rayyan-11, Norasia Hamburg-08, APL Arabia-04, ANL Hamburg-04, Norasia Hamburg-03, Cosco Bremerhaven-01, Honour-00, OOCL Honour-00, APL Arabia-97, OOCL Honour-96
8819952	Mytilini	Pan	1991	52,181	60,350	294	32	23	ucc	4,814 teu: ex Maersk Mytilini-11, Madison Maersk-06
9256212	SNL Colombo	Lbr	2004	41,855	53,610	264	32	24	ucc	4,334 teu: ex YM Colombo-12, Norasia Integra-07, E.R. Auckland-04, I/a E.R. Wellington
9360910	Taiwan Express	Cyp	2007	40,030	50,813	260	32	23	ucc	4,526 teu: ex YM Seattle-11
9438523	YM Mandate	Lbr	2010	73,675	83,200	299	40	25	ucc	6,572 teu
9438535	YM Maturity	Lbr	2010	73,675	83,200	299	40	25	ucc	6,572 teu
9256224	YM Singapore	Lbr	2004	41,855	53,611	264	32	24	ucc	4,334 teu; ex Norasia Atria-08, E.R. Wellington-04, I/a E.R. Auckland
9363364	YM Vancouver	Cyp	2007	40,030	50,632	260	32	23	ucc	4,253 teu
9391268	Zim Dalian	Mlt	2009	40,030	50,829	260	32	32	ucc	4,526 teu
9389693	Zim Kingston	Mlt	2008	40,030	50,550	260	32	24	ucc	4,526 teu
9403229	Zim Luanda	Mlt	2009	40,030	50,550	260	32	24	ucc	4,526 teu
9389708	Zim Monaco	Mlt	2009	40,030	50,842	260	32	24	ucc	4,526 teu
9363376	Zim Rio Grande	Cyp	2008	40,030	50,842	260	32	24	ucc	4,526 teu
9289681	Zim Sao Paolo	Mlt	2008	40,030	50,818	260	32	24	ucc	4,526 teu

newbuildings:

Dannebrog Rederi A/S   Denmark

Funnel: *Yellow with houseflag, white cross on red penant flag, on broad blue band. Joint venture formed with Jutha Maritime (2006)*
Hull: *Grey with red boot-topping.* **History**: *Formed 1883 as A/S Dannebrog to 1970.* **Web**: *www.dannebrog.com*

IMO#	name	flag	year	grt	dwt	loa	bm	kts	type	former names
9261657	Amalienborg *	Dnk	2004	24,663	40,059	175	31	15	tco	ex Southern Unity-08

Danaos Shipping Co. : ZIM RIO GRANDE : *Chris Brooks*

IMO#	name	flag	year	grt	dwt	loa	bm	kts	type	former names
9488061	Clipper Amber	Pan	2011	9,627	12,731	139	21	15	ggc	ex Ellensborg-12
9488047	Billesborg	Sgp	2011	9,627	12,696	139	21	15	ggc	ex Clipper Angela-12, Billesborg-11
9488035	Brattingsborg	Sgp	2010	9,627	12,705	139	21	15	ggc	
9488061	Clipper Amber	Sgp	2011	9,627	12,731	139	21	15	ggc	ex Ellensborg-12
9488059	Elsborg	Sgp	2011	9,627	12,671	139	21	15	ggc	
9465394	Fredensborg	Sgp	2011	9,627	12,667	139	21	15	ggc	
9431434	SE Panthia	Sgp	2009	9,627	12,840	139	21	15	ggc	ex Elsborg-10
9453781	SE Pelagica	Sgp	2010	9,627	12,738	139	21	15	ggc	ex Billesborg-10
9431460	SE Pacifica	Sgp	2009	9,627	12,649	139	21	15	ggc	ex Ellensborg-09
9316593	Kronborg *	Lbr	2007	25,400	40,208	176	31	15	tco	
9453793	Marselisborg	Lbr	2010	9,627	12,696	139	21	15	ggc	
7725166	Schackenborg +	Pan	1979	14,805	10,470	161	24	15	urc	ex Dana Caribia-84
7725154	Skanderborg +	Pan	1979	14,805	10,470	161	24	15	urc	ex Dana Arabia-84 (len-04)
7725142	Skodsborg +	Pan	1979	14,805	10,470	161	24	15	urc	ex Dana Africa-84
8508369	Stjerneborg +	Sgp	1994	20,370	14,163	174	26	15	urc	ex Medcoa Lome-12, Frederiksborg-09, Global Africa-07 (len-12)

newbuildings:
* owned by Difko Kronborg K/S, + owned by Nordana Shipping (Singapore), managed by Jutha Maritime

Herm Dauelsberg GmbH & Co. KG   Germany

Funnel: *White with black 'D' on cream band between narrow blue bands, or charterers colours.* **Hull:** *Black or grey with red boot-topping.* **History:** *Formed 1857 as shipbrokers and started shipowning in 1857.* **Web:** *www.dauelsberg.de*

IMO#	name	flag	year	grt	dwt	loa	bm	kts	type	former names
9064322	Altavia	Lbr	1995	23,691	30,743	188	30	21	ucc	1,918 yeu: ex Safmarine Tugela-07, Altavia-03, Safmarine Tugela-03, Maersk Nagoya-01, Maersk Santos-99, Choyang Fortune-97, Altavia-95
9290440	Bellavia	Mhl	2005	53,807	66,501	294	32	25	ucc	5,117 teu
9064334	Bonavia	Lbr	1995	23,691	30,743	188	30	21	ucc	1,918 teu: ex CMA CGM Oryx-09, Bonavia-08, Cap Sunion-08, Bonavia-04, Safmarine Maluti-04, Maersk Algeciras-01, Contship Auckland-97, Bonavia-95
9570838	Cervia	Lbr	2010	50.697	92,500	230	38	14	bbu	
9570840	Elvia	Lbr	2010	50.697	92,500	230	38	14	bbu	
9570852	Fulvia	Lbr	2010	50.697	92,500	230	38	14	bbu	
9122435	Lindavia	Lbr	1996	23,825	30,615	188	30	21	ucc	2,078 teu: ex ACX Jasmine-10, Lindavia-06, Maersk Sydney-00, Lindavia-98, Sea Lindavia-98, Lindavia-96
9228564	Lobivia	Lbr	2001	23,652	30,375	188	30	21	ucc	1,918 teu: ex Fathulkhair-09, Cala Pintada-08, Lobivia-04
9122447	Magnavia	Lbr	1996	23,825	30,743	188	30	21	ucc	2,078 teu: ex TS Incheon-09, Magnavia-08, MOL Waratah-02, Alligator Unity-01, Maersk Oceania-00, Magnavia-97
9228576	Marivia	Lbr	2001	23,652	30,375	188	30	21	ucc	2,078 teu: ex SCI Trust-10, Marivia-09
9101508	Novia	Lbr	1995	14,968	20,176	167	25	19	ucc	1,388 teu: ex Melfi Iberia-10, Cala Providencia-08, Novia-04, P&O Nedlloyd Slauerhoff-03, P&O Nedlloyd Mumbai-02, Novia-01, Sea Novia-97, Novia-95
9290452	Octavia	Mhl	2005	53,807	66,501	294	32	25	ucc	5,117 teu
9101510	Olivia	Lbr	1995	14,936	20,416	167	25	19	ucc	1,388 teu: ex P&O Nedlloyd Mahe-02, Olivia-01
9579864	Piavia	Lbr	2011	50.697	92,500	230	38	14	bbu	
9295206	YM Ningbo	Mhl	2005	40,952	55,490	261	32	24	ucc	4,130 teu: ex Cherokee Bridge-07, I/a Clivia
9280811	YM Taichung	Mhl	2005	40,952	55,497	261	32	24	ucc	4,130 teu: ex Chesapeake Bay Bridge-07, I/a Silvia

Diamond Ship Management N.V.   Belgium

Funnel: *Operators colours.* **Hull:** *white with red boot-topping.* **History:** *Founded 2007.* **Web:** *www.diamondship.be*

IMO#	name	flag	year	grt	dwt	loa	bm	kts	type	former names
9015204	Chiquita Belgie *	Bhs	1992	13,049	13,930	158	24	22	grf	
9014755	Chiquita Bremen **	Bhs	1992	10,842	12,890	157	23	21	grf	
9015187	Chiquita Deutschland *	Bhs	1991	13,049	13,930	158	24	22	grf	
9030137	Chiquita Italia *	Bhs	1992	13,049	13,930	158	24	22	grf	
9015199	Chiquita Nederland *	Bhs	1991	13,049	13,930	158	24	21	grf	
9014767	Chiquita Rostock **	Bhs	1993	10,842	12,850	157	24	21	grf	
9030149	Chiquita Scandinavia *	Bhs	1992	13,049	13,930	159	24	21	grf	
9015216	Chiquita Schweiz *	Bhs	1992	13,049	13,930	158	24	22	grf	

* operated by Chiquita Brands (successor to United Fruit Co.) ** chartered to Seatrade

IMO#	name	flag	year	grt	dwt	loa	bm	kts	type	former names

Diana Shipping Services
Greece

Funnel: *White with red cross on white panel between narrow red bands.* **Hull:** *Blue or operators colours.* **History:** *Company founded 2010, associated with Diana Shipping Services which operates a large fleet of bulkers.* **Web:** *www.dcontainerships.com*

IMO#	name	flag	year	grt	dwt	loa	bm	kts	type	former names
9077460	APL Garnet	Mhl	1995	53,519	66,618	294	32	24	ucc	4,729 teu: ex Hyundai Garnet-09, APL Garnet-05, MOL Vigor-05, MSC Louisiana-03,
9077458	APL Sardonyx	Mhl	1995	53,519	65,598	294	32	24	ucc	4,729 teu: ex MOL Vision-09, MSC Maryland-03, APL Sardonyx-02, NOL Sardonyx-98, Neptune Sardonyx-96
9081215	APL Spinel	Mhl	1996	53,519	66,511	294	32	24	ucc	4,729 teu: ex MOL Velocity-09, APL Spinel-05, MOL Velocity-04, APL Spinel-04, MOL Velocity-03, APL Spinel-02, NOL Spinel-98
9215672	Cap Domingo	Lbr	2001	40,085	51,087	257	32	23	ucc	3,739 teu: ex Cap San Marco-12
9227285	Cap Doukato	Lbr	2002	40,085	51,059	257	32	22	ucc	3,739 teu: ex Cap San Raphael-12
9401178	Centaurus	Mhl	2010	36,087	42,604	229	32	23	ucc	3,414 teu: ex Frisia Cottbus-10
8808628	Maersk Madrid	Mhl	1989	50,538	59,285	290	32	23	ucc	4,206 teu: ex Peninsular Bay-06
8904123	Maersk Malacca	Mhl	1990	49,779	56,049	294	32	24	ucc	4,714 teu: ex MSC Malacca-09, Maersk Malacca-08, Munkebo Maersk-03, Alsia-93
8904111	Maersk Merlion	Mhl	1990	49,874	55,971	294	32	24	ucc	4,714 teu: ex MISC Merlion-09, Maersk Merlion-07, Marstal Maersk-03, Arosia-93
9401166	Sagitta	Mhl	2010	36,087	42,614	229	32	23	ucc	3,414 teu: ex Frisia Brussel-10

Dioryx Maritime Corp.
Greece

Funnel: *Blue with blue 'P' on white band, or charterers colours.* **Hull:** *Blue or red with red boot topping.* **History:** *Formed 1947.* **Web:** *none found*

IMO#	name	flag	year	grt	dwt	loa	bm	kts	type	former names
9397614	CMA CGM Jasper	Lbr	2009	40,560	52,427	259	32	24	ucc	4,308 teu
9386495	CMA CGM Lapis	Lbr	2009	40,560	52,513	259	32	24	ucc	4,308 teu
9386483	CMA CGM Opal	Lbr	2009	40,560	52.408	259	32	24	ucc	4,308 teu
9385611	CMA CGM Quartz	Lbr	2008	40,560	52,523	259	32	24	ucc	4,308 teu: ex Argolikos-08
9397602	CMA CGM Topaz	Lbr	2009	40,560	52,366	259	32	24	ucc	4,308 teu
9386471	CMA CGM Turquoise	Lbr	2009	40,560	52,513	259	32	24	ucc	4,308 teu: l/a Kossiakos
9114191	Dorikos	Cyp	1996	19,147	24,074	171	28	19	ucc	1,561 teu: ex CMA CGM Quetzal-12, Dorikos-04, Columbia-04, MSC Africa-01, Dorikos-99, P&O Nedlloyd Bahrain-98. Nedlloyd Seoul-98, Dorikos-96
9464247	Maliakos	Lbr	2012	41,391	51,310	262	32	24	ucc	4,400 teu: ex CCNI Austral-12, STX Maliakos-12
9444417	STX Corinthiakos	Lbr	2010	41,391	51,570	262	32	24	ucc	4,334 teu
9464214	STX Pagasitikos	Lbr	2012	41,391	51,570	262	32	24	ucc	4,334 teu
9442172	STX Patraikos	Lbr	2010	41,391	51,570	262	32	24	ucc	4,334 teu
9114189	Thermaikos	Cyp	1996	19,147	24,457	171	28	19	ucc	1,561 teu: ex CMA CGM Colibri-12, Thermaikos-04, Norsia Punjab-04, Thermaikos-03, Puerto Cabello-03, Thermaikos-02, P&O Nedlloyd Santos-01, Zim Buenos Aires-98, Thermaikos-96, l/a Alvaro Diaz
9236638	Vitality	Cyp	2001	27,093	34,622	210	30	23	ucc	2,602 teu: ex CMA CGM Vitality-06, Laconikos-04, MOL Santiago-02, Laconikos-02

Dockwise Shipping B.V.
Netherlands

Funnel: *Dark blue with black 'D' on white disc on light blue square on white band.* **Hull:** *Black, orange or green with 'DOCKWISE', red boot-topping.* **History:** *Formed by 1994 merger of Wijsmuller Transport BV (formed 1914) with Dock Express Shipping BV (formed 1977) and owned by their respective parents Heerema (70%) and Royal Vopak (formerly Van Ommeren) (30%). Merged with Offshore Heavy Transport ASA, Norway (part owned by Wilh. Wilhelmsen and Dyvi) in 2001. Reported sold to equity group 3i in Jan. 2007.* **Web:** *www.dockwise.com*

IMO#	name	flag	year	grt	dwt	loa	bm	kts	type	former names
9186326	Black Marlin *	Ant	2000	37,938	57,021	218	42	14	ohl	
9186338	Blue Marlin *	Ant	2000	51,821	76,051	218	63	14	ohl	(wid-03)
9618783	Dockwise Vanguard	Nld	2013	91,284	116,173	275	78	14	ohl	L - 07:10:2012
8130875	Mighty Servant 1 (me2)	Nld	1983	29,193	40,910	190	45	14	ohl	(len/wid-98)
8130899	Mighty Servant 3 (me2)	Ant	1984	22,123	27,720	181	40	14	ohl	(rbt-09 – following sinking off Luanda)
8025331	Super Servant 3 (2) **	Ant	1982	10,224	14,138	140	32	13	ohl	
8025343	Super Servant 4 (2) **	Ant	1982	12,642	14,138	140	32	13	ohl	
8001000	Swan	Ant	1981	22,788	30,060	181	32	16	ohl	ex Sea Swan-96, Swan H.L.-89, Dyvi Swan-88
8113554	Swift *	Ant	1983	22,835	32,187	183	32	15	ohl	ex Sea Swift-96, Swift H.L.-89, Dyvi Swift-88
8918942	Talisman *	Ant	1993	42,515	53,000	216	45	14	ohl	ex Front Comor-08, Comor-99 (conv/sht tcr-08)

IMO#	name	flag	year	grt	dwt	loa	bm	kts	type	former names
8617938	Target *	Ant	1990	42,515	53,806	217	45	14	ohl	ex Front Target-07, Genmar Centaur-04, Crude Target-03, Nord-Jahre Target-00, Jahre Target-93 (conv/sht tcr-08)
8113566	Teal	Ant	1984	22,835	32,101	181	32	15	ohl	ex Sea Teal-96, Teal H.L.-89, Dyvi Teal-88
8000977	Tern	Ant	1982	22,788	30,060	181	32	16	ohl	ex Sea Tern-96, Tern H.L.-89, Dyvi Tern-88
8918930	Transporter	Ant	1992	42,609	53,806	217	45	14	ohl	ex Front Sunda-08, Sunda-99 (conv/sht tcr-08)
8512279	Transshelf (me2)	Ant	1987	26,547	34,030	173	40	15	ohl	
8617940	Treasure *	Ant	1990	42,515	53,818	217	45	14	ohl	ex Front Traveller-08, GenmarTraveller-04, Crude Traveller-03, Nord-Jahre Traveller-00, Jahre Traveller-93 (conv/sht tcr-08)
8902967	Triumph *	Ant	1992	42,515	53,818	269	45	14	ohl	ex Marble-08 (conv tcr-08)
8902955	Trustee *	Ant	1991	42,515	54,013	269	45	14	ohl	ex Front Granite-08, Granite-01 (conv tcr-08)
9346029	Yacht Express **	Ant	2007	17,951	12,500	209	32	18	ohl	

*managed by Anglo-Eastern (UK) Ltd., UK (www.angloeasterngroup.com). ** managed by Dockwise Yacht Transport*

Peter Döhle Schiffahrts-KG   Germany

Funnel: *Black with black 'PD' on white diamond on broad red band bordered by narrow white bands, black with yellow 'ICL' above yellow wave inside yellow rectangular outline (Independent) or charterers colours.* **Hull:** *Grey or dark blue with red boot-topping.*
History: *Formed 1956 as Robert Bornhofen KG until 1962, then Peter Döhle to 1973.* **Web:** *www.doehle.de*

IMO#	name	flag	year	grt	dwt	loa	bm	kts	type	former names
9306079	Adelina D.	Iom	2006	15,487	20,580	179	28	21	ucc	1,579 teu: ex TS Keelung-09, I/a Adeline
9400215	Aglaia	Lbr	2011	42,609	52,788	269	33	24	ucc	4,250 teu: ex UASC Zamzam-12, I/a Aglaia
9217553	Altonia	Deu	2000	16,803	22,968	184	25	20	ucc	1,728 teu: ex MOL Ultimate-12, German Senator-08, Safmarine Mgeni-06, Altonia-04, Safmarine Buffalo-03, Maersk Felixstowe-01, CSAV Marsella-00, I/a Altonia
9217565	Amanda	Atg	2000	16,803	22,967	184	25	19	ucc	1,728 teu: ex NYK Lotus-12, Amanda-11, YM Santos-08, MOL Americas-06, Amanda-04, Libra Livorno-03, I/a Amanda
9295945	Anguila	Lbr	2006	66,280	68,228	276	40	25	ucc	5,527 teu: ex Chaiten-12, I/dn Anguila
9219367	Anke	Atg	2002	35,824	42,200	220	32	22	ucc	3,104 teu: ex CSAV Moema-09, Norasia Makalu-06, APL Portugal-05, Antonia-02, I/a Chloe
9306201	Annaba	Lbr	2006	15,487	20,615	168	25	20	ucc	1,579 teu: TS Shenzhen-12, I/a Annaba
9306225	Ava D.	Lbr	2007	15,487	20,647	168	25	20	ucc	1,579 teu: ex TS Hochiminh-12, I/a Ava

Dioryx Maritime Corp. : THERMAIKOS : *Chris Brooks*

IMO#	name	flag	year	grt	dwt	loa	bm	kts	type	former names
9327683	Arelia	Lbr	2008	32,161	39,000	211	32	21	ucc	2,732 teu: ex Maruba Victory-10, Arelia-08
9327671	Ariana	Lbr	2006	32,161	38,700	211	32	21	ucc	2,732 teu: ex Amerigo Vespucci-06
9306067	Calisto	Lbr	2005	15,487	20,615	168	25	20	ucc	1,578 teu: ex Independent Pursuit-10, Heide E-06
9295957	Chacabuco †	Lbr	2006	66,280	68,228	276	40	25	ucc	5,527 teu
9334375	CSAV Itajai	Lbr	2008	35,824	42,213	220	32	22	ucc	3,104 teu: l/dn Hebe
9298648	Daphne	Lbr	2006	35,881	41,748	220	32	22	ucc	3,104 teu: ex CCNI Arica-11, l/dn Daphne
9298636	Demeter	Lbr	2005	35,645	41,850	220	32	22	ucc	3,104 teu: ex CCNI Antillanca-11, Demeter-06
9333369	Emirates Dar es Salaam	Lbr	2006	17,189	22,300	179	28	21	ucc	1,719 teu: ex Viona-12, Safmarine Mbashe-09, Viona-06
9502910	Hanjin Africa	Iom	2012	141,754	140,973	366	48	24	ucc	13,092 teu: c/a Rio Lilly
9502946	Hanjin America	Iom	2012	141,754	140,973	366	48	24	ucc	13,092 teu: c/a Rio Lucy
9502867	Hanjin Asia	Iom	2012	141,754	140,974	366	48	24	ucc	13,092 teu: l/a Rio Eliza
9502972	*Hanjin Blue Ocean*	Iom	2013	141,754	140,900	366	48	24	ucc	13,092 teu: l/a Rio Ragna
9502908	Hanjin Europe	Iom	2012	141,754	140,973	366	48	24	ucc	13,092 teu: l/a Rio Lara
9502958	*Hanjin Harmony*	Iom	2013	141,754	140,900	366	48	24	ucc	13,092 teu: l/a Rio Marie
9501239	Hanjin Sooho	Iom	2012	141,754	140,973	366	48	24	ucc	13,092 teu: l/a Rio Elena
9306237	Independent Accord	Lbr	2007	15,345	20,955	168	25	20	ucc	1,578 teu
9306213	Independent Concept	Lbr	2007	15,345	20,994	168	25	20	ucc	1,578 teu
9477359	Jamila	Lbr	2010	16,137	17,152	161	25	20	ucc	1,388 teu
9477335	Jan	Lbr	2009	16,137	17,121	161	25	19	ucc	1,388 teu
9477347	Jost	Lbr	2010	16,137	17,157	161	25	20	ucc	1,388 teu
9477294	Juliana	Lbr	2009	16,137	17,197	161	25	20	ucc	1,388 teu
9311880	Leto	Lbr	2006	35,881	42,200	220	32	22	ucc	3,104 teu: ex CCNI Antofagasta-11, l/dn Leto
9290816	Limari †	Lbr	2005	42,382	51,870	268	32	25	ucc	4,043 teu
9294824	Lircay	Lbr	2006	42,300	51,870	268	32	25	ucc	4,043 teu: l/dn Ariba
9290804	Loa	Lbr	2005	42,382	51,870	268	32	25	ucc	4,043 teu: l/a Adda
9294836	Longavi †	Lbr	2006	42,300	51,870	268	32	25	ucc	4,043 teu
9395525	Malleco	Lbr	2009	75,572	81,002	306	40	25	ucc	6,589 teu
9400095	Mataquito	Lbr	2010	75,572	81,002	306	40	25	ucc	6,589 teu
9400071	Maullin	Lbr	2010	75,572	81,002	306	40	25	ucc	6,589 teu
9246712	Minna	Lbr	2005	35,881	41,800	220	32	22	ucc	3,104 teu: ex Emirates Liberty-09, Minna-06, Zeus-05
9202481	MOL Amazonia	Lbr	2000	17,167	21,331	169	27	20	ucc	1,600 teu: ex Clou Island-11, Mira-08, Cala Paestum-07, YM Hakata-04, P&O Nedlloyd Canterbury-03, Mira-02
9535151	MOL Garland	Lbr	2011	59,307	71,409	275	40	24	ucc	5,605 teu
9535137	MOL Gateway	Lbr	2011	59,307	71,429	275	40	24	ucc	5,605 teu
9535216	MOL Generosity	Lbr	2012	59,307	71,416	275	40	24	ucc	5,605 teu
9535199	MOL Genesis	Lbr	2012	59,307	71,416	275	40	24	ucc	5,605 teu

Peter Döhle Schiffahrts-KG : AMANDA : *Chris Brooks*

IMO#	name	flag	year	grt	dwt	loa	bm	kts	type	former names
9535175	MOL Guardian	Lbr	2011	59,307	71,416	275	40	24	ucc	5,605 teu
9327669	MSC Davos	Lbr	2006	32,161	39,600	212	32	21	ucc	2,732 teu: ex Vasco da Gama-06, Arosia-06, I/a Vasco da Gama
9447847	MSC Fabiola	Lbr	2010	140,259	146,093	366	48	25	ucc	12,552 teu
9447885	MSC Faustina	Lbr	2011	140,259	146,148	366	48	25	ucc	12,552 teu
9447902	MSC Fillippa	Lbr	2011	140,259	146,073	366	48	25	ucc	12,552 teu
9447861	MSC Filomena	Lbr	2010	140,259	146,161	366	48	25	ucc	12,552 teu
9237486	Norasia Alya	Lbr	2004	35,881	41,748	220	32	22	ucc	3,104 teu: ex Renata-04
9306196	Palena †	Lbr	2006	73,934	81,248	304	40	25	ucc	6,539 teu
9306160	Pangal	Lbr	2006	73,934	81,236	304	40	25	ucc	6,539 teu: I/dn Alda
9306184	Petrohue	Lbr	2006	73,934	81,236	304	40	25	ucc	6,539 teu
9144031	Postojna ‡	Lbr	1998	25,537	46,570	183	31	14	bbu	ex Tristan-08, Glen Helen-08, Alicahue-04
9306158	Pucon †	Lbr	2006	73,934	81,099	304	40	25	ucc	6,539 teu: I/dn Paine
9306287	Puelche	Lbr	2007	73,934	81,243	304	40	25	ucc	6,539 teu
9306172	Puelo †	Lbr	2006	73,934	81,250	304	40	25	ucc	6,539 teu
9144043	Slavnik ‡	Lbr	1998	25,537	46,570	183	31	14	bbu	ex Glen Mooar-09, Antuco-05
9294812	Tabea	Lbr	2006	66,280	68,228	276	40	25	ucc	5,527 teu: ex MSC Turchia-10, Cholguan-06
9290787	Talassa	Lbr	2005	66,280	68,228	276	40	25	ucc	5,527 teu: ex MSC Malta-10, Choapa-06
9290945	Tamina	Lbr	2004	66,280	68,228	276	40	25	ucc	5,527 teu: ex MSC France-10, Copiapo-06, Amazonia-04
9290779	Tessa	Lbr	2005	66,280	67,970	276	40	25	ucc	5,527 teu: ex MSC Egypt-10, Chillan-05, I/dn Arizona
9574729	Teamworth No.1	Lbr	2011	15,392	22,733	159	25	14	bbu	I/a Minika

Peter Döhle Schiffahrts-KG : LOA : *ARO*

Peter Döhle Schiffahrts-KG : MSC DAVOS : *ARO*

IMO#	name	flag	year	grt	dwt	loa	bm	kts	type	former names
9643477	Teamworth No.2	Lbr	2012	15,461	22,631	159	25	14	bbu	
9348493	TS Hongkong	Pan	2006	15,487	20,599	168	25	20	ucc	1,579 teu: l/a Hammonia Xenia
9339595	TS Korea	Lbr	2008	26,358	34,439	209	30	22	ucc	2,504 teu: ex Artemis-08
9360697	TS Singapore	Lbr	2008	26,358	34,282	209	30	22	ucc	2,504 teu: ex Apollon-08
9603506	TW Beijing *	Lbr	2012	51,265	93,243	229	38	14	bbu	
9603520	TW Hamburg *	Lbr	2012	51,265	93,225	229	38	14	bbu	
9603562	TW Jiangsu *	Lbr	2012	51,265	93,225	229	38	14	bbu	
9594121	TW Manila *	Lbr	2012	51,265	93,250	229	38	14	bbu	
9397913	UASC Sitrah	Mhl	2009	42,609	52,788	269	33	24	ucc	4,250 teu: l/a Amalthea
9131216	Valbella	Deu	1998	28,148	46,376	185	32	15	gpc	1,830 teu: ex CCNI Atacama-08, l/a Valbella
9333395	Valdivia	Mhl	2006	17,360	22,229	179	28	21	ucc	1,875 teu
9344722	Valentina	Mhl	2007	17,360	22,263	179	28	21	ucc	1,875 teu
9290177	Vera D.	Lbr	2004	17,188	22,513	179	28	21	ucc	1,719 teu: ex Maersk Vera Cruz09, l/a Pyxis
9290165	Victoria	Lbr	2004	17,188	22,506	179	28	21	ucc	1,719 teu: ex Maersk Victoria-09, l/a Palomar
9344710	Violetta	Mhl	2007	17,360	22,267	179	28	21	ucc	1,875 teu: ex DAL Madagascar-10, Violetta-09, CMA CGM Providencia-08, MOL Drakensberg-07, l/a Violetta
9144055	Vipava ‡	Lbr	1998	25,537	46,570	183	31	14	bbu	ex Isolde-08, Glen Maye-06, Allipen-05
9236535	YM Portland	Lbr	2003	51,364	58,255	286	32	25	ucc	4,444 teu: ex Norasia Enterprise-07, Amaranta-03

newbuildings: 8 x 10,000 teu container ships [Yangzijiang SY]
also owns/manages a large number of smaller vessels and has a 13% minority interest in Navieros Group controlled Compania Chilena de Navegacion Interoceanica SA, Chile (CCNI)
* managed by Döhle IOM Ltd, UK (formed 1994 as Midocean Maritime Ltd to 2001 - www.doehle-iom.com)
† managed by Southern Shipmanagement (Chile) Ltd, Chile (www.ssm.cl) or ‡ by Splosna Plovba, Slovenia.

Hammonia Reederei GmbH & Co. KG

Funnel: *Charterers colours.* **Hull:** *Red with red boot-topping.* **History:** *Founded 2003 jointly by Peter Döhle and HCI Hanseatische Capital AG.* **Web:** *www.hammonia.org*

IMO#	name	flag	year	grt	dwt	loa	bm	kts	type	former names
9316323	Apulia	Lbr	2005	30,047	35,741	208	32	22	ucc	2,763 teu: ex CCNI Punta Arenas-11, l/d Amasia
9149316	Austria	Cyp	1997	25,608	34,015	208	30	21	ucc	2,468 teu: ex CSAV Chicago-10, Maersk Freeport-99, Liberta-99, Montebello-99, l/a Liberta
9149304	Belgica	Deu	1997	25,608	34,015	208	30	21	ucc	2,468 teu: ex Emirates Rafiki-11, Belgica-10, Cap Egmont-08, Cap Norte-06, Santos Express-03, Sea Ocelot-02, Transroll Argentina-00, Cap Norte-99, Impala-98, Brasil Star-98, Impala-97
9280665	CMA CGM Wagner	Lbr	2004	65,247	73,235	277	40	24	ucc	5,770 teu
9219355	CS Discovery	Lbr	2001	35,645	42,089	220	32	22	ucc	3,104 teu: ex Norasia Balkans-10, Norasia Taurus-05, APL Mexico-04, l/a Katjana, l/dn Celine
9477309	CSAV La Ligua	Lbr	2010	40,541	50,488	260	32	24	ucc	4,253 teu: c/a Hammonia Calabria
9477311	CSAV Laraquete	Lbr	2010	40,541	50,488	260	32	24	ucc	4,253 teu: c/a Hammonia Granada

Peter Döhle Schiffahrts-KG : MSC FILOMENA : *Hans Kraijenbosch*

IMO#	name	flag	year	grt	dwt	loa	bm	kts	type	former names
9301483	CSAV Paris	Lbr	2006	89,941	102,761	334	43	25	ucc	7,928 teu: ex-MSC Paris-11, c/a Hammonia Hamburg
9301471	CSAV Valencia	Lbr	2006	89,941	102,756	335	43	25	ucc	7,928 teu: ex MSC Valencia-12, Hammonia Jork-06
9219393	Emirates Ganges *	Lbr	2003	35,645	42,062	220	32	22	ucc	3,104 teu: ex TS Dubai-12, Azalea-06, APL Shanghai-07, Azalea-03, l/a Clarissa
9219418	Emirates Kabir	Deu	2003	35,645	41,850	220	32	22	ucc	3,104 teu: ex APL Jakarta-06, Julia-03, Alessa-03, l/a Carmen
9326823	Emirates Nile	Lbr	2006	26,836	34,248	210	30	21	ucc	2,556 teu: ex Libra Ipanema-11, l/a Hammonia Emden
9336165	Emirates Zambezi	Lbr	2006	26,435	34,305	209	30	22	ucc	2,546 teu: ex Hammonia Palatium-11, MOL Stability-09, CCNI Ningbo-09, l/dn Hammonia Palatium
9071480	Hammonia Adriaticum †	Gib	1993	9,581	12,721	150	23	17	ucc	1,016 teu: ex Mare Adriaticum-12, Mekong Stream-03, Mare Adriaticum-03, ACX Wagle-02, Mare Adriaticum-00, Rotterdam Stad-98, Mare Adriaticum-97, Sea Nordic-95, Independent Trader-94, Mare Adriaticum-94
9141314	Hammonia Africum †	Lbr	1997	29,383	34,670	196	32	22	ucc	2,859 teu: ex-Kota Ekspres-12, Mare Africum-02
8910108	Hammonia Balticum †	Gib	1993	9,584	12,715	150	23	17	ucc	1,016 teu: ex Mare Balticum-12 X-Press Konkan-02, Mare Balticum-01, Saudi Dammam-99, Mare Balticum-99, Maersk Euro Octavo-94, Mare Balticum-93
9376012	Hammonia Bavaria	Lbr	2009	26,435	34,000	209	30	22	ucc	2,504 teu
9336177	Hammonia Berolina	Lbr	2007	26,435	34,236	209	30	22	ucc	2,546 teu
9110951	Hammonia Caspium †	Gib	1995	29,383	34,625	196	32	21	ucc	2,859 teu: ex Mare Caspium-12, CMA CGM Beirut-11, Maersk Portland-07, Mare Caspium-04, ANL China-02, NYK Minerva-01, Mare Caspium-00
9400186	Hammonia Galicia	Lbr	2010	42,609	52,788	268	32	24	ucc	4,178 teu
9122394	Hammonia Gallicum †	Lbr	1996	29,383	34,671	196	32	22	ucc	2,959 teu: ex Mare Gallicum-12, YM Hiroshima-10, Mare Gallicum-06, Ipex Emperor-02, OOCL Haven-01, Mare Gallicum-00, Acapulco-98, TMM Acapulco-97, Mare Gallicum-96
9326835	Hammonia Husum	Lbr	2006	26,836	34,253	210	30	21	ucc	2,546 teu: ex Libra Copacabana-11, l/a Hammonia Husum
9175975	Hammonia Internum	Lbr	1997	29,383	34,705	196	32	22	ucc	2,959 teu: ex Mare Internum-12, Maersk Pittsburg-07, Mare Internum-04
9143518	Hammonia Ionium †	Lbr	1997	29,750	34,800	196	32	21	ucc	2,959 teu: ex Mare Ionium-12, Tiger Star-11, Mare Ionium-10, Maersk Peterhead-09, OOCL Harmony-04, Mare Ionium-00
9515759	Hammonia Korsika	Lbr	2010	32,987	56,722	205	32	14	bbu	
9515747	Hammonia Malta	Lbr	2010	32,987	56,700	205	32	14	bbu	
9383261	Hammonia Massilia	Lbr	2008	26,435	34,000	209	30	22	ucc	2,546 teu: ex TS India-10, Hammonia Massilia-08
9336191	Hammonia Pacificum	Lbr	2007	26,435	34,242	209	30	22	ucc	2,546 teu
9335983	Hammonia Pomerenia	Lbr	2007	25,320	34,191	209	30	22	ucc	2,504 teu: ex CCNI Busan-09
9383259	Hammonia Roma	Lbr	2009	25,320	33,800	209	30	22	ucc	2,546 teu: ex TS Malaysia-10, l/a Hammonia Roma
9151527	Hammonia Thracium	Lbr	1997	29,383	34,705	196	32	22	ucc	2,959 teu: ex Mare Thracium-12, Maersk Petersburg-07, Mare Thracium-04, MSC Oregon-01, Mare Thracium-00
9477385	*Hammonia Toscana*	Lbr	2013	39,941	57,750	255	37	22	ucc	4,785 teu
9383247	Hammonia Teutonica	Lbr	2008	26,435	34,376	209	30	22	ucc	2,546 teu: ex MOL Serenity-10, Hammonia Teutonica-08
9400203	Hammonia Venetia	Lbr	2010	42,609	52,788	268	32	24	ucc	4,178 teu: ex Valparaiso Express-12, c/a Hammonia Venetia
9149328	Helvetia	Deu	1998	25,608	34,015	208	30	21	ucc	2,468 teu: ex CCNI Guayas-12, Alianca Hong Kong-06, Columbus Chile-04, Alianca Rotterdam-02, Lykes Traveler-01, CMA CGM Gaugain-01, CGM Gaugain-00, Charlotta-98
9273806	HR Constellation	Lbr	2006	10,899	12,476	157	22	17	ghl	cr: 2(240): ex Beluga Constellation-11, l/a Beluga Constitution
9273791	HR Constitution	Atg	2006	10,899	12,479	157	22	17	ghl	cr: 2(240); ex Beluga Constitution-11, l/a Beluga Constellation
9214563	HR indication	Lbr	2000	11,434	13,289	162	20	17	ghl	cr: 2(350), 1(150): ex Beluga Indication-11, Nirint Iberia-07, Beluga Indication-06, CEC Apollon-04 (len-07)

IMO#	name	flag	year	grt	dwt	loa	bm	kts	type	former names
9214551	HR Intonation	Lbr	2000	11,434	13,426	162	20	17	ghl	cr: 2(350), 1(150): ex Beluga Intonation-11, Nirint Atlas-07, Beluga Intonation-05, Nirint Atlas-04, TMC Atlas-03, Atlas-02, Industrial Atlas-02, CEC Atlas-01 (len-07)
9187033	HR Margaretha	Lbr	1999	11,894	17,539	143	22	16	ggc	ex SE Verdant-12, Margaretha Green-10, Newpac Cumulus-05, Margaretha Green-04, Nirint Voyager-02, Coral Green-01, Margaretha Green-00
9164017	HR Maria	Lbr	1998	11,894	17,539	143	22	16	ggc	ex SE Viridian-12, Maria Green-10, BBC India-08, Maria Green-04
9164029	HR Marion	Lbr	1999	11,894	17,539	143	22	16	ggc	ex SE Verdigris-12, Marion Green-10, BBC Malaysia-08, Marion Green-06
9336189	Independent Pursuit	Lbr	2007	26,435	34,282	209	30	22	ucc	2,546 teu: ex Hammonia Fortuna-11
9481532	Independent Voyager	Lbr	2011	28,561	39,164	225	30	22	ucc	2,790 teu: I/a Hammonia Baltica, I/d Positano
9246683	Letavia	Lbr	2005	35,881	42,157	220	32	22	ucc	3,104 teu: ex Emirates Freedom-09, Letavia-06, Norasia Atlas-05, I/a Cosima
9246695	Lutetia	Lbr	2005	35,881	41,802	220	32	22	ucc	3,104 teu: ex Emirates Marina-11, CSAV Rio Trancura-06, Coletta-05
9085558	Maersk Karlskrona	Lbr	1996	81,488	82,135	318	43	25	ucc	7,908 teu: ex Karen Maersk-08
9085546	Maersk Kleven	Lbr	1996	81,488	84,900	318	43	25	ucc	7,908 teu: ex Kate Maersk-08
9085534	Maersk Kotka	Lbr	1996	81,488	84,900	318	43	25	ucc	7,908 teu: ex Knud Maersk-08
9301495	MSC Bilbao	Lbr	2006	89,941	102,759	334	43	25	ucc	7,928 teu: I/dn Hammonia Bremen
9219379	Polonia	Lbr	2003	35,645	41,850	221	32	22	ucc	3,104 teu: ex Libra Rio-12, I/a Katharina, I/dn Albona
9383235	TS Qingdao	Lbr	2008	26,435	34,331	209	30	22	ucc	2,546 teu: ex APL Qingdao-10, Hyundai Qingdao-09 Hammonia Holsatia-08
9401051	UASC Shuwaikh	Lbr	2009	39,900	50,849	260	32	24	ucc	4,526 teu: I/a Benjamin Schulte-09

* owned by Saxonia Schiffahrts, † managed for Hansa Mare Reedrei

Dole Food Co.   Costa Rica

Funnel: *Dark blue with with red 'Dole' symbol on white band or charterers colours.* **Hull:** *White or cream with red 'Dole' symbol above blue line, blue boot-topping.* **History:** *Founded 1851 and 1975 merged with Castle & Cook Inc to 1991.* **Web:** *www.dole.com*

9046328	Dole Africa	Bhs	1994	10,584	10,288	150	23	21	grf	
9046502	Dole America	Bhs	1994	10,584	10,288	150	23	21	grf	
9046526	Dole Asia	Bhs	1994	10,584	10,288	150	23	21	grf	
8513467	Dole California	Bhs	1989	16,488	11,800	179	27	20	ucc	890 teu
9185281	Dole Chile	Bhs	1999	31,779	30,145	205	32	21	ucc	2,046 teu
9185293	Dole Colombia	Bhs	1999	31,779	30,145	205	32	21	ucc	2,046 teu
8900335	Dole Costa Rica	Bhs	1991	16,488	11,800	179	27	20	ucc	890 teu
8513479	Dole Ecuador	Bhs	1989	16,488	11,800	179	27	20	ucc	890 teu
9046514	Dole Europa	Bhs	1994	10,584	10,288	150	23	21	grf	
8900323	Dole Honduras	Bhs	1991	16,488	11,800	179	27	20	ucc	910 teu
8408868	Tropical Mist	Bhs	1986	9,749	11,998	149	22	20	grf	
8408882	Tropical Sky	Bhs	1986	9,749	11,998	149	22	20	grf	
8408894	Tropical Star	Bhs	1986	9,749	11,998	149	22	20	grf	

managed by subsidiary Reefership Marine Services Ltd, Costa Rica (formed 1976 as Intercontinental Transportation Services Ltd to 1991 and Dole Fresh Fruit International Ltd to 2000)

DT-Bereederungs GmbH & Co. KG   Germany

Funnel: *Yellow or charterers colours.* **Hull:** *Black, green, blue and grey with red boot-topping.* **History:** *Controlled by Danz (shipowners since 1870) and Tietjens (since 1824) families formed as Danz und Tietjens Schiffahrts KG in 1982, being renamed in 2003.* **Web:** *www.danz-tietjens.com*

9105009	Alemania	Atg	1995	8,633	9,200	133	23	18	ucc	913 teu: ex Sea Gale-07 , Sophie Rickmers-97
9010079	Arminia *	Atg	1994	9,601	12,310	150	22	17	ucc	1,012 teu: ex CMA CGM Tobruk-10, Arminia-08, MOL Elite-05, Arminia-04, MOL Loyalty-04, P&O Nedlloyd Cartagena-04, Griffin Africa-02, Maersk Harare-09, Gamtoos-98, Bulwark-97, Maersk Santos-96, I/a Bulwark
9071272	Austria *	Atg	1993	10,742	14,111	163	22	17	ucc	1,162 teu: ex Zim Houston III-08, Lukas-99, Kaedi-99, Kano-98, Lukas-98
9113446	Bavaria *	Atg	1996	14,473	18,355	159	24	19	ucc	1,205 teu: ex CSAV Cedar-09, Bavaria-08, ANL Yanderra-08, Bavaria-07, TS Kelang-06, ACX Primrose-04, Doris Wulff-03, Sakura-01, Norasia Montreal-00, Direct Jabiru-99, OOCL Amity-98, Doris Wulff-97, Nuova Ionia-96, Doris Wulff-96, Nuova Ionia-96, I/a Doris Wulff

IMO#	name	flag	year	grt	dwt	loa	bm	kts	type	former names
9497323	Burgia	Atg	2010	43,717	79,403	229	32	15	bbu	
9230787	Gloria *	Atg	2001	16,803	22,967	185	25	20	ucc	1,728 teu: ex P&O Nedlloyd Pessoa-04, P&O Nedlloyd Lagos-02, I/a Gloria
9277400	Oland	Mlt	2003	7,519	8,621	137	21	19	ucc	822 teu: I/a Frisia
9497335	Selandia	Atg	2011	43,717	79,508	229	32	14	bbu	

* owned or managed by associated BBC-Burger Bereederungs Contor GmbH & Co KG, Germany

Ecuadorian Line Inc.   U.S.A.

Funnel: *Dark blue with yellow 'EL' on red disc.* **Hull:** *Orange with red boot-topping.* **History:** *Founded 1988.*
Web:*www.ecuadorianline.com*

9059602	Albemarle Island	Bhs	1993	14,061	14,160	179	25	21	grf	
9059614	Barrington Island	Bhs	1993	14,061	14,140	179	25	21	grf	
9059616	Charles Island	Bhs	1993	14,061	14,140	179	25	21	grf	
9059638	Duncan Island	Bhs	1993	14,061	14,140	179	25	21	grf	
9059640	Hood Island	Bhs	1994	14,601	14,140	179	25	21	grf	

managed by Trireme Vessel Management n.v., Belgium

Eitzen Group   Norway

Funnel: *Black with white 'E' inside blue 'C' on broad red band or * white with broad blue band beneath broad black top, some with 'ESO' below band.* **Hull:** *Black or red with white 'EITZEN' or 'EITZEN CHEMICAL', red boot-topping.* **History:** *Founded 1883 and traded as Tschudi & Eitzen from 1936 until joint venture terminated in 2003. Sichem Shipping merged with Blystad's Songa Shipholding in 2006 to form Eitzen Chemical, which acquired Mosvold Chemical AS in 2007.* **Web:** *www.eitzen-group.com or www.ems-shipmanagement.com*

9416020	Sichem Contester *	Sgp	2007	11,757	19,822	147	24		tco	
9358632	Sichem Defender *	Pan	2006	11,660	19,999	144	24	-	tco	
9388704	Sichem Eagle	Sgp	2008	17,789	25,421	170	26	-	tco	
9396012	Sichem Falcon	Sgp	2009	17,500	25,418	170	26	-	tco	
9396000	Sichem Hawk	Sgp	2008	17,789	25,385	170	26	-	tco	
9396024	Sichem Osprey	Sgp	2009	17,500	25,418	170	26	-	tco	
9340415	Sichem Pace	Mlt	2006	11,568	19,982	146	24	11	tco	
9326914	Siteam Adventurer	Sgp	2007	26,751	46,190	183	32	-	tco	
9111058	Siteam Anja	Mhl	1997	28,027	44,640	183	32	14	tco	ex Team Anja-07, Simunye-05, Engen Simunye-00
9326938	Siteam Discoverer	Mhl	2008	26,571	46,005	183	32	-	tco	
9326902	Siteam Explorer	Mhl	2007	27,199	46,190	183	32	-	tco	
9343194	Siteam Leader	Sgp	2009	27,139	46,190	183	32	-	tco	
9326926	Siteam Voyager	Sgp	2008	27,139	46,190	183	32	-	tco	

also operates a large number of smaller tankers
vessels owned by Eitzen Chemical Singapore Pte. Ltd. except * managed by Eitzen Chemical A/S, Denmark

Eletson Corp.   Greece

Funnel: *Buff base with red-edged blue five-pointed star on broad white band edged with narrow blue bands, beneath black top.* **Hull:** *Black with red boot-topping.* **History:** *Formed 1966 as Eletson Maritime Services Inc to 1982.* **Web:** *www.eletson.com*

9232448	Agathonissos	Grc	2002	57,062	106,149	244	42	15	tco	
9031959	Alkyonis	Grc	1992	39,265	66,895	228	32	14	tco	
9250531	Alonissos	Grc	2004	57,062	106,149	244	42	15	tco	
9411733	Anafi	Grc	2009	22,971	26,577	173	28	16	lpg	35,000 m³
9176773	Angistri	Grc	2000	39,283	76,019	213	37	15	tcr	
9281853	Antikeros	Grc	2004	40,038	69,714	228	32	14	tco	ex LMZ Artemis-07
9306562	Dhonoussa	Grc	2005	40,038	69,180	228	32	15	tco	ex LMZ Afroditi -07
9254850	Erikoussa	Grc	2003	41,679	70,142	228	32	15	tco	
9405564	Fourni	Grc	2010	29,663	51,611	183	32	15	tco	
9081813	Kandilousa	Grc	1995	28,507	46,700	183	32	14	tco	
9405552	Kastos	Grc	2010	29,663	51,589	183	32	15	tco	
9405540	Kimolos	Grc	2010	29,663	51,522	183	32	15	tco	
9405538	Kinaros	Grc	2009	29,663	51,601	183	32	15	tco	
9232450	Makronissos	Grc	2002	57,062	106,149	244	42	15	tcr	
9250543	Megalonissos	Grc	2004	57,062	106,290	244	42	15	tco	
9412062	Nisyros	Grc	2009	22,971	26,540	173	28	16	lpg	35,000 m³
9176761	Pelagos	Grc	1999	39,283	76,020	213	37	15	tcr	
9306574	Polyaigos	Grc	2005	40,038	69,509	228	32	15	tco	ex LMZ Nefeli-07
9081825	Serifopoulo	Grc	1995	28,507	46,700	183	32	14	tco	
9081837	Serifos	Grc	1995	28,507	46,700	183	32	14	tco	
9254862	Skopelos	Grc	2003	41,679	70,146	228	32	15	tco	
9035137	Sporades	Grc	1993	39,265	66,895	228	32	14	tco	
9074585	Stavronisi	Grc	1996	38,667	68,232	243	32	14	tco	
9319545	Strofades	Grc	2006	40,038	69,431	228	32	15	tco	ex LMZ Nafsika-07
9406269	Symi	Grc	2012	22,971	26,597	173	28	16	lpg	35,000 m³

IMO#	name	flag	year	grt	dwt	loa	bm	kts	type	former names
9412086	Telendos	Grc	2010	22,971	26,634	173	28	16	lpg	35,000 m³
9412074	Tilos	Grc	2009	22,971	26,587	173	28	16	lpg	35,000 m³
9031961	Velopoula	Grc	1993	39,265	66,895	228	32	14	tco	

newbuildings:

Enesel S.A. Greece

Funnel: *Blue with white logo.* **Hull:** *Grey with red boot topping.* **History:** *Derivative of the Lemos Shipping dynasty. Enesel formed 2003 by merger of Avra Shipmanagement & Sealuck Shg. Corp.* **Web :** *eneselsa.com*

IMO#	name	flag	year	grt	dwt	loa	bm	kts	type	former names
9224295	Antonis	Grc	2001	160,100	309,371	333	58	14	tcr	
9285823	Irene SL	Grc	2004	161,175	319,247	333	60	14	tcr	
9274616	Pantelis	Cyp	2004	62,877	114,500	250	44	14	tcr	
9274800	Sparto	Cyp	2004	62,877	114,549	250	44	14	tcr	
9315367	Spyros	Grc	2007	161,175	319,247	333	60	14	tcr	
9452490	Thalassini Axia	Mlt	2010	34,374	58,608	196	32	14	bbu	
9452517	Thalassini Kyra	Mlt	2010	34,374	58,609	196	32	14	bbu	
9452505	Thalassini Niki	Mlt	2010	34,374	58,923	196	32	14	bbu	
9633939	*Hyundai 2527*		2014	119,000	123,730	332	48		ucc	9,814 teu
9633941	*Hyundai 2528*								ucc	9,814 teu
9633953	*Hyundai 2529*								ucc	9,814 teu
9633965	*Hyundai 2539*								ucc	9,814 teu

newbuildings : 10 x 13,806 teu containerships, 368 x 51m. [Hyundai 2614-19, 2623-29(2013/14)] for 5 year lease to Evergreen

Enterprises Shipping & Trading S.A. Greece

Funnel: *Light grey with black top or * black with gold anchor on broad white band below narrow green band and black top or ** grey with narrow white band on broad blue band.* **Hull:** *Black or red with red boot-topping, * black with with yellow 'GOLDEN ENERGY' or ** brown with white 'SafOre'.* **History:** *Formed 1973 and part of Restis Group, who acquired bulk shipping interest of Safmarine (founded 1948) in 1999.* **Web:** *www.estsa.gr*

IMO#	name	flag	year	grt	dwt	loa	bm	kts	type	former names
9082683	African Jaguar	Bhs	1996	16,041	26,477	169	26	14	bbu	ex Handy Roseland-05
9082609	African Lion	Bhs	1995	16,041	26,300	169	26	14	bbu	ex Handy Gunner-05
9125217	African Puma	Bhs	1997	16,041	26,412	169	26	14	bbu	ex Pacific Selesa-05, l/a Selesa
9125229	African Wildcat	Bhs	1997	16,041	26,391	169	26	14	bbu	ex Marquisa-05
9164627	Antwerp Max	Iom	1998	38,489	73,144	225	32	14	bbu	ex Bunga Saga Lima-05
9431503	Assos Striker	Bhs	2010	33,044	56,819	190	32	14	bbu	
9070723	Bay Ranger	Bhs	1996	24,550	43,125	185	31	14	bbu	ex Bunga Melor Dua-05
9050383	Bergen Max	Iom	1994	39,012	72,338	225	32	14	bbu	ex Bunga Saga Tiga-05
9398682	Braverus	Iom	2009	88,479	170,015	287	45	15	bbu	
9050369	Bremen Max	Iom	1993	39,012	73,503	225	32	14	bbu	ex Bunga Saga Satu-05
9164639	Brugge Max	Iom	1998	38,489	73,056	225	32	14	bbu	ex Bunga Saga Enam-05
9070735	Channel Ranger	Bhs	1995	24,550	43,108	185	31	14	bbu	ex Bunga Melor Tiga-05
9074511	Choulex	Bmu	1996	77,211	150,961	274	45	14	bbu	ex Sanko Spark-10, World Spark-04
9398694	Citius	Iom	2009	88,479	170,024	287	45	14	bbu	
9398709	Colossus	Iom	2010	88,479	170,060	287	45	14	bbu	
9132686	Constantia	Bhs	1996	83,658	171,039	289	45	14	bbu	ex Cape Mercury-00, First Mercury-99
9438030	Davakis G	Bhs	2008	31,137	53,800	190	32	14	bbu	

Enesel S.A. : PANTELIS : *ARO*

IMO#	name	flag	year	grt	dwt	loa	bm	kts	type	former names
9438042	Delos Ranger	Bhs	2008	31,091	54,057	190	32	14	bbu	
9438054	Delphi Ranger	Bhs	2009	31,091	53,800	190	32	14	bbu	
9071595	Delta Ranger	Bhs	1995	24,550	43,108	185	31	14	bbu	ex Bunga Melor Empat-05
9398711	Divinus	Iom	2010	88,479	170,022	287	45	15	bbu	
9493652	Dynamic Striker	Bhs	2010	33,044	56,736	190	32	14	bbu	
9171278	Elbe Max	Iom	1999	38,972	73,548	225	32	14	bbu	ex Bunga Saga 10-05
9387281	Energy Centaur	Iom	2008	42,296	74,995	228	32	14	tco	
9387970	Energy Centurion *	Iom	2008	42,998	74,471	228	32	14	tco	
9259329	Energy Century	Iom	2003	41,397	70,470	228	32	14	tco	
9288265	Energy Challenger	Iom	2005	42,172	70,675	228	32	14	tco	
9288356	Energy Champion	Iom	2005	42,172	70,681	228	32	14	tco	
9292606	Energy Chancellor	Iom	2005	42,172	70,558	228	32	14	tco	
9275658	Energy Commander	Iom	2004	42,172	70,691	228	32	14	tco	
9275660	Energy Conqueror	Iom	2004	42,172	70,616	228	32	14	tco	
9388015	Energy Panther	Iom	2008	29,494	46,846	183	32	14	tco	
9388003	Energy Patriot *	Iom	2008	29,494	46,606	183	32	14	tco	
9281920	Energy Pioneer	Iom	2004	30,008	51,224	183	32	14	tco	
9281932	Energy Power	Iom	2004	30,008	51,383	183	32	14	tco	
9278052	Energy Pride **	Iom	2004	30,008	51,318	183	32	14	tco	
9387279	Energy Progress *	Iom	2008	29,494	46,606	183	32	14	tco	
9278064	Energy Protector **	Iom	2004	30,008	51,314	183	32	14	tco	
9388027	Energy Puma	Iom	2008	29,494	49,549	183	32	14	tco	
9117325	Energy Ranger	Iom	1996	26,330	45,950	190	32	14	bbu	ex Energy Saver-02, Cape Infanta-02
9297515	Energy Skier	Iom	2005	81,345	159,089	274	48	15	tco	
9297503	Energy Sprinter	Iom	2005	81,345	159,089	274	48	15	tco	
9391646	Eternus	Iom	2010	88,479	170,018	287	45	15	bbu	
9117313	Force Ranger	Iom	1996	26,330	45,950	189	32	14	bbu	ex Cape Agulhas-02
9398735	Furious	Iom	2010	88,479	170,037	287	45	15	bbu	
9398747	Generous	Iom	2010	88,479	170,024	287	45	15	bbu	
9398759	Genius	Iom	2010	88,479	170,057	287	45	15	bbu	
9164641	Ghent Max	Iom	1998	38,489	73,220	225	32	14	bbu	ex Bunga Saga Tujuh-05
9605853	Gladiator	Bhs	2012	33,044	57,000	190	32	14	bbu	
9266944	Glorius	Iom	2004	87,720	171,314	289	45	14	bbu	
9304241	Good Hope Max	Iom	2005	40,039	76,739	225	32	14	bbu	ex Georgios F-06, Ocean Lady-05
9050395	Hamburg Max	Iom	1994	39,012	72,338	225	32	14	bbu	ex Bunga Saga Empat-05
9588603	Helvetia One	Lbr	2012	51,195	92,737	229	38	14	bbu	ex Trans Beijing-12
9493676	Heroic Striker	Bhs	2010	33,044	56,820	190	32	14	bbu	
9403504	Imperius	Iom	2011	93,196	179,062	292	45	15	bbu	
9169249	Iron Baron **	Iom	1999	88,385	169,981	289	45	14	bbu	ex Philippe LD-04
9108300	Iron King **	Iom	1996	81,155	161,167	280	45	14	bbu	ex Kalahari-02
9116747	Iron Queen **	Iom	1996	81,155	161,183	280	43	14	bbu	ex Karoo-02
9070711	Island Ranger	Bhs	1994	24,550	42,427	185	31	14	bbu	ex Bunga Melor Satu-05
9589140	Jaguar Max	Bhs	2012	44,326	81,309	229	32	14	bbu	
8610277	Hainan Baosha 001	Lbr	1989	32,096	10,200	179	28	15	fff	ex Vsevolod Sibirtsev-11
9063665	Hainan Baosha 011	Bhs	1996	9,438	9,000	138	22	22	grf	ex Louis Pasteur-11, Mont Blanc-96
9063653	Hainan Baosha 012	Bhs	1995	9,438	9,357	138	22	21	grf	ex Pierre Doux-11
9493664	Magic Striker	Bhs	2010	33,044	56,803	190	32	14	bbu	
9403516	Maximus	Iom	2011	93,196	179,238	292	45	15	bbu	
9050371	Miden Max	Iom	1993	39,012	74,696	225	32	14	bbu	ex Bunga Saga Dua-05
9493688	Mystic Striker	Bhs	2010	33,044	56,884	190	32	14	bbu	
9159567	Newcastle Max	Iom	1997	38,364	73,786	225	32	14	bbu	ex Nadia F-06, Agate-05, National Progress-04
8122828	Ntabeni	Pan	1984	25,005	37,425	183	30	15	ggc	ex Recife-96, Tellus-88
9266956	Olympius	Iom	2004	87,720	171,314	289	45	14	bbu	
9164653	Ostende Max	Iom	1998	38,489	73,207	225	32	14	bbu	ex Bunga Saga Lapan-05
9593402	Panther Max	Bhs	2012	44,326	81,283	229	32	14	bbu	
9453987	Paramount Halifax	Iom	2009	62,851	114.062	250	44	14	tcr	
9426207	Paramount Hamilton	Iom	2010	62,851	114,022	250	44	14	tcr	
9498723	Paramount Hanover	Iom	2010	62,851	114,014	250	44	14	tcr	
9453975	Paramount Hatteras	Iom	2010	62,851	114,028	250	44	14	tcr	
9453963	Paramount Helsinki	Iom	2010	62,851	114,165	250	44	14	tcr	
9453999	Paramount Hydra	Iom	2011	62,851	113,968	250	44	14	tcr	
9123740	Power Ranger	Iom	1996	26,330	45,946	189	32	14	bbu	ex Cape Recife-02
9589152	Puma Max	Bhs	2012	44,326	81,339	229	32	14	bbu	
9221205	SA Altius	Bhs	2001	87,542	171,480	289	45	14	bbu	
9221217	SA Fortius	Bhs	2001	87,542	171,509	289	45	14	bbu	
9303528	Spartacus	Iom	2011	93,196	179,156	292	45	15	bbu	
9082738	Storm Ranger	Bhs	1995	26,071	45,744	190	31	14	bbu	ex Lorenzina-03, Brilliance-00
9403530	Taurus	Iom	2011	93,169	179,067	292	45	15	bbu	
9273375	Victorius	Iom	2004	87,720	171,314	289	45	14	bbu	
9493690	Virtuous Striker	Bhs	2010	33,044	56,822	190	32	14	bbu	
9605865	Warrior	Bhs	2012	33,044	56,800	190	32	14	bbu	

newbuildings:

* operated by subsidiaries Golden Energy Management SA, Greece (formed 2003) or ** South African Marine Corp, South Africa.
Also operates chartered bulk carriers as SwissMarine.

John T. Essberger GmbH & Co. KG   Germany

Funnel: Buff, narrow red band on black-edged broad white band and black top or buff with broad green band. **Hull:** Black with red boot-topping or light grey with blue 'DEUTSCHE AFRIKA-LINIEN'. **History:** Formed 1924 and now managed by third generation of Essberger/von Rantzau family. Acquired Deutsche Afrika Linien in 1941. **Web:** www.rantzau.de

IMO#	name	flag	year	grt	dwt	loa	bm	kts	type	former names
9294408	DAL Kalahari	Lbr	2005	50,736	62,994	266	37	24	ucc	5,057 teu
9170652	Sanaga	Lbr	1997	17,784	28,215	169	27	14	bbu	ex Paclogger-98
9235957	Hibernia *	Lbr	2001	17,784	28,107	169	27	14	bbu	ex Sag Bulk Australia-11, Selinda-09
9235969	Tremonia *	Lbr	2001	17,784	28,083	169	27	14	bbu	ex Sag Bulk Canada-11, Swakop-10
9124392	UAFL Zanzibar	Mhl	1996	16,264	22,386	178	25	19	ucc	1,684 teu: ex R Sea-12, Nordsea-11, CSAV Maya-08, Nordsea-07, Nordseas-06, MOL Sprinter-04, Malacca Star-03, Nordsea-01, Nordseas-01, Pacific Voyager-01, Nordsea-00, Panaustral-98, Nordsea-97

* managed for Salamon AG, Germany. also operates a fleet of small tankers

Eurobulk Ltd.   Greece

Funnel: Black with broad white band with black 'E' inside five-pointed star, **Hull:** Black with red boot topping. **History:** Established 1994, but initial family origins date back to 1873. **Web:** www.eurobulk.gr

IMO#	name	flag	year	grt	dwt	loa	bm	kts	type	former names
9146302	Aggeliki P.	Lbr	1998	23,809	30,360	188	30	21	ucc	2,078 teu: ex Oder Trader-10, Maruba Cathay-07, Oder Trader-05, Zim Lisbon I-03, Oder Trader-02, Cielo d'America-02, Maersk Rio Grande-99, c/a Oder Trader
8918241	Anking	Mhl	1990	17,331	22,568	177	27		ggc	ex Tasman Trader-12, El Dorado-01
9043990	Aristides N.P.	Mhl	1993	36,952	69,268	225	32	14	bbu	ex Torm Tekla-06
9334351	Cap Egmont	Lbr	2007	35,824	41,850	221	32	22	ucc	3,104 teu: ex Cap Norte-12
8919001	Captain Costas	Mhl	1992	21,053	30,007	182	29	19	ucc	1,742 teu: ex Oel Transworld-09, Clan Gladiator-08, Alberta-05, Fesco Enterprise-00, Nedlloyd Singapore-99, Santa Victoria-96, MSC Victoria-95, Muscat Bay-94, l/a Santa Victoria
8901391	Despina P.	Pan	1990	22,712	33,667	188	28	18	ucc	1,932 teu: ex Beauty River-07, l/a Belstar
9146314	Diamantis P.	Lbr	1998	23,809	30,340	188	30	21	ucc	2,078 teu : Arkona Trader-10, CMA CGM Tucano-08, Arkona Trader-03
9128025	Eleni P.	Lbr	1997	37,707	72,119	224	32	14	bbu	ex Glorious Wind-00
9259379	EM Andros	Lbr	2003	27,227	33,216	200	32	22	ucc	2,495 teu: ex Torge S-12, Maersk Nassau-08, Torge S-04, l/a Superior Container
9243617	EM Astoria	Lbr	2004	30,024	35,600	208	32	22	ucc	2,672 teu: ex Mate-11, Kota Perkasa-07, Mate-04

John T. Essberger GmbH : DAL KALAHARI : *Chris Brooks*

IMO#	name	flag	year	grt	dwt	loa	bm	kts	type	former names
9203538	EM Athens	Mhl	2000	25,294	32,350	207	30	22	ucc	2,506 teu: ex Santa Adriana-10, P&O Nedlloyd Algoa-05, MOL Parana-02, P&O Nedlloyd Algoa-01, I/a Santa Adriana
9203514	EM Chios	Mhl	2000	25,294	32,321	207	30	22	ucc	2,506 teu; ex Santa Arabella-10, P&O Nedlloyd Accra-06, MOL Salvador-02, P&O Nedlloyd Accra-01, Santa Arabella-00
9338937	EM Hydra	Lbr	2005	18,334	23,679	176	27	20	ucc	1,740 teu: ex Lambert Schulte-10, Cap Agulhas-08, I/a Lambert Schulte
9178537	EM Ithaki	Lbr	1999	25,497	28,917	194	32	20	ucc	2,135 teu: ex MOL Volta-12, Santos Challenger-01
9301988	EM Psara	Lbr	2007	32,903	37,125	206	32	22	ucc	2,785 teu: ex CMA CGM Telopea-12, Artus-10, MSC Cameroun-10, Cala Pancaldo-09
9403413	EM Spetses	Cyp	2007	18,321	23,579	175	27	20	ucc	1,740 teu: ex Leopold Schulte-10, Cap Andreas-09,
8802210	Irini	Mhl	1988	36,177	69,734	225	32	14	bbu	ex Dooyang Hope-02
8907943	Jolly	Mhl	1992	27,103	25,904	178	32	18	ucc	1,762 teu; ex Kota Setia-02, Jolly-01, Jolly Topazi-00, Jolly Oro-99, Croatia Express-98
9055448	Kuo Hsiung	Pan	1993	15,183	18,154	167	27	17	ucc	1,169 teu:
9231494	Maersk Nairobi	Cyp	2001	26,582	34,649	210	30	22	ucc	2,556 teu: ex Donata Schulte-06
9231482	Maersk Noumea	Lbr	2001	26,582	34,717	210	30	22	ucc	2,556 teu: ex Elisabeth Schulte-06
9101493	Manolis P.	Mhl	1995	14,962	20,346	167	25	18	ucc	1,388 teu: ex Birthe Richter-07, Cala Piedad-02, Kaduna-00, TNX Express-98, Zim Argentina II-98, CCNI Anakena-96, c/a Birte Richter
9053232	Marinos	Lbr	1993	16,236	23,596	163	28	18	ucc	1,597 teu: ex YM Port Kelang-11, Mastro Nicos-09, YM Xingang I-09, MSC France-04, Conti France-03, Maersk Jakarta-00, Conti France-98, Contship France-98
9179218	Monica P.	Lbr	1998	27,011	46,667	190	31	14	bbu	ex Solar Europe-09, Solar Bay-02
8909082	Ninos	Pan	1990	15,122	18,253	167	27	16	ucc	998 teu: ex YM Qingdao I-07, Kuo Jane-04
9207730	Pantelis	Lbr	2000	38,380	74,010	225	32	14	bbu	ex Four Coal-09
8901884	Tiger Bridge	Mhl	1990	24,495	30,400	182	31	18	ucc	2,024 teu: ex City of Hamburg-07, Astrid Schulte-03, Ibn Al Kadi-98, American Senator-97, Choyang Green-97, American Senator-94, I/a Astrid Schulte

Evergreen Marine Corp. (Taiwan) Ltd   Taiwan

Funnel: *Black with green eight-pointed star above 'EVERGREEN' within brown globe outline on broad white band or * green 'H' above 'HATSU' on globe outline.* **Hull:** *Black or dark green with white 'EVERGREEN', red or green boot-topping.* **History:** *Founded 1968. Formerly part-owned Uniglory Marine Corp merged 2002.* **Web:** www.evergreen-marine.com or www.hatsu-marine.com

9134232	Ever Dainty	**	Sgp	1997	52,700	55,604	294	32	25	ucc	4,211 teu
9134244	Ever Decent	**	Sgp	1997	52,090	55,604	294	32	25	ucc	4,211 teu
9142162	Ever Delight		Pan	1998	52,090	55,515	294	32	25	ucc	4,211 teu

Eurobulk Ltd. : AGGELIKI P. : *ARO*

IMO#	name	flag	year	grt	dwt	loa	bm	kts	type	former names
9234256	Ever Deluxe **	Sgp	1998	52,090	54,300	294	32	25	ucc	4,211 teu
9142174	Ever Develop	Pan	1998	52,090	55,515	294	32	25	ucc	4,211 teu
9134268	Ever Devote **	Spp	1998	52,090	55,604	294	32	25	ucc	4,211 teu
9134270	Ever Diadem **	Sgp	1998	52,090	55,604	294	32	25	ucc	4,211 teu
9142186	Ever Diamond	Pan	1998	52,090	55,515	294	32	25	ucc	4,211 teu
9134282	Ever Divine **	Sgp	1998	52,090	55,604	294	32	25	ucc	4,211 teu
9142198	Ever Dynamic	Pan	1998	52,090	55,515	294	32	25	ucc	4,211 teu
9241310	Ever Eagle *	Gbr	2001	76,022	75,898	300	43	25	ucc	6,332 teu: ex Hatsu Eagle-08, l/a Ever Eagle
9241281	Ever Elite *	Gbr	2002	76,022	75,898	300	43	25	ucc	6,332 teu: ex Hatsu Elite-07
9241308	Ever Envoy *	Gbr	2002	76,067	75,898	300	43	25	ucc	6,332 teu: ex Hatsu Envoy-10, l/a Ever Envoy
9241293	Ever Ethic *	Gbr	2002	76,067	75,898	300	43	24	ucc	6,332 teu: ex Hatsu Ethic-08
9241322	Ever Excel *	Gbr	2002	76,022	75,898	300	43	25	ucc	6,332 teu: ex Hatsu Excel-10
9595448	Ever Laden	Pan	2012	98,882	104,409	337	46	24	ucc	8,452 teu
9595436	Ever Lambent *	Gbr	2012	98,882	104,409	337	46	24	ucc	8,452 teu
9595450	Ever Lasting *	Gbr	2012	98,882	104,409	337	46	24	ucc	8,452 teu
9595474	Ever Laurel	Sgp	2012	98,882	104,409	337	46	24	ucc	8,452 teu
9595498	Ever Lawful	Sgp	2012	98,882	104,409	337	46	24	ucc	8,452 teu
9595503	Ever Leader		2013			337	46	24	ucc	8,452 teu
9595462	Ever Leading	Gbr	2012	98,882	104,409	337	46	24	ucc	8,452 teu
9595515	Ever Legacy	Sgp	2013	98,882	109,409	337	46	24	ucc	8,452 teu
9604093	Ever Legend		2013			337	46	24	ucc	8,452 teu
9604110	Ever Legion		2014			337	46	24	ucc	8,452 teu
9595486	Ever Libra	Twn	2012	98,882	104,409	337	46	24	ucc	8,452 teu
9629122	Ever Lifting		2015			337	46	24	ucc	8,452 teu
9629043	Ever Linking		2013			337	46	24	ucc	8,452 teu
9629079	Ever Lissome		2014			337	46	24	ucc	8,452 teu
9604134	Ever Lively		2014			337	46	24	ucc	8,452 teu
9629031	Ever Living	Sgp	2013	98,892	104,409	337	46	24	ucc	8,452 teu
9629081	Ever Loading		2014			337	46	24	ucc	8,452 teu
9629110	Ever Lovely		2015			337	46	24	ucc	8,452 teu
9629067	Ever Lucent		2013			337	46	24	ucc	8,452 teu
9629055	Ever Lucid		2014			337	46	24	ucc	8,452 teu
9629093	Ever Lunar		2014			337	46	24	ucc	8,452 teu
9629108	Ever Lyric		2015			337	46	24	ucc	8,452 teu
9249207	Ever Peace	Pan	2002	17,887	19,309	182	28	18	ucc	1,618 teu: ex LT Peace-04, l/a Ever Peace
9249219	Ever Pearl	Pan	2002	17,887	19,309	182	28	18	ucc	1,618 teu: ex LT Pearl-04
9249221	Ever Power	Pan	2002	17,887	19,309	182	28	19	ucc	1,618 teu: ex LT Power-05, l/a Ever Power
9249233	Ever Pride *	Gbr	2003	17,887	19,309	182	28	19	ucc	1,618 teu: ex Hatsu Pride-08
9249245	Ever Prima *	Gbr	2003	17,887	19,309	182	28	18	ucc	1,618 teu: ex Hatsu Prima-08
9088110	Ever Racer	Pan	1994	53,359	57,904	294	32	23	ucc	4,229 teu
9055474	Ever Radiant	Pan	1994	53,101	58,912	294	32	23	ucc	4,229 teu: ex Ever Renown-07
9088122	Ever Reach	Pan	1994	53,359	57,904	294	32	23	ucc	4,229 teu
9061124	Ever Refine	Pan	1995	53,103	58,912	266	32	23	ucc	4,229 teu
9061136	Ever Respect	Pan	1995	53,103	58,912	294	32	23	ucc	4,229 teu: ex Ever Repute-07
9061112	Ever Result	Pan	1994	53,103	58,912	294	32	23	ucc	4,229 teu
9055462	Ever Reward	Pan	1994	53,103	58,912	294	32	23	ucc	4,229 teu
9300465	Ever Safety	Pan	2007	75,246	78,618	300	43	25	ucc	7,024 teu

Evergreen Marine Corp. : EVER LAMBENT : *J. Kakebeeke*

IMO#	name	flag	year	grt	dwt	loa	bm	kts	type	former names
9300477	Ever Salute	Pan	2008	75,246	78,733	300	43	25	ucc	7,024 teu
9300386	Ever Shine *	Gbr	2005	75,246	78,693	300	43	25	ucc	7,024 teu: ex Hatsu Shine-08
9300398	Ever Sigma *	Gbr	2005	75,246	78,693	300	43	25	ucc	7,024 teu: ex Hatsu Sigma-08
9300403	Ever Smart *	Gbr	2006	75,246	78,693	300	43	25	ucc	7,024 teu: ex Hatsu Smart-08
9300415	Ever Smile *	Gbr	2006	75,246	78,796	300	43	25	ucc	7,024 teu: ex Hatsu Smile-09
9300439	Ever Steady	Pan	2006	75,246	78,664	300	43	25	ucc	7,024 teu
9300441	Ever Strong	Pan	2007	75,246	78,715	300	43	25	ucc	7,024 teu
9300453	Ever Summit	Pan	2007	75,246	78,612	300	43	25	ucc	7,024 teu
9300427	Ever Superb	Pan	2006	75,246	78,661	300	43	25	ucc	7,024 teu: l/a Ever Spring
9168831	Ever Uberty **	Sgp	1999	69,246	63,216	285	40	25	ucc	5,652 teu
9116577	Ever Ultra	Pan	1996	69,218	63,388	285	40	24	ucc	5,364 teu
9196955	Ever Ulysses **	Sgp	2000	69,200	62,700	285	40	25	ucc	5,652 teu: ex LT Ulysses-05, l/a Ever Ulysses
9196967	Ever Unicorn **	Sgp	2000	69,246	63,400	285	40	25	ucc	5,652 teu: ex LT Unicorn-05, l/a Ever Unicorn
9168843	Ever Unific **	Sgp	1999	69,246	63,216	285	40	25	ucc	5,652 teu
9116618	Ever Union	Pan	1997	69,218	63,388	285	40	24	ucc	5,364 teu
9116606	Ever Unique **	Sgp	1997	69,218	63,388	285	40	24	ucc	5,364 teu
9116591	Ever Unison **	Sgp	1996	69,218	63,388	285	40	24	ucc	5,364 teu
9116589	Ever United **	Sgp	1996	69,218	62,386	285	40	24	ucc	5,364 teu: ex LT United-03, Ever United-00
9169158	Ever Unity	Pan	1999	69,246	62,700	285	40	25	ucc	5,652 teu: ex LT Unity-04, Ever Unity-00
9168855	Ever Uranus	Pan	1999	69,246	63,216	285	40	24	ucc	5,652 teu
9169160	Ever Urban	Pan	2000	69,246	63,216	285	40	24	ucc	5,652 teu
9168867	Ever Ursula	Pan	1999	69,246	62,700	285	40	25	ucc	5,652 teu: ex LT Ursula-04, Ever Ursula-00
9168879	Ever Useful	Pan	1999	69,246	62,700	285	40	24	ucc	5,652 teu
9188154	Ever Utile	Pan	2000	69,246	63,216	285	40	25	ucc	5,652 teu: ex LT Utile-05, Ever Utile-00

* owned by subsidiary Evergreen Marine (UK) Ltd, UK (formed 2002 as Hatsu Marine Ltd to 2007), **Evergreen Marine Singapore
newbuildings :a total of 30 'Ever L' class: Samsung (20) 2012-14 and CSBC (10) 2013-15. Also 10 x 13,800 teu containerships to lease from
Enesel S.A.(Hyundai) 2013-14
The company also operates 24 smaller container feeder ships (Ever-A, Uni-A and Uni-P classes) mainly in Far East services.

Italia Marittima SpA, Italy
Funnel: Cream with blue 'LT' below narrow blue band, blue top. **Hull:** Blue with white 'ITALIA' or 'L TRIESTINO', red boot-topping.
History: Founded in 1836 as Linee Triestine per l'Oriente SA di Nav Oriens, then Lloyd Austriaco to 1918 and formed as Lloyd Triestino
di Navigazione SpA in 1937. Acquired from Italian state-owned Finmare in 1998 and renamed 2006. **Web:** www.italiamarittima.it

9308039	Ital Florida	Ita	2007	36,483	42,950	239	32	23	ucc	3,451 teu
9330496	Ital Fortuna	Ita	2007	36,483	42,969	239	32	23	ucc	3,451 teu
9330501	Ital Fulgida	Ita	2007	36,483	42,930	239	32	23	ucc	3,451 teu
9315953	Ital Massima *	Pan	2007	42,020	53,728	264	32	23	ucc	4,363 teu: l/a E.R. Napier
9315915	Ital Mattina	Ita	2007	42,020	53,644	264	32	23	ucc	4,363 teu: l/a E.R. Nelson
9315965	Ital Melodia *	Pan	2007	42,020	53,697	264	32	23	ucc	4,363 teu: ex E.R. Tauranga
9349617	Ital Milione	Ita	2008	42,020	53,641	264	32	24	ucc	4,363 teu: l/a E.R. Cook
9349629	Ital Moderna	Ita	2009	42,020	53,685	264	32	24	ucc	4,353 teu: l/a E.R. Bounty
9196981	Ital Unica	Ita	2001	68,888	63,216	285	40	25	ucc	5,652 teu: ex LT Unica-08
9196993	Ital Universo	Ita	2001	68,888	63,216	285	40	25	ucc	5,652 teu: ex LT Universo-06
9196979	Ital Usodimare	Ita	2000	68,888	63,216	285	40	25	ucc	5,652 teu: ex LT Usodimare-08

* formerly owned now on charter from Wisdom Marine Lines, Taiwan

Exmar N.V.   Belgium
Funnel: Blue with red 'E' on broad white band. **Hull:** Red with dark red boot-topping. **History:** Formed 1991 following demerger from
CMB Group. **Web:** www.exmar.be

9318321	Antwerpen	Hkg	2005	22,901	26,361	174	28	16	lpg	35,223 m³
9237747	Bastogne	Bel	2002	22,902	26,616	174	28	16	lpg	35,229 m³ ex BW Hugin-11, Berge Hugin-07, Lancashire-05
9265548	Berlian Ekuator	Pan	2004	22,209	26,776	170	29	16	lpg	35,437 m³
9132789	Brugge Venture *	Hkg	1997	22,352	26,777	170	27	16	lpg	35,418 m³
9142150	Brussels	Bel	1997	22,323	26,943	170	27	16	lpg	35,454 m³ ex Oxfordshire-05
8818843	Chaconia	Bel	1990	19,643	29,271	166	27	16	lpg	28,070 m³
8804725	Courcheville	Bel	1989	19,719	29,171	166	27	16	lpg	28,006 m³ ex Nyhall-96
8414178	Donau	Bel	1985	23,508	32,339	183	30	15	lpg	30,207 m³ ex Gaz Nordsee-96, Donau-91
9102198	Eeklo	Bel	1995	23,519	29,458	179	27	16	lpg	37,450 m³
9102203	Elversele	Bel	1996	23,519	28,993	179	27	18	lpg	37,511 m³
9177806	Eupen	Bel	1999	23,952	29,121	180	27	18	lpg	38,961 m³
9230050	Excalibur (st)	Bel	2002	93,786	77,822	268	43	19	lng	138,034 m³
9246621	Excel (st)	Bel	2003	93,786	77,774	277	43	19	lng	138,107 m³ l/a Peace River
9322255	Excelerate (st)	Bel	2006	93,786	77,822	277	43	19	lng	138,074 m³
9252539	Excellence (st)	Bel	2005	93,937	77,348	277	43	19	lng	138,120 m³
9239616	Excelsior (st)	Bel	2005	93,719	76,500	277	43	19	lng	138,060 m³
9389643	Expedient (st)	Bel	2010	100,361	83,166	291	43	19	lng	151,015 m³
9444649	Exemplar (st)	Bel	2010	100,361	83,125	291	43	19	lng	151,072 m³
9361445	Express (st)	Bel	2009	114,987	83,200	277	43	19	lng	151,116 m³
9361079	Explorer (st)	Bel	2008	100,325	82,500	291	43	19	lng	150,981 m³
9381134	Exquisite (st)	Bel	2009	114,987	77,822	277	43	19	lng	151,017 m³

IMO#	name	flag	year	grt	dwt	loa	bm	kts	type	former names
9002908	Flanders Harmony	Bel	1992	47,597	64,220	228	36	19	lpg	85,826 m³
9113379	Flanders Tenacity	Bel	1996	47,027	54,155	230	36	19	lpg	84,270 m³
9045807	Kemira Gas	Bel	1995	10,018	13,289	143	21	16	lpg	12,030 m³
9292761	Libramont	Bel	2006	25,994	29,328	180	29	16	lpg	38,466 m³
7357452	Methania (st)	Bel	1978	81,792	67,879	280	42	19	lng	131,235 m³
9292113	Sombeke (st)	Bel	2006	25,994	29,213	180	29	19	lng	38,447 m³ ex BW Sombeke-11, Berge Sombeke-06
9014432	Temse	Bel	1994	22,521	30,761	170	27	18	lpg	35,058 m³ ex BW Helga-11, Helga-09
9134165	Touraine *	Hkg	1996	25,337	30,309	196	29	19	lpg	39,270 m³ ex Antwerpen Venture-97

newbuildings : 4 x 38,000 m³ [Hyundai Mipo (2014)]
managed by subsidiary Exmar Marine NV, * managed by Wah Kwong Ship Management HK
Also operates LNG tankers in joint venture with Golar and Lpg tankers in Pool with Moller and Bergesen.

ExxonMobil Corp.   U.S.A.

History: Formed by 1999 amalgamation of Exxon Corp (formerly Standard Oil Co. of New Jersey to 1892 and Standard Oil Co until 1972) with Mobil Oil Corp (founded 1888 as Socony-Vacuum Oil to 1955 and Socony Mobil Oil Co until 1966)
Web: www.exxon.mobil.com

SeaRiver Maritime Inc., U.S.A.

Funnel: Blue with white band separated from upper broad red band by further white band, narrow black top. **Hull:** Black with red or blue boot-topping. **History:** Founded 1920 as Humble Oil & Refining Co to 1973, later Exxon Shipping Co to 1993 and Exxon Co.

IMO#	name	flag	year	grt	dwt	loa	bm	kts	type	former names
7408081	Kodiak (st)	Usa	1978	64,329	124,644	265	42	17	tcr	ex Tonsina-05
9118628	S/R American Progress	Usa	1997	26,092	45,435	183	32	14	tcr	ex Despotico-97
7408093	Sierra (st)	Usa	1979	64,329	125,091	265	42	17	tcr	ex Kenai-06

newbuildings: two 115,000dwt tankers on order from Aker Philadelphia for 2014 delivery

International Marine Transportation Ltd., U.K.

Funnel: Black with white 'IMT' on blue rectangle on large white disc. **Hull:** Black or dark grey with red boot-topping.
History: Amalgamation in 1999 of Standard Marine Services Ltd (formerly Esso International Shipping to 1994) and Mobil Shipping Co Ltd (formerly Mobil Transportation Co Ltd to 1957). **Web:** None found.

IMO#	name	flag	year	grt	dwt	loa	bm	kts	type
9183324	Alrehab	Mhl	1999	160,279	301,620	335	58	15	tcr
9178757	Osprey	Mhl	1999	160,279	284,893	335	58	16	tcr

Also see Chevron Corp, USA

Fednav Ltd.   Canada

Funnel: White, red design incorporating part of maple leaf with interlinked 'F' and 'C', broad black top. **Hull:** Red or dark blue with red boot-topping. **History:** Founded 1946 as Federal Commerce & Navigation Ltd to 1984. **Web:** www.fednav.com

IMO#	name	flag	year	grt	dwt	loa	bm	kts	type	former names
7517507	Arctic	Can	1978	20,236	28,418	221	23	15	cbo	
8316522	Federal Agno	Hkg	1985	17,821	29,643	183	23	14	bbu	ex Federal Asahi-89
9200419	Federal Asahi	Hkg	1999	20,659	36,500	200	24	14	bbu	
9304095	Federal Baffin ‡	Pan	2007	30,721	55,309	190	32	14	bbu	
9271511	Federal Danube ††	Cyp	2004	22,654	37,116	200	24	14	bbu	
9230000	Federal Elbe ††	Cyp	2003	22,654	37,038	200	24	14	bbu	
9229984	Federal Ems ††	Cyp	2002	22,654	37,058	200	24	14	bbu	
9317547	Federal Franklin	Pan	2008	30,721	55,303	190	32	14	bbu	
8321931	Federal Fuji +	Bhs	1986	17,814	29,531	183	23		bbu	
9205902	Federal Hudson *	Hkg	2000	20,659	36,563	200	24	14	bbu	
9205938	Federal Hunter *	Hkg	2001	20,659	36,563	200	24	14	bbu	
9293923	Federal Katsura	Pan	2005	19,165	32,594	190	24	14	bbu	
9205885	Federal Kivalina *	Hkg	2000	20,659	36,563	200	24	14	bbu	
9244257	Federal Kumano ‡	Hkg	2003	20,661	36,489	200	24	14	bbu	
9284702	Federal Kushiro ‡	Mhl	2004	19,200	32,762	190	24	14	bbu	
9229996	Federal Leda ††	Cyp	2003	22,665	37,180	200	24	14	bbu	
9118135	Federal Maas	Brb	1997	20,837	34,372	200	24	14	bbu	
9299460	Federal Mackinac	Mhl	2004	18,825	27,638	185	24	14	bbu	
9299460	Federal Mackinac **	Lbr	2004	18,825	27,785	185	24	14	bbu	
9299472	Federal Margaree **	Lbr	2005	18,825	25,781	185	24	14	bbu	
9315537	Federal Mattawa **	Lbr	2005	18,825	27,779	185	24	14	bbu	
9299472	Federal Margaree	Mhl	2005	18,825	27,787	185	24	14	bbu	
9315537	Federal Mattawa	Lbr	2005	18,825	27,782	185	24	14	bbu	
9315549	Federal Miramichi †	Lbr	2006	18,825	27,781	185	24	14	bbu	ex Lake St. Clair-05
9278791	Federal Nakagawa ‡	Hkg	2005	20,661	36,489	200	24	14	bbu	
9200330	Federal Oshima *	Hkg	1999	20,659	36,563	200	24	14	bbu	
8321929	Federal Polaris +	Mhl	1985	17,815	29,536	183	23	14	bbu	
9190119	Federal Power ††	Cyp	2000	12,993	17,451	143	23	15	ggc	ex Seaboard Power-07, Atlantic Power-01
8806864	Federal Progress	Hkg	1989	21,469	36,445	177	30	14	bbu	
9110925	Federal Rhine	Brb	1997	20,837	34,372	200	23	14	bbu	
9200445	Federal Rideau *	Hkg	2000	20,659	36,563	200	24	14	bbu	
9595888	Federal Sable	Mhl	2012	24,196	37,169	190	28		bbu	

IMO#	name	flag	year	grt	dwt	loa	bm	kts	type	former names
9288291	Federal Sakura	Pan	2005	19,165	32,594	190	24	14	bbu	
9110913	Federal Saguenay	Brb	1996	20,837	34,167	200	23	14	bbu	
9118147	Federal Schelde	Brb	1997	20,837	34,372	200	23	14	bbu	
9267209	Federal Seto ‡	Hkg	2004	20,861	36,300	200	23	14	bbu	
9606821	Federal Severn	Hkg	2012	24,200	37,200	190	28		bbu	
9218404	Federal Shimanto ‡	Pan	2001	19,125	32,787	190	24	14	bbu	
9595890	Federal Skeena	Mhl	2012	24,196	37,168	190	28		bbu	
9606833	Federal Skye	Hkg	2012	24,200	37,200	190	28		bbu	
9110896	Federal St. Laurent	Brb	1996	20,837	34,372	200	23	14	bbu	
9595917	Federal Sutton	Mhl	2012	24,200	37,200	190	28		bbu	
9595905	Federal Swift	Hkg	2012	24,200	37,200	190	28		bbu	
8806852	Federal Venture	Hkg	1989	21,469	36,445	177	30	14	bbu	ex Northern Venture-02
9205916	Federal Welland *	Hkg	2000	20,659	35,750	200	24	14	bbu	
9229972	Federal Weser ††	Cyp	2002	22,654	37,372	200	24	14	bbu	
9218416	Federal Yoshino ‡	Mhl	2001	19,125	32,845	190	24	14	bbu	
9476977	Federal Yukina	Hkg	2010	20,465	35,868	200	24	14	bbu	
9205897	Federal Yukon *	Hkg	2000	20,659	36,563	200	24	14	bbu	
9364813	Maple Hill ‡	Pan	2006	30,002	53,452	190	32	14	bbu	
9350070	Maple Grove	Pan	2006	30,002	53,474	190	32	14	bbu	
9308247	Neptune Pioneer ‡	Pan	2007	31,236	55,921	190	32	14	bbu	
9309667	Ocean Breeze ‡	Hkg	2006	30,067	52,289	190	32	14	bbu	
9110901	Orsula ‡	Mhl	1996	20,837	34,198	200	24	14	bbu	ex Federal Calumet-97
9324150	Triton Seagull ‡	Pan	2007	31,247	56,058	190	32	14	bbu	
9334715	Umiak I	Can	2006	22,462	31,992	189	27	-	bbu	
8212099	Utviken +	Bhs	1987	17,191	30,052	189	23	14	bbu	ex C. Blanco-95, Bijelo Polje-92
9339959	Windsor Adventure ‡	Pan	2008	31,247	55,975	190	32	14	bbu	
9336866	Vega Rose ‡	Pan	2007	30,847	55,711	190	32	14	bbu	

newbuildings: one 20,500 grt 35,300 dwt bulk carrier for 2012 delivery.
*Owned ships and * owned by subsidiary Fednav International Ltd, managed by Anglo-Eastern Ship Management Ltd. Hong Kong*
*(www.aesm.com.hk). ** owned by Baffin Investments Ltd. + owned by Viken Lakers II AS, Montreal*
† chartered from Sunship Schiffahrts subsidiary of Reederei M Lauterjung KG, Germany or †† from Athena Marine Co Ltd, Cyprus.
‡ chartered from various other owners (nearly 20 others chartered without Federal prefix). See others with 'Federal' prefix in index.

Foreland Shipping Ltd.   U.K.

Funnel: *Yellow with 4-coloured 'propeller' on green band, black top.* **Hull:** *Green with red boot-topping.* **History:** *Founded 2001 as equal partnership between Andrew Weir, Bibby Line, Hadley Shipping and James Fisher plc* **Web:** *www.foreland-shipping.co.uk*

9248540	Anvil Point *	Gbr	2003	23,235	13,274	193	26	17	urr	
9234094	Beachy Head **	Gbr	2003	23,235	13.256	193	26	17	urr	
9234070	Eddystone *	Gbr	2002	23,235	13,274	193	26	17	urr	
9248538	Hartland Point *	Gbr	2002	23,235	13,274	193	26	17	urr	
9234068	Hurst Point *	Gbr	2002	23,235	13,274	193	26	17	urr	
9234082	Longstone **	Gbr	2003	23,235	13,274	193	26	17	urr	

*vessels managed by Andrew Weir Shipping Ltd. (www.aws.co.uk) * on charter to UK Government and ** in European trades.*

Fednav Ltd. : FEDERAL SETO : *ARO*

Frontline Ltd.   Bermuda

Funnel: *White with light blue 'f' symbol on dark blue vertical rectangle above 'FRONTLINE'.* **Hull:** *Black, brown or light blue with red or dark blue boot-topping.* **History:** *Originally founded1986 as Uddevalla Shipping AB by Swedish government, privatised 1989, controlling interest acquired in 1996 by John Fredriksen through Hemen Holdings and 1998 amalgamated with London & Overseas Freighters Ltd (founded 1949).* **Web:** *www.frontmgt.no*

IMO#	name	flag	year	grt	dwt	loa	bm	kts	type	former names
9179646	DS Crown	Bhs	1999	157,863	311,176	334	58	15	tcr	ex Front Crown-12
9150834	Front Ardenne **	Mhl	1998	79,633	153,152	258	46	15	tcr	ex Ardenne-00
9196606	Front Ariake §	Iom	2001	158,397	298,530	333	60	15	tcr	ex Oliva-12, Ariake-06, Berge Ariake-01
9155808	Front Brabant **	Nis	1998	79,633	152,550	269	46	15	tcr	ex Brabant-00
9400681	Front Cecilie #	Hkg	2010	156,988	296,995	330	60	15	tcr	
9166675	Front Century ††	Mhl	1998	157,976	311,189	334	58	15	tcr	ITM
9166687	Front Champion ††	Bhs	1998	157,976	311,286	334	58	15	tcr	
9169691	Front Chief †	Bhs	1999	157,863	311,224	334	58	15	tcr	V Ships gmbh
9166742	Front Circassia **	Mhl	1999	163,346	306,009	333	58	15	tcr	ex Omala-06, New Circassia-04, I/a Golden Circassia
9172674	Front Comanche #	Lbr	1999	159,423	300,133	333	60	15	tcr	ex Ovatella-12, Front Comanche-10, Stena Comanche-01
9158264	Front Commerce ††	Lbr	1999	159,423	300,144	333	60	16	tcr	ex Ocana-12, Front Commerce-04, Stena Commerce-01
9176993	Front Commodore †	Lbr	2000	159,397	298,620	333	60		tcr	
9353802	Front Eminence **	Mhl	2009	162,198	321,300	333	60	15	tcr	
9353797	Front Endurance **	Mhl	2009	162,198	321,300	333	60	15	tcr	
9192228	Front Energy **	Cyp	2004	164,300	305,318	330	60	15	tcr	ex Sea Energy-05, I/a Mt. Pertamina 2
9238856	Front Falcon §	Bhs	2002	160,904	308,875	333	58	-	tcr	I/a Mosfalcon
9292163	Front Force §	Mhl	2004	156,873	305,442	330	60	15	tcr	ex Onobo-12, Front Force-09, Sea Force-05, I/a Mt. Pertamina 1
9087972	Front Glory *	Nis	1995	79,979	149,834	269	46	15	tcr	ex London Glory-97
9196644	Front Hakata #	Bhs	2002	159,383	298,465				tcr	
9384590	Front Kathrine *	Mhl	2009	156,651	297,974				tcr	
9249312	Front Melody †	Lbr	2001	79,525	150,500	272	46		tcr	
9408205	Front Njord #	Hkg	2010	83,805	156,760	274	48		tcr	
9406001	Front Odin #	Hkg	2010	83,805	156,840	274	48		tcr	
9172844	Front Opalia ††	Mhl	1999	159,756	302,193	333	60	15	tcr	ex Opalia-06
9248497	Front Page §	Lbr	2002	156,916	299,164	330	60	15	tcr	I/a Front Saga Thome SM
9018464	Front Pride *	Mhl	1993	79,978	149,686	269	46	15	tcr	ex London Pride-98
9384605	Front Queen *	Mhl	2009	156,651	297,936	330	60		tcr	
9172856	Front Scilla ††	Mhl	2000	160,805	302,561	333	60	16	tcr	ex Oscilla-05
9248473	Front Serenade †	Lbr	2002	157,000	298,300	333	60	16	tcr	Thome SM
9410997	Front Signe #	Hkg	2010	156,991	297,007	330	60		tcr	
9104885	Front Splendour *	Nis	1995	79,979	148,835	269	46	15	tcr	ex London Splendour-97
9248485	Front Stratus ††	Lbr	2002	156,916	299,517	330	60		tcr	
9249324	Front Symphony †	Lbr	2001	79,525	149,995	272	46		tcr	
9153513	Front Vanguard ††	Mhl	1998	159,423	300,058	333	60	14	tcr	ex New Vanguard-04
9169421	Mindanao **	Sgp	1998	81,265	147,447	274	48	15	tcr	
9439539	Sea Bay #	Hkg	2009	60,193	108,760	243	42	-	tcr	
9439541	Sea Hope #	Hkg	2009	60,193	108,701	243	42	-	tcr	
9164835	Ulriken #	Bhs	1998	160,036	309,996	333	58	16	tcr	ex Antares Voyager-11, Frank A. Shrontz-03

Frontline Ltd. : Front Circassia : *Hans Kraijenbosch*

IMO#	name	flag	year	grt	dwt	loa	bm	kts	type	former names

newbuildings: 2 x 160,000 dwt tankers [Rongsheng yard # 1161/2 (2013)]
* managed by Orion Tankers/V. Ships (UK) Ltd. ** Orion Tankers/V. Ships Norway † owned by German KG companies and managed by Orion Tankers/V. Ships Germany †† International Tanker Management Holdings Ltd. UAE, # by Seateam Management Pte., Singapore § by Thome Ship Managemen tPte. Ltd.
Also see Euronav SA (under CMB) and other chartered ships with 'Front' prefix in index.

Golar LNG Ltd., Bermuda

Funnel: Blue with white swallowtail flag having blue 5-point star inside blue ring or * black with three narrow white bands. **Hull:** Black with white 'LNG', red boot-topping. **History:** Founded 1940 as T Gotaas & Co, renamed Gotaas-Larsen Shipping Corp in 1946. Golar Management (formed 1969) acquired by Singapore-based Osprey Maritime Ltd in 1997, then purchased by World Shipholding (indirectly controlled by John Fredriksen) in 2001. **Web:** www.golar.com

IMO#	name	flag	year	grt	dwt	loa	bm	kts	type	former names
7361934	Gandria (st)	Mhl	1977	96,011	66,999	288	43	19	lng	125,000 m³ ex Hoegh Gandria-08
7382732	Gimi (st)	Mhl	1976	96,235	72,703	293	42	19	lng	125,000 m³
9253105	Golar Arctic	Mhl	2003	94,934	80,800	280	43	19	lng	138,500 m³ ex Granatina-09
9303560	Golar Grand	Mhl	2006	97,491	84,894	277	43	19	lng	145,700 m³ ex Grandis-10, I/a Golar Asia
9320374	Golar Maria	Mhl	2006	97,491	84,823	277	43	19	lng	145,700 m³ ex Granosa-09
9165011	Golar Mazo (st)	Lbr	2000	111,835	76,210	290	47	19	lng	135,000 m³
9256767	Golar Viking (st)	Mhl	2005	93,899	80,810	280	43	19	lng	140,000 m³ ex Gracilis-09, Golar Viking-06
7382720	Hilli (st)	Mhl	1975	96,235	72,703	293	42	19	lng	125,000 m³ ex Golar Glacier-75
9253715	Methane Princess (st)	Mhl	2003	93,899	77,707	277	43	19	lng	138,000 m³

newbuildings: 9 x 160,000 m³ (Samsung) 2013/14, 4 x 160,000 m³ (Hyundai Samho) 2014/15
vessels managed by Golar Wilhelmsen Management. Also operates LNG vessels in joint venture with Exmar q.v.

GasLog Logistics Ltd.   Monaco

Funnel: Black with blue company logo on broad white band, or, BG owned vessels, black with three narrow white bands. **Hull:** dark blue with pink boot topping or BG vessels, black with white 'LNG' and red boot-topping. **Web:** gaslogltd.com

IMO#	name	flag	year	grt	dwt	loa	bm	kts	type	former names
9352860	GasLog Savannah	Bmu	2010	97,818	82,339	285	43		lng	154,800 m³
9355604	GasLog Singapore	Bmu	2010	97,818	82,339	285	43		lng	154,800 m³
9600528	GasLog Shanghai	Lbr	2013	97,818	83,300	285	43		lng	154,800 m³
9321768	Methane Alison Victoria (st) *	Bmu	2007	95,753	79,058	283	43	20	lng	145,000 m³
9516129	Methane Becki Anne (tf) *	Bmu	2010	109,004	86,269	290	45		lng	170,000 m³
9321744	Methane Heather Sally (st) *	Bmu	2007	95,753	79,085	283	43	20	lng	145,000 m³
9307190	Methane Jane Elizabeth (st) *	Bmu	2006	95,753	78,984	283	43	20	lng	145,000 m³
9412880	Methane Julia Louise (tf) *	Bmu	2010	109,004	86,125	290	45		lpg	170,000 m³
9256793	Methane Kari Elin (st) *	Bmu	2004	93,410	73,989	279	43	19	lng	138,000 m³
9307205	Methane Lydon Volney (st) *	Bmu	2006	95,753	78,957	283	43	20	lng	145,000 m³
9520376	Methane Mickie Harper (tf) *	Bmu	2010	109,004	86,170	290	45		lng	170,000 m³
9321770	Methane Nile Eagle (st) *	Bmu	2007	95,753	79,006	283	43	20	lng	145,000 m³
9425277	Methane Patricia Camila (tf) *	Bmu	2010	109,004	86,272	290	45		lng	170,000 m³
9307188	Methane Rita Andrea (st) *	Bmu	2006	95,753	79,046	283	43	20	lng	145,000 m³
9321756	Methane Shirley Elisabeth (st) *	Bmu	2007	95,753	78,997	283	43	20	lng	145,000 m³

* managed by GasLog LNG Services for BG Group (UK) www.bg-group.com
newbuildings: seven 155,000 m³ lng tankers [Samsung yd # 1947, 2016/7, 2041-44 (2013/5)]

Genco Shipping & Trading   U.S.A.

Funnel: Dark blue with white 'G' in white diamond on broad light blue band between two narrow white bands, black top **Hull:** Black with red boot-topping. **History:** US based company founded 2004. **Web:** www.gencoshipping.com

IMO#	name	flag	year	grt	dwt	loa	bm	kts	type	former names
9176711	Genco Acheron	Hkg	1999	37,695	72,495	225	32	14	bbu	ex Anita-06, Monviken-04, Far Eastern Jennifer-00
9490624	Genco Aquitaine	Mhl	2009	32,837	57,970	190	32	14	bbu	ex Major-10
9490636	Genco Ardennes	Mhl	2009	32,837	57,970	190	32	14	bbu	ex Tabor-10
9361249	Genco Augustus	Hkg	2007	90,106	180,151	288	45	14	bbu	I/a Ferro Goa
9557123	Genco Auvegne	Mhl	2009	32,837	58,020	190	32	14	bbu	ex Molitor-10
9450753	Genco Avra	Lbr	2011	23,456	34,391	180	32	14	bbu	
9450715	Genco Bay	Lbr	2010	23,456	34,296	180	30	14	bbu	I/a Handy Bay
9200380	Genco Beauty	Hkg	1999	38,646	73,941	225	32	14	bbu	ex Top Beauty-06
9490662	Genco Bourgogne	Mhl	2010	32,837	58,020	190	32	14	bbu	I/a Sefor

IMO#	name	flag	year	grt	dwt	loa	bm	kts	type	former names
9490698	Genco Brittany	Mhl	2010	32,837	58,020	190	32	14	bbu	l/a Matador
9149392	Genco Carrier	Hkg	1998	26,098	47,180	186	31	14	bbu	ex Top Carrier-04
9345818	Genco Cavalier	Mhl	2007	31,261	53,617	190	32	14	bbu	ex CMB Yangtze-08, Nikomarine-07
9287429	Genco Challenger	Hkg	2003	16,978	28,428	169	27	14	bbu	ex Orchid Bay-08
9350094	Genco Champion	Hkg	2006	16,960	28,445	169	27	14	bbu	ex Stentor-08
9324710	Genco Charger	Hkg	2005	16,960	28,398	169	27	14	bbu	ex Captain Adams-08
9444819	Genco Claudius	Mhl	2010	88,397	169,025	288	45	14	bbu	
9422079	Genco Commodus	Mhl	2009	88,397	167,025	288	45	14	bbu	
9361251	Genco Constantine	Hkg	2008	90,106	180,200	288	45	14	bbu	
9199842	Genco Explorer *	Hkg	1999	18,036	29,952	170	27	14	bbu	ex Top Explorer-04
9422067	Genco Hadrian	Mhl	2008	88,397	169,694	288	45	14	bbu	
9368871	Genco Hunter	Mhl	2007	32,379	57,982	190	32	14	bbu	ex Tomahawk-08
9200378	Genco Knight	Hkg	1999	38,646	73,941	225	32	14	bbu	ex Top Knight-05
9490686	Genco Languedoc	Mhl	2010	32,837	58,020	190	32	14	bbu	l/d Tenor
9200366	Genco Leader	Hkg	1999	38,646	73,941	225	32	14	bbu	ex Top Leadrr-05
9511820	Genco Loire	Mhl	2009	31,117	53,100	190	32	14	bbu	ex Fructidor-10
9430038	Genco London	Hkg	2007	91,373	177,852	292	45	14	bbu	
9474785	Genco Lorraine	Mhl	2009	31,117	53,146	190	32	14	bbu	ex Nantor-10
9450765	Genco Mare	Lbr	2011	23,456	34,428	180	30	14	bbu	l/a Handy Mare
9125906	Genco Marine	Hkg	1996	26,040	45,222	188	31	14	bbu	ex Lucky Marine-05
9422081	Genco Maximus	Mhl	2009	88,397	167,025	288	45	14	bbu	
9234214	Genco Muse	Hkg	2001	28,097	48,913	190	32	14	bbu	ex Western Muse-05, l/a Muse Venture

Genco Shipping & Trading : GENCO CHARGER : *ARO*

Genco Shipping & Trading : GENCO OCEAN : *F. de Vries*

IMO#	name	flag	year	grt	dwt	loa	bm	kts	type	former names
9347877	Genco Normandy	Mhl	2007	31,107	53,500	190	32	14	bbu	ex Thermidor-10
9450739	Genco Ocean	Lbr	2010	23,456	34,402	180	30	14	bbu	l/a Handy Ocean
9301720	Genco Picardy	Mhl	2005	31,264	55,257	190	32	14	bbu	ex Dalior-10
9197935	Genco Pioneer *	Hkg	1998	18,036	29,952	170	27	14	bbu	ex Top Pioneer-05
9316165	Genco Predator	Mhl	2005	31,069	55,407	190	32	14	bbu	ex Predator-07
9199830	Genco Progress *	Hkg	1998	18,036	29,952	170	27	14	bbu	ex Top Progress-05
9121742	Genco Prosperity	Hkg	1997	26,094	47,180	186	31	14	bbu	ex Top Prosperity-05
9316220	Genco Provence	Mhl	2004	31,264	55,317	190	32	14	bbu	ex Messidor-10
9511832	Genco Pyrenees	Mhl	2010	32,837	58,018	190	32	14	bbu	c/a Chun He 56, l/d Pearlor
9330812	Genco Raptor	Mhl	2007	41,115	76,499	225	32	14	bbu	ex CMB Laetitia
9200407	Genco Reliance *	Hkg	1999	18,036	29,952	170	27	14	bbu	ex Top Reliance-05
9490832	Genco Rhone	Mhl	2011	32,839	57,970	190	32	14	bbu	
9450777	Genco Spirit	Lbr	2011	23,456	34,393	180	30	14	bbu	
9121730	Genco Success	Hkg	1997	26,094	47,186	186	31	14	bbu	ex Top Success-05
9191034	Genco Sugar *	Hkg	1998	18,036	29,952	170	27	14	bbu	ex Top Sugar-05
9184914	Genco Surprise	Hkg	1998	37,695	72,495	225	32	14	bbu	ex Koby-06, Norviken-04, Far Eastern Wendy-00
9331555	Genco Tiberius	Hkg	2007	88,675	175,874	292	45	14	bbu	l/a Ferro Fos
9410959	Genco Titus	Hkg	2007	91,373	177,729	292	45	14	bbu	
9332212	Genco Thunder	Mhl	2007	41,115	76,499	225	32	14	bbu	ex CMB Aurelie-08
9200392	Genco Vigour	Hkg	1999	38,646	73,941	225	32	14	bbu	ex Top Vigour-04
9316153	Genco Warrior	Mhl	2005	31,069	55,435	190	32	14	bbu	ex Innovator-07
9149380	Genco Wisdom	Hkg	1997	26,094	47,000	186	31	14	bbu	ex Top Wisdom-05

* operated by Lauritzen Bulkers, most vessels chartered out

Baltic Trading Ltd., Marshall Islands
Funnel: *Dark blue with white 'B' on broad light blue band between two narrow white bands.* **Hull:** *Black with red boot-topping.*
History: *formed as subsidiary of Gencon in 2010.* **Web:** www.baltictrading.com

IMO#	name	flag	year	grt	dwt	loa	bm	kts	type	former names
9469259	Baltic Bear	Mhl	2010	91,373	177,700	292	45	14	bbu	ex Inna-10
9450741	Baltic Breeze	Lbr	2010	23,456	34,386	180	30	14	bbu	ex Handy Breeze-10
9387358	Baltic Cougar	Mhl	2009	31,117	53,100	190	32	14	bbu	ex Spice-10
9450727	Baltic Cove	Lbr	2009	23,456	34,403	180	30	14	bbu	ex Handy Cove-10
9387360	Baltic Jaguar	Mhl	2009	31,117	53,100	190	32	14	bbu	ex Inta-10
9387334	Baltic Leopard	Mhl	2009	31,117	53,100	190	32	14	bbu	ex Borak-10
9387346	Baltic Panther	Mhl	2009	31,117	53,100	190	32	14	bbu	ex Sinova-10
9450703	Baltic Wind	Lbr	2009	23,456	34,408	180	30	14	bbu	ex Handy Wind-10
9492335	Baltic Wolf	Mhl	2010	91,373	177,752	292	45	14	bbu	ex Smyrna-10

General Maritime Corp.   U.S.A.
Funnel: *Black with yellow 'G' inside yellow edged green diamond on yellow edged broad dark blue band or charterers colours.*
Hull: *Black with red boot-topping.* **History:** *Formed 1997. Acquired Soponata SA in 2004 and merged with Arlington Tankers (27%) in 2008.* **Web:** www.generalmaritimecorp.com

IMO#	name	flag	year	grt	dwt	loa	bm	kts	type	former names
9083304	GenMar Agamemnon	Lbr	1995	53,829	96,214	243	42	14	tcr	ex Emilie-98
9108702	GenMar Ajax	Lbr	1996	53,829	96,183	243	42	14	tcr	ex Julie-98
9185530	GenMar Argus	Mhl	2000	81,151	159,901	274	48	15	tcr	ex Crude Tria-03
9322281	GenMar Atlas	Mhl	2007	157,844	306,506	332	58	15	tcr	ex Crudesky-10
9255933	GenMar Companion *	Bmu	2004	41,589	72,637	229	32	15	tcr	ex Stena Companion-09
9255945	GenMar Compatriot *	Bmu	2004	41,589	72,000	229	32	15	tcr	ex Stena Compatriot-09
9258600	GenMar Concord *	Mhl	2004	27,357	47,171	183	32	14	tcr	ex Stena Concord-09
9258612	GenMar Consul *	Bmu	2004	27,357	47,171	183	32	14	tcr	ex Stena Consul-09
9223318	Genmar Daphne *	Mhl	2002	57,683	106,548	241	42	15	tcr	ex Fidelity-08
9247974	GenMar Defiance	Lbr	2002	56,225	105,538	239	42	14	tcr	ex Peneda-04
9336971	Genmar George T.	Mhl	2007	79,235	149,847	274	48	15	tcr	
9233313	Genmar Elektra *	Mhl	2002	57,683	106,560	241	42	14	tcr	ex Fantasy-08
9302982	GenMar Harriet G.	Lbr	2006	79,325	150,205	274	48	15	tcr	
9322279	GenMar Hercules	Mhl	2007	157,844	306,506	332	58	15	tcr	ex Crudesun-10
9173745	GenMar Hope	Sgp	1999	81,526	159,539	274	48	15	tcr	ex Crude Hope-03, Nord Hope-00
9173757	GenMar Horn	Mhl	1999	81,526	159,474	274	48	15	tcr	ex Crude Horn-03, Nord Horn-00
9302994	GenMar Kara G.	Lbr	2007	79,235	150,296	274	48	15	tcr	
9461764	GenMar Maniate	Mhl	2010	84,735	164,716	274	50	15	tcr	ex Crude Zita-10
9083316	GenMar Minotaur	Lbr	1995	53,829	96,213	243	42	14	tcr	ex Stephanie-98
9224271	GenMar Orion	Mhl	2002	81,381	159,992	274	48	15	tcr	ex Crude Okto-03, Antares-02
9182746	GenMar Phoenix	Mhl	1999	80,058	153,015	269	46	15	tcr	ex Crude Ena-03
9236250	GenMar Poseidon	Mhl	2002	154,348	305,796	332	58	15	tcr	ex Crude Progress-10, Poros-04
9461776	GenMar Spartiate	Mhl	2011	84,735	164,714	274	50	15	tcr	l/a Crude Ita
9185528	GenMar Spyridon	Mhl	2000	81,151	159,959	274	48	15	tcr	ex Crude Dio-03
9336983	GenMar St. Nikolas	Mhl	2008	79,235	149,876	274	48	15	tcr	
9247986	GenMar Strength	Lbr	2003	56,225	105,674	239	42	15	tcr	ex Portel-04

IMO#	name	flag	year	grt	dwt	loa	bm	kts	type	former names
9254082	GenMar Ulysses	Mhl	2003	160,889	318,692	333	60	15	tcr	ex Crudestar-10
9205093	GenMar Victory	Bmu	2001	163,761	312,679	335	70	16	tcr	ex Stena Victory-09
9205081	GenMar Vision	Bmu	2001	163,761	312,679	335	70	16	tcr	ex Stena Vision-09
9411032	GenMar Zeus	Mhl	2010	160,502	318,325	333	60	15	tcr	ex Crudemed-10

operated by subsidiaries General Maritime Management LLC, USA or General Maritime Management (Portugal) Lda (formerly Soponata SA to 2004) or affiliate Concordia Maritime..

German Tanker Shipping GmbH & Co. KG   Germany
Funnel: *Yellow with red 'GT' on white segments of white/blue diagonally quartered flag, narrow black top.* **Hull:** *Black with red boot-topping.* **History:** *Company founded 1998 in Bremen.* **Web:** *www.german-tanker.de*

9251640	Seabass	Lbr	2001	21,353	32,480	178	28	14	tco	
9352315	Seacod	Deu	2006	26,548	40,558	188	32	16	tco	
9352298	Seaconger	Deu	2005	21,329	32,200	178	28	16	tco	
9255488	Seahake	Deu	2003	21,329	32,480	178	28	16	tco	
9251652	Sealing	Deu	2003	21,356	32,480	178	28	16	tco	
9380489	Seamarlin	Deu	2007	26,548	40,550	188	32	15	tco	
9204776	Seamullet	Deu	2001	21,353	32,230	178	28	15	tco	
9423449	Seapike	Lbr	2009	28,449	43,550	188	32	16	tco	
9255490	Searay	Deu	2004	21,353	32,310	178	28	16	tco	
9298193	Seashark	Deu	2004	21,329	32,310	178	28	16	tco	
9380477	Seasprat	Deu	2007	26,548	40,597	188	32	16	tco	
9352303	Seatrout	Deu	2006	26,548	40,600	188	32	15	tco	
9204764	Seaturbot	Deu	2000	21,353	32,230	178	28	14	tco	

Goldenport Holdings Inc.   Greece
Funnel: *White with gold 'G' above the right of two blue waves, black top.* **Hull:** *Black with red boot-topping.* **History:** *Founded 1975 as Goldenport Cia. Nav. (Cyprus) until 1992.* **Web:** *www.goldenport.biz*

9438028	Alpine Trader	Mlt	2009	30,669	53,800	190	32	14	bbu	
9134490	Conti Seattle	Lbr	1997	24,053	28,370	205	27	20	ucc	2,109 teu: ex Delmas Libreville-12, Tiger Bay-07, APL Melbourne-06, Vancouver-04, Ivory Star 1-03, Conti Seattle-02, CCNI Antartico-02, Sea Lynx-00, Conti Seattle-97
9587453	D. Skalkeas	Lbr	2011	51,225	93,281	229	38	14	bbu	
9577410	Eleni D.	Lbr	2010	34,374	58,429	196	32	14	bbu	
9472103	Erato	Lbr	2011	26,374	34,162	209	30	22	ucc	2,546 teu
9041459	Golden Trader	Mlt	1994	28,420	48,170	192	32	14	bbu	ex Arctic Trader-10, Goldstar-94
9634969	Ioanna D.	Lbr	2012	22,434	35,000	180	28	24	bbu	
9577422	Maria	Lbr	2011	34,335	58,407	186	32	14	bbu	
9438016	Marie-Paule	Mlt	2009	30,669	53,800	190	32	14	bbu	
9472098	Milos	Lbr	2010	32,983	56,988	190	32	14	bbu	

General Maritime Corp. : GENMAR COMPANION : *Hans Kraijenbosch*

IMO#	name	flag	year	grt	dwt	loa	bm	kts	type	former names
8408844	MSC Accra	Mhl	1985	22,667	33,857	188	28	18	ucc	1,889 teu: ex Nautic-07, Hellas Macedonia-03, MSC Africa-03, Hellas Macedonia-02, MSC Recife-02, P&O Nedlloyd Peru-01, MSC Caracas-00, Hellas Macedonia-99, Canmar Pride-96, Canmar Fortune -95, Sea Macedonia-94, Hellas Macedonia-94, Hellas Senator-92, Bremen Senator-92, ScanDutch Honshu-88, Modern Trader-87, Alameda-86, World Success-85 (conv ggc)
9031064	MSC Ada	Nld	1993	19,573	20,027	174	29	18	ucc	1,648 teu: ex Rhoneborg-10, MSC Java-03, European Express-02, Zim Australia-00, European Express-99, Freshwater Bay-96, European Express-94
9003304	MSC Anafi	Lbr	1994	30,526	34,079	205	32	19	ucc	2,283 teu: ex Anafi-08, Ajama-07, CP Pathfinder-06, Lykes Pathfinder-05, DAL East London-04, Ajama-02, Sea Star-99, Choyang Grace-97, Delaware Bay-95, Sea Musketeer-94, Ajama-94, I/a Charles de Foucauld
9112272	MSC Fortunate	Pan	1996	64,054	68,363	275	40	25	ucc	5,551 teu: ex Fortune-09, Hyundai Fortune-06
8913461	MSC Scotland	Lbr	1992	37,071	47,120	237	32	21	ucc	ex Bengal Sea-06, SCI Gaurav-04, German Senator-02, Choyang Volga-98
9074004	MSC Socotra	Pan	1995	60,117	63,179	300	38	22	ucc	4,812 teu: ex Procyon I-09, NYK Procyon-09
9108398	Paris JR	Mlt	1996	14,241	18,400	159	24	18	ucc	1,129 teu: ex HC Maria-11, Delmas Anemone-09, Saturn-06, TMM Leon-01, CMB Endurance-97, Saturn-96
9456367	Pisti	Lbr	2011	32,983	56,898	190	32	14	bbu	
9456379	Sifnos	Lbr	2010	32,983	57,050	190	32	14	bbu	
9472086	Sofia	Lbr	2011	32,983	56,899	190	32	14	bbu	
8902802	Vasos	Mlt	1990	77,655	152,065	270	43	14	bbu	ex Orient Alliance-06, Partagas-03, Polycarp-01

vessels operated by Goldenport Shipmanagement Ltd, Greece
newbuilding : 40,300gt container ship (2012) [Sungdong 4006]IMO9608283

Green Management Sp.z.o.o.   Poland

Funnel: *Dark green.* **Hull**: *Dark green with white 'GREEN REEFERS', red boot-topping.* **History**: *Founded 1989 as Nomadic Shipping ASA to 2003. Green Reefers ASA sold to parent company Caiano Gp., May 2012, renamed Transit Invest ASA, merged with Reach Subsea AS, November 2012.* **Web**: *www.greenreefers.no*

IMO#	name	flag	year	grt	dwt	loa	bm	kts	type	former names
9045792	Green Brazil *	Bhs	1994	7,743	7,721	131	20	19	grf	ex Pittsburg-05, Pioneer-96, Crystal Pioneer-96
8912156	Green Chile *	Bhs	1992	7,743	7,726	131	20	19	grf	ex Privilege-06, Crystal Privilege-03
9011038	Green Concordia	Bhs	1991	5,617	7,072	120	19	17	grf	
8912120	Green Costa Rica *	Bhs	1991	7,743	7,726	131	20	19	grf	ex Prince-06, Crystal Prince-04
8912144	Green Guatemala *	Bhs	1992	7,743	7,726	131	20	19	grf	ex Primadonna-05, Crystal Primadonna-04
8912132	Green Honduras *	Bhs	1992	7,743	7,721	131	20	19	grf	ex Pride-06, Cyystal Pride-03
9045780	Green Italia *	Bhs	1994	7,743	7,721	131	20	19	grf	ex Pilgrim-06, Crystal Pilgrim-96

German Tanker Shipping : SEAMULLET : *ARO*

IMO#	name	flag	year	grt	dwt	loa	bm	kts	type	former names
8822583	Green Magic	Bhs	1989	5,103	6,116	136	16	20	grf	ex Magic-06
9011492	Green Magnific #	Bhs	1992	5,103	6,116	136	16	20	grf	ex Magnific-06
9043055	Green Maveric	Bhs	1993	5,103	6,105	136	16	20	grf	ex Maveric-06
8822595	Green Music	Bhs	1990	5,103	6,116	136	16	20	grf	ex Music-07
9015785	Green Toledo	Bhs	1991	5,617	7,075	120	19	17	grf	

vessels owned by Transit Invest ASA, (Caiano Group),Norway, formerly Green Reefers ASA until May 2012: also operates smaller vessels
* chartered to SeaTrade b.v. # laid up, Istanbul 04:05:2012

Grieg Star Shipping   Norway

Funnel: *Yellow with two blue stars on white panel with blue top and bottom edges.* **Hull:** *Blue, red or grey with red or blue boot-topping.* **History:** *Formed 1961 as Star Shipping, restructured 1984 as Grieg Shipping Group until June 2012.*
Web: *www.griegstar.com*

IMO#	name	flag	year	grt	dwt	loa	bm	kts	type	former names
8221777	Star Alabama	Nis	1985	20,916	30,204	169	27	15	boh	ex Hawaiian Rainbow-92
8508280	Star America	Nis	1985	20,929	30,168	169	27	15	boh	ex Canadian Rainbow-91, Star Canadian-90, Canadian Rainbow-89
9497880	Star Athena	Nis	2012	32,839	58,000	190	32	14	bbu	
8502834	Star Atlantic	Nis	1986	20,125	30,402	165	26	15	boh	ex Höegh Mistral-03, Star Atlantic-03, Höegh Mistral-03, Star Texas-90, Texas Rainbow-89
9228144	Star Canopus ‡	Grc	2002	25,388	45,635	180	31	14	bbu	ex Star Mizuho-07
9228071	Star Capella ‡	Grc	2001	25,388	45,601	180	31	14	bbu	
7507265	Star Dieppe	Nis	1977	27,104	43,082	183	31	15	boh	ex Star Shiraz-79, Star Dieppe-77
7507293	Star Dover	Nis	1977	27,911	43,082	183	31	15	boh	ex Star Estahan-79, Star Dover-77
8005109	Star Eagle	Nis	1981	24,479	39,749	180	29	15	boh	
9499450	Star Eracle	Nis	2012	32,839	58,000	190	32	14	bbu	c/a Chun He 125
8011330	Star Evviva	Nis	1982	24,479	39,718	180	29	15	boh	
8309828	Star Florida	Nis	1985	25,345	40,790	187	29	15	boh	
8309842	Star Fraser	Nis	1985	25,345	40,840	187	29	15	boh	
8309830	Star Fuji	Nis	1985	25,345	40,850	187	29	15	boh	
8420799	Star Gran	Nis	1986	27,192	43,759	198	29	16	boh	ex Triton-86
8420787	Star Grip	Nis	1986	27,192	43,712	198	29	16	boh	
9103128	Star Hansa	Nis	1996	32,749	46,580	198	31	16	boh	
9103130	Star Harmonia	Nis	1998	32,749	46,604	198	31	16	boh	
9071557	Star Herdla	Nis	1994	32,744	47,942	198	31	16	boh	
9071569	Star Hidra	Nis	1994	32,749	46,547	198	31	16	boh	
9182978	Star Isfjord	Nis	2000	29,898	41,749	185	31	16	boh	
9182966	Star Ismene	Nis	1999	28,897	41,777	185	31	16	boh	
9182954	Star Istind	Nis	1999	29,898	41,749	185	31	16	boh	
9254654	Star Japan	Nis	2004	32,844	46,387	198	31	16	boh	
9310513	Star Java	Nis	2006	32,879	46,387	198	31	16	boh	
9254642	Star Juventus	Nis	2004	32,844	44,837	198	31	16	boh	
9316139	Star Kilimanjaro	Nis	2009	37,158	49,862	208	32	16	boh	
9396141	Star Kinn	Nis	2010	37,158	49,850	209	32	16	boh	
9316927	Star Kirkenes	Nis	2009	37,158	49,924	208	32	16	boh	
9396153	Star Kvarven	Nis	2010	37,158	49,924	209	32	16	boh	
9593854	Star Laguna	Nis	2012	37,190	50,827	204	32		boh	
9593866	Star Lima	Nis	2012	37,190	50,761	204	32		boh	
9593878	Star Lindesnes	Nis	2013	37,447	50,748	204	32		boh	
9593880	Star Louisiana	Nis	2013	37,447	50,748	204	32		boh	
9593892	Star L…	Nis	2013	37,447					boh	
9593907	Star L…	Nis	2013	37,447					boh	
9496135	Star Manx	Iom	2009	32,354	58,133	190	32	14	bbu	

newbuildings: 4 further 50,000dwt boh 'L' class (Hyundai Mipo 2012/14)

Grimaldi Group   Italy

Funnel: *Blue with either white 'G', 'I' or 'A' symbol or white 'S' within white ring.* **Hull:** *Yellow with black 'GRIMALDI LINES' on white upperworks, red boot-topping.* **History:** *Founded 1941 as Fratelli Grimaldi Armatori to 1993.* **Web:** *www.grimaldi.napoli.it*

IMO#	name	flag	year	grt	dwt	loa	bm	kts	type	former names
9030852	Fides *	Ita	1993	33,825	16,802	178	27	19	mve	2,350 ceu
9143702	Gran Bretagna *	Ita	1999	51,714	18,461	181	32	20	urc	716 teu, 4,650 ceu
9117900	Grand Benelux *	Ita	2001	37,712	12,594	176	31	20	mve	4,300 ceu
9246607	Grande Amburgo †	Ita	2003	56,642	26,170	214	32	19	urc	1,321 teu, 3,515 ceu
9130937	Grande America †	Ita	1997	56,642	26,169	214	32	18	urc	1,321 teu, 3,515 ceu
9343156	Grande Angola †	Ita	2008	47,115	26,881	211	32	21	urc	1,360 teu
9287417	Grande Anversa *	Ita	2004	38,651	12,353	177	31	20	mve	4,300 ceu
9130951	Grande Atlantico	Ita	1999	56,640	26,170	214	32	18	urc	1,321 teu, 3,515 ceu
9343170	Grande Benin †	Ita	2009	47,218	26,097	211	32	20	urc	1,360 teu: 3,890 ceu
9253210	Grande Buenos Aires	Ita	2004	56,642	26,169	214	32	19	urc	1,321 teu, 3,515 ceu
9377482	Grande Cameroon †	Ita	2010	47,218	26,652	211	32	20	urc	1,360 teu, 3,890 ceu
9318527	Grande Colonia †	Ita	2007	38,651	12,292	177	31	20	mve	4,300 ceu
9437921	Grande Congo †	Ita	2010	47,658	25,682	211	32	20	urc	1,360 teu, 3,890 ceu

IMO#	name	flag	year	grt	dwt	loa	bm	kts	type	former names
9465382	Grande Costa									
	d'Avorio	Ita	2011	47,218	24,800	211	32	20	urc	1,360 teu, 3,890 ceu
9293272	Grande Detroit	Ita	2005	38,651	12,420	177	31	20	mve	4,300 ceu
9220627	Grande Ellade *	Ita	2001	52,485	18,440	181	32	20	urc	716 teu, 4,650 ceu
9138381	Grande Europa *	Ita	1998	51,714	18,461	181	32	20	urc	716 teu, 4,650 ceu
9246592	Grande Francia †	Ita	2002	56,642	26,170	214	32	19	urc	1,321 teu, 3,515 ceu
9437933	Grande Gabon †	Ita	2011	47,658	24,400	211	32		urc	1,360 teu, 3,890 ceu
9343168	Grande Ghana †	Ita	2009	47,115	25,000	211	32		urc	1,360 teu, 3,890 ceu
9437919	Grande Guinea †	Ita	2010	47,658	25,799	211	32		urc	1,360 teu, 3,890 ceu
9227912	Grande Italia *	Ita	2001	37,712	12,594	176	31	20	mve	4,300 ceu
9437907	Grande Marocco †	Ita	2010	47,635	24,400	211	32	20	urc	1,360 teu: 3,890 ceu
9138393	Grande									
	Mediterraneo *	Ita	1998	51,714	18,427	181	32	20	urc	716 teu, 4,650 ceu
9247924	Grande Napoli *	Ita	2003	44,408	14,565	197	31	20	mve	5,300 ceu
9246580	Grande Nigeria †	Ita	2002	56,642	26,170	214	32	19	urc	1,321 teu, 3,515 ceu
9245598	Grande Portogallo *	Ita	2002	37,712	12,594	176	31	20	mve	4,300 ceu
9247936	Grande Roma *	Ita	2003	42,600	14,900	201	31	20	mve	5,300 ceu
9253208	Grande San Paolo	Ita	2003	56,642	26,170	214	32	18	urc	1,321 teu, 3,515 ceu
9220615	Grande Scandinavia *	Ita	2001	52,487	18,440	181	32	20	urc	716 teu, 4,650 ceu
9377470	Grande Senegal †	Ita	2010	47,218	26,653	211	32		urc	1,360 teu, 3,890 ceu
9437945	Grande									
	Sierra Leone †	Ita	2011	47,658	24,400	211	32		urc	1,360 teu, 3,890 ceu
9312092	Grande Sicilia	Ita	2006	38,651	12,353	177	31	20	mve	4,300 ceu
9227924	Grande Spagna *	Ita	2002	37,712	12,594	176	31	20	mve	4,300 ceu
9465370	Grande Togo	Ita	2011	47,218	26,650	211	32		urc	1,360 teu, 3,890 ceu
9138410	Repubblica									
	Argentina †	Ita	1998	51,925	23,882	206	30	20	urc	800 teu,1,200 ceu
9138422	Repubblica									
	del Brasile †	Ita	1998	51,925	23,800	206	30	20	urc	800 teu,1,200 ceu
8521218	Repubblica di Amalfi	Ita	1989	42,574	25,450	216	30	18	urc	1,316 teu, 3,400 ceu: (len 1990)
9009504	Repubblica									
	di Roma †	Ita	1992	42,001	19,287	184	30	19	urc	890 teu, 2,200 ceu: (len 1995)
9030864	Spes *	ita	1993	33.823	16,806	178	27	19	mve	2,350 ceu

*ships owned by related Italian companies Grimaldi Compagnia di Navigazione SpA, * by Atlantica SpA di Navigazione or † by Industria Armamento Meridionale SpA (INARME)*

ACL Shipmanagement AB, Sweden

Funnel: *White with blue 'ACL' over wavy line, black top.* **Hull:** *Black with white 'ACL' symbol.* **History:** *Originally formed 1965 as Atlantic Container Line by Wallenius, Swedish-America, Transatlantic and Holland-America, Cunard-Brocklebank and CGT added 1967. Consortium dissolved 1990 and ACL acquired by Transatlantic (Bilspedition subsidiary). Grimaldi acquired 44% share in 2000 and balance in 2001.* **Web:** *www.aclcargo.com*

IMO#	name	flag	year	grt	dwt	loa	bm	kts	type	former names
8215481	Atlantic Cartier	Swe	1985	58,358	51,648	292	32	17	urc	2,908 teu: (len-87)
8214152	Atlantic Companion	Swe	1984	57,255	51,648	292	32	17	urc	2,908 teu: ex Companion Express-94, Atlantic Companion-87 (len-87)
8214176	Atlantic Compass	Swe	1984	57,255	51,648	292	32	17	urc	2,908 teu: (len-87)
8214164	Atlantic Concert	Swe	1984	57,255	51,648	292	32	17	urc	2,908 teu: ex Concert Express-94, Atlantic Concert-87 (len-87)

Grimaldi Group (Industrie Arm. Meridionale) : GRANDE AMBURGO : *ARO*

IMO#	name	flag	year	grt	dwt	loa	bm	kts	type	former names
8215534	Atlantic Conveyor	Swe	1985	58,438	51,648	292	32	17	urc	2,908 teu: (len-87)
9130949	Grande Africa *	Gib	1998	56,642	26,195	214	32	18	urc	1,321 teu, 3,515 ceu
9198135	Grande Argentina *	Gib	2001	56,642	26,170	214	32	18	urc	1,321 teu, 3,515 ceu
9198123	Grande Brasile *	Gib	2000	56,642	26,170	214	32	18	urc	1,321 teu, 3,515 ceu
9293272	Grande Detroit *	Ita	2005	38,651	12,353	176	31	20	mve	4,300 ceu
9312092	Grande Sicilia *	Ita	2006	38,651	12,353	176	31	20	mve	4,300 ceu

* owned by ACL Invest, managed and operated by Grimaldi
newbuildings : 5 x 296m 3,800 teu,1,307 ceu con-ro vessels [Hudong-Zhonghua SB Co.(2015)]

Reederei Hamburger Lloyd GmbH & Co. KG   Germany

Funnel: *black with broad white band and red top or charterers colours.* **Hull:** *Dark blue, red or black with black or red boot-topping.*
History: *Founded 2007 and financially linked to Hansa Hamburg Shg. International GmbH & Co KG .* **Web:** *www.hamburger-lloyd.com*

IMO#	name	flag	year	grt	dwt	loa	bm	kts	type	former names
9313228	Barmbek	Lbr	2005	16,324	15,955	169	27	21	ucc	1,600 teu
9539688	CCNI Andes	Lbr	2012	48,799	58,189	260	37	23	ucc	4,620 teu: I/a RHL Concordia
9539664	CCNI Aysen	Lbr	2012	48,799	58,197	260	37	23	ucc	4,620 teu: ex RHL Conscientia-12
9313199	Eilbek	Lbr	2005	16,324	15,952	169	27	21	ucc	1,600 teu ex Cast Prosperity-06, Eilbek-05
9313216	Flottbek	Lbr	2005	16,324	15,952	169	27	21	ucc	1,600 teu
9357846	Mell Sentosa	Lbr	2007	18,480	23,745	177	27	20	ucc	1,732 teu: ex CSAV Venezuela-11, G. W. Lessing-07
9313204	Reinbek	Lbr	2005	16,324	15,952	169	27	21	ucc	1,600 teu: ex Cast Prestige-06, Reinbek-05
9373486	RHL Agilitas	Lbr	2007	18,480	23,664	177	27	20	ucc	1,732 teu: ex Wilhelm Busch-07
9373498	RHL Aqua	Lbr	2007	18,480	23,732	177	27	20	ucc	1,732 teu: ex Theodor Fontane-07
9334844	RHL Astrum	Lbr	2006	18,480	23,640	177	27	20	ucc	1,732 teu: ex Heinrich Heine-11
9334832	RHL Aurora	Lbr	2006	18,480	23,685	177	27	20	ucc	1,721 teu: ex Matthias Claudias-11
9495777	RHL Calliditas	Lbr	2013	48,799	58,000	260	37	23	ucc	4,620 teu
9495765	RHL Constantia	Lbr	2012	48,799	58,000	260	37	23	ucc	4,620 teu
9426790	RHL Felicitas	Lbr	2010	54,182	63,059	294	32	25	ucc	5,086 teu
9426805	RHL Fidelitas	Lbr	2010	54,182	62,920	294	32	25	ucc	5,086 teu
9426817	RHL Fiducia	Lbr	2010	54,182	63,069	294	32	25	ucc	5,086 teu

newbuildings:
managed by Wappen Reederei GmbH & Co KG, Germany. see also vessels managed by Ernst Jacob GmbH, Leonhardt & Blumberg Reederei GmbH and Reederei Karl Schluter GmbH.

Hanjin Shipping Co. Ltd.   South Korea

Funnel: *Orange with white 'H' inside white ring.* **Hull:** *Black with white 'HANJIN', red boot-topping.* **History:** *Formed 1988. Senator Lines GmbH (formed 1987 as Senator Linie, a subsidiary of Bremer Vulkan shipyard), later merged with former East German company Deutsche Seerederei Rostock and became 80% owned affiliate in 1997, before closing in early 2009.* **Web:** *www.hanjin.com*

IMO#	name	flag	year	grt	dwt	loa	bm	kts	type	former names
9383974	Atlantic Canyon	Hkg	2009	23,342	36,677	184	27	15	tco	
9597795	Blue Matterhorn	Pan	2011	44,102	81,391	229	32	15	bbu	
9039145	Empress **	Pan	1992	76,925	151,662	274	45	13	bbu	
9039157	Frontier **	Pan	1992	76,925	151,492	274	45	13	bbu	
9037745	Goodwill **	Pan	1992	75,277	149,401	269	43	14	bbu	
9268930	Great River	Kor	2004	19,829	33,745	169	28	15	bbu	
9613666	Hanjin Albany	Pan	2011	32,537	55,648	188	32	14	bbu	
9389394	Hanjin Atlanta	Pan	2009	40,487	51,733	261	32	24	ucc	4,275 teu

Reederei Hamburger Lloyd GmbH : RHL FIDUCIA : *ARO*

IMO#	name	flag	year	grt	dwt	loa	bm	kts	type	former names
9539731	Hanjin Balikpapan	Pan	2012	63,993	114,531	255	43	14	bbu	
9115731	Hanjin Beijing *	Kor	1996	65,893	67,115	279	40	25	ucc	5,302 teu
9412828	Hanjin Belewan †	Hkg	2007	17,225	21,973	172	28	19	ucc	1,700 teu
9115743	Hanjin Berlin *	Kor	1997	66,403	67,236	279	40	25	ucc	5,302 teu
9110315	Hanjin Bombay	Kor	1994	16,252	27,029	167	26	14	bbu	
9493066	Hanjin Brazil	Pan	2011	152,219	299,688	340	55	14	bor	
9312779	Hanjin Bremerhaven	Pan	2006	74,962	80,855	304	40	26	ucc	6,655 teu
9128142	Hanjin Brisbane	Kor	1997	16,252	27,327	167	26	14	bbu	
9312937	Hanjin Budapest	Pan	2006	74,962	80,866	304	40	26	ucc	6,655 teu
9537563	Hanjin Buchanan	Pan	2011	63,993	114,688	255	43	14	bbu	
9444039	Hanjin Cape Lambert	Pan	2009	93,152	179,147	292	45	15	bbu	
9054224	Hanjin Capetown	Kor	1993	76,954	147,631	274	45	13	bbu	
9532276	Hanjin Chennai +	Pan	2010	27,061	33,380	200	32	22	ucc	2,553 teu
9408865	Hanjin China	Pan	2011	113,412	118,835	350	46	25	ucc	9,954 teu
9347449	Hanjin Chongqing	Pan	2008	74,962	80,855	304	40	26	ucc	6,622 teu
9458389	Hanjin Dalrymple Bay	Pan	2010	93,152	179,147	292	45	15	bbu	
9490894	Hanjin Dangjin	Pan	2010	93,152	179,255	292	45	15	bbu	
9532288	Hanjin Dalian +	Pan	2011	27,061	33,381	200	32	22	ucc	2,553 teu
9375513	Hanjin Durban	Pan	2008	40,487	51,750	261	32	24	ucc	4,275 teu
9454515	Hanjin Fos	Pan	2010	93,152	179,147	292	45	15	bbu	
9389409	Hanjin Gdynia	Pan	2009	40,487	51,733	261	32	24	ucc	4,275 teu
8821620	Hanjin Gladstone	Kor	1990	110,541	207,391	309	50	13	bbu	
9461491	Hanjin Hamburg	Pan	2011	91,621	102,455	336	43	24	ucc	8,580 teu
8821668	Hanjin Haypoint	Kor	1990	77,650	151,431	274	45	13	bbu	
9604768	Hanjin Hinase †	Pan	2011	17,019	28,386	169	27	14	bbu	
9442536	Hanjin Hirose	Pan	2011	44,372	83,494	229	32	15	bbu	
9626314	Hanjin Isabel	Pan	2012	22,664	36,798	186	28	14	bbu	
9536973	Hanjin Jebel Ali +	Pan	2011	27,061	33,417	200	32	22	ucc	2,552 teu
8913667	Hanjin Kaohsiung ‡	Cyp	1990	37,134	43,925	243	32	22	ucc	2,932 teu
9389382	Hanjin Kingston	Pan	2008	40,487	51,733	261	32	24	ucc	4,275 teu
9408853	Hanjin Korea	Pan	2010	113,412	118,800	350	46	25	ucc	9,954 teu
9616302	Hanjin Liverpool	Pan	2012	22,664	36,767	186	28	15	bbu	
9111383	Hanjin London	Kor	1996	66,687	67,298	279	40	26	ucc	5,302 teu
9461465	Hanjin Long Beach	Pan	2010	91,621	102,518	336	43	25	ucc	8,580 teu
9128130	Hanjin Los Angeles	Kor	1997	51,754	62,700	290	32	24	ucc	4,024 teu
9021679	Hanjin Malta	Kor	1993	51,299	62,649	290	32	24	ucc	4,024 teu
9412816	Hanjin Manila †	Pan	2007	17,225	21,976	172	28	19	ucc	1,700 teu
9536985	Hanjin Manzanillo +	Pan	2011	27,061	33,407	200	32	22	ucc	2,553 teu:
9015541	Hanjin Marseilles	Kor	1993	51,299	62,681	290	32	24	ucc	4,024 teu

Hanjin Shipping Co. : HANJIN HINASE : *M. Lennon*

IMO#	name	flag	year	grt	dwt	loa	bm	kts	type	former names
9464522	Hanjin Marugame †	Pan	2008	17,018	28,343	170	27	14	bbu	
9514030	Hanjin Matsue †	Pan	2011	31,540	55,868	190	32	14	bbu	
9576296	Hanjin Matsuyama †	Mhl	2011	93,169	179,166	292	45	15	bbu	
9389411	Hanjin Monaco	Pan	2009	40,487	51,733	261	32	24	ucc	4,275 teu
9347425	Hanjin Mumbai	Pan	2007	74,962	85,250	304	40	26	ucc	6,622 teu
9155078	Hanjin Muscat (st)	Pan	1999	93,765	75,463	280	43	20	lng	138,366 m³
9155028	Hanjin Nagoya	Pan	1998	51,754	62,688	290	32	24	ucc	4,024 teu
9079133	Hanjin New Orleans	Kor	1994	37,550	70,337	225	32	13	bbu	
9408841	Hanjin Netherlands	Pan	2011	113,515	118,712	350	46	25	ucc	9,954 teu
9461505	Hanjin New York	Pan	2011	91,621	102,518	336	43	25	ucc	8,580 teu
9618812	Hanjin Newcastle	Mhl	2011	93,597	179,905	292	45	15	bbu	
9404194	Hanjin Newport	Mhl	2009	40,542	50,574	261	32	24	ucc	4,250 teu
9470765	Hanjin Nhava Sheva +	Pan	2008	17,280	21,438	172	28	19	ucc	1,577 teu
9375496	Hanjin Norfolk	Pan	2008	40,487	51,752	261	32	24	ucc	4,275 teu
9539729	Hanjin Odessa	Pan	2012	64,110	114,536	255	43	14	bbu	
9161778	Hanjin Oslo	Pan	1998	65,469	68,993	279	40	25	ucc	5,302 teu
9128128	Hanjin Paris	Kor	1997	66,687	68,500	279	40	25	ucc	5,302 teu
9375501	Hanjin Piraeus	Pan	2008	40,487	50,542	261	32	24	ucc	4,275 teu
8821644	Hanjin Pittsburg	Kor	1990	25,461	38,393	186	28	15	bbu	ex Pittsburg-93
9454527	Hanjin Port Headland	Pan	2010	93,152	179,283	292	45	15	bbu	
9312949	Hanjin Port Kelang	Pan	2006	75,061	80,811	304	40	26	ucc	6,655 teu
9019729	Hanjin Port Kembla	Kor	1993	68,243	126,267	264	41	13	bbu	
9618824	Hanjin Port Walcott	Mhl	2012	93,597	180,000	292	45	15	bbu	
9061928	Hanjin Pyeong Taek (st)	Pan	1995	90,004	71,041	269	43	19	lng	130,000 m³
9176008	Hanjin Ras Laffan (st)	Pan	2000	93,769	75,079	280	43	20	lng	138,214 m³
9519717	Hanjin Ras Tanura	Pan	2011	160,493	309,988	333	60	16	tcr	
9141338	Hanjin Richards Bay	Kor	1997	75,752	149,322	269	43	14	bbu	
9375305	Hanjin Rio de Janiero	Pan	2008	40,487	51,648	261	32	24	ucc	4,275 teu
9490882	Hanjin Rizhao	Pan	2010	93,152	179,194	292	45	15	bbu	
9077329	Hanjin Roberts Bank	Kor	1994	73,706	135,069	268	43	14	bbu	
9161766	Hanjin Rome	Pan	1998	65,469	68,955	280	40	25	ucc	5,302 teu
9613678	Hanjin Rostock	Pan	2011	32,537	55,625	188	32	14	bbu	
9461489	Hanjin Rotterdam	Pan	2011	91,621	102,539	336	43	25	ucc	8,580 teu
9513749	Hanjin Saijo ++	Pan	2010	104,729	206,291	300	50		bbu	
9458377	Hanjin Saldanha Bay	Pan	2010	93,152	179,147	292	45	15	bbu	
9537551	Hanjin Samarinda	Pan	2011	63,993	114,536	255	43	14	bbu	
9131058	Hanjin San Francisco *	Kor	1996	50,792	62,681	290	32	24	ucc	4,024 teu
9597111	Hanjin Santana	Pan	2012	34,531	58,627	196	32	14	bbu	
9461477	Hanjin Seattle	Pan	2011	91,621	102,529	336	43	25	ucc	8,580 teu
9088251	Hanjin Shanghai	Kor	1995	50,792	62,799	290	32	24	ucc	4,024 teu
9347437	Hanjin Shenzhen	Pan	2008	74,962	80,855	304	40	26	ucc	6,622 teu
9446532	Hanjin Shikoku	Pan	2011	92,725	181,502	292	45	15	bbu	
9444027	Hanjin Sines	Pan	2009	93,152	179,147	252	45	15	bbu	

Hanjin Shipping Co. : HANJIN LONG BEACH : *Douglas Cromby*

IMO#	name	flag	year	grt	dwt	loa	bm	kts	type	former names
9408877	Hanjin Spain	Pan	2011	113,412	118,814	350	46	25	ucc	9,954 teu
9176010	Hanjin Sur (st)	Pan	2000	93,769	75,193	280	43	20	lng	138,333 m³
9079145	Hanjin Tacoma	Pan	1994	37,550	70,347	225	32	13	bbu	
9312767	Hanjin Tianjin	Pan	2007	74,962	80,855	304	40	25	ucc	6,655 teu
9493054	Hanjin Tubarao	Pan	2011	152,219	299,688	340	55	15	bor	
9406738	Hanjin United Kingdom	Pan	2011	113,412	118,888	350	46	25	ucc	9,954 teu
9142485	Hanjin Valencia	Pan	1998	51,754	62,799	290	32	24	ucc	4,024 teu
8820822	Hanjin Vancouver ‡	Cyp	1990	35,745	44,764	241	32	20	ucc	2,900 teu: ex Hanjin Hamburg-90
9111395	Hanjin Washington	Kor	1997	65,643	67,272	279	40	25	ucc	5,302 teu
9142473	Hanjin Wilmington	Kor	1997	50,792	62,799	290	32	24	ucc	4,024 teu
9312755	Hanjin Xiamen	Pan	2007	74,962	80,855	304	40	26	ucc	6,655 teu
9039195	Innovator **	Pan	1993	75,277	149,298	269	43	14	bbu	
9131072	Keoyang Majesty	Pan	1997	43,181	48,618	221	32	15	bwc	
9131084	Keoyang Noble	Pan	1997	43,181	51,662	221	32	15	bwc	
9141326	Keoyang Orient	Pan	1997	75,752	149,322	269	43	14	bbu	
9597812	Orion Pride	Pan	2011	44,102	81,323	229	32	15	bbu	
9037733	Pos Ambition	Pan	1992	75,277	149,330	269	43	14	bbu	
9037721	Pos Bravery	Kor	1992	110,593	207,096	309	50	13	bbu	
9039171	Pos Challenger	Pan	1992	75,277	140,302	269	43	13	bbu	
9037719	Pos Dedicator	Kor	1993	110,627	208,393	312	50	13	bbu	
9039183	Pos Harvester	Pan	1992	75,277	140,302	269	43	13	bbu	
9597800	Unity Pride	Pan	2011	44,102	81,393	229	32	15	bbu	

newbuildings: five 13,000 teu container ships [Daewoo]
* owned by Korea French Banking Corp. (formed jointly with Société Génerale SA) and by subsidary ** Keoyang Shipping Co. Ltd (formed 1990).
formerly owned now chartered ‡ from Samartzis Maritime Enterprises Co. SA, both Greece, + chartered from Santoku Senpaku, † chartered from other owners

Hansa Heavy Lift Germany

Funnel: *White.* **Hull:** *Red with white 'Hansa Heavy Lift', red boot-topping.* **History:** *Founded 2011 with acquired various interests from former Beluga Shipping GmbH founded 1995.* **Web:** *www.hansaheavylift.com*

IMO#	name	flag	year	grt	dwt	loa	bm	kts	type	former names
9466996	HHL Amazon	Lbr	2009	9,611	12,662	138	21	17	ghl	cr: 2(180): ex Beluga Fairy-11
9435753	HHL Amur	Atg	2009	9,611	12,678	138	21	15	ghl	cr: 2(180): ex Beluga Fidelity-11
9418999	HHL Bilbao	Atg	2010	15,377	16,523	166	23	17	ghl	cr: 2(400) 1(120): ex Beluga Sao Paulo-12, l/a Beluga Participation
9467005	HHL Congo	Atg	2011	9,616	12,546	138	21	15	ghl	cr: 2(180): ex Beluga Fealty-11
9448360	HHL Fremantle	Atg	2011	17,644	19,382	169	25	17	ghl	cr: 2(700) 1(180): l/a Beluga Protection
9419008	HHL Hamburg	Atg	2009	15,377	16,577	166	23	17	ghl	cr: 2(400) 1(120): ex Beluga Cape Town-11, Beluga Profession-10
9424572	HHL Hong Kong	Lbr	2010	17,634	19,348	169	25	17	ghl	cr: 2(700) 1(180): ex Beluga Shanghai-11, l/a Beluga Preparation
9448384	HHL Kobe	Atg	2012	17,644	19,864	169	25	17	ghl	cr: 2(700) 1(180)
9448358	HHL Lagos	Atg	2011	17,644	19,379	169	25	17	ghl	cr: 2(700) 1(180): ex Beluga Progression-11

Hansa Heavy Lift : HHL Amazon : *Chris Brooks*

IMO#	name	flag	year	grt	dwt	loa	bm	kts	type	former names
9418975	HHL Lisbon	Lbr	2010	15,377	18,388	166	23	16	ghl	cr: 2(400) 1(120): ex Singapore-12, Beluga Singapore-12, Beluga Persuasion-10
9424560	HHL Macao	Gib	2010	17,634	19,366	169	25	17	ghl	cr: 2(700) 1(180): ex Beluga Stavanger-11, I/a Beluga Provocation
9448372	HHL New York	Atg	2011	17,644	19,866	169	25	17	ghl	cr: 2(700) 1(180): I/a Beluga Publication
9443669	HHL Nile	Gib	2009	9,611	12,744	138	21	15	ghl	cr: 2(180): ex Beluga Faculty-11
9435765	HHL Mississippi	Atg	2009	9,611	12,669	138	21	15	ghl	cr: 2(180): ex OXL Fantasy-11, Beluga Fantasy-11
9467017	HHL Rhine	Lbr	2009	9,616	12,951	138	21	15	ghl	cr: 2(180): ex Beluga Feasibility-11
9448308	HHL Richards Bay	Atg	2010	17,644	19,329	169	25	17	ghl	cr: 2(700) 1(180): ex Beluga London-11, I/a Beluga Passion
9424546	HHL Rio di Janiero	Lbr	2009	17,628	20,171	169	25	17	ghl	cr: 2(700) 1(180)ex Beluga Houston-11, Beluga H-10, Beluga Houston-10, I/d Beluga Presentation
9448346	HHL Tokyo	Atg	2011	17,644	19,496	169	25	17	ghl	cr: 2(700) 1(180): ex Beluga Toyko-11, Beluga Procession-11
9424558	HHL Valparaiso	Lbr	2010	17,634	19,413	169	25	17	ghl	cr: 2(700) 1(180)ex Beluga Bremen-11, I/a Beluga Perfection
9418987	HHL Venice	Atg	2010	15,377	18,373	166	23	17	ghl	cr :2(400) 1(120): ex Beluga Mumbai-11, I/a Beluga Promotion
9381392	HHL Volga	Lbr	2007	9,611	12,782	138	21	15	ghl	cr: 2(180): ex Volga-11, Beluga Family-11

newbuildings:

Hansa Treuhand Schiffsbeteiligungs AG & Co. KG   Germany

Funnel: White with blue houseflag or charterers colours. **Hull:** Dark blue, red or black with black or red boot-topping.
History: Founded 1983. **Web:** www.hansatreuhand.de

IMO#	name	flag	year	grt	dwt	loa	bm	kts	type	former names
9124512	Hansa Century *	Deu	1997	31,730	34,954	193	32	22	ucc	2,507 teu: ex Kota Perdana-04, Zim Pusan I-02, Hansa Century-98, Ibn Duraid-98, Hansa Century-97
9124524	Hansa Constitution *	Deu	1997	31,730	34,954	193	32	22	ucc	2,507 teu: ex Norasia Alps-10, Hansa Constitution-05, MSC Florida-03, Hansa Constitution-98, Ibn Al Akfani-98, Hansa Constitution-97
9217034	Hansa Liberty *	Lbr	2000	25,369	33,912	207	30	21	ucc	2,470 teu: ex CSCL Yantian-07, Hansa Liberty-00
9217022	Hansa Victory *	Lbr	2000	25,369	33,899	207	30	21	ucc	2,470 teu: ex Alianca Gavea-09, Cala Palos-08, CSCL Xiamen-07, Hansa Victory-00
9221970	HS Alcina *	Lbr	2001	83,723	160,183	274	48	14	tcr	ex Somjin-06
9323015	HS Bach *	Lbr	2007	38,320	44,985	247	32	23	ucc	3,500 teu
9252266	HS Beethoven *	Lbr	2002	50,243	58,213	282	32	24	ucc	4,350 teu: ex APL Italy-09, MSC Arizona-05, HS Voyager-03, I/a Hansa Voyager
9315343	HS Berlioz *	Lbr	2007	38,320	46,288	247	32	23	ucc	3,500 teu
9315355	HS Bizet *	Lbr	2007	38,320	46,313	247	32	23	ucc	3,500 teu
9392559	HS Bruckner *	Lbr	2009	35,981	42,004	231	32	22	ucc	3,534 teu
9242120	HS Carmen *	Lbr	2003	62,254	113,033	250	44	-	tcr	ex Avor-06
9243605	HS Challenger *	Lbr	2004	30,024	35,924	207	32	22	ucc	2,672 teu: ex Hansa Challenger-04
9323027	HS Chopin *	Lbr	2007	38,320	46,345	247	32	23	ucc	3,500 teu
9436484	HS Debussy *	Lbr	2009	36,007	41,973	231	32	23	ucc	3,534 teu: ex SCI New Delhi-12, HS Debussy-09
9243590	HS Discoverer *	Deu	2003	30,123	35,600	207	32	22	ucc	2,672 teu: ex Zim Charleston-07, HS Discoverer-06, Hansa Discoverer-04
9178329	HS Elektra *	Lbr	1998	57,009	105,994	244	42	13	tcr	ex Nordasia-07
9392561	HS Haydn *	Lbr	2010	35,981	41,989	231	32	23	ucc	3,534 teu
9292151	HS Humboldt *	Mlt	2004	54,271	66,672	294	32	23	ucc	4,367 teu: ex Maersk Dortmund-09, HS Humboldt-04
9368742	HS Liszt *	Lbr	2008	16,162	17,350	161	24	20	ucc	1,347 teu
9292149	HS Livingstone *	Mlt	2004	54,271	68,187	294	32	23	ucc	4,367 teu: ex Maersk Darmstadt-09, HS Livingstone-04, I/dn Maersk Dunkirk
9242118	HS Medea *	Lbr	2003	62,254	113,033	250	44	14	tcr	ex Sinova-06
9252254	HS Mozart *	Lbr	2002	50,243	58,486	282	32	24	ucc	4,350 teu: ex APL Australia-09, MSC Lausanne-04, HS Explorer-02, I/a Hansa Explorer
9337597	HS Schubert *	Lbr	2006	18,480	23,690	177	27	20	ucc	1,740 teu: Viking Osprey-09
9308194	HS Scott *	Lbr	2007	32,968	38,547	213	32	23	ucc	2,800 teu: ex CMA CGM Newton-09, HS Scott-07
9312652	HS Smetana *	Lbr	2006	18,327	23,377	176	27	20	ucc	1,740 teu: ex Viking Merlin-09
9288851	HS Tosca *	Lbr	2004	62,796	115,635	250	44	15	tcr	
9436472	HS Wagner *	Lbr	2008	36,007	42,100	231	32	23	ucc	3,534 teu: ex Maruba America-10, HS Wagner-08
9300984	Ital Oceano	Lbr	2006	32,968	38,686	214	32	23	ucc	2,800 teu: ex HS Cook-06

IMO#	name	flag	year	grt	dwt	loa	bm	kts	type	former names
9308182	Ital Onesta	Lbr	2007	32,968	38,617	214	32	23	ucc	2,800 teu: l/a HS Magellan
9300972	Ital Onore ‡	Lbr	2006	32,968	38,609	214	32	23	ucc	2,800 teu: ex HS Amundsen-06
9248083	Maersk Dampier *	Lbr	2002	50,242	58,399	282	32	24	ucc	4,367 teu: ex CMA CGM Neptune-06, l/a HS Colon-02, l/dn Hansa Colon
9248095	Maersk Drammen *	Lbr	2002	50,242	58,512	282	32	24	ucc	4,367 teu: ex CMA CGM Mercure-06, HS Caribe-02, l/a Hansa Caribe
9368730	Mell Stamford *	Lbr	2007	16,162	17,350	161	25	20	ucc	1,347 teu: ex HS Puccini-12
9225079	MSC Brindisi *	Lbr	2001	65,131	67,955	275	40	26	ucc	5,447 teu: ex CSCL Seattle-09, l/a HS Columbia, l/dn Hansa Columbia
9565338	Niledutch Leopard *	Lbr	2012	39,753	46,020	228	32	22	ucc	l/a HS Rossini

newbuildings:
* owned/managed by subsidiary Hansa Shipping GmbH & Co KG.
† managed by Leonhardt & Blumberg Schiffahrts GmbH & Co KG, Germany and †† chartered out to Seatrade Groningen BV,
See also Norddeutsche Reederei H Schuldt GmbH, KG Projex-Schiffahrts GmbH & Co, F A Vinnen & Co and Oskar Wehr KG.

Hanseatic Lloyd AG   Switzerland

Funnel: Black with red dot over blue wave on broad white band or charterers colours. **Hull:** Blue or light grey with red boot-topping.
History: Formed 2003. **Web:** www.hanseatic-lloyd.com

IMO#	name	flag	year	grt	dwt	loa	bm	kts	type	former names
9345972	APL Atlanta	Atg	2008	43,071	55,482	267	32	25	ucc	4,250 teu: l/a HLL Adriatic
9345960	APL Denver	Atg	2008	43,071	55,612	267	32	25	ucc	4,250 teu: l/a HLL Pacific
9345958	APL Los Angeles	Atg	2008	43,071	55,387	267	32	25	ucc	4,250 teu
9332550	APL Oakland	Atg	2008	43,071	55,476	267	32	25	ucc	4,250 teu
9252230	APL Peru	Atg	2002	41,834	53,554	266	32	25	ucc	4,200 teu: ex Delaware Bridge-05, HLL Atlantic-02
9316244	Ashley Sea	Lbr	2007	42,052	73,933	229	32	15	tco	
9173094	MCT Alioth *	Lbr	1999	12,358	19,996	149	24	15	tco	ex Alioth-04
9173109	MCT Almak *	Lbr	1999	12,358	17,561	149	24	15	tco	ex Almak-03
9173082	MCT Altair *	Lbr	1999	12,358	17,553	149	24	15	tco	ex Altair-03
9173111	MCT Arcturus *	Lbr	1999	12,358	17,575	149	24	15	tco	ex Arcturus-03
9298375	MCT Breithorn *	Che	2007	12,776	20,635	164	27	15	tco	l/a HLL Celtic
9298351	MCT Matterhorn *	Che	2006	12,776	20,677	164	23	15	tco	l/a HLL Arctic
9298363	MCT Monte Rosa *	Che	2007	12,776	20,718	164	27	15	tco	
9356816	MCT Rhine *	Lbr	2013	12,000	19,953	164	27	15	tco	l/a HLL Black Sea
9298307	MCT Stockhorn *	Che	2008	12,776	20,610	164	23	15	tco	l/a HLL Caspian
9316232	Sharon Sea	Lbr	2006	42,167	73,870	229	32	15	tco	

newbuildings, 3 x 19,800dwt tco [Amur Shipbuilding Co. IMO 9374466, 9374478, 9374480 to be named MCT Mississippi, MCT Yangtze and MCT Amazon (2013)]
owned by subsidiaries of Hanseatic Lloyd Schiffahrt GmbH & Co KG, Germany. * managed by Mega Chemicals Schiffahrts AG, Switzerland

Hanseatic Lloyd AG : APL ATLANTA : *Hans Kraijenbosch*

IMO#	name	flag	year	grt	dwt	loa	bm	kts	type	former names

Hansa Mare Reederei GmbH & Co. KG, Germany

Funnel: Black with red dot over blue wave on broad white band or charterers colours. **Hull:** Blue or light grey with red boot-topping.
History: Formed 1991 and jointly owned by Hanseatic Lloyd Reederei and Schlüssel Reederei KG (founded 1950).
Web: www.hansamare.de

IMO#	name	flag	year	grt	dwt	loa	bm	kts	type	former names
9169134	Alvsborg Bridge *	Atg	1998	40,306	52,357	261	32	25	ucc	4,038 teu: ex Maersk Dulles-09, Maersk Tangier-06, P&O Nedlloyd Tiger-05, Weser Bridge-04, I/a Mare Siculum
9213284	Mare Arcticum *	Gib	2000	40,306	52,250	261	32	22	ucc	4,038 teu: ex APL Chile-12, Mare Arcticum-04, YM New York-04, Trade Tesia-03, Mare Arcticum-01
9213272	Mare Atlanticum *	Atg	2000	40,306	52,250	261	32	24	ucc	4,038 teu: ex MSC Scandinavia-11, Donau Bridge-04, Mare Atlanticum-01
9235074	Mare Britannicum *	Gib	2000	40,306	52,250	261	32	22	ucc	4,038 teu: ex APL Kaohsiung-12, Kaohsiung-09, APL Kaohsiung-08, APL Panama-06, APL Britannicum-04, YM Wilmington-04, Trade Freda-03, I/a Mare Britannicum
9235086	Mare Caribicum *	Gib	2000	40,306	52,250	261	32	22	ucc	4,038 teu: ex APL Argentina-12, YM Savannah-04, Trade Hallie-03, Mare Caribicum-01
9101819	Mare Doricum **	Gib	1995	9,590	12,705	150	22	17	ucc	1,016 teu: ex MSC Belize-09, Mare Doricum-07, ACX Falcon-02, Mare Doricum-00, Breda Stad-98, Mare Doricum-97, Sea Nordic-95, Mare Doricum-95
9193238	Mare Lycium *	Atg	1999	40,306	47,660	261	32	24	ucc	4,038 teu: ex Libra Mexico-11, Mumbai Express-07, Mare Lycium-06, P&O Nedlloyd Cobra-05, Mare Lycium-03, Mosel Bridge-02, I/a Mare Lycium
9193226	Mare Phoenicium *	Gib	1999	40,306	52,330	261	32	24	ucc	4,038 teu: ex Ems Bridge-01, I/a Mare Phoenicium
9169122	Mare Superum *	Gib	1998	40,306	52,329	261	32	24	ucc	4,038 teu: ex Maersk Tirana-09, Dalian Express-07, Maersk Tirana-06, P&O Nedlloyd Cartagena-05, Elbe Bridge-04, Mare Superum-98

* managed by Schlüssel Reederei

Hapag-Lloyd AG Germany

Funnel: Orange with blue 'HL' symbol. **Hull:** Black or red with white 'Hapag-Lloyd' and red boot-topping. **History:** Formed in 1970 by amalgamation of Hamburg-Amerika Linie (founded 1847) and Norddeutscher Lloyd (founded 1857). Rickmers Linie became wholly owned subsidiary in 1987 (part-owned since 1974), later being resold to Rickmers family. Control of Hapag acquired by Preussag AG in 1997 and Hapag acquired control of TUI Group in 1998, Preussag (now TUI) acquiring remaining shares in 2002 and in 2005 TUI acquired CP Ships (originally founded 1883 as Canadian Pacific Railway Co, first ship chartered 1886, later Canadian Pacific Steamships (founded 1922) and Canadian Pacific Ltd from 1981. Canada Maritime founded 1987, jointly with CMB (43%) whose share was acquired 1993. Acquired Cast (1983) Ltd in 1995, Lykes Bros Steamship Co (founded 1900) and Contship in 1997, Ivaran Lines and ANZDL in 1998, TMM and CCAL in 2000 and Italia Line in 2002). **Web:** www.hapag-lloyd.com

IMO#	name	flag	year	grt	dwt	loa	bm	kts	type	former names
8501426	Altamira Express *	Bmu	1987	40,436	40,845	270	32	20	ucc	3,266 teu: ex CP Ambassador-06, Lykes Ambassador-05, Ming Plenty-01
9612997	Antwerpen Express	Deu	2013			366	48	24	ucc	13,092 teu
8902577	Atlanta Express	Deu	1992	53,833	67,680	294	32	23	ucc	4,639 teu: ex Ludwigshafen Express-12
8406286	Barcelona Express *	Bmu	1987	40,439	40,744	270	32	20	ucc	3,266 teu: ex CP Sinaloa-06, TMM Sinaloa-05, Ming Promotion-01
9501344	Basle Express	Deu	2012	142,295	127,100	366	48	24	ucc	13,092 teu
9613006	Beijing Express	Deu	2013			366	48	24	ucc	13,092 teu
9229855	Berlin Express	Deu	2003	88,493	100,019	320	43	26	ucc	7,179 teu
8711368	Bonn Express	Deu	1989	35,919	45,977	236	32	20	ucc	2,803 teu
9343728	Bremen Express	Deu	2008	93,750	103,567	336	43	25	ucc	8,749 teu
9450430	Budapest Express	Deu	2010	93,750	103,662	336	43	25	ucc	8,749 teu
9307023	Canada Express +	Sgp	2006	66,462	66,940	281	40	21	ucc	5,888 teu: ex OOCL Dubai-10
9224049	Canberra Express	Deu	2000	23,652	29,841	188	30	20	ucc	2,078 teu: ex CP Eagle-06, Lykes Eagle-05, Clivia-00
9243162	Charleston Express †	Usa	2002	40,146	36,644	243	32	20	ucc	3,237 teu: ex CP Everglades-07, Lykes Ranger-05
9295268	Chicago Express	Deu	2006	93,811	103,691	336	43	25	ucc	8,749 teu
9295244	Colombo Express	Deu	2005	93,750	103,800	335	43	25	ucc	8,749 teu
9229829	Dalian Express	Deu	2001	88,493	100,006	320	43	26	ucc	7,506 teu: ex Hamburg Express-11
9193288	Dallas Express	Deu	2000	54,437	67,145	294	32	24	ucc	4,864 teu: ex Antwerpen Express-12, Tokyo Express-99
8902553	Dresden Express	Deu	1991	53,883	67,680	294	32	23	ucc	4,409 teu
9232577	Dublin Express	Deu	2002	46,009	54,157	281	32	25	ucc	4,121 teu: ex Maersk Dale-08, CP Australis-06, Contship Australis-05
9143556	Düsseldorf Express	Deu	1998	53,523	66,525	294	32	23	ucc	4,616 teu

IMO#	name	flag	year	grt	dwt	loa	bm	kts	type	former names
9036909	Essen Express	Deu	1993	53,815	67,680	294	32	23	ucc	4,422 teu
9613018	*Essen Express*	Deu	2013			366	48	24	ucc	13,092 teu
9450442	Frankfurt Express	Deu	2010	93,750	103,994	335	43	25	ucc	8,749 teu
9062996	Fremantle Express *	Gbr	1995	23,540	30,645	187	30	19	ucc	2,074 teu: ex CP Voyager-06, Lykes Voyager-05, P&O Nedlloyd Bandar Abbas-01, P&O Nedlloyd Yafo-99, Pax-98, CMBT Melbourne-97, Contship Melbourne-97, I/a Pax
8501452	Genoa Express	Bmu	1988	40,436	40,845	270	32	20	ucc	3,266 teu: ex CP Jalisco-06, TMM Jalisco-05, Ming Progress-01
9232589	Glasgow Express	Deu	2002	46,009	54,221	281	32	25	ucc	4,121 teu: ex Maersk Dayton-08, CP Borealis-06, Contship Borealis-05
9461051	Hamburg Express	Deu	2012	142,295	142,092	366	48	23	ucc	13,169 teu
9343716	Hanover Express	Deu	2007	93,750	103,760	336	43	25	ucc	8,749 teu
8711370	Heidelberg Express	Deu	1989	35,919	45,977	236	32	20	ucc	2,803 teu: ex Ville De Verseau-91, Heidelberg Express-91
8902565	Hoechst Express	Deu	1991	53,833	67,680	294	32	23	ucc	4,409 teu
9501356	*Hong Kong Express*	Deu	2013			366	48	24	ucc	13,092 teu
9306990	Italy Express +	Pan	2006	66,462	66,940	281	40	25	ucc	5,888 teu: ex OOCL Vancouver-10
8902539	Kiel Express	Deu	1991	53,783	67,680	294	32	23	ucc	4,626 teu: ex Hannover Express-07
9143544	Kobe Express	Deu	1998	53,523	67,537	294	32	23	ucc	4,612 teu: ex Shanghai Express-02
9343730	Kuala Lumpur Express	Deu	2008	93,811	103,538	336	43	25	ucc	8,749 teu
9295256	Kyoto Express	Deu	2005	93,750	103,890	335	43	25	ucc	8,749 teu
9613020	*Leverkusen Express*	Deu	2013			366	48	24	ucc	13,092 teu
9108128	Lisbon Express	Bmu	1995	33,735	34,330	216	32	20	ucc	2,298 teu: ex CP Prospect-06, Cast Prospect-05, CanMar Fortune-03
9232565	Liverpool Express	Deu	2002	46,009	54,156	281	32	25	ucc	4,121 teu: ex Maersk Dexter-07, CP Aurora-06, Contship Aurora-05
8905969	Livorno Express	Bmu	1991	37,474	43,084	242	32	21	ucc	2,846 teu: ex Lykes Motivator-06, Jupiter-01, Ville de Jupiter-01, CGM Pascal-00, Nedlloyd Pascal-98, CGM Pascal-95
9143568	London Express	Deu	1998	53,523	66,577	294	32	23	ucc	4,612 teu
9501370	*Ludwigshaven Express*	Deu	2013			366	48	24	ucc	13,092 teu
8406262	Madrid Express	Bmu	1986	40,447	40,744	270	32	20	ucc	3,266 teu: ex CP Hermosillo-06, TMM Hermosillo-05, Ming Propitious-01
9112296	Milan Express *	Bmu	1996	33,663	33,659	216	32	20	ucc	2,486 teu: ex CP Los Angeles-06, Cielo di Los Angeles-05, Cast Premier-05, OOCL Canada-03
9165358	Mississauga Express *	Bmu	1998	39,174	40,881	245	32	21	ucc	2,808 teu: ex CP Pride-06, CanMar Pride-05
9253741	Montreal Express	Gbr	2003	55,994	62,300	294	32	22	ucc	4,402 teu: ex CP Spiri-06, CanMar Spirit-05
9450428	Nagoya Express	Deu	2010	93,750	103,646	335	43	25	ucc	8,749 teu: ex Basle Express-12
8714229	New Orleans Express *	Gbr	1989	35,958	42,976	240	32	21	ucc	3,032 teu: ex CP Campeche-06, TMM Campeche-05, Choyang Park-01

Hapag-Lloyd AG : HAMBURG EXPRESS : *John Davidson*

IMO#	name	flag	year	grt	dwt	loa	bm	kts	type	former names
9501332	New York Express	Deu	2012	142,295	142,028	367	48	24	ucc	13,169 teu
9229843	Ningbo Express	Deu	2002	88,493	100,016	320	43	26	ucc	7,179 teu: ex Hong Kong Express-12, Berlin Express-02
9104902	Norfolk Express	Deu	1995	36,606	45,362	245	32	24	ucc	3,607 teu: ex OOCL Atlantic-03, Norfolk Express-02, Hong Kong Express-02, Northern Majesty-96
9320697	Osaka Express	Deu	2007	93,750	103,662	336	43	25	ucc	8,749 teu
9165360	Ottawa Express *	Bmu	1998	39,174	40,120	245	32	21	ucc	2,808 teu: ex CP Honour-06, CanMar Honour-05
9038919	Paris Express	Deu	1994	53,815	67,613	294	32	23	ucc	4,639 teu: ex Hamburg Express-01
9243203	Philadelphia Express †	Usa	2003	40,146	40,478	243	32	22	ucc	3,237 teu: ex CP Yosemite-06, TMM Yucatan-05
8902541	Portland Express	Deu	1991	53,783	67,680	294	32	23	ucc	4,639 teu: ex Leverkusen Express-12
9450399	Prague Express	Deu	2010	93,750	104,014	336	43	25	ucc	8,749 teu
8406274	Rome Express *	Bmu	1986	40,439	40,856	270	32	20	ucc	3,266 teu: ex CP Challenger-06, Lykes Challenger-05, Ming Peace-01
9193317	Rotterdam Express	Deu	2000	54,465	66,975	294	32	24	ucc	4,843 teu
9193305	Seoul Express	Deu	2000	54,465	66,971	294	32	24	ucc	4,890 teu: ex Bremen Express-07
9501368	Shanghai Express	Deu	2013			366	48	24	ucc	13,092 teu
9450404	Sofia Express	Deu	2010	93,750	104,007	336	43	25	ucc	8,749 teu
9243286	St. Louis Express †	Usa	2002	40,146	40,478	244	32	22	ucc	3,237 teu: ex CP Yellowstone-06, TMM Guanajuato-05
9038907	Stuttgart Express	Deu	1993	53,815	67,640	294	32	23	ucc	4,639 teu
9062984	Sydney Express *	Gbr	1994	23,540	30,621	187	30	19	ucc	2,074 teu : ex CP Dynasty-06, CanMar Dynasty-05, TMM Guadalajara-03, P&O Nedlloyd Melbourne-01, Coral Seatel-98, Contship Sydney-98, Coral Seatel-94
9367188	Thailand Express +	Pan	2007	66,462	66,940	281	40	24	ucc	5,888 teu: ex OOCL Seattle-10
9193290	Tokyo Express	Deu	2000	54,465	67,145	294	32	24	ucc	4,843 teu
9253727	Toronto Express *	Gbr	2003	55,994	47,840	294	32	22	ucc	4,402 teu: ex CP Venture-06, CanMar Venture-05
9320702	Tsingtao Express	Deu	2007	93,750	103,631	336	43	25	ucc	8,749 teu
9108130	Valencia Express	Bmu	1996	33,735	34,330	216	32	20	ucc	2,298 teu: ex CP Performer-06, Lykes Performance-05, Cast Prominence-05, CanMar Courage-03
8406298	Veracruz Express *	Bmu	1987	40,439	40,870	270	32	20	ucc	3,266 teu: ex CP Achiever-06, Lykes Achiever-05, Ming Pleasure-01
9450416	Vienna Express	Deu	2010	93,750	103,648	335	43	25	ucc	8,749 teu
9367205	Vietnam Express +	Hkg	2007	66,462	66,940	281	40	25	ucc	5,888 teu: ex OOCL Italy-10
9243198	Washington Express †	Gbr	2003	40,146	40,478	243	32	22	ucc	3,237 teu: ex CP Denali-06, Lykes Flyer-05
9224051	Wellington Express	Deu	2001	23,652	29,894	188	30	21	ucc	2,078 teu: ex CP Tabasco-06, TMM Tabasco-05, Silvia-01
9229831	Yantian Express	Deu	2002	88,493	100,003	320	43	26	ucc	7,179 teu: ex Shanghai Express-12, l/a Berlin Express
9243174	Yorktown Express †	Usa	2002	40,146	40,478	243	32	21	ucc	3,237 teu: ex CP Shenandoah-07, TMM Colima-05, Contship Tenacity-02

Hapag-Lloyd AG : ROTTERDAM EXPRESS : *ARO*

118

newbuildings: included in list above
* owned by subsidiary Hapag-Lloyd Ships Ltd, UK and managed by Anglo-Eastern Ship Management Ltd., Hong Kong (China) or ** by Hapag-Lloyd (Eastwind) Pte. Ltd., Singapore. † owned by Hapag-Lloyd USA LLC and managed by Marine Transport Management, USA or + managed by Shoei Kisen Kaisha
See other chartered ships with 'Express' suffix under Costamare Shipping Co SA, Norddeutsche Vermogensanlage GmbH & Co KG, NSB Niederelbe Schiffahrts GmbH & Co KG and Ofer Brothers (Zodiac Maritime Agencies).
NB in late December 2012, believed to be in merger talks with Hamburg-Süd.

Harren & Partner Schiffahrts GmbH   Germany

Funnel: Cream with two dark sails above three waves. **Hull:** Light grey, black, green or blue ** with red boot-topping.
History: Formed 1989. **Web:** www.harren-partner.de

IMO#	name	flag	year	grt	dwt	loa	bm	kts	type	former names
9400485	OIG Giant (2)	Atg	2008	18,169	10,480	169	25	16	urh	cr: 1(200, 2(350) ex Blue Giant-11, Combi Dock II-08
9509970	OIG Giant II (2)	Atg	2010	18,118	10,025	179	25	16	urh	ex Combi Dock IV-11
9400473	Combi Dock I (2)	Atg	2008	17,341	10,480	169	25	15	urh	cr: 1(200), 2(350)
9432828	Combi Dock III (2)	Atg	2008	18,169	10,480	169	25	15	urh	cr: 1(200), 2(350)
9538892	EIT Palmina *	Atg	2009	12,679	9,391	142	23	17	urh	cr: 2(350): ex Hyundai Britania-11, Scan Britania-09
9305180	Maersk Newport **	Mlt	2005	11,935	16,664	144	23	14	tco	ex Patalya-05
9305178	Maersk Nordenham **	Mlt	2005	11,935	16,716	144	23	14	tco	ex Patrona-05
9614842	Pabal	Atg	2012	41,213	75,377	225	32	15	bbu	
9614854	Pabur	Atg	2012	41,000	75,500	225	32	15	bbu	
9312080	Patagonia **	Cyp	2006	11,935	16,772	144	23	14	tco	ex Maersk Nairn-10, I/a Patagonia
9373644	Patani **	Mlt	2008	11,935	16,611	144	23	14	tco	ex Marida Patani-11, Patani-09
9344423	Patara	Mlt	2007	12,164	16,979	144	23	14	tco	ex Gan-Ocean-10
9373622	Patea **	Mlt	2008	11,935	16,651	144	23	14	tco	ex Marida Patea-11
9365477	Paterna **	Cyp	2006	11,935	16,748	149	22	15	tco	ex Marida Paterna-11
9365489	Patnos **	Cyp	2006	11,935	16,714	149	22	14	tco	ex Marida Patnos-10
9348297	Patras **	Mlt	2007	12,137	16,744	144	23	14	tco	ex Gan-Sword-10
9312078	Patricia **	Cyp	2005	11,935	16,642	144	23	14	tco	ex Maersk Naantali-10, Patricia-05
9262534	Pochard †	Atg	2003	22,655	37,384	199	24	14	bbu	I/a Panarea
9262522	Puffin	Jam	2003	22,654	37,641	199	24	14	bbu	
9267429	Ultra Paguera	Atg	2003	29,985	53,609	190	32	14	bbu	ex U-Sea Paguera-12, Paguera-11, Sibulk Premier-08, Paguera-03

vessels owned or managed by Harren & Partners Ship Management GmbH & Co KG.
† managed for H&H Schiffahrts GmbH or * managed for EIT European Investment & Trading or ** managed by Brostrom AB

Hartmann Schiffahrts GmbH & Co. KG   Germany

Funnel: White with blue 'h' symbol or charterers colours. **Hull:** Blue or red, with white 'UCC' (Frisia vessels) or UBC (UBC vessels) or (GasChem)or Italia (Ital vessels), red boot-topping. **History:** Formed 1981. **Web:** www.hartmann-reederei.de

IMO#	name	flag	year	grt	dwt	loa	bm	kts	type	former names
9470961	Frisia Bonn	Lbr	2010	21,842	28,632	190	28	21	ucc	1,970 teu: ex CCNI Columbia-12, Frisia Bonn-11
9299044	Frisia Helsinki	Lbr	2005	25,406	33,750	207	30	21	ucc	2,478 teu; ex Libra Santa Catarina-11, Santos Star-09, Frisia Helsinki-05
9302437	Frisia Kiel	Lbr	2004	25,406	33,847	207	30	21	ucc	2,478 teu: ex Cap Doukato-09, I/a Frisia Kiel
9299020	Frisia Lissabon	Lbr	2004	25,406	33,829	207	30	22	ucc	2,478 teu: ex CSAV Santos-11, Frisia Lissabon-09, Cap Flinders-08, Cabo Prior-06, I/a Frisia Lissabon
9320001	Frisia Loga	Lbr	2005	25,406	33,900	207	30	22	ucc	2,478 teu: ex Paranagua Express-11, Frisia Loga-06
9302449	Frisia Lübeck	Lbr	2004	25,406	33,781	207	30	22	ucc	2,478 teu: ex CSAV Rio Lontue-11, Frisia Lübeck-09, Libra Santa Catarina-09, Frisia Lübeck-04
9470973	Frisia Nürnberg	Lbr	2010	21.842	28,520	190	28	21	ucc	1,970 teu
9311842	Frisia Rostock	Lbr	2004	25,406	33,900	207	30	21	ucc	2,478 teu: ex CSAV Santos-09, I/a Frisia Rostock
9299032	Frisia Rotterdam	Deu	2004	25,406	33,784	207	30	21	ucc	2,478 teu: ex Cap Saray-09, I/a Frisia Rotterdam
9311830	Frisia Wismar	Lbr	2004	25,406	27,400	207	30	21	ucc	2,478 teu: ex CSAV Rio Lontue-09, I/a Frisia Wismar
9402586	Gaschem Adriatic	Lbr	2010	13,879	18,775	156	23		lpg	17,000 m³
9402598	Gaschem Antarctic	Lbr	2010	13,879	18,110	156	23		lpg	17,000 m³
9471032	Gaschem Bremen	Lbr	2010	22,977	26,645	173	28		lpg	35,000 m³
9471018	Gaschem Hamburg	Lbr	2010	22,977	26,599	173	28		lpg	35,000 m³
9471123	Gaschem Stade	Lbr	2010	22,977	26,618	173	28		lpg	35,000 m³
9223904	HAL Patriot *	Cyp	2003	12,993	17,471	143	23	15	ggc	ex Federal Patriot-10, BBC Russia-08, Atlantic Progress-03
9223899	HAL Pendant *	Cyp	2003	12,993	17,477	143	23	15	ggc	ex Federal Pendant-10, BBC Korea-08, Atlantic Pendant-05

IMO#	name	flag	year	grt	dwt	loa	bm	kts	type	former names
9320013	Itajai Express	Lbr	2006	25,406	33,743	207	30	22	ucc	2,478 teu: l/a Frisia Hannover
9337250	Ital Ordine	Lbr	2006	27,779	38,345	222	30	23	ucc	2,824 teu
9338058	Ital Oriente	Lbr	2007	27,779	39,269	222	30	23	ucc	2,824 teu
9337262	Ital Ottima	Lbr	2007	27,779	39,332	222	30	23	ucc	2,824 teu
9395238	UBC Laguna	Lbr	2009	31,094	53,477	190	32	14	bbu	l/a Dessau
9395226	UBC Lemessos	Lbr	2008	31,094	53,571	190	32	14	bbu	ex Daewoo Challenge-09, l/a Cuxhaven
9395252	UBC Limas	Grc	2009	31,094	53,406	190	32	14	bbu	l/a Gerolstein
9395264	UBC Livorno	Lbr	2009	31,094	53,428	190	32	14	bbu	l/a Husum
9395214	UBC Longkou	Lbr	2008	31,094	53,408	190	32	14	bbu	ex Dawoo Brave-09, l/a Handorf
9395240	UBC Luzon	Lbr	2009	31,094	53,507	190	32	14	bbu	l/a Flensburg
9463671	UBC Odessa **	Nld	2011	65,976	118,585	260	43	14	bbu	
9462366	UBC Ohio **	Nld	2011	65,976	118,532	260	43	14	bbu	
9464669	UBC Olimbus **	Gib	2011	65,976	118,472	260	43	14	bbu	
9463645	UBC Onsan **	Nld	2011	65,976	118,590	260	43	14	bbu	
9463657	UBC Oristano **	Gib	2011	65,976	118,467	260	43	14	bbu	
9463633	UBC Ottawa **	Nld	2011	65,976	118,626	260	43	14	bbu	
9426881	UBC Salaverry *	Cyp	2010	21,018	33,305	182	28	14	bbu	
9380805	UBC Santa Marta †	Cyp	2008	19,748	31,582	172	27	14	bbu	
9287340	UBC Stavanger *	Cyp	2004	19,748	31,751	172	27	14	bbu	
9285354	UBC Tampico *	Cyp	2004	24,140	37,821	182	29	14	ggc	
9300752	UBC Tokyo †	Cyp	2005	24,140	37,865	182	29	14	ggc	

newbuildings
*owned by associated * Intership Navigation Co. Ltd (formed 1988 - www.intership-cyprus.com), Cyprus, ** managed by Feederlines b.v.*
† owned by Athena Marine Co. Ltd., Cyprus
'Frisia' vessels operate in United Container Carrier (UCC) pool formed in 2004. The company also operates smaller container ships in the Mini-Container Pool (MCP). Also see United Product Tanker (UPT) pool under Schoeller Holdings Ltd

Horn-Linie (GmbH & Co.)   Germany

Funnel: *Grey with white 'H' on blue above red bands.* **Hull:** *White with red boot-topping.* **History:** *Founded 1864 and shipping company formed 1951 as Heinrich C Horn.* **Web:** *www.hornlinie.com*

8802002	Hornbay	Lbr	1990	12,887	9,069	154	23	20	grf	
8802014	Horncap	Lbr	1991	12,887	9,069	154	23	20	grf	
9012041	Horncliff	Lbr	1992	12,877	9,184	154	23	20	grf	

managed by Norbulk Shipping UK Ltd (www.norbulkshipping.com).

Leif Höegh & Co. Ltd.   Norway

Funnel: *White with blue/grey top and houseflag interrupting white band or ** dark blue/grey 'A' on broad white band between blue/grey bands above white base.* **Hull:** *Dark grey with dark blue 'HÖEGH AUTOLINERS' on white superstructure, red boot-topping.*
History: *Founded 1927 as Leif Höegh & Co. to 1938, Leif Höegh & Co ASA to 2003 and Leif Höegh & Co AS to 2006. Formed Höegh-Ugland Auto Liners (HUAL) in 1968 jointly with Ugland International, but took complete control in 2000 and renamed as Höegh Autoliners in 2005. Tanker and OBO vessels demerged into Bona Shipping AS in 1992. Acquired Cool Carriers in 1994, renamed Unicool in 1997 as joint venture with Safmarine, who withdrew in 1999, Cool Carriers subsequently sold to Lauritzen in 2001. Open-hatch activities transferred to Saga Forest Carriers and liner business sold in 2001. Moller-Maersk acquired 37.5% share in Höegh Autoliners in 2008.* **Web:** *www.Höeghautoliners.com*

Hartmann Schiffahrts GmbH : ITAL ORIENTE : *Hans Kraijenbosch*

IMO#	name	flag	year	grt	dwt	loa	bm	kts	type	former names

Höegh Autoliners Shipping AS, Norway

IMO#	name	flag	year	grt	dwt	loa	bm	kts	type	former names
8507664	City of Mumbai *	Sgp	1987	27,887	7,894	158	27	19	mve	2,300 ceu: ex Höegh Mumbai-08, Maersk Sun-08
9153783	CSAV Rio Serrano *	Sgp	1998	44,219	13,695	179	32	19	mve	4,300 ceu: ex Höegh Pusan-11, Maersk Taiki-08
9191876	Höegh Asia	Bhs	2000	68,060	27,000	229	32	19	mve	7,859 ceu: ex Hual Asia-06 (len-08)
9318474	Höegh Bangkok ***	Nis	2007	55,775	16,632	200	32	20	mve	6,500 ceu
9431836	Höegh Beijing	Nis	2010	47,232	12,250	183	32		mve	4,300 ceu
9295842	Höegh Berlin †	Bhs	2005	68,871	27,176	229	32	19	mve	7,850 ceu (len-08)
9368895	Höegh Brasilia ****	Pan	2007	51,731	17,252	180	32	19	mve	5,400 ceu
8507652	Höegh Chennai	Sgp	1987	27,887	7,902	158	27	19	mve	3,000 ceu: ex Maersk Sea-08
9420057	Höegh Copenhagen	Nis	2010	68,392	27,351	229	32		mve	7,850 ceu
9318462	Höegh Delhi ***	Nis	2007	55,775	16,890	200	32	20	mve	6,500 ceu
9312470	Höegh Detroit	Nis	2006	68,871	27,100	229	32	20	mve	7,850 ceu: (len-08)
9088249	Höegh Inchon	Sgp	1997	44,219	12,490	179	32	19	mve	4,300 ceu: ex Maersk Tide -08
9330616	Höegh Kobe	Sgp	2006	52,691	21,500	199	32	19	mve	5,400 ceu: ex Maersk Wizard-08
9088237	Höegh Kunsan +	Sgp	1996	44,219	13,778	179	32	19	mve	4,300 ceu; ex Maersk Taiyo-08
9368912	Höegh Manila	Nis	2007	51,964	17,252	180	32	19	mve	5,400 ceu
9431850	Höegh Maputo	Nis	2011	47,266	12,250	183	32		mve	4,300 ceu
9166704	Höegh Masan *	Sgp	1998	44,219	12,490	179	32	19	mve	4,300 ceu: ex CSAV Rio Salado-12, Höegh Masan-11, Maersk Teal-08
9185463	Höegh Osaka	Sgp	2000	51,770	12,473	180	32	20	mve	5,400 ceu: ex Maersk Wind-11
9382396	Höegh Oslo	Nis	2008	51,964	17,252	180	32	19	mve	5,400 ceu
9312482	Höegh Shanghai	Nis	2007	68,871	27,178	229	32	20	mve	7,850 ceu: (len-09)
9420045	Höegh St. Petersburg	Nis	2009	68,392	27,352	229	32		mve	7,850 ceu
9431862	Höegh Singapore	Nis	2011	47,266	12,250	183	32		mve	4,300 ceu
9368900	Höegh Sydney ****	Jpn	2007	51.731	17,311	180	32	19	mve	5,400 ceu
9171280	Höegh Trader	Bhs	1998	68,060	27,100	229	32	20	mve	7,850 ceu: ex Hual Trader-06 (len-09)
8013613	Höegh Transit +	Nis	1981	45,596	17,650	190	32	19	mve	5,400 ceu: ex Hual Transit-05, Hual Transita-00, Kyushu-96, Kyushu Maru-88
9176395	Höegh Transporter	Nis	1999	57,757	21,300	200	32	20	mve	6,600 ceu: ex Hual Transporter-07
8130966	Höegh Trapeze	Nis	1983	41,871	15,500	180	31	17	mve	3,900 ceu: ex Hual Trapeze-06, Hual Carmencita-00
9184859	Höegh Treasure	Bhs	1999	58,684	21,199	200	32	19	mve	6,500 ceu: ex Hual Treasure-06, Hual Carolita-00
9075709	Höegh Trident	Bhs	1995	56,164	21,423	200	32	20	mve	6,500 ceu: ex Hual Trident—06
8608080	Höegh Triton +	Nis	1988	52,422	23,052	200	32	18	mve	6,000 ceu: ex Morning Meridian-10, Hual Triton-04, Auto Diana-00, l/a Auto Daewoo
9075711	Höegh Trooper	Bhs	1995	56,164	21,414	200	32	20	mve	6,500 ceu; ex Hual Trooper-05
7903093	Höegh Tropicana	Nis	1980	33,359	12,003	180	32	17	mve	3,300 ceu: ex Hual Tropicana-05, Hual Lisita-00, Lisita-82
9186302	Höegh Trove	Bhs	2000	58,684	21,200	200	32	19	mve	6,500 ceu: ex Hual Trove-05, Hual Maritita-00
9285495	Höegh Seoul	Nis	2004	68,871	27,178	228	32	20	mve	7,600 ceu: ex Hual Seoul-09, len-09
9431848	Höegh Xiamen	Nis	2010	47,232	12,250	183	32		mve	4,300 ceu
9185451	Maersk Wave +	Sgp	2000	51,770	12,473	180	32	20	mve	5,400 ceu
8608078	Morning Mercator +	Nis	1988	52,422	23,096	200	32	18	mve	6,000 ceu: ex Hual Tricorn-04, Hual Champ-00, Auto Champ-00

Leif Höegh & Co. (Höegh Autoliners Shipping AS) : HÖEGH TREASURE : *C. Lous*

IMO#	name	flag	year	grt	dwt	loa	bm	kts	type	former names
9295830	Prestige New York **	Usa	2005	57,280	15,990	200	32	20	mve	6,500 ceu: ex Alliance New York-10, Höegh New York-05, Hual New York-05

newbuildings: 2 x 6,500 ceu vessels to be chartered from Ocean Yield and built by Daewoo Mangalia [2014]
*managed by Höegh Fleet Services AS, Norway (formed 1995), * Moller Singapore,, ** by Liberty Maritime Corp, USA or † by Pacific Basin Ship Management Ltd, Hong Kong. ‡ jointly owned with Mitsui OSK Lines Ltd., Japan q.v. † managed for Marenav Schiffahrts AG*
*** managed for P D Gram & Co AS, Norway (founded 1974 – www.pdgram.com) **** owned by subsidiary of Tsuneishi Holdings Corp, Japan and managed by Astro Shipmanagement Inc, Philippines. + chartered to Hyundai Glovis See also Cido Shipping.*

Höegh LNG AS, Norway

Funnel: *White with houseflag interrupting white band on broad blue band, red top or owners colours.* **Hull:** *Red, black or blue with red boot-topping.* **Web:** *www.hoeghlng.com*

9284192	Arctic Lady (st)	Nis	2006	121,597	84,878	288	49	19	lng	147,835 m³
9271248	Arctic Princess (st)	Nis	2006	121,597	84,878	288	49	19	lng	147,835 m³
9390680	GDF Suez Cape Ann (df)	Nis	2010	96,153	80,780	283	43	19	lng	145,130 m³
9385673	GDF Suez Neptune (df)	Nis	2009	96,153	80,986	283	43	19	lng	145,130 m³
7413232	LNG Libra (st)	Mhl	1979	95,084	72,650	274	44	19	lng	126,400 m³
7391214	Matthew (st)	Nis	1979	88,919	64,991	289	41	19	lng	126,538 m³ ex Suez Matthew-09, Matthew, Gamma-88, El Paso Howard Boyd
7320344	Norman Lady (st)	Nis	1973	71,469	50,922	250	40	18	lng	86,234 m³
9390185	STX Frontier (df)	Sgp	2010	100,374	86,778	289	44	19	lng	153,600 m³

Hyundai Merchant Marine Co. Ltd.   South Korea

Funnel: *White with yellow edged green triangle.* **Hull:** *Blue with white 'HYUNDAI', red or pink boot-topping.* **History:** *Founded 1976 as subsidiary of Hyundai Corporation.* **Web:** *www.hmm21.com or www.hyundaicorp.com*

9293155	Asian Jade	Pan	2005	57,164	106,062	244	42	14	tcr	ex KWK Jade-05
9387138	Atlantic Mirage	Hkg	2009	29,733	51,476	183	32	15	tco	
9374301	Atlantic Muse	Hkg	2009	29,733	51,149	183	32	15	tco	
9459527	FEG Success	Pan	2010	93,104	182,619	292	45	15	bbu	
9179581	Hyundai Aquapia (st)	Pan	2000	113,998	77,564	289	48	20	lng	135,000m³
9087295	Hyundai Atlas	Kor	1995	76,068	149,310	270	43	13	bbu	
9323510	Hyundai Bangkok	Pan	2007	74,651	80,108	304	40	26	ucc	6,800 teu
9346304	Hyundai Brave **	Pan	2008	94,511	99,123	340	46	27	ucc	8,652 teu
9323508	Hyundai Colombo	Pan	2007	74,651	80,108	340	40	26	ucc	6,800 teu
9278985	Hyundai Concord	Pan	2002	13,267	18,067	162	26	18	ucc	1,032 teu
9154848	Hyundai Confidence	Pan	2003	64,845	68,114	275	40	25	ucc	5,680 teu
9155157	Hyundai Cosmopia (st)	Pan	2000	113,998	77,591	289	48	20	lng	135,000 m³
9347542	Hyundai Courage	Pan	2008	94,511	99,052	340	46	27	ucc	8,562 teu: ex CMA CGM Courage-09, Hyundai Courage-08
9347578	Hyundai Dynasty	Pan	2008	52,581	63,254	294	32	25	ucc	4,922 teu
9372999	Hyundai Ecopia (st)	Kor	2008	100,545	83,959	288	44	20	lng	149,745 m³
9347554	Hyundai Faith **	Pan	2008	94,511	98,967	340	46	27	ucc	8,750 teu

Leif Höegh & Co. (Höegh LNG AS) : GDF SUEZ NEPTUNE : *Chris Brooks*

IMO#	name	flag	year	grt	dwt	loa	bm	kts	type	former names
9347566	Hyundai Force	Pan	2008	94,511	99,043	340	46	27	ucc	8,750 teu: ex CMA CGM Force-09, Hyundai Force-08
9330707	Hyundai Forward **	Pan	2007	52,581	63,439	294	32	25	ucc	4,922 teu
9112260	Hyundai Freedom	Pan	1996	64,054	68,363	275	40	25	ucc	5,551 teu: ex MSC Liberty-11, Hyundai Freedom-09
9112284	Hyundai General	Pan	1996	64,054	68,363	275	40	25	ucc	5,551 teu: ex APL General-09, Hyundai General-07
9267936	Hyundai Glory	Pan	2004	53,352	63,404	294	32	25	ucc	4,648 teu
9347607	Hyundai Goodwill	Pan	2008	52,581	63,439	294	32	25	ucc	4,922 teu
9330721	Hyundai Grace **	Pan	2007	52,581	63,439	294	32	25	ucc	4,922 teu
9075333	Hyundai Greenpia (st)	Pan	1996	103,764	71,684	274	47	18	lng	135,000 m³
9128166	Hyundai Highness	Kor	1996	64,054	68,379	275	40	25	ucc	5,551 teu: MSC Highness-11. Hyundai Highness-09
9347592	Hyundai Integral	Kor	2008	52,581	63,157	294	32	25	ucc	4,922 teu
9323522	Hyundai Jakarta	Pan	2007	74,651	80.108	304	40	26	ucc	6,800 teu
9183269	Hyundai Oceanpia (st)	Pan	2000	113,998	77,513	288	48	20	lng	135,000 m³
8519019	Hyundai Olympia	Kor	1987	93,005	186,330	292	46	13	bbu	
9625542	Hyundai Paramount †	Lbr	2013	52,467	62,335	255	37		ucc	5,000 teu
9398101	Hyundai Pioneer	Bhs	2009	106,367	207,955	300	50	14	bbu	
9637155	Hyundai Platinum †	Lbr	2013	52,467	62,335	255	37		ucc	5,000 teu
9164586	Hyundai Power	Pan	1998	76,068	149,322	269	43	14	bbu	
9625530	Hyundai Premium †	Lbr	2013	52,467	62,335	255	37		ucc	5,000 teu
9625528	Hyundai Prestige †	Lbr	2013	52,467	62,335	255	37		ucc	5,000 teu
9625554	Hyundai Privilege †	Lbr	2013	52,467	62,335	255	37		ucc	5,000 teu
8821632	Hyundai Prosperity	Kor	1990	77,650	151,257	274	45	13	bbu	
9021461	Hyundai Spirit	Kor	1993	68,093	126,051	263	41	18	bbu	
9490911	Hyundai Success	Pan	2011	93,153	179,156	292	45	15	bbu	
9158898	Hyundai Sun	Pan	1998	156,692	301,178	330	58	15	tcr	
9347619	Hyundai Supreme	Pan	2008	52,581	63,384	294	32	25	ucc	4,922 teu
9591739	Hyundai Talent	Pan	2012	92,865	178,896	292	45	15	bbu	
9155145	Hyundai Technopia (st)	Pan	1999	113,998	77,584	289	48	20	lng	135,000 m³
9589970	Hyundai Trust	Pan	2011	92,865	179,019	292	45	15	bbu	
9330719	Hyundai Unity **	Pan	2007	52,581	63,439	294	32	25	ucc	4,922 teu
8821591	Hyundai Universal	Kor	1990	101,604	200,052	309	50	13	bbu	
9018555	Hyundai Utopia (st)	Kor	1994	103,764	71,909	274	47	18	lng	125,182 m³
9490909	Hyundai Vision	Pan	2011	93,153	179,135	292	45	15	bbu	
9347580	Hyundai Voyager	Pan	2008	52,581	64,220	294	32	25	ucc	4,922 teu
9399868	Oriental Diamond	Pan	2008	30,110	50,323	183	32		tco	
9399870	Oriental Gold	Pan	2010	30,110	50,591	183	32		tco	
9292577	Oriental Ruby *	Pan	2005	30,971	50,375	189	32	15	tcr	ex Ocean Jupiter-05
9605724	Pacific Ace	Pan	2012	35,297	59,840	200	32	14	bbu	
9413779	Paciific Jewel	Hkg	2009	28,754	48,012	181	32		tco	
8821656	Pacific Success	Kor	1989	24,790	38,412	186	28	14	bbu	
9307645	Universal Crown *	Pan	2005	163,465	309,316	333	60	15	tcr	
9002611	Universal Hope *	Pan	1993	158,475	299,700	344	56	14	tcr	ex Eugen Maersk-04, British Vigilance-02, Emma Maersk-97
9002635	Universal Peace **	Pan	1995	158,475	299,700	344	56	14	tcr	ex Emma Maersk-04, Ellen Maersk-97
9307633	Universal Queen *	Pan	2005	163,465	309,373	333	60	15	tcr	

newbuildings:
* managed by subsidiary Haeyoung Maritime Services Co. Ltd., South Korea, ** for Korea Ship Finance Co Ltd
† owned by Container Carrier Corp. (Capital Ship Management Corp),Greece : See also Eukor Car Carriers Inc (under Wallenius Wilhelmsen)

Glovis Co. Ltd.
Funnel: *White with blue 'Glovis'.or owners colours.* **Hull:** *Blue with blue 'Glovis' on cream upperworks,, red boot-topping.*
History: *Founded 2001 as subsidiary of Hyundai/Kia Motor Group.* **Web:** *www.glovis.net*

IMO#	name	flag	year	grt	dwt	loa	bm	kts	type	former names
9158604	Asian Chorus *	Pan	1997	55,729	21,505	200	32	19	mve	6,000 ceu
9122930	Asian Grace *	Pan	1996	55,680	21,421	200	32	19	mve	6,000 ceu
9122942	Asian Legend *	Pan	1996	55,680	21,421	200	32	19	mve	6,000 ceu
9114165	Asian Sun *	Pan	1995	44,891	13,292	184	32	18	mve	4,200 ceu
9114177	Asian Venture *	Pan	1995	44,891	13,241	184	32	18	mve	4,200 ceu
9039169	Alexander Carl	Pan	1993	110,627	208,189	312	50	13	bbu	
9454517	Cosco Shengshi **	Pan	2011	51,671	14,868	200	32	20	mve	5,000 teu
9590606	Glovis Advance *	Pan	2012	93,313	179,217	292	45	15	bbu	
9590589	Glovis Century *	Pan	2012	58,288	20,895	200	32	20	mve	6,000 ceu
9590591	Glovis Challenge *	Pan	2012	58,288	20,895	200	32	19	mve	6,000 ceu
9293583	Glovis Composer ††	Hkg	2005	58,631	18,881	200	32	19	mve	5,213 ceu: ex Excellent Ace-12
9293909	Glovis Conductor ††	Pan	2006	60,118	17,709	200	32	19	mve	5,231 ceu; ex Favorite Ace-12
9116553	Glovis Master *	Pan	1995	25,789	45,304	190	30	14	bbu	ex New Harmony-12
9543603	Glovis Mermaid *	Bhs	2012	32,545	55,705	188	32	14	bbu	

IMO#	name	flag	year	grt	dwt	loa	bm	kts	type	former names
8709119	GMT Polaris ***	Pan	1987	31,367	9,694	174	28	17	mve	3,400 ceu: ex Hyundai 201-10
8211514	GMT Venus ***	Pan	1983	29,886	12,507	176	27	16	mve	2,900 ceu: ex Sea Venus-10, Kazahaya-89, Orchid Ace-88
8517944	Hyundai No.103 †	Pan	1986	40,772	12,893	184	31	17	mve	4,800 ceu
9043691	Jade Arrow	Pan	1993	47,367	12,271	180	32	19	mve	4,215 ceu
8321905	Princess VII ††	Pan	1984	47,747	15,940	190	32	21	mve	4,700 ceu: ex Prince No.1-08
9414876	STX Dove ††	Mhl	2011	60,396	22,351	199	32	19	mve	6,000 ceu

newbuidings 3 x 6,700 ceu PCTC [Hyundai (06:2012)]
* owned or managed by subsidiary Haeyoung Maritime Services Co. Ltd., South Korea
chartered from ** COSCO HK Investment, *** Doriko, Korea, † Wilhelmsen Ship Management Korea, †† other Japanese/Korean owners
see also, Cido Shipping, Leif Höegh & Co., Ray Car Carriers, Rickmers Reederei, Zodiac Maritime Agencies

International Shipholding Corporation   U.S.A.

Central Gulf Lines Inc., U.S.A.
Funnel: White with blue symbol within blue ring, narrow black top or buff with 8-pointed white star on white edged broad red band or green with two broad white bands. **Hull:** Black with red boot-topping. **History:** Founded 1947 as Central Gulf SS Corp to 1974. **Web:** www.intship.com or www.waterman-steamship.com

IMO#	name	flag	year	grt	dwt	loa	bm	kts	type	former names
9176632	Asian Emperor ††	Pan	1999	55,729	21,479	200	32	20	mve	6,402 ceu
9203291	Asian King ††	Pan	1998	55,729	21,511	200	32	19	mve	6,402 ceu
8106068	Bali Sea (2) ++	Sgp	1982	24,201	22,268	175	36	13	urr	ex Super Servant 5-95, Dan Lifter-85 (len-95)
8106056	Banda Sea (2) ++	Sgp	1982	24,201	13,282	175	36	13	urr	ex Super Servant 6-95, Dan Mover-85 (len-95)
9476721	CSAV Rio Geike +†	Mhl	2010	60,213	18,701	200	32	19	mve	6,340 ceu
9576727	EGS Crest +	Mhl	2011	23,054	35,914	178	28	14	bbu	
9576739	EGS Tide +	Mhl	2011	23,054	35,916	178	28	14	bbu	
9576741	EGS Wave +	Mhl	2011	23,054	35,921	178	28	14	bbu	
8026799	Energy Enterprise (st)	Usa	1983	28,250	33,373	203	29	15	bbu	ex Energy Independence-96
9339818	Green Bay	Usa	2007	59,217	18,090	200	32	19	mve	6,402 ceu
9181560	Green Cove	Usa	1999	57,566	22,747	200	32	19	mve	5,053 ceu: ex Pegasus Leader-13
9181376	Green Dale	Usa	1999	50,087	15,894	179	32	19	mve	4,148 ceu: ex Altair Leader-99
9158288	Green Lake	Usa	1998	57,623	22,799	200	32	19	mve	5,055 ceu: ex Cygnus Leader-01
9056296	Green Point	Usa	1994	51,819	14,930	180	32	19	mve	5,120 ceu: ex Triton Diamond-98
9177428	Green Ridge	Usa	1998	57,449	21,523	200	32	19	mve	6,000 ceu: ex Hercules Leader-05
9190092	Green Wave *	Usa	2000	12,993	17,451	143	23	15	ggc	ex Federal Patroller-11, African Patroller-06, Atlantic Patroller-05, Forest Patroller-03, Atlantic Patroller-01

managed by LMS Shipmanagement Inc (founded 1997 as Lash Marine Services Inc) including for ISC subsidiaries * Waterman Steamship Corp (founded 1920) and ** LCI Shipholding Inc (founded 1997). + owned by East Gulf Shipholding, ++ owned by Gulf South Shg. Pte. chartered to † Hyundai Glovis, †† Eukor

Interorient Navigation Co. Ltd.   Cyprus
Funnel: Buff with blue 'IN' symbol inside blue ring. **Hull:** Black or light grey with red boot-topping. **History:** Formed 1977. **Web:** www.interorient.com

IMO#	name	flag	year	grt	dwt	loa	bm	kts	type	former names
9257010	ACS Brave	Sgp	2003	56,172	105,672	239	42	14	tcr	ex Sanko Brave-12
9295347	Baltic Ambition ††	Cyp	2006	23,240	37,343	183	27	14	tco	
9327360	Baltic Faith ††	Cyp	2006	23,337	37,067	183	27	14	tco	
9327384	Baltic Force ††	Cyp	2006	23,337	37,039	183	27	14	tco	
9314832	Baltic Marshall ††	Cyp	2006	23,240	37,304	183	27	14	tco	
9314806	Baltic Merchant ††	Cyp	2006	23,240	37,304	183	27	14	tco	
9137894	Conti Harmony *	Cyp	1997	31,207	38,421	210	32	22	ucc	2,890 teu: ex San Pedro Bay Dragon-10, Conti Harmony-10, Contship Innovator-02, Contship Harmony-99, Conti Harmony-97, l/a Timarchos
9346433	Ice Base	Cyp	2008	38,899	63,605	228	32	15	tco	
9212400	Nordamerika +	Mhl	2000	23,740	35,775	183	27	14	tco	
9301964	Nave Ariadne +	Cym	2007	42,403	74,875	228	32	14	tco	ex Ariadne Jacob-11
9301976	Nave Cielo +	Cym	2007	42,514	74,896	228	32	14	tco	ex Colin Jacob-11
9410882	Northern Spirit	Cyp	2009	62,775	112,827	250	44	14	tco	
9467627	Orient Accord	Mlt	2010	23,426	33,755	180	30	14	bbu	
9496329	Orient Adventure	Cyp	2009	23,426	33,755	180	30	14	bbu	
9496331	Orient Alliance	Mlt	2012	23,426	33,755	180	30	14	bbu	
9496434	Orient Approach	Mlt	2012	23,368	33,500	180	30	14	bbu	
9436460	Orient Cavalier	Cyp	2009	63,993	114,751	255	43	14	bbu	
9464572	Orient Centaur	Cyp	2010	63,993	114,841	255	43	14	bbu	
9464584	Orient Champion	Cyp	2010	63,993	115,000	255	43	14	bbu	
9464596	Orient Crusader	Cyp	2010	63,993	114,861	255	43	14	bbu	
9522881	Orient Defender	Cyp	2011	22,683	36,892	186	28	14	bbu	
9522893	Orient Delivery	Cyp	2012	22,83	36,746	186	28	14	bbu	

IMO#	name	flag	year	grt	dwt	loa	bm	kts	type	former names
9464663	Orient Strength	Cyp	2012	63,993	115,000	255	43	14	bbu	
9464675	Orient Sun	Cyp	2013	63,993	115,000	255	43	14	bbu	
9467548	Orient Target	Cyp	2009	23,426	33,755	180	30	14	bbu	
9467550	Orient Tide	Cyp	2010	23,426	33,755	180	30	14	bbu	
9467562	Orient Tiger	Mlt	2011	23,426	33,500	180	30	14	bbu	
9467574	Orient Trader	Cyp	2009	23,426	33,757	180	30	14	bbu	
9467586	Orient Trail	Mlt	2011	23,426	33,762	180	30	14	bbu	
9467598	Orient Transit	Cyp	2010	23,426	33,755	180	30	14	bbu	
9467603	Orient Tribune	Cyp	2011	23,426	33,500	180	30	14	bbu	
9163269	Peterpaul ‡	Cyp	1998	19,257	35,994	175	30	15	tch	ex Formosa Nine-07
9299563	Polar †	Pan	2005	40,690	72,825	229	32	15	tco	
9410894	Southern Spirit	Mlt	2009	62,775	113,043	250	44	15	tco	

newbuildings:

*managed by Interorient Marine Services Ltd, Cyprus, except * owned or managed by subsidiary Interorient Navigation (Germany) GmbH & Co KG, Germany (formed 1995 as Interorient Navigation Hamburg GmbH to 2000 and INC Interorient Navigation Hamburg GmbH & Co KG to 2007). Also operate vessels in Norient Product Pool ApS which see*
** managed for Gebab Conzeptions-und Emissions GmbH, Germany or ‡ for Locat Locazione Attrezzature SpA, Italy.
† managed by Paradise Navigation SA, Greece. See also König & Cie GmbH & Co KG., †† managed by Scorpio Shipmanagement SAM

Ernst Jacob GmbH & Co. KG   Germany

Funnel: *Black, white diagonal cross on broad blue band with blue 'J' on white centre diamond or charterers colours.* **Hull:** *Grey or red with red boot-topping or white with blue boot-topping.* **History:** *Founded 1955.* **Web:** *www.ernstjacob.de*

IMO#	name	flag	year	grt	dwt	loa	bm	kts	type	former names
9164213	Andre Jacob	Lbr	1999	40,705	60,913	229	32	14	tco	ex Margara-09
9482873	Cordula Jacob	Lbr	2012	43,904	75,619	229	32	15	tco	
9482859	Georg Jacob	Lbr	2011	43,904	75,618	229	32	15	tco	
9164201	Jacques Jacob	Gib	2000	40,705	71,345	229	32	15	tco	ex Chaleur Bay-09
9257498	Jill Jacob *	Lbr	2003	40,037	72,909	229	32	15	tco	ex Four Clipper-04
9189134	Johann Jacob *	Lbr	2000	40,037	73,001	229	32	15	tco	ex Four Brig-04
9159660	Kim Jacob *	Lbr	1998	81,265	159,211	274	48	15	tcr	ex Celebes-98
9482847	Konstantin Jacob	Lbr	2011	43,904	76,547	229	32	15	tco	
9188788	Max Jacob *	Deu	2000	81,565	157,449	274	48	14	tcr	ex Soyang-01
9233741	Nell Jacob *	Lbr	2003	81,236	160,292	274	48	14	tcr	ex Four Sun-08
9175078	Oliver Jacob **	Lbr	1999	81,565	157,326	274	48	14	tcr	ex Columbia-02
9037159	Santa Ana *	Cym	2002	24,252	39,768	190	28	14	tco	ex Greenock-02, I/a Diamant
9257503	Tanya Jacob *	Lbr	2003	40,037	73,004	229	32	15	tco	ex Four Ketch-07
9482861	Till Jacob	Lbr	2012	43,904	75,564	229	32	15	tco	
9179622	Yves Jacob	Lbr	2000	40,705	61,130	229	32	15	tcr	ex Los Roques-09

* managed for Hansa Hamburg Shipping International GmbH & Co KG, ** for Salamon AG or † for Hamburg Tankers GmbH, all Germany.

Kristian Gerhard Jebsen Skipsrederi AS   Norway

Gearbulk Holding Ltd., Bermuda

Funnel: *Black with large white 'G'.* **Hull:** *Black with white 'GEARBULK', red boot-topping.* **History:** *Associated company founded 1968 as Gearbulk Ltd. to 1991 and 49% owned by Mitsui OSK. Acquired Borgestad Shipping AS in 2006.* **Web:** *www.gearbulk.com*

IMO#	name	flag	year	grt	dwt	loa	bm	kts	type	former names
9008706	Aracari Arrow *	Bhs	1992	29,369	46,956	199	31	15	boh	ex Bridge Arrow-08, Westwood Bridge-05, Saga River-03, Sea River-92

Ernst Jacob GmbH : GEORG JACOB : *Nico Kemps*

IMO#	name	flag	year	grt	dwt	loa	bm	kts	type	former names
8309397	Auk Arrow	Bhs	1984	27,962	43,952	188	29	13	boh	ex Heina-91
8324373	Barbet Arrow	Bhs	1985	27,470	39,218	199	30	15	boh	ex City of New Westminster-98, Belforest-93
9339947	Bulk Jupiter #	Bhs	2006	31,256	56,009	190	32		bbu	
9389215	Bulk Leo #	Pan	2008	31,258	55,679	190	32	14	bbu	
9017318	Canelo Arrow	Bhs	1997	32,520	48,077	187	31	14	boh	
9232802	Cedar Arrow	Bhs	2001	32,458	47,818	190	31	14	boh	
7342469	CHL Innovator †	Sgp	1976	19,426	26,931	175	26	15	bbu	ex Rodney-86, Cape Rodney-85
8130681	CHL Progressor †	Sgp	1985	32,333	48,251	189	32	14	bbu	ex Therassia-89
9552886	Condor Arrow #	Pan	2012	37,046	61,860	200	32		ggc	
9385477	Corella Arrow	Bhs	2009	44,684	72,863	225	32		boh	
8400634	Cormorant Arrow	Bhs	1986	28,005	43,074	188	29	13	boh	
8512982	Cotinga Arrow	Bhs	1987	28,805	45,252	200	31	15	boh	ex Westwood Anette-07
8308147	Crane Arrow	Bhs	1984	27,818	42,913	188	29	14	boh	ex Chelsfield-89
9529592	Eagle Arrow #	Pan	2011	37,046	61,860	200	32	15	ggc	
9144392	Emu Arrow	Bhs	1997	36,008	51,419	200	32	14	boh	

Ernst Jacob GmbH : JACQUES JACOB : *Chris Brooks*

Kristian Gerhard Jebsen Skipsrederi AS (Gearbulk Holdings) : CORELLA ARROW :
Hans Kraijenbosch

IMO#	name	flag	year	grt	dwt	loa	bm	kts	type	former names
8512956	Falcon Arrow	Bhs	1986	28,805	45,295	200	31	15	boh	ex Norsul Europa-04, Westwood Belinda-03
8207329	Finch Arrow	Bhs	1984	26,130	39,273	183	29	13	boh	ex Francois LD-90
9077070	Grebe Arrow	Bhs	1997	35,998	51,633	200	32	16	boh	
8918215	Grouse Arrow	Bhs	1991	44,398	42,276	185	30	15	boh	
8308159	Harefield	Bhs	1985	27,818	41,651	188	29	13	boh	
8313685	Hawk Arrow	Bhs	1985	28,092	40,269	188	29	14	boh	
8313702	Ibis Arrow	Bhs	1986	28,239	42,497	188	29	14	boh	ex Singapore Express-91, Ibis Arrow-91
9007532	Jacamar Arrow *	Bhs	1992	29,369	46,998	199	31	15	boh	ex Borg Arrow-06, Westwood Borg-04, Spero-98, Saga Ocean-95
9215347	Jaeger Arrow	Bhs	2001	29,103	24,101	171	25	18	ggc	
9077082	Kite Arrow	Bhs	1997	36,008	51,800	200	32	16	boh	
9282730	Kuljak Arrow	Bhs	2003	30,054	52,408	190	32		bbu	ex Bulk Saturn-12
9105035	Mandarin Arrow	Bhs	1996	35,998	51,733	200	32	16	boh	
9155303	Merlin Arrow *	Bhs	1999	36,008	51,459	200	32	15	boh	ex Tolten-04
8918227	Mozu Arrow	Bhs	1992	44,398	42,276	185	30	15	boh	
9529280	Nandu Arrow #	Pan	2011	37,046	61,860	200	32		ggc	
8313697	Osprey Arrow	Bhs	1985	27,938	42,596	188	29	13	boh	
9151814	Penguin Arrow	Bhs	1997	36,008	51,738	200	32	16	boh	
8309713	Petersfield	Bhs	1985	27,818	41,646	188	29	13	boh	
9107306	Pine Arrow	Bhs	1996	32,520	48,041	190	31	14	boh	
9552898	Pipit Arrow #	Pan	2012	37,046	61,860	200	32		ggc	
9144407	Plover Arrow	Bhs	1997	36,008	51,880	200	32	14	boh	
9235141	Poplar Arrow	Bhs	2005	35,250	47,818	190	31	14	boh	
9566605	Puffin Arrow #	Pan	2011	36,925	62,967	200	32		ggc	
9007544	Quetzal Arrow	Nis	1992	29,369	46,908	199	31	15	boh	ex Breeze Arrow-08, Westwood Breeze-03, Saga Breeze-98
9232814	Spruce Arrow	Bhs	2002	32,458	47,818	190	31	14	boh	
9323821	Sunbird Arrow	Bhs	2005	12,959	15,002	144	24	14	tas	
8512970	Swan Arrow	Bhs	1987	28,805	45,295	200	31	15	boh	ex Norsul America-04, Westwood Jago-03
8918239	Swift Arrow	Bhs	1992	44,398	42,276	185	30	15	boh	
9401879	Tawa Arrow #	Pan	2008	30,983	53,560	190	32	-	ggc	
8309402	Teal Arrow	Bhs	1984	27,962	43,002	188	29	13	boh	ex Lista-91
8316710	Tern Arrow	Bhs	1986	28,239	42,570	188	29	14	boh	
8512944	Tinamou Arrow *	Bhs	1986	28,805	45,295	200	31	15	boh	ex Westwood Marianne-07
9434539	Toki Arrow #	Pan	2010	36,925	62,942	200	32		ggc	
9105023	Toucan Arrow	Bhs	1996	35,998	51,880	200	32	16	boh	
8512968	Tsuru Arrow *	Bhs	1987	28,805	45,295	200	31	15	boh	ex Norsul Vancouver-04, Westwood Cleo-02
9151826	Weaver Arrow	Bhs	1997	36,008	51,364	200	32	14	boh	
8316704	Westfield	Bhs	1985	27,818	41,619	188	29	13	boh	
8316699	Wren Arrow	Bhs	1985	27,824	41,637	188	29	13	boh	ex Charles LD-90

newbuildings:
*vessels owned by Gearbulk Shipowning Ltd, Norway or * by Gearbulk Shipping AS, Norway † managed for CHL Shipping BV, Netherlands (subsidiary of TNT Shipping & Development Ltd., Australia) # chartered vessels*

SKS Tankers Ltd., Bermuda

Funnel: Pale green with white 'SKS' on broad red band, narrow black top. Hull: Red with green boot-topping. History: Founded 1996 jointly with Nordship AS subsidiary of CSAV to 2004. Web: www.sksobo.com

IMO#	name	flag	year	grt	dwt	loa	bm	kts	type
9248813	SKS Saluda *	Nis	2003	81,270	159,438	274	50	15	tcr
9301524	SKS Satilla	Nis	2006	81,380	158,842	274	48	15	tcr
9326718	SKS Segura	Nis	2007	81,380	158,784	274	48	15	tcr
9248825	SKS Senne *	Mhl	2003	81,270	159,385	274	48	15	tcr
9232931	SKS Sinni	Nis	2003	81,270	159,385	274	48	15	tcr
9232929	SKS Sira *	Mhl	2002	81,270	159,453	274	48	15	tcr
9301536	SKS Skeena	Nis	2006	81,380	158,943	274	48	15	tcr
9326720	SKS Spey	Nis	2007	81,380	158,842	274	48	15	tcr

SKS OBO Ltd., Bermuda

Funnel: Pale green with white 'SKS' on broad red band, narrow black top. Hull: Red with green boot-topping. History: Founded 1996 jointly with Nordship AS subsidiary of CSAV to 2004. Web: www.sksobo.com

IMO#	name	flag	year	grt	dwt	loa	bm	kts	type
9461843	SKS Darent	Bhs	2011	65,830	119,456	250	45	15	tco
9428994	SKS Dee	Nis	2010	65,830	119,456	250	45	15	tco
9426312	SKS Delta	Nis	2010	65,380	119,456	250	45	15	tco
9531636	SKS Demini	Nis	2012	65,830	119,456	250	45	15	tco
9531648	SKS Doda	Nis	2012	65,380	119,456	250	45	15	tco
9461831	SKS Dokka	Nis	2010	65,830	119,456	250	45	15	tco
9461855	SKS Donggang	Bhs	2011	65,830	119,456	250	45	15	tco
9428982	SKS Douro	Nis	2010	65,830	119,456	250	45	15	tco
9429003	SKS Doyles	Nis	2010	65,830	119,456	250	45	15	tco
9428970	SKS Driva	Nis	2010	65,830	119,456	250	45	15	tco
9240445	SKS Mersey	Nis	2003	70,933	120,499	250	44	15	cbo
9240433	SKS Mosel	Nis	2003	70,933	120,670	250	44	15	cbo

IMO#	name	flag	year	grt	dwt	loa	bm	kts	type	former names
9133458	SKS Tagus	Nis	1997	63,515	109,933	244	42	15	cbo	
9116967	SKS Tana	Nis	1996	63,515	109,906	244	42	14	cbo	
9172662	SKS Tanaro	Nis	1999	63,515	109,787	244	42	14	cbo	
9172650	SKS Tiete	Nis	1999	63,515	109,773	244	42	14	cbo	
9161273	SKS Torrens	Nis	1999	63,515	109,846	244	42	14	cbo	
9133446	SKS Trent	Nis	1997	63,515	109,832	244	42	15	cbo	
9161285	SKS Trinity	Nis	1999	63,515	109,798	244	42	14	cbo	
9133460	SKS Tugela	Nis	1997	63,515	109,913	244	42	15	cbo	
9122928	SKS Tweed	Nis	1996	63,515	109,832	244	42	15	cbo	
9116955	SKS Tyne	Nis	1996	63,515	109,891	244	42	14	cbo	

newbuildings:
managed by Columbia Shipmanagement (Deutschland) GmbH.
* 40% owned by subsidiaries of König & Cie GmbH & Co KG (managed by Columbia Shipmanagement (Deutschland) GmbH)

Jüngerhans Maritime Services GmbH & Co. KG   Germany

Funnel: *White with pale blue 'J' inside pale blue diamond outline between two narrow pale blue bands or charterers colours.*
Hull: *Black or grey with red boot-topping.* **History:** *Founded 1983 as Reederei Heinrich Jungerhans to 1995, then Jungerhans & Co Reedereiverwaltung OHG to 2003.* **Web:** *www.juengerhans.de*

IMO#	name	flag	year	grt	dwt	loa	bm	kts	type	former names
9242314	Antares J	Atg	2002	14,062	18,400	156	25	18	ucc	1,201 teu: ex Maersk Rotterdam-12, I/a Antares J
9242302	Auriga J	Atg	2001	14,062	18,400	156	25	18	ucc	1,150 teu: ex Maersk Ravenna-12, I/a Auriga J
9238686	Corona J	Atg	2002	16,129	16,794	161	25	19	ucc	1,209 teu: ex Maersk Rio Grande-08, Corona J-02
9238698	Crux J	Atg	2003	16,129	16,824	161	25	19	ucc	1,209 teu: ex Maersk Rosario-08, Crux J-03
9138238	Helene J	Atg	1997	18,233	26,260	178	28	20	ucc	1,900 teu: ex CMA CGM Montenegro-11 Helene J-07, Clan Praetorian-07, Helene J-05, ANL Oryx-03, Helene J-02, Fesco Express-00, Maersk Manzanillo-99, TNX Sprint-98, Antares-97, Helene J-97
9506758	Industrial Faith	Atg	2011	12,810	14,288	153	23	17	ggc	I/a Senda J
9506734	Industrial Fighter	Atg	2010	12,810	14,360	153	23	17	ggc	I/a Eris J
9506746	Industrial Force	Atg	2011	12,810	14,360	153	23	17	ggc	I/a Ran J
9138240	Klaus J	Deu	1997	18,233	26,260	177	28	20	ucc	1,900 teu: ex ACX Salvia-10, ACX Plumeria-09, City of Stuttgart-05, Klaus J-02, Irma Delmas-02, Maersk San Antonio-99, TNX Express-98, Aldebaren-97, I/a Klaus J
9203904	Libra J	Atg	1998	12,004	14,174	149	23	19	ucc	1,116 teu: ex Tausala Samoa-05, I/a Libra J
9457000	Polaris J	Lbr	2012	50,885	61,962	249	37	24	ucc	4,334 teu

Kristian Gerhard Jebsen Skipsrederi AS (SKA OBO Ltd.) : SKS DEE : *Nico Kemps*

IMO#	name	flag	year	grt	dwt	loa	bm	kts	type	former names
9248916	Taurus J	Atg	2002	14,062	18,832	156	25	19	ucc	1,201 teu: ex Delmas Lisboa-10, Maersk Rostock-07, I/a Taurus J-03
9456977	Zim Colombo	Lbr	2009	41,331	51,535	262	32	24	ucc	4,300 teu: I/a Atlas J

also owns a fleet of smaller vessels, mostly container feeder ships

Kahn Scheepvaart B.V.   Netherlands
Funnel: *White with red elephant and red/blue eight-pointed star between narrow green bands.* **Hull:** *Dark blue with white web address, red boot-topping.* **History:** *Founded 1956 and subsidiary Jumbo Shipping Co formed 1969.* **Web:** *www.jumboshipping.nl*

IMO#	name	flag	year	grt	dwt	loa	bm	kts	type	former names
9243849	Fairpartner	Ant	2004	15,022	11,350	143	27	17	uhl	cr : 2(800)
9371579	Fairplayer	Ant	2008	15,027	13,278	145	27	17	uhl	cr : 2(900)
9243837	Jumbo Javelin	Ant	2004	15,022	12,870	143	27	17	uhl	cr : 2(800)
9371581	Jumbo Jubilee	Nld	2008	15,022	12,870	145	27	17	uhl	cr : 2(900)

also owns smaller heavy-lift vessels.

Kawasaki Kisen K.K. ('K' Line)   Japan
Funnel: *Bright red with white 'K', above grey base.* **Hull:** *Grey with red boot-topping.* **History:** *Formed 1919 as Kawasaki Kisen Kaisha and merged 1964 with Iino Kisen Kaisha (formed 1918). Taiyo Nippon Kisen subsidiary formed 2000 by merger of Taiyo Kaiun KK with Kobe Nippon KK (founded 1917).* **Web:** *www.kline.co.jp*

IMO#	name	flag	year	grt	dwt	loa	bm	kts	type	former names
9442885	Adriatic Highway **	Pan	2008	58,990	18,869	200	32	20	mve	6,237 ceu
9464388	Aegean Highway **	Jpn	2008	60,320	18,867	200	32	20	mve	6,237 ceu
9224532	Akinada Bridge	Pan	2001	68,687	71,366	285	40	25	ucc	5,610 teu
9409039	Alexandria Bridge	Pan	2009	40,839	51,314	261	32	24	ucc	4,228 teu
9409027	Ambassador Bridge	Phl	2009	40,839	51,314	261	32	24	ucc	4,228 teu
9205976	American Highway	Pan	2000	49,212	16,750	179	32	20	mve	5,052 ceu
9078842	Arcadia Highway	Pan	1994	49,012	15,507	180	32	20	mve	5,008 ceu
9451484	Arica Bridge	Pan	2010	27,213	32,997	200	32	22	ucc	2,450 teu
9409041	Astoria Bridge	Pan	2009	40,839	51,314	261	32	24	ucc	4,228 teu
9409053	Athens Bridge	Pan	2009	40,839	51,314	261	32	24	ucc	4,228 teu
9443073	Athens Highway **	Pan	2008	59,440	18,809	200	32	20	mve	6,237 ceu
9250232	Atlantic Highway	Pan	2002	55,493	17,232	200	32	20	mve	6,015 ceu
8612251	Atlas Highway	Lbr	1987	45,742	14,487	180	32	20	mve	4,857 ceu
9463346	Bai Chay Bridge	Pan	2011	44,234	52,452	267	35	24	ucc	4,432 teu
9243461	Baltic Highway	Pan	2001	42,238	17,828	179	32	20	mve	4,004 ceu
9463281	Baltimore Bridge	Pan	2010	44,234	52,184	267	35	24	ucc	4,432 teu
9506710	Bangkok Highway **	Pan	2009	48,927	15,306	180	32	20	mve	5,036 ceu
9437282	Baogang Spirit	Pan	2010	152,311	297,902	327	55	14	bor	
9463267	Bay Bridge	Pan	2010	44,234	52,118	267	35	24	ucc	4,432 teu
9463293	Bear Mountain Bridge	Pan	2011	44,234	52,118	267	35	24	ucc	4,432 teu
9409340	Bishu Highway **	Pan	2009	56,978	17,649	200	32	20	mve	6,135 ceu
9519107	Bosporus Highway	Pan	2009	59,440	18,792	200	32	20	mve	6,237 ceu
9247546	Bremen Bridge †	Pan	2001	66,332	67,170	279	40	25	ucc	4,492 teu: ex YM Bridge-06, Bremen Bridge-04
9519119	Brasilia Highway	Pan	2009	59,440	18,793	200	32	20	mve	6,327 ceu
9458999	Brooklyn Bridge	Pan	2010	44,459	52,055	267	35	24	ucc	4,432 teu
9463310	Brussels Bridge	Pan	2011	44,234	52,452	267	35	24	ucc	4,432 teu
9574078	California Highway **	Pan	2010	59,447	18,644	200	32	18	mve	6,215 ceu
9574066	Canadian Highway **	Pan	2010	59,447	18,581	200	32	18	mve	6,215 ceu
9281906	Cape Acacia	Pan	2005	104,732	206,237	300	50	15	bbu	
9463308	Cape Althea	Pan	2011	93,227	179,250	292	45	15	bbu	
9374038	Cape Alliance	Pan	2007	104,732	206,190	300	50	15	bbu	
9552410	Cape Amanda **	Pan	2011	93,235	182,741	292	45	15	bbu	
9311828	Cape Apricot	Pan	2004	90,091	180,310	289	45	14	bbu	
9538749	Cape Aster	Pan	2012	91,412	176,217	292	45	15	bbu	
9113915	Cape Awoba	Jpn	1996	87,803	171,978	289	45	14	bbu	ex Cape Acacia-05
9223590	Cape Camellia	Pan	2000	87,322	172,502	289	45	14	bbu	ex Cape Daisy-04
9409144	Cape Celtic **	Pan	2011	92,249	178,342	292	45	15	bbu	
9350800	Cape Dover *	Pan	2006	92,993	185,805	290	47	14	bbu	
9463322	Cape Dream	Pan	2011	93,227	179,250	292	45	15	bbu	
9241669	Cape Enterprise	Pan	2003	92,993	185,909	290	47	14	bbu	
9603362	Cape Eternity	Pan	2011	106,251	207,855	300	50	14	bbu	
9182629	Cape Flora	Pan	2000	83,056	164,361	280	47	14	bbu	
9241657	Cape Future	Pan	2002	92,993	185,820	290	47	14	bbu	
9271391	Cape Glory	Pan	2003	89,525	177,173	289	45	14	bbu	
9437270	Cape Infinity	Pan	2011	132,589	250,847	330	57	14	bor	
9446594	Cape Jacaranda	Pan	2011	92,752	181,452	292	45	14	bbu	
9463334	Cape Keystone	Pan	2011	93,227	179,250	292	45	15	bbu	
9333797	Cape Liberty	Pan	2005	92,993	185,897	290	47	14	bbu	
9201695	Cape Lotus	Pan	2000	83,849	170,780	289	45	16	bbu	
9573757	Cape Magnolia	Pan	2011	92,752	181,461	292	45	15	bbu	

IMO#	name	flag	year	grt	dwt	loa	bm	kts	type	former names
9281918	Cape Maple	Pan	2005	104,932	206,204	300	50	14	bbu	
9316828	Cape Med *	Pan	2006	93,003	185,827	290	47	14	bbu	
9125451	Cape Olive	Pan	1996	85,663	169,963	290	46	14	bbu	
9238571	Cape Orchid **	Pan	2001	87,322	172,569	289	45	14	bbu	
9300570	Cape Provence	Pan	2005	89,651	177,022	289	45	14	bbu	
9603398	Cape Rainbow	Pan	2012	106,251	207,886	300	50	17	bbu	
9327736	Cape Riviera *	Pan	2005	93,006	185.879	290	47	14	bbu	
9273985	Cape Rosa	Pan	2005	101,911	203,163	300	50	14	bbu	
9573763	Cape Sakura **	Jpn	2010	92,697	181,529	292	45	14	bbu	
9218832	Cape Salvia	Pan	2002	87,341	172,559	289	45	14	bbu	
9558220	Cape Sampagita	Pan	2011	92,376	180,646	292	45	14	bbu	
9293739	Cape Sentosa	Sgp	2003	89,545	177,346	289	45	14	bbu	
9342891	Cape Sophia	Pan	2005	55,285	99,047	250	43	14	bbu	
9565558	Cape Town Highway **	Pan	2011	58,535	21,676	200	32	19	mve	6,249 ceu
9254692	Cape Triumph	Pan	2004	88,594	176,343	289	45	15	bbu	
9482249	Cape Tsubaki	Pan	2010	92,977	182,718	292	45		bbu	
9603386	Cape Universe	Pan	2012	106,251	207,856	300	50	17	bbu	
9374052	Cape Vanguard	Pan	2006	104,732	206,180	300	50	14	bbu	
9482524	Cape Victory	Pan	2003	89,492	177,359	289	45	14	bbu	
9243473	Caribbean Highway	Pan	2002	42,238	17,866	179	32	20	mve	4,004 ceu
8319718	Century Highway No. 2	Pan	1985	44,616	15,509	186	32	18	mve	5,401 ceu
9565546	Chesapeake Highway **	Pan	2010	58,535	21,643	200	32		mve	6,249 ceu
9247558	Chicago Bridge	Pan	2001	66,332	67,170	279	40	25	ucc	5,570 teu: ex YM Chicago-06, Chicago Bridge-04
9224544	Chiswick Bridge	Pan	2001	68,687	68,280	285	40	25	ucc	5,610 teu
9323780	Colorado Highway **	Pan	2005	44,382	12,806	183	30	20	mve	4,318 ceu
9238519	Continental Highway	Pan	2001	55,493	17,201	200	32	20	mve	6,249 ceu
9565560	Dalian Highway **	Pan	2011	58,535	21,616	200	32	20	mve	6,249 ceu
9536959	Delhi Highway **	Pan	2011	58,997	18,891	200	32	20	mve	6,120 ceu
9574107	Dover Highway **	Jpn	2011	59,030	18,720	200	32	21	mve	6,215 ceu
9536961	Durban Highway **	Pan	2011	58,997	18,906	200	32	20	mve	6,120 ceu
9325764	Eastern Highway **	Pan	2006	39,422	12,991	188	28	20	mve	3,893 ceu
8602828	Emden	Pan	1987	38,062	13,898	178	29	17	mve	3,788 ceu
9604938	Euphrates Highway **	Pan	2012	59,447	18,709	200	32	21	mve	6,215 ceu
9604938	Eurasian Highway **	Jpn	2012	59,029	18,709	200	32	21	mve	6,215 ceu
9206011	European Highway	Pan	1999	48,039	15,057	180	32	20	mve	5,064 ceu
9442861	Florida Highway †	Pan	2008	59,493	18,930	200	32	20	mve	6,237 ceu
9262168	Fujikawa	Pan	2004	159,929	299,984	333	60	15	tcr	
9267651	Genoa Bridge	Pan	2002	66,292	67,197	279	40	25	ucc	5,570 teu
9302073	George Washington Bridge	Pan	2006	68,687	71,309	285	40	25	ucc	5,642 teu
9339820	Georgia Highway **	Jpn	2007	56,973	17,685	200	32	20	mve	6,135 ceu
9302097	Glen Canyon Bridge	Pan	2006	68,687	71,291	285	40	25	ucc	5,642 teu
9224506	Golden Gate Bridge	Pan	2001	68,687	71,376	285	40	25	ucc	5,642 teu
9322023	Grande Progresso **	Pan	2008	151,137	297,351	327	55	14	bor	
9302085	Greenwich Bridge	Pan	2006	68,687	71,270	285	40	25	ucc	5,642 teu
9302102	Guang Dong Bridge	Pan	2006	68,687	71,283	285	40	25	ucc	5,642 teu
9294367	Guangzhou Highway **	Pan	2006	48,927	15,301	180	32	20	mve	5,036 ceu
9351159	Hamburg Bridge	Pan	2009	98,747	98,849	336	46	25	ucc	9,040 teu
9395147	Hammersmith Bridge	Pan	2009	98,747	98,849	336	46	25	ucc	9,040 teu
9302138	Hannover Bridge	Pan	2006	98,747	99,214	336	46	25	ucc	9,040 teu
9588093	Hanoi Bridge	Pan	2012	98,800	97,000	335	46	25	ucc	8,930 teu
9302152	Harbour Bridge	Pan	2007	98,747	98,849	336	46	25	ucc	9,040 teu
9588081	Helsinki Bridge	Pan	2012	96,801	96,980	335	46	24	ucc	8,930 teu
9302176	Henry Hudson Bridge	Pan	2008	98,747	99,214	336	46	24	ucc	9,040 teu
8612316	Hercules Highway	Jpn	1987	46,875	14,977	180	32	18	mve	4,925 ceu
9395161	Hong Kong Bridge	Sgp	2009	98,747	98,849	336	46	25	ucc	8,212 teu
9588079	Honolulu Bridge	Pan	2012	96,790	96,980	335	46	24	ucc	8,930 teu
9566382	Houston Bridge	Pan	2012	96,801	96,980	335	46	24	ucc	8,930 teu
9302140	Humber Bridge	Pan	2006	98,747	98,849	336	46	24	ucc	8,212 teu
9302164	Humen Bridge	Pan	2007	98,747	98,849	336	46	24	ucc	8,212 teu
9272888	Indiana Highway **	Jpn	2003	55,457	17,442	200	32	20	mve	6,043 ceu
9262156	Isuzugawa	Pan	2004	159,929	299,984	333	60	15	tcr	
9224520	James River Bridge	Pan	2001	68,687	71,336	285	40	25	ucc	5,610 teu
8616958	Kentucky Highway **	Jpn	1987	50,320	15,587	180	32	19	mve	5,640 ceu
9490612	King Ore	Pan	2010	89,605	176,944	289	45	14	bbu	
9206035	Kumanogawa	Lbr	2001	159,566	299,988	333	60	15	tcr	
9224518	Lions Gate Bridge	Pan	2001	68,687	71,395	285	40	25	ucc	5,610 teu

L : 22:06:2012

IMO#	name	flag	year	grt	dwt	loa	bm	kts	type	former names
9362267	London Highway	Pan	2006	55,600	17,765	200	32	20	mve	6,057 ceu
8604292	Manhattan Bridge	Pan	1987	42,394	40,934	241	32	22	ucc	3,032 teu
9250220	Mediterranean Highway **	Pan	2002	55,493	17,228	200	32	20	mve	6,015 ceu
9339832	Michigan Highway **	Jpn	2008	56,951	17,673	200	32	20	mve	6,135 ceu
9391775	Nagaragawa	Pan	2010	159,941	301,583	333	60	15	tcr	
9330745	Neva River (st)	Pan	2007	117,895	77,163	290	50	19	lng	147,804 m³: ex Celestine River-10
9205964	Nippon Highway	Pan	1999	49,212	16,827	179	32	20	mve	5,052 ceu
9205988	Ocean Highway	Pan	2000	49,212	16,733	179	32	20	mve	5,052 ceu
9082324	Olympian Highway *	Pan	1995	47,077	14,226	180	32	20	mve	5,060 ceu
9381665	Oregon Highway **	Pan	2007	57,147	17,699	200	32	20	mve	6,135 ceu
9206023	Pacific Highway	Pan	2000	48,039	15,127	180	32	20	mve	5,064 ceu
9078830	Pegasus Highway	Pan	1994	49,012	15,553	180	32	18	mve	5,008 ceu
9334894	Rigel **	Jpn	2009	150,836	297,571	327	55	17	bor	
9391751	Sakuragawa	Pan	2009	160,068	299,982	333	60	15	tcr	
9560376	San Diego Bridge	Pan	2010	71,787	72,912	293	40	25	ucc	6,350 teu
9560364	San Francisco Bridge	Pan	2010	71,787	72,890	293	40	25	ucc	6,350 teu
9615195	Sargam **	Jpn	2012	50,624	95,671	235	38	14	bbu	
9560352	Seattle Bridge	Pan	2010	71,787	72,890	293	40	25	ucc	6,350 teu
9391763	Setagawa	Pan	2009	159,936	299,998	333	60	15	tcr	
9238521	Seven Seas Highway **	Pan	2001	55,493	17,232	200	32	22	mve	6,015 ceu

Kawasaki Kisen K.K. : FLORIDA HIGHWAY : *M. Lennon*

Kawasaki Kisen K.K. : HELSINKI BRIDGE : *J. Kakebeeke*

IMO#	name	flag	year	grt	dwt	loa	bm	kts	type	former names
9294343	Shanghai Highway **	Pan	2005	48,927	15,413	180	32	22	mve	5,036 ceu
9043689	Shenandoah Highway	Pan	1992	47,368	12,308	180	32	18	mve	4,211 ceu
9325439	Sierra Nevada Highway **	Pan	2007	44,364	12,851	183	30	20	mve	4,318 ceu
9338632	Southern Highway **	Pan	2008	39,422	12,892	188	28	20	mve	3,893 ceu
9552379	Stenia Colossus	Sgp	2009	33,096	58,731	197	32		bbu	
9230311	Suez Canal Bridge	Pan	2002	68,687	71,359	285	40	25	ucc	5,610 teu
9313149	Tamagawa	Pan	2007	160,231	314,237	333	60	15	tcr	
9272890	Texas Highway **	Jpn	2003	55,458	17,481	200	32	20	mve	6,043 ceu
9294355	Tianjin Highway **	Pan	2005	48,927	15,461	180	32	19	mve	5,036 ceu
9319404	Trinity Arrow (st)	Pan	2008	101,080	79,556	278	44	19	lng	154,982 m³
9350927	Trinity Glory (st)	Pan	2009	101,126	79,605	278	44	19	lng	154,200 m³
8602263	Triton Highway	Jpn	1987	45,783	14,484	180	32	18	mve	4,857 ceu
9230309	Tsing Ma Bridge	Pan	2002	68,687	71,310	285	40	25	ucc	5,610 teu
9292254	Valencia Bridge	Pan	2004	54,519	65,006	294	32	23	ucc	4,738 teu
9292230	Vancouver Bridge	Pan	2005	54,519	65,002	294	32	23	ucc	4,738 teu
9293454	Vecchio Bridge	Pan	2005	54,519	64,983	294	32	23	ucc	4,738 teu
9293442	Venice Bridge	Pan	2005	54,519	64,989	294	32	23	ucc	4,738 teu
9292175	Verrazano Bridge	Pan	2004	54,519	65,038	294	32	23	ucc	4,738 teu
9293466	Victoria Bridge	Pan	2005	54,519	64,986	294	32	23	ucc	4,738 teu
9292266	Vincent Thomas Bridge	Pan	2005	54,519	65,023	294	32	23	ucc	4,738 teu
9292242	Virginia Bridge	Pan	2004	54,519	64,990	294	32	23	ucc	4,738 teu
9623829	Vivace	Pan	2012	40,354	74,933	225	32	14	bbu	
9325776	Western Highway **	Pan	2007	39,422	12,980	188	28	19	mve	3,893 ceu
9313137	Yamatogawa	Pan	2006	160,231	302,488	333	60	15	tcr	

newbuilldings:
*managed by 'K' Line Ship Management Co Ltd, Japan or by subsidiaries * Stargate Shipmanagement GmbH, Germany or ** Taiyo Nippon Kisen (founded 1944 as Kobe Nippon KK and merged 2000 with Taiyo Kaiun KK - www.nipponkisen.co.jp) † owned by Shoei Kisen Kaisha, Japan. The company and its many subsidiaries own or manage over 210 vessels, only the larger container ships, tankers, bulk carriers and vehicle carriers being listed. The owned and managed fleet also includes over 35 'panamax' or 'handy' bulk carriers, 10 wood-chip carriers, 10 product and Lpg tankers, 23 Lng tankers and several smaller vehicle carriers. Doun Kisen K.K.*
Also see Cido Shipping and various chartered container ships with 'Bridge' suffix in index.

Klaveness Maritime Logistics AS   Norway

Funnel: *Yellow with blue 'K' on white disc and blue edged narrow white band.* **Hull:** *Grey or orange with red boot-topping.*
History: *Founded 1946 as Gorrissen & Klaveness A/S to 1958 and as Torvald Klaveness & Co AS to 2005.* **Web:** *www.tk-group.com or www.klaveness.com*

IMO#	name	flag	year	grt	dwt	loa	bm	kts	type	former names
9228057	Al Mansour	Mhl	2002	38,889	72,562	225	32	14	bbu	

Kawasaki Kisen K.K. : RIGEL : *Chris Brooks*

IMO#	name	flag	year	grt	dwt	loa	bm	kts	type	former names
9289051	Amundsen *	Sgp	2004	18,334	23,679	175	27	20	ucc	1,740 teu: ex Oceanlady-10, Ocean Progress I-09, Cap Arnauti-09, Philipp Schulte-04
9308728	Bakkedal	Mhl	2007	38,883	72,450	225	32	14	bbu	
	Balao		2013						ucc	2,500 teu
	Balchen		2013		71,900				bsd	
9233416	Balder	Mhl	2002	30,739	48,184	190	32	14	bsd	
7926148	Baldock	Mhl	1982	46,068	75,569				bsd	
	Baleares		2013						ucc	2,500 teu
	Ballerita		2013						ucc	2,500 teu
	Balsa		2013						ucc	2,500 teu
	Balto	Mhl	2012	41,500	71,900				bsd	
9214135	Banasol	Mhl	2001	38,889	72,562	225	32	14	bbu	
9228045	Banastar	Mhl	2001	38,889	72,700	225	32	16	bbu	
9228057	Bangor	Mhl	2002	38,889	72,562	225	32	14	bbu	ex Al Mansour-12
9214147	Baniyas	Nis	2001	38,889	72,562	225	32	14	bbu	
9304067	Bantry	Mhl	2005	38,883	72,562	225	32	14	bbu	
9233404	Barkald	Mhl	2002	28,912	49,900	190	32	14	bsd	
9237503	Barry *	Sgp	2004	35,881	41,800	220	32	22	ucc	3,091 teu: ex Anke Ritscher-10, CSAV Sao Paulo-09, Norasia Andes-06, Anke Ritscher-04
8413851	Baru	Mhl	1986	43,733	83,970	229	32	14	tco	
9086071	Trans Bay ††	Mhl	1996	37,550	70,120	225	32	13	bsd	ex Balsfjord-07, Sumava-98
9059951	Trans Emirates ††	Mhl	1993	37,550	70,456	225	32	13	bsd	ex Bakra-07, Bakar-99, Beskydy-98

* managed by Klaveness Asia Pte. Ltd., † formerly owned, now chartered by Bulk Transloading AS to 2012 (†† to 2022) from Norwegian KS company managed by Pioneer Ship Management, UAE. Also operates time-chartered vessels in Bulkhandling and Baumarine Pools

Knutsen OAS Shipping AS   Norway

Funnel: Black with two red bands. **Hull**: Orange (larger vessels with white 'KNUTSEN OAS'), red boot-topping. **History**: Founded 1896 as Knut Knutsen OAS until 1982. **Web**: www.knutsenoas.com

IMO#	name	flag	year	grt	dwt	loa	bm	kts	type	former names
9176929	Anneleen Knutsen	Nis	2002	24,242	35,140	183	27	15	tco	
9401295	Barcelona Knutsen	Cni	2010	110,920	97,730	290	46	19	lng	173,400 m³
9483516	Birgit Knutsen	Nis	2010	11,889	16,536	144	23	13	tco	
9236432	Bilbao Knutsen (st)	Cni	2004	90,835	68,530	284	43	19	lng	135,049 m³
9246578	Cadiz Knutsen (st)	Cni	2003	90,835	68,411	284	43	19	lng	135,240 m³
9409261	Eli Knutsen	Gbr	2009	11,889	16,544	144	23	13	tco	
9005780	Helene Knutsen	Iom	1992	11,737	14,848	142	23	13	tco	
9326603	Iberica Knutsen (st)	Nis	2006	93,915	77,541	277	43	19	lng	135,230 m³
9141405	Kristin Knutsen	Nis	1998	12,184	19,152	148	23	15	tco	
9409273	Liv Knutsen	Gbr	2009	11,899	16,585	144	23	13	tco	
9442249	Louise Knutsen	Gbr	2010	11,889	16,512	144	23	13	tco	
9070905	Pascale Knutsen	Gbr	1993	11,688	14,848	142	23	13	tco	
9477593	Ribera del Duero Knutsen (df)	Nis	2010	111,109	96,740	290	46	19	lng	173,400 m³
9338797	Sestao Knutsen (st)	Cni	2007	90,583	68,530	284	43	19	lng	135,357 m³
9414632	Sevilla Knutsen (df)	Cni	2010	110,920	97,730	290	46	19	lng	166,600 m³
9007207	Synnøve Knutsen	Nis	1992	11,433	17,071	142	23	13	tco	
9039884	Turid Knutsen	Nis	1993	15,689	22,617	142	23	13	tco	
9343266	Valencia Knutsen (df)	Cni	2010	110,920	97,730	290	46	19	lng	173,400 m³

newbuildings:

Knutsen NYK Offshore Tankers, Norway

Funnel: Black with two red bands or * yellow with white 'BR' on green square, black top. **Hull**: Orange with white 'KNOT' or * black with red boot-topping. **History**: founded 2010, j/v between Knutsen OAS (50%) and NYK (50%)

IMO#	name	flag	year	grt	dwt	loa	bm	kts	type	former names
9172870	Betty Knutsen	Nis	1999	24,185	35,309	183	27	14	tcs	
9472529	Bodil Knutsen	Iom	2011	93,147	157,644	285	50	14	tcs	
8714994	Catherine Knutsen †	Nis	1992	77,352	141,200	277	43	14	tcs	ex Tanana-99, Wilomi Tanana-98, Tanana-98, Wilomi Tanana-97
9131357	Elisabeth Knutsen (me2)	Nor	1997	71,880	124,788	265	43	14	tcs	
9499876	Fortaleza Knutsen *	Bhs	2011	63,560	106,316	247	42	14	tcs	
9041057	Gerd Knutsen	Iom	1996	79,244	134,510	277	44	14	tcs	ex Knock An-03
9313527	Gijon Knutsen	Gbr	2006	24,242	35,309	187	27	15	tcs	
9190638	Hanne Knutsen (2)	Gbr	2000	72,245	123,851	265	43	15	tcs	
9273064	Heather Knutsen †	Can	2005	80,918	148,644	277	46	14	tcs	l/a Rose Knutsen
9273557	Jasmine Knutsen †	Nis	2005	80,918	148,706	277	46	14	tcs	
9169615	Karen Knutsen (2)	Iom	1999	87,827	154,390	276	50	14	tcs	ex Knock Whillan-03
9160619	Loch Rannoch + (2)	Gbr	1998	75,526	130,031	270	46	14	tcs	
9499888	Recife Knutsen *	Bhs	2011	63,560	105,928	247	42	14	tcs	
9169627	Sallie Knutsen (2)	Iom	1999	87,827	154,390	276	50	14	tcs	ex Knock Sallie-03

IMO#	name	flag	year	grt	dwt	loa	bm	kts	type	former names
9247168	Siri Knutsen	Gbr	2004	24,242	35,309	187	27	15	tcs	
9032496	Tordis Knutsen	Nor	1993	66,671	123,848	265	43	14	tcs	
8715546	Tove Knutsen	Nis	1989	60,719	112,508	246	43	14	tcs	laid up Galang, Indonesia, 04:12
9052989	Vigdis Knutsen	Nor	1993	66,671	123,423	265	43	14	tcs	
9316115	Windsor Knutsen *	Nis	2007	87,146	162,258	281	50	14	tcs	(conv tcr-11)

newbuildings: one 157,000dwt and two 123,000dwt shuttle tankers (HHI late-2012), one from Chinese builder
* operated by Petrobras Transportes S.A., Brazil, † by Canship Ugland Ltd (formed jointly by A/S Ugland Rederi and Canship Ltd),
Canada (www.canship.com) or + BP Shipping Ltd.

König & Cie. GmbH & Co. KG   Germany

Funnel: *Operator or charterers colours.* **Hull**: *Operator or charterers colours.* **History**: *Investment organisation founded 1999 and 40% owned by Schoeller Holdings Ltd.* **Web**: *www.emissionshaus.com*

IMO#	name	flag	year	grt	dwt	loa	bm	kts	type	former names
9357808	King Basil	Mlt	2008	17,964	24,092	183	25	19	ucc	1,706 teu
9357793	King Brian	Lbr	2008	17,964	24,150	182	25	19	ucc	1,710 teu
9357810	King Bruce	Mlt	2008	17,964	24,150	183	25	19	ucc	1,706 teu
9357781	King Byron	Mlt	2007	17,964	24,161	183	25	20	ucc	1,674 teu
9407287	King Daniel *	Mhl	2008	42,010	73,720	229	32	14	tco	
9417251	King Darius *	Mhl	2007	42,010	73,634	229	32	14	tco	
9347856	King Darwin *	Mhl	2007	42,010	73,604	229	32	14	tco	
9374844	King Dorian *	Mhl	2007	42,010	73,611	229	32	14	tco	ex King David-08
9407275	King Douglas *	Mhl	2008	42,010	73,666	229	32	14	tco	
9407263	King Duncan *	Mhl	2008	42,010	73,720	229	32	14	tco	
9384100	King Edgar *	Mhl	2008	24,112	38,402	183	27	14	tco	l/a Meriom Gem
9290490	King Edward *	Mhl	2004	23,240	37,384	183	27	14	tco	ex Ruby-06, Baltic Admiral-04
9267027	King Emerald *	Mhl	2004	25,507	38,875	183	27	14	tco	ex Meriom Breeze-08
9228849	King Eric *	Mhl	2001	23,217	37,270	183	27	14	tco	ex Ashley-07
9305532	King Ernest *	Mhl	2004	23,246	37,106	183	28	14	tco	ex Ganges-07
9228837	King Everest *	Mhl	2001	23,217	37,230	183	27	14	tco	ex Marne-06, l/a Ruby Star
9567441	King Felipe *	Mhl	2011	33,032	57,000	190	32	14	bbu	
9567453	King Fraser *	Mhl	2011	33,032	57,000	190	32	14	bbu	
9490442	King Hadley *	Mhl	2011	43,507	79,642	229	32	14	bbu	
9490466	King Hakan *	Mhl	2011	43,506	79,642	229	32	14	bbu	
9488803	King Harold *	Mhl	2011	43,507	79,642	229	32	14	bbu	
9108362	King Julius *	Mhl	1995	14,241	18,395	159	24	18	ucc	1,129 teu: ex Astor-12, APL CaracAs-01, Astor-00, Infanta-97, l/a Astor
9421843	King Robert *	Mhl	2008	89,510	169,676	291	45	14	bbu	
9295335	Mare Action **	Mhl	2005	23,240	37,467	183	27	14	tco	ex Baltic Action-07
9190505	Mare Ambassador **	Mhl	2005	23,240	37,371	183	27	14	tco	ex Baltic Ambassador-07
9216559	Mare Atlantic **	Mlt	2001	39,085	68,467	229	32	14	tco	ex Latgale-07, Inca-01
9384095	Mare Baltic **	Mhl	2008	24,112	38,402	183	27	14	tco	l/a Meriom Ruby
9276004	Mare Caribbean **	Mhl	2004	29,327	46,718	183	32	14	tco	ex Cape Bauld-07
9216547	Mare Pacific **	Mlt	2001	39,085	68,467	229	32	14	tco	ex Zemgale-07, Maya-01
9567439	Mare Tracer **	Mhl	2011	33,032	57,000	190	32	14	bbu	
9567415	Mare Trader **	Mhl	2010	33,032	56,745	190	32	14	bbu	
9567403	Mare Transporter **	Mhl	2011	33,033	56,745	190	32	14	bbu	
9567427	Mare Traveller **	Mhl	2011	33,032	56,745	190	32	14	bbu	

Knutsen OAS Shipping (Knutsen NYK Offshore Tankers) : BODIL KNUTSEN : *Chris Dornom*

IMO#	name	flag	year	grt	dwt	loa	bm	kts	type	former names
9215048	SC Laura +	Bhs	2001	61,764	109,325	245	42	15	tcr	ex Maersk Pointer-07
9230971	SC Sara †	Lbr	2001	56,346	105,322	239	42	15	tcr	ex Nordatlantic-07

newbuildings:
* managed by subsidiaries Scorship Navigation, Germany (formed jointly with Scorpio Ship Management SAM, Monaco) or ** by Marenave Schiffahrts AG, Germany (managed by Columbia Shipmanagement (Deutschland) GmbH), † by H Clarkson or + by Taurus Tankers Ltd. See other vessels managed by Columbia Shipmanagement (Deutschland) GmbH (under Schoeller Holdings Ltd.), SKS OBO Holding Ltd (under Kristian Gerhard Jebsen Skipsrederi AS), Thien & Heyenga GmbH and Oskar Wehr KG (GmbH & Co). Also see United Product Tanker (UPT) pool under Schoeller Holdings Ltd

Kuwait Oil Tanker Co. (SAK)   Kuwait

Funnel: *Red with gold Arabic characters on green oval disc on broad white band beneath black top.* **Hull:** *Black with red or grey boot-topping.* **History:** *Founded 1957 as subsidiary of Kuwait Petroleum Corp.* **Web:** *www.kotc.com.kw*

IMO#	name	flag	year	grt	dwt	loa	bm	kts	type	former names
9004803	Al Awdah	Kwt	1991	149,647	284,533	322	56	14	tcr	
8619443	Al Badiyah	Kwt	1989	26,356	35,643	183	32	13	tco	
8619455	Al Deerah	Kwt	1989	26,356	35,643	183	32	13	tco	
9329708	Al Jabriyah II	Kwt	2007	161,113	317,250	333	60	-	tcr	
8619429	Al Kuwaitiah	Kwt	1988	26,351	35,643	183	32	13	tco	
9534808	Al Riqqa	Kwt	2011	162,625	319,704	332	60		tcr	
8619431	Al Sabiyah	Kwt	1988	26,356	35,644	183	32	13	tco	
9328168	Al Salam II	Kwt	2007	42,798	69,790	228	32	-	tco	
9162875	Al Salheia	Kwt	1998	158,503	310,453	334	58	15	tcr	
9534793	Al Salmi	Kwt	2011	162,625	319,634	332	60		tcr	
9005261	Al Samidoon	Kwt	1992	149,719	284,889	322	57	14	tcr	
9162887	Al Shegaya	Kwt	1998	158,503	310,433	334	58	15	tcr	
9013311	Al Shuhadaa	Kwt	1992	149,719	285,116	322	57	14	tcr	
9329784	Al Soor II	Kwt	2007	42,798	69,835	228	32	-	tco	
9016868	Al Tahreer	Kwt	1991	149,719	284,532	322	56	14	tcr	
8619479	Arabiyah	Kwt	1988	75,029	121,109	250	43	13	tcr	
9595008	Bahra	Kwt	2012	62,925	110,751	250	42		tcr	
9595010	Bneider	Kwt	2012	62,925	110,587	250	42		tcr	
9534779	Dar Salwa	Kwt	2011	162,625	319,761	332	60		tcr	
9005065	Gas Al-Gurain	Kwt	1993	44,868	49,874	230	37	16	lpg	76,893 m³
9329710	Gas Al Kuwait II	Kwt	2007	48,104	57,738	225	37	16	lpg	80,607 m³
9005053	Gas Al Mutlaa	Kwt	1993	44,868	49,874	230	37	16	lpg	76,905 m³
9329722	Gas Al Negeh	Kwt	2007	48,104	57,748	225	37	16	lpg	80,681 m³
8619467	Hadiyah	Kwt	1988	75,029	121,109	250	43	16	tcr	
9329693	Kazimah II	Kwt	2006	161,113	317,250	333	60	15	tcr	
9534781	Umm Al Aish	Kwt	2011	162,625	319,634	332	60		tcr	
9328170	Wafrah	Kwt	2007	63,440	113,849	250	44	-	tcr	

Reederei F. Laeisz GmbH & Co. KG   Germany

Funnel: *Yellow or charterers colours.* **Hull:** *Black with red boot-topping or white with blue boot-topping.* **History:** *Founded 1824 as F Laeisz until 1982 and F Laeisz Schiffahrts GmbH to 1993. Fleet merged in 1993 with privatised East German state fleet of Deutsche Seereederei Rostock as joint venture with Hamburg business associate until 1999, when fully taken-over.* **Web:** *www.laeiszline.de*

IMO#	name	flag	year	grt	dwt	loa	bm	kts	type	former names
9334519	ANL Benalla †	Lbr	2006	28,270	32,900	213	32	22	ucc	2,646 teu: ex Pontremoli-11, Gulf Bridge-10, I/a Pontremoli
9123398	Chrismir +	Lbr	1997	81,329	159,829	280	45	14	bbu	I/a Mathilde
9427952	CSAV Rio Bueno	Lbr	2010	47,057	11,314	183	32	20	mve	5,000 ceu: I/a Pagna
9427926	CSAV Rio Illapel	Lbr	2009	47,020	11,453	183	32	21	mve	5,000 ceu: I/a Paganella
9427938	CSAV Rio Itata	Lbr	2009	47,020	11,372	183	32	20	mve	5,000 ceu: I/a Paganino
9082960	Hanjin Colombo	Pan	1994	50,792	62,850	290	32	24	ucc	4,024 teu
9141273	Hanjin Haiphong	Deu	1997	53,324	63,527	294	32	23	ucc	4,545 teu: ex Peking Senator-09, Cho Yang Ark-00
9139490	Hanjin Mundra	Deu	1997	53,324	63,533	294	32	23	ucc	4,545 teu: ex Penang Senator-09, Cho Yang Atlas-01
9232101	Hanjin Philadephia †	Lbr	2002	50,242	58,810	282	32	24	ucc	4,389 teu: I/a Philadelphia
9232084	Hanjin Phoenix †	Lbr	2002	50,242	58,423	282	32	24	ucc	4,389 teu: I/a Phoenix
9021681	Hanjin Portland	Lbr	1993	50,792	62,716	290	32	24	ucc	4,024 teu
9232072	Hanjin Praha *	Lbr	2001	50,242	58,423	280	32	24	ucc	4,389 teu: I/a Praha
9232113	Hanjin Pretoria *	Lbr	2002	50,242	58,768	282	32	24	ucc	4,389 teu
9141302	Hanjin San Diego	Deu	1997	53,324	63,645	294	32	23	ucc	4,545 teu: ex Portland Senator-09, Cho Yang Alpha-01
9330549	Kaya	Lbr	2007	28,616	39,338	222	30	21	ucc	2,824 teu: ex Valentia Schulte-13, Cap Capricorn-12, Valentia Schulte-07
9141261	MSC Tanzania	Deu	1997	53,324	62,057	294	32	23	ucc	4,545 teu: ex Pudong Senator-07
9141285	MSC Uganda	Deu	1997	53,324	63,645	294	32	23	ucc	4,545 teu: ex Punjab Senator-07
9427950	Paglia	Lbr	2010	47,057	11,368	183	32	20	mve	5,000 ceu: ex CSAV Rio Blanco-12, I/a Paglia
9149794	Paradise N ***	Lbr	1997	155,051	322,398	332	58	13	bor	ex Peene Ore-02
9427964	Parana	Gib	2012	47,053	12,868	183	32	20	mve	5,000 ceu

IMO#	name	flag	year	grt	dwt	loa	bm	kts	type	former names
9491874	Passama	Gib	2012	47,053	12,806	183	32	20	mve	5,000 ceu
9491886	Passero	Gib	2012	47,053	12,800	183	32	20	mve	5,000 ceu
9491898	Patara	Gib	2012	47,053	12,800	183	32	20	mve	5,000 ceu
9293430	Pazific	Gib	2005	25,852	42,937	205	32	16	lpg	60,000 m³ ex Pacific-12, BW Hesiod-11, Pacific Viking-06
9139282	Piro †	Lbr	1997	38,215	73,726	225	32	15	bbu	ex Babitonga-09, William Oldendorff-06, Wiltrader-03, Win Trader-02
9147071	Pohang	Gib	1998	53,334	63,537	294	32	23	ucc	4,545 teu: ex CSAV Pyrennes-13, Pohang Senator-08
9292216	Polar	Gib	2004	35,853	42,854	205	32	16	lpg	60,000 m³ ex BW Herdis-11, Polar Viking-06
9349875	Pona	Lbr	2007	27,968	37,570	222	30	22	ucc	2,741 teu: ex CMA CGM Copernic-09, Pona-07
9334521	Pontresina	Lbr	2008	28,270	32,949	213	32	22	ucc	2,646 teu: ex Kota Permas-12, Pontresina-08
9481520	Porto	Lbr	2010	28,561	39,267	225	30	22	ucc	2,790 teu
9147083	Portugal	Deu	1998	53,324	63,645	294	32	23	ucc	4,545 teu: ex CSAV Jura-12, CMA CGM Asia-08, Portugal Senator-06
9349887	Posen †	Lbr	2007	27,968	37,570	222	30	22	ucc	2,790 teu: ex OOCL Bremen-09, Posen-07
9105578	Powhatan †	Lbr	1995	36,615	69,045	225	32	15	bbu	
9074133	Premnitz †	Lbr	1994	38,513	72,873	225	32	14	bbu	ex Luise Oldendorff-08
9158965	Priwall	Lbr	1997	28,701	32,500	202	31	20	ucc	2,604 teu: ex MSC Chile-09, Priwall-04, MSC Chile-04, Priwall-02, Sea Panther-01, Priwall-97
9141297	Pugwash	Deu	1997	53,334	62,200	294	32	23	ucc	4,545 teu: ex CSAV Appennini-12, Pugwash Senator-07
9139488	Pusan	Deu	1997	53,324	63,584	294	32	23	ucc	4,545 teu: ex MSC Kenya-11, Pusan Senator-07

newbuildings:

owned or managed by Reederei F. Laeisz GmbH or † by associated company Hamburgische Seehandlung GmbH
* managed for Dr. Peters KG fund, , *** for Gebab GmbH & Co KG, all Germany. + managed by OSG Shipmgmt.
also see managed vessels under BW Gas and NSB Niederelbe Schiffahrt GmbH.

Latvian Shipping Company   Latvia
Funnel: *Red with red 'Lat' symbol on broad white band.* **Hull:** *Black or red with red boot-topping.* **History:** *Government controlled and formed 1940.* **Web:** *www.lk.lv or www.lscsm.lv*

9323405	Ainazi	Mhl	2008	30,641	52,606	195	32	14	tco	
9323314	Ance	Mhl	2006	30,641	52,622	195	32	14	tco	
9323326	Jurkalne	Mhl	2006	30,641	52,622	195	32	14	tco	
9253234	Kaltene	Mhl	2003	23,217	37,261	183	27	14	tco	ex Pink Star-04
9314856	Kandava	Mhl	2007	23,315	37,258	183	27	14	tco	
9314868	Kazdanga	Mhl	2007	23,315	37,312	183	27	14	tco	
9253246	Kolka	Mhl	2003	23,217	37,211	183	27	14	tco	ex Purple Star-04
9314844	Kraslava	Mhl	2007	23,315	37,258	183	27	14	tco	
9314870	Krisjanis Valdemars	Mhl	2007	23,315	37,266	183	27	14	tco	
9253258	Kuldiga	Mhl	2003	23,217	37,237	183	27	14	tco	ex Coral Star-04
9482550	Latgale	Mhl	2011	29,694	51,408	183	32	14	tco	
9323376	Piltene	Mhl	2007	30,641	52,648	195	32	14	tco	
9323338	Puze	Mhl	2006	30,641	52,622	195	32	14	tco	
9221657	Riga	Mhl	2001	39,085	68,467	229	32	14	tco	ex Aztec-01
9323390	Salacgriva	Mhl	2008	30,641	52,620	195	32	14	tco	
9323340	Targale	Mhl	2007	30,641	52,622	195	32	14	tco	
9323352	Ugale	Mhl	2007	30,641	52,642	195	32	14	tco	
9323364	Usma	Mhl	2007	30,641	52,684	195	32	14	tco	
9323388	Uzava	Mhl	2008	30,541	52,650	195	32	14	tco	
9482562	Zemgale	Mhl	2011	29,694	51,406	183	32	14	tco	

newbuildings:

managed by LSC Shipmanagement Sia, Latvia (formed 1999)

J. Lauritzen A/S   Denmark

Lauritzen Bulkers A/S
Funnel: *As above or red upper part with white 'LB', white lower part with red over blue 'ivs' logo or black with red over blue 'ivs' logo on white square.* **Hull:** *Red (owned vessels), black or grey with white 'Lauritzen Bulkers',or black with white 'IVS', red boot-topping.* **History:** *Subsidiary formed in 1997 to re-enter the bulk carrier trade. Operates mainly chartered vessels, including a 'Handysize' joint venture with South African-based Island View Shipping (acquired by Grindrod Group in 1999).* **Web:** *www.lauritzenbulkers.com*

9270907	Achiles Bulker	Pan	2003	19,891	32,729	177	28	14	bbu	ex Apex Bulker-12, Irene Oldendorff-09
9470820	Admiral Bulker **	Pan	2008	17,023	28,320	170	27	14	bbu	
9336763	Alpha Bulker **	Pan	2006	19,885	32,741	177	28	14	bbu	ex Crystal Ocean-11
9310599	Amine Bulker **	Mlt	2007	17,663	28,700	177	26	14	bbu	
9544152	Anne Mette Bulker	Iom	2012	23,950	38,191	185	31	14	bbu	

IMO#	name	flag	year	grt	dwt	loa	bm	kts	type	former names
9459151	Apollo Bulker **	Hkg	2011	21,483	33,124	177	29	14	boh	
9527180	Asahi Bulker **	Pan	2012	21,483	33,179	177	29	14	boh	
9527192	Azure Bulker **	Pan	2012	21,483	33,179	177	29	14	boh	
9270919	Aurora Bulker **	Pan	2004	19,891	32,723	177	28	14	bbu	
9293870	Bumbi **	Pan	2004	17,951	29,870	171	27	14	bbu	
9455961	Camilla Bulker	Pan	2009	93,216	179,362	292	45	14	bbu	
9527910	Cassiopeia Bulker	Mlt	2011	93,715	179,398	292	45	14	bbu	
9446570	Catharina Bulker **	Pan	2011	92,752	181,458	292	45	14	bbu	
9335874	Charlotte Bulker **	Hkg	2007	19,831	32,132	176	29	14	bbu	
9527922	Christina Bulker	Mlt	2011	93,717	179,431	292	45	14	bbu	
9564097	Christine **	Mhl	2010	90,095	180,274	289	45	14	bbu	
9476848	Churchill Bulker	Mlt	2011	93,216	179,362	292	45	14	bbu	
9476836	Corona Bulker	Mlt	2011	93,216	179,362	292	45	14	bbu	
9281944	DHL Forester	Mlt	2003	16,966	28,481	169	27	14	bbu	ex Tilda Bulker-10, Triton Seagull-06
9300219	Durban Bulker **	Pan	2005	19,889	32,545	177	28	14	bbu	
9441295	Egret Bulker **	Mhl	2010	33,045	57,809	190	32	14	bbu	
9424132	Elvira Bulker	Iom	2011	19,812	31,858	176	29	14	bbu	
9497177	Emilie Bulker	Iom	2010	20,809	32,691	180	28	14	bbu	
9242091	Emma Bulker	Pan	2010	19,812	31,887	176	29	14	bbu	
9277668	Ermis **	Grc	2004	29,990	52,810	190	32	14	bbu	
9544164	Eva Bulker	Iom	2012	23,950	38,191	180	30	14	bbu	
9441300	Gannet Bulker **	Mhl	2010	33,045	57,809	190	32	14	bbu	

J. Lauritzen A/S (Lauritzen Bulkers) : EMILIE BULKER : *J. Kakebeeke*

J. Lauritzen A/S (Lauritzen Bulkers) : GREBE BULKER : *Chris Brooks*

IMO#	name	flag	year	grt	dwt	loa	bm	kts	type	former names
9496147	Geraldine Manx	Iom	2010	32,354	58,058	190	32	14	bbu	
9602174	Graig Cardiff **	Gbr	2012	23,444	34,827	180	30	14	bbu	
9602186	Graig Rotterdam **	Gbr	2012	23,444	35,898	180	30	14	bbu	
9441312	Grebe Bulker **	Mhl	2010	33,045	57,809	190	32	14	bbu	
9462512	Gry Bulker	Pan	2009	91,508	174,788	290	45	14	bbu	
9424120	Hedvig Bulker	Pan	2011	19,812	31,872	176	29	14	bbu	
9441324	Ibis Bulker **	Mhl	2010	33,045	57,809	190	32	14	bbu	
9590929	IVS Beachwood **	Pan	2011	34,795	61,418	200	32	14	bbu	
9604744	IVS Ibis **	Sgp	2012	17,019	28,240	169	27	14	bbu	
9295567	IVS Kanda *	Sgp	2004	19,885	32,621	177	28	14	bbu	
9303376	IVS Kawana *	Sgp	2005	19,885	32,642	177	28	14	bbu	
9251078	IVS Kestrel **	Hkg	2002	19,872	32,537	177	28	14	bbu	
9336787	IVS Kingbird **	Pan	2007	19,885	32,561	177	28	14	bbu	
9459149	IVS Kinglet *	Sgp	2011	21,483	33,132	177	29	14	boh	
9250696	IVS Kite **	Pan	2002	19,885	32,556	177	28	14	bbu	
9310769	IVS Kittiwake **	Pan	2007	19,885	32,555	177	28	14	bbu	
9459137	IVS Knot *	Sgp	2010	21,483	33,143	177	29	14	boh	
9300178	IVS Kwaito **	Pan	2004	19,885	32,573	177	28	14	bbu	
9250701	IVS Kwela **	Pan	2002	19,872	32,473	177	28	14	bbu	
9604732	IVS Magpie **	Sgp	2011	17,019	28,240	169	27	14	bbu	
9303429	IVS Nightjar *	Sgp	2004	20,283	32,328	173	29	14	boh	
9528029	IVS Orchard *	Sgp	2011	20,928	32,535	180	28	14	bbu	
9528005	IVS Sentosa *	Sgp	2010	20,809	32,755	180	28	14	bbu	
9370329	IVS Shikra **	Pan	2007	17,979	29,664	171	27	14	bbu	
9385087	Karine Bulker **	Pan	2008	20,236	32,271	177	28	14	boh	
9379662	Laura Bulker	Sgp	2008	19,825	31,890	176	29	14	bbu	
9288540	Lauretta **	Pan	2004	17,951	29,870	170	27	14	bbu	
9424089	Louise Bulker **	Pan	2010	19,812	31,881	176	29	14	bbu	
9338589	Maren Bulker	Pan	2008	19,822	31,945	176	29	14	bbu	
9528861	Maritime Fidelity **	Sgp	2010	19,724	32,000	183	26	14	bbu	
9544138	Milau Bulker **	Sgp	2012	38,191	47,233	185	31	14	bbu	
9544140	Nicoline Bulker	Iom	2012	38,191	47,233	185	31	14	bbu	
9379674	Nona Bulker **	Pan	2009	19,825	31,922	176	29	14	bbu	
9528017	Orchard Bulker *	Sgp	2010	20,928	32,535	180	28	14	bbu	
9147758	Pacific Bulker **	Pan	1997	17,075	27,865	177	26	14	bbu	
9311191	Palma Bulker **	Pan	2009	40,033	75,843	225	32	14	bbu	
9300207	Paola **	Pan	2004	19,885	32,565	177	28	14	bbu	
9288411	Penda Bulker **	Pan	2005	39,969	76,520	225	32	14	bbu	
9311177	Perla Bulker **	Pan	2007	40,033	75,884	225	32	14	bbu	
9441398	Petrel Bulker **	Mhl	2011	33,045	57,809	190	32	14	bbu	ex Petrel-11
9441403	Puffin Bulker **	Mhl	2011	33,045	57,809	190	32	14	bbu	
9441415	Roadrunner Bulker **	Mhl	2011	33,045	57,809	190	32	14	bbu	
9441427	Sandpiper Bulker **	Mhl	2011	33,045	57,809	190	32	14	bbu	
9527996	Sentosa Bulker *	Sgp	2010	20,809	32,755	180	28	14	bbu	
9599913	Shanghai Bulker **	Sgp	2012	32,987	56,719	190	32	14	bbu	
9497165	Signe Bulker	Pan	2010	20,809	32,755	180	28	14	bbu	
9599901	Singapore Bulker **	Sgp	2012	32,987	56,719	190	32	14	bbu	
9310604	Sofie Bulker	Mlt	2007	17,663	28,682	177	26	14	bbu	
9140528	Super Adventure	Pan	1996	17,977	28,630	172	27	14	bbu	ex IVS Super Adventure-02, Super Adventure-01
9140530	Super Challenge	Pan	1996	17,977	28,581	172	27	14	bbu	ex IVS Super Challenge-02, Super Challenge-01
9619892	Taizhou Pioneer **	Hkg	2011	20,954	32,453	180	28	14	bbu	
9423578	Tanager Bulker	Iom	2011	32,309	57,991	190	32	14	bbu	
9322736	Tenna Bulker *	Sgp	2005	16,960	28,391	169	27	14	bbu	
9423255	Tess Bulker	Iom	2011	32,309	57,991	190	32	14	bbu	
9423580	Thunderbird Bulker	Iom	2011	32,309	57,991	190	32	14	bbu	
9605023	Tokyo Bulker **	Pan	2012	34,795	61,439	200	32	14	bbu	
9423592	Toucan Bulker	Iom	2011	32,309	57,991	190	32	14	bbu	
9409077	Triton Bulker **	Pan	2009	31,251	55,651	190	32	14	bbu	
9606546	Uni Challenge	Sgp	2012	18,465	29,078	170	27	14	bbu	
9383508	Vigor SW **	Pan	2009	20,236	32,227	177	28	14	boh	

newbuildings: 1 x 31,800 dwt bulk carriers (Hakodate # 584 (2013)]
*owned by J. Lauritzen Singapore Pte.Ltd. * owned by IVS Bulk Owning Pvt. Ltd., Singapore*
*** chartered in from various Japanese, Hong Kong, Singapore, Greek, US or UK owners*

Lauritzen Tankers A/S

Funnel: Red with white 'J' above and 'L' below ivory band. **Hull:** Red with white 'Lauritzen', red boot-topping. **History:** Subsidiary formed in 2004 to re-enter the tanker trade. **Web:** www.lauritzentankers.com

IMO#	name	flag	year	grt	dwt	loa	bm	kts	type	former names
9419723	Alam Budi †	Mys	2001	28,539	47,065	183	32	15	tco	
9419723	Anja Kirk *	Gbr	2009	29,955	51,332	183	32	15	tco	ex Blue Emerald-11
9382700	Belaia †	Gbr	2007	28,799	48,673	180	32	14	tco	
9414292	Christina Kirk *	Gbr	2010	31,510	53,540	186	32	14	tco	ex Freja Scandia-10
9513440	Dan Cisne +	Dis	2012	36,303	59,335	207	32	14	tcs	
9183609	Dan Eagle +	Dis	1999	28,448	46,185	183	32	14	tcs	ex Freja Pacific-08, Soundless-06, Hellas Serenity-05
9513438	Dan Sabia +	Dis	2012	36,303	59,317	207	32	14	tcs	
9302657	Edith Kirk *	Gbr	2004	23,244	37,255	183	28	14	tco	ex Kerlaz-10
9461661	Freja Andromeda	Gbr	2011	30,241	50,386	183	32	14	tco	
9278519	Freja Atlantic	Dis	2004	30,004	45,967	183	32	14	tco	ex Crozon-04
9367683	Freja Baltic †	Pan	2008	26,897	47,538	183	32	14	tco	
9461697	Freja Crux	Dis	2012	30,241	52,550	183	32	14	tco	
9343986	Freja Fionia †	Pan	2007	31,433	53,714	186	32	14	tco	
9311036	Freja Hafnia †	Pan	2006	31,433	53,712	186	32	14	tco	
9461685	Freja Lupus	Dis	2012	30,241	52,550	183	32	14	tco	
9426283	Freja Nordica	Pan	2010	31,510	53,520	186	32	14	tco	
9461659	Freja Pegasus	Gbr	2010	30,241	50,391	183	32	14	tco	
9461673	Freja Taurus	Gbr	2011	30,241	50,385	183	32	14	tco	
9476812	Gunhild Kirk *	Gbr	2009	30,241	50,436	183	32	14	tco	ex Stealth Argentina-10
9555307	Leopard †	Pan	2010	28,798	47,991	180	32	14	tco	
9419735	Marianne Kirk *	Gbr	2009	29,955	51,291	183	32	14	tco	ex Blue Jade-11
9425526	Unique Explorer †	Hkg	2010	28,465	50,090	183	32	14	tco	

newbuildings: 3 x 52,300dwt tco (2013).
*† time chartered from various owners   * managed for Hafnia Tankers,.   + shuttle tankers operated by Lauritzen Offshore AS*

C. M. Lemos & Co. Ltd.   U.K.
Funnel: *Yellow with blue 'L' on white houseflag, black top.* **Hull:** *Black or grey with red boot-topping.* **History:** *Parent founded 1950 and subsidiary formed 1967.*   **Web:** *none found for either Lemos or Nereus Shipping*

IMO#	name	flag	year	grt	dwt	loa	bm	kts	type	former names
9541813	Asiatic	Grc	2012	34,456	58,451	196	32	14	bbu	
9290933	Authentic	Grc	2004	78,922	150,249	274	48	15	tcr	
9194983	Cosmic	Grc	2000	78,918	150,284	274	48	15	tcr	
9510187	Epic	Grc	2010	93,360	182,060	292	45	14	bbu	
9326067	Gloric	Grc	2006	156,933	298,495	330	60	15	tcr	
9510199	Heroic	Grc	2010	93,360	182,060	292	45	14	bbu	
9541825	Laconic	Grc	2012	34,375	58,474	196	32	14	bbu	
9194995	Majestic	Grc	2000	78,918	150,284	274	48	15	tcr	
9114593	North Star	Grc	1996	79,832	148,561	269	46	15	tcr	
9239848	Poetic	Grc	2003	78,922	150,103	274	48	15	tcr	
9303247	Romantic	Grc	2004	78,922	150,247	274	48	15	tcr	
9326055	Symphonic	Grc	2006	156,933	298,522	330	60	15	tcr	

operated by subsidiary Nereus Shipping SA, Greece.

Leonhardt & Blumberg Schiffahrts GmbH & Co. KG   Germany
Funnel: *Black with red 'x' and black '+' combined on broad white band, * black with blue single wave on white rectangle with white 'Maltese Cross' on dark blue square in top corner or charterers colours.* **Hull:** *Dark grey, blue or black with red boot-topping or white with blue boot-topping.* **History:** *Original company founded 1903 by Adolf Leonhardt and Arthur Blumberg to succeed Leonhardt & Heeckt (formed 1899). Present company formed in 1987as joint venture with Hansa Treuhand (25%).* **Web:** *www.leonhardt-blumberg.com*

IMO#	name	flag	year	grt	dwt	loa	bm	kts	type	former names
9256418	H Fyn	Mlt	2003	16,145	20,367	170	25	19	ucc	1,581 teu: ex Maersk Vaasa-07, I/a H. Fyn
9221061	Hansa Aalesund †	Lbr	2001	15,988	20,461	170	25	20	ucc	1,552 teu: ex Al Yamamah-08, Hansa Aalesund-04, MSC New Plymouth-04, I/a Hansa Aalesund
9134517	Hansa Africa †	Lbr	1997	37,398	43,378	243	32	22	ucc	3,398 teu; ex Maruba Simmons-10, Hansa Africa-08, ANL Excellence-03, Ville de Venus-02, Ibn Zaidoun-00, Hansa Africa-97
9516739	Hansa Altenburg	Lbr	2011	18,358	23,370	175	27	18	ucc	1,740 teu
9221059	Hansa Arendal †	Lbr	2001	15,988	20,700	170	25	16	ucc	1,262 teu: ex TMM Chiapas-05, Hansa Arendal-02
9112571	Hansa Atlantic †	Deu	1996	50,644	62,422	292	32	24	ucc	4,322 teu: ex Maersk Dresden-10, MSC Dresden-10, Maersk Dresden-09, MSC Dresden-09, Maersk Dresden-08, Dagmar Maersk-04, Hansa Atlantic-96
9373474	Hansa Augsburg	Lbr	2008	18,327	23,388	176	27	18	ucc	1,740 teu: ex NileDutch Tianjin-09, Hansa Augsburg-08
9155391	Hansa Augustenburg *	Lbr	2003	18,335	23,606	175	27	18	ucc	1,740 teu: ex Maersk Vilnius-07, Hansa Augustenburg-03

IMO#	name	flag	year	grt	dwt	loa	bm	kts	type	former names
9128477	Hansa Bergen *	Deu	1997	15,988	20,887	170	25	20	ucc	1,550 teu: ex Columbus Bondi-01, Hansa Bergen-00, Maersk Windhoek-99, Maersk Gothenburg-98, Hansa Bergen-98
8910081	Hansa Berlin †	Lbr	1993	9,609	12,582	150	22	17	ucc	1,012 teu: ex P&O Nedlloyd Orinoco-05, APL Manaus-05, MB Caribe-04, Melbridge Berlin-03, EWL Venezuela-99, Hansa Berlin-98, Eagle Wisdom-95, Hansa Berlin-93
9236236	Hansa Brandenburg †	Lbr	2003	18,334	23,493	176	27	18	ucc	1,740 teu: ex Tiger Jade-11, Maersk Auckland-07, Hansa Brandenburg-03
9152583	Hansa Caledonia †	Deu	1998	16,927	21,563	168	27	19	ucc	1,601 teu; ex Maersk Malaga-07, Hansa Caledonia-03, CSAV Suape-98, Hansa Caledonia-98
9153612	Hansa Calypso †	Lbr	1998	16,915	21,480	168	27	19	ucc	1,601 teu: ex Maersk Pireaus-07, Hansa Calypso-00, CMA Hakata-00, Hansa Calypso-99
9152595	Hansa Castella †	Lbr	1998	16,915	21,480	168	27	19	ucc	1,601 teu: ex Damaskus-06, CMA Mersin-00, Hansa Castella-99
9148659	Hansa Centaur †	Lbr	1998	16,927	20,860	168	27	19	ucc	1,601 teu: ex Pacific Merchant-01, CMA Qingdao-00, P&O Nedlloyd Luanda-99, l/a Hansa Centaur
9152600	Hansa Centurion †	Lbr	1998	16,915	21,473	168	27	19	ucc	1,601 teu: ex Maersk Athens-07, Hansa Centurion-00, CMA Kobe-00, Hansa Centurion-99
9357860	Hansa Cloppenburg	Lbr	2007	18,327	23,396	176	27	18	ucc	1,740 teu: ex NileDutch Singapore-10, l/a Hansa Cloppenburg
9334920	Hansa Coburg	Lbr	2007	18,327	23,452	176	27	18	ucc	1,740 teu: ex NileDutch Asia-10, Hansa Coburg-07
9535096	Hansa Duburg *	Lbr	2012	18,296	23,500	175	27	18	ucc	1,740 teu
9459412	Hansa Europe	Lbr	2012	38,388	47,267	240	32		ucc	3,646 teu
9155365	Hansa Flensburg *	Lbr	2000	18,335	23,579	175	27	18	ucc	1,740 teu: ex Melbourne Express-06, CP Condor-06, Direct Condor-05, Hansa Flensburg-00
9256389	Hansa Freyburg *	Lbr	2003	18,334	23,508	175	27	19	ucc	1,740 teu: ex Maersk Volos-08, l/a H.Freyburg, l/dn Hansa Freyburg
9118501	Hansa Greifswald *	Mlt	1996	9,605	12,559	150	22	17	ucc	1,150 teu: ex EWL West Indies-04, Hansa Greifswald-96
9241449	Hansa Kirkenes *	Lbr	2002	15,988	20,463	175	27	18	ucc	1,550 teu; ex Zim Itajai-11, H Kirkenes-08, l/a Hansa Kirkenes
9226815	Hansa Kristiansand †	Lbr	2001	15,988	20,700	170	25	16	ucc	1,262 teu: ex Zim Santos-11, MOL Focus-08, Hansa Kristiansand-07, Kota Machan-03, Hansa Kristiansand-02
9256406	Hansa Langeland *	Lbr	2003	16,145	20,170	170	25	19	ucc	1,581 teu: ex MOL Accord-10, H. Langeland-06, CSAV Ilha Bela-05, Cap Pilar-04, H. Langeland-03
9323481	Hansa Limburg	Lbr	2008	18,327	23,447	175	27	18	ucc	1,740 teu
9516741	Hansa Ludswigsburg	Lbr	2011	18,358	23,305	175	27	18	ucc	1,740 teu
9256377	Hansa Magdeburg *	Lbr	2003	18,334	23,454	175	27	18	ucc	1,740 teu: ex Maersk Voshod-09, Cap Aguilar-05, Hansa Augustenburg-03
9334818	Hansa Marburg	Lbr	2007	18,327	23,419	175	27	18	ucc	1,740 teu
9373462	Hansa Meersburg	Lbr	2007	18,327	23,419	176	27	18	ucc	1,740 teu: ex NileDutch Hong Kong-10, Hansa Meersburg-07
9151864	Hansa Narvik †	Lbr	1998	15,988	20,630	170	25	20	ucc	1,270 teu: ex Kota Serikat-03, Hansa Narvik-02, Direct Eagle-00, Hansa Narvik-99
9236212	Hansa Nordburg †	Lbr	2002	18,334	23,493	175	27	18	ucc	1,740 teu: ex Cap Azul-09, P&O Nedlloyd Nelson-04, l/a Hansa Nordburg
9516765	Hansa Offenburg *	Lbr	2011	18,358	23,314	175	27	18	ucc	1,740 teu
9236224	Hansa Oldenburg †	Lbr	2002	18,334	23,493	175	27	18	ucc	1,740 teu: ex ex Delmas Kerguelen-09, l/a Hansa Oldenburg
9105920	Hansa Pacific †	Deu	1996	50,644	62,400	277	32	24	ucc	4,322 teu: ex Maersk Duisburg-10, Dorthe Maersk-04, Hansa Pacific-96
9357858	Hansa Papenburg	Lbr	2007	18,327	23,579	176	27	18	ucc	1,740 teu: ex Niledutch Shenzhen-10, Maruba Aldebaran-09, l/a Hansa Papenburg
9435246	Hansa Ravensburg	Lbr	2008	18,327	23,415	176	27	18	ucc	1,740 teu
9435258	Hansa Reggensburg	Lbr	2008	18,327	23,357	175	27	18	ucc	1,740 teu
9155377	Hansa Rendsburg *	Lbr	2000	18,335	23,992	175	27	18	ucc	1,740 teu: ex CP Jabiru-06, Direct Jabiru-05, Hansa Rendsburg-01
9060285	Hansa Riga †	Lbr	1994	16,927	21,480	168	27	19	ucc	1,400 teu: ex Maersk Marseille-07, CMA Inchon-00, P&O Nedlloyd Accra-99, Nedlloyd River Plate-97, Hansa Riga-94
9256391	Hansa Ronneburg †	Lbr	2004	18,334	23,508	175	27	19	ucc	1,740 teu: ex Maruba Parana-10, Maersk Ventspils-07, l/a H. Ronneburg
8910093	Hansa Rostock †	Lbr	1994	9,606	12,575	150	23	18	ucc	1,016 teu : ex Selandia-, l/d Fiona II

IMO#	name	flag	year	grt	dwt	loa	bm	kts	type	former names
9516753	Hansa Salzburg *	Lbr	2011	18,358	23,301	175	27	18	ucc	1,740 teu

* owned by Leonhardt & Blumberg Reederei GmbH   † managed for Hansa Hamburg Shipping International GmbH & Co KG (founded 1999 – www.hansahamburg.de) or its subsidiary HHSI Flottenfonds GmbH & Co KG (founded 2003)

Livanos Group   Greece

*Funnel: Black with red 'Λ' between 'Greek key' borders on broad white band. **Hull**: Black or grey with red boot-topping.
History: Formed 1920. **Web**: www.sunenterprises.gr*

IMO#	name	flag	year	grt	dwt	loa	bm	kts	type	former names
9458494	Achilleas	Grc	2010	81,278	158,370	274	48	15	tcr	
9305051	Aliakmon	Grc	2006	30,020	46,792	183	32	14	tco	
9275969	Amazon Beauty	Grc	2003	43,075	72,909	228	40	15	tco	
9294678	Amazon Brilliance	Grc	2005	43,075	72,910	228	40	15	tco	
9231511	Amazon Explorer	Grc	2002	43,075	72,910	228	40	15	tco	
9222132	Amazon Gladiator	Grc	2001	43,075	72,910	228	40	15	tco	
9197739	Amazon Guardian	Grc	1999	43,075	72,910	228	40	15	tco	
9228069	Atlantic Hawk	Bhs	2002	38,727	74,204	225	32	14	bbu	ex Jin Kang-04
9291119	Atlantic Hero	Bhs	2005	38,871	75,804	225	32	14	bbu	
9303106	Atlantic Horizon	Bhs	2006	38,877	75,709	225	32	14	bbu	
9294666	Axios	Grc	2006	30,020	46,792	183	32	14	tco	
9175080	Christina	Grc	1999	158,110	309,344	335	58	16	tcr	
9290921	Evros	Grc	2005	30,020	47,120	183	32	14	tco	
9247285	Ioannis Zafirakis	Bhs	2004	38,700	74,000	225	32	14	bbu	
9197909	Meandros	Grc	2000	157,883	309,498	335	58	15	tcr	
9290919	Strymon	Grc	2005	30,020	47,120	183	32	14	tco	
9346160	Tubarao	Bhs	2007	32,474	53,350	190	32	14	bbu	

*newbuildings:
operated by subsidiary Sun Enterprises Ltd, Greece, established 1968*

Lomar Shipping Ltd.   U.K.

*Funnel: Dark blue with two narrow white bands, upper interrupted by pointed peak or charterers colours. **Hull**: Black, dark blue or light grey with red boot-topping. **History**: Founded 1976 by Logothetis family to own and operate reefers. Subsidiary of Libra Group since 2003. In 2009 acquired Allocean Ltd, formed 1993 as Allco UK, subsidiary of Allco Finance Group (established 1979 in Australia), the ship-owning vehicle for Andreas Ugland & Sons, being renamed Allocean when UB Shipping acquired in 2002.
Web: www.lomarshipping.com*

IMO#	name	flag	year	grt	dwt	loa	bm	kts	type	former names
9070175	Athens Trader *	Deu	1995	29,195	35,534	196	32	20	ucc	2,227 teu: ex Belem 2-11, MSC Belem-10, Trade Harvest-02
9111474	Acapulco ‡	Gbr	1996	10,730	14,148	163	22	17	ucc	1,162 teu: ex MSC Acapulco-10, MOL Faithful-08, Sophie Schulte-05, Marfret Guyane-03, Sophie Schulte-03, CMA CGM Oyapock-02, X-press Annapurna-01, Sophie Schulte-00
9316098	Hamburg Trader	Sgp	2005	9,957	13,710	148	23	20	ucc	1,102 teu: Stadt Celle-10, Delmas Tomboti-07, I/a Stadt Celle
9162617	MSC Provider	Gbr	1999	24,836	14,169	217	27	25	ucc	1,733 teu: ex Ocean Provider-08, Hertford-08, Lykes Competitor-05, Hertford-04, ADCL Selina-01, Norasia Selina-00
9064786	Nairobi	Mlt	1995	28,892	41,624	203	31	20	ucc	2,480 teu: ex MSC Nairobi-10, MSC Amsterdam-08, Trade Selene-03, MSC Amsterdam-02, Trade Selene-01
9059963	Ocean Preface	Hkg	1993	37,550	70,255	225	32	13	bbu	ex Geeta-04, De Poterne-95
9249257	Ocean Prefect	Gbr	2003	29,323	53,035	189	32	14	bbu	ex Scandinavian Express-06, Anni Selmer-04
9254458	Ocean Prelate	Gbr	2002	30,011	52,433	190	32	15	bbu	ex John Oldendorff-05
9227998	Ocean President	Hkg	2001	28,647	50,913	190	32	14	bbu	ex Sea Angel-04
9108233	Ocean Probe	Hkg	1995	15,095	18,585	169	27	17	ucc	1,471 teu; ex TS Colombo-09, Andalusian Express-08, Young Chance-02, Choyang Challenger-01
9162605	Ocean Producer	Gbr	1999	24,836	14,367	217	27	25	ucc	1,733 teu; ex MSC Kiwi-08, Ocean Producer-08, Perth-08, CP Master-06, Lykes Master-05, Perth-04, ADCL Sultana-01, Norasia Sultana-00
9108221	Ocean Prologue	Hkg	1995	15,095	18,294	169	27	17	ucc	1,471 teu: ex Algerian Express-09, Syms Express I-08, Algerian Express-07, Young Liberty-05, Choyang Leader-01, Kuo Fah-95
9215892	Ocean Promise	Gbr	2001	26,718	33,871	210	30	22	ucc	ex Henrika Schulte-07, P&O Nedlloyd Atacama-05, I/a Henrika Schulte
9064798	Ocean Protector	Mlt	1995	28,892	41,553	203	31	20	ucc	2,480 teu: ex MSC Protector-09, Trade Eternity-04, MSC London-02, Trade Eternity-01
9070163	Sima Singapore *	Mlt	1995	29,195	35,551	196	32	20	ucc	2,227 teu: ex Ocean Promoter-11, MSC Greece-09, Trade Maple-02, MSC Hamburg-02, Trade Maple-01

IMO#	name	flag	year	grt	dwt	loa	bm	kts	type	former names
9041174	Singapore Trader	Mlt	1992	10,837	15,566	158	23	17	ucc	1,066 teu: ex Eastern Glory-11, Cape Arago-10, Silver Sky-02, Maersk Singapore-98, Silver Sky-98, Global Bahana-96

newbuildings : 6 x 2,200teu container ships [Guangzhou Wenchong SY yd # 427-30 (2015/6), 438/9 (2014)], 6 x 1,100teu containerships [Jiangsu Yiangzijiang SY, 1031-36 (2014/15)], 6 x 63,000dwt bulk carriers [COSCO Zhoushan yd # 505-510 (2014/5)]
also owns smaller container ships, tankers and LPG tankers
* managed by subsidiary Lomar Deutschland GmbH, ‡ managed by Bernhard Schulte Shipmanagement companies.

Louis Dreyfus Armateurs SAS   France

Funnel: *Black with blue 'LD & C' on white band between two narrow red bands.* **Hull:** *Black.* **History:** *Founded 1851 as Louis-Dreyfus et Cie to 1972 taking the current company name in 1995.* **Web:** *www.lda.fr*

| 9311593 | Jean LD | Atf | 2005 | 89,076 | 171,908 | 289 | 45 | 14 | bbu | |
| 9311608 | Pierre LD | Atf | 2006 | 89,070 | 171,877 | 289 | 45 | 14 | bbu | |

Joint Stock Co. LUKoil   Russia

Murmansk Shipping Co., Russia

Funnel: *Blue with white polar bear, (or white with polar bear on broad blue band) and black top.* **Hull:** *Grey, black or red with red boot-topping.* **History:** *Established in 1939 and controlled since 1998 by LUKoil (founded 1997 and controlled by Russian government).* **Web:** *www.msco.ru*

7721251	Admiral Ushakov	Rus	1979	16,257	23,169	181	23	14	bbu	(len-06)
7721237	Aleksandr Suvorov	Rus	1979	16,257	23,169	181	23	14	bbu	(len-06)
9385879	Grumant	Rus	1978	15,868	22,945	181	23	14	bbu	ex Co-operation-06, Emelyan Pugachev-06 (len/rbt-06) [ex IMO 7721287]
8837928	Ivan Papanin	Rus	1990	14,184	10,105	166	23	17	urc	
8406729	Kapitan Danilkin	Rus	1987	18,574	19,763	174	25	17	urc	
8218706	Kapitan Sviridov	Rus	1982	16,253	23,357	181	23	14	bbu	(len-06)
8610887	Khatanga	Rus	1987	14,937	23,050	158	26	15	tco	ex Bauska-04, Nord Skagerrak-87
7721263	Kuzma Minin	Rus	1980	16,257	23,169	181	23	14	bbu	(len-06)
7721249	Mikhail Kutuzov	Rus	1979	16,257	23,169	181	23	14	bbu	(len-06)
8131881	Mikhail Strekalovskiy	Rus	1981	16,253	23,357	181	23	14	bbu	(len-06)
8915794	Nataly	Rus	1993	77,470	142,498	274	43	14	tcr	ex Velez-Blanco-05
9549281	Novaya Zemlya	Rus	1977	15,868	23,645	181	23	14	bbu	ex North Way-08, Fourth-08, Aleksandr Nevskiy-08 (len/rbt-09) [ex IMO 7721213]
8131893	Pavel Vavilov	Rus	1981	16,253	23,357	181	23	15	bbu	(len-06)
9428499	Pomorye	Rus	1977	15,868	23,645	181	23	14	bbu	ex Goodwill-07, Yuriy Dolgorukiy-06 (len/rbt-07) [ex IMO 7721299]
7721225	Pyotr Velikiy	Rus	1978	16,257	23,169	181	23	14	bbu	(len-06)
9551923	Severnaya Zemlya	Rus	1977	15,868	23,645	181	23	15	bbu	ex Victory-09, Fifth-08, Dimitriy Donskoy-07 (len/rbt-09) [ex IMO 7721196]
7500401	Varzuga	Rus	1977	11,290	15,954	164	22	14	tco	ex Uikku-03
8131934	Viktor Tkachyov	Rus	1981	14,141	19,240	162	23	15	bbu	
8406705	Yuriy Arshenevskiy	Rus	1986	18,574	19,724	177	25	17	urc	

Lomar Shipping Ltd : NAIROBI : *ARO*

IMO#	name	flag	year	grt	dwt	loa	bm	kts	type	former names
9524205	Zapolyarye	Rus	1977	15,868	23,645	181	23	14	bbu	ex Perseverence-08,Third-08, Ivan Bogun-08 (len/rbt-08) [ex IMO 7721304]

newbuildings:
* owned by subsidiary NB Shipping (managed by NB Maritime Management (Cyprus) Ltd.).

Lundqvist Rederierna AB   Finland

Funnel: *White with yellow diamond interrupting thin blue band on blue edged broader yellow band.* **Hull:** *Brown or black with red boot-topping.* **History:** *Founded 1917 as Hugo Lundqvist to 1937, Arthur Karlsson to 1955 and Fraenk Lundqvist to 1959.* **Web:** *www.lundqvist.aland.fi*

IMO#	name	flag	year	grt	dwt	loa	bm	kts	type
9154232	Alfa Britannia	Bhs	1998	56,115	99,222	248	43	14	tcr
9158551	Alfa Germania	Bhs	1998	56,115	99,193	248	43	14	tcr
9255880	Alfa Italia	Bhs	2002	59,719	105,588	249	43	15	tcr
9194139	Hildegaard	Bhs	1999	56,115	99,122	248	43	14	tcr
9105906	Katja	Bhs	1995	52,067	97,220	232	42	15	tcr
9325908	Penelop	Bhs	2006	62,448	115,091	254	44	15	tcr
9238052	Sarpen	Bhs	2002	59,719	105,655	248	43	15	tcr
9116970	Thornbury	Bhs	2001	56,115	99,220	248	43	15	tcr

MACS - Maritime Carrier AG   Switzerland

Funnel: *Blue with white 'macs'.* **Hull:** *Black with white rhinoceros symbol and 'macs', some with white band above red boot-topping.* **History:** *Formed 1987.* **Web:** *www.macship.com*

IMO#	name	flag	year	grt	dwt	loa	bm	kts	type	
9138123	Amber Lagoon	Mhl	1997	23,401	31,916	187	27	17	gpc	1,486 teu
9262572	Atacama **	Mlt	2004	24,960	35,200	177	27	17	ggc	1,874 teu
9231107	Golden Isle *	Mhl	2002	23,132	30,537	193	28	19	gpc	cr: 2(100): 1,680 teu: ex Pacific Dream-09, Tasman Voyager-08, CCNI Shanghai-06, Cape Don-04
9151905	Grey Fox	Lbr	1998	23,401	33,684	192	27	16	gpc	1,486 teu
9038135	Purple Beach	Lbr	1998	23,401	31,916	187	27	17	gpc	1,486 teu

operated by MACS - Maritime Carrier Shipping GmbH & Co, Germany
* managed by Columbia Shipmanagement Deutschland, ** managed by Bertling Reederei

Marconsult Schiffahrt (GmbH & Co.) KG   Germany

Funnel: *Charterers colours.* **Hull:** *Black or grey with red boot-topping.* **History:** *Founded 2003 following end of merger between Marconsult Gesellschaft fur Reedereiberatung (formed 1991) and Johs Thode GmbH (founded 1890).* **Web:** *www.mc-schiffahrt.de*

IMO#	name	flag	year	grt	dwt	loa	bm	kts	type	
9013282	Lugano	Atg	1992	17,726	21,850	177	27	18	ggc	ex MarChallenger-12, Tasman Challenger-12, Margret Oldendorff-04, NDS Proteus-03, MSC Damas-03, Margret Oldendorff-02, CCNI Austral-99
9113458	MarCajama	Atg	1996	14,473	18,323	159	24	18	ucc	1,205 teu: ex Delmas Leixoes-08, Steindeich-07, Guatemala-06, P&O Nedlloyd Mobasa-01, Steindeich-98
9489986	MarCarolina	Atg	2010	23,548	33,741	185	30	14	bbu	

Joint Stock Co. LUKoil (Murmansk Shipping Co.) : SEVERNAYA ZEMLYA : *ARO*

IMO#	name	flag	year	grt	dwt	loa	bm	kts	type	former names
9186754	MarCherokee	Atg	1999	13,066	20,567	153	24	17	ggc	ex NileDutch Prestige-09, MSC Maracaibo-06, Georg Oldendorff-03, Libra Ecuador-02, CSAV Estambul-00, Georg Oldendorff-00
9202053	MarChicora *	Atg	2000	13,066	20,140	153	24	17	ggc	ex NileDutch Kuito-09, MSC Toulouse-07, Trina Oldendorff-04, Cielo del Caribe-03, Trina Oldendorff-01
9489974	MarColorado	Atg	2010	23,548	33,712	185	30	14	bbu	ex Colorado-12, I/a MarColorado
9161170	MarComanche	Atg	1998	13,066	20,526	153	24	17	ggc	ex Niledutch Antwerp-09, Lydia Oldendorff-08

* managed for subsidiary of HCI Capital AG

Compagnie Maritime Marfret   France
Funnel: Blue with red 'MF', black top. **Hull:** *Black or light grey with red or pink boot-topping.* **History:** *Formed 1957 as Armement Marseille-Fret SA until 1989.* **Web:** *www.marfret.fr*

IMO#	name	flag	year	grt	dwt	loa	bm	kts	type	former names
9256365	BG Freight Iberia	Fra	2003	18,334	23,579	175	27	18	ucc	1,740 teu: ex Marfret Durande-12, Delmas Forbin-06, Durande-03, I/a Hansa Sonderburg
9362334	Marfret Guyane *	Fra	2007	17,594	18,860	170	27	19	ucc	1,691 teu
9431360	Marfret Marajo *	Rif	2008	17,594	21,260	170	27	19	ucc	1,691 teu
9231157	Marfret Sormiou	Lux	2001	27,093	33,220	210	30	22	ucc	2,622 teu: ex Sormiou-10, Rodin-07, CMA CGM Rodin-06, I/a Ansgaritor

* owned by subsidiary Marseilles Fret S.A.

Martime-Gesellschaft für Maritime Diens GmbH   Germany
Funnel: Large blue 'M' or charterers colours. **Hull:** *Grey with red boot-topping.* **History:** *Formed 1994.* **Web:** *www.martime.de*

IMO#	name	flag	year	grt	dwt	loa	bm	kts	type	former names
9251846	ANL Binburra	Lbr	2002	25,587	33,940	201	30	21	ucc	2,452 teu: ex Cap Spencer-08, Alianca Bahia-07, Kassandra-02
9374595	Cap Castillo	Lbr	2008	28,097	37,763	215	30	21	ucc	2,702 teu: I/a Pandora
9308390	Cape Melville	Mhl	2005	27,786	37,883	222	30	22	ucc	2,742 teu: ex Cosco Melbourne-10, I/a Cape Melville
9308429	Cape Mollini †	Mhl	2006	27,786	37,882	222	30	22	ucc	2,742 teu: ex CMA CGM Jefferson-08, Cape Molloni-06
9308417	Cape Mondego †	Mhl	2006	27,786	37,854	222	30	22	ucc	2,742 teu: ex DAL Reunion-09, YM Mondego-07, Cape Mondego-06
9308405	Cape Moreton	Mhl	2005	27,786	38,882	222	30	22	ucc	2,742 teu: ex Cosco Dammam-10
9313242	Conti Emden *	Lbr	2006	27,915	37,900	215	30	21	ucc	2,702 teu: ex Medusa-06, Zim Norfolk-07, Conti Emden-06
9372872	CSAV Romeral	Lbr	2008	36,087	42,566	229	32	24	ucc	3,428 teu: ex Quadriga-08
9372860	CSAV Rungue	Lbr	2008	36,087	42,600	229	32	24	ucc	3,428 teu
9070644	Eyrene **	Lbr	1993	21,034	29,931	182	28	19	ucc	1,806 teu: ex Clan Tribune-07, Eyrene-05, Norasia Seoul-03, CSAV Seattle-00, P&O Nedlloyd San Jose-00, Nedlloyd San Jose-98, Eyrene-94
9166651	Gallia **	Lbr	1998	25,499	34,116	200	30	21	ucc	2,452 teu: ex Alianca Shanghai-09, P&O Nedlloyd Eagle-03, Columbus Texas-01, Gallia-98

Martime-Ges. für Maritime Diens : CSAV RUNGUE : *Hans Kraijenbosch*

IMO#	name	flag	year	grt	dwt	loa	bm	kts	type	former names
9166649	Gemini **	Lbr	1998	25,500	34,362	199	30	21	ucc	2,452 teu: ex Cap Ortegal-09, CMA CGM Delacroix-02, Cap Ortegal-00, Gemini-98
9176682	Hispania **	Deu	1996	16,211	20,976	168	28	21	ucc	1,651 teu: ex Alianca Andes-09, Cap Reinga-06, Columbus Coromandel-04, I/a Hispania
9187863	Isodora **	Lbr	1999	25,535	33,917	200	30	21	ucc	2,452 teu: ex Cap Bonavista-09, P&O Nedlloyd La Spezia-02, I/a Cap Bonavista
9187875	Isolde **	Lbr	2000	25,535	34,026	200	30	21	ucc	2,452 teu: ex Cap Delgado-09, P&O Nedlloyd Salerno-02, Cap Delgado-00
9226516	Janus **	Lbr	2001	25,535	33,894	200	30	21	ucc	2,452 teu: ex Cap Stewart-10, CSCL Yantai-08, I/a Jasmin
9226504	Jupiter **	Lbr	2001	25,535	33,917	200	30	21	ucc	2,452 teu: ex Cap Reinga-10, CSCL Longkou-07, Juturna-01
9312432	Larentia	Lbr	2005	27,915	38,121	215	30	21	ucc	2,702 teu: ex Cosco Brisbane-10
9320142	Minerva	Lbr	2005	27,915	37,900	215	30	21	ucc	2,702 teu: Cosco Panama-11
9236652	MOL Symphony **	Lbr	2001	25,535	35,976	200	30	21	ucc	2,452 teu: ex CSCL Lianyungang-08, Katharina-01
9326706	Najade	Lbr	2007	27,915	38,131	215	30	21	ucc	2,702 teu: ex Europa Bridge-09, Najade-07
9321471	Nona **	Lbr	2006	27,915	38,133	215	30	21	ucc	2,702 teu: ex YM Mundra-12, ANL Bindana-11, Nona-10
9374571	Olivia	Lbr	2007	28,050	38,096	215	30	21	ucc	2,702 teu: ex Cap Campbell-12, Americas Bridge-09, I/a Olivia
9374583	Olympia	Lbr	2007	28,050	38,013	215	30	21	ucc	2,702 teu: ex APL Chennai-11, Olympia-10, Cap Campbell-09, Olympia-07
9077290	Sea Bright **	Lbr	1994	22,738	33,520	188	28	19	ucc	1,932 teu: ex Tiger Shark-12, Sea Bright-06, Med Kaohsiung-95, Ming Bright-95
9101522	Sea Navigator	Lbr	1995	14,981	20,406	167	25	19	ucc	1,492 teu: ex CMA CGM Maasai-11,Sea Navigator-08, Indamex Mississippi-01, Sea Navigator-00, Nauplius-99, TNX Sprint-98, Zim Brazil-97, Energy-97, Nauplius-95

*managed for Conti Holdings GmbH & Co KG, ** for Gebab Conzeptions-und Emissions GmbH, † for Salamon AG*

Mediterranean Shipping Co. S.A.   Switzerland

Funnel: Cream with cream 'MSC' on black disc, narrow black band below black top. **Hull:** Black with cream 'MSC', red boot-topping.
History: Formed 1970. **Web:** www.mscgva.ch

IMO#	name	flag	year	grt	dwt	loa	bm	kts	type	former names
9625970	Anastasia	Pan	2012	51,168	92,216	230	38	14	bbu	ex MSC Anastasia-12
8519186	HMS Laurence	Nld	1985	13,769	18,155	166	23	15	ucc	950 teu: ex MSC Selma-07, Mina-02, Kuang Ming Taichung-00, Sinar Nusa-96, Tiger Cape-94, Impala-91, Ruhland-85
8512906	MSC Adele	Pan	1986	21,633	31,205	187	28	17	ucc	1,742 teu: ex Norasia Sharjah-94
9169055	MSC Adriana	Pan	1998	25,219	18,779	216	27	25	ucc	1,388 teu: ex MSC Malaysia-04, Warwick-03, ADCL Sheba-02, Norasia Sheba-00
8119376	MSC Agata	Pan	1982	20,345	28,422	174	28	18	ucc	1,346 teu: ex DAL Madagascar-03, SEAL Usaramo-00, Sea Trade-97, Usaramo-87
9123166	MSC Alabama	Pan	1996	37,518	42,966	243	32	23	ucc	3,424 teu: ex APL Italy-01, Chetumal-00, TMM Chetumal-97
9129873	MSC Alexa	Pan	1996	42,307	51,111	244	32	22	ucc	3,301 teu
9461374	MSC Alexandra	Pan	2010	153,115	165,908	366	51	25	ucc	14,000 teu
9235050	MSC Alyssa	Pan	2001	43,575	61,487	274	32	23	ucc	4,340 teu
9008603	MSC America *	Pan	1993	34,231	45,696	216	32	19	ucc	2,680 teu: ex American Senator-04, DSR-America-00
9351593	MSC Angela	Pan	2008	41,225	50,568	265	32	24	ucc	4,254 teu
9203942	MSC Aniello	Pan	2000	40,631	56,916	260	32	23	ucc	4,056 teu
8414752	MSC Anna *	Pan	1985	5,974	9,535	113	19	10	ggc	ex Palmgracht-04
8521402	MSC Annamaria	Pan	1987	21,633	31,205	187	28	17	ucc	1,742 teu: ex Norasia Al-Mansoorah-94
8609589	MSC Annick *	Pan	1988	13,315	16,768	159	23	15	ucc	928 teu: ex Promotor N-04, Contship Asia-03, NDS Benguela-02, Contship Asia-02, Tiger Wave-98, Jurong Express-96, Columbus Ohio-96
9282261	MSC Ans	Pan	2004	54,304	68,588	294	32	24	ucc	4,900 teu
8408832	MSC Antonia	Pan	1985	22,667	33,864	188	28	18	ucc	1,802 teu: ex Mixteco-94, Birthe Oldendorff-93, Ville de Castor-92, DSR Oakland-92, London Senator-91, ScanDutch Hispania-89, Commander-87, Astoria-86, World Champion-85
9484443	MSC Ariane	Pan	2012	143,521	154,503	366	48	25	ucc	13,100 teu
9162631	MSC Asli	Mlt	2000	24,836	14,150	217	27	25	ucc	1,388 teu: ex Lincoln-04, ADCL Salwa-02, Norasia Salwa-00
9263344	MSC Astrid *	Pan	2004	35,954	42,186	231	32	22	ucc	3,400 teu: ex MSC Delhi-07, Northern Distinction-04
9339296	MSC Asya	Pan	2008	107,849	112,063	337	46	26	ucc	9,200 teu

IMO#	name	flag	year	grt	dwt	loa	bm	kts	type	former names
8913447	MSC Atlantic	Pan	1991	37,071	46,975	237	32	21	ucc	2,668 teu: ex Rostock Senator-02, DSR-Rostock-00
8512891	MSC Augusta	Pan	1986	21,648	31,205	187	28	17	ucc	1,879 teu: ex Norasia Pearl-94
9484481	MSC Aurora	Pan	2012	143,521	154,494	366	48	25	ucc	13,100 teu
8413033	MSC Ayala *	Pan	1985	36,124	35,382	215	32	20	ucc	1,399 teu: ex Alen-04, Oasis Altair-03, Ligwa-03, Great Rizal-96, Oasis Altair-90
9263332	MSC Banu *	Pan	2004	35,954	42,186	231	32	22	ucc	3,400 teu: ex MSC Queensland-07, l/a Northern Devotion
9226932	MSC Barbara	Pan	2002	73,819	85,250	304	40	25	ucc	6,730 teu
9399014	MSC Beatrice	Pan	2009	151,559	156,085	366	51	25	ucc	13,300 teu
9399038	MSC Bettina	Pan	2010	151,559	156,131	366	51	25	ucc	13,300 teu
8410952	MSC Brianna *	Pan	1986	40,177	43,288	244	32	19	ucc	3,268 teu: ex Neptune Jade-97
9169043	MSC Caitlin	Pan	1998	25,219	18,779	216	27	25	ucc	1,388 teu: ex Oxford-05, ADCL Shamsaa-01, Norasia Shamsaa-00, Norasia Salome-99
9404651	MSC Camille	Pan	2009	153,092	165,844	366	51	25	ucc	13,300 teu
9102722	MSC Canberra	Pan	1995	29,181	41,583	203	31	19	ucc	2,604 teu: ex Joseph-01, TMM Puebla-01, Joseph-00, Zim Venezia I-98, Med Fos-97, Joseph Lykes-96
9339284	MSC Candice	Pan	2007	107,849	111,749	337	46	26	ucc	9,200 teu
9465289	MSC Capella	Pan	2012	141,635	141,103	366	48	24	ucc	13,102 teu
8419714	MSC Carla *	Pan	1986	35,953	43,300	241	32	20	ucc	3,044 teu: ex Hanjin Longbeach-01
9349813	MSC Carmen	Pan	2008	50,963	63,359	275	32	23	ucc	4,860 teu
9295397	MSC Carolina	Pan	2005	65,483	72,037	275	40	26	ucc	5,599 teu
8420892	MSC Chiara	Pan	1988	31,430	41,815	199	32	18	ucc	2,078 teu: ex TMM Morelos-01, Morelos-00 (conv bbu-02)
8803410	MSC Claudia *	Pan	1989	50,538	59,285	291	32	23	ucc	4,038 teu: ex Montreal-11, Maersk Montreal-10, Oriental Bay-06
8511316	MSC Clementina	Pan	1986	39,892	43,567	244	32	21	ucc	3,016 teu: ex COSCO Chiwan-09, Hyundai Innovator-06, Sydney Star I-03, Hyundai Innovator-02
9484429	MSC Clorinda	Pan	2012	153,115	165,960	366	51	25	ucc	13,050 teu
9453298	MSC Cristiana *	Pan	2011	59,835	21,500	200	32	19	mve	5,500 ceu
9399002	MSC Daniela	Pan	2008	151,559	156,301	366	51	25	ucc	13,798 teu:
9404649	MSC Danit	Pan	2009	153,092	165,517	366	46	25	ucc	13,798 teu
9461415	MSC Deila	Pan	2012	153,115	166,093	366	51	24	ucc	14,000 teu
8509375	MSC Denisse	Pan	1987	31,430	41,771	199	32	18	ucc	2,072 teu: ex MSC Alexandra-10, MSC Orinoco-99, Toluca-99, MSC Nicole-99, Toluca-98
8517891	MSC Didem *	Pan	1987	35,598	43,108	241	32	21	ucc	3,032 teu: ex Savannah-05, SCI Asha-03, Savannah-02, Hanjin Savannah-01
9202649	MSC Diego	Pan	1999	40,631	56,889	260	32	23	ucc	4,056 teu
9102746	MSC Don Giovanni *	Pan	1996	29,181	41,583	203	31	19	ucc	2,604 teu: ex Jean-96, l/a Jean Lykes
9237151	MSC Donata *	Lbr	2002	40,108	52,806	258	32	24	ucc	4,132 teu
9169029	MSC Edith	Pan	1998	25,219	18,779	216	27	25	ucc	1,384 teu: ex Lykes Crusader-05, Ayrshire-04, Safmarine Prime-04, Ayrshire-03, ADCL Samantha-01, Norasia Samantha-00
9282259	MSC Ela	Pan	2004	54,304	68,307	294	32	24	ucc	5,048 teu
9051480	MSC Elena	Pan	1994	30,971	36,887	202	32	21	ucc	2,394 teu: ex TMM Sonora-04, Houston Express-00, Sonora -99
9278143	MSC Eleni	Pan	2004	54,881	68,254	294	32	24	ucc	5,048 teu
9064750	MSC Eleonora *	Pan	1994	28,892	41,667	203	31	20	ucc	2,604 teu: ex MSC Beijing-03, Trade Cosmos-02, Sea Excellence-96, Trade Cosmos-95
8917778	MSC Eloise *	Pan	1991	37,902	44,541	241	32	18	ucc	2,440 teu: ex Maersk Niigata-07, Arafura-06
9399052	MSC Emanuela	Pan	2010	151,559	156,078	366	51	25	ucc	13,978 teu
9043756	MSC Erminia *	Pan	1993	48,220	47,384	277	32	25	ucc	3,720 teu: ex Newport Bridge-11
9304411	MSC Esthi	Lbr	2006	107,849	110,838	337	46	26	ucc	9,178 teu
9000493	MSC Eugenia	Pan	1992	53,521	65,535	275	37	24	ucc	4,469 teu: ex Bunga Pelangi-07
9401130	MSC Eva	Pan	2010	151,559	156,097	366	51	25	ucc	13,798 teu
8201648	MSC Eyra *	Pan	1982	21,586	21,370	203	25	20	ucc	1,254 teu: ex Pelineo-04, Miden Agan-02, Maersk Toronto-00, Miden Agan-97, CMA Le Cap-95, Kapitan Kozlovskiy-95 (len-89)
9279965	MSC Fabienne	Pan	2004	54,774	66,825	294	32	24	ucc	5,050 teu
8715869	MSC Federica	Pan	1990	52,181	60,189	294	32	25	ucc	4,814 teu: ex Marie Maersk-11
9369758	MSC Fiammetta	Pan	2008	66,399	73,355	277	40	24	ucc	5,762 teu
9467433	MSC Flavia	Pan	2012	140,096	139,467	366	48	22	ucc	12,400 teu
9251705	MSC Florentina	Pan	2003	75,590	85,832	304	40	25	ucc	6,750 teu
8521397	MSC Floriana	Pan	1986	21,648	31,205	187	28	17	ucc	1,879 teu: ex Princess-95, Norasia Princess-94
9401116	MSC Francesca	Pan	2008	131,771	131,356	366	46	25	ucc	11,660 teu

Mediterranean Shipping Co. S.A. : MSC ANS : *ARO*

Mediterranean Shipping Co. S.A. : MSC ASTRID : *J. Kakebeeke*

Mediterranean Shipping Co. S.A. : MSC AURORA : *Hans Kraijenbosch*

147

IMO#	name	flag	year	grt	dwt	loa	bm	kts	type	former names
8413875	MSC Gabriella	Pan	1985	21,887	31,290	189	28	17	ucc	1,893 teu: ex Safmarine Europe-11, CMBT Europe-00, Norasia Susan-94, Norasia Helga-85 (len-89)
9401141	MSC Gaia	Pan	2010	151,559	156,084	366	51	25	ucc	13,798 teu
7925493	MSC Gianna ·	Pan	1983	27,758	42,077	209	30	18	ucc	1,721 teu: ex Hellen C-03, Jolly Ebano-01, Hellen C-00, Ellen Hudig-97 (conv bbu)
9202663	MSC Gina	Pan	1999	40,631	56,889	260	32	23	ucc	4,056 teu
8408818	MSC Giorgia	Pan	1985	22,667	33,823	188	28	18	ucc	1,923 teu: ex Maya-94, DSR Yokohama-93, Tokyo Senator-91, ScanDutch Massilia-88, Azuma-87, Pacific Pride-86
8505836	MSC Giovanna	Pan	1987	27,103	25,904	178	32	18	ucc	1,762 teu: ex MSC Provence-99, Dubrovnik Express-99, Koper Express-96
8918057	MSC Grace *	Pan	1991	13,258	24,330	155	23	16	ucc	ex Putney Bridge-02, Melanesian Chief-00, Putney Bridge-99, Mikhail Tsarev-97, Zim Rio-96, Mikhail Tsarev-94, Contship Columbus-93, Mikhail Tsarev-93
9309473	MSC Heidi	Pan	2006	94,489	107,895	332	43	25	ucc	8,402 teu
8201686	MSC Hina *	Pan	1984	21,585	21,370	203	25	20	ucc	1,254 teu: ex Leixoes-03, MSC Melbourne-01, Leixoes-98, Tikhon Kiselyev-95
7925508	MSC Imma *	Pan	1983	27,758	42,077	209	30	17	ucc	1,721 teu: ex Princess Stefanie-04, Jolly Avorio-01, Princess Stefanie-00, Prince Nicolas-00, Cornelis Verolme-97
9305714	MSC Ines	Lbr	2006	107,551	108,461	337	46	25	ucc	9,115 teu
9181651	MSC Ingrid *	Pan	1999	53,208	67,678	294	32	25	ucc	4,400 teu: ex Saudi Jeddah-02
9399040	MSC Irene	Pan	2010	151,559	156,082	366	51	25	ucc	13,798 teu
8201624	MSC Iris *	Pan	1982	21,586	21,370	203	25	20	ucc	1,254 teu: ex Pelat-04, MSC Eyra-04, Pelat-04, Lisboa-02, P&O Nedlloyd Ottawa-00, Sea-Land Canada-99, Lisboa-97, Kapitan Gavrilov-95 (len-89)
8414740	MSC Isabelle *	Pan	1985	5,974	9.498	113	19	10	ggc	ex Prinsengracht-04
9398371	MSC Ivana	Pan	2009	131,771	131,489	364	46	25	ucc	11,660 teu
8419726	MSC Jade *	Pan	1986	36,514	43,293	241	32	20	ucc	3,044 teu: ex Hanjin Yokohama-01
9110975	MSC Japan	Grc	1996	37,518	42,938	243	32	23	ucc	3,424 teu: ex APL Panama-01, Manzanillo-00, TMM Manzanillo-97, Manzanillo-96, Carmen-96
8420907	MSC Jasmine	Pan	1988	31,430	41,771	199	32	18	ucc	2,078 teu: ex TMM Oaxaca-00, Contship Houston-97, Oaxaca-96
9051478	MSC Jemima	Pan	1994	30,971	36,887	202	32	20	ucc	2,394 teu: ex Nuevo Leon-05, TMM Nuevo Leon-03, Nuevo Leon-00
8709169	MSC Jenny *	Pan	1988	39,990	43,537	245	32	21	ucc	3,016 teu: ex Hyundai Commander-04, NYK Pride-04, Hyundai Commander-00
8502717	MSC Jilhan *	Pan	1986	14,068	19,560	162	25	18	ucc	1,317 teu: ex Kapitan Kurov-04, Contship Italy-93, Red Sea Europa-91, CGM Roussillon-90, Sandra K-88, Sea Merchant-88, JSS Scandinavia-88, I/a Sandra K
9304435	MSC Joanna	Lbr	2006	107,849	110,800	337	46	25	ucc	9,178 teu
8918980	MSC Jordan	Lbr	1993	37,071	47,120	237	32	21	ucc	3,005 teu: ex Sovcomflot Senator-03

Mediterranean Shipping Co. S.A. : MSC ELENI : *ARO*

IMO#	name	flag	year	grt	dwt	loa	bm	kts	type	former names
9039250	MSC Joy	Mlt	1992	30,567	31,160	203	31	19	ucc	1,939 teu: ex Northern Joy-10, Canada Senator-08, Northern Joy-01, CMA Xingang-01, Contship Mexico-99, Northern Joy-98, Sea Vigor-97, Hyundai Tacoma-96, Sea Hawk-94, Northern Joy-93
9299549	MSC Judith	Pan	2006	89,954	105,083	325	43	25	ucc	8,089 teu
9399026	MSC Kalina	Pan	2009	151,559	156,086	366	52	25	ucc	13,798 teu
9467457	MSC Katie	Pan	2012	140,096	139,287	366	48	22	ucc	12,400 teu
9467445	MSC Katrina	Pan	2012	140,096	139,439	366	48	22	ucc	12,400 teu
9062960	MSC Kerry	Pan	1995	37,323	45,530	240	32	22	ucc	3,501 teu: ex Ville de Norma-98
9351581	MSC Kim	Pan	2008	41,225	50,547	265	32	24	ucc	4,254 teu
9123154	MSC Korea	Grc	1996	37,518	42,938	243	32	23	ucc	3,424 teu: ex APL Spain-01, Sinaloa-00, TMM Sinaloa-97, Sinaloa-96
9051507	MSC Krittika	Pan	1994	30,971	36,999	202	32	21	ucc	2,394 teu: ex Lykes Commander-05, TMM Mexico-01, Sea Guardian-96, Mexico-94
9372470	MSC Krystal	Pan	2008	66,399	72,900	277	40	24	ucc	5,762 teu
8130019	MSC Lana *	Pan	1983	31,403	32,631	218	32	21	ucc	1,830 teu: ex Pacific Quest-08, Richmond Bridge-98, Hyundai Portland-97, Maersk Rotterdam-94, Richmond Bridge-93
9064748	MSC Lara *	Pan	1994	28,892	38,270	203	31	20	ucc	2,604 teu: ex MSC Bruxelles-04, Trade Apollo-02, Jadroplov Trader-95, Chesapeake Bay-95, Sea Excellence-94, Trade Sol-94
9225665	MSC Laura	Pan	2002	75,590	85,928	300	40	24	ucc	6,750 teu
9467407	MSC Lauren	Pan	2011	140,096	139,324	366	48	23	ucc	12,400 teu
9467419	MSC Laurence	Pan	2011	140,096	139,408	366	48	23	ucc	12,400 teu
9162643	MSC Lea	Mlt	2000	24,836	14,150	217	27	25	ucc	1,350 teu: ex Shropshire-04, ADCL Sabrina-01, I/a Norasia Sabrina
9320439	MSC Leigh	Pan	2006	50,963	63,411	275	32	23	ucc	4,884 teu
8608200	MSC Levina *	Pan	1989	36,420	43,140	241	32	21	ucc	2,670 teu: ex Hanjin Le Havre-98
8201674	MSC Lieselotte *	Pan	1983	21,586	21,370	203	25	20	ucc	1,438 teu: ex Aveiro-03, Tiger Sea-02, Aveiro-02, Nikolay Tikhonov-95 (len-89)
9281279	MSC Lisa	Pan	2004	54,304	68,577	294	32	24	ucc	5,048 teu
9320403	MSC Lorena	Pan	2006	50,963	59,587	261	32	24	ucc	4,860 teu
9230490	MSC Loretta	Pan	2002	73,819	85,801	304	40	25	ucc	6,750 teu
8413887	MSC Lucia	Pan	1985	21,887	31,290	189	28	17	ucc	1,893 teu: ex Safmarine Asia-11, CMBT Asia-00, Norasia Samantha-84 (len-89)
9398383	MSC Luciana	Pan	2009	131,771	131,463	364	46	24	ucc	11,660 teu
9289104	MSC Lucy	Pan	2005	89,954	104,954	325	43	25	ucc	8,034 teu
9251690	MSC Ludovica *	Pan	2003	75,590	85,882	304	40	25	ucc	6,750 teu
9225677	MSC Luisa	Pan	2002	75,590	84,920	304	40	25	ucc	6,750 teu
9305702	MSC Madeleine	Lbr	2006	107,551	108,637	337	46	25	ucc	9,100 teu: I/a Ambika
9289128	MSC Maeva	Pan	2005	89,954	105,007	325	43	25	ucc	8,034 teu
8201636	MSC Malin *	Pan	1982	21,586	21,370	203	25	20	ucc	1,438 teu: ex Pelado-04, Tavira-03, Maersk Montreal-00, Tavira-97, Kapitan Kanlevskiy -95 (len-89)
8918966	MSC Mandy	Pan	1993	37,071	47,120	237	32	21	ucc	2,668 teu: ex SCI Vaibhav-04, Bremen Senator-03

Mediterranean Shipping Co. S.A. : MSC FLAVIA : *Hans Kraijenbosch*

IMO#	name	flag	year	grt	dwt	loa	bm	kts	type	former names
9302578	MSC Mara [2]	Mhl	2006	54,214	68,165	294	32	24	ucc	5,060 teu
9304423	MSC Maria Elena	Pan	2006	107,849	108,200	337	46	25	ucc	9,178 teu: ex MSC Fiorenza-06
8616520	MSC Maria Laura	Pan	1988	36,389	42,513	229	32	20	ucc	2,631 teu: ex Sea Cheetah-00, Cap Verde-00, CGM La Perouse-98, Ville de la Fontaine-93, La Fontaine-92, CGM La Perouse-91
9155107	MSC Maria Pia	Pan	1997	29,115	40,117	196	32	22	ucc	2,808 teu: ex MSC Bremen-04, Lykes Innovator-03, Safmarine Erebus-02, CMBT Erebus-01, Northern Vision-97
9467421	MSC Maria Saveria	Pan	2011	140,096	139,295	366	48	23	ucc	12,400 teu
9226920	MSC Marianna	Pan	2002	73,819	85,250	304	40	25	ucc	6,750 teu: l/a MSC Loraine
9275971	MSC Marina	Pan	2003	73,819	85,806	304	40	24	ucc	6,750 teu
9295385	MSC Marta	Pan	2005	65,483	72,044	275	40	26	ucc	5,599 teu
9060637	MSC Martina	Pan	1993	37,398	43,436	243	32	22	ucc	3,398 teu: ex Maersk Hong Kong-97, Hansa America-93
9169031	MSC Marylena	Mlt	1998	25,219	23,487	216	27	25	ucc	1,388 teu: ex Cheshire-05, ADCL Savannah-01, Norasia Savannah-00
9181663	MSC Matilde *	Pan	1999	53,208	67,615	294	32	25	ucc	4,400 teu: ex Saudi Jubail-02
9251717	MSC Maureen	Pan	2003	75,590	85,832	304	40	25	ucc	6,750 teu
8714190	MSC Maya	Pan	1988	35,598	43,184	242	32	21	ucc	3,032 teu: ex Maersk Levant-04, MSC Jamie-02, Hanjin Seattle-98
9102710	MSC Mediterranean	Pan	1995	29,181	41,583	203	31	19	ucc	2,604 teu: ex Nautic II-04, CMA CGM Monet-02, James-00, James Lykes-96
9404675	MSC Melatilde	Pan	2010	153,092	165,478	366	51	24	ucc	14,000 teu
9226918	MSC Melissa	Pan	2002	73,819	85,250	304	40	25	ucc	6,750 teu
9256755	MSC Methoni	Pan	2003	73,819	85,250	304	40	25	ucc	6,750 teu: ex MSC Viviana-11
9169067	MSC Mia Summer	Pan	1999	25,219	18,779	216	27	25	ucc	1,388 teu: ex Buckinghamshire-05, ADCL Scarlet-01, Norasia Scarlet-00
9230488	MSC Michaela	Pan	2002	73,819	85,797	304	40	25	ucc	6,750 teu
8709640	MSC Mirella	Pan	1989	27,103	25,904	178	32	18	ucc	1,762 teu: ex Zagreb Express-99,
9060649	MSC Monica	Pan	1993	37,398	43,378	243	32	22	ucc	3,424 teu: ex Ville d'Aquila-97, Hansa Asia-93
8410940	MSC Natalia *	Pan	1986	40,177	43,403	244	32	21	ucc	3,268 teu: ex MSC California-01, Vision-99, Choyang Vision-98, Neptune Garnet-96
8918954	MSC Nederland	Pan	1992	37,071	47,120	237	32	21	ucc	2,668 teu: ex Vladivostok Mariner-03, Vladivostok Senator-02
9278155	MSC Nerissa	Pan	2004	54,881	68,178	294	32	24	ucc	5,048 teu
8509387	MSC Nicole	Pan	1989	31,430	41,787	199	32	18	ucc	2,073 teu: ex Contship America-00, Monterrey-00, MSC Lima-98, Nedlloyd Montevideo-98, Monterrey-97
9051492	MSC Nilgun	Pan	1994	30,971	36,887	202	32	20	ucc	2,394 teu: ex P&O Nedlloyd Pinta-05, Contship Inspiration-02, TMM Yucatan-01, Yucatan-00
8419702	MSC Noa *	Pan	1986	35,953	43,270	241	32	20	ucc	3,044 teu: ex Hanjin Newyork-02
9349825	MSC Nuria	Pan	2008	50,963	63,377	275	32	23	ucc	4,884 teu
9372482	MSC Oriane	Pan	2008	66,399	72,900	277	40	24	ucc	5,762 teu
9281267	MSC Ornella	Pan	2004	54,304	68,372	294	32	24	ucc	5,048 teu
9441001	MSC Paloma	Pan	2010	153,092	165,564	366	51	24	ucc	14,000 teu

Mediterranean Shipping Co. S.A. : MSC LAURENCE : *J. Kakebeeke*

IMO#	name	flag	year	grt	dwt	loa	bm	kts	type	former names
9290531	MSC Pamela	Pan	2005	107,849	110,592	337	46	26	ucc	9,178 teu
9161297	MSC Paola *	Cyp	1998	37,579	56,902	243	32	23	ucc	3,398 teu: ex MSC Christina-11, P&O Nedlloyd Chicago-04
8209729	MSC Perle *	Pan	1983	17,414	25,329	166	29	18	ucc	1,429 teu: ex Corona-03, Nautic I-02, City of Dublin-00, City of Antwerp-98, City of London-97, Pacific Span-93, Incotrans Pacific-90, ScanDutch Arcadia-90, Korean Senator-88, Corona-87, Atlantic Corona-85, Corona-84, ScanDutch Corona-84, Corona-83
8715871	MSC Pilar	Pan	1990	52,181	60,350	294	32	23	ucc	4,814 teu: ex Magelby Maersk-11, Magelby-10, Magelby Maersk-10
9339272	MSC Pina	Pan	2007	107,849	112,053	337	46	25	ucc	9,580 teu
9279977	MSC Poh Lin	Pan	2004	54,774	66,786	294	32	24	ucc	5,050 teu
9290282	MSC Rachele	Pan	2005	90,745	101,874	335	43	25	ucc	8,238 teu
9129885	MSC Rafaela	Pan	1996	42,307	51,210	243	32	22	ucc	3,301 teu
9309447	MSC Rania	Pan	2006	94,489	107,898	332	43	25	ucc	8,402 teu
9139505	MSC Rebecca *	Pan	1997	37,579	42,954	243	32	22	ucc	3,200 teu: ex Grand Concord-97
9202651	MSC Regina	Pan	1999	40,631	56,890	260	32	23	ucc	4,056 teu
9465291	MSC Regulus	Pan	2012	141,635	140,951	366	48	24	ucc	13,102 teu: I/a E.R. Regulus

Mediterranean Shipping Co. S.A. : MSC MARIA PIA : *ARO*

Mediterranean Shipping Co. S.A. : MSC PALOMA : *Hans Kraijenbosch*

IMO#	name	flag	year	grt	dwt	loa	bm	kts	type	former names
9289116	MSC Rita	Pan	2005	89,954	104,850	325	43	25	ucc	8,089 teu
8905878	MSC Ronit *	Pan	1990	18,000	26,288	177	28	18	ucc	1,743 teu; ex Conti Arabian-08, YM Cairo I-04, Conti Arabian-04, Delmas Mascareignes-03, Kaedi-02, Conti Arabian-00, Maruba Challenger-00, Conti Arabian-97, Arabian Senator-97
9461398	MSC Rosa M	Pan	2010	153,115	165,991	366	51	24	ucc	14,000 teu
9320453	MSC Rosaria	Pan	2007	50,963	63,427	275	32	23	ucc	4,884 teu
9065443	MSC Rossella	Pan	1993	37,398	43,604	243	32	22	ucc	3,424 teu: ex Ville de Carina-97, Hansa Europe-93
8714205	MSC Sabrina	Pan	1989	35,598	43,078	243	32	21	ucc	3,032 teu: ex Hanjin Oakland-98
9203965	MSC Sandra	Pan	2001	43,575	61,468	274	32	23	ucc	4,340 teu
8913411	MSC Santhya	Pan	1991	37,071	46,600	237	32	21	ucc	2,668 teu: ex Baykal Senator-04, DSR Senator-00, Vladivostok-91
9181675	MSC Sarah *	Pan	1999	53,208	67,795	294	32	24	ucc	4,400 teu: ex Saudi Yanbu-02
8715857	MSC Sariska	Pan	1990	52,181	60,639	294	32	23	ucc	4,814 teu: ex Majestic-11, Majestic Maersk-10
8511328	MSC Sena *	Pan	1986	39,892	43,567	244	32	21	ucc	3,016 teu: ex Hyundai Pioneer-06, MSC Pioneer-04, Hyundai Pioneer-04, P&O Nedlloyd Miami-03, Hyundai Pioneer-02
8913423	MSC Shannon	Pan	1991	37,071	47,120	237	32	21	ucc	2,668 teu; ex Berlin Senator-04
9036002	MSC Shaula *	Pan	1992	51,836	61,153	275	37	26	ucc	4,651 teu: ex MSC Idil-12, Hyundai Emperor-11, APL Emperor-08
9180968	MSC Sheila	Pan	1999	12,396	16,211	150	23	14	ggc	ex Atlantik Trader-05
9309459	MSC Silvana	Pan	2006	94,489	107,964	332	43	25	ucc	8,402 teu
9336048	MSC Sindy	Pan	2007	107,849	111,894	337	46	26	ucc	9,580 teu
9401104	MSC Sola	Pan	2008	131,771	131,346	366	46	25	ucc	11,660 teu
9404663	MSC Sonia	Pan	2010	153,092	165,691	366	51	24	ucc	14,000 teu
9073062	MSC Sophie	Pan	1993	37,398	43,294	243	32	22	ucc	3,424 teu: ex Maersk Colombo-97, Hansa Australia-93
9372494	MSC Soraya	Pan	2008	66,399	73,262	277	40	24	ucc	5,762 teu
9279989	MSC Stella	Pan	2004	73,819	85,680	304	40	24	ucc	6,724 teu
8918978	MSC Suez	Pan	1993	37,071	47,120	237	32	21	ucc	3,005 teu: ex Hamburg Senator-02
9290543	MSC Susanna	Pan	2005	107,849	110,623	337	46	25	ucc	9,178 teu
9008574	MSC Tasmania *	Pan	1993	34,231	45,696	216	32	19	ucc	2,700 teu; ex Japan Senator-04, Choyang Elite-98, DSR-Asia-96
9469560	MSC Teresa	Pan	2011	153,115	166,101	366	51	24	ucc	14,000 teu
9309461	MSC Tomoko	Pan	2006	94,489	107,915	332	43	25	ucc	8,402 teu
9461439	MSC Valeria	Pan	2012	153,115	165,967	366	51	24	ucc	14,000 teu
9484467	MSC Vandya	Pan	2012	143,521	154,185	366	48	24	ucc	13,050 teu
9251688	MSC Vanessa *	Pan	2003	75,590	85,844	300	40	25	ucc	6,570 teu
9299551	MSC Vittoria	Pan	2006	89,954	105,101	325	43	25	ucc	8,089 teu

newbuildings: numerous large container ships on order.
* managed by MSC Ship Management (Hong Kong) Ltd., Hong Kong
World's second largest container carrier (by vessels and capacity) - see other chartered ships in index with 'MSC' prefix

Metrostar Management Corp.   Greece

Funnel: *white with blue 'M' surmounted with red 6–pointed star and black top.* **Hull:** *Black with red boot topping.* **History:** *Formed 1996.* **Web:** *www.metrostar.gr*

IMO#	name	flag	year	grt	dwt	loa	bm	kts	type	former names
9210050	Carlotta Star	Lbr	2000	37,113	40,018	243	32	23	ucc	3,430 teu: ex Santa Carlotta-11, P&O Nedlloyd Olinda-05, I/a Santa Carlotta
9210062	Carolina Star	Lbr	2000	37,113	40,125	243	32	22	ucc	3,430 teu: ex Santa Carolina-11, P&O Nedlloyd Surat-05, Santa Carolina-01
9210074	Catalina Star	Lbr	2001	37,113	40,102	243	32	23	ucc	3,430 teu: ex Santa Catalina-11, P&O Nedlloyd Dejima-05, I/a Santa Catalina
9210086	Celina Star	Lbr	2001	37,113	40,018	243	32	23	ucc	3,430 teu: ex Santa Celina-11, P&O Nedlloyd Chusan-05, Santa Celina-01
9210098	Cristina Star	Lbr	2001	37,113	39,978	243	32	23	ucc	3,430 teu: ex Santa Cristina-11, P&O Nedlloyd Bantam-05, I/a Santa Cristina

newbuildings: four 3,600 teu container ships [SPP Shipyard]

Mibau Holding GmbH   Germany

Funnel: *White with yellow 'H' over yellow wave on blue square, narrow black top.* **Hull:** *Blue with yellow 'mibau+stema', red boot-topping* **History:** *Formed 2003.* **Web:** *www.mibau.de*

IMO#	name	flag	year	grt	dwt	loa	bm	kts	type	former names
9432206	Beltnes	Atg	2009	20,234	33,173	176	26	14	bsd	
9384370	Bulknes	Atg	2009	20,234	33,171	176	26	14	bsd	
9490105	Fitnes	Atg	2010	20,234	33,169	176	26	14	bsd	
9306029	Sandnes	Atg	2005	17,357	28,000	167	25	15	bsd	
9101730	Splittnes (2)	Pan	1994	9,855	16,073	148	21	14	bsd	ex Kari Arnhild-02
9226396	Stones	Atg	2001	17,357	28,115	166	25	14	bsd	

Jointly owned by Heidelberg Zement GmbH and Hans-Jurgen Hartmann, operated by Mibau & Stema and managed by HJH Shipmanagement

Minerva Marine Inc. Greece

Funnel: *White with light blue over dark blue trianges.* **Hull:** *Black or dark grey with blue 'MINERVA' or red with red boot-topping.*
History: *Formed 1996 and associated with Thenamaris (Ships Management) Inc.* **Web:** *wwwminervatank.gr*

IMO#	name	flag	year	grt	dwt	loa	bm	kts	type	former names
9619555	Afales	Mlt	2012	91,407	177,935	292	45	15	bbu	
9298650	Amalthea	Grc	2006	60,007	107,115	248	43	14	tcr	
9455973	Amphitrite	Grc	2010	162,203	320,137	333	60		tcr	
9352561	Andromeda	Grc	2008	162,198	321,300	333	60	-	tcr	l/a Mars Glory
9419474	Apolytares	Grc	2009	160,619	316,679	336	60		tcr	
9282792	Atalandi	Grc	2004	59,781	105,306	244	42	14	tcr	ex Valpiave-04
9442378	Fiskardo	Mlt	2010	44,348	83,448	229	32		bbu	
9198094	Minerva Alexandra	Grc	2000	58,125	104,643	244	42	14	tcr	
9309435	Minerva Alice	Grc	2006	63,619	114,850	253	44		tcr	ex Urals Star-11
9380398	Minerva Antonia	Grc	2008	29,295	46,923	183	32		tco	
9298507	Minerva Anna	Grc	2005	30,053	50,939	183	32	14	tco	
9230098	Minerva Astra	Grc	2001	59,693	105,830	248	43	15	tcr	l/a Stromness
9297333	Minerva Clara	Grc	2006	58,156	104,500	244	42	14	tcr	
9271406	Minerva Concert	Grc	2003	56,477	105,817	241	42	15	tcr	

Metrostar Management Corp : CARLOTTA STAR : *ARO*

Mibau Holding GmbH : SANDNES : *C. Lous*

IMO#	name	flag	year	grt	dwt	loa	bm	kts	type	former names
9304617	Minerva Doxa	Grc	2007	83,722	159,438	277	50	15	tcr	
9276573	Minerva Eleonora	Grc	2004	58,156	104,875	244	42	14	tcr	
9297321	Minerva Ellie	Grc	2005	58,156	103,194	244	42	14	tcr	
9296195	Minerva Emma	Grc	2003	58,118	107,597	247	42		tcr	ex Domua Aurea-11
9332157	Minerva Georgia	Grc	2008	84,914	163,417	274	50	-	tcr	
9382750	Minerva Gloria	Grc	2009	61,341	115,873	249	44		tcr	
9305855	Minerva Grace	Grc	2005	30,053	50,922	183	32	14	tcr	
9276561	Minerva Helen	Grc	2004	58,156	104,875	244	42	14	tcr	
9285861	Minerva Iris	Grc	2004	58,156	103,124	244	42	14	tcr	
9280386	Minerva Joanna	Grc	2008	29,295	46,968	183	32		tco	
9380831	Minerva Julie	Grc	2008	28,960	50,922	183	32	14	tcr	
9317951	Minerva Libra	Grc	1999	58,156	105,344	244	42	15	tcr	l/a Al Bizzia
9276597	Minerva Lisa	Grc	2004	58,156	103,622	244	42	14	tcr	
9411939	Minerva Marina	Grc	2009	81,467	157,954	274	48		tcr	
9233234	Minerva Maya	Grc	2002	57,508	105,709	244	42	14	tcr	
9255696	Minerva Nike	Grc	2004	57,301	105,330	244	42	14	tcr	
9309423	Minerva Nounou	Grc	2006	63,619	114,850	253	44		tcr	ex Urals Princess-11
9305867	Minerva Rita	Mlt	2005	30,050	50,922	183	32	14	tco	
9276585	Minerva Roxanne	Grc	2004	58,156	103,622	244	42	14	tcr	
9382762	Minerva Sophia	Grc	2009	61,341	115,873	249	44		tcr	
9304605	Minerva Symphony	Grc	2006	83,722	159,450	277	50	15	tcr	
9018008	Minerva Vaso	Grc	2006	28,960	50,921	183	32	14	tco	

Minerva Marine Inc. : MINERVA XANTHE : *Nico Kemps*

Minerva Marine Inc. : SAPIENTZA : ARO

IMO#	name	flag	year	grt	dwt	loa	bm	kts	type	former names
9411941	Minerva Vera	Grc	2009	81,478	158,016	274	48		tcr	
9307827	Minerva Virgo	Grc	2006	28,960	50,921	183	32	14	tco	
9318010	Minerva Xanthe	Grc	2006	28,960	50,921	183	32	14	tco	
9410909	Minerva Zen	Grc	2009	29,442	52.941	183	32		tco	ex Torm Lana-09
9236248	Minerva Zenia	Grc	2002	59,693	105,946	248	43	15	tcr	ex Torness-02, l/a Wrabness
9255684	Minerva Zoe	Grc	2004	57,301	105,330	244	42	14	tcr	
9455686	Monemvasia	Grc	2009	91,373	177,933	292	45	15	bbu	
9469869	Parapola	Mlt	2008	91,373	177,736	292	45	15	bbu	
9469871	Sapienza	Mlt	2008	91,373	177,730	292	45	15	bbu	
9276016	Surfer Rosa	Mlt	2004	29,327	46,719	183	32	14	tco	ex Kazbek-04

Associated with Thenamaris (Ships Management) Inc.

MISC Berhad   Malaysia

Funnel: *Blue, broad red band divided by white band with 14-pointed yellow star.* **Hull:** *Black or red with white 'MISC' or 'MISC MALAYSIA', red or grey boot-topping.* **History:** *Founded 1968 as Malaysian International Shipping Corporation Berhad to 1995, then Malaysia International Shipping Corp Berhad to 2005. Government's majority share sold in 1997 to national oil company Petronas Group (Petroleum Nasional Berhad) founded 1974.* **Web:** *www.misc.com.my*

IMO#	name	flag	year	grt	dwt	loa	bm	kts	type
9389497	Bunga Akasia	Mys	2009	25,709	37,961	180	32		tco
9389502	Bunga Alamanda	Mys	2009	25,709	37,961	180	32		tco
9389514	Bunga Allium	Mys	2010	25,709	37,961	180	32		tco
9389526	Bunga Angelica	Mys	2010	25,710	38,001	180	32		tco
9399349	Bunga Angsana	Mys	2010	25,613	38,001	180	32		tco
9399351	Bunga Aster	Mys	2010	25,710	37,933	180	32		tco
9399363	Bunga Azalea	Mys	2010	25,710	37,959	180	32		tco
9148808	Bunga Bakawali	Mys	2010	29,124	45,553	183	32		tco
9458822	Bunga Balsam	Mys	2010	29,124	45,612	183	32		tco
9458834	Bunga Banyan	Mys	2011	29,124	45,444	183	32		tco
9458858	Bunga Begonia	Mys	2011	29,124	45,444	183	32		tco
9529645	Bunga Laurel	Pan	2010	11,908	19,992	146	24	16	tco
9542130	Bunga Lavender	Pan	2010	11,908	19,997	146	24	16	tco
9542166	Bunga Lilac	Pan	2011	11,908	19,992	146	24	16	tco
9542178	Bunga Lily	Pan	2011	11,908	19,991	146	24	16	tco
9499486	Bunga Lotus	Sgp	2012	11,925	19,992	146	24	16	tco
9327140	Bunga Kantan Dua *	Sgp	2005	11,590	19,766	144	24	14	tco
9327138	Bunga Kantan Satu *	Sgp	2005	11,590	19,774	144	24	14	tco
9333228	Bunga Kantan Tiga *	Sgp	2005	11,590	19,734	144	24	14	tco
9123661	Bunga Melati Dua	Mys	1997	22,254	32,169	177	30	14	tco
9123659	Bunga Melati Satu	Mys	1997	22,254	32,127	177	30	14	tco
9172234	Bunga Melati 3	Mys	1999	22,116	31,967	177	30	14	tco
9172248	Bunga Melati 4	Mys	1999	22,116	30,000	177	30	15	tco

MISC Berhad : BUNGA MELATI DUA : *Chris Brooks*

IMO#	name	flag	year	grt	dwt	loa	bm	kts	type	former names
9172258	Bunga Melati 5	Mys	1999	22,116	31,986	177	30	15	tco	
9172260	Bunga Melati 6	Mys	2000	22,116	31,980	177	30	15	tco	
9172272	Bunga Melati 7	Mys	2000	22,116	31,972	177	30	15	tco	
9459632	Bunga Raya Tiga +	Pan	2010	40,165	50,713	260	32	24	ucc	4,334 teu: ex Cosco Kawasaki-11
9157662	Bunga Teratai	Mys	1998	21,339	24,612	184	27	19	ucc	1,735 teu: ex Bunga Teratai Satu-01
9157674	Bunga Teratai Dua	Mys	1998	21,339	24,554	184	27	19	ucc	1,735 teu
9158949	Bunga Teratai 3	Mys	1998	21,339	24,554	184	27	19	ucc	1,735 teu
9159658	Bunga Teratai 4	Mys	1998	21,339	24,561	184	27	19	ucc	1,735 teu: ex Bunga Teratai Empat-05
9030814	Puteri Delima (st)	Mys	1995	86,205	73,519	274	43	21	lng	130,405 m³
9211872	Puteri Delima Satu (st) †	Mys	2002	93,038	76,190	276	43	21	lng	137,100 m³
9030840	Puteri Firus (st)	Mys	1997	86,205	73,519	274	43	21	lng	130,405 m³
9248502	Puteri Firus Satu (st) †	Mys	2004	94,446	76,197	276	43	21	lng	137,100 m³
9030802	Puteri Intan (st)	Mys	1994	86,205	73,519	274	43	21	lng	130,405 m³
9213416	Puteri Intan Satu (st) †	Mys	2002	93.038	76,110	276	43	19	lng	137,100 m³
9261205	Puteri Mutiara Satu (st) †	Mys	2005	94,446	76,229	276	43	21	lng	137,100 m³
9030826	Puteri Nilam (st)	Mys	1995	86,211	73,519	274	43	21	lng	130,405 m³
9229647	Puteri Nilam Satu (st)	Mys	2003	94,446	76,110	276	43	21	lng	137,100 m³
9030838	Puteri Zamrud (st)	Mys	1996	86,205	73,519	274	43	21	lng	130,405 m³
9245031	Puteri Zamrud Satu (st)	Mys	2003	94,446	76,144	276	43	21	lng	137,100 m³
9293832	Seri Alam (st)	Mys	2005	95,729	73,351	283	43	19	lng	138,000 m³ l/a Puteri Intan Dua
9293844	Seri Amanah (st)	Mys	2006	95,729	83,400	283	43	19	lng	145,000 m³
9321653	Seri Anggun (st) †	Mys	2006	95,729	83,395	283	43	19	lng	145,000 m³
9321665	Seri Angkasa (st) †	Mys	2006	95,729	71,500	283	43	19	lng	145,000 m³
9329679	Seri Ayu (st)	Mys	2007	95,729	83,365	283	43	19	lng	145,000 m³
9331634	Seri Bakti (st) †	Mys	2007	105,335	90,065	290	47	19	lng	152,300 m³
9331660	Seri Balhaf	Mys	2009	107,633	91,201	295	47	19	lng	152,300 m³
9331672	Seri Balqis	Mys	2009	107,633	91,198	295	47	19	lng	152,300 m³
9331646	Seri Begawan (st) †	Mys	2007	105,335	89,953	290	47	19	lng	152,300 m³
9331658	Seri Bijaksana (st) †	Mys	2008	104,881	89,953	290	47	19	lng	152,300 m³
9567661	Seroja Lima +	Pan	2011	86,682	90,388	316	46	24	ucc	8,540 teu
7428469	Tenaga Dua (st) †	Mys	1981	80,510	70,949	281	42	20	lng	130,000 m³
7428433	Tenaga Empat (st)†	Mys	1981	80,510	71,555	281	42	20	lng	130,000 m³
7328445	Tenaga Lima (st) †	Mys	1981	80,510	72.319	281	42	20	lng	130,000 m³
7428471	Tenaga Tiga (st) †	Mys	1981	80,510	70,949	281	42	20	lng	130,000 m³ laid up 2010

newbuildings:

managed by subsidiary AET Inc, * by MSI Ship Management Pte Ltd, Singapore or † by parent Petronas Tankers Sdn Bhd, Malaysia
+ chartered from Japanese owners

AET Inc. Ltd., Bermuda

Funnel: White with grey eagle-head symbol on grey edged blue disc. **Hull:** Orange with red boot-topping. **History:** Subsidiary of MISC founded 1994 as American Eagle Tankers by Neptune Orient Lines and acquired in 2003. **Web:** www.aetweb.com

IMO#	name	flag	year	grt	dwt	loa	bm	kts	type	former names
9273337	Bunga Kasturi *	Mys	2003	156,967	299,999	330	60	15	tcr	
9292632	Bunga Kasturi Dua *	Mys	2005	157,008	300,542	330	60	15	tcr	
9337133	Bunga Kasturi Empat *	Mys	2007	156,967	300,325	330	60	17	tcr	
9327554	Bunga Kasturi Enam *	Mys	2008	157,209	299,319	330	60	15	tcr	
9327114	Bunga Kasturi Lima *	Mys	2007	157,209	300,246	330	60	17	tcr	
9302968	Bunga Kasturi Tiga *	Mys	2006	156,967	300,398	330	60	17	tcr	
9131125	Bunga Kelana Dua *	Mys	1997	57,017	105,575	244	42	14	tcr	
9131113	Bunga Kelana Satu *	Mys	1997	57,017	105,575	244	42	14	tcr	
9178331	Bunga Kelana 3 *	Mys	1998	57,017	105,784	244	42	14	tcr	
9178343	Bunga Kelana 4 *	Mys	1999	57,017	105,815	244	42	14	tcr	
9169706	Bunga Kelana 5 *	Mys	1999	57,017	105,811	244	42	14	tcr	
9169718	Bunga Kelana 6 *	Mys	1999	57,017	105,400	244	42	14	tcr	
9284582	Bunga Kelana 7 *	Mys	2004	58,194	105,193	244	42	14	tcr	
9284594	Bunga Kelana 8 *	Mys	2004	58,194	105,193	244	42	14	tcr	
9292979	Bunga Kelana 9 *	Mys	2004	58,194	105,200	244	42	14	tcr	
9189122	Bunga Kenanga *	Mys	2000	40,037	73,083	229	32	15	tcr	ex Four Cutter-00
9182928	Eagle Albany	Sgp	1998	57,929	107,160	247	42	14	tcr	
9182942	Eagle Anaheim	Sgp	1999	57,929	107,160	247	42	14	tcr	
9182930	Eagle Atlanta *	Sgp	1999	57,929	107,160	247	42	14	tcr	
9176034	Eagle Augusta	Sgp	1999	58,156	105,345	244	42	14	tcr	
9008744	Eagle Auriga	Sgp	1993	55,962	102,352	241	42	14	tcr	ex Neptune Auriga-94
9176022	Eagle Austin	Sgp	1998	58,156	105,000	244	42	14	tcr	
9111632	Eagle Baltimore	Sgp	1996	57,456	99,405	253	44	14	tcr	
9111644	Eagle Beaumont	Sgp	1996	57,456	99,448	253	44	14	tcr	

IMO#	name	flag	year	grt	dwt	loa	bm	kts	type	former names
9123192	Eagle Birmingham	Sgp	1997	57,456	99,343	253	44	14	tcr	
9111620	Eagle Boston	Sgp	1996	57,456	99,328	253	44	14	tcr	
9042441	Eagle Carina	Sgp	1993	52,504	95,639	247	42	14	tcr	ex Neptune Carina-94
9042439	Eagle Centaurus	Sgp	1992	52,504	95,644	247	42	14	tcr	ex Neptune Centaurus-94
9136046	Eagle Columbus	Sgp	1997	57,949	107,166	247	42	14	tcr	
9042453	Eagle Corona	Sgp	1993	52,504	79,993	235	42	14	tcr	ex Neptune Corona-94
9417024	Eagle Kangar	Sgp	2010	60,379	107,481	244	42		tcr	
9422196	Eagle Kinabalu	Sgp	2011	60,379	107,481	244	42		tcr	
9422201	Eagle Kinarut	Sgp	2011	60,379	107,481	244	42		tcr	
9417892	Eagle Klang	Sgp	2010	60,379	107,481	244	42		tcr	
9417012	Eagle Kuantan	Sgp	2010	60,379	107,481	244	42		tcr	
9417000	Eagle Kuching	Sgp	2009	60,379	107,481	244	42		tcr	
9518892	Eagle Louisiana	Sgp	2011	60,379	107,481	244	42		tcr	
9443865	Eagle Miri +	Pan	2008	30,027	46,195	183	32	14	tco	
9051351	Eagle Otome	Sgp	1994	52,504	95,663	247	42	14	tcr	ex Neptune Otome-00
9598256	Eagle Paraiba	Mys	2012	62,912	105,153	248	42	14	tcs	
9598268	Eagle Parana	Mys	2012	62,912	105,048	248	42	14	tcs	
9161259	Eagle Phoenix	Sgp	1998	56,346	106,127	241	42	14	tcr	ex Paola I-01
9594822	Eagle San Antonio	Sgp	2012	80,783	157,661	274	49	14	tcr	
9594834	Eagle San Diego	Sgp	2012	80,783	157,900	274	49	14	tcr	
9594846	Eagle San Juan	Sgp	2012	80,872	157,850	274	49	14	tcr	
9594858	Eagle San Pedro	Sgp	2012	80,782	157,850	274	49	14	tcr	
9198082	Eagle Seville	Sgp	1999	58,125	105,365	244	42	14	tcr	ex Minerva Emma-08
9412995	Eagle Stavanger	Pan	2009	55,898	105,355	229	42		tcr	
9235000	Eagle Stealth	Mhl	2001	56,346	105,322	239	42	14	tcr	ex Nord Stealth-07
9413004	Eagle Sydney	Pan	2009	55,898	105,419	229	42	14	tcr	
9051363	Eagle Subaru *	Sgp	1994	52,504	95,675	247	42	14	tcr	ex Neptune Subaru-99
9257802	Eagle Tacoma	Sgp	2002	57,950	107,123	247	42	14	tcr	
9253076	Eagle Tampa	Sgp	2003	58,166	107,123	247	42	14	tcr	
9518907	Eagle Texas	Mhl	2011	60,379	107,481	244	42	14	tcr	
9250892	Eagle Toledo	Sgp	2002	58,166	107,092	247	42	14	tcr	
9360453	Eagle Torrance	Sgp	2007	58,168	107,123	247	42	14	tcr	
9250907	Eagle Trenton	Sgp	2003	58,166	107,123	247	42	14	tcr	
9253064	Eagle Tucson	Sgp	2003	58,166	107,123	247	42	14	tcr	
9360465	Eagle Turin	Sgp	2008	58,168	107,123	247	42	14	tcr	
9292486	Eagle Valencia	Sgp	2005	160,046	306,999	333	58	15	tcr	
9597240	Eagle Vancouver	Sgp	2013	161,974	320,299	333	60	15	tcr	
9597252	Eagle Varna	Sgp	2013	161,974	320,000	333	60	15	tcr	
9292498	Eagle Venice	Mys	2005	160,046	309,164	333	58	15	tcr	
9234654	Eagle Vermont	Sgp	2002	161,233	318,338	333	60	16	tcr	

MISC Berhad (AET Inc. Ltd.) : EAGLE TORRANCE : *Chris Brooks*

157

IMO#	name	flag	year	grt	dwt	loa	bm	kts	type	former names
9290775	Eagle Vienna	Sgp	2004	161,233	306,999	333	60	15	tcr	
9230878	Eagle Virginia	Sgp	2002	161,233	318,338	333	60	16	tcr	
9412036	Stealth Skyros †	Mhl	2011	62,884	115,000	250	44		tcr	

newbuildings: further 320,000dwt crude oil tankers (Daewoo)
* owned by AET Petroleum Tanker, Malaysia: vessels managed by AET Shipmanagemen Pte. Ltd. Singapore
managed for : † Stealth Maritime Corp SA (Brave Maritime Corp Inc), Greece. + Pos Maritime, Norway

Mitsui OSK Lines Japan

Funnel: *Bright red.* **Hull:** *Light blue with white 'MOL' or grey with green waterline and red boot-topping.* **History:** *Formed 1884 as Osaka Shosen Kaisha, merged in 1964 with Mitsui Senpaku KK to form Mitsui OSK. Merged 1999 with Navix Line which had been formed by 1989 merger of Japan Line (founded 1930 and 1964 merger of Nitto Shosen KK with Daido Kaiun KK) and Yamashita-Shinnihon Steamship Co (founded 1903 and 1964 merger of Yamashita Kisen KK with Shinnihon Kisen KK).* **Web:** www.mol.co.jp

IMO#	name	flag	year	grt	dwt	loa	bm	kts	type	former names
9370202	Alstroemeria	Pan	2010	49,720	64,500	210	37	15	bwc	
9397999	Amethyst Ace †	Cym	2008	60,143	18,700	200	32	20	mve	6,334 ceu
9370812	Anemona	Pan	2010	39,895	49,442	200	32	15	bwc	
9297987	Aquamarine Ace	Cym	2008	60,143	18,772	200	32	20	mve	6,334 ceu
9150339	Aquarius Ace *	Pan	1998	36,615	14,353	175	29	15	mve	3,027 ceu
8600208	Asian Spirit †	Lbr	1988	53,578	21,835	200	32	18	mve	5,501 ceu: ex Hual Tribute-04
9182368	Astral Ace	Pan	2000	36,615	14,280	175	29	18	mve	3,027 ceu
9542283	Azalea Ace	Lbr	2011	43,810	15,154	180	30	18	mve	3,930 ceu
9278636	Azul Cielo	Pan	2005	101,933	203,195	300	50	14	bbu	
9271561	Azul Fortuna	Pan	2005	101,933	203,095	300	50	14	bbu	
9403281	Bergamot Ace	Cym	2010	42,401	14,996	186	28	19	mve	4,216 ceu
9207120	Bravery Ace *	Pan	2000	52,276	17,686	189	32	20	mve	4,518 ceu
9598012	Brilliant Ace	Cym	2011	59,022	18,448	200	32	17	mve	6,172 ceu
9103180	Camellia Ace *	Pan	1994	55,336	18,938	200	32	18	mve	
9544920	Carnation Ace	Cym	2011	60,975	16,416	200	32	21	mve	6,282 ceu
9544918	Cattleya Ace †	Cym	2011	60,975	16,384	200	32	21	mve	6,282 ceu
9328728	Celestial Wing *	Pan	2005	45,232	14,962	180	30	19	mve	4,537 ceu
9363950	Clover Ace *	Bhs	2008	60,065	17,280	200	32	20	mve	6,287 ceu
9182356	Comet Ace	Pan	2000	36,615	14,283	175	29	18	mve	3,027 ceu
9153563	Cosmos Ace *	Pan	1998	46,346	15,439	182	31	19	mve	4,095 ceu
9051375	Cougar Ace †	Sgp	1993	55,328	18,922	200	32	19	mve	5,542 ceu
9252204	Courageous Ace †	Pan	2003	56,439	19,927	198	32	20	mve	5,281 ceu
9539224	Crystal Ace †	Mhl	2011	60,131	18,381	161	27	16	mve	6,312 ceu
9363118	Crystal Pioneer	Cym	2008	49,720	64,510	210	37	15	bwc	
9370800	Dalia	Jpn	2008	39,894	49,411	200	32	15	bwc	
9561265	Elegant Ace	Cym	2010	58,939	18,833	200	32	19	mve	6,233 ceu
9539236	Emerald Ace	Mhl	2012	60,154	18,334	200	32	19	mve	6,312 ceu
9293571	Eminent Ace *	Pan	2005	58,616	18,947	200	32	20	mve	5,213 ceu
9606479	Eternal Ace *	Pan	2011	59,022	18,418	200	32	19	mve	6,163 ceu
9293595	Euphony Ace	Pan	2005	58,631	18,944	200	32	20	mve	5,214 ceu
9293911	Felicity Ace *	Pan	2006	60,118	17,738	200	32	20	mve	5,232 ceu
9293894	Firmament Ace *	Pan	2006	60,118	17,713	200	32	20	mve	5,232 ceu
9293662	Freedom Ace †	Pan	2005	60,175	19,093	200	32	20	mve	6,354 ceu
9209271	Frontier Ace †	Pan	2000	52,276	17,693	189	32	20	mve	4,518 ceu
9624237	Galaxy Ace	Lbr	2012	59,583	22,250	200	32	19	mve	6,233 ceu

Mitsui OSK Lines : ALSTROEMERIA : *Nico Kemps*

IMO#	name	flag	year	grt	dwt	loa	bm	kts	type	former names
9502568	Genciana	Pan	2008	40,269	49,775	200	32	15	bwc	
9610418	Genuine Ace	Lbr	2012	59,022	18,900	200	32	19	mve	6,163 ceu
9561277	Glorious Ace *	Cym	2010	58,939	18,836	200	32	19	mve	6,233 ceu
9047996	Harmony Ace *	Pan	1992	47,519	14,256	180	32	19	mve	4,774 ceu
9252216	Heroic Ace *	Pan	2002	56,439	19,879	198	32	20	mve	5,281 ceu
9515474	Iris Ace *	Cym	2011	43,709	14,349	188	28	19	mve	4,064 ceu
9363948	Lavender Ace †	Bhs	2008	60,065	17,262	200	32	20	mve	6,287 ceu
9293650	Liberty Ace †	Pan	2004	60,175	19,106	200	32	20	mve	6,354 ceu
9406465	London Courage	Mhl	2007	104,721	206,366	300	50	14	bbu	
9110107	Luminous Ace	Phl	1995	45,796	15,181	188	31	18	mve	4,095 ceu
9303118	Luminous Sky	Pan	2005	45,011	54,514	204	37	15	bwc	ex Mulberry-10
9014808	Maple Ace II *	Lbr	1992	38,349	15,361	188	28	18	mve	3,241 ceu
8610526	Marina Ace †	Pan	1987	54,332	17,319	200	32	19	mve	5,272 ceu
9267675	Martorell	Pan	2003	57,789	19,531	200	32	20	mve	5,342 ceu
9426386	Marguerite Ace	Cym	2009	60,067	17,237	200	32	19	mve	5,214 ceu
9293519	Marvelous Ace †	Pan	2006	59,422	18,900	200	32	20	mve	6,141 ceu
9591052	Mercury Ace	Pan	2011	59,409	19,110	200	32	19	mve	6,109 ceu
9209518	Meridian Ace †	Pan	2000	55,878	20,144	200	32	19	mve	5,059 ceu
9561289	Mermaid Ace †	Pan	2010	58,939	18,828	200	32	19	mve	6,233 ceu
9293521	Miraculous Ace †	Cym	2006	59,422	19,381	200	32	20	mve	6,141 ceu
9245005	MOL Advantage	Pan	2001	66,332	66,532	279	40	25	ucc	5,220 teu: ex APL Advantage-08, MOL Advantage-08
9101596	MOL Bravery	Pan	1995	41,114	39,788	245	32	23	ucc	2,852 teu: ex Alligator Bravery-01
9321251	MOL Celebration †	Bhs	2008	86,692	90,649	316	46	25	ucc	8,110 teu
9321249	MOL Charisma	Bhs	2008	86,692	90,649	316	46	25	ucc	8,110 teu: ex APL France -10, MOL Charisma-07
9358761	MOL Comfort *	Bhs	2008	86,692	90,613	316	46	25	ucc	8,110 teu: ex APL Russia-12
9339662	MOL Competence †	Pan	2008	86,692	90,613	316	46	25	ucc	8,110 teu
9388352	MOL Continuity	Pan	2008	88,089	90,466	320	46	25	ucc	8,110 teu: ex APL Finland-12
9388340	MOL Cosmos	Pan	2008	88,089	90,466	320	46	25	ucc	8,110 teu
9321263	MOL Courage	Bhs	2008	86,692	90,634	316	46	25	ucc	8,110 teu: ex APL Poland-12, l/a MOL Comfort
9321237	MOL Creation †	Bhs	2007	86,692	90,678	316	46	25	ucc	8,110 teu
9333840	MOL Earnest	Pan	2007	54,098	56,100	294	32	24	ucc	4,803 teu: ex APL Earnest-10, MOL Earnest-08
9251365	MOL Efficiency †	Pan	2002	53,822	63,160	294	32	24	ucc	4,646 teu
9261712	MOL Encore †	Pan	2003	53,096	61,441	294	32	24	ucc	4,578 teu
9261724	MOL Endeavor †	Pan	2003	53,096	61,441	294	32	24	ucc	4,578 teu
9333852	MOL Endowment †	Pan	2007	54,098	62,949	294	32	24	ucc	4,803 teu
9261736	MOL Endurance †	Pan	2003	53,096	61,441	294	32	24	ucc	4,578 teu
9261748	MOL Enterprise †	Pan	2004	53,600	61,441	294	32	24	ucc	4,578 teu
9251377	MOL Excellence	Pan	2003	53,822	63,096	294	32	24	ucc	4,636 teu
9251389	MOL Expeditor *	Pan	2003	53,822	63,098	294	32	24	ucc	4,646 teu: ex APL Expeditor-10, MOL Expeditor-08
9333838	MOL Experience	Pan	2007	54,098	62,953	294	32	23	ucc	4,803 teu: ex APL Experience-10, MOL Experience-08
9333826	MOL Explorer	Pan	2007	53,822	62,958	294	32	24	ucc	4,803 teu
9251391	MOL Express *	Pan	2003	53,822	63,046	294	32	24	ucc	4,646 teu

Mitsui OSK Lines : EMERALD ACE : *J. Kakebeeke*

IMO#	name	flag	year	grt	dwt	loa	bm	kts	type	former names
9245017	MOL Integrity	Pan	2001	66,332	66,800	279	40	25	ucc	5,220 teu
9110042	MOL Loire *	Pan	1995	58,531	61,470	300	37	24	ucc	4,706 teu: ex APL Ningpo-09, MOL Loire-02, La Loire-01
9415727	MOL Maestro †	Mhl	2010	78,316	79,423	302	43	24	ucc	6,724 teu
9424900	MOL Magnificence	Mhl	2010	78,316	79,417	302	43	24	ucc	6,724 teu
9424912	MOL Majesty †	Mhl	2010	78,316	79,443	302	43	24	ucc	6,724 teu
9475648	MOL Maneuver †	Mhl	2011	78,316	79,423	302	43	24	ucc	6,724 teu
9574612	MOL Marvel †	Mhl	2010	78,316	79,460	302	43	24	ucc	6,724 teu
9424924	MOL Matrix †	Mhl	2010	78,316	79,312	302	43	24	ucc	6,724 teu
9424936	MOL Maxim	Mhl	2010	78,316	79,373	302	43	24	ucc	6,724 teu
9475650	MOL Mission †	Mhl	2011	78,316	79,491	302	43	24	ucc	6,724 teu
9475636	MOL Modern	Mhl	2011	78,316	79,283	302	43	24	ucc	6,724 teu
9475624	MOL Motivator	Mhl	2011	78,316	79,278	302	43	24	ucc	6,724 teu
9307047	MOL Paradise	Pan	2005	71,902	72,968	293	40	25	ucc	6,350 teu: ex APL Paradise-12, MOL Paradise-11
9307059	MOL Paramount	Pan	2005	71,892	72,968	293	40	25	ucc	6,350 teu
9307035	MOL Partner	Pan	2005	71,902	72,968	293	40	25	ucc	6,350 teu
9250971	MOL Performance *	Pan	2001	74,071	74,453	294	40	27	ucc	6,402 teu
9236470	MOL Precision	Pan	2002	71,902	73,063	293	40	25	ucc	6,350 teu: ex APL Precision-12, MOL Precision-11
9444261	MOL Premium	Pan	2008	71,776	72,912	293	40	25	ucc	6,350 teu
9250995	MOL Priority *	Pan	2002	74,071	74,453	294	40	26	ucc	6,402 teu
9250983	MOL Progress *	Pan	2002	71,902	74,453	293	40	25	ucc	6,402 teu
9236482	MOL Promise	Pan	2002	71,902	73,063	293	40	25	ucc	6,350 teu
9245029	MOL Solution	Pan	2001	71,902	72,300	293	40	25	ucc	5,220 teu
9087946	MOL Tyne *	Pan	1995	59,622	63,440	299	37	24	ucc	4,713 teu: ex APL Chiwan-12, MOL Tyne-02, Tyne-01
9187289	Mona Century *	Pan	2000	87,523	172,036	289	45	15	bbu	
9008689	Mona Liberty †	Sgp	1992	77,195	151,533	273	43	14	bbu	ex Kohju-01
9201736	Mona Linden *	Jpn	2000	84,507	170,473	289	45	14	bbu	
9177052	Mosel Ace	Pan	2000	37,237	12,761	177	31	19	mve	3,919 ceu
9584059	Neptune Ace †	BHs	2010	59,006	18,436	200	32	19	mve	6,172 ceu
9539212	Onyx Ace †	Cym	2012	60,131	18,529	200	32	19	mve	6,312 ceu
9539183	Opal Ace †	Cym	2011	60,131	18,507	200	32	19	mve	6,312 ceu
9381677	Orchid Ace	Jpn	2008	59,262	17,289	200	32	20	mve	6,287 ceu
9270567	Pacific Glory †	Pan	2004	118,230	233,694	317	55	17	bor	
9207388	Palmela †	Pan	2000	55,926	20,581	200	32	19	mve	5,080 ceu
9293648	Paradise Ace	Pan	2004	60,175	19,080	200	32	20	mve	6,354 ceu
9051818	Pearl Ace *	Pan	1994	45,796	15,194	188	31	18	mve	4,095 ceu
9150341	Pegasus Ace *	Pan	1998	36,615	14,348	175	29	19	mve	3,027 ceu
9014810	Planet Ace *	Pan	1992	38,349	15,327	188	28	18	mve	3,241 ceu
9153549	Polaris Ace *	Pan	1997	46,346	15,522	182	31	19	mve	4,095 ceu
9554200	Precious Ace	Cym	2010	59,402	19,045	200	32	19	mve	6,124 ceu
9213454	Prestige Ace †	Pan	2000	55,878	20,202	200	32	19	mve	5,059 ceu
9355185	Primrose Ace †	Cym	2007	59,952	17,339	200	32	20	mve	5,213 ceu

Mitsui OSK Lines : MOL COSMOS : *Chris Brooks*

IMO#	name	flag	year	grt	dwt	loa	bm	kts	type	former names
9267687	Progress Ace	Pan	2003	57,789	19,512	200	32	20	mve	5,342 ceu
9267699	Prominent Ace	Pan	2004	57,789	19,550	200	32	20	mve	5,342 ceu
8712324	Queen Ace †	Pan	1988	55,423	18,777	200	32	19	mve	5,542 ceu
9130614	Rubin Artemis †	Pan	1997	77,065	151,982	273	43	14	bbu	
9146584	Rubin Phoenix	Pan	1997	83,658	171,080	289	45	14	bbu	
9476757	Ruby Ace	Cym	2010	60,148	18,724	200	32	19	mve	6,334 ceu
9279757	Ruby Express **	Pan	2004	57,468	106,516	241	42	14	tco	
9338876	Salvia Ace	Cym	2008	42,401	15,013	186	28	19	mve	4,216 ceu
9409481	Sanderling Ace †	Cym	2007	58,684	18,865	200	32	19	mve	5,222 teu
9051806	Sapphire Ace	Pan	1993	45,796	15,204	188	31	18	mve	4,055 ceu
9519092	Sincerity Ace	Pan	2009	59,408	19,265	200	32	19	mve	6,141 ceu
8708244	Solar Wing *	Lbr	1988	41,604	13,224	187	32	19	mve	4,518 ceu
9252228	Splendid Ace †	Pan	2003	56,439	19,893	198	32	19	mve	5,281 ceu
9102148	Sunny Amazon *	Lbr	1995	60,133	62,905	300	37	23	ucc	4,743 teu: ex MOL Maas-10, Maas-01
9102150	Sunny Oasis *	Pan	1995	60,133	62,905	300	37	24	ucc	4,743 teu: ex APL Rhine-10, Hyundai Dubai-09, APL Dubai-08, MOL Rhine-02, Rhine-01
9338864	Sunlight Ace	Bhs	2009	58,911	18,855	200	32	19	mve	5,220 ceu
9338840	Sunrise Ace	Bhs	2009	58,685	18,864	200	32	19	mve	5,220 ceu
9338852	Sunshine Ace †	Bhs	2009	58,917	18,858	200	32	19	mve	5,220 ceu
9610391	Supreme Ace *	Pan	2011	59,022	18,384	200	32	19	mve	6,163 ceu
9338620	Swallow Ace *	Bhs	2007	58,685	18,864	200	32	20	mve	6,237 ceu
9338826	Swan Ace *	Bhs	2008	58,685	18,867	200	32	20	mve	6,237 ceu
9338838	Swift Ace *	Bhs	2008	58,685	18,865	200	32	20	mve	6,237 ceu
9213169	Tachibana	Pan	2000	83,528	154,324	275	47	14	bbu	
9561253	Tranquil Ace	Cym	2009	58,939	18,840	200	32	19	mve	6,233 ceu
9519121	Triton Ace	Pan	2009	60,876	22,723	200	32	19	mve	6,502 ceu
9209506	Triumph Ace †	Pan	2000	55,880	20,131	194	32	20	mve	5,059 ceu
9205990	Tsunomine	Pan	2000	83,496	152,400	275	47	14	bbu	
9370214	Universal Pioneer	Pan	2010	49,720	64,538	210	37	15	bwc	
9293636	Utopia Ace	Pan	2004	60,175	19,086	200	32	20	mve	6,354 ceu
9610420	Valiant Ace	Mhl	2012	59,022	18,143	200	32	20	mve	6,163 ceu
9610406	Victorious Ace	Pan	2011	59,022	18,396	200	32	20	mve	6,163 ceu
9355197	Wisteria Ace †	Cym	2007	59,952	17,325	200	32	20	mve	6,287 ceu

newbuildings:

*owned or managed by MOL Ship Management Co. Ltd., Japan, † by New Asian Shipping Co., Hong Kong or ** by Thome Ship Management, Singapore. One of the world's largest shipping groups with many subsidiaries owning or managing over 500 vessels. Only the largest container, tanker, bulk carrier and vehicle carriers are listed, in addition to which there are many other bulk carriers, wood-chip carriers, product tankers and lng carriers.*

MOL Ocean Expert Co., Japan

Funnel: *Bright red.* **Hull:** *Light blue with white 'MOL' or grey with green waterline and red boot-topping founded 2011 by merger of MOL Tankship Management Co (founded 1917) and International Marine Transport Co. (founded 1937)*

IMO#	name	flag	year	grt	dwt	loa	bm	kts	type	former names
9307176	Al Deebel (st)	Bhs	2005	95,824	78,594	283	43	20	lng	
9294331	Altair Trader *	Iom	2005	160,216	299,985	333	60	15	tcr	
9191400	Asian Progress II **	Sgp	2000	160,079	314,026	333	60	15	tcr	
9294290	Asian Progress III **	Sgp	2004	159,875	306,352	333	60	14	tcr	
9316701	Asian Progress IV **	Bhs	2006	160,292	313,992	333	60	15	tcr	
9397157	Azumasan +	Sgp	2010	159,943	302,241	333	60	15	tcr	
9197832	Bandaisan **	Pan	2000	149,282	281,037	330	60	15	tcr	
9177143	Diamond Jasmine	Pan	1999	152,041	281,050	330	60	16	tcr	
9562685	Chokaisan **	Iom	2011	160,137	308,221	333	60	16	tcr	
9410387	Duqm **	Pan	2008	160,160	310,084	333	60	16	tcr	
9562697	Gassan **	Pan	2012	160,137	308,209	333	60	16	tcr	
9405227	Grand Sea †	Hkg	2008	160,216	310,444	333	60	15	tcr	
9376878	Hakkaisan +	Jpn	2009	160,080	309,916	333	60	15	tcr	
9535058	Hakusan	Iom	2011	160,059	305,360	333	60	16	tcr	
9607875	Horaisan	Pan	2013	160,202	303,400	333	60	15	tcr	
9191412	Ibukisan **	Pan	2000	160,079	299,999	330	60	15	tcr	
9191424	Ikomasan +	Pan	2000	160,079	299,986	333	60	15	tcr	
9262754	Iwatesan **	Jpn	2003	159,912	300,667	333	60	16	tcr	
9250622	Kaimon II **	Pan	2002	160,079	314,014	333	60	15	tcr	
9259331	Kaminesan **	Jpn	2003	159,813	303,896	333	60	16	tcr	
9324100	Kasagisan **	Bhs	2006	160,216	302,478	333	43	15	tcr	
9513402	Kazusa **	Mhl	2010	160,151	310,406	333	60	15	tcr	
9329863	Kashimasan	Bhs	2007	159,840	306,033	333	60	15	tcr	
9294240	Katsuragisan +	Pan	2005	160,292	311,620	333	60	15	tcr	
9562673	Libra Trader	Mhl	2011	160,149	310,339	333	60	15	tcr	
9567659	Omega Trader **	Iom	2011	160,059	305,206	333	60	15	tcr	
9294305	Oriental Jade +	Pan	2004	159,875	306,352	333	60	14	tcr	
9294252	Otowasan **	Pan	2005	160,292	302,477	333	60	15	tcr	
9290309	Pacific Alliance *	Iom	2004	57,226	105,941	244	42	14	tco	

IMO#	name	flag	year	grt	dwt	loa	bm	kts	type	former names
9290294	Pacific Partner	Pan	2004	57,226	105,946	244	42	14	tco	
9251597	Perseus Trader +	Pan	2003	160,066	299,992	333	60	15	tcr	
9352559	Phoenix Vanguard +	Sgp	2007	157,844	306,506	333	60	15	tcr	
9513751	Phoenix Vigor +	Sgp	2009	160,160	309,887	333	60	15	tcr	
9251602	Rokkosan **	Pan	2003	160,066	300,257	333	60	15	tcr	
9197844	Ryuohsan **	Pan	2000	149,282	281,050	330	60	16	tcr	
9262766	Selene Trader **	Pan	2000	159,912	299,991	333	60	15	tcr	
9259343	Vega Trader	Pan	2003	159,813	299,985	333	60	15	tcr	
9222455	Washusan **	Pan	2000	152,041	281,050	330	60	16	tcr	
9362877	Yakumosan +	Mhl	2008	159,943	302,165	333	60	15	tcr	
9294329	Yufusan **	Pan	2005	160,216	311,389	330	60	15	tcr	

* owned or managed by subsidiaries MOL Tankship Management (Europe) Ltd, UK (founded 1992 as MOL Tankship Management Ltd to 2006) or ** by MOL Tankship Management (Asia) Pte Ltd, Singapore (formerly International Energy Transport Co Ltd to 2006), including † jointly owned by Sinotrans, China. + operates in Nova Tankers Pool (established January 2012 between Mitsui OSK, A P Moller Maersk, Phoenix Tankers Pte., Samco Shipholding and Ocean Tankers.

A. P. Møller   Denmark

A. P. Møller-Maersk A/S, Denmark
Funnel: Black with white seven-pointed star on broad light blue band. **Hull:** Light blue with black 'Maersk Line', red boot-topping.
History: Formed 2003 by merger of A/S Dampskibs Svendborg (founded 1904) and Dampskibs af 1912 A/S (founded 1912). Acquired liner services of Chargeurs Reunis and CMB (both 1987), also Torm (2002) and the container lines of Sea-Land and Safmarine (both 1999) and P&O Nedlloyd (2005). Acquired Brostrom AB in 2009. **Web:** www.maersk.com or www.maerskline.com

IMO#	name	flag	year	grt	dwt	loa	bm	kts	type	former names
9214898	A. P. Moller	Dis	2000	91,560	104,750	347	43	25	ucc	7,226 teu
9260457	Adrian Maersk	Dis	2004	93,496	109,000	353	43	25	ucc	7,370 teu
9260469	Albert Maersk	Dis	2004	93,496	105,750	352	43	25	ucc	7,370 teu
9164237	Alexander Maersk	Dis	1998	14,120	17,375	155	25	18	ucc	1,092 teu: ex Adrian Maersk-04
9260421	Anna Maersk	Dis	2003	93,496	109,000	352	43	25	ucc	7,370 teu
9260433	Arnold Maersk	Dis	2003	93,496	109,000	352	43	25	ucc	7,370 teu
9260445	Arthur Maersk	Dis	2003	93,496	105,750	352	43	25	ucc	7,370 teu
9260419	Axel Maersk	Dis	2003	93,496	109,000	352	43	25	ucc	7,370 teu
9313929	Bentonville	Dis	2006	48,853	53,201	294	32	29	ucc	4,196 teu: ex Maersk Bentonville-10
9340582	Brigit Maersk	Dis	2006	19,758	29,017	175	29	14	tco	
9341433	Britta Maersk	Dis	2007	19,758	29,017	175	29	14	tco	
9150614	Bro Anton +	Dnk	1999	11,375	16,376	144	23	15	tco	ex United Anton-00
9160932	Bro Atland +	Dnk	1999	11,377	16,326	144	23	15	tco	ex United Atland-00, United Albert-99
9313096	Bro Deliverer +	Dis	2006	11,344	14,766	147	22	13	tco	
9313101	Bro Designer +	Dis	2006	11,344	14,846	147	22	13	tco	
9313125	Bro Developer +	Dis	2006	11,344	14,737	147	22	13	tco	
9313113	Bro Distributor +	Dis	2007	11,344	14,907	147	22	13	tco	
9323584	Bro Nakskov +	Dis	2007	12,105	16,427	144	23	14	tco	ex Nakskov Maersk-12
9322700	Bro Nibe +	Dis	2007	12,105	16,534	144	23	14	tco	ex Nibe Maersk-10
9322695	Bro Nyborg +	Dis	2007	12,105	16,564	144	23	14	tco	ex Nakskov Maersk-12
9171498	Camilla Maersk ++	Dis	1999	29,289	44,999	183	32	14	tco	ex Bro Premium-10, Iver Exact-06
9178678	Caribe	Ven	2000	17,980	20,815	159	26	18	lpg	20,815 m³ ex Maersk Holyhead-06
9171503	Carla Maersk ++	Dnk	1999	29,289	45,790	183	32	15	tco	ex Bro Promotion-10, Iver Example-06
9214903	Caroline Maersk	Dis	2000	92,198	104,750	347	43	25	ucc	7,226 teu
9219795	Carsten Maersk	Dis	2000	92,198	104,750	347	43	25	ucc	7,226 teu
9064401	Cecilie Maersk	Dis	1994	20,842	28,550	190	28	18	ucc	1,827 teu
9245744	Charlotte Maersk	Dis	2002	92,198	104,000	347	43	25	ucc	7,226 teu
9219800	Chastine Maersk	Dis	2001	91,560	104,750	347	43	25	ucc	7,226 teu
9064396	Claes Maersk	Dis	1994	20,842	28,550	190	28	18	ucc	1,827 teu
8820016	Clara Maersk	Dis	1992	18,979	25,275	176	28	18	ucc	1,658 teu
9245770	Clementine Maersk	Dis	2002	91,921	104,750	347	43	25	ucc	7,226 teu
9198575	Clifford Maersk	Dis	1999	91,560	104,700	348	43	25	ucc	7,226 teu
9245768	Columbine Maersk	Dis	2002	91,921	110,000	347	43	25	ucc	7,226 teu
9245756	Cornelia Maersk	Dis	2002	91,921	104,750	347	43	25	ucc	7,226 teu
9198587	Cornelius Maersk	Dis	2000	92,198	104,700	347	43	25	ucc	7,226 teu
9321524	Ebba Maersk	Dis	2007	170,794	156,900	398	56	25	ucc	12,508 teu
9321548	Edith Maersk	Dis	2007	170,794	156,907	398	56	25	ucc	12,508 teu
9321500	Eleonora Maersk	Dis	2007	170,794	156,900	398	56	25	ucc	12,508 teu
9321536	Elly Maersk	Dis	2007	170,794	156,907	398	56	25	ucc	12,508 teu
9321483	Emma Maersk	Dis	2006	170,794	156,907	398	56	25	ucc	12,508 teu
9321495	Estelle Maersk	Dis	2006	170,794	156,907	398	56	25	ucc	12,508 teu
9321550	Eugen Maersk	Dis	2008	170,794	156,907	398	56	25	ucc	12,508 teu
9321512	Evelyn Maersk	Dis	2007	170,794	156,907	398	56	25	ucc	12,508 teu
9219276	Freja Maersk ++	Dnk	2001	21,517	31,632	177	28	14	tco	ex Bro Provider-10, Iver Prosperity-06
9219264	Frida Maersk ++	Dnk	2001	21,517	31,687	177	28	14	tco	ex Bro Priority-10, Iver Progress-05
9320257	Georg Maersk	Dis	2006	97,900	115,700	367	43	25	ucc	7,668 teu
9320245	Gerd Maersk	Dis	2006	97,900	115,700	367	43	25	ucc	7,668 teu
9320233	Gjertrud Maersk	Dis	2005	97,933	115,700	367	43	25	ucc	7,668 teu

IMO#	name	flag	year	grt	dwt	loa	bm	kts	type	former names
9302889	Grete Maersk	Dis	2005	97,933	115,700	367	43	25	ucc	7,668 teu
9302877	Gudrun Maersk	Dis	2005	97,933	115,700	367	43	25	ucc	7,668 teu
9302891	Gunvor Maersk	Dis	2005	97,933	115,700	367	43	25	ucc	7,668 teu
9215177	Jens Maersk	Dis	2001	30,166	27,300	216	32	23	ucc	2,833 teu
9215165	Jepperson Maersk	Dis	2001	30,166	35,097	216	32	22	ucc	2,833 teu
9215189	Johannes Maersk	Dis	2001	30,166	27,300	216	32	23	ucc	2,833 teu
9215191	Josephine Maersk	Dis	2002	30,166	27,300	216	32	23	ucc	2,833 teu
9423712	Karen Maersk	Dis	2010	24,412	39,708	183	28	15	tco	
9431276	Kate Maersk	Dis	2010	24,412	39,756	183	28	15	tco	
9294379	Lars Maersk	Dis	2004	50,657	62,994	267	37	24	ucc	4,045 teu
9190731	Laura Maersk	Dis	2001	50,721	63,200	266	37	24	ucc	4,045 teu
9190743	Laust Maersk	Dis	2001	50,721	63,000	266	37	24	ucc	4,045 teu
9190755	Leda Maersk	Dis	2001	50,721	63,200	266	37	24	ucc	4,045 teu
9190767	Lexa Maersk	Dis	2001	50,721	63,400	266	37	24	ucc	4,045 teu
9190779	Lica Maersk	Dis	2001	50,721	63,400	266	37	24	ucc	4,045 teu
9190781	Luna Maersk	Dis	2002	50,721	63,400	266	37	25	ucc	4,045 teu
9619945	*Madison Maersk*	Dis	2013	174,500	196,000	399	59	22	ucc	18,100 teu
9164225	Maersk Ahram **	Egy	1998	14,063	17,728	155	25	18	ucc	1,092 teu
9299458	Maersk Barry	Dis	2006	19,758	29,040	176	29	14	tco	
9299434	Maersk Bristol	Dis	2006	19,758	29,050	176	29	14	tco	
9525493	Maersk Cabinda	Sgp	2012	50,869	61,570	249	37	21	ucc	4,500 teu
9525479	Maersk Cairo	Hkg	2012	50,869	61,561	249	37	21	ucc	4,500 teu

A. P. Møller (A. P. Møller-Maersk A/S) : CLARA MAERSK : *Andy McAlpine*

A. P. Møller (A. P. Møller-Maersk A/S) : EBBA MAERSK : *Hans Kraijenbosch*

IMO#	name	flag	year	grt	dwt	loa	bm	kts	type	former names
9274630	Maersk Edgar	Dnk	2004	26,634	37,188	186	31	15	tco	ex Bro Edgar -10, Geestestern-06
9274628	Maersk Erin	Dnk	2004	26,634	37,178	186	31	15	tco	ex Bro Erin -10, Huntestern-07
9235579	Maersk Garonne	Dnk	2003	50,698	61,636	282	32	24	ucc	4,318 teu
9235555	Maersk Gironde	Dnk	2002	50,757	61,636	292	32	24	ucc	4,318 teu
9153862	Maersk Kalmar *	Nld	1998	80,942	88,669	300	43	24	ucc	6,674 teu: ex P&O Nedlloyd Rotterdam-06
9215311	Maersk Kampala *	Nld	2001	80,654	88,967	300	43	24	ucc	6,674 teu: ex P&O Nedlloyd Houtman-06
9526899	Maersk La Paz	Mhl	2011	88,237	94,267	300	46	22	ucc	7,450 teu
9526942	Maersk Laguna	Sgp	2012	88,237	94,300	300	46	22	ucc	7,450 teu
9526978	Maersk Laberinto	Hkg	2012	89,505	94,300	300	46	22	ucc	7,450 teu
9526930	Maersk Lebu	Hkg	2011	88,237	94,267	300	46	22	ucc	7,450 teu
9526916	Maersk Leticia	Hkg	2011	88,237	94,267	300	46	22	ucc	7,450 teu
9526875	Maersk Lima	Mhl	2011	88,237	94,267	300	46	22	ucc	7,450 teu
9526887	Maersk Lirquen	Mhl	2011	88,237	94,267	300	46	22	ucc	7,450 teu
9526904	Maersk Luz	Hkg	2011	88,237	94,267	300	46	22	ucc	7,450 teu
9619945	Maersk Mc-Minlay Moller	Dis	2013	174,500	196,000	399	59	22	ucc	18,100 teu
9356127	Maersk Newport	Dis	2008	25,888	35,483	210	30	22	ucc	2,474 teu
9236987	Maersk Rosyth	Dis	2003	22,184	34,811	171	27	14	tco	
9352016	Maersk Salalah	Dis	2008	94,127	102,311	334	46	25	ucc	8,750 teu
9352028	Maersk Savannah	Dis	2008	94,127	102,367	334	46	25	ucc	8,750 teu
9352004	Maersk Stepnica	Dis	2008	91,427	102,367	334	46	25	ucc	8,750 teu
9619957	Magelby Maersk	Dis	2013	174,500	196,000	399	59	22	ucc	18,100 teu

A. P. Møller (A. P. Møller-Maersk A/S) : EDITH MAERSK : *ARO*

A. P. Møller (A. P. Møller-Maersk A/S) : FRIDA MAERSK : *Nico Kemps*

IMO#	name	flag	year	grt	dwt	loa	bm	kts	type	former names
9359014	Marchen Maersk	Dis	2008	98,268	115,993	367	43	25	ucc	10,150 teu
9359026	Maren Maersk	Dis	2009	98,268	115,993	367	43	25	ucc	10,150 teu
9359002	Margrethe Maersk	Dis	2008	98,268	115,993	367	43	25	ucc	10,150 teu
9619969	Maribo Maersk	Dis	2014	174,500	196,000	399	59	22	ucc	18,100 teu
9619933	Marin Maersk	Dis	2014	174,500	196,000	399	59	22	ucc	18,100 teu
9359040	Marit Maersk	Dis	2009	98,268	115,993	367	43	25	ucc	10,150 teu
9619971	Marstal Maersk	Dis	2014	174,500	196,000	399	59	22	ucc	18,100 teu
9359052	Mathilde Maersk	Dis	2009	98,268	116,100	367	43	25	ucc	10,150 teu
9619921	Mary Maersk	Dis	2014	174,500	196,000	399	59	22	ucc	18,100 teu
9619983	Matz Maersk	Dis	2014	174,500	196,000	399	59	22	ucc	18,100 teu
9619995	Mayview Maersk	Dis	2014	174,500	196,000	399	59	22	ucc	18,100 teu
9359038	Mette Maersk	Dis	2009	98,268	115,993	367	43	25	ucc	10,150 teu
9106481	Nedlloyd de Liefde *	Nld	1995	10,917	13,700	151	24	18	ucc	1,170 teu: ex P&O Nedlloyd de Liefde-06, Milena-05, Sigrid Wehr-04, Washington Express-01, Sigrid Wehr-00, Independent Venture-98, Sigrid Wehr-96, Cape Scott-95
9192442	Nele Maersk	Dis	2000	27,733	30,194	199	30	21	ucc	2,240 teu
9220885	Nexø Maersk	Dis	2001	27,733	30,420	199	30	21	ucc	2,240 teu

A. P. Møller (A. P. Møller-Maersk A/S) : JOHANNES MAERSK : *Chris Brooks*

A. P. Møller (A. P. Møller-Maersk A/S) : MAERSK LABERINTO : *Hans Kraijenbosch*

IMO#	name	flag	year	grt	dwt	loa	bm	kts	type	former names
9192454	Nicolai Maersk	Dis	2000	27,733	30,420	199	30	21	ucc	2,240 teu
9192466	Nicoline Maersk	Dis	2000	27,733	30,191	199	30	21	ucc	2,240 teu
9340623	Nissum Maersk	Dis	2008	12,105	16,400	144	23	14	tco	
9192478	Nora Maersk	Dis	2000	27,733	30,194	199	30	21	ucc	2,240 teu
9322712	Nordby Maersk	Dis	2007	12,105	16,511	144	23	14	tco	
9323819	Nuuk Maersk	Dis	2008	12,105	16,631	144	23	14	tco	
9220897	Nysted Maersk	Dis	2001	27,733	30,194	197	30	21	ucc	2,240 teu
9251614	Olga Maersk	Dis	2003	34,202	41,028	237	32	24	ucc	3,028 teu
9251638	Olivia Maersk	Dis	2003	34,202	41,097	237	32	24	ucc	3,028 teu
9251626	Oluf Maersk	Dis	2003	34,202	41,028	237	32	24	ucc	3,028 teu
9236999	Ras Maersk	Dis	2003	22,181	34,999	171	27	14	tco	
9265407	Ribe Maersk	Dis	2004	22,181	35,000	171	27	14	tco	
9214757	Richard Maersk	Dis	2001	22,184	34,909	171	27	14	tco	
9298820	Rita Maersk	Dis	2004	22,184	35,199	171	27	14	tco	
9237008	Robert Maersk	Dis	2003	22,181	34,801	171	27	14	tco	
9251406	Romø Maersk	Dis	2003	22,161	34,808	171	27	14	tco	
9306940	Rosa Maersk	Dis	2005	22,184	35,192	171	27	14	tco	
9306938	Roy Maersk	Dis	2005	22,184	35,190	171	27	14	tco	
9120865	Sally Maersk	Dis	1998	91,560	104,696	348	43	25	ucc	7,226 teu
9313905	Seago Antwerp †	Dis	2006	48,808	53,701	294	32	29	ucc	4,196 teu: ex Maersk Boston-12, Boston-12, Maersk Boston
9313967	Seago Bremerhaven †	Dis	2007	48,853	53,890	294	32	29	ucc	4,196 teu: ex Maersk Beaumont-12, Beaumont-12, Maersk Beaumont-10
9313917	Seago Felixstowe †	Dis	2006	48,853	53,634	294	32	29	ucc	4,196 teu: ex Baltimore-12, Maersk Baltimore-10
9313943	Seago Istanbul †	Dis	2007	48,853	53,701	294	32	29	ucc	4,196 teu: ex Maersk Buffalo-12, Buffalo-12, Maersk Buffalo-11
9313955	Seago Piraeus †	Dis	2007	48,853	53,807	294	32	29	ucc	4,196 teu: ex Maersk Brownsvill-13, Brownsville-12, Maersk Brownsvill-11
9146455	Sine Maersk	Dis	1998	92,158	104,696	348	43	25	ucc	7,226 teu
9166792	Skagen Maersk	Dis	1999	91,500	104,700	348	43	25	ucc	7,226 teu
9146479	Sofie Maersk	Dis	1999	92,198	104,696	348	43	25	ucc	7,226 teu

A. P. Møller (A. P. Møller-Maersk A/S) : NEDLLOYD DE LIEFDE : *Roy Fenton*

IMO#	name	flag	year	grt	dwt	loa	bm	kts	type	former names
9166780	Sorø Maersk	Dis	1999	91,500	104,696	348	43	25	ucc	7,226 teu
9120841	Sovereign Maersk	Dis	1997	91,560	104,886	348	43	25	ucc	7,226 teu
9120853	Susan Maersk	Dis	1997	92,198	104,886	348	43	25	ucc	7,226 teu
9166778	Svend Maersk	Dis	1999	92,198	104,896	348	43	25	ucc	7,226 teu
9146467	Svendborg Maersk	Dis	1998	91,560	104,696	348	43	25	ucc	7,226 teu
9064684	Tåsinge Maersk	Dis	1994	20,842	28,550	190	28	18	ucc	1,827 teu: ex Maersk California-02, Caroline Maersk-97
8819990	Thies Maersk	Dis	1992	16,982	21,825	162	28	18	ucc	1,446 teu: ex Cornelia Maersk-01
9064267	Thomas Maersk	Dis	1994	18,859	25,368	176	28	18	ucc	1,446 teu: ex Maersk Tennesse-02, Thomas Maersk-97
8819976	Thurø Maersk	Dis	1991	16,982	21,825	162	28	18	ucc	1,446 teu: ex Chastine Maersk-01
9064279	Tinglev Maersk	Dis	1994	18,859	25,431	176	28	18	ucc	1,325 teu: ex Maersk Texas-02, Tinglev Maersk-97
8819988	Tove Maersk	Dis	1992	16,982	21,825	162	28	18	ucc	1,446 teu: ex Charlotte Maersk-01
8820004	Troense Maersk	Dis	1992	16,982	21,825	162	28	18	ucc	1,446 teu: ex Maersk Colorado-03, Clifford Maersk-97

newbuildings: 11 x 18,000teu containerships, 400 x 59m. [Daewoo (2013-2015)]
*vessels are owned or managed by subsidiaries * by Maersk BV, Netherlands, ** by Maersk Egypt SAE, Egypt*
† operated by Seago Line, 100% Maersk subsidiary, web: www.seagoline.com
≠ owned/managed by Eastwind Group or ‡‡ by MC Shipping See also MPC Munchmeyer Petersen & Co.
managed by + Brostrom AB, ++ Hanytankers K/S

Maersk Shipping Hong Kong Ltd.
Hull and **Funnel:** *As above.* **History:** *Founded 1975.* **Web:** *www.maerskline.com*

IMO#	name	flag	year	grt	dwt	loa	bm	kts	type	former names
9175793	Maersk Aberdeen	Hkg	1999	14,130	17,720	155	25	18	ucc	1,092 teu
9164249	Maersk Arizona	Hkg	1998	14,120	17,375	155	25	18	ucc	1,092 teu: ex Agnete Maersk-08
9175781	Maersk Antwerp	Hkg	1999	14,063	17,720	155	25	18	ucc	1,092 teu
9164245	Maersk Arun	Hkg	1999	14,063	14,175	155	25	18	ucc	1,092 teu
9175808	Maersk Atlantic	Hkg	1999	14,063	17,720	155	25	18	ucc	1,092 teu: ex Swan River Bridge-00, Maersk Atlantic-99
9164275	Maersk Avon	Hkg	1999	14,063	17,728	155	25	18	ucc	1,092 teu
9525455	Maersk Cabo Verde	Hkg	2012	50,869	61,643	249	37	21	ucc	4,500 teu
9525479	Maersk Cairo	Hkg	2012	50,869	61,561	249	37	21	ucc	4,500 teu
9525467	Maersk Casablanca	Hkg	2012	50,869	61,588	249	37	21	ucc	4,500 teu
9525481	Maersk Cubango	Hkg	2012	50,869	61,608	249	37	21	ucc	4,500 teu
9162215	Maersk Karachi	Hkg	1998	80,600	82,700	300	43	24	ucc	6,674 teu: ex P&O Nedlloyd Kobe-06
9153850	Maersk Kiel	Hkg	1998	80,942	88,669	300	43	24	ucc	6,674 teu: ex P&O Nedlloyd Southampton-06
9211482	Maersk Klaipeda	Hkg	2001	80,654	87,343	300	43	24	ucc	6,802 teu: ex Maersk Kingston-07, P&O Nedlloyd Stuyvesant-06
9211494	Maersk Kyrenia	Hkg	2001	80,654	87,343	300	43	24	ucc	6,802 teu: ex P&O Nedlloyd Shackleton
9526978	Maersk Laberinto	Hkg	2012	89,505	93,912	300	45	24	ucc	8,700 teu
9527063	Maersk Labrea	Hkg	2013	89,500	93,840	300	45	24	ucc	8,700 teu
9527051	Maersk Lamanai	Hkg	2013	89,500	93,840	300	45	24	ucc	8,700 teu
9527049	Maersk Lanco	Hkg	2013	89,500	93,840	300	45	24	ucc	8,700 teu
9526928	Maersk Lavras	Hkg	2011	88,237	94,267	300	45	24	ucc	7,450 teu
9527025	Maersk Lins	Hkg	2012	89,505	94,112	300	45	24	ucc	8,700 teu
9527037	Maersk Londrina	Hkg	2012	89,505	93,827	300	45	24	ucc	8,700 teu
9332690	Maersk Ronneby	Hkg	2007	9,957	13,769	148	24	16	ucc	1,118 teu
9355367	Safmarine Benguela	Hkg	2009	35,835	43,197	223	32	22	ucc	2,787 teu
9525388	Safmarine Chachai	Hkg	2012	50,869	61,614	249	37	21	ucc	4,500 teu
9525376	Safmarine Chambal	Hkg	2012	50,869	62,557	249	37	21	ucc	4,500 teu
9525364	Safmarine Chilka	Hkg	2012	50,869	61,614	249	37	21	ucc	4,500 teu
9356103	Safmarine Nakuru	Hkg	2008	25,904	35,137	211	30	21	ucc	2,478 teu
9356098	Safmarine Nile	Hkg	2008	25,904	35,181	211	30	21	ucc	2,478 teu
9294381	Safmarine Nomazwe	Hkg	2004	50,657	62,994	266	37	25	ucc	4,045 teu
9356115	Safmarine Nuba	Hkg	2008	25,904	35,144	211	30	21	ucc	2,478 teu
9356086	Safmarine Nyassa	Hkg	2008	25,800	35,292	211	30	21	ucc	2,478 teu

vessels managed by Moller-Maersk A/S

The Maersk Co. Ltd., U.K.
Hull and **Funnel:** *As above.* **History:** *Formed 1972.* **Web:** *www.maersk.co.uk*

IMO#	name	flag	year	grt	dwt	loa	bm	kts	type	former names
9193276	Grasmere Maersk	Gbr	2000	50,698	62,007	292	32	24	ucc	4,338 teu
9394882	Maersk Bogor	Sgp	2009	35,835	43,177	223	32	22	ucc	3,194 teu
9394894	Maersk Bratan	Sgp	2009	35,835	43,114	223	32	22	ucc	3,194 teu
9313931	Maersk Brooklyn	Dis	2007	48,853	53,201	294	32	29	ucc	4,196 teu: ex Brooklyn-12, Maersk Brooklyn-10
9235565	Maersk Gairloch	Gbr	2002	50,698	62,242	292	32	24	ucc	4,318 teu
9235543	Maersk Gateshead	Gbr	2002	50,686	62,242	292	32	24	ucc	4,318 teu
9348170	Maersk Innoshima	Gbr	2008	35,491	41,337	232	32	22	ucc	3,364 teu

IMO#	name	flag	year	grt	dwt	loa	bm	kts	type	former names
9348156	Maersk Inverness	Gbr	2008	35,491	41,350	232	32	22	ucc	3,364 teu
9348168	Maersk Izmir *	Nld	2008	35,491	41,238	232	32	22	ucc	3,364 teu
9333008	Maersk Kelso	Gbr	2007	74,642	84,783	300	43	24	ucc	6,188 teu
9332999	Maersk Kendal	Gbr	2007	74,642	84,771	300	43	24	ucc	6,188 teu
9333010	Maersk Kensington	Gbr	2007	74,642	84,897	300	43	24	ucc	6,188 teu
9162227	Maersk Kimi †	Nld	1998	80,942	88,669	300	43	24	ucc	6,930 teu: ex P&O Nedlloyd Kowloon-06
9333022	Maersk Kinloss	Gbr	2008	74,642	84,835	299	40	24	ucc	6,188 teu
9215323	Maersk Kithira	Gbr	2001	80,654	88,700	300	43	24	ucc	5,618 teu: ex P&O Nedlloyd Cook-06
9356139	Maersk Norfolk	Dnk	2008	25,888	35,205	207	30	22	ucc	2,474 teu
9167150	Maersk Rapier	Iom	2000	22,181	34,985	171	27	15	tco	ex Robert Maersk-00
9189366	Nedlloyd Barentsz †	Nld	2000	66,526	67,785	278	40	25	ucc	5,618 teu: ex P&O Nedlloyd Barentsz-05
9189500	Nedlloyd Drake †	Gbr	2000	66,526	67,712	278	40	25	ucc	5,618 teu: ex P&O Nedlloyd Drake-06
9189354	Nedlloyd Hudson †	Gbr	2000	66,526	67,515	278	40	24	ucc	5,618 teu: ex P&O Nedlloyd Houston-06
9189495	Nedlloyd Mercator †	Nld	2000	66,526	67,785	278	40	25	ucc	5,618 teu: ex P&O Nedlloyd Mercator-06
9189342	Nedlloyd Tasman †	Gbr	1999	66,526	67,900	278	40	24	ucc	5,618 teu: ex P&O Nedlloyd Tasman-06

*vessels managed by Moller-Maersk A/S   * owned by Maersk BV ** owned by Mundan Mobilienges.operated by Handytankers KS,   † owned by various Finance Houses*

A. P. Møller (Maersk Shipping Hong Kong) : SAFMARINE NAKURU : *Chris Brooks*

A. P. Møller (Maersk Line Ltd. U.S.A.) : MAERSK RHODE ISLAND : *Chris Brooks*

Maersk Line Ltd., U.S.A.

Hull *and* Funnel: *As above.* History: *Formed 1947.* Web: *www.maersklinelimited.com*

IMO#	name	flag	year	grt	dwt	loa	bm	kts	type	former names
9285483	Alliance Beaumont *	Usa	2004	68,871	21,500	229	32	20	mve	7,850 ceu: ex Höegh Tokyo-10, Hual Tokyo-07 (len-08)
9342205	Alliance Charleston *	Usa	2008	68,871	21,500	229	32	20	mve	6,000 ceu: ex Höegh London-10 (len-08)
9303546	Alliance Fairfax	USA	2005	52,691	21,500	199	32	19	mve	5,400 ceu: ex Höegh Kyoto-13, Maersk Willow-08
9303558	Alliance Richmond	Usa	2006	52,691	21,500	199	32	19	mve	5,400 ceu: ex Höegh Chiba-12, Maersk Welkin-08
9332547	Alliance Norfolk *	Usa	2007	57,280	15,880	200	32	20	mve	ex Höegh Madrid-07
9285500	Alliance St. Louis *	Usa	2006	57,280	15,972	200	32	20	mve	ex Höegh Paris-08, Hual Paris-06
9164263	Maersk Alabama	Usa	1998	14,120	17,375	155	25	18	ucc	1,092 teu: ex Alva Maersk-04
9164251	Maersk Arkansas	Usa	1998	14,120	17,375	155	25	18	ucc	1,092 teu: ex Angelica Maersk-04, Albert Maersk-04
8820195	Maersk California	Usa	1992	18,979	25,375	176	28	18	ucc	1,394 teu: ex Christian Maersk-08
9155133	Maersk Carolina	Usa	1998	50,698	62,229	292	32	24	ucc	4,306 teu: ex Grete Maersk-02
9155119	Maersk Georgia	Usa	1997	50,698	62,242	292	32	24	ucc	4,306 teu: ex Gudrun Maersk-02
9193264	Maersk Idaho	Usa	2000	50,698	61,986	292	32	24	ucc	4,338 teu: ex Gosport Maersk-09
9469778	Maersk Illinois	Usa	2011	13,816	19,600	148	23	16	ghl	cr: 2(240)
9298686	Maersk Iowa	Usa	2006	50,686	61,454	292	32	24	ucc	4,154 teu: ex Maersk Greenock-07
9193240	Maersk Kentucky	Usa	1999	50,698	61,986	292	32	24	ucc	4,338 teu: ex Glasgow Maersk-09
9155121	Maersk Missouri	Usa	1998	50,698	62,226	292	32	24	ucc	4,306 teu: ex Gerd Maersk-02
9255244	Maersk Michigan	Usa	2003	28,517	47,047	183	32	14	tco	ex Marco-08, St. Marco-08
9305312	Maersk Montana	Usa	2006	50,686	61.499	292	32	24	ucc	4,154 teu: ex Maersk Guernsey-07
9298698	Maersk Ohio	Usa	2006	50,686	61,454	292	32	24	ucc	4,154 teu: ex Maersk Gosforth-07
9278492	Maersk Peary	Usa	2004	25,487	38,177	183	32	14	tco	ex Jutul-11
9236975	Maersk Rhode Island	Usa	2002	22,161	34,801	171	27	14	tco	l/a Maersk Ramsey
9469780	Maersk Texas	Usa	2011	13,816	19,638	148	23	16	ghl	cr: 2(240)
9305300	Maersk Utah	Usa	2006	50,686	62,000	292	32	25	ucc	4,154 teu: ex Maersk Gloucester-09
9235531	Maersk Virginia	Usa	2002	50,686	62,009	292	32	24	ucc	4,318 teu: ex Maersk Geelong-03
9193252	Maersk Wisconsin	Usa	2000	50,698	62,441	292	32	24	ucc	4,338 teu: ex Greenwich Maersk-09
9105932	Maersk Wyoming	Usa	1996	50,698	61,927	292	32	24	ucc	3,614 teu: ex Dirch Maersk-09
9106170	Sea-Land Champion	Usa	1995	49,985	59,840	292	32	24	ucc	4,082 teu
9143001	Sea-Land Charger	Usa	1997	49,985	59,961	292	32	24	ucc	4,082 teu
9106182	Sea-Land Comet	Usa	1995	49,985	59,840	292	32	24	ucc	4,082 teu
9143013	Sea-Land Eagle	Usa	1997	49,985	59,840	292	32	24	ucc	4,082 teu
9143025	Sea-Land Intrepid	Usa	1997	49,985	59,840	292	32	24	ucc	4,082 teu
9116890	Sea-Land Racer	Usa	1996	49,985	59,964	292	32	24	ucc	4,082 teu: ex MSC Everest-09, Sea-Land Racer-07
9143037	Sea-Land Lightning	Usa	1996	49,985	59,938	292	32	24	ucc	4,082 teu
9106194	Sea-Land Mercury	Usa	1995	49,985	59,961	292	32	24	ucc	4,082 teu: ex CSX Mercury-03, Sea-Land Mercury-00
9106209	Sea-Land Meteor	Usa	1996	49,985	59,938	292	32	24	ucc	4,082 teu

* owned by Wilmington Trust Co., USA and operated by Farrell Lines   also owns twelve other vessels long-term chartered to US military fleet

A. P. Møller (Maersk Line Ltd. U.S.A.) : MAERSK IDAHO : *Chris Brooks*

Maersk Tankers France SAS

Hull *and* Funnel: *As above.* History: Web: *www.maersktankers.com*

IMO#	name	flag	year	grt	dwt	loa	bm	kts	type	former names
9079171	Maersk Cameron	Gbr	1995	28,226	46,802	183	32	14	tco	ex Bro Arthur-10, Port Arthur-00
9133070	Maersk Catherine	Atf	1997	29,083	44,922	180	32	14	tco	ex Bro Catherine-10, Port Catherine-00
9116917	Maersk Christiansbro	Lux	1996	29,083	44,885	180	32	14	tco	ex Cilaos-09, Port Christine-98
9116905	Maersk Claire	Atf	1995	29,083	45,014	183	32	14	tco	ex Bro Caroline-10, Port Caroline-00
9133068	Maersk Clarissa	Atf	1997	29,083	44,970	181	32	14	tco	ex Bro Charlotte-10, Port Charlotte-00
9274654	Maersk Edward	Atf	2005	26,659	37,300	184	30	14	tco	ex Bro Edward-10
9210892	Maersk Elizabeth	Atf	2001	24,099	37,026	184	30	15	tco	ex Bro Elizabeth-10
9210907	Maersk Ellen	Atf	2002	24,100	37,000	184	30	15	tco	ex Bro Ellen-10
9274678	Maersk Elliot	Atf	2005	26,659	37,300	184	30	14	tco	ex Bro Elliot-10
9274642	Maersk Etienne	Atf	2004	26,659	37,300	184	30	14	tco	ex Bro Etienne-10

Maersk Tankers Singapore Pte., Singapore

Hull *and* Funnel: *As above.* Web: *www.maersktankers.com*

IMO#	name	flag	year	grt	dwt	loa	bm	kts	type
9447732	Gan-Trophy	Sgp	2010	29,669	51,551	183	32	14	tco
9340594	Maersk Beaufort	Sgp	2006	19,758	29,015	175	29	14	tco
9299446	Maersk Belfast	Sgp	2005	19,758	29,031	175	29	14	tco
9299422	Maersk Bering	Sgp	2005	19,758	29,057	176	29	14	tco

A. P. Møller (Maersk Tankers Singapore) : MAERSK KATARINA : *Nico Kemps*

A. P. Møller (Maersk Tankers Singapore) : MAERSK NAUTILUS : *Chris Brooks*

IMO#	name	flag	year	grt	dwt	loa	bm	kts	type	former names
9341445	Maersk Borneo	Sgp	2007	19,758	29,013	176	29	14	tco	
9133082	Maersk Caitlin	Sgp	1997	29,083	44,936	180	32	14	tco	ex Bro Cecile-10, Port Cecile-00
9200847	Maersk Eli *	Sgp	2000	159,187	308,491	330	60	14	tcr	ex Eli Maersk-11
9398084	Maersk Hakone *	Sgp	2010	159,806	302,624	333	60	14	tcr	
9395290	Maersk Hayama *	Sgp	2011	156,915	297,221	330	60	14	tcr	
9395496	Maersk Heiwa *	Sgp	2011	156,915	297,274	330	60	14	tcr	l/a Pacific Jade
9377420	Maersk Hirado *	Sgp	2011	159,806	302,550	333	60	14	tcr	
9588392	Maersk Ilma *	Sgp	2012	160,716	318,395	333	60	14	tcr	l/a Vasant J. Sheth
9529956	Maersk Ingrid *	Sgp	2012	160,716	318,478	333	60	14	tcr	l/a Maneklal Ujamshi Sheth
9529968	Maersk Isabella *	Sgp	2012	161,500	318,478	333	60	14	tcr	l/a Ardeshir H. Bhiwandiwalla
9256298	Maersk Kalea	Sgp	2004	25,507	38,850	168	29	14	tco	ex Meriom Pride-08
9431317	Maersk Katalin	Sgp	2012	24,412	39,724	183	27	14	tco	
9431290	Maersk Katarina	Sgp	2011	24,412	39,724	183	27	14	tco	
9431288	Maersk Kaya	Sgp	2011	24,412	39,729	183	27	14	tco	
9431305	Maersk Kiera **	Sgp	2011	24,412	39,724	183	27	14	tco	
9315056	Maersk Marmara	Sgp	2006	30,029	51,182	183	32	14	tco	ex Gan-Sure-11
9314911	Maersk Mediterranean	Sgp	2007	29,348	46,616	183	32	14	tco	ex Gan-Voyager-12
9312509	Maersk Navarin *	Sgp	2007	159,911	307,284	333	58	16	tcr	
9323948	Maersk Nautica *	Sgp	2008	159,911	307,284	333	58	16	tcr	
9312494	Maersk Nautilus *	Sgp	2006	159,911	307,284	333	58	16	tcr	
9323936	Maersk Nectar *	Sgp	2008	159,911	307,284	333	58	16	tcr	
9312511	Maersk Neptune *	Sgp	2007	159,911	307,284	333	58	16	tcr	
9358292	Maersk Newton	Sgp	2009	159,911	307,284	333	58	16	tcr	
9358290	Maersk Noble *	Sgp	2008	159,911	307,284	333	58	16	tcr	
9322293	Maersk Nucleus *	Sgp	2007	159,911	307,284	333	58	16	tcr	
9315446	Maersk Pearl	Sgp	2005	61,764	109,570	245	42	15	tco	
9319674	Maersk Penguin	Sgp	2007	61,724	109,647	245	42	15	tco	
9306639	Maersk Petrel	Sgp	2007	61,724	109,672	245	42	15	tco	ex Torm Mette-11
9283291	Maersk Phoenix	Sgp	2005	61,764	109,571	245	42	15	tco	
9319703	Maersk Piper	Sgp	2008	61,724	109,672	245	42	15	tco	ex Torm Marianne-11
9180920	Maersk Prime	Sgp	1999	61,764	109,529	245	42	15	tco	ex Dromus-10, Maersk Prime-04
9308948	Maersk Princess	Sgp	2005	61,724	109,637	245	42	15	tco	
9263643	Maersk Privilege	Sgp	2003	56,285	105,483	248	43	15	tco	ex Unique Privilege-07
9308950	Maersk Producer	Sgp	2006	61,724	109,647	248	43	15	tco	
9315458	Maersk Promise	Sgp	2006	61,724	109,647	248	43	15	tco	
9215050	Maersk Prosper	Sgp	2001	61,784	109,326	245	42	15	tco	ex Donax-10, Maersk Prosper-04
9283289	Maersk Progress	Sgp	2005	61,764	109,181	248	43	15	tco	
9537745	Maersk Sara *	Sgp	2011	164,641	323,182	332	60	14	tcr	
9537757	Maersk Sandra	Sgp	2011	164,641	323,183	332	60	14	tcr	
9537769	Maersk Simone *	Sgp	2012	164,641	323,182	332	60	14	tcr	

*crude oil tankers operated within the Nova Tankers pool, ** operated by Stena Weco*

Moller Singapore AP Pte. Ltd., Singapore

Hull *and* **Funnel:** *As above.* **History:** *Formed 1978 as Maersk Co. (Singapore) Pte Ltd to 1989.* **Web:** *www.apmsingapore.com.sg*

IMO#	name	flag	year	grt	dwt	loa	bm	kts	type	former names
9342516	Maersk Alfirk	Sgp	2008	108,393	110,401	338	46	25	ucc	9,580 teu
9342528	Maersk Algol	Sgp	2008	108,393	110,228	338	46	25	ucc	9,580 teu
9342499	Maersk Altair	Sgp	2007	108,393	110,295	338	46	25	ucc	9,580 teu
9342504	Maersk Antares	Sgp	2007	108,393	110,271	338	46	25	ucc	9,580 teu
9394870	Maersk Bali	Sgp	2008	35,835	43,206	224	32	22	ucc	3,194 teu
9355331	Maersk Batam	Sgp	2008	35,835	43,133	224	32	22	ucc	3,194 teu
9402029	Maersk Batur	Sgp	2009	35,835	43,273	224	32	22	ucc	3,194 teu
9355288	Maersk Bintan	Sgp	2008	35,835	43,097	224	32	22	ucc	3,194 teu
9409352	Maersk Brani	Sgp	2010	35,835	43,239	223	32	22	ucc	3,194 teu
9355343	Maersk Balam	Sgp	2008	35,836	43,177	224	32	22	ucc	3,194 teu
9392925	Maersk Buton	Sgp	2008	35,835	43,123	224	32	22	ucc	3,194 teu
9525302	Maersk Calabar	Sgp	2011	50,869	61,614	249	37	21	ucc	4,500 teu
9525326	Maersk Cameroun	Sgp	2011	50,869	61,614	249	37	21	ucc	4,500 teu
9525314	Maersk Cape Coast	Sgp	2011	50,869	61,614	249	37	21	ucc	4,500 teu
9525352	Maersk Cape Town	Sgp	2011	50,869	61,614	249	37	21	ucc	4,500 teu
9525338	Maersk Chennai	Sgp	2011	50,869	61,614	249	37	21	ucc	4,500 teu
9525390	Maersk Colombo	Sgp	2012	50,869	61,614	249	37	21	ucc	4,500 teu
9525285	Maersk Conokry	Sgp	2011	50,869	61,614	249	37	21	ucc	4,500 teu
9525340	Maersk Congo	Sgp	2011	50,869	61,614	249	37	21	ucc	4,500 teu
9525405	Maersk Copenhagen	Sgp	2012	50,869	61,120	249	37	21	ucc	4,500 teu
9525297	Maersk Cotonou	Sgp	2011	50,869	61,614	249	37	21	ucc	4,500 teu
9561497	Maersk Cuanza	Sgp	2012	50,869	61,614	249	37	21	ucc	4,500 teu
9561485	Maersk Cunene	Sgp	2011	50,869	61,614	249	37	21	ucc	4,500 teu
9348649	Maersk Kowloon	Sgp	2006	74,642	84,676	299	40	25	ucc	6,477 teu
9332975	Maersk Kuantan	Sgp	2007	74,642	84,775	299	40	25	ucc	6,477 teu

IMO#	name	flag	year	grt	dwt	loa	bm	kts	type	former names
9332987	Maersk Kushiro	Sgp	2007	74,642	84,704	299	40	25	ucc	6,477 teu
9348651	Maersk Kwangyang	Sgp	2007	74,642	84,676	299	40	25	ucc	6,477 teu
9526966	Maersk Leon	Sgp	2012	89,505	93,907	300	45	22	ucc	8,600 teu
9526954	Maersk Lota	Sgp	2012	88,237	94,121	300	45	22	ucc	8,600 teu
9315056	Maersk Marmara	Sgp	2006	30,029	52,182	183	32	14	tco	ex Gan-Sure-11
9168207	Maersk Palermo	Nld	1998	31,333	38,250	210	32	22	ucc	2,890 teu: ex P&O Nedlloyd Auckland-06
9168221	Maersk Patras	Gbr	1998	31,333	37,845	210	32	22	ucc	2,890 teu: ex P&O Nedlloyd Marseille-06
9319686	Maersk Pelican	Sgp	2007	61,724	109,647	245	42	14	tco	
9168180	Maersk Pembroke	Nld	1998	31,333	38,400	210	32	22	ucc	2,890 teu: ex P&O Nedlloyd Sydney-06
9168192	Maersk Penang *	Nld	1998	31,333	38,170	210	32	22	ucc	2,890 teu: ex P&O Nedlloyd Jakarta-06
9168219	Maersk Phuket	Gbr	1998	31,333	37,845	210	32	22	ucc	2,890 teu: ex P&O Nedlloyd Genoa-06
9352030	Maersk Salina	Hkg	2008	91,427	102,148	334	43	25	ucc	8,086 teu
9315238	Maersk Sebarok	Sgp	2007	79,702	87,534	318	40	25	ucc	5,648 teu
9315197	Maersk Seletar	Sgp	2007	79,702	87,545	318	40	25	ucc	5,648 teu
9315252	Maersk Semakau	Sgp	2007	79,702	87,621	318	40	25	ucc	5,648 teu
9315226	Maersk Sembawang	Sgp	2007	79,702	87,534	318	40	25	ucc	5,648 teu
9315240	Maersk Senang	Sgp	2007	79,702	87,608	318	40	25	ucc	5,648 teu
9315202	Maersk Sentosa	Sgp	2007	79,702	87,618	318	40	25	ucc	5,648 teu
9315214	Maersk Serangoon	Sgp	2007	79,702	87,624	318	40	25	ucc	5,648 teu
9352042	Maersk Stockholm	Hkg	2008	91,427	102,238	334	43	25	ucc	8,086 teu
9334662	Maersk Taikung	Sgp	2007	94,193	107,329	332	43	24	ucc	8,086 teu
9332511	Maersk Tanjong	Sgp	2007	94,193	107,500	332	43	24	ucc	8.086 teu
9334674	Maersk Taurus	Sgp	2008	94,193	107,266	332	43	24	ucc	8,086 teu
9334686	Maersk Tukang	Sgp	2008	94,193	107,404	332	43	24	ucc	8,086 teu
9411381	Maersk Vallvik	Sgp	2011	20,927	25,500	180	28	20	ucc	1,800 teu
9320752	Maersk Value	Sgp	2008	47,386	59,423	225	37	16	lpg	80,645 m³
9411379	Maersk Varna	Sgp	2011	20,927	25,500	180	28	20	ucc	1,800 teu
9320764	Maersk Venture	Sgp	2008	47,386	58,159	225	37	16	lpg	80,606 m³
9408956	Maersk Vilnius	Sgp	2010	20,927	26,036	180	28	20	ucc	1,800 teu
9320740	Maersk Virtue	Sgp	2007	47,386	58,123	225	37	16	lpg	80,656 m³
9320738	Maersk Visual	Sgp	2007	47,386	58,063	225	37	16	lpg	80,656 m³
9411367	Maersk Visby	Sgp	2010	20,927	26,036	180	28	20	ucc	1,800 teu
9289180	Safmarine Cameroun	Sgp	2004	24,488	28,936	196	32	20	ucc	2,096 teu
9333034	Safmarine Kariba	Sgp	2008	74,642	84,626	299	40	25	ucc	6,188 teu
9342176	Safmarine Komati	Sgp	2008	74,642	84,688	299	40	25	ucc	6,188 teu
9289207	Safmarine Kuramo	Sgp	2004	24,488	28,844	196	32	20	ucc	2,096 teu
9314210	Safmarine Mafadi	Sgp	2007	50,698	61,433	292	32	25	ucc	4,154 teu
9318319	Safmarine Makutu	Sgp	2007	50,698	61,407	292	32	25	ucc	4,154 teu
9311696	Safmarine Meru	Sgp	2006	50,686	61,392	292	32	25	ucc	4,154 teu
9311701	Safmarine Mulanje	Sgp	2007	50,686	61,447	292	32	25	ucc	4,154 teu
9356074	Safmarine Ngami	Sgp	2008	25,904	35,119	211	30	21	ucc	2,478 teu
9289192	Safmarine Nimba	Sgp	2004	24,488	28,897	196	32	20	ucc	2,096 teu
9356165	Mercosul Manaus **	Bra	2009	25,888	35,220	207	30	22	ucc	2,474 teu
9356153	Mercosul Santos ***	Bra	2009	25,888	35,239	207	30	22	ucc	2,487 teu
9356141	Mercosul Suape ***	Bra	2008	25,888	35,221	207	30	22	ucc	2,474 teu

A. P. Møller (Møller Singapore AP Pte) : Maersk Bali : *Chris Brooks*

*owned by Maersk B.V., ** owned by Maersk BV and operated by Mercosul Line Navegacao, Brasil
*** owned by Mercosul Line Navegacao, Brasil and managed by Moller Singapore AP Pte. Ltd.

Safmarine Container Lines, Belgium

Funnel: Blue with 'Safmarine' houseflag (white with orange cross) on large white disc. **Hull:** White with blue 'Safmarine',or blue with white 'Safmarine', red or green boot-topping. **History:** Container subsidiary founded 1996 as Safmarine & CMBT Lines NV to 1998 and acquired 1999. **Web:** www.safmarine.com

IMO#	name	flag	year	grt	dwt	loa	bm	kts	type	teu
9355355	Safmarine Bayete	Gbr	2009	35,835	43,197	223	32	22	ucc	2,787 teu
9294393	Safmarine Nokwanda	Gbr	2005	50,657	62,994	266	37	24	ucc	4,045 teu
9538880	Safmarine Sahara +	Gbr	2011	14,859	17,884	162	25		ggc	
9539365	Safmarine Sahel +	Hkg	2011	14,859	17,954	162	25		ggc	
9539389	Safmarine Suguta +	Hkg	2012	14,859	17,907	162	25		ggc	
9423516	Safmarine Sumba +	Hkg	2010	14,859	18,019	162	25		ggc	

+ managed by Enzian Ship Mgmt., Zurich
also see other chartered vessels with 'Safmarine' prefix in index.

A/S J. Ludwig Mowinckels Rederi   Norway

Funnel: Cream with narrow blue band on white band on broad red band beneath black top. **Hull:** Black, grey or brown with red boot-topping. **History:** Originally founded 1898 and split into separate family operating subsidiaries Viken and Vista in 2002.

Web: www.jlmr.no

IMO#	name	flag	year	grt	dwt	loa	bm	kts	type	former names
9389825	Goya	Nis	2008	41,655	75,750	225	32	14	bbu	
9348447	Grena	Bhs	2003	81,141	148,553	278	46	14	tcs	
9039597	Mire*	Lbr	1994	52,157	96,347	238	42	14	tco	ex- Molda-09
9413418	Ogna	Nis	2009	40,500	75,750	225	32	14	bbu	

operated by Mowinckel Ship Management AS (formerly Vista Ship Management to 2008) *managed for Eurotankers, Greece

MPC Münchmeyer Petersen Steamship Gmbh & Co. KG
Germany

Funnel: Black with houseflag (red/black diagonally divided with white 'MPC') or charterers colours. **Hull:** Grey with red boot-topping. **History:** founded 1999 and subsidiary MPC Capital AG in 2000 (holds 40% interest in HCI Capital). **Web:** www.mpc-marine.com or www.mpc-steamship.de

IMO#	name	flag	year	grt	dwt	loa	bm	kts	type	former names
9135901	Alianca Pearl	Lbr	1998	25,791	44,144	199	30	14	bbu	ex Pearl River-11, Hugo Oldendorff-06
9135913	Alianca River	Lbr	1998	25,791	44,114	199	30	15	bbu	ex Yangtze River-11 Gerdt Oldendorff-05
9216987	Buenos Aires Express	Lbr	2000	65,059	68,122	275	40	26	ucc	5,551 teu: ex Rio Blackwater-10,MSC Shanghai-10, CSCL Shanghai-08
9131242	CCNI Ancud ††	Mhl	1998	28,148	44,596	185	32	15	bcb	ex CSAV Valencia-03, CCNI Ancud-01
9344564	CMA CGM Auckland	Lbr	2006	27,322	34,200	212	30	22	ucc	2,492 teu: ex Rio Ardeche-06
9339868	CMA CGM Comoe	Lbr	2008	23,633	27,155	191	29	20	ucc	2,007 teu: ex Rio San Francisco-08
9344552	CMA CGM Iguacu	Lbr	2006	27,322	34,200	212	30	22	ucc	2,492 teu: ex Rio Adour-06
9362449	CSAV Lonquimay	Lbr	2008	40,807	55,313	261	32	24	ucc	4,334 teu
9216999	Navegantes Express	Lbr	2001	65,059	68,122	275	40	26	ucc	5,551 teu: ex Rio Barrow-11, MSC Hong Kong-10, CSCL Hong Kong-08

A. P. Møller (Safmarine Container Line) : SAFMARINE BAYETE : *Hans Kraijenbosch*

IMO#	name	flag	year	grt	dwt	loa	bm	kts	type	former names
9304734	MCC Shanghai	Lbr	2004	27,059	34,415	212	30	22	ucc	2,492 teu: ex Rio Alster-10, Maersk Naples-09
9506382	Rio Anna	Lbr	2012	26,374	34,116	209	30	22	ucc	2,546 teu
9506394	*Rio Angelina*	Lbr	2013	26,374	34,000	209	30	22	ucc	2,546 teu
9360764	Rio Cadiz	Lbr	2008	40,807	55,301	261	32	24	ucc	4,334 teu: ex CSAV Lonquen-12
9456953	Rio Cardiff	Lbr	2010	41,331	51,693	262	32	24	ucc	4,334 teu
9456965	Rio Chicago	Lbr	2010	41,331	51,687	262	32	24	ucc	4,334 teu
9304746	Rio Eider	Lbr	2005	27,059	34,444	212	30	22	ucc	2,492 teu: ex Maersk Narvik-10, I/a Rio Eider
9304629	Rio Genoa †	Lbr	2007	83,722	159,395	277	50	14	tcr	
9536155	Rio Manaus	Lbr	2012	93,789	179,023	292	45	14	bbu	
9537848	Rio Montevideo	Lbr	2012	93,789	179,000	292	45	14	bbu	
9337028	Rio Stora	Lbr	2007	23,666	28,325	191	29	20	ucc	2,007 teu; ex CMA CGM Togo-12, Rio Stora-07
9261815	Rio Valiente	Deu	2003	25,703	33,673	208	30	21	ucc	2,524 teu: ex Cap Valiente-09, Cabo Creus-07, I/a Rio Valiente
9261827	Rio Verde	Deu	2003	25,703	33,741	208	29	21	ucc	2,524 teu: ex Cap Verde-09, Alianca Sao Paulo-07, Rio Verde-03

newbuildings:.
† by Bernard Schulte Shipmanagement (Deutschland) GmbH, †† by Uniteam Marine Shipping GmbH or ‡ by Rickmers Reederei GmbH & Cie KG
Also other ships under Reederei Claus-Peter Offen GmbH & Co and Seatrade Groningen BV (Triton Schiffahrts GmbH))

A/S J. Ludwig Mowinckels Rederi : GRENA : *M. Lennon*

MPC Münchmeyer Petersen Steamship : RIO STORA : *Hans Kraijenbosch*

IMO#	name	flag	year	grt	dwt	loa	bm	kts	type	former names

The National Shipping Company of Saudi Arabia   Saudi Arabia

Funnel: *White with yellow palm tree above crossed swords between two narrow green bands, narrow black top.* **Hull:** *Green or red some with yellow 'NSCSA', red or blue boot-topping.* **History:** *Formed 1979 as Saudi National Shipping Co. with 25% owned by Saudi government. Acquired 30% share of Petredec in 2005. Now being referred to as Bahri and in late June 2012 a Memorandum of Understanding was signed regarding merger with Vela International.* **Web:** *www.bahri.sa*

IMO#	name	flag	year	grt	dwt	loa	bm	kts	type	former names
9247182	Abqaiq	Bhs	2002	159,990	302,986	333	58	16	tcr	
9620944	Bahri Abha	Sau	2013	50,714	26,000	220	32	17	urc	364 teu
9620956	Bahri Hofuf	Sau	2013	50,714	26,000	220	32	17	urc	364 teu
9620970	Bahri Jazan	Sau	2013	50,714	26,000	220	32	17	urc	364 teu
9626522	Bahri Jeddah	Sau	2013	50,714	26,000	220	32	17	urc	364 teu
9620968	Bahri Tobuk	Sau	2013	50,714	26,000	220	32	17	urc	364 teu
9626534	Bahri Yanbu	Sau	2014	65,000	26,000	220	32	17	urc	364 teu
9386964	Dorra	Bhs	2009	160,782	317,458	333	60	15	tcr	
9102241	Ghawar	Bhs	1996	163,882	300,361	340	56	15	tcr	
9387009	Ghazal	Sau	2009	160,782	317,664	333	60	15	tcr	
9386940	Habari	Bhs	2008	160,782	317,693	333	60	15	tcr	
9220952	Harad	Bhs	2001	159,990	303,115	333	58	17	tcr	l/a Hellespont Burnside
9102265	Hawtah	Bhs	1996	163,882	300,361	340	56	15	tcr	ex TI Hawtah-11, Hawtah-07
9386938	Jana	Bhs	2007	160,782	318,000	333	60	15	tcr	
9386952	Kahla	Bhs	2009	160,782	317,521	333	60	15	tcr	
9330698	Layla	Bhs	2007	160,782	317,788	333	60	15	tcr	
9220964	Marjan	Bhs	2002	159,990	303,115	333	58	17	tcr	
9102239	Ramlah	Bhs	1996	163,882	300,361	340	56	15	tcr	
9102277	Safaniyah	Bhs	1997	163,882	300,361	340	56	15	tcr	
9223887	Safwa	Bhs	2002	159,990	302,977	333	58	16	tcr	
9288273	Sahba	Bhs	2009	160,782	317,563	333	60	15	tcr	
8121757	Saudi Diriyah	Sau	1983	44,171	42,600	249	32	18	urc	
8121769	Saudi Hofuf	Sau	1983	44,171	42,600	249	32	18	urc	
8121771	Saudi Tabuk	Sau	1983	44,171	42,600	249	32	18	urc	
9102253	Watban	Bhs	1996	163,882	300,361	340	56	15	tcr	ex TI Watban-11, Watban-07
9332535	Wafrah	Bhs	2007	160,782	317,788	333	60	15	tcr	

newbuildings: six further 318,000 dwt crude oil tankers

managed by Mideast Ship Management Ltd, UAE (formed 1996 jointly by NSCSA and V.Ships (UK) Ltd - www.msml.com)

National Chemical Carriers, Saudi Arabia

Funnel: *White 'NCC' in green, between two narrow green bands, narrow black top.* **Hull:** *Red with red boot-topping.* **History:** *Company, 80% owned by NSCSA, 20% by SABIC, formed 1990.* **Web:** *ncc-riyadh.com*

IMO#	name	flag	year	grt	dwt	loa	bm	kts	type	former names
9087025	Bow Jubail *	Nis	1996	23,197	37,449	183	32	16	tco	ex NCC Jubail-09
9047752	Bow Mekka *	Nis	1995	23,197	37,272	183	32	16	tco	ex NCC Mekka-09

National Shipping Co. of Saudi Arabia : DORRA : *ARO*

IMO#	name	flag	year	grt	dwt	loa	bm	kts	type	former names
9047506	Bow Riyad *	Nis	1994	23,197	37,252	183	32	16	tco	ex NCC Riyad-09
9295282	NCC Abha	Pan	2006	29,575	45,958	183	32	14	tco	
9411317	NCC Amal	Pan	2011	29,168	45,544	183	32	14	tco	
9335056	NCC Dammam	Pan	2008	29,575	45,965	183	32	14	tco	
9419541	NCC Danah	Pan	2011	29,168	45,579	183	32	14	tco	
9335068	NCC Haiel	Pan	2008	29,575	45,953	183	32	14	tco	
9399272	NCC Huda	Pan	2011	29,168	45,459	183	32	14	tco	
9299886	NCC Hijaz	Pan	2005	29,575	45,956	183	32	14	tco	
9299874	NCC Najd	Pan	2005	29,575	45,998	183	32	14	tco	
9459022	NCC Najem	Pan	2012	28,300	45,499	183	32	14	tco	
9459008	NCC Nasma	Pan	2011	29,168	45,550	183	32	14	tco	
9399260	NCC Noor	Pan	2011	29,165	45,565	183	32	14	tco	
9306811	NCC Qassim	Pan	2008	29,575	46,038	183	32	14	tco	
9335032	NCC Rabigh	Sau	2006	29,575	46,038	183	32	14	tco	
9459034	NCC Reem	Pan	2012	28,300	45,498	183	32	14	tco	
9411329	NCC Safa	Pan	2011	29,168	45,471	183	32	14	tco	
9480150	NCC Sama	Pan	2012	29.168	45,471	183	32	14	tco	
9480162	NCC Bader	Pan	2012	29,168	45,000	183	32	14	tco	launched : 10:12:2011
9459010	NCC Shams	Pan	2012	29,168	45,468	183	32	14	tco	
9335044	NCC Sudair	Pan	2007	29,575	46,012	183	32	14	tco	
9306809	NCC Tabuk	Pan	2006	29,575	45,963	183	32	14	tco	
9295270	NCC Tihama	Pan	2005	29,575	45,948	183	32	14	tco	

newbuilding : 1 x 75,000dwt tank [Daewoo (2013)]
* bareboat chartered to Odfjell SE, Norway (www.odfjell.com) until 2019, other vessels commercially operated by NCC Odfjell Chemical Tankers JLT, Dubai managed by Mideast Ship Management Ltd, UAE (formed 1996 jointly by NSCSA and V.Ships (UK) Ltd - www.msml.com)

Navalmar (U.K.) Ltd. **U.K.**

Funnel: *Black.* **Hull:** *Black or grey with white 'NAVALMAR', red boot-topping.* **History:** *Founded 1990.* **Web:** *www.navalmar.co.uk*

IMO#	name	flag	year	grt	dwt	loa	bm	kts	type	former names
9102485	Arundel Castle	Pan	1997	30,928	48,139	200	31	14	ggc	ex Meghna Pride-12, Syrena-10, Seaboard Syrena-00, Syrena-98
9137428	Colchester Castle	Mlt	1996	27,552	45,300	190	31	14	bbu	ex Getaldic-11, Unterwalden-05
8215778	East Castle	Pan	1983	8,328	11,754	133	20		ggc	ex Ameglia Star-09, Range-08, Eagle Prosperity-99, David Bluhm-93, OOCL Affluence-92, David Bluhm-90, Eagle Sea-90, David Bluhm-88, Annapurna-88, Ville d'Aurore-83, I/a David Bluhm
8100882	Hastings Castle	Vct	1984	22,076	37,612	188	28	14	bbu	ex Alda-10, Catherine C.-03, Theotoko-99, Youssoufia-93
9137430	Rochester Castle	Mlt	1997	27,552	45,269	190	32	14	bbu	ex Gundulic-11, Luzem-05, Skaugum-97

managed by B Navi Shipmanagement Srl. Italy (www.bnavi.it)

National Shipping Co. of Saudi Arabia (National Chemical Carriers) : NCC NASMA :
Hans Kraijenbosch

IMO#	name	flag	year	grt	dwt	loa	bm	kts	type	former names

Navigation Maritime Bulgare

Bulgaria

Funnel: *Yellow with broad red band, narrow black top.* **Hull:** *Black with red boot-topping.* **History:** *Founded 1892 and Government controlled, but with 43% owned since 2000 by British Orient Holdings.* **Web:** *www.navbul.com*

IMO#	name	flag	year	grt	dwt	loa	bm	kts	type	former names
8417766	Alexander Dimitrov	Bgr	1985	23,609	38,524	199	28	15	bbu	
9158159	Balgarka	Mlt	2004	25,065	41,425	186	30	14	bbu	ex Dolly-03
8417754	Baltic Star	Bgr	1985	23,409	38,498	199	29	15	bbu	ex General Grot-10, General Grot-Rowecki-10
9498262	Belasitza	Mlt	2011	19,906	30,685	186	24	14	bbu	
9132492	Bogdan	Mlt	1997	10,220	13,960	142	22	13	bbu	
9404431	Bulgaria	Mlt	2010	24,165	37,852	189	28	14	bbu	ex Cordoba-10
8510934	Dimitrovsky Komsomol	Bgr	1985	23,444	38,545	201	28	15	bbu	
8507509	Georgi Grigorov	Mlt	1986	23,540	38,518	199	28	15	bbu	
9354791	Hemus	Mlt	2008	25,327	42,704	186	30	14	bbu	
9132480	Kom	MLt	1997	10,220	13,971	142	22	13	bbu	
8325901	Koznitsa	Bgr	1984	16,502	24,100	185	23	14	bbu	
9498248	Lyulin	Mlt	2011	19,906	30,685	186	24	14	bbu	
8203359	Malyovitza	Bgr	1983	16,188	24,456	184	23	14	bbu	
9015656	Midjur	Bgr	1992	13,834	21,537	168	25	13	bbu	
9498250	Osogovo	Mlt	2011	19,906	30,692	186	24	14	bbu	
9123507	Perelik	Bgr	1998	10,220	13,902	142	22	13	bbu	
9132519	Persenik	Bgr	1998	10,220	13,900	142	22	13	bbu	
9381861	Pirin	Mlt	2007	13,965	21,211	169	25	14	bbu	
9004176	Plana	Mlt	1991	13,834	19,985	169	25	13	bbu	
9404429	Rodina	Mlt	2009	24,165	37,852	190	28	14	bbu	
9498274	Rodopi	Mlt	2012	19,857	30,685	186	24	14	bbu	
9104811	Sakar	Mlt	1995	13,957	21,591	168	25	13	bbu	
9381873	Stara Planina	Mlt	2007	25,327	42,704	186	30	14	bbu	
9565140	Strandja	Mlt	2010	19,865	30,682	186	24		bbu	
9145231	Trapezitsa	Bgr	2003	13,967	21,250	169	25	-	bbu	
9145229	Tzarevetz	Mlt	1998	13,965	21,470	169	25	-	bbu	
9136931	Verila	Bgr	1996	14,431	23,723	151	26	-	bbu	
9564138	Vitosha	Mlt	2010	19,865	30,692	186	24		bbu	
9044700	Vola 1	Mlt	1992	13,834	20,620	168	25	13	bbu	ex Vola-03
8515532	Yordan Lutibrodski	Bgr	1986	23,589	38,519	198	28	15	bbu	

newbuildings:.

Navigator Gas LLC

U.K.

Funnel: *Light blue with blue 'N' over gold anchor on broad white band.* **Hull:** *Red with maroon boot-topping.* **History:** *Company restructured after emerging from Chapter 11 bankruptcy in 2006.* **Web:** *www.navigatorgas.com*

IMO#	name	flag	year	grt	dwt	loa	bm	kts	type	former names
9403762	Navigator Aires	Idn	2008	18,311	23,333	160	24	16	lpg	20,750 m³
9536363	Navigator Galaxy	Sgp	2011	16,823	16,686	154	26		lpg	22,500 m³ ex Maersk Galaxy-13
9404780	Navigator Gemini	Lbr	2009	18,311	23,358	160	24	16	lpg	20,750 m³

Navigation Maritime Bulgare : KOZNITSA : *ARO*

IMO#	name	flag	year	grt	dwt	loa	bm	kts	type	former names
9531519	Navigator Genesis	Sgp	2011	16,823	16,687	154	26		lpg	22,500 m³ ex Maersk Genesis-13
9531507	Navigator Gusto	Sgp	2011	16,823	16,686	154	26		lpg	22,500 m³ ex Maersk Gusto-13
9482574	Navigator Leo	Lbr	2011	18,321	22,844	160	24	16	lpg	20,600 m³
9482586	Navigator Libra	Lbr	2012	18,321	22,911	160	24	16	lpg	20,600 m³
9177545	Navigator Mars	Lbr	2000	17,840	23,495	170	24	16	lpg	22,085 m³
9177583	Navigator Neptune	Lbr	2000	17,840	23,495	170	24	16	lpg	22,085 m³
9407328	Navigator Pegasus	Lbr	2009	17,840	23,640	170	24	16	lpg	22,200 m³ ex Desert Orchid-12
9407330	Navigator Phoenix	Lbr	2009	17,807	23,618	170	24	16	lpg	22,200 m³ ex Dancing Brave-12
9177571	Nanigator Pluto	Idn	2000	17,849	23,484	170	24	16	lpg	22,085 m³
9177569	Navigator Saturn	Lbr	2000	17,840	23,495	170	24	16	lpg	22,085 m³
9404807	Nabigator Taurus	Lbr	2009	18,311	23,316	160	24	16	lpg	20,750 m³
9177557	Navigator Venus	Lbr	2000	17,849	23,503	170	24	16	lpg	22,085 m³

following purchased from Maersk Handy Gas Tankers, 11:2012 and to be transferred, likely renamed, during 2013

IMO#	name	flag	year	grt	dwt	loa	bm	kts	type	former names
9157478	Maersk Humber	Sgp	1998	17,980	23,292	159	26		lpg	20,928 m³ ex Burgos-05, Maersk Humber-00
9536375	Maersk Global	Sgp	2011	16,823	16,819	154	26		lpg	22,500 m³
9531466	Maersk Glory	Sgp	2010	16,823	16,819	154	26		lpg	22,500 m³
9531478	Maersk Grace	Sgp	2010	16,823	16,687	154	26		lpg	22,500 m³
9157478	Maersk Humber	Sgp	1998	17,980	20,815	159	26	18	lpg	20,928 m³ ex Burgos-05, Maersk Humber-00
9403774	Maersk Harmony	Sgp	2009	18,311	23,333	159	26		lpg	20,657 m³
9404792	Maersk Heritage	Sgp	2009	18,311	23,333	159	26		lpg	20,657 m³
9404819	Maersk Honour	Sgp	2009	18,311	23,273	159	26		lpg	20,657 m³

newbuildings: Jiangnan Shipyard hull 2530-32 21,000 m³ (2014)

Neptune Orient Lines Ltd.   Singapore

Funnel: *Blue with horizontal blue and diagonal green triple wave design on broad white band, narrow black top or blue with white 'eagle' symbol on red band (APL).* **Hull:** *Light grey with blue 'NOL' or black with white 'APL' with red or dark grey boot-topping.* **History:** *Singapore government controlled and founded 1969. American President Lines (founded 1896 and 1973 amalgamation with American Mail Lines) acquired 1997.* **Web:** *www.nol.com.sg or www.apl.com*

IMO#	name	flag	year	grt	dwt	loa	bm	kts	type	former names
9631979	APL Accolade	Sgp	2013	151,200	150,936	367	51	23	ucc	13,900teu
9631967	APL Accolade	Sgp	2013	151,200	150,936	367	51	23	ucc	13,900teu
9631979	APL Achiever #	Sgp	2013	151,200	150,936	367	51	23	ucc	13,900teu
9631981	APL Advance #	Sgp	2013	151,200	150,936	367	51	23	ucc	13,900teu
9631993	APL Advisor	Sgp	2013	151,200	150,936	367	51	23	ucc	13,900teu
9139713	APL Agate *	Usa	1997	65,475	63,693	272	40	24	ucc	5,020 teu: ex MOL Freedom-09, APL Agate-08, NOL Agate-00
9632002	APL Agile #	Sgp	2013	151,200	150,936	367	51	23	ucc	13,900teu
9015498	APL Almandine	Sgp	1993	49,716	59,560	288	32	23	ucc	3,821 teu: ex Tokyo Bay-98, Neptune Almandine-96
9007958	APL Amazonite	Sgp	1993	49,716	59,603	288	32	24	ucc	3,821 teu: ex APL Sweden-01, NOL Amazonite-00, Osaka Bay-97, NOL Amazonite-96, Neptune Amazonite-95
9632014	APL Ambassador	Sgp	2013	151,200	150,936	367	51	23	ucc	13,900teu
9632026	APL Ambition #	Sgp	2013	151,200	150,936	367	51	23	ucc	13,900teu
9632038	APL Ascent	Sgp	2013	151,200	150,936	367	51	23	ucc	13,900teu
9632040	APL Aspire #	Sgp	2013	151,200	150,936	367	51	23	ucc	13,900teu
9444285	APL Austria **	Lbr	2007	71,867	72,807	295	40	26	ucc	6,350 teu
9462043	APL Barcelona	Sgp	2012	128,929	131,400	348	46	25	ucc	10,700 teu
9218686	APL Belgium	Sgp	2002	65,792	67,500	277	40	24	ucc	5,514 teu
9234109	APL Cairo	Sgp	2001	25,305	34,133	207	30	21	ucc	2,506 teu
9074389	APL China *	Usa	1995	64,502	67,432	276	40	24	ucc	4,832 teu
9461867	APL Chongxing	Sgp	2011	113,735	122,200	349	46	25	ucc	10,106 teu
9139749	APL Coral *	Sgp	1998	65,475	64,145	275	40	24	ucc	5,020 teu: ex NOL Coral-01
9139725	APL Cyprine *	Sgp	1997	65,475	64,156	275	40	24	ucc	5,020 teu: ex NOL Cyprine-00
9234135	APL Dalian	Sgp	2002	25,305	34,133	207	30	21	ucc	2,506 teu: ex Indamex Dalian-04, APL Dalian-03
9601314	APL Dublin	Sgp	2012	128,929	131,400	349	46	24	ucc	10,100 teu
9218650	APL England	Sgp	2001	65,792	67,967	277	40	24	ucc	5,514 teu
9350032	APL Florida	Lbr	2008	71,787	72,300	293	40	25	ucc	6,350 teu
9077460	APL Garnet	Sgp	1995	53,519	66,565	294	32	24	ucc	4,392 teu: ex Hyundai Garnet-09, APL Garnet-05, MOL Vigor-05, MSC Louisiana-03, APL Garnet-02, NOL Seginus-98, l/a Neptune Seginus
9288394	APL Germany **	Lbr	2003	66,462	67,109	281	40	25	ucc	5,588 teu
9461879	APL Gwangyang	Sgp	2011	113,735	122,200	349	46	25	ucc	10,106 teu
9218674	APL Holland	Sgp	2001	65,792	67,500	277	40	24	ucc	5,514 teu
9260902	APL Hong Kong **	Lbr	2002	66,573	67,009	279	40	25	ucc	5,588 teu
9144756	APL Iolite	Sgp	1997	63,900	62,693	272	40	26	ucc	4,918 teu: ex MSC Hudson-04, APL Iolite-03, NOL Iolite-00
9260914	APL Ireland **	Lbr	2002	66,462	67,009	280	40	25	ucc	4,588 teu
9144768	APL Iris	Sgp	1998	63,900	62,693	272	40	24	ucc	4,918 teu; ex NOL Iris-01

IMO#	name	flag	year	grt	dwt	loa	bm	kts	type	former names
9081203	APL Jade	Sgp	1995	53,519	66,647	294	32	24	ucc	4,392 teu: ex Hyundai Grace-05, APL Jade-04, NOL Sheratan-98, l/a Neptune Sheratan
9074391	APL Japan *	Sgp	1995	64,502	66,520	276	40	24	ucc	4,832 teu; ex Hyundai Japan-09, APL Japan-07
9234111	APL Jeddah	Sgp	2001	25,305	34,122	207	30	21	ucc	2,506 teu: ex Indamex Malabar-04, APL Jeddah-03
8616295	APL Kennedy	Sgp	1988	61,926	54,665	275	39	24	ucc	4,340 teu: ex Hyundai Kennedy-09, APL Kennedy-07, President Kennedy-03
9074535	APL Korea *	Usa	1995	64,502	66,370	276	40	24	ucc	4,832 teu
9461881	APL Le Havre	Sgp	2012	113,735	123,127	349	46	25	ucc	10,100 teu
9350018	APL Minnesota **	Lbr	2008	71,787	72,912	293	40	26	ucc	6,350 teu
9350020	APL New Jersey **	Lbr	2008	71,787	72.912	293	40	26	ucc	6,350 teu
9597484	APL New York	Sgp	2013	109,712	112,000	332	42	25	ucc	9,200 teu
9495040	APL Ningbo **	Pan	2010	86,679	90,488	316	46	26	ucc	8,540 teu
9403621	APL Norway **	Lbr	2007	71,867	72,807	293	40	26	ucc	6,350 teu
9532783	APL Oregon **	Pan	2010	71,787	72,912	293	40	26	ucc	6,350 teu
9139737	APL Pearl *	Sgp	1998	65,475	64,050	275	40	24	ucc	5,020 teu: ex NOL Pearl-99
9234123	APL Pusan	Sgp	2002	25,305	34,122	207	30	21	ucc	2,506 teu: ex Indamex Chesapeake-04, APL Pusan-02
9077276	APL Philippines *	Usa	1996	64,502	66,370	276	40	24	ucc	4,832 teu
9461893	APL Qingdao	Sgp	2012	113,735	123,137	349	46	25	ucc	10,100 teu
9462029	APL Salalah	Spg	2012	128,929	131,477	347	45	25	ucc	10,700 teu

Neptune Orient Lines : APL FLORIDA : *ARO*

Neptune Orient Lines : APL SALALAH : *Chris Dornom*

IMO#	name	flag	year	grt	dwt	loa	bm	kts	type	former names
9218662	APL Scotland	Sgp	2001	65,792	67,500	277	40	24	ucc	5,514 teu
9074547	APL Singapore *	Usa	1995	64,502	66,370	276	40	24	ucc	4,832 teu
9462017	APL Southampton	Sgp	2012	128,929	131,358	347	45	25	ucc	10,700 teu
9288409	APL Spain **	Lbr	2004	66,300	66,100	281	40	25	ucc	5,888 teu
9631955	APL Temasek	Sgp	2013	151,200	150,936	367	51	23	ucc	13,900teu: l/d APL Absolute
9077123	APL Thailand *	Usa	1995	64,502	66,370	276	40	24	ucc	4,832 teu
9082336	APL Tourmaline	Sgp	1995	52,086	60,323	294	32	24	ucc	4,369 teu: ex MOL Innovation-10, APL Tourmaline-04, MOL Innovation-04, MOL Tourmaline-03, APL Tourmaline-02, NOL Tourmaline-98
9532771	APL Turkey **	Lbr	2009	71,787	72,912	293	40	26	ucc	6,350 teu
9082348	APL Turquoise *	Sgp	1996	52,086	60,323	294	32	24	ucc	4,369 teu: ex NOL Turquoise-98
9597472	APL Vancouver	Sgp	2013	109,712	112,000	332	42	25	ucc	9,200 teu
9462031	APL Yangshan	Sgp	2012	128,929	131,400	347	45	25	ucc	10,700 teu
9495038	APL Zeebrugge **	Pan	2010	86,679	90,414	316	46	24	ucc	8,540 eu: l/a Bunga Seroja Tiga
8616934	President Adams *	Usa	1988	61,296	53,613	275	39	24	ucc	4,340 teu
8616300	President Jackson *	Usa	1988	61,296	53,613	275	39	24	ucc	4,340 teu
8616922	President Polk *	Usa	1988	61,296	53,613	275	39	24	ucc	4,340 teu
8616283	President Truman *	Usa	1988	61,296	53,613	275	39	24	ucc	4,340 teu

newbuildings: upgrade of ten 8,400 to 9,200 teu container ships [Daewoo]
 # to be chartered to MOL for 3 years and will probably be completed with MOL names
*managed by Neptune Shipmanagement Services (Pte) Ltd, Singapore, except * owned by subsidiary APL Maritime Ltd, USA (founded 1984 as American Automar Inc to 2005) and managed by American Ship Management LLC, USA ** chartered from Japanese owners or banks.*

Neste Oil Corporation   Finland
Funnel: *Black with diamond divided green over blue.* **Hull:** *Black or dark blue, some with pale green or white 'NESTESHIP', red or pink boot-topping.* **History:** *Subsidiary of Fortum Oy, founded 1948 as government controlled Neste Oil to 1999, then Fortum Oil Oy until 2005.* **Web:** *www.nesteoil.com*

IMO#	name	flag	year	grt	dwt	loa	bm	kts	type	former names
9255282	Futura	Fin	2004	15,980	25,084	170	24	14	tco	
9255270	Jurmo	Fin	2004	15,980	25,049	169	24	14	tco	
9235892	Mastera (me2)	Fin	2003	64,259	106,208	252	44	14	tci	
9255294	Neste	Fin	2004	15,980	25,117	170	24	14	tco	
9334703	Palva *	Fin	2007	42,810	74,940	229	32	14	tco	l/a Neste Polaris
9255268	Purha	Fin	2003	15,980	25,000	170	24	14	tco	
9305556	Stena Arctica *	Fin	2005	65,293	117,099	250	44	14	tcr	
9334698	Stena Poseidon *	Fin	2006	42,810	74,927	229	32	14	tco	l/a Stena Polaris
9235880	Tempera (me2)	Fin	2002	64,259	106,034	252	44	14	tci	

* owned jointly with Concordia Maritime AB (see under Stena AB)

Niki Shipping Co. Inc.   Greece
Funnel: *charterer's colours.* **Hull:** *Charterer's colours.* **History:** *founded 2001*

IMO#	name	flag	year	grt	dwt	loa	bm	kts	type	former names
9322463	Ital Laguna	Ita	2006	54,152	68,038	294	32	24	ucc	5,090 teu
9322475	Ital Libera	Ita	2007	54,152	67,986	294	32	24	ucc	5,090 teu
9322487	Ital Lirica	Ita	2007	54,152	68,138	294	32	24	ucc	5,090 teu
9322499	Ital Lunare	Ita	2007	54,152	68,009	294	32	24	ucc	5,090 teu
9467392	MSC Beryl	Pan	2010	140,096	139,419	366	48	23	ucc	12,400 teu
9463205	MSC Immacolata	Pan	2012	59,835	22,196	299	22	19	mve	6,700 ceu

newbuildings : further four 12,400 teu container ships (STX Shipyard) 1 x 106,600dwt bulker [STX Dalian (2013)]

NileDutch Africa Line   Netherlands
Funnel: *Blue base below broad white band with orange flash above blue 'NileDutch', deep orange top.* **Hull:** *Black, dark grey or blue with red or black boot-topping.* **History:** *Founded 1988.* **Web:** *www.niledutch.com*

IMO#	name	flag	year	grt	dwt	loa	bm	kts	type	former names
9539482	NileDutch Beijing *	Lbr	2011	39,753	46,020	228	32	22	ucc	3,405 teu
9334387	NileDutch Luanda **	Mlt	2011	34,642	41,850	221	32	22	ucc	3,104 teu: ex Port Gdynia-11, l/a Albert

*managed or owned by * Nordic Hamburg Shipmanagement, ** POL-Levant Shipping Lines*
See other chartered vessels in index with NDS or NileDutch prefixes.

Nippon Yusen Kaisha (NYK)   Japan
Funnel: *Black with two narrow red bands on broad white band.* **Hull:** *Black or dark blue (vehicle carriers) with white/grey/pale blue diagonal stripes and white 'NYK LINE' with red boot-topping.* **History:** *Founded 1870 asTsukumo Shokai being renamed Mitsukawa Shokai in 1872, Mitsubishi Shokai in 1873, Mitsubishi Kisen then Mitsubishi Mail Steamship Co in 1875. Merged in 1885 with Kyodo Unyu Kaisha to form NYK. Became joint-stock corporation in 1893 and name changed to Nippon Yusen Kabushiki Kaisha. Acquired Dai-ni Tokyo Kisen Kaisha in 1926 and Kinkai Yusen Kaisha in 1939. Merged with Mitsubishi Shipping in 1964 and Showa Line in 1998. Web: www.nykline.com*

IMO#	name	flag	year	grt	dwt	loa	bm	kts	type	former names
9054119	Aegean Leader	Pan	1993	47,171	13,157	180	32	18	mve	4,736 ceu: ex Ocean Beluga-99, Mercury Diamond-96
9166895	Alioth Leader +	Pan	1998	51,790	14,909	180	32	19	mve	4,305 ceu

IMO#	name	flag	year	grt	dwt	loa	bm	kts	type	former names
9539171	Altair Leader *	Jpn	2011	60,295	18,688	200	32		mve	6,341 ceu
9273909	Andromeda Leader *	Pan	2004	62,195	21,443	200	32	20	mve	5,427 ceu
9539169	Antares Leader *	Jpn	2011	60,294	18,646	200	32		mve	6,341 ceu
9335953	Aphrodite Leader +	Pan	2007	62,571	21,443	200	32	19	mve	6,333 ceu
9402706	Apollon Leader *	Pan	2008	60,213	18,573	200	32	20	mve	6,341 ceu
9158276	Aquarius Leader *	Pan	1998	57,623	22,815	200	32	19	mve	5,055 ceu
9355202	Artemis Leader	Pan	2009	62,571	21,424	200	32	20	mve	6,333 ceu
9531741	Asteria Leader	Jpn	2010	63,084	21,349	200	32	19	mve	6,341 ceu
9531739	Atlas Leader	Jpn	2010	63,085	21,323	200	32	19	mve	6,341 ceu
9402718	Auriga Leader *	Sgp	2008	60,213	18,686	200	32	19	mve	6,341 ceu
9367607	Canopus Leader *	Sgp	2009	51,917	17,382	180	32	19	mve	5,195 ceu
9313008	Capricornus Leader	Pan	2004	61,854	20,120	200	32	20	mve	6,501 ceu
9182277	Cassiopeia Leader +	Pan	1999	57,455	21,547	200	32	19	mve	5,066 ceu
9284740	Centaurus Leader +	Pan	2004	62,195	21,471	200	32	20	mve	5,427 ceu
8502468	Century Leader No.3	Jpn	1986	44,830	14,154	179	32	18	mve	4,726 ceu
8513510	Century Leader No.5	Jpn	1986	50,867	15,293	200	32	18	mve	4,880 ceu
9308883	Cepheus Leader *	Pan	2006	62,571	21,402	200	32	20	mve	6,333 ceu
9291133	Cetus Leader	Pan	2005	62,195	21,466	200	32	20	mve	5,427 ceu
9345623	Champion Pleasure	Pan	2008	56,362	105,852	241	42	15	tco	
9157777	Champion Pride	Pan	1998	58,141	99,997	244	42	13	tco	
9318486	Coral Leader †	Bhs	2006	40,986	12,164	176	31	20	mve	4,750 ceu
9464455	Cronus Leader	Pan	2008	61,804	20,096	200	32	19	mve	6,501 ceu

Niki Shipping Co. Inc. : MSC BERYL : *Hans Kraijenbosch*

Nippon Yusen Kaisha (NYK) : CANOPUS LEADER : *ARO*

IMO#	name	flag	year	grt	dwt	loa	bm	kts	type	former names
9426362	Daedalus Leader	Jpn	2009	62,993	21,423	200	32	19	mve	6,332 ceu
9566629	Daio Southern Cross	Pan	2012	49,098	60,434	210	37	15	bwc	
9174282	Delphinus Leader	Pan	1998	57,391	21,514	200	32	19	mve	5,066 ceu
9477921	Demeter Leader +	Pan	2009	61,804	20,019	200	32	19	mve	5,415 ceu
9426350	Dionysus Leader	Jpn	2009	62,993	21,438	200	32	19	mve	6,332 ceu
9308895	Dorado Leader *	Pan	2006	62,571	21,410	200	32	29	mve	6,333 ceu
9361811	Emerald Leader †	Bhs	2008	40,986	10,819	176	31	20	mve	4,750 ceu
9342906	Equuleus Leader *	Pan	2005	61,804	20,141	200	32	20	mve	6,501 ceu
9332834	Forward Bright *	Hkg	2007	59,164	115,577	244	42	15	tcr	
9498602	Eridanus Leader *	Pan	2010	59,637	18,056	200	32		mve	6,400 ceu
9536818	Gaia Leader	Sgp	2011	62,838	21,286	200	32	20	mve	6,331 ceu
9194969	Gas Diana	Lbr	2000	46,021	49,999	230	37	16	lpg	78,888 m³
9225342	Gas Taurus	Lbr	2001	46,021	48,500	230	37	16	lpg	78,921 m³
9515216	Glorious Hibiscus	Pan	2012	49,097	60,411	210	32	15	bwc	
9515204	Glorious Jasmine	Pan	2012	43,823	53,995	210	32	15	bwc	
9357913	Glorious Lotus	Sgp	2007	39,904	49,602	200	32	15	bwc	
9357925	Glorious Maple	Sgp	2007	39,901	49,131	200	32	15	bwc	
9311139	Glorious Peony	Pan	2007	40,393	49,798	200	32	15	bwc	
9357901	Glorious Plumeria	Sgp	2007	39,904	49,636	200	32	15	bwc	
9363699	Glorious Sakura	Pan	2009	49,192	60.500	210	37	15	bwc	
8905426	Heijin *	Pan	1989	47,521	14,366	180	32	18	mve	4,264 teu
9476745	Helios Leader *	Jpn	2009	60,212	18.692	200	32	19	mve	6,341 ceu
9531753	Hercules Leader *	Jpn	2011	63,083	21,385	300	32	19	mve	6,331 ceu
9355226	Hestia Leader *	Jpn	2008	63,007	21,419	200	32	19	mve	6,324 ceu
8916267	Hojin *	Vut	1990	57,871	18,273	200	32	19	mve	4,681 ceu
8607749	Hudson Leader	Pan	1987	47,707	14,104	180	32	18	mve	ex Green Lake-01
9403279	Hyperion Leader	Pan	2010	41,886	14,381	190	28	19	mve	3,921 ceu
9021423	Jingu *	Jpn	1992	42,164	17,216	196	32	18	mve	4,508 ceu: ex Jingu Maru-10
8913514	Jinsei Maru	Jpn	1990	55,489	17,914	199	32	19	mve	4,985 ceu
9402756	Jupiter Leader	Sgp	2008	44,412	12,889	183	31	19	mve	4,318 ceu
9053505	Kaijin *	Pan	1994	41,931	17,183	196	29	18	mve	4,513 ceu
9186950	Kassel +	Pan	1999	51,204	17,297	180	32	19	mve	4,300 ceu
9181546	Kou-Ei	Pan	1999	149,371	279,999	330	60	15	tcr	
9181558	Leo Leader +	Pan	1999	57,566	22,733	200	32	19	mve	5,055 ceu
9206396	Linden Pride *	Pan	2001	46,021	49,999	230	37	16	lpg	78,921 m³
9367578	Lord Vishnu	Pan	2008	51,917	17,341	180	32	19	mve	5,195 ceu
9284752	Lyra Leader *	Pan	2005	62,510	21,453	200	32	20	mve	5,427 ceu
9392353	Mercury Leader *	Pan	2010	42,487	15,045	186	28	20	mve	4,115 ceu
9052343	MG Shipping	Jpn	1993	151,447	250,903	332	58	15	bor	ex Takayama-09 (conv tcr-09)
9021332	New Nada *	Pan	1992	47,519	14,180	180	32	19	mve	4,760 ceu
9237527	Nippon *	Pan	2002	159,613	298,399	333	60	15	tcr	
9468293	NYK Adonis	Pan	2010	105,644	89,692	332	45	24	ucc	9,592 teu
9468308	NYK Altair	Pan	2010	105,644	89,692	332	45	24	ucc	9,592 teu
9162497	NYK Andromeda *	Pan	1998	75,637	81,819	300	40	23	ucc	6,492 teu
9162485	NYK Antares *	Pan	1997	75,637	81,819	300	40	23	ucc	6,492 teu

Nippon Yusen Kaisha (NYK) : GLORIOUS HIBISCUS : *Chris Brooks*

IMO#	name	flag	year	grt	dwt	loa	bm	kts	type	former names
9247754	NYK Aphrodite *	Pan	2003	75,484	81,171	300	40	25	ucc	6,492 teu
9247730	NYK Apollo *	Pan	2002	75,484	81,171	300	40	25	ucc	6,492 teu
9262704	NYK Aquarius *	Pan	2003	75,484	81,171	300	40	25	ucc	6,492 teu
9262716	NYK Argus *	Pan	2004	75,484	81,171	300	40	25	ucc	6,492 teu
9247742	NYK Artemis ‡	Pan	2003	75,484	81,171	300	40	25	ucc	6,492 teu
9247786	NYK Athena ‡	Pan	2003	75,484	81,171	300	40	25	ucc	6,492 teu
9262728	NYK Atlas *	Pan	2004	75,519	81,171	300	40	25	ucc	6,492 teu
9152296	NYK Canopus	Pan	1998	76,847	82,275	300	40	23	ucc	6,208 teu
9152284	NYK Castor *	Pan	1998	76,847	82,275	300	40	23	ucc	6,208 teu
9355408	NYK Clara *	Sgp	2008	27,051	34,578	210	30	23	ucc	2,846 teu
9337614	NYK Daedalus *	Pan	2007	55,534	65,867	294	32	25	ucc	4,882 teu
9355410	NYK Daniella	Sgp	2008	27,051	34,536	210	30	23	ucc	2,846 teu
9337652	NYK Delphinus *	Pan	2007	55,534	65,950	294	32	25	ucc	4,888 teu
9337664	NYK Demeter	Pan	2008	55,534	65,965	294	32	25	ucc	4,888 teu
9337676	NYK Deneb *	Pan	2008	55,534	65,953	294	32	25	ucc	4,882 teu
9337688	NYK Diana *	Pan	2008	55,534	65,976	294	32	25	ucc	4,888 teu
9229302	NYK Leo *	Pan	2002	75,201	77,900	300	40	27	ucc	6,178 teu
9229348	NYK Libra ‡	Pan	2002	75,201	77,900	300	40	26	ucc	6,178 teu
9229300	NYK Loadstar *	Pan	2001	75,201	77,900	300	40	27	ucc	6,178 teu
9229324	NYK Lynx ‡	Pan	2002	75,201	77,950	300	40	26	ucc	6,178 teu
9229336	NYK Lyra *	Pan	2002	75,201	77,950	300	40	26	ucc	6,178 teu
9312975	NYK Oceanus *	Pan	2007	98,799	99,563	336	46	25	ucc	8,628 teu
9312987	NYK Olympus ‡	Pan	2008	98,799	99,563	336	40	25	ucc	8,628 teu
9312999	NYK Orion *	Pan	2008	98,799	99,563	336	40	25	ucc	9,050 teu
9313008	NYK Orpheus *	Jpn	2008	99,543	99,563	336	40	25	ucc	9,050 teu
9267637	NYK Pegasus *	Pan	2003	76,199	80,270	300	40	25	ucc	6,586 teu
9267649	NYK Phoenix *	Pan	2003	76,199	80,270	300	40	25	ucc	6,586 teu
9416965	NYK Remus *	Pan	2009	55,534	65,981	294	32	23	ucc	4,888 teu
9416977	NYK Rigel *	Pan	2009	55,534	66,051	294	32	23	ucc	4,888 teu
9416989	NYK Romulus	Sgp	2009	55,534	65,883	294	32	23	ucc	4,888 teu
9419644	NYK Rosa ‡	Sgp	2009	27,051	34,528	210	30	23	ucc	2,664 teu
9416991	NYK Rumina ‡	Sgp	2010	55,534	66,171	294	32	23	ucc	4,999 teu
9168324	NYK Sirius	Pan	1998	76,847	82,271	300	40	23	ucc	6.148 teu
9354167	NYK Terra *	Pan	2008	76,928	80,282	300	40	25	ucc	6,661 teu
9356696	NYK Themis *	Pan	2008	76,928	80,282	300	40	25	ucc	6,661 teu
9356701	NYK Theseus *	Pan	2008	79,280	79,030	300	40	25	ucc	6,661 teu
9356713	NYK Triton ‡	Pan	2008	76,614	79,280	300	40	25	ucc	6,661 teu
9312781	NYK Vega *	Pan	2006	97,825	103,310	338	46	25	ucc	9,012 teu
9312793	NYK Venus *	Pan	2007	97,825	100,900	338	46	25	ucc	9,012 teu
9419668	NYK Veronica ‡	Pan	2009	27,051	34,567	210	30	23	ucc	2,664 teu
9312808	NYK Vesta ‡	Pan	2007	97,825	103,260	338	46	26	ucc	9,012 teu
9312810	NYK Virgo *	Pan	2007	97,825	103,284	338	46	25	ucc	8,100 teu
9165516	Ocean Ceres	Sgp	1999	88,385	171,850	289	45	14	bbu	ex Charles LD-04
9300582	Ocean Cygnus	Pan	2006	89,603	178,996	289	45	15	bbu	
9318498	Opal Leader †	Bhs	2007	40,986	12,200	176	31	20	mve	4,750 ceu
9182289	Orion Leader	Pan	1999	57,513	21,526	200	32	19	mve	5,066 ceu
9177430	Perseus Leader	Pan	1999	57,449	21,503	200	32	19	mve	5,066 ceu

Nippon Kaisha Kaisha (NYK) : NYK OCEANUS : *ARO*

IMO#	name	flag	year	grt	dwt	loa	bm	kts	type	former names
9283875	Phoenix Leader *	Pan	2004	61,804	20,146	200	32	20	mve	5,415 ceu
9426374	Pleiades Leader *	Jon	2009	62,994	21,462	200	32	21	mve	6,332 ceu
9335965	Poseidon Leader *	Jpn	2007	63,001	21,449	200	32	20	mve	6,324 ceu
9207754	Procyon Leader *	Pan	2000	51,259	17,361	180	32	19	mve	4,666 ceu
9338888	Prometheus Leader +	Sgp	2008	41,886	14,382	190	28	20	mve	3,305 ceu
9284738	Pyxis Leader +	Pan	2004	62,195	21,466	200	32	20	mve`	5,427 ceu
8712324	Queen Ace	Pan	1988	55,423	18,777	200	32	19	mve	5,542 ceu
9355214	Rhea Leader *	Jpn	2008	63,004	21,428	200	32	19	mve	5,371 ceu
9604940	Rigel Leader *	Pan	2012	59,692	18,884	200	32	21	mve	6,153 ceu
9055486	Ryujin	Pan	1993	47,737	14,080	180	32	19	mve	4,759 ceu
9283887	Sagittaurus Leader +	Pan	2005	61,804	20,098	200	32	20	mve	6,501 ceu
9498597	Selene Leader	Pan	2010	59,637	18,082	200	32		mve	6,400 ceu
9271597	Shin Onoe	Pan	2004	101,953	203,248	300	50	15	bbu	
9073701	Shohjin	Pan	1994	50,308	16,178	179	32	19	mve	4,148ceu: ex Green Cove-12, Shohjin-00
9213806	Sirius Leader	Pan	2000	51,496	16,451	180	32	19	mve	4,323 ceu
9536909	Spica Leader	Sgp	2012	41,886	14,378	190	28		mve	3,921 ceu
8613188	Straits Voyager +	Mys	1987	38,659	13,491	182	30	18	mve	4,013 ceu: ex Columbia Leader-10 Green Bay-01
9294563	Taga *	Pan	2004	160,007	303,430	333	60	15	tcr	
9244635	Taizan	Pan	2002	160,084	300,405	333	60	15	tcr	
9183348	Takachiho II	Pan	1998	149,376	280,889	330	60	16	tcr	
9321304	Takahashi *	Pan	2007	160,295	314,020	333	60	15	tcr	
9295593	Takamine	Pan	2004	150,084	306,206	333	60	15	tcr	
9183350	Takasago Maru	Jpn	1999	149,376	281,050	330	60	15	tcr	
9320831	Takasaki	Pan	2005	159,939	300,390	333	60	15	tcr	
9177686	Takasuzu *	Pan	2000	152,139	279,989	330	60	16	tcr	
9343495	Tamba	Pan	2009	159,927	302,107	333	60	15	tcr	
9454486	Tango	Pan	2009	159,927	301,662	333	60	15	tcr	
9244623	Tateyama	Pan	2002	160,072	300,373	333	60	15	tcr	
9343390	Tenjun	Pan	2008	159,927	302,107	333	60	15	tcr	
9321299	Tenki *	Pan	2007	160,295	316,021	333	60	15	tcr	
9177155	Tenryu	Lbr	1999	152,139	281,050	330	60	16	tcr	
9222443	Tenyo *	Sgp	2000	152,139	281,050	330	60	15	tcr	
9553115	Themis Leader	Pan	2010	61,804	20,037	200	32	19	mve	5,415 ceu
9304655	Toba	Pan	2004	160,068	299,980	333	60	15	tcr	
9320843	Tohshi	Pan	2007	159,939	300,363	333	60	15	tcr	
9183374	Tokachi *	Pan	1999	149,376	280,973	330	60	16	tcr	
9311270	Tokio	Pan	2005	159,953	306,206	333	60	15	tcr	
9568809	Tokitsu Maru	Jpn	2011	159,963	305,484	333	60	15	tcr	
9343388	Tosa	Pan	2008	159,927	302,150	333	60	15	tcr	
9321213	Towada *	Pan	2006	159,982	305,801	333	60	15	tcr	
9304667	Toyo *	Pan	2005	160,096	310,309	333	60	15	tcr	
9553103	Triton Leader +	Pan	2010	60,876	22,657	200	32	19	mve	6,502 teu
9454498	Tsugaru *	Sgp	2010	160,145	301,498	333	60	15	tcr	
9439058	Tsuruga *	Pan	2009	160,068	309,960	333	60	15	tcr	
9264893	Tsurumi *	Pan	2003	159,960	300,838	333	60	15	tcr	
9213818	Vega Leader +	Pan	2000	51,496	16,396	180	32	19	mve	4,323 ceu
9392341	Venus Leader *	Pan	2010	42,487	15,031	186	28	20	mve	4,115 ceu
9273894	Virgo Leader *	Pan	2004	61,854	20,111	200	32	20	mve	5,415 ceu
9381237	Volans Leader	Pan	2007	61,775	20,168	200	32	20	mve	5,415 ceu
9476733	Zeus Leader *	Jpn	2009	60,212	18,697	200	32	20	mve	6,341 ceu

newbuildings: 4 x 7,000 ceu car carriers 2014/5 (Imabari x 2, Shin Kurushima x 2)
* managed by NYK Ship Management Co. Ltd, Singapore (formed 2001) or ** NYK Ship Management, Hong Kong (formed 1989). † managed by UECC,. + managed by Wilhelmsen SM Send. Ber. ‡ managed by Columbia Shipmanagement Ltd., Cyprus
The company and its numerous subsidiaries own or manage over 410 vessels with many others on charter. Only the largest container ships, bulk carriers, vehicle carriers and tankers are listed. Tthe company also owns, manages or operates 22 large LNG tankers, 46 wood-chip carriers, many other bulk carriers, tankers and smaller container ships and vehicle carriers. See also Ray Shipping, Stolt-Nielsen, Torm and Vroon.

NYK Cool AB, Sweden

Funnel: Deep red base and broad blue top with blue and red arcs on broad white central band. **Hull:** Red, cream or white with red/blue 'NYKCool', red or blue boot-topping. **History:** Formed 2007, when the reefer operations of LauritzenCool AB (formed 2001 following acquisition of Cool Carriers AB (formed 1984) from Leif Höegh) were acquired, having previously been a joint venture since 2005. **Web:** www.nyklc.com

IMO#	name	flag	year	grt	dwt	loa	bm	kts	type	former names
9194476	Atlantic Erica	Pan	1999	9,649	11,791	145	22	21	grf	
9038835	Autumn Wave +	Bhs	1993	13,077	13,981	158	24	22	grf	ex Dominica-09, Geest Dominica-97
9038323	Autumn Wind +	Bhs	1993	13,077	13,981	158	24	22	grf	ex St. Lucia-08, Geest St. Lucia-97
8300365	Belgian Reefer **	Bhs	1983	12,383	14,786	145	24	18	grf	ex Anne B-92
8300377	Brazilian Reefer **	Bhs	1984	12,383	14,786	145	24	16	grf	ex Betty B-92
8700230	Chaiten **	Lbr	1988	13,312	12,838	152	24	18	grf	
8917546	Chilean Reefer	Bhs	1992	7,944	11,095	141	20	22	grf	ex Carelian Reefer-97
9128037	Crown Emerald *	Pan	1996	10,519	10,351	152	23	18	grf	
9128049	Crown Garnet *	Pan	1996	10,519	10,322	152	23	21	grf	

IMO#	name	flag	year	grt	dwt	loa	bm	kts	type	former names
9128051	Crown Jade *	Pan	1997	10,519	10,332	152	23	21	grf	
9128063	Crown Opal *	Pan	1997	10,519	10,332	152	23	21	grf	
9159103	Crown Ruby *	Pan	1997	10,519	10,338	152	23	21	grf	
9159115	Crown Sapphire *	Pan	1997	10,519	10,334	152	23	21	grf	
9191498	Crown Topaz +	Pan	1999	10,527	10,318	152	23	21	grf	
8819926	Ditlev Reefer	Bhs	1990	14,406	16,950	164	24	20	grf	ex Ditlev Lauritzen-11
8819938	Ivar Reefer	Bhs	1990	14,406	16,950	165	24	20	grf	ex Ivar Lauritzen-11
9008732	Ivory Dawn	Bhs	1991	10,412	10,713	150	23	20	grf	
9143099	Ivory Girl	Vut	1996	11,438	10,432	154	24	21	grf	
9007489	Jorgen Reefer	Bhs	1991	14,406	16,950	164	24	19	grf	ex Jorgen Lauritzen-11
8903167	Knud Reefer	Bhs	1991	14,406	16,950	164	24	19	grf	ex Knud Lauritzen-11
8917572	Peruvian Reefer	Bhs	1992	7,944	11,092	141	20	22	grf	ex Savonian Reefer-97
8917560	Scandinavian Reefer	Bhs	1992	7,944	11,054	141	20	22	grf	
8907876	Swan Chacabuco **	Bhs	1990	13,099	12,974	152	24	18	grf	ex Chacabuco-97
8911102	Triton Reefer *	Lbr	1990	8,818	9,683	144	22	18	grf	
9181132	Wild Cosmos +	Pan	1998	9,859	10,097	150	22	20	grf	
9181144	Wild Heather	Pan	1998	9,859	10,114	150	22	20	grf	

Nippon Yusen Kaisha (NYKCool AB) : CROWN RUBY : *M. Lennon*

Nippon Yusen Kaisha (NYKCool AB) : JORGEN REEFER : *Chris Brooks*

IMO#	name	flag	year	grt	dwt	loa	bm	kts	type	former names
9181168	Wild Lotus +	Pan	1998	9,859	10,139	150	22	20	grf	
9191474	Wild Peony +	Pan	1998	9,859	10,110	150	22	20	grf	

* managed by Wallem Shipmanagement Ltd, Hong Kong.
chartered from various owners/managers including ** from Chartworld Shipping Corp., Greece (www.chartworld.gr), + Norbulk Shipping, UK

Nissan Motor Car Carriers   Japan

Funnel: *white with red 'NISSAN' above grey pane topped by red line, narrow black top'.* **Hull:** *grey with white upperworks separated by red line, red boot-topping.* **History:** *company founded 1965, originally for export of Nissan cars to US market.* **web:** *nissancarrier.co.jp*

IMO#	name	flag	year	grt	dwt	loa	bm	kts	type	former names
9372327	Andromeda Spirit	Pan	2007	43,810	15,261	180	30	19	mve	3,505 ceu
9153551	Euro Spirit	Lbr	1988	46,346	15,483	188	31	20	mve	5,100 ceu
8517279	Global Spirit	Lbr	1987	47,500	16,493	191	32	20	mve	4,733 ceu: ex Tochigi-99, Tochigi Maru-96
9509401	Jupiter Spirit	Lbr	2011	45,961	13,954	183	30	19	mve	5,000 ceu
9620295	Leo Spirit	Pan	2012	60,825	16,758	200	32	20	mve	6,400 ceu
9372315	Luna Spirit	Pan	2007	43,810	15,261	180	30	19	mve	3,505 ceu
9409326	Pleiades Spirit	Pan	2008	60,330	17,424	200	32	19	mve	6,400 ceu
9185047	United Spirit	Lbr	2000	37,949	14,067	175	29	20	mve	3.200 ceu
9505900	Venus Spirit	Lbr	2011	45,959	13,951	183	30	20	mve	5,000 ceu
9175925	World Spirit	Lbr	2000	37,949	14,101	175	29	19	mve	3,200 ceu

vessels managed for World Car Carrier Co.

Norddeutsche Vermogensanlage GmbH & Co. KG   Germany

Norddeutsche Reederei H. Schuldt GmbH & Co KG, Germany

Funnel: *White with red 'S' on white triange on blue square or charterers colours.* **Hull:** *Black or red with red boot-topping.* **History:** *Parent founded 1984 and subsidiary 2002 following merger of 'NRG' Norddeutsche Reederei Beteiligungs GmbH with H Schuldt OHG (founded 1868) and Engineering Consulting & Management GmbH which had merged in 1989.* **Web:** *www.norddeutsche.de*

IMO#	name	flag	year	grt	dwt	loa	bm	kts	type	former names
9450351	Alianca Charrua	Lbr	2010	94,419	108,836	333	43	24	ucc	8,400 teu: ex Northern Justice-12
9466984	Alianca Urca	Lbr	2010	94,407	108,622	334	43	24	ucc	8,400 teu: ex Northern Jupiter-12
9196890	APL Arabia	Lbr	2000	54,415	66,895	294	32	24	ucc	4,843 teu: ex MOL Vigilance-03, Vantage-03, MOL Vantage-02, APL Arabia-02, I/a Northern Grace
9196905	APL Egypt	Lbr	2000	54,415	66,922	294	32	24	ucc	4,843 teu: ex MOL Virtue-03, APL Egypt-02
9196917	APL Malaysia	Lbr	2000	54,415	66,910	294	32	24	ucc	4,843 teu; ex MOL Value-03, APL Malaysia-02, I/a Northern Glance
9252553	Bangkok Express	Deu	2003	75,590	85,810	300	40	25	ucc	6,732 teu: ex Northern Magnitude-04
9252577	Busan Express	Deu	2004	75,590	85,810	300	40	25	ucc	6,732 teu: I/a Northern Monument
9344708	Cap Gabriel	Lbr	2008	41,835	53,870	264	32	24	ucc	4,319 teu: I/dn Northern General
9348431	Cap George	Lbr	2008	41,835	53,874	264	32	24	ucc	4,319 teu: I/dn Northern Genius
9348443	Cap Gilbert	Lbr	2008	41,835	53,874	264	32	24	ucc	4,319 teu: I/dn Northern Gleam
9348455	Cap Graham	Lbr	2008	41,835	53,870	264	32	24	ucc	4,319 teu: I/dn Northern Guard
9348467	Cap Gregory	Lbr	2008	41,835	53,870	264	32	24	ucc	4,319 teu: I/dn Northern Guild
9450313	Cap Irene	Lbr	2009	47,855	59,368	264	32	24	ucc	4,319 teu: ex Northern Priority-11, Bunga Raya Sebelas-10, I/a Northern Priority

Nissan Motor Car Carriers : VENUS SPIRIT : *Nico Kemps*

IMO#	name	flag	year	grt	dwt	loa	bm	kts	type	former names
8908715	Carola E.	Lbr	1991	12,997	17,610	150	25	17	ucc	1,208 teu: ex YM Mersin-10, Independent Trader-06, Carola E-97, Caroline-96, America-96, Carolina-91
9147095	CSAV Cantabrian	Lbr	1998	53,324	63,615	294	32	23	ucc	4,688 teu: ex ANL Hong Kong-08, Yokohama Senator-06, Cho Yang Ace-01
9405033	CSAV Ranco	Lbr	2008	36,007	42,054	231	32	23	ucc	3,534 teu
9391799	CSAV Rauten	Lbr	2008	36,007	41,977	231	32	23	ucc	3,534 teu: I/a Northern Discovery
9329643	CSAV Renaico	Lbr	2007	35,975	42,121	231	32	23	ucc	3,400 teu: I/a Northern Defender
9346017	CSAV Rupanco	Lbr	2008	36,007	42,011	231	32	23	ucc	3,534 teu: I/a Northern Decision
9450349	CSAV Taltal	Lbr	2009	94,419	108,828	333	43	25	ucc	8,400 teu: ex APL Manila-12, Northern Juvenile-11
9294991	Houston Express	Deu	2005	94,483	108,106	332	43	25	ucc	8,411 teu: I/dn Northern Jade
9064762	Independent Venture	Lbr	1993	14,849	20,480	167	25	19	ucc	1,578 teu: ex Sea Voyager-99, Nautique-98
9252541	Los Angeles Express	Lbr	2003	75,590	85,810	300	40	25	ucc	6,732 teu: I/a Northern Magnum
9062972	Luetjenburg *	Deu	1995	37,323	45,530	239	32	22	ucc	3,501 teu: ex Garden Bridge-03, Heaven River-00, Lutjenburg-98
9253301	MSC Prague	Lbr	2003	41,078	48,874	260	32	23	ucc	3,963 teu: ex Barcelona Bridge-06, I/a Northern Delicacy
9253296	MSC Vienna	Lbr	2003	41,078	48,923	260	32	23	ucc	3,963 teu: ex Potomac Bridge-06, I/a Northern Decency
9353228	Northern Debonair	Lbr	2007	35,975	42,183	231	32	23	ucc	3,400 teu: ex NYK Lyttelton-12, Northern Debonair-11 CSAV Rahue-07
9391787	Northern Democrat	Lbr	2009	35,954	41,986	231	32	23	ucc	3,534 teu
9353230	Northern Diplomat	Lbr	2009	36,007	42,106	231	32	23	ucc	3,534 teu
9147112	Northern Diversity	Lbr	1997	36,606	45,131	245	32	23	ucc	3,607 teu: ex Indamex Godavari-09, MSC Bursa-04, P&O Nedlloyd Barcelona-02, Northern Diversity-98
9147100	Northern Divinity	Lbr	1997	36,606	44,117	245	32	23	ucc	3,607 teu; ex P&O Nedlloyd Damietta-05, OOCL Europe-02, P&O Nedlloyd Damietta-01, Northern Divinity-97
9230074	Northern Endeavour	Lbr	2001	25,713	33,900	208	30	21	ucc	2,456 teu: ex Cap Frio-08, Northern Endeavour-03, Andhika Loreto-01
9230086	Northern Endurance	Lbr	2001	25,713	33,838	208	30	21	ucc	2,456 teu: ex Cap Matapan-08, Alianca Singapore-07, Cap Matapan-04, Northern Endurance-03, Andhika Fatima-01
9235401	Northern Enterprise	Lbr	2001	25,713	33,836	208	30	21	ucc	2,456 teu: ex Cap Salinas-08, NYK Freesia-05, Cap Salinas-04, Northern Enterprise-03, Andhika Lourdes-02
9466972	Northern Jaguar	Lbr	94,407	108,731	334	43	25	ucc		8,400 teu: ex APL Dhaka-12, Northern Jaguar-12
9450363	Northern Jamboree	Lbr	2010	94,419	108,827	333	43	25	ucc	8,400 teu
9466960	Northern Jasper	Lbr	2009	94,407	108,804	334	43	25	ucc	8,400 teu: ex APL Portugal-12, Northern Jasper-11
9465095	Northern Javelin	Lbr	2009	94,407	108,677	334	43	25	ucc	8,400 teu ex APL Italy-12, Northern Javelin-11
9450337	Northern Jubilee	Lbr	2009	94,419	108,770	333	43	25	ucc	8,400 teu
9467055	Northern Power	Lbr	2010	47,855	59,346	264	32	24	ucc	4,600 teu

Norddeutsche Vermogensanlage (Norddeutsche Reederei H. Schuldt) : APL ARABIA : *ARO*

IMO#	name	flag	year	grt	dwt	loa	bm	kts	type	former names
9450301	Northern Practise	Lbr	2009	47,855	59,352	264	32	24	ucc	4,600 teu: ex APLXingang-11, Ankara Bridge-10
9450296	Northern Precision	Lbr	2009	47,855	59,431	264	32	24	ucc	4,319 teu: ex CCNI Patagonia-12, Northern Precision-10, Adriatic Bridge-10
9450325	Northern Prelude	Lbr	2009	47,855	59,404	264	32	24	ucc	4,600 teu
9467043	Northern Promotion	Lbr	2010	47,855	59,483	264	32	24	ucc	4,600 teu
9304693	Northern Valence	Lbr	2005	27,437	37,921	222	30	22	ucc	2,742 teu: Sinotrans Shanghai-11, l/a Northern Valence
9304708	Northern Vigour	Lbr	2005	27,437	37,901	222	30	22	ucc	2,742 teu: ex CMA CGM Qingdao-12, Sinotrans Qingdao-09
9304966	Northern Vivacity	Lbr	2005	27,437	37,856	222	30	22	ucc	2,742 teu: ex Sinotrans Tianjin-12, l/a Northern Vivacity
9304978	Northern Volition	Lbr	2006	27,437	37,813	222	30	22	ucc	2,742 teu: ex Sinotrans Dalian-12, APL Yokohama-09, Northern Volition-06, Sinotrans Dalian-06, l/a Northern Volition
9346005	NYK Lyttelton	Lbr	2008	36,007	42,002	231	32	23	ucc	3,534 teu ; CSAV Ranquil-12, l/a Northern Delegation
9252565	San Francisco Express	Deu	2004	75,590	85,400	300	40	25	ucc	6,732 teu: l/a Norther Majestic
9294989	Savannah Express	Deu	2005	94,483	101,500	332	43	25	ucc	8,411 teu: l/dn Northern Julie
9452854	Tasman Castle	Mlt	2011	32,987	56,868	190	32	14	bbu	
9112806	Wilhelm E.	Lbr	1995	14,923	20,406	167	25	19	ucc	1,388 teu: ex YM Osaka-10, Independent Endeavor-08, Astoria D-00, Libra New York-99, Libra Valencia-97, l/a Astoria
9405033	X-Press Makalu	Lbr	2010	40,541	42,054	231	32	23	ucc	3,534 teu: ex CSAV Ranco-12, l/a Northern Diamond

* managed for Hansa Treuhand Schiffsbeteiligungs GmbH & Co KG. Also see vessels managed by F. Laeisz Schiffahrts GmbH

Dampskibsselskabet 'Norden' A/S   Denmark

Funnel: *Black with narrow red band on broad white band.* **Hull:** *Black or dark blue with red boot-topping.* **History:** Formed 1871 and now 32% owned by A/S Dampskibsselskabet Torm. **Web:** www.ds-norden.com

IMO#	name	flag	year	grt	dwt	loa	bm	kts	type
9595254	Nord Aarhus *	Sgp	2012	21,934	33,221	179	29	14	bbu
9544750	Nord Auckland *	Sgp	2011	22,683	36,782	186	28	14	bbu
9544748	Nord Barcelona *	Sgp	2011	22,683	35,746	186	28	14	bbu
9448023	Nord Delphinus *	Sgp	2010	63,864	114,167	250	43	14	bbu
9448035	Nord Dorado *	Sgp	2010	63,864	114,167	250	43	14	bbu
9314090	Nord-Energy *	Sgp	2004	90,085	180,319	289	45	14	bbu
9403114	Nord Express *	Sgp	2007	32,379	58,785	190	32	14	bbu
9479046	Nord Fuji *	Sgp	2011	31,250	55,628	190	32	14	bbu
9599004	Nord Hong Kong *	Sgp	2011	20,969	32,289	180	28	14	bbu
9543251	Nord Houston *	Sgp	2011	20,924	32,389	180	28	14	bbu
9599016	Nord London *	Sgp	2011	20,969	32,312	180	28	14	bbu
9284491	Nord Maru *	Sgp	2006	30,684	55,745	190	32	14	bbu
9577898	Nord Melbourne *	Bhs	2011	20,924	32,417	180	28	14	bbu

Dampskibsselskabet 'Norden' A/S : NORDKAP : *ARO*

IMO#	name	flag	year	grt	dwt	loa	bm	kts	type	former names
9612284	Nord Montreal *	Sgp	2012	22,850	37,000	180	28	14	bbu	
9612313	Nord Mumbai *	Sgp	2012	22,746	36,612	187	28	14	bbu	
9310537	Nord Neptune	Dis	2006	38,892	75,726	225	32	14	bbu	
9566564	Nord Peak *	Sgp	2011	33,990	61,649	200	32	14	bbu	
9448059	Nord Pisces *	Sgp	2010	63,864	114,167	250	43	14	bbu	
9271626	Nord Power *	Sgp	2005	88,594	176,346	289	45	14	bbu	
9448047	Nord Pyxis *	Sgp	2010	63,864	114,167	250	43	14	bbu	
9544762	Nord Rotterdam *	Sgp	2011	22,683	36,599	186	28	14	bbu	
9544736	Nord Seoul *	Sgp	2010	22,683	36,781	186	29	14	bbu	
9612325	Nord Shanghai *	Sgp	2012	22,746	36,746	187	28	14	bbu	
	Nord Treasure		2013		56,000	190	32	14	bbu	
9598995	Nord Vancouver *	Sgp	2011	20,969	32,353	180	28	14	bbu	
9253181	Nordkap	Dis	2002	40,066	77,229	225	32	14	bbu	
9253193	Nordpol	Dis	2002	40,066	77,195	225	32	14	bbu	
9233923	Nordtramp	Dis	2001	85,379	171,199	289	45	14	bbu	

newbuildings: 6 x Panamax bulkers (2013/4). 2 x 37,000dwt bulkers (2013/4)
* owned by subsidiary Norden Shipping (Singapore) Pte Ltd.
Including charters, the Company currently operates many bulkers within the Norden Post-Panamax and Handysize Pools (formed 2010 with Interorient Navigation Co Ltd)

Nordic American Tankers Ltd.   Bermuda

Funnel: *White with blue and red coloured/striped rectangle, black top.* **Hull:** *Black or red with red or green boot-topping.* **History:** *Formed 1995 as Navion ASA to 2003, when it was acquired from Statoil ASA.* **Web:** *www.nat.bm*

IMO#	name	flag	year	grt	dwt	loa	bm	kts	type	former names
9248423	Nordic Apollo	Mhl	2003	81,310	159,988	274	48	14	tcr	ex Glyfada Spirit-06, Euro Spirit-03
9159672	Nordic Aurora +	Lbr	1999	80,668	147,262	274	48	14	tcr	ex Hellespont Trust-11
9588445	Nordic Breeze	Bhs	2011	86,266	158,597	274	48	14	tcr	
9233765	Nordic Cosmos	Mhl	2003	81,310	159,999	274	48	14	tcr	ex Calm Sea-06, Euro Sea-03
9157727	Nordic Discovery	Nis	1998	79,669	153,328	269	46	14	tcr	ex Front Hunter-05
9157715	Nordic Fighter	Nis	1998	79,669	153,328	269	46	14	tcr	ex Front Fighter-05
9288887	Nordic Freedom	Bhs	2005	83,594	159,331	274	48	14	tcr	ex Santiago Spirit-05
9230892	Nordic Grace	Nis	2002	84,598	149,921	274	50	14	tcr	ex Seagrace-09
9131137	Nordic Harrier **	Iom	1997	80,187	151,459	274	46	14	tcr	ex Gulf Scandic-10, British Harrier-04
9131149	Nordic Hawk	Iom	1997	80,187	151,400	274	46	14	tcr	ex British Hawk-04
9131151	Nordic Hunter *	Bhs	1997	80,100	151,400	274	46	14	tcr	ex British Hunter-04
9160205	Nordic Jupiter	Mhl	1998	81,565	157,411	274	48	14	tcr	ex Sacramento-06
9322310	Nordic Mistral ‡	Mhl	2002	84,586	164,236	274	50	15	tcr	ex Pentathlon-09, Cape Balboa-08, Pentathlon-03
9224283	Nordic Moon	Mhl	2002	81,310	160,200	274	48	14	tcr	ex Summer Sky-06, Euro Sky-03
9229386	Nordic Passat ‡	Mhl	2002	84,586	164,487	274	50	15	tcr	ex Decathlon-10, Cape Baker-08, Decathlon-03
9167198	Nordic Saturn	Mhl	1998	81,565	157,331	274	48	14	tcr	ex Sabine-05
9159684	Nordic Sprite	Nis	1999	80,668	147,188	274	48	14	tcr	ex Seasprite-09
9412581	Nordic Vega	Bhs	2010	86,266	163,940	275	48	14	tcr	
9102930	Nordic Voyager *	Nis	1996	79,494	149,775	270	45	15	tcr	ex Wilma Yangtze-07
9588469	Nordic Zenith	Lbr	2011	81,509	158,645	274	48	14	tcr	

newbuildings:
*managed by V.Ships Norway AS, except * by Teekay Marine Services AS, Norway, ** by Gulf Navigation Ship Management, UAE, + by Gemini pool LLC, ‡ by Columbia Shipmanagement Deutschland*

Norient Product Pool ApS   Denmark

Funnel: owners colours. **History:** *limited company founded in Denmark as 50/50 joint venture between Interorient Navigation Co. and Dampskibsselskabet Norden A/S. Also manages vessels for third party owners.*

IMO#	name	flag	year	grt	dwt	loa	bm	kts	type	former names
9418119	Abu Dhabi Star	Sgp	2008	29,734	51,069	183	32	14	tco	
9376945	Acor	Mlt	2007	23,248	37,900	184	27	14	tco	
9318034	Arctic Bay +	Mlt	2006	30,053	50,921	183	32	14	tco	ex West Point-06
9350862	Arctic Blizzard +	Mlt	2006	30,053	50,922	183	32	14	tco	ex Baltic Point-06
9350850	Arctic Breeze +	Mlt	2006	30,053	50,922	183	32	14	tco	ex Ice Point-06
9307815	Arctic Bridge +	Mlt	2005	30,053	50,930	183	32	14	tco	ex Ice Point-06
9271591	Ardmore Seamaster	Mhl	2004	28,114	45,840	180	32	14	tco	
9222168	Atlantic Latvia +	Lbr	2001	23,740	35,770	183	27	14	tco	ex AS Latvia-12, Nordscot-09
9192777	Atlantic Levantia +	Lbr	1999	23,843	35,953	183	27	14	tco	ex AS Levantia-12, Montreux-09
9192741	Atlantic Liguria +	Lbr	1999	23,843	35,966	183	27	14	tco	ex AS Liguria-12, Robin-09
9192765	Atlantic Livadia +	Lbr	1999	23,843	35,841	183	27	14	tco	ex AS Livadia-12,Melide-09
9230426	Atlantic Lobelia	Lbr	2001	23,232	37,263	183	27	14	tco	ex Lobelia-12, Kersaint-08
9208485	Atlantic Lombardia	Lbr	2000	23,842	35,841	183	27	14	tco	ex Lombardia-12, Silvia-08
9192753	Atlantic Lutetia +	Lbr	1999	23,843	35,966	183	27	14	tco	ex AS Lutetia-12, Magpie-09
9425552	Axel	Pan	2010	28,465	50,090	183	32	15	tco	
9299862	Baltic Advance +	Cyp	2006	23,240	37,332	183	27	14	tco	
9208112	Baltic Commander I +	Cyp	2000	23,235	37,418	183	27	14	tco	ex Baltic Commander-02, I/a Antifon

IMO#	name	flag	year	grt	dwt	loa	bm	kts	type	former names
9260017	Baltic Commodore +	Mlt	2003	23,240	37,343	183	27	14	tco	ex British Engineer-07, Baltic Commodore-05
9260029	Baltic Champion +	Mlt	2003	23,240	37,333	183	27	14	tco	ex British Experience-07, Baltic Champion-05
9327372	Baltic Favour +	Cyp	2006	23,337	37,106	183	27	14	tco	
9327396	Baltic Freedom +	Cyp	2006	23,337	37,048	183	27	14	tco	
9327401	Baltic Frost +	Cyp	2006	23,337	37,340	183	27	14	tco	ex Baltic Front-11
9314820	Baltic Mariner	Cyp	2006	23,240	37,304	183	27	14	tco	
9314818	Baltic Monarch +	Cyp	2006	23,240	37,273	183	27	14	tco	
9443425	Baltic Sapphire +	Cyp	2009	23,339	37,250	184	27	14	tco	
9228801	Baltic Sky I +	Mlt	2001	23,235	37,272	183	27	14	tco	ex Flores-06, Flores I-01
9228813	Baltic Soul +	Mlt	2001	23,235	37,244	183	27	14	tco	ex Sicilia-06
9286059	Baltic Sun II +	Mlt	2005	23,235	37,305	183	27	15	tco	ex Baltic Sun-05
9464376	Baltic Swift +	Cyp	2010	23,339	37,565	184	27	14	tco	
9259991	Baltic Wave +	Mlt	2003	23,235	37,300	183	27	15	tco	ex Prostar-05, Ice Point-03
9261401	Baltic Wind +	Mlt	2003	23,235	37,296	183	27	15	tco	ex Prosky-05
9215115	Blue Marlin	Lbr	2001	23,682	35,970	183	25	15	tco	ex Blu Star-12, Blue Star-08, British Energy-06
9561370	Bright Fortune	Pan	2010	28,777	48,009	180	32	14	tco	
9380570	Cargo	Mlt	2008	23,248	37,923	183	27	14	tco	
9377652	Carry	Mlt	2007	23,248	37,847	183	27	14	tco	
9251286	Dukhan	Qat	2003	25,408	37,284	176	31	14	tco	
9433834	FPMC 25	Lbr	2011	28,458	50,085	183	32	15	tco	
9433846	FPMC 26	Lbr	2011	28,458	50,076	183	32	15	tco	
9302669	Freja Polaris	Gbr	2004	23,244	37,217	186	27	14	tco	ex Kermaria-07
9286047	Giannutri +	Mlt	2004	23,235	37,272	183	27	14	tco	
9346445	Ice Beam +	Cyp	2008	38,899	63,495	228	32	15	tco	
9346457	Ice Blade +	Cyp	2008	38,899	63,599	228	32	15	tco	
9241695	Kerel +	Mlt	2002	23,235	37,272	183	27	14	tco	
9561382	New Breeze	Pan	2010	28,777	48,064	180	32	15	tco	
9309980	Nord Bell	Dis	2007	24,048	38,461	183	27	14	tco	
9448310	Nord Butterfly	Dis	2008	24,048	38,431	183	27	14	tco	
9293947	Nord Farer *	Sgp	2005	25,382	40,083	176	31	14	tco	ex F.D. Nord Farer-10, Nord Farer-08
9316608	Nord Fast *	Sgp	2008	25,382	40,083	176	31	14	tco	ex F.D. Nord Fast-10, Nord Fast-08
9448724	Nord Gainer	Dis	2011	30,241	50,281	183	32	14	tco	
9448334	Nord Goodwill	Dis	2009	30,241	50,326	183	32	14	tco	
9448712	Nord Guardian	Dis	2011	30,241	50,420	183	32	14	tco	
9352195	Nord Hummock	Dis	2007	23,204	37,159	183	27	14	tco	ex Payal-11, Jag Payal-09
9547506	Nord Imagination	Pan	2009	28,777	48,006	180	32	15	tco	
9568043	Nord Independence	Pan	2010	28,777	48,005	180	32	15	tco	
9555292	Nord Innovation	Pan	2010	28,777	47,981	180	32	15	tco	
9441855	Nord Inspiration	Pan	2010	28,798	47,987	180	32	15	tco	
9568031	Nord Integrity	Pan	2010	28,777	48,026	180	32	15	tco	
9561368	Nord Intelligence	Sgp	2010	28,813	47,975	180	32	15	tco	
9303730	Nord Mermaid	Dis	2007	24,048	38,461	183	27	14	tco	
9376816	Nord Nightingale *	Dis	2008	24,048	38,461	183	27	14	tco	
9338814	Nord Observer	Lbr	2007	26,900	47,344	183	32	14	tco	
9367671	Nord Obtainer	Pan	2008	26,897	47,522	183	32	14	tco	
9338802	Nord Optimiser	Lbr	2007	26,900	47,407	183	32	14	tco	

Norient Product Pool : BALTIC SUN II : *ARO*

190

IMO#	name	flag	year	grt	dwt	loa	bm	kts	type	former names
9367748	Nord Organiser	Pan	2008	26,900	47,399	183	32	14	tco	
9303728	Nord Princess	Dis	2007	24,048	38,500	183	27	14	tco	
9536820	Nord Sakura	Mhl	2012	28,736	45,953	182	32	16	tco	
9376828	Nord Snow Queen *	Dis	2008	24,066	38,500	183	27	14	tco	
9448322	Nord Swan	Dis	2009	24,066	38,431	183	27	14	tco	
9309978	Nord Thumbelina	Dis	2006	24,048	38,461	183	27	14	tco	
9394040	Norient Saturn +	Cyp	2007	25,864	40,435	180	32	15	tco	l/a Nordic Saturn
9436678	Norient Scorpius +	Mlt	2009	25,814	40,400	180	32	15	tco	
9396373	Norient Solar +	Mlt	2008	25,864	40,429	180	32	15	tco	
9396385	Norient Star +	Mlt	2008	25,814	40,400	180	32	15	tco	
9380582	Rock	Mlt	2008	23,248	37,889	183	27	14	tco	
9380594	Rocket	Mlt	2008	23,248	37,889	183	27	14	tco	
9325611	Star Falcon	Pan	2007	31,433	53,815	186	32	14	tco	ex Freja Selandia-12
9325609	Star Merlin	Pan	2007	31,500	53,755	186	32	14	tco	ex Freja Dania-13
9414278	Torm Helsingor	Pan	2009	28,054	45,997	183	32	15	tco	
9402809	Unique Developer	Hkg	2010	26,914	47,366	183	32	15	tco	
9540821	Unique Guardian	Hkg	2012	29,411	50,475	183	32	15	tco	

newbuildings: four x 49,600dwt tankers (2013), two x 40,000dwt tankers (2014) :

Norient Product Pool : NORD INTELLIGENCE : *Roy Fenton*

Norient Product Pool : NORD NIGHTINGALE : *Chris Brooks*

Norwegian Car Carriers ASA   Norway

Funnel: *White with large blue square divided by white diagonal.* **Hull:** *Blue with red boot-topping.* **History:** *Founded 1930 by Ditlev-Simonsen & Co as A/S Eidsiva, becoming Eidsiva Rederi ASA in 1996. Renamed 2010 after acquisition of Dyvi Holdings AS, formed 1955 as Jan-Erik Dyvi to 2003 and now 32% shareholders.* **Web:** *www.nocc.no or www.eidsiva.nor*

IMO#	name	flag	year	grt	dwt	loa	bm	kts	type	former names
9430519	NOCC Atlantic *	Nis	2009	60,868	22,500	200	32	19	mve	6,754 ceu: Dyvi Atlantic-11
8709145	NOCC Caspian **	Sgp	1987	42,247	12,706	184	31	19	mve	5,387 ceu: ex Morning Mermaid-11, Hyundai No. 205-07, Eurasian Beauty-93, Hyundai No. 205-90
8709157	NOCC Coral *	Sgp	1987	42,247	12,706	184	31	18	mve	5,387 ceu: ex Hyundai No. 206-11, Oriental Beauty-93, Hyundai No. 206-90
9279812	NOCC Kattegat +	Mhl	2004	44,408	14,650	197	30	19	mve	5,379 ceu: ex Grande Lagos-10
9624029	NOCC Oceanic *	Nis	2012	57,600	15,770	200	32		mve	6,500 ceu
9177038	NOCC Pamplona †	Nis	1999	37,237	12,778	180	31	19	mve	4,287 ceu; ex Dyvi Pamplona-10
9177026	NOCC Puebla †	Nis	1999	37,237	12,780	180	31	19	mve	4,287 ceu: ex Dyvi Puebla-11
9070931	Vinni	Nis	1994	23,409	13,480	170	24	17	mve	2,300 ceu: ex Novorossiysk-04 (conv urr-08)
9065182	Vibeke #	Nis	1996	23,409	13,480	170	24	17	mve	2,300 ceu: ex Sochi-05 (conv urr-08)

newbuilding:
*vessels chartered out to * Höegh, ** Eukor, † K Line, + Hyundai Glovis # laid up Labuan, Malaysia 29:11:2011*

NSB Niederelbe Schiffahrts GmbH & Co. KG   Germany

Funnel: *Blue with blue 'NSB' on white diamond or blue 'N' on square on broad white band or charterers colours.* **Hull:** *Black, dark blue or dark grey with red boot-topping.* **History:** *Formed 1982 and associated with W. Harms GmbH & Co KG and Conti Holding GmbH & Co KG.* **Web:** *www.reederei-nsb.com*

IMO#	name	flag	year	grt	dwt	loa	bm	kts	type	former names
9410648	Alpine Alaska *	Lbr	2010	57,221	105,291	244	42	14	tcr	l/d Conti Alaska
9410650	Alpine Athelia *	Lbr	2010	57,221	105,291	244	42	14	tcr	l/d Conti Madagaskar
9221815	Buxcliff **	Deu	2001	72,760	79,501	300	40	26	ucc	6,456 teu: ex CMA CGM Verlaine-12, l/a Buxcliff
9221827	Buxcoast **	Deu	2001	72,760	79,559	300	40	26	ucc	6,546 teu: CMA CGM Voltaire-12, l/a Buxcoast
9235828	Buxcontact **	Deu	2002	25,375	33,864	207	30	21	ucc	2,478 teu: ex CMA CGM Pacifico-11, APL Osaka-08, Cap Ferrato-06
9150212	Buxfavourite **	Deu	1997	25,713	34,083	206	30	21	ucc	2,468 teu: ex CSCL Yingkou-03, Sea Puma-01, Buxfavourite-98
9150195	Buxhansa **	Lbr	1998	25,713	33,995	206	30	21	ucc	2,468 teu: ex ANL Esprit-09, CMA CGM Falcon-04, CSCL Nantong-03, Sea Leopard-01, Buxhansa-98
9377133	Buxharmony *	Deu	2007	28,050	38,070	215	30	22	ucc	2,702 teu: ex Maruba Europa-07, l/a Buxharmony
9111565	Buxhill	Deu	1995	16,259	23,465	163	30	18	ucc	1,684 teu: ex CSAV Santos-04, Buxhill-03, Indamex Malabar-03, Buxhill-02, Contship Ticino-98
9109029	Buxlagoon	Deu	1994	16,270	23,130	163	28	17	ucc	1,684 teu: ex YM Surabaya-04, Indamex New Delhi-03, Kota Perwira-00, Contship Italy-98
9235816	Buxlink	Deu	2002	25,375	33,817	207	30	23	ucc	2,470 teu: ex APL Jebel Ali-08, Buxlink-06, P&O Nedlloyd Hunter Valley-05
9377145	Buxmelody **	Lbr	2008	28,050	38,092	215	30	22	ucc	2,702 teu: Maruba Maxima-10, l/a Buxmelody
9109017	Buxmoon	Lbr	1995	16,270	23,130	163	28	18	ucc	1,687 teu: ex YM Kwang Yang-12, Buxmoon-10, St. John Grace-09, Buxmoon-09, Melbourne Star I-06, YM Kwang Yang-04, Buxmoon-03, Maersk Osaka-02, Contship Lavagna-98
9070022	Buxsailor	Deu	1993	16,282	23,465	163	28	19	ucc	1,599 teu: ex Marfret Caraibes-06, Buxsailor-05, City of York-03, Buxsailor-01, CSAV Salerno-00, Libra Houston-00, CMBT Amboseli-98, Contship Atlantic-97
9150200	Buxstar **	Deu	1997	40,465	49,308	259	32	23	ucc	3,962 teu: ex ANL Georgia-06, Ville de Mimosa-04
9150183	Buxtaurus **	Lbr	1997	40,465	49,238	259	32	23	ucc	3,961 teu: ex Kohala-11, Buxtaurus-10, Ville de Taurus-10
9108295	Caribbean Sea	Mlt	1996	37,549	44,731	241	32	24	ucc	3,681 teu: ex MOL Wish-11, Caribbean Sea-06, MSC Madrid-03, Sea-Land Endeavour-01, Sea Endeavour-96, Caribbean Sea-96
9128180	CMA CGM Alabama	Deu	1997	31,730	34,731	193	32	22	ucc	2,758 teu: ex Indamex Alabama-04, Conti Wellington-03, Contship Vision-03, l/a Conti Wellington
9222273	CMA CGM Balzac	Deu	2001	73,172	77,941	300	40	26	ucc	6,627 teu: ex Conti Paris-01
9222285	CMA CGM Baudelaire	Deu	2001	73,172	77,946	300	40	26	ucc	6,627 teu: ex Conti Lyon-01
9409170	CMA CGM Corneille	Lbr	2009	73,339	85,408	299	40	24	ucc	6,500 teu

IMO#	name	flag	year	grt	dwt	loa	bm	kts	type	former names
9286231	CMA CGM Hugo *	Deu	2004	90,745	101,662	334	43	25	ucc	8,238 teu: I/a Conti Everest
9354923	CMA CGM Vela *	Deu	2008	128,600	131,938	347	46	24	ucc	10,960 teu: I/a Conti jupiter
9391361	Conti Agulhas	Lbr	2008	23,403	37,606	184	27	15	tco	
9326768	Conti Anping *	Deu	2006	41,899	53,682	264	32	23	ucc	4,298 teu: ex YM Anping-11, YM Chiwan-06
9357119	Conti Arabella *	Lbr	2007	22,801	30,562	204	28	22	ucc	2,710 teu: ex CMA CGM Fortuna-12, I/a Conti Arabella
9391373	Conti Benguela	Lbr	2008	23,403	37,606	184	27	15	tco	
9154191	Conti Bilbao	Lbr	1997	25,713	34,083	206	30	22	ucc	2,468 teu: ex Tiger Speed-11, Kota Pertama-07, CMA CGM Albatross-04, Conti Bilbao-03, Brasilia-02, Sea-Land Brasil-99, I/a Conti Bilbao
9128192	Conti Brisbane	Lbr	1997	31,730	34,894	193	32	22	ucc	2,758 teu: ex YM Ibiza-10, P&O Nedlloyd Newark-05, Contship Nobility-03, Conti Brisbane-97
9154206	Conti Cartagena	Deu	1997	25,713	34,083	205	27	20	ucc	2,468 teu: ex MOL Splendor-09, Cap Pilar-07, Conti Cartagena-05, CMA CGM Eagle-04, Conti Cartagena-03, MSC Provence-01, Sea-Land Argentina -00, I/a Conti Cartagena
9357121	Conti Daphne *	Lbr	2007	22,801	30,580	204	28	21	ucc	2,127 teu: ex Maruba Asia-11, I/a Conti

NSB Niederelbe Schiffahrts : BUXSAILOR : *C. Lous*

NSB Niederelbe Schiffahrts : CONTI CARTAGENA : *Chris Brooks*

IMO#	name	flag	year	grt	dwt	loa	bm	kts	type	former names
										Daphne
9357092	Conti Elektra	Lbr	2007	22,801	30,607	204	28	21	ucc	2,127 teu: ex Maruba Africa-10, I/a Conti Elektra
9391385	Conti Equator	Lbr	2008	23,403	37,527	184	27	15	tco	
9124500	Conti Esperance	Deu	1996	31,730	34,800	193	32	22	ucc	2,758 teu: ex MSC Kirari-11, Conti Esperance-10, Contship Romance-03, I/a Conti Esperance
9391397	Conti Greenland	Lbr	2008	23,403	37,606	184	27	15	tco	
9391402	Conti Guinea	Lbr	2008	23,403	37,554	184	27	15	tco	
8808587	Conti Hong Kong	Mhl	1989	18,000	26,288	177	28	19	ucc	1,793 teu: ex YM Pearl River I-07, Conti Hong Kong-03, MSC Guayaquil-01, Conti Hong Kong-99, MSC Guayaquil-98, Nedlloyd Zaandam-97, Buxmerchant-95, Choyang Star-94, Hongkong Senator-91
9391414	Conti Humboldt	Lbr	2008	23,403	37,602	184	27	15	tco	
9357080	Conti Salome	Lbr	2007	22,801	30,573	204	28	21	ucc	2,127 teu
9154220	Conti Valencia	Deu	1998	25,713	34,051	206	30	21	ucc	2,460 teu: ex MSC Malaga-08, Conti Valencia-06, MSC Spain-05, Conti Valencia-03, Lykes Hunter-01, Ivaran Hunter-99, Sea Tiger-98, Conti Valencia-98
9293765	Ever Champion *	Deu	2005	90,449	100,949	334	43	25	ucc	8,073 teu
9293777	Ever Charming *	Deu	2005	90,465	100,887	334	43	25	ucc	8,073 teu
9293791	Ever Chilvary *	Deu	2006	90,465	100,902	334	43	25	ucc	8,073 teu
9293818	Ever Conquest *	Deu	2006	90,465	100,909	334	43	25	ucc	8,073 teu
8614194	Frontier	Lbr	1987	10,811	13,464	147	23	15	ucc	1,022 teu: ex Doria-07, ANL Pioneer-04, MSC Kiwi-02, Everett Express-01, Doria-00, OOCL Admiral-98, Doria-97, Sea-Land Mexico-94, Doria-94, Contship Asia-91, Ocean Asia-88, Doria-88
9402562	Gaschem Nordsee	Deu	2009	13,878	18,846	156	23	17	lpg	17,000 m³
9402574	Gaschem Pacific	Deu	2009	13,879	18,919	156	23	17	lpg	17,000 m³
9200677	Hanjin Amsterdam	Deu	1999	66,278	68,824	279	40	26	ucc	5,618 teu: I/a Conti Canberra
9200706	Hanjin Athens	Deu	2000	66,278	68,819	279	40	26	ucc	5,618 teu: ex YM Athens-05, Hanjin Athens-03, Conti Fremantle-00
9290488	Hanjin Baltimore *	Deu	2005	83,133	92,964	300	43	24	ucc	7,471 teu
9248136	Hanjin Basel	Deu	2003	65,918	68,200	279	40	26	ucc	5,752 teu: ex Hanjin Lisbon-03
9290464	Hanjin Boston *	Deu	2005	83,133	92,964	300	43	24	ucc	7,471 teu
9200691	Hanjin Brussels **	Deu	2000	66,278	68,790	279	40	26	ucc	5,618 teu
9248162	Hanjin Chicago **	Deu	2003	65,918	68,037	278	40	26	ucc	5,752 teu
9200689	Hanjin Copenhagen	Deu	1999	66,278	68,996	279	40	26	ucc	5,618 teu: ex Conti Darwin-99
9295220	Hanjin Dallas *	Deu	2005	83,133	92,964	300	43	24	ucc	7,471 teu
9215646	Hanjin Geneva *	Deu	2000	65,918	68,263	279	40	26	ucc	5,752 teu: ex Cosco Tianjin-05, Hanjin Geneva-03, Conti Porto-00
9235103	Hanjin Gothenburg	Deu	2002	65,131	68,063	275	40	25	ucc	5,551 teu: ex CMA CGM Seattle-09, I/a Conti Gothenburg
9071521	Hanjin Lima	Deu	1994	34,454	45,455	216	32	20	ucc	3,017 teu: ex Washington Senator-09, Tabuk-08, Washington Senator-06, Maersk Antwerp-95, Tor Bay-94, Washington Senator-94
9248148	Hanjin Lisbon **	Deu	2003	65,918	67,979	279	40	26	ucc	5,752 teu
9248150	Hanjin Madrid *	Deu	2003	65,918	67,979	279	40	26	ucc	5,752 teu
9290476	Hanjin Miami *	Deu	2005	83,133	92,964	300	43	24	ucc	7,471 teu
9200718	Hanjin Ottawa *	Deu	2000	66,278	68,834	278	40	26	ucc	5,618 teu: ex Conti Melbourne-00
9056090	Hanjin Palermo	Deu	1994	34,454	45,696	216	32	24	ucc	3,017 teu: ex London Senator-09, Sea Endeavour-95, Delaware Bay-94, London Senator-94
9110561	Hanjin Punta Arenas	Deu	1995	34,617	45,470	216	32	21	ucc	3,017 teu: Hongkong Senator-09
9231755	Hanjin Taipei *	Deu	2002	65,131	68,086	275	40	25	ucc	5,551 teu
9215634	Hanjin Vienna *	Deu	2000	65,918	68,263	279	40	26	ucc	5,752 teu: ex CMA CGM Vancouver-09, Hanjin Vienna-09, Conti Lissabon-00
9295218	Hanjin Yantian *	Deu	2005	82,794	92,964	300	43	24	ucc	7,471 teu
9293789	Hatsu Courage *	Deu	2005	90,465	98,700	334	43	25	ucc	8,073 teu
9293820	Hatsu Crystal *	Deu	2006	90,465	98,700	334	43	25	ucc	8,073 teu
9235098	Helsinki *	Deu	2002	65,131	68,045	275	40	25	ucc	5,551 teu: ex Hanjin Helsinki-11
9326744	Hyundai Tianjin *	Deu	2006	41,899	53,627	264	32	23	ucc	4,298 teu: ex YM Tianjin-11
9056088	Ibn Sina	Deu	1993	34,454	45,470	216	32	24	ucc	3,017 teu: ex Tokyo Senator-97, Sea Progress-96, Tokyo Senator-94
9293806	Ital Contessa *	Deu	2006	90,465	101,007	334	43	25	ucc	8,073 teu: I/a LT Contessa
9293753	LT Cortesia *	Deu	2005	90,449	100,863	334	43	25	ucc	8,073 teu
9225653	MSC Alessia	Deu	2001	75,590	85,891	304	40	25	ucc	6,732 teu
9320441	MSC Carouge	Deu	2007	50,963	63,428	275	32	24	ucc	4,860 teu: I/a Buxpost
9349801	MSC Cordoba	Lbr	2008	50,963	63,428	275	32	24	ucc	4,860 teu: I/a Conti Cordoba

IMO#	name	flag	year	grt	dwt	loa	bm	kts	type	former names
9225615	MSC Flaminia	Deu	2001	75,590	85,823	304	40	24	ucc	6,732 teu: I/a Buxclipper
9128207	MSC Fuji	Lbr	1997	31,730	34,790	193	32	22	ucc	2,758 teu: ex Conti Albany-10, Emirates Spring-09, Conti Albany-06, ANL Albany-03, Conti Albany-03, Contship Optimism-02, I/a Conti Albany
9320427	MSC Geneva	Deu	2006	50,963	63,505	275	32	24	ucc	4,860 teu: I/a Buxsong
9225641	MSC Ilona	Deu	2001	75,590	85,890	304	40	25	ucc	6,732 teu: I/a Buxcomet
9320398	MSC Lausanne **	Deu	2005	50,963	63,638	275	32	24	ucc	4,890 teu: I/a Buxhai
9154218	MSC Malaga *	Deu	1997	25,713	24,083	205	27	20	ucc	2,468 teu: ex Conti Malaga-08, MSC Chile-02, Sea-Land Uruguay-01, Conti Malaga-98
9349796	MSC Monterey	Deu	2007	50,963	63,300	275	32	24	ucc	4,860 teu: I/a Buxvillage
9286243	MSC Texas *	Deu	2004	90,745	101,898	334	43	25	ucc	8,238 teu
9357107	NileDutch Kudu *	Lbr	2007	22,801	30,608	204	28	22	ucc	2,130 teu: ex Conti Ariadne-12, CMA CGM Esperanza-12, c/a Conti Ariadne
9082374	Northern Delight	Lbr	1994	19,819	22,246	174	27	19	ucc	1,709 teu: ex P&O Nedlloyd Rumba-05, Kairo-05, P&O Nedlloyd Dubai-03, Kairo-03, Northern Delight-03, Zim Chicago II-01, Kota Sejati-00, Northern Delight-99, P&O Nedlloyd Dubai-99, Dubai Bay-98, Nedlloyd Sao Paulo-96, Northern Delight-94
9070759	Northern Happiness	Lbr	1994	19,819	22,273	174	27	19	ucc	1,709 teu: ex Cap Velas-04, Northern Happiness-03, Kairo-00, DNOL Kairo-99, Kairo-98, Northern Happiness-94
9064853	Northern Pioneer	Deu	1994	35,595	42,673	240	32	22	ucc	3,538 teu: ex CMA CGM Vernet-10, Northern Pioneer-02, Ville de Sagitta-01, I/a Northern Pioneer
9326756	NYK Galaxy *	Deu	2006	41,899	53,704	264	32	23	ucc	4,298 teu: ex CMA CGM Galaxy-09, NYK Galaxy-08
9286255	Pacific Link *	Deu	2004	90,745	101,661	334	43	25	ucc	8,238 teu
9256535	Queen Zenobia	Lbr	2002	16,770	19,621	156	25	-	lpg	22,952 m³
9115717	Sargasso Sea	Mlt	1996	37,549	44,690	241	32	24	ucc	3,681 teu: ex San Pedro Bridge-09, Sea-Land Initiative-00, Sea Initiative-96, Sargasso Sea-96
9125592	White Sea *	Deu	1996	37,549	44,647	241	32	24	ucc	3,681 teu: ex Rialto Bridge-10, Safmarine Kimley-03, Sea-Land Mistral-02, I/a White Sea
9115729	Yellow Sea *	Deu	1996	37,549	44,765	241	32	24	ucc	3,681 teu: ex Jilfar-09, Yellow Sea-06, City of Edinburgh-03, Humen Bridge-02, Sea-Land Victory-00, Yellow Sea-96
9400112	Zim San Francisco	Deu	2009	50,963	63,355	275	32	24	ucc	4,860 teu
9400136	Zim Ontario	Deu	2009	50,963	63,350	275	32	24	ucc	4,860 teu

newbuildings:
* managed for associated Conti Reederei (Conti Holding GmbH & Co KG – www.conti-gruppe.de) or ** for Gebab Konzeptions-und Emissions GmbH. + managed by STX Pan Ocean   Also see United Product Tanker (UPT) pool (under Schoeller Holdings), BBG-Bremer GmbH & Co KG and Martime—Gesellschaft GmbH

NSB Niederelbe Schiffahrts : MSC CORDOBA : *ARO*

NSC Schiffahrts GmbH & Cie. KG Germany

Funnel: *lower half dark blue and top half light blue with white star, separated with white band and white with white 'NSC' on dark blue/grey houseflag or charterers colours.* **Hull:** *Blue or red (bbu) with red boot-topping.* **History:** *Formed 2004.*
Web: *www.nsc-ship.com*

IMO#	name	flag	year	grt	dwt	loa	bm	kts	type	former names
9399789	Algarrobo	Lbr	2009	32,901	34,700	224	31	21	ucc	2,797 teu
9399791	Angeles	Lbr	2010	32,901	35,377	224	31	21	ucc	2,797 teu
9399806	Angol	Lbr	2010	32,901	35,446	224	31	21	ucc	2,797 teu
9231145	Anhui **	Mhl	2003	23,132	30,345	193	28	19	ghl	cr: 2(100): ex Cape Darnley-11
9112973	Anthea	Lbr	1996	34,885	49,370	196	32	15	ggc	ex Skauboard-06
9235983	Antonio **	Mhl	2002	23,132	30,586	193	28	15	ghl	cr: 2(100): ex Hyundai Jumbo-11, CCNI Magallanes-07, Cape Dyer-03
9395927	APL Bahrain	Lbr	2010	40,741	52,383	260	32	24	ucc	4,308 teu: l/a Bermuda
9322504	APL Brisbane **	Lbr	2006	35,573	44,133	223	32	22	ucc	3,388 teu: c/a Newark
9333072	APL Chicago	Lbr	2007	35,573	44,234	223	32	22	ucc	3,388 teu: c/a Natal
9395941	APL Doha	Lbr	2010	40,741	51,400	260	32	24	ucc	4,308 teu: c/a Bahamas
9322516	APL Guangzhou **	Lbr	2007	35,573	44,165	223	32	22	ucc	3,398 teu: ex Guangzhou-07, c/a Noro
9395939	APL Riyadh	Lbr	2010	40,741	52,326	260	32	24	ucc	4,308 teu: l/a Barbados
9333046	APL Seattle	Lbr	2007	35,573	44,239	223	32	22	ucc	3,388 teu: ex Seattle-07, l/a Cape Rexton, l/d Nelson
9395953	APL Seoul	Lbr	2010	40,741	51,400	260	32	24	ucc	4,308 teu: l/a Bonaire
9131266	Atalanta	Lbr	1999	28,148	44,593	185	32	15	gpc	1,830 teu: ex CCNI Arauco-05
9334351	Cap Norte †	Lbr	2007	35,824	41,850	220	32	22	ucc	3,091 teu: ex Alegra-07
9419230	Catamarca	Lbr	2009	35,240	53,021	196	32	15	ggc	ex Alcmene-12, Andromeda-09, l/a Bodega Sea
9304758	Coral Bay *	Deu	2005	27,059	34,426	212	30	22	ucc	2,492 teu: ex Maersk Narbonne-11, l/a Caroline E, l/dn Coral Bay
9419254	Corrientes	Lbr	2010	35,240	53,035	196	32	15	ggc	ex Athena-12, Artemis-10, l/a Beagle Sea
9304760	Crystal Bay *	Lbr	2005	27,059	34,393	212	30	22	ucc	2,492 teu: ex Maersk Nashville-11, l/a Andres E, l/dn Crystal Bay
9235359	Fernando	Mhl	2003	23,132	30,345	193	28	19	ghl	cr: 2(100): ex Cape Delgardo-12
9334349	Fesco Amalthea **	Deu	2007	35,824	41,850	220	32	22	ucc	3,091 teu: ex Amalthea-11, Cap Prior-10, l/a Almathea
9348675	Maersk Damietta	Lbr	2008	54,675	68,463	294	32	24	ucc	5,085 teu: l/a Memphis
9348687	Maersk Danang	Lbr	2008	54,675	68,411	294	32	24	ucc	5,085 teu: l/a Chicago
9348663	Maersk Denpasar	Lbr	2008	54,675	68,463	294	32	24	ucc	5,085 teu: l/a Miami
9348699	Maersk Dhahran	Lbr	2008	54,675	67,410	294	32	24	ucc	5,085 teu: l/a Las Vegas
9399741	Maersk Jakobstad *	Lbr	2007	32,901	34,700	225	31	21	ucc	2,872 teu: ex Arica-07
9399777	Maersk Jambi	Lbr	2008	32,901	35,556	224	31	21	ucc	2,872 teu: ex Austral-08
9399765	Maersk Jefferson	Lbr	2008	32,901	35,391	225	31	21	ucc	2,872 teu: ex Andino-08
9399739	Maersk Jena	Lbr	2007	32,901	34,345	225	31	21	ucc	2,872 teu: ex Andes-07
9399753	Maersk Jennings	Lbr	2008	32,901	35,534	225	31	21	ucc	2,872 teu: ex Antofagasta-08
9289556	Manhattan	Lbr	2005	54,592	66,633	294	32	25	ucc	5,015 teu: ex APL New York-10, l/a E.R.Savannah
9418640	Pago	Lbr	2009	35,998	41,982	231	32	23	ucc	3,554 teu
9419785	Partici	Lbr	2010	35,998	41,974	231	32	23	ucc	3,554 teu
9419797	Pescara	Lbr	2010	35,998	42,011	231	32	23	ucc	3,554 teu

NSC Schiffahrts : ANTONIO : *J. Kakebeeke*

IMO#	name	flag	year	grt	dwt	loa	bm	kts	type	former names
9419773	Praia	Lbr	2009	35,998	41,996	231	32	23	ucc	3,554 teu
9419242	Salta	Lbr	2009	35,240	52,998	196	32	15	ggc	ex Aphrodite-11, I/a Botany Sea
9235361	San Pablo **	Mhl	2004	23,132	30,343	193	28	19	ghl	cr: 2(100) ex Cape Delfaro-12
9231133	San Rafael **	Mhl	2003	23,132	30,490	193	28	19	ghl	cr: 2(100) ex Cape Donington-12, Golden Isle-04, Cape Donington-03
9423566	Santa Fe	Lbr	2010	35,240	52,928	196	32	15	ggc	ex Asteria-12, I/a Biscay Bay
9358888	STX Bluebird	Deu	2008	40,628	12,303	176	31	20	mve	4,870 ceu: ex Andino-11
9382097	STX Oriole	Lbr	2008	40,619	12,245	176	31	20	mve	4,870 ceu: ex Montreal-09
9498846	Tana Sea	Lbr	2011	50,729	92,500	229	38	14	bbu	
9484704	Tango Sea	Lbr	2011	51,253	93,028	229	38	14	bbu	
9498810	Thira Sea	Lbr	2010	50,697	92,500	229	38	14	bbu	
9498834	Tonda Sea	Lbr	2011	50,729	92,500	229	38	14	bbu	
9622916	Tonic Sea	Lbr	2012	51,253	93,005	229	38	14	bbu	
9498822	Tosa Sea	Lbr	2010	50,697	92,500	229	38	14	bbu	
9231121	Vicente **	Mhl	2002	23,132	30,490	193	28	19	ghl	cr: 2(100): ex Hyundai Rhino-11, CCNI Antartico-08, CSAV Genova-04, Cape Dorchester-03
9289568	Virginia **	Lbr	2005	54,592	66,644	294	32	25	ucc	5,015 teu: ex APL Virginia-10
9401776	Zim Moskva	Lbr	2009	40,741	52,316	259	32	24	ucc	4,300 teu
9403396	Zim Ukrayina	Lbr	2009	40,741	52,316	259	32	24	ucc	4,300 teu

newbuildings:
* managed for FHH Fonds Haus Hamburg GmbH & Co KG or ** for Lloyd Fonds AG. † managed by Columbus Shipmanagement.

Odfjell ASA
Norway

Funnel: *White with blue diagonal chain link symbol, black top.* **Hull:** *Orange with blue 'ODFJELL SEACHEM', red or black boot-topping.* **History:** *Formed 1914 as Storli ASA to 1998; Seachem merged 1989 and Ceres Hellenic merged 2000. Acquired 50% of Flumar Brazil in 1999 and remainder in 2008 from Kristian Gerhard Jebsen Skips.* **Web:** *www.odfjell.com*

IMO#	name	flag	year	grt	dwt	loa	bm	kts	type	former names
9304306	Bow Americas ‡	Pan	2004	11,924	19,707	146	24	13	tco	
9319480	Bow Architect ‡	Pan	2005	18,405	30,058	170	26	14	tco	
9102928	Bow Atlantic	Sgp	1995	10,369	17,480	142	23	14	tco	ex Brage Atlantic-07
9407079	Bow Cape	Pan	2008	11,722	19,975	144	24	14	tco	
9114244	Bow Cardinal	Nis	1997	23,196	37,479	183	32	16	tco	
9143219	Bow Cecil **	Nis	1998	23,206	37,545	183	32	16	tco	
9087013	Bow Cedar	Nis	1996	23,196	37,455	183	32	16	tco	
9214317	Bow Chain	Nis	2002	23,190	37,518	183	32	16	tco	
8709298	Bow Cheetah +	Sgp	1988	22,637	40,257	171	32	14	tco	ex Santa Anna-00, Falkanger-91, Fort Cheetah-89, Northern Cheetah-88
9047518	Bow Clipper	Nis	1995	23,197	37,221	183	32	16	tco	
8112914	Bow Eagle	Nis	1985	15,829	24,728	172	28	14	tco	ex Northern Eagle-89, Mangueira-88
9388302	Bow Elm +	Sgp	2011	26,327	46,098	183	32	14	tco	
9317860	Bow Engineer	Pan	2006	18,405	30,086	170	26	14	tco	
9339351	Bow Europe ‡	Pan	2005	11,690	19,728	144	24	14	tco	ex North Contender-05
9047764	Bow Fagus	Nis	1995	23,197	37,221	183	32	16	tco	
9114232	Bow Faith	Nis	1997	23,196	37,479	183	32	16	tco	
9250751	Bow Firda	Nis	2003	23,190	37,000	183	32	16	tco	
9143207	Bow Flora	Nis	1998	23,206	37,369	183	32	16	tco	
9047491	Bow Flower	Nis	1994	23,197	37,221	183	32	16	tco	
9168635	Bow Fortune	Nis	1999	23,206	37,395	183	32	16	tco	
9379909	Bow Harmony	Pan	2008	19,420	33,619	170	27	14	tco	
9363493	Bow Hector §	Phl	2009	20,145	33,694	174	28	15	tco	
9363481	Bow Heron §	Phl	2008	20,145	33,707	174	28	15	tco	
9379894	Bow Kiso	Pan	2008	19,420	33,641	170	27	14	tco	
9407043	Bow Lima	Pan	2007	11,722	19,971	144	24	14	tco	
9388314	Bow Lind	Sgp	2011	26,327	46,047	183	32	14	tco	ex Stolt Gulf Mizhar-11, I/a Gulf Mizhar
9143321	Bow Oceanic	Sgp	1997	10,369	16,094	142	23	14	tco	ex Brage Pacific-07
9215309	Bow Saga **	Nis	2007	29,965	40,085	183	32	15	tco	
9379911	Bow Sagami	Pan	2008	19,420	33,614	170	27	14	tco	
9303651	Bow Santos *	Pan	2004	11,986	19,997	148	24	14	tco	
9215282	Bow Sea	Sgp	2006	29,965	40,036	183	32	15	tco	
9215295	Bow Sirius	Nis	2006	29,965	40,048	183	32	15	tco	
9215268	Bow Sky	Sgp	2005	29,965	40,005	183	32	15	tco	
9215256	Bow Spring	Nis	2004	29,965	39,942	183	32	15	tco	
9197296	Bow Star	Nis	2004	29,971	39,832	183	32	15	tco	
9215270	Bow Summer	Sgp	2005	29,965	40,036	183	32	15	tco	
9197284	Bow Sun	Sgp	2003	29,965	39,942	183	32	15	tco	I/a George L., I/d Multicarrier

Majority owned or managed by Odfjell SE, Norway (formed 2007), * by Odfjell Asia II Pte Ltd, Singapore (formed 2000) or ** Odfjell (UK) Ltd (formed 2002).+ by NCC Odfjell Chemical Tankers, † jointly owned by Compania SudAmericana de Vapores SA, managed by Southern Shipmanagement (Chile) Ltd (www.ssm.cl).
§ owned by Safemarine Corp. and managed by Victoria Ship Management Inc, Philippines or ‡ chartered from other owners.
Also see chartered vessels under The National Shipping Company of Saudi Arabia.

J. O. Odfjell A/S   Norway

JO Tankers A/S, Norway

Funnel: *Blue with white interlinked 'JO' symbol.* **Hull:** *Orange some with blue 'JO TANKERS', red boot-topping.*
History: *Parent founded 1977, Dutch subsidiary JO Tankers BV in 1981 as Winterport Tankers to 1990 and JO Management BV to 1996, Norwegian subsidiary JO Tankers AS in 1989 as JO Management A/S to 1996.* **Web:** *www.jotankers.com*

IMO#	name	flag	year	grt	dwt	loa	bm	kts	type	former names
8919049	Cedar +	Nis	1994	22,415	36,733	182	32	15	tco	ex Jo Cedar-10
9272668	Jo Acer *	Nis	2004	18,703	29,709	170	26	14	tco	
9266267	Jo Betula *	Nis	2003	15,992	25,032	159	25	15	tco	
9505936	Jo Ilex	Nis	2010	11,668	19,735	144	24	14	tco	ex Golden Topstar-11
9266243	Jo Kashi	Pan	2003	15,895	25,148	159	26	14	tco	
9266231	Jo Kiri	Pan	2003	11,769	19,508	145	24	14	tco	
9592680	Jo Pinari	Nis	2012	42,420	74,455	228	32	14	tco	
9592692	Jo Provol	Nis	2013	42,392	74,450	228	32	14	tco	
8919051	Selje +	Nld	1993	22,380	36,800	182	32	15	tco	ex Jo Selje-10
9235062	Sequoia * +	Nis	2003	23,129	37,622	183	32	15	tco	ex Jo Sequoia-10
8919037	Spruce +	Nld	1993	22,415	36,778	182	32	15	tco	ex Jo Spruce-10
9198563	Sycamore * +	Nis	2000	23,200	37,500	183	32	15	tco	ex Jo Sycamore-10
9150315	Sypress +	Nld	1998	22,415	36,752	182	32	15	tco	ex Jo Sypress-10

newbuildings : 2 x 30,000 tankers [Mingde H.I yd 159.160 (2013/14)] 2 x 74,500 product tankers [New Times SB yd 307369/70 (2013)])
* managed by JO Tankers UK Ltd (formed 2003)   Also see A/S Borgestad ASA and Knutsen O.A.S. Shipping A/S, both Norway.
+ time chartered to Stolt-Nielsen Joint Service

Odfjell ASA : BOW CEDAR : *ARO*

Odfjell ASA : BOW SIRIUS : *Hans Kraijenbosch*

Rudolf A. Oetker   Germany

Hamburg-Südamerikanische Dampfschiffahrts-ges (HSDG)

Funnel: *White with red top or yellow 'CCL' on blue/red diagonally divided with black top.* **Hull:** *Red with white 'HAMBURG SÜD' red boot-topping.* **History:** *HSDG founded 1871. Dr August Oetker acquired an interest in 1934 and Rudolf A Oetker (founded 1951) took control in 1952, amalgamating the companies in 1973. Acquired 50% of Ybarra Cia Sudamericana in 1989, Furness-Withy (Shipping) Ltd from CY Tung (OOCL) in 1990, Laser Lines from Nordstjernan (Johnson Line) in 1991, Alianca in 1998, Transroll in 1999, Ellerman in 2003, the balance of Ybarra in 2005 and Costa Container Lines (formed 1947) in 2007.* **Web:** *www.hamburgsud.com*

IMO#	name	flag	year	grt	dwt	loa	bm	kts	type	former names
9360752	Bahia	Lbr	2007	41,483	53,125	254	32	21	ucc	3,630 teu
9362396	Bahia Blanca	Deu	2007	41,483	53,094	254	32	21	ucc	3,630 teu
9362401	Bahia Castillo	Deu	2007	41,483	53,124	254	32	21	ucc	3,630 teu
9362413	Bahia Grande	Deu	2007	41,483	53,176	254	32	21	ucc	3,630 teu
9391660	Bahia Laura	Deu	2007	41,483	53,139	254	32	21	ucc	3,630 teu
9391672	Bahia Negra	Deu	2007	41,483	53,142	254	32	21	ucc	3,630 teu: ex CCNI Shenzhen-10, Bahia Negra-08
9311775	Cap Blanche **	Cyp	2006	28,371	37,883	222	30	22	ucc	2,742 teu: ex Fesco Baykal-06, I/a CapeMartin
9484560	Cap Jackson	Lbr	2010	47,877	59,336	264	32	22	ucc	4,600 teu
9484572	Cap Jervis	Lbr	2010	47,877	59,266	264	32	22	ucc	4,600 teu
9273959	Cap Melville	Lbr	2003	25,705	33,836	207	30	22	ucc	2,524 teu
9273947	Cap Palmas	Lbr	2003	25,709	33,795	208	30	21	ucc	2,524 teu: ex NYK Fantasia-05, Cap Palmas-03
9311799	Cap Pasado **	Cyp	2006	27,786	37,883	222	30	22	ucc	2,742 teu: ex Fesco Bratsk-06
9311787	Cap Vilano **	Cyp	2006	27,786	37,883	222	30	22	ucc	2,742 teu: ex Fesco Barguzin-06
9348077	Monte Aconcagua	Deu	2009	69,132	64,847	272	40	23	ucc	5,568 teu
9348065	Monte Alegre	Deu	2008	69,132	71,273	272	40	23	ucc	5,560 teu
9348053	Monte Azul	Deu	2008	69,132	71,256	272	40	23	ucc	5,568 teu
9283186	Monte Cervantes	Deu	2004	69,132	64,963	272	40	23	ucc	5,560 teu: ex P&O Nedlloyd Salsa-06, Monte Cervantes-05
9283198	Monte Olivia	Deu	2004	69,132	64,730	272	40	23	ucc	5,560 teu
9283203	Monte Pascoal	Deu	2004	69,132	65,066	272	40	23	ucc	5,560 teu: ex P&O Nedlloyd Lambada-06, Monte Pascoal-05
9283215	Monte Rosa	Deu	2004	69,132	64,888	272	40	23	ucc	5,560 teu
9283227	Monte Sarmiento	Deu	2004	69,132	65,028	272	40	23	ucc	5,560 teu
9357949	Monte Tamaro	Deu	2007	69,132	71,588	272	40	23	ucc	5,560 teu
9283239	Monte Verde	Deu	2005	69,132	65,005	272	40	23	ucc	5,560 teu: ex Alianca Maua-11, Monte Verde-05
9444728	Paranagua Express	Deu	2010	85,676	93,603	300	43	22	ucc	7,090 teu: ex Leblon-12, Santa Isabel-11
9348089	Rio Blanco	Lbr	2009	73,899	80,115	287	40	23	ucc	5,905 teu
9348091	Rio Bravo	Lbr	2009	73,899	80,226	287	40	23	ucc	5,905 teu
9357963	Rio de Janeiro	Deu	2008	73,899	80,398	287	40	23	ucc	5,905 teu
9357951	Rio de la Plata	Deu	2008	73,899	80,455	287	40	23	ucc	5,905 teu
9348106	Rio Madeira	Deu	2009	73,899	80,294	287	40	23	ucc	5,905 teu
9357975	Rio Negro	Deu	2008	73,899	80,410	287	40	23	ucc	5,905 teu
9430399	Santa Barbara	Lbr	2012	86,601	93,430	300	43	22	ucc	7,090 teu
9444730	Santa Catarina	Lbr	2011	85,676	93,592	300	43	22	ucc	7,090 teu
9444716	Santa Clara	Deu	2010	85,676	93,552	300	43	22	ucc	7,090 teu
9444742	Santa Cruz	Lbr	2011	85,676	93,424	300	43	22	ucc	7,090 teu
9444845	Santa Ines	Lbr	2012	86,601	92,910	300	43	22	ucc	7,090 teu
9425382	Santa Rita	Deu	2011	85,676	93,404	300	43	22	ucc	7,090 teu
9430363	Santa Rosa	Lbr	2011	85,676	93,398	300	43	22	ucc	7,090 teu
9430375	Santa Teresa	Lbr	2011	85,676	93,591	300	43	22	ucc	7,090 teu
9430387	Santa Ursula	Deu	2012	86,601	93,430	300	43	22	ucc	7,090 teu

newbuildings:
managed by Columbus Shipmanagement GmbH (formed 1998)
*** chartered by HSDG until 2012 from Premium Capital Emissionshaus GmbH & Co KG (founded 2004) and managed by Reederei Alnwick Harmstorf & Co GmbH & Co KG, Germany (formed 1950 as A F Harmstorf & Co GmbH to 2000 - www.harmstorf-co.com)*

Alianca Navegacao e Logistica Ltda., Brazil

Funnel: *Yellow with broad white over red bands beneath black top, black triangular 'A' on white band or HSDG colours.* **Hull:** *Blue with white 'ALIANCA', red boot-topping.* **History:** *Founded 1950 as Alianca Transportes Maritimos SA to 2000.* **Web:** *www.alianca.com.br*

IMO#	name	flag	year	grt	dwt	loa	bm	kts	type	former names
9000730	Alianca Brasil	Bra	1994	28,397	32,984	200	32	18	ucc	2,303 teu
9000742	Alianca Europa	Bra	1994	28,397	32,984	200	32	18	ucc	2,303 teu
9273961	Alianca Manaus	Bra	2004	25,709	33,925	208	30	21	ucc	2,524 teu: ex Cap Nelson-08, Santos Express-05, I/a Cap Nelson
9273923	Alianca Santos	Bra	2003	25,709	33,890	208	30	21	ucc	2,524 teu: ex Cap Carmel-09
8223000	Copacabana	Bra	1984	20,995	26,848	179	31	18	ucc	1,402 teu
8223012	Flamengo	Bra	1985	20,994	26,868	179	31	18	ucc	1,402 teu

IMO#	name	flag	year	grt	dwt	loa	bm	kts	type	former names

Maritime Services Aleuropa GmbH, Germany

Funnel: White with red half-circle on broad blue top above broad green band. **Hull:** White. **History:** Formed 1980. **Web:** None found.

IMO#	name	flag	year	grt	dwt	loa	bm	kts	type	former names
9230995	Carlos Fischer *	Lbr	2002	33,005	43,067	204	32	20	tfj	
9018646	Ouro do Brasil *	Lbr	1993	15,218	19,519	173	26	20	tfj	
9242089	Premium do Brasil	Lbr	2003	33,005	43,002	205	32	20	tfj	
9018658	Sol do Brasil *	Lbr	1994	15,218	19,563	173	26	20	tfj	

* managed for Group Fischer, Brazil (founded 1932) **web** : citrosuco.com.br

Reederei Claus-Peter Offen GmbH & Co. Germany

Funnel: Black with white Maltese Cross on broad blue band edged with narrow white bands, or charterers colours. **Hull:** Light grey, black or red with red boot-topping. **History:** Founded in Hamburg, 1971. **Web:** www.offenship.de

IMO#	name	flag	year	grt	dwt	loa	bm	kts	type	former names
9365790	Butterfly	Lbr	2008	111,249	120,934	350	43	25	ucc	9,661 teu: CMA CGM Butterfly-12, l/a Santa Laurina
9439498	Cap Hamilton	Lbr	2009	41,358	51,745	262	32	24	ucc	4,255 teu: l/a CPO Boston
9440772	Cap Harald	Lbr	2009	41,358	51,808	262	32	24	ucc	4,255 teu: l/a CPO New York
9440784	Cap Harriett	Lbr	2009	41,358	51,780	262	32	24	ucc	4,255 teu: l/a CPO Philadelphia
9440796	Cap Harrisson	Lbr	2009	41,358	51,699	262	32	24	ucc	4,255 teu: l/a CPO Baltimore
9440801	Cap Harvey	Lbr	2009	41,358	51,744	262	32	24	ucc	4,255 teu: l/a CPO Richmond
9440813	Cap Henri	Lbr	2009	41,358	51,727	262	32	24	ucc	4,255 teu: l/a CPO Norfolk
9344679	Cap Palliser *	Lbr	2007	22,914	28,219	186	28	21	ucc	1,819 teu: l/a San Alfredo
9344643	Cap Palmerston *	Lbr	2007	22,914	28,203	186	28	21	ucc	1,819 teu: l/a San Alberto
9344655	Cap Pasley *	Lbr	2007	22,914	28,142	186	28	21	ucc	1,819 teu: l/a San Allessandro
9344667	Cap Patton *	Lbr	2007	22,914	28,179	186	28	21	ucc	1,819 teu: ex Tasman Crusader-09, San Alfonso-07
9344631	Cap Portland *	Lbr	2007	22,914	28,142	186	28	21	ucc	1,819 teu: l/a San Albano
9227326	Cap Roberta *	Lbr	2002	45,803	53,462	281	32	25	ucc	4,112 teu: ex Maersk Dominica-10, Sydney Express-06, P&O Nedlloyd Pegasus-03, l/a Santa Roberta
9238741	Cap Verde *	Lbr	2002	65,289	67,644	277	40	24	ucc	5,762 teu: ex Santa Virginia-10, OOCL Thailand-09, l/a Santa Virginia
9238739	CCNI Angamos	Deu	2001	66,500	67,796	277	40	24	ucc	5,762 teu: ex Cap Valiente-12, Santa Victoria-10, OOCL Korea-09, l/a Santa Victoria
9469572	CMA CGM Alaska	Lbr	2011	140,259	146,112	366	48	25	ucc	12,562 teu: l/a CPO Marseille
9365805	CMA CGM Ivanhoe	Lbr	2009	111,249	120,944	350	43	25	ucc	9,661 teu: l/a Santa Luciana
9471408	CMA CGM Nevada	Lbr	2011	140,259	146,182	366	48	26	ucc	12,562 teu; l/a CPO Toulon
9364992	CMA CGM Orfeo	Lbr	2008	111,249	120,892	350	43	25	ucc	9,661 teu: l/a Santa Laetitia
9522647	CPO America †	Lbr	2011	94,250	179,570	292	45	15	bbu	
9522635	CPO Asia †	Lbr	2011	94,250	179,558	292	45	15	bbu	
9353149	CPO England **	Lbr	2008	23,353	37,313	184	28	15	tco	
9522087	CPO Europe †	Lbr	2010	94,250	179,448	292	45	15	bbu	
9353101	CPO Finland **	Lbr	2008	23,353	37,293	184	28	15	tco	
9347308	CPO France **	Lbr	2008	23,353	37,304	184	28	15	tco	
9353096	CPO Germany **	Lbr	2008	23,270	37,297	184	28	15	tco	
9353137	CPO Italy **	Lbr	2008	23,270	37,282	184	28	15	tco	
9353113	CPO Norway **	Lbr	2008	23,270	37,321	184	28	15	tco	

Rudolf A. Oetker (Maritime Services Aleuropa GmbH) : CARLOS FISCHER : *Hans Kraijenbosch*

IMO#	name	flag	year	grt	dwt	loa	bm	kts	type	former names
9522099	CPO Oceana †	Lbr	2010	94,250	179,701	292	45	15	bbu	
9353125	CPO Russia **	Lbr	2008	23,353	37,296	184	28	15	tco	
9353084	CPO Sweden **	Lbr	2008	23,353	37,280	184	28	15	tco	
9326794	Maersk Dieppe	Lbr	2005	54,809	67,310	294	32	25	ucc	4,839 teu: ex P&O Nedlloyd Doha-05, l/a Santa Placida
9326782	Maersk Dunedin	Lbr	2005	54,809	67,247	295	32	25	ucc	4,839 teu: ex P&O Nedlloyd Detroit-05, l/a Santa Pamina
9330070	Maersk Semarang *	Lbr	2007	94,322	108,448	332	43	25	ucc	8,400 teu
9330068	Maersk Surabaya	Lbr	2006	94,322	108,351	332	43	25	ucc	8,400 teu: l/a Santa Laura
9293179	MOL Caledon	Lbr	2005	58,289	64,519	294	32	25	ucc	4,922 teu: ex P&O Nedlloyd Livingstone-06, l/a Santa Regula
9293167	MOL Cullinan *	Lbr	2005	58,289	64,519	294	32	25	ucc	4,922 teu: ex P&O Nedlloyd Heemskerck-06
9480174	MSC Alicante	Lbr	2011	61,870	74,477	270	40	23	ucc	5,568 teu: l/a CPO Alicante
9480186	MSC Barcelona	Lbr	2011	61,870	74,456	270	40	23	ucc	5,568 teu: l/a CPO Barcelona
9461441	MSC Bari	Lbr	2011	153,115	154,906	366	51	24	ucc	14,000 teu: l/a CPO Napoli
9289099	MSC Beijing	Lbr	2005	89,954	105,034	325	43	25	ucc	8,034 teu: l/a Santa Laurentia
9290567	MSC Bruxelles *	Lbr	2005	107,849	110,860	337	46	25	ucc	9,178 teu: l/a Santa Loretta
9289087	MSC Busan	Lbr	2005	89,954	104,904	325	43	25	ucc	8,034 teu: l/a Santa Larissa
9480203	MSC Cadiz	Lbr	2011	61,870	74,526	270	40	23	ucc	5,568 teu: l/a CPO Cadiz
9299537	MSC Charleston *	Lbr	2006	89,954	105,014	325	43	25	ucc	8,034 teu: l/a Santa Leopalda
9290555	MSC Chicago *	Lbr	2005	107,849	110,852	337	46	25	ucc	9,178 teu: l/a Santa Linea
9480215	MSC Coruna	Lbr	2011	62,870	74,506	270	40	23	ucc	5,568 teu: l/a CPO Valencia
9461415	MSC Deila	Pan	2012	153,115	166,093	366	51	24	ucc	14,000 teu
9461386	MSC Genova	Lbr	2010	153,115	166,041	366	51	24	ucc	14,000 teu: l/a CPO Genova
9461403	MSC La Spezia	Deu	2010`	153,115	165,978	366	51	24	ucc	14,000 teu: l/a CPO La Spezia
9304459	MSC Lisbon	Lbr	2007	107,849	110,697	337	46	25	ucc	9,178 teu: l/a Santa Lucilla
9461427	MSC Livorno	Deu	2010	153,115	165,918	366	51	24	ucc	14,000 teu: l/a CPO Livorno
9480198	MSC Madrid	Lbr	2011	61,870	74,376	270	40	23	ucc	5,568 teu: l/a CPO Bilbao
9484455	MSC Rapallo	Lbr	2011	143,521	154,539	366	48	24	ucc	13,050 teu
9484431	MSC Ravenna	Lbr	2011	153,115	165,963	366	51	24	ucc	14,000 teu: l/a CPO Ancona
9304447	MSC Roma	Lbr	2006	107,849	110,634	337	46	25	ucc	9,178 teu: l/a Santa Louisa
9461398	MSC Rosa M	Pan	2010	153,115	165,991	366	51	24	ucc	14,000 teu
9460356	MSC Savona	Lbr	2010	153,115	165,887	366	51	24	ucc	14,000 teu: l/a CPO Savona
9295373	MSC Shanghai	Lbr	2005	65,483	72,064	275	40	26	ucc	5,606 teu: l/a Santa Viola
9475258	MSC Taranto	Lbr	2011	153,115	166,085	366	51	24	ucc	14,000 teu: l/a CPO Palermo
9469560	MSC Teresa	Pan	2011	153,115	166,101	366	51	24	ucc	14,000 teu
9295361	MSC Tokyo *	Lbr	2005	65,483	71,949	275	40	26	ucc	5,606 teu: l/a Santa Vanessa
9299525	MSC Toronto *	Lbr	2006	89,954	105,084	325	43	25	ucc	8,034 teu: l/a Santa Leonarda
9484479	MSC Trieste	Lbr	2011	143,521	154,664	366	48	24	ucc	13,050 teu: l/a CPO Trieste
9480227	MSC Vigo	Lbr	2012	61,870	73,840	270	40	23	ucc	5,600 teu: l/a CPO Vigo
9365788	Pelleas	Lbr	2008	111,249	120,853	350	43	25	ucc	9,661 teu: ex CMA CGM Pelleas-12, l/a Santa Liana
9344681	Rio Tamanaco *	Lbr	2007	22,914	28,123	186	28	21	ucc	1,819 teu: ex Cap Preston-12, l/a San Alvaro
9347279	San Adriano	Lbr	2008	22,914	28,300	186	28	21	ucc	1,819 teu: ex Ibn Qutaibah-09, l/a San Adriano
9347293	San Alessio	Lbr	2008	22,914	28,142	186	28	21	ucc	1,819 teu
9344693	San Amerigo *	Lbr	2008	22,914	28,186	186	28	21	ucc	1,819 teu

Reederei Claus-Peter Offen : MAERSK DUNEDIN : *Chris Brooks*

IMO#	name	flag	year	grt	dwt	loa	bm	kts	type	former names
9347255	San Andres *	Lbr	2008	22,914	28,300	186	28	21	ucc	1,819 teu
9347267	San Antonio *	Lbr	2008	22,914	28,197	186	28	21	ucc	1,819 teu; ex Ibn Rushd-09, l/a San Antonio
9347281	San Aurelio	Lbr	2008	22,914	28,170	186	28	21	ucc	1,819 teu
9046227	San Vicente +	Lbr	1993	15,778	20,278	167	28	19	ucc	1,512 teu: ex Mercosul Palometa-08, P&O Nedlloyd Zanzibar-01, San Vicente-99, CGM Santos Dumont-98, San Vicente-97
9105126	Santa Ana	Deu	1995	36,028	45,170	246	32	24	ucc	3,467 teu: ex Pos Hongkong-12, Santa Ana-10,Maersk Ipanema-10, P&O Nedlloyd Seattle-05, Chesapeake Bay-98, l/a Santa Ana
9330513	Santa Balbina *	Lbr	2006	28,616	39,360	222	30	23	ucc	2,824 teu: ex Maersk Jackson-11, l/a Santa Balbina
9006502	Santa Barbara +	Lbr	1991	21,049	30,007	182	28	19	ucc	1,742 teu: ex Ibn Malik-09, Santa Barbara-07, CCNI Tokyo-07, Santa Barbara I-04, Indfex SCI-02, Santa Barbara I-01, P&O Nedlloyd Bahrain-01, Santa Barbara I-98, Santa Barbara-97, Sea Jade-97, Khaleej Bay-96, Maersk Kanagawa-95, Santa Barbara-94, Puebla-94, Santa Barbara-93
9330525	Santa Belina *	Lbr	2006	28,616	39,359	222	30	23	ucc	2,824 teu: ex Maersk Jamestown-11, l/a Santa Belina
9338084	Santa Bettina *	Lbr	2007	28,616	39,277	222	30	23	ucc	2,824 teu: ex Cap Byron-11, l/a Santa Bettina
9341110	Santa Bianca *	Lbr	2007	28,616	37,053	222	30	23	ucc	2,824 teu: ex Cap Bianco-12, l/a Santa Bianca
9341122	Santa Brunella *	Lbr	2008	28,616	39,337	222	30	23	ucc	2,824 teu: ex Cap Beaufort-12, l/a Santa Brunella
9113616	Santa Elena I *	Lbr	1995	36,028	45,170	246	32	24	ucc	3,467 teu: ex MSC Johannesburg-07, Santa Elena-04, Maersk Rotterdam-01, New York Senator-98, Santa Elena-95
9162277	Santa Felicita *	Lbr	1999	21,583	30,135	183	30	20	ucc	2,169 teu: ex P&O Nedlloyd Seoul-02, l/dn Santa Felicita
9188219	Santa Francesca	Deu	1998	21,583	30,029	183	30	20	ucc	2,169 teu: ex CMA CGM Volta-09, Santa Francesca-07, P&O Nedlloyd Sao Paulo-02, l/a Santa Francesca
9141780	Santa Giannina *	Lbr	1997	21,531	30,173	182	30	20	ucc	2,061 teu: ex Cala Palamos-08, P&O Nedlloyd Salsa-05, Santa Giannina-02, P&O Nedlloyd Kingston-02, l/a Santa Giannina
9141792	Santa Giorgina *	Lbr	1997	21,531	30,202	182	30	20	ucc	2,061 teu: ex CMA CGM Lagos-09, Canmar Promise-06, Santa Giorgina-03, P&O Nedlloyd Rio Grande-02, l/a Santa Giorgina
9126479	Santa Giovanna	Deu	1996	21,531	30,201	182	30	20	ucc	2,061 teu: ex CMA CGM Tema-09, Santa Giovanna-06, P&O Nedlloyd Amazonas-01, Santa Giovanna-01, P&O Nedlloyd Amazonas-01, Nedlloyd Amazonas-99, Santa Giovanna-96

Reederei Claus-Peter Offen : MSC TRIESTE : *Hans Kraijenbosch*

IMO#	name	flag	year	grt	dwt	loa	bm	kts	type	former names
9126481	Santa Giuliana *	Lbr	1996	21,531	30,201	182	30	19	ucc	2,061 teu: ex Delmas Bouake-09, Clan Tangun-08, Santa Giuliana-05, P&O Nedlloyd Orinoco-01, Nedlloyd Orinoco-99, Santa Giuliana-96
9141778	Santa Giulietta	Deu	1997	21,531	30,252	182	30	20	ucc	2,061 teu: ex Delmas Abuja-09, Santa Giulietta-07, P&O Nedlloyd Parana-02, I/a Santa Giulietta
9290402	Santa Paola *	Lbr	2005	54,809	67,310	294	32	25	ucc	ex Maersk Driscoll-10, P&O Nedlloyd Dalian-05
9297864	Santa Pelagia	Deu	2005	54,771	66,821	294	32	25	ucc	4,112 teu: ex Cap Serrat-12, Santa Pelagia-10, Maersk Detroit-10, I/a Santa Pelagia
9297876	Santa Petrissa	Deu	2005	54,771	66,799	294	32	25	ucc	5,043 teu: ex UASC Sharjah-12, Maersk Douglas-10, I/a Santa Petrissa
9290426	Santa Philippa	Deu	2005	54,809	67,310	294	32	25	ucc	4,839 teu: ex Cap Stephens-12, Maersk Durham-10, P&O Nedlloyd Dover-05, I/a Santa Philippa

Reederei Claus-Peter Offen : SAN ANTONIO : *ARO*

Reederei Claus-Peter Offen : SANTA GIORGINA : *J. Kakebeeke*

IMO#	name	flag	year	grt	dwt	loa	bm	kts	type	former names
9297474	Santa Priscilla	Lbr	2005	54,771	67,222	294	32	25	ucc	5,043 teu: ex UACC Dammam-12, Maersk Donegal-10, P&O Nedlloyd Dublin-05, l/dn Santa Paula
9227297	Santa Rafaela	Lbr	2002	45,803	53,328	281	32	25	ucc	4,112 teu: ex Southampton Express-09, Maersk Denia-07, P&O Nedlloyd Remuera-06, l/a Santa Rafaela
9227302	Santa Rebecca	Deu	2002	45,803	53,410	281	32	25	ucc	4,112 teu: ex Maersk Decartur-11, P&O Nedlloyd Encounter-06, l/a Santa Rebecca
9227314	Santa Ricarda	Deu	2002	45,803	53,452	281	32	25	ucc	4,112 teu: ex Maersk Dunafare-10, P&O Nedlloyd Botany-05, l/a Santa Ricarda
9227338	Santa Romana	Deu	2002	45,803	53,081	281	32	25	ucc	4,112 teu: ex Maersk Damascus-11, P&O Nedlloyd Palliser-06, l/a Santa Romana
9227340	Santa Rosanna	Deu	2002	45,803	52,800	281	32	25	ucc	4,112 teu: ex Maersk Duffield-10, Columbus New Zealand-06, P&O Nedlloyd Resolution-02, l/a Santa Rosanna
9244881	Santa Rufina	Lbr	2002	45,803	53,115	281	32	25	ucc	4,112 teu: ex Maersk Denton-10, MSC Marbella-09, Maersk Denton-08, P&O Nedlloyd Mairangi-06, Santa Rufina-02
9290414	SCI Nhava Sheva	Deu	2005	54,809	67,255	294	32	25	ucc	4,839 teu: ex Santa Patricia-12, Cap Scott-12, Maersk Dolores-10, P&O Nedlloyd Delft-05, l/dn Santa Patricia
9450375	Seattle Express	Lbr	2009	91,203	103,845	334	43	25	ucc	8,580 teu: l/a CPO Hamburg
9445576	UASC Jeddah	Lbr	2009	41,358	51,687	262	32	24	ucc	4,255 teu: l/a CPO Jacksonville
9445588	UASC Khor Fakkan	Lbr	2009	41,358	51,738	262	32	24	ucc	4,255 teu: l/a CPO Miami
9440825	UASC Ramadi	Lbr	2009	41,358	51,671	262	32	24	ucc	4,255 teu: l/a CPO Charleston
9440837	UASC Shuaiba	Lbr	2009	41,358	51,701	262	32	24	ucc	4,255 teu: l/a CPO Savannah
9450387	Vancouver Express	Lbr	2009	91,203	103,773	334	43	25	ucc	8,598 teu: l/a CPO Bremen
9173135	Westwood Cascade	Lbr	1999	21,583	30,135	183	30	20	ucc	2,048 teu: ex Santa Fabiola-11, CMA CGM Nyala-09, Santa Fabiola-08, P&O Nedlloyd Singapore-05, l/dn Santa Fabiola
9162253	Westwood Discovery	Lbr	1998	21,583	30,007	183	30	20	ucc	2,048 teu: ex Santa Fiorenzo-11, CMA CGM Niger-09, Santa Fiorenzo-07, P&O Nedlloyd Arica-02, l/a Santa Fiorenzo
9162265	Westwood Pacific	Deu	1998	21,583	29,700	182	30	20	ucc	2,048 teu: ex Santa Federica-11, P&O Nedlloyd Santiago-02, l/a Santa Fredericia

* managed for MPC Munchmeyer Petersen & Co GmbH qv or + for Gebab Konzeptions-und Emissions GmbH ** managed by subsidiary Claus-Peter Offen Tankschiffreederei GmbH & Co KG, † managed by Offen Bulkers

Egon Oldendorff OHG   Germany

Funnel: Grey with white 'EO' on broad blue band, or charterers colours. Hull: Grey, black or red with red boot-topping. History: Founded 1921 as Nordische Dampfer Reederei (Lillenfeld & Oldendorff) GmbH to 1936. Oldendorff Express Lines (formerly CEC) 60% owned from 2006 other 40% Flamar, Belgium. Web: www.oldendorff.com

IMO#	name	flag	year	grt	dwt	loa	bm	kts	type	former names
9272773	Albert Oldendorff	Lbr	2004	19,883	31,647	172	27	14	ggc	
9183776	Alice Oldendorff *	Lbr	2000	28,747	48,000	190	32	14	bsd	
9240809	Anna Oldendorff *	Mlt	2002	29,369	52.466	190	32	14	bbu	ex Vega Pioneer-12
8602476	Beate Oldendorff	Mlt	1988	112,895	227,183	325	52	14	bor	ex Kazusa-10, Kazusa Maru-95

Egon Oldendorff OHG : BEATE OLDENDORFF : *Hans Kraijenbosch*

IMO#	name	flag	year	grt	dwt	loa	bm	kts	type	former names
8900529	Bernhard Oldendorff	Lbr	1991	43,332	77,548	245	32	14	bsd	ex Yeoman Burn-94
9232058	Bulk Asia *	Lbr	2001	87,590	170,578	289	45	14	bbu	
9232060	Bulk Europe *	Lbr	2001	87,590	169,770	289	45	14	bbu	
9484807	C. Prosperity *	Hkg	2011	92,050	175,611	292	45	14	bbu	
9249025	Carl Oldendorff *	Pmd	2002	19,822	31,350	172	27	14	bbu	
8900517	Caroline Oldendorff	Lbr	1991	43,332	77,548	245	32	14	bsd	ex Yeoman Brook-11
9255074	Cathrin Oldendorff *	Lbr	2003	19,883	31,643	172	27	14	bbu	
9149689	Clipper Freeway *	Lbr	1998	18,597	29,227	181	26	14	ggc	ex Freeway-07, DS Freeway-07, Mirande-04
8007808	E. Oldendorff *	Lbr	1982	45,777	78,488	243	32	14	bsd	ex Nobel Fountain-07, Fountain Spirit-04, Teekay Fountain-03, Bona Fountain-99, Höegh Fountain-92 (conv cbo-05)
9125786	Ernst Oldendorff *	Lbr	1997	16,405	26,045	172	25	14	bbu	ex Jan Hus-98
9168154	Fiesta *	Bhs	1997	19,354	29,516	181	26	14	ggc	ex DS Fiesta-06, Clipper Fiesta-01
9120334	Harmen Oldendorff *	Lbr	2005	39,568	69,700	225	32	14	bsd	
9138628	Henry Oldendorff *	Lbr	1998	16,405	26,031	172	25	14	bbu	ex Jan Zelivsky-98
9057446	Johanna Oldendorff *	Lbr	1998	37,978	67,508	225	32	14	bsd	ex Sofia III-06, Aifos-03, Ever Victory-02
9225005	John Oldendorff	Lbr	2001	86,201	169,229	289	45	14	bbu	ex Lowlands Prosperity-12, Lowlands Prosperous-04
9268083	Lily Oldendorff *	Lbr	2003	19,883	31,350	172	27	14	bbu	
9246308	Lucas Oldendorff *	Lbr	2002	19,882	31,643	172	27	14	bbu	
9587166	Lucy Oldendorff *	Lbr	2011	20,867	32,491	180	28	14	bbu	
9317705	Maria Oldendorff	Lbr	2006	22,698	37,534	178	29	14	bbu	
9123099	Ocean Trader *	Lbr	1996	19,354	29,516	181	26	14	ggc	ex Pacific Faithful-09, Christiane Oldendorff-04, Tamaya-99, Christiane Oldendorff-96
9117600	Pacific Fantasy *	Lbr	1996	19,354	29,538	181	26	14	ggc	ex DS Fantasy-04, Cielo di Spagna-01, Clipper Fantasy-00, Paipote-98, Clipper Fantasy-97, Paipote-97, Clipper Fantasy-96
9177624	Pacific Fighter *	Lbr	1998	18,597	29,538	181	26	14	ggc	ex Clipper Fighter-04, Dolisle-04
9233492	Paul Oldendorff *	Prt	2001	38,928	74,247	225	32	14	bbu	ex Goldbeam Trader-12
9147617	Ocean Hope *	Lbr	1996	19,354	29,512	181	26	14	ggc	ex Pacific Freedom-09, Ilsabe Oldendorff-05, CSAV Livorno-02, Ilsabe Oldendorff-01, Cielo di Monfalcone-99, Andacollo-98, Ilsabe Oldendorff-97
9317690	Regina Oldendorff ‡	Pmd	2006	22,698	37,504	178	29	14	bbu	
9138109	Sophie Oldendorff *	Lbr	2000	41,428	70,037	225	32	14	bsd	
9243564	Zella Oldendorff *	Mlt	2007	27,989	50,326	190	32	14	bbu	ex Violet-12

also operate a large number of time-chartered vessels and some operated in joint Pool with CSL Group Inc., Canada
* managed by subsidiary Oldendorff Carriers GmbH & Co. KG (formed 2001) and ** managed by Pacific King Shipping Pte Ltd, Singapore.
† managed by Oldendorff Carriers GmbH for Investeringsgruppen Danmark A/S, Denmark or ‡ for Buchanan Maritime Corp.

Reederei 'Nord' Klaus E. Oldendorff   Cyprus

Funnel: *Grey with white 'N' inside white ring on broad blue band or charterers colours.* **Hull:** *Dark grey with red boot-topping.*
History: *Founded 1964 in Germany, relocated to Cyprus in 1987. Recently divided business into two operating divisions, one for dry cargo based in Hamburg, the other for tankers and based in Cyprus.* **Web:** *www.reederei-nord.com*

Reederei Nord GmbH, Germany

IMO#	name	flag	year	grt	dwt	loa	bm	kts	type	former names
9294549	Australia Express	Cyp	2001	26,611	34,704	210	30	22	ucc	2,602 teu: ex Nordwoge-11
9323039	Autumn E	Cyp	2008	38,332	45,309	247	32	23	ucc	3,586 teu: ex Nordautumn-11
9241475	Baltic	Iom	2003	25,407	33,850	207	30	22	ucc	2,506 teu: ex Nordbaltic-11, CMA CGM Romania-08, Nordbaltic-03
9212694	Elbe	Cyp	2001	40,605	75,259	225	32	14	bbu	ex Nordelbe-11
9224685	Ems	Cyp	2001	40,605	75,253	225	32	14	bbu	ex Nordems-11
9134505	Kota Megah	Cyp	1997	24,053	27,100	206	27	20	ucc	2,045 teu: ex Nordeagle-11, CMA CGM Aguila-09, Nordeagle-06, Libra Houston-01, CSAV Seoul-00, Panatlantic-99, Nordeagle-97
9144316	Kota Mesra	Cyp	1997	24,053	27,100	206	27	20	ucc	2,086 teu: ex Nordfalcon-11, CMA CGM Carioca-09, Nordfalcon-04, CSAV Taipei-01, Panamerican-99, Nordfalcon-97
9144328	Kota Mewah	Cyp	1997	24,053	27,100	206	27	20	ucc	2,045 teu: ex Nordhawk-11, CMA CGM Colombie-09, CSAV Livorno-03, Nordhawk-02, Libra Buenos Aires-01, Zim Sao Paulo-99, Panbrasil-98, I/a Nordhawk
9241487	Med	Cyp	2003	25,407	33,900	207	30	22	ucc	2,506 teu: ex MCC Jakarta-12, Normed-10, CMA CGM Intensity-08, Nordmed-04
9321897	MOL Spring	Cyp	2007	38,212	45,230	247	32	23	ucc	3,586 teu: ex Spring R.-12, Nordspring-11
9323041	MOL Winter	Cyp	2008	38,332	46,212	247	32	23	ucc	3,586 teu: ex Winter D.-12, Nordwinter-11
9596026	N Loire	Mlt	2013	24,195	37,211	189	28	14	bbu	
9596038	N Schelde	Mlt	2013	24,195	37,200	189	28	14	bbu	

IMO#	name	flag	year	grt	dwt	loa	bm	kts	type	former names
9241451	NileDutch Impala	Cyp	2003	25,407	33,853	207	30	22	ucc	2,506 teu: ex Atlantic-12, Nordatlantic-11, Libra Niteroi-10, Nordatlantic-05, Cala Palos-04, Nordatlantic-03
9057173	Nordlake	Cyp	1994	16,202	22,450	179	25	19	ucc	1,524 teu: ex X-Press Khyber-09, Nordlake-08, YM Okinawa-08, Nordlake-05, CSAV Lonquimay-98, Nordlake-96
9224714	Mosel	Cyp	2001	40,605	75,080	225	32	14	bbu	ex Nordmosel-11
9224702	Rhine	Cyp	2001	40,605	75,080	225	32	14	bbu	ex Nordrhine-11
9321902	Summer E.	Cyp	2007	38,332	46,321	247	32	23	ucc	3,586 teu: ex MOL Summer-12, Nordsummer-11, Orange River Bridge-11, Nordsummer-07
9224697	Trave	Cyp	2001	40,605	75,080	225	32	14	bbu	ex Nordtrave-11
9134684	Vento di Grecale	Cyp	1997	16,264	22,350	179	25	19	ucc	1,684 teu: ex Coast-12, Nordcoast-11, Cala Puebla-09, Nordcoast-05, Safmarine Nahoon-02, DAL East London-02, Nordcoast-01, Alianca Parana-00, Nordcoast-00, CSAV Buenos Aires-99, Nordcoast-97
9294537	Welle	Cyp	2005	26,611	34,740	210	30	22	ucc	2,602 teu: ex Nordwelle-11
9212709	Weser	Cyp	2001	40,605	75,321	225	32	14	bbu	ex Nordweser-11

newbuildings : 8 x 1,700teu box boats: 2 further 37,500dwt bulk carriers (Zhejiang Ouhou)

Reederei Nord Ltd., Cyprus

IMO#	name	flag	year	grt	dwt	loa	bm	kts	type	former names
9241114	Energy R.	Cyp	2003	161,306	319,174	333	60	16	tcr	ex Nordenergy-11
9319870	Nordbay	Cyp	2007	62,241	116,104	249	44	15	tcr	
9277761	Merkur O.	Cyp	2004	42,432	74,999	225	32	14	tco	ex Nordmerkur
9277759	N. Mars	Cyp	2004	42,432	74,999	225	32	14	tco	ex Nordmars-11
9277773	Neptun D	Cyp	2004	42,432	74,999	225	32	14	tco	ex Nordneptun-11
9147447	Nordmark	Cyp	1998	57,148	105,337	244	42	15	tcr	
9521435	Nordrose	Cyp	2012	56,320	104,583	244	42	14	tcr	
9144067	Nordstrength	Cyp	1998	57,148	105,212	244	42	15	tcr	
9241102	Power D	Cyp	2003	161,308	319,012	333	60	16	tcr	ex Nordpower-11
9521447	Tulip	Cyp	2013	57,081	104,280	244	42	14	tcr	ex Nordtulip-13
9334571	Two Million Ways	Cyp	2008	40,865	73,965	228	32	14	tcr	ex Eagle Hope-11
9277747	Venus R.	Cyp	2004	42,432	74,999	225	32	14	tco	ex Nordvenus-11

newbuildings:
See also Nordcapital Holding GmbH & Cie KG (ER Schiffahrt GmbH & Cie KG)

D. Oltmann GmbH & Co.   Germany

Funnel: *Mainly in charterers colours.* **Hull:** *Dark grey with red boot-topping.* **History:** *Founded 1871.* **Web:** *www.oltmann.com*

IMO#	name	flag	year	grt	dwt	loa	bm	kts	type	former names
9623673	Cap Ferrato	Mlt	2012	52,464	63,007	256	37	21	ucc	4,975 teu: l/a RDO Fortune
9623661	Cap Frio	Mlt	2012	52,464	62,997	256	37	21	ucc	4,975 teu: l/a RDO Favour
9280809	CSAV Lirquen	Bhs	2004	40,952	55,461	261	32	24	ucc	4,130 teu: ex APL Brazil-11, l/a RDO Harmony
9369734	MSC Bremen	Lbr	2007	54,605	67,033	294	32	25	ucc	5,029 teu: l/a RDO Bremen
9232890	MSC England	Lbr	2001	39,812	51,020	258	32	24	ucc	4,132 teu: ex CMA CGM Vega-07, l/a RDO England

Reederei ;Nord' Klaus E. Oldendorff (Reederei Nord GmbH) : N. MARS : *C. Lous*

IMO#	name	flag	year	grt	dwt	loa	bm	kts	type	former names
9305635	NYK Cosmos	Lbr	2006	40,952	55,483	261	32	24	ucc	4,130 teu: l/a RDO Honour
9401283	RDO Concord	Lbr	2009	73,819	85,626	304	40	25	ucc	6,969 teu: ex CMA CGM Flaubert-11, l/a RDO Concord
9415844	RDO Concert	Lbr	2009	75,604	85,622	304	40	25	ucc	6,969 teu: ex UASC Yanbu-12, l/a RDO Concert

Schiffahrts Oltmann Verwaltung GmbH   Germany

Funnel: *Mainly in charterers colours.* **Hull:** *Dark grey with red boot-topping.* **History:** *Founded 1962 as Rederei Gerhard Oltmann KG to 1989.* **Web:** *www.oltship.de*

IMO#	name	flag	year	grt	dwt	loa	bm	kts	type	former names
9220328	JPO Aires	Atg	2001	25,361	33,900	207	30	22	ucc	2,466 teu: ex MOL Dream-12, Trade Rainbow-05, TCL Challenger-02, JPO Aries-01
9220316	JPO Aquarius	Atg	2000	25,361	33,937	207	30	22	ucc	2,466 teu: ex CMA CGM Bahia-12, Libra Buenos Aires-06, CMA CGM Chili-02, JPO Aquarius-01
9495402	JPO Cancer *	Lbr	2005	41,359	52,450	264	32	24	ucc	4,132 teu: ex Maersk Dabou-12, Seattle Express-07, Maersk Dabou-06, P&O Nedlloyd Cardenas-05, JPO Cancer-05
9495414	JPO Capricornus *	Lbr	2005	41,359	52,786	264	32	24	ucc	4,132 teu: ex Maersk Danville-12, P&O Nedlloyd Cardigan-05, JPO Capricornus-05
9455648	JPO Delphinus	Lbr	2009	32,987	56,819	190	32	14	bbu	
9455650	JPO Dorado	Lbr	2009	32,987	56,686	190	32	14	bbu	
9294020	JPO Gemini	Deu	2005	25,630	33,742	207	30	22	ucc	2,474 teu: ex CSAV Yokohama-10, JPO Gemini-05
9246700	JPO Leo	Lbr	2005	35,881	41,743	220	32	22	ucc	3,104 teu: ex Hyundai Renaissance-09, MOL Renaissance-08, JPO Leo-05
9307267	JPO Sagittarius **	Lbr	2006	27,100	34,532	210	30	22	ucc	2,602 teu
9307279	JPO Scorpius **	Lbr	2006	27,100	34,537	210	30	22	ucc	2,602 teu
9400198	JPO Tucana	Lbr	2009	42,609	52,788	269	32	24	ucc	4,250 teu
9406180	JPO Vela	Lbr	2009	41,225	50,420	265	32	24	ucc	4,250 teu: ex Bunga Raya Sembilan-10, l/a JPO Vela
9430765	JPO Virgo	Lbr	2009	41,225	50,361	265	32	24	ucc	4,250 teu
9430777	JPO Volans	Lbr	2010	41,225	50,041	265	32	24	ucc	4,250 teu
9430789	JPO Vulpecula	Lbr	2010	41,225	50,425	265	32	24	ucc	4,250 teu
9297840	Maersk Dunbar	Lbr	2006	41,359	52,450	264	32	24	ucc	4,132 teu: ex P&O Nedlloyd Carolinas-06, JPO Libra-05
9297852	Maersk Duncan	Lbr	2006	41,359	52,786	264	32	24	ucc	4,132 teu: ex P&O Nedlloyd Carthago-06, JPO Pisces-05

Schiffahrts Oltmann Verwaltung GmbH : JPO Gemini : *Andy McAlpine*

IMO#	name	flag	year	grt	dwt	loa	bm	kts	type	former names
9138288	MSC Caracas	Deu	1998	25,361	33,919	207	30	21	ucc	2,470 teu: ex Montebello-06, Anika Oltmann-99, Montebello-99, Anika Oltmann-98
9400174	UASC Ajman	Lbr	2010	42,609	52,300	269	32	24	ucc	4,250 teu: I/a JPO Taurus
9153408	Ute Oltmann	Deu	1998	25,359	33,964	207	30	20	ucc	2,474 teu: ex CP Rangitoto-06, Contship Rangitoto-05, Cielo di San Francisco-05, Ute Oltmann-99

newbuildings: .
* managed for HCI Capital AG or ** for HCI Hanseatische Schiffstreuhand GmbH.

Olympic Shipping and Management SA   Greece

Funnel: *Orange, large white disc containing blue/yellow pennant flag with five interlocking coloured rings above and below.* **Hull:** *Black with red boot-topping.* **History:** *Founded 1951 as Olympic Maritime SA to 1992.* **Web:** *www.onassis.gr*

IMO#	name	flag	year	grt	dwt	loa	bm	kts	type	former names
8913954	Olympic Faith	Grc	1991	81,192	147,457	274	45	14	tcr	
9271341	Olympic Flag	Grc	2004	80,591	155,099	274	47	16	tcr	
8913966	Olympic Flair	Grc	1991	81,192	147,396	274	45	14	tcr	
9271353	Olympic Future	Grc	2004	80,591	155,039	274	47	16	tcr	
9212864	Olympic Hawk	Mhl	2000	159,414	306,324	335	58	14	tcr	ex Hawk-12
9088689	Olympic Legacy	Grc	1996	160,129	302,789	332	58	14	tcr	
9238868	Olympic Legend	Grc	2003	160,083	308,500	333	60	15	tcr	
9233791	Olympic Liberty	Grc	2003	160,083	304,992	333	60	15	tcr	
8912613	Olympic Serenity	Grc	1991	52,127	96,733	232	42	13	tcr	
9133587	Olympic Spirit II	Grc	1997	52,197	96,773	232	42	13	tcr	
9060601	Olympic Sponsor	Grc	1994	52,196	96,547	232	42	13	tcr	

owned by Alexander S. Onassis Public Benefit Foundation and managed by subsidiary Springfield Shipping Co. (Panama) SA, Greece.

Orient Overseas International Ltd   Hong Kong (China)

Orient Overseas Container Line Ltd., Hong Kong (China)

Funnel: *Yellow with red and gold 'plum blossom' symbol.* **Hull:** *Light grey with red 'OOCL', orange with white 'OOCL' or black with red boot-topping.* **History:** *Parent founded in 1946 as CY Tung Group and OOCL formed in 1969. CY Tung acquired Furness, Withy & Co in 1980, but resold to Rudolf A Oetker in 1990.* **Web:** *www.oocl.com*

IMO#	name	flag	year	grt	dwt	loa	bm	kts	type	former names
9622588	NYK Helios *	Hkg	2013	141,003	143,521	366	48	25	ucc	13,000 teu
9622631	NYK Hermes *	Hkg	2013	141,000	143,500	366	48	25	ucc	13,000 teu
9627980	NYK Hyperion *	Hkg	2013	141,000	143,500	366	48	25	ucc	13,000 teu
9102291	OOCL America	Hkg	1995	66,047	67,741	276	40	24	ucc	5,344 teu
9307011	OOCL Antwerp †	Pan	2006	66,462	66,940	281	40	25	ucc	5,888 teu
9300790	OOCL Asia	Hkg	2006	89,097	99,602	323	43	25	ucc	8,063 teu
9285005	OOCL Atlanta	Hkg	2005	89,097	99,620	323	43	25	ucc	8,063 teu
9332200	OOCL Australia	Hkg	2006	41,479	52,217	263	32	24	ucc	4,583 teu
9627978	OOCL Bangkok	Hkg	2013	141,000	143,500	366	48	25	ucc	13,000 teu
9477878	OOCL Beijing	Hkg	2011	91,563	101,589	335	43	25	ucc	8,888 teu
9169419	OOCL Belgium	Hkg	1998	39,174	40,972	245	32	21	ucc	2,808 teu

Olympic Shipping and Management : OLYMPIC SPONSOR : *M. Lennon*

IMO#	name	flag	year	grt	dwt	loa	bm	kts	type	former names
9622605	OOCL Berlin	Hkg	2013	141,000	143,500	366	48	25	ucc	13,000 teu
9445502	OOCL Brisbane	Hkg	2009	40,168	50,575	260	32	24	ucc	4,526 teu
9102318	OOCL Britain	Hkg	1996	66,046	67,958	276	40	24	ucc	5,344 teu
9622590	OOCL Brussels	Hkg	2013	141,000	143,500	366	48	25	ucc	13,000 teu
9329540	OOCL Busan	Hkg	2008	40,168	50,567	260	32	23	ucc	4,526 teu
9102289	OOCL California	Hkg	1995	66,046	67,765	276	40	24	ucc	5,344 teu
9477880	OOCL Canada	Hkg	2011	91,563	101,412	335	43	25	ucc	8,888 teu
9461790	OOCL Charleston	Hkg	2010	40,168	50,518	260	32	24	ucc	4,526 teu
9199270	OOCL Chicago	Hkg	2000	66,677	67,278	277	40	25	ucc	5,714 teu
9622628	OOCL Chongxing	Hkg	2013	141,000	143,500	366	48	25	ucc	13,000 teu
9445526	OOCL Dalian	Hkg	2009	40,168	50,554	260	32	24	ucc	4,526 teu
9300805	OOCL Europe	Hkg	2006	89,097	99,618	323	43	25	ucc	8,063 teu
9404869	OOCL Guangzhou	Hkg	2010	40,168	50,486	260	32	24	ucc	4,526 teu
9252008	OOCL Hamburg	Hkg	2004	89,097	99,618	323	43	25	ucc	8,063 teu
9355757	OOCL Houston	Hkg	2007	40,168	50,585	260	32	23	ucc	4,526 teu
9404883	OOCL Jakarta	Hkg	2010	40,168	50,560	260	32	24	ucc	4,526 teu: ex OOCL Ho Chi Minh-10
9307009	OOCL Kaohsiung †	Sgp	2006	66,462	66,940	281	40	25	ucc	5,888 teu
9329526	OOCL Kobe	Hkg	2007	40,168	50,554	260	32	23	ucc	4,526 teu
9367176	OOCL Kuala Lumpur †	Hkg	2007	66,462	66,940	281	40	25	ucc	5,888 teu
9404857	OOCL Le Havre	Hkg	2010	40,168	50,580	260	32	24	ucc	4,526 teu
9417268	OOCL London	Hkg	2010	89,097	99,636	323	43	25	ucc	8,063 teu
9243409	OOCL Long Beach	Hkg	2003	89,097	99,508	323	43	25	ucc	8,063 teu
9417270	OOCL Luxembourg	Hkg	2010	89,097	99,654	323	43	25	ucc	8,063 teu
9477892	OOCL Miami	Hkg	2013	90,757	101,000	335	43	25	ucc	8,888 teu
9253739	OOCL Montreal	Hkg	2003	55,994	47,840	294	32	24	ucc	4,404 teu
9445538	OOCL Nagoya	Hkg	2009	40,168	50,501	260	32	24	ucc	4,526 teu
9445514	OOCL New Zealand	Hkg	2009	40,168	50,554	260	32	24	ucc	4,526 teu
9198109	OOCL New York †	Lbr	1999	66,289	67,660	277	40	26	ucc	5,762 teu: l/a E.R. Hong Kong
9256482	OOCL Ningbo	Hkg	2004	89,097	99,500	323	43	25	ucc	8,063 teu
9440045	OOCL Norfolk	Hkg	2009	40,168	50,489	260	32	24	ucc	4,526 teu
9367170	OOCL Oakland †	Pan	2007	66,462	66,940	281	40	25	ucc	5,888 teu
9355769	OOCL Panama	Hkg	2008	40,168	50,633	260	32	24	ucc	4,526 teu
9256470	OOCL Qingdao	Hkg	2004	89,097	99,600	323	43	25	ucc	8,063 teu
9251999	OOCL Rotterdam	Hkg	2004	89,097	99,522	323	43	25	ucc	8,063 teu
9199268	OOCL San Francisco	Hkg	2000	66,677	67,286	277	40	25	ucc	5,888 teu
9404871	OOCL Savannah	Hkg	2010	40,168	50,490	260	32	24	ucc	4,526 teu
9417244	OOCL Seoul	Hkg	2010	89,097	99,635	323	43	25	ucc	8,063 teu
9198111	OOCL Shanghai †	Lbr	1999	66,289	67,473	277	40	26	ucc	5,762 teu: l/a E.R. Shanghai
9243394	OOCL Shenzhen	Hkg	2003	89,097	99,518	323	43	25	ucc	8,063 teu
9310240	OOCL Southampton	Hkg	2007	89,097	99,678	323	43	25	ucc	8,063 teu
9329552	OOCL Texas	Hkg	2008	40,168	50,610	260	32	23	ucc	4,526 teu
9285471	OOCL Tianjin	Hkg	2005	89,097	99,500	323	43	25	ucc	8,063 teu
9310238	OOCL Tokyo	Hkg	2007	89,097	99,706	323	43	25	ucc	8,063 teu
9417256	OOCL Washington	Hkg	2010	89,097	99,631	323	43	25	ucc	8,063 teu
9329538	OOCL Yokohama	Hkg	2007	40,168	50,634	260	32	23	ucc	4,526 teu

Orient Overseas International Ltd. (Orient Overseas Container Line) : OOCL SOUTHAMPTON : ARO

IMO#	name	flag	year	grt	dwt	loa	bm	kts	type	former names
9332195	OOCL Zhoushan	Hkg	2006	41,479	52,214	263	32	24	ucc	4,583 teu

newbuildings: 5 further 8,888teu (Hudong-Zhonghua) 2013, further 3 x 13,000teu (Samsung) 2013/14 (1 to be chartered to NYK)
* chartered to Nippon Yusen Kaisha or † on charter from various Japanese owners or finance houses and managed by Anglo-Eastern Shipmanagement, by Fleet Management Ltd, Hong Kong, by Orient Marine Co Ltd or by Bernhard Schulte Shipmanagement (China) Co Ltd.

Associated Maritime Co. (Hong Kong) Ltd., Hong Kong (China)

History: *Formed 1946 jointly by CY Tung as Island Navigation Corp. (until 1978) and by Hong Kong Ming Wah Shipping Co. Ltd, Hong Kong (founded 1980 and wholly owned by China Merchants Group).* **Web:** *www.hkmw.com.hk*

IMO#	name	flag	year	grt	dwt	loa	bm	kts	type	former names
9361512	New Ability	Lbr	2008	55,898	105,381	229	42	14	tcr	
9487172	New Accord	Lbr	2009	61,736	109,804	245	42	14	tco	
9361524	New Activity	Lbr	2008	55,898	105,342	229	42	14	tcr	
9337212	New Advance	Lbr	2007	56,172	105,544	229	42	14	tcr	
9177947	New Alliance	Lbr	1998	56,311	106,118	241	42	14	tcr	
9177820	New Amity	Lbr	1998	56,311	106,120	241	42	14	tc	
9487184	New Award	Lbr	2010	61,735	109,804	245	42	14	tco	
9288083	New Century	Lbr	2004	156,973	299,031	330	60	14	tcr	
9340635	New Creation	Lbr	2009	152,727	297,259	330	60	14	tcr	
8907333	New Fortuner	Lbr	1992	78,958	146,041	277	44	14	tcr	
9398060	New Paradise	Lbr	2010	156,921	297,863	330	60	14	tcr	
9398058	New Prospect	Lbr	2009	156,921	297,934	330	60	14	tcr	
9434620	New Resource	Lbr	2010	157,039	297,101	330	60	14	tcr	
9288095	New Spirit	Lbr	2005	156,973	298,972	330	60	14	tcr	
9434632	New Success	Lbr	2010	157,039	297,027	330	60	14	tcr	
8919271	New Valor	Lbr	1992	156,317	281,598	328	57	13	tcr	
9445631	New Vanguard	Lbr	2011	157,039	297,115	330	60	14	tcr	
9006617	New Venture	Lbr	1992	156,307	291,640	328	57	13	tcr	
9014418	New Victory	Lbr	1993	156,307	291,613	328	57	14	tcr	
9458614	New Vista	Lbr	2011	157,039	297,252	330	60	14	tcr	
9014470	New Vitality	Lbr	1993	153,808	290,691	330	56	15	tcr	

Chinese Maritime Transport Ltd., Taiwan

Funnel: *Green with red and gold 'plum blossom' symbol on broad white band, blue top.* **Hull:** *Black with red boot-topping.*
History: *Founded by CY Tung in Taiwan, 1940.* **Web:** *www.cmt.tw*

IMO#	name	flag	year	grt	dwt	loa	bm	kts	type	former names
9329447	China Peace	Hkg	2005	88,930	174,413	289	45	14	bbu	
9588768	China Pioneer	Hkg	2012	106,884	206,079	300	50	14	bbu	
9558799	China Pride	Hkg	2011	91,373	177,856	292	45	14	bbu	
9378319	China Progress	Hkg	2006	88,900	174,322	289	45	14	bbu	
9592434	China Prosperity	Hkg	2012	104,361	203,028	300	50	14	bbu	
9592422	China Triumph	Hkg	2011	104,361	203,028	300	50	14	bbu	

newbuildings: one 206,000dwt bbu Shanghai Wugaoqiao ShipbuildingCo. H1219 (2013)

Overseas Shipholding Group Inc.   U.S.A.

Funnel: *Blue with white 'OSG' ('S' having waves in lower part), black top.* **Hull:** *Black with red boot-topping.* **History:** *Formed 1969 Acquired Stelmar Shipping in 2005.* **Web:** *www.osg.com*

IMO#	name	flag	year	grt	dwt	loa	bm	kts	type	former names
9337705	Al Gattara (st) §	Mhl	2007	136,410	106,898	315	50	19	lng	266,000 m³
9337717	Al Gharrafa (st) §	Mhl	2008	136,410	107,000	315	50	19	lng	266,000 m³
9337743	Al Hamla (st) §	Mhl	2008	136,410	106,983	315	50	19	lng	266,000 m³
9244661	Alaskan Explorer †	Usa	2005	110,693	193,049	287	50	15	tcr	
9244659	Alaskan Frontier †	Usa	2004	110,693	193,049	287	50	15	tcr	
9271432	Alaskan Legend †	Usa	2006	110,693	193,048	287	50	15	tcr	
9244673	Alaskan Navigator †	Usa	2005	110,693	193,048	287	50	15	tcr	l/dn Alaskan Adventurer
9274725	Cabo Hellas *	Mhl	2003	40,038	69,636	228	32	14	tco	
9275737	Cabo Sounion *	Mhl	2004	40,038	69,636	228	32	14	tco	
9389679	Overseas Acadia *	Mhl	2008	62,775	113,005	250	44	-	tcr	
9265861	Overseas Alcesmar	Mhl	2004	30,018	46,215	183	32	14	tco	ex Alcesmar-06
9265873	Overseas Alcmar	Mhl	2004	30,018	46,245	183	32	14	tco	ex Alcmar-06
9231626	Overseas Ambermar	Mhl	2002	23,843	35,970	183	27	14	tco	ex Ambermar-05
9353591	Overseas Anacortes ‡	Usa	2010	29,252	46,666	183	32		tco	
9265885	Overseas Andromar	Mhl	2004	30,018	46,195	183	32	14	tco	ex Andromar-06
9271834	Overseas Antigmar	Mhl	2004	30,018	46,168	183	32	14	tco	ex Antigmar-06
9273624	Overseas Ariadmar	Mhl	2004	30,018	46,205	183	32	14	tco	ex Ariadmar-06
9273636	Overseas Atalmar	Mhl	2004	30,018	46,177	183	32	15	tco	ex Atalmar-05
9470260	Overseas Athens	Mhl	2012	30,031	50,342	183	32	14	tco	
9043043	Overseas Beryl *	Mhl	1994	53,341	94,797	245	42	14	tcr	ex Beryl-06
9353565	Overseas Boston	Usa	2009	29,242	46,802	183	32		tco	
9432218	Overseas Chinook	Usa	2010	29,234	46,666	183	32		tco	
9053660	Overseas Eliane *	Mhl	1994	53,341	94,813	245	42	14	tcr	ex Eliane-06
9116400	Overseas Equatorial +	Mhl	1997	156,880	273,539	330	58	15	tcr	ex Equatorial Lion-06
9400679	Overseas Everest +	Mhl	2010	156,651	296,907	333	60	15	tcr	ex Front Emperor-10

IMO#	name	flag	year	grt	dwt	loa	bm	kts	type	former names
9394935	Overseas Everglades *	Mhl	2008	62,775	113,005	250	44	14	tcr	
9213313	Overseas Fran *	Mhl	2001	62,385	112,118	250	44	14	tcr	
9239628	Overseas Goldmar *	Mhl	2002	40,343	69,684	228	32	14	tcr	ex Goldmar-05, l/a LMZ Mandi
9351062	Overseas Houston ‡	Usa	2007	29,242	46,815	183	32	14	tco	
9232606	Overseas Jademar *	Mhl	2002	40,343	69,697	228	32	14	tcr	ex Jademar-05
9213301	Overseas Josefa Camejo *	Mhl	2001	62,385	112,200	250	44	14	tcr	
9563237	Overseas Kilimanjiro	Mhl	2012	157,048	296,999	330	60		tcr	
9384019	Overseas Kimolos	Mhl	2008	30,010	51,218	183	32	14	tco	
9569841	Overseas Kythnos	Mhl	2010	30,021	50,284	183	32		tco	
9470272	Overseas Leyte	Mhl	2011	42,153	73,944	229	32		tco	
9121003	Overseas Limar *	Mhl	1996	28,357	46,170	183	32	14	tco	ex Limar-05, Osprey Lyra-01
9353527	Overseas Long Beach ‡	Usa	2007	29,242	42,994	183	32	14	tco	
9353530	Overseas Los Angeles ‡	Usa	2007	29,242	46,817	183	32	14	tco	l/a Overseas San Francisco
9129940	Overseas Luxmar ‡	Usa	1997	28,357	46,162	183	32	14	tco	ex Luxmar-05, Petrobulk Pollux-01
9301940	Overseas Luzon	Mhl	2006	42,403	74,908	228	32	14	tco	ex Amalia Jacob-07
9165293	Overseas Maremar	Mhl	1998	28,400	47,225	183	32	15	tco	ex Maremar-05, Alam Belia-02
9353589	Overseas Martinez	Usa	2010	29,242	46,666	183	32		tco	
9530228	Overseas McKinley	Mhl	2011	157,048	296,971	330	60		tcr	
9470258	Overseas Milos	Mhl	2011	30,031	50,378	183	32		tco	
9441207	Overseas Mindoro	Mhl	2009	42,010	73,677	229	32		tco	
9230880	Overseas Mulan +	Mhl	2002	161,233	319,029	333	60	16	tcr	
9435894	Overseas Mykonos	Mhl	2010	29,433	51,711	183	32		tco	
9085390	Overseas Nedimar	Mhl	1996	28,326	43,999	183	32	14	tco	ex Nedimar-05
9353541	Overseas New York ‡	Usa	2008	29,242	46,810	183	32	14	tco	
9219056	Overseas Newcastle *	Mhl	2001	82,250	164,626	274	50	15	tcr	ex Besiktas-07
9353577	Overseas Nikiski	Usa	2009	29,242	46,666	183	32		tco	
9401233	Overseas Palawan	Mhl	2008	42,010	73,796	229	32	-	tco	
9232591	Overseas Pearlmar *	Mhl	2002	40,043	69,697	228	32	14	tcr	ex Pearlmar-05
9222170	Overseas Petromar	Mhl	2001	23,740	35,768	183	27	14	tco	ex Petromar-05, l/a Nordafrika
9213325	Overseas Portland *	Mhl	2001	62,385	112,139	250	44	14	tcr	
9197894	Overseas Raphael +	Mhl	2000	157,883	308,700	335	58	15	tcr	ex Raphael-10
9275749	Overseas Reymar *	Mhl	2004	40,038	69,636	228	32	14	tcr	ex Reymar-05
9234666	Overseas Rosalyn +	Mhl	2003	161,233	317,972	333	60	15	tcr	
9232620	Overseas Rosemar *	Mhl	2002	40,343	69,697	228	32	14	tcr	ex Rosemar-05
9232618	Overseas Rubymar *	Mhl	2002	40,343	69,697	228	32	14	tcr	ex Rubymar-05
9196618	Overseas Sakura +	Mhl	2001	159,397	298,641	333	60	15	tcr	ex Sakura I-06, Berge Sakura-01
9470284	Overseas Samar	Mhl	2011	42,153	74,192	229	32		tco	
9435909	Overseas Santorini	Mhl	2010	29,433	51,711	183	32		tco	
9384021	Overseas Serifos	Mhl	2008	30,010	51,257	183	32	14	tco	
9213296	Overseas Shirley *	Can	2001	62,385	112,056	250	44	14	tcr	
9384033	Overseas Sifnos	Mhl	2008	30,010	51,225	183	32	14	tco	
9239630	Overseas Silvermar *	Mhl	2002	40,343	69,609	228	32	14	tcr	ex Overseas-05, l/a LMZ Zacvi
9478638	Overseas Skopelos	Mhl	2009	29,826	50,222	183	32	14	tco	l/a Hope I

Overseas Shipholding Group : OVERSEAS LONG BEACH : Hans Kraijenbosch

IMO#	name	flag	year	grt	dwt	loa	bm	kts	type	former names
9118381	Overseas Sovereign *	Mhl	1996	164,371	309,892	330	58	16	tcr	ex Sovereign Unity-06
9353606	Overseas Tampa	Usa	2011	29,242	46,666	183	32		tco	
9196632	Overseas Tanabe +	Mhl	2002	159,383	298,561	333	60	16	tcr	ex Tanabe-07
9353553	Overseas Texas City ‡	Usa	2008	29,242	46,801	183	32	14	tco	
9301952	Overseas Visayas	Mhl	2006	42,403	74,933	228	32	-	tco	l/a Carl Jacob
9394947	Overseas Yellowstone *	Mhl	2008	62,775	112,990	250	44	-	tcr	
9394959	Overseas Yosemite *	Mhl	2009	62,775	112,905	250	44	-	tcr	
9337731	Tembek §	Mhl	2007	136,410	107,514	315	50	-	lng	266,000 m³
9246633	TI Oceania +	Mhl	2002	234,006	441,585	380	68	16	tcr	ex Hellespont Fairfax-04

owned by OSG Ship Management (GR)Ltd, Greece (formerly Stelmar Tankers Management Ltd to 2005) or * by OSG Ship Management (UK) Ltd (formerly Souter Hamlet Ltd to 1981 and Souter Shipping Ltd to 2001)
+ managed by Tankers (UK) Agencies Ltd vessels operate in Tankers International Pool.
§ owned by Qatar Gas Transport, managed by OSG Ship Management UK Ltd.
† managed by subsidiary Alaska Tanker Co. LLC (formed jointly with Keystone Shipping Co, USA and BP Shipping Ltd, UK)
‡ managed by OSG Ship Management Inc, USA
See also Navion ASA (under Teekay) and Tanker International Pool under CMB (Euronav Luxembourg SA).

Pacific International Lines (Pte.) Ltd.　　　　Singapore

Funnel: Red with black 'PIL' on broad white band. **Hull:** Black or grey with red boot-topping. **History:** Formed 1967.
Web: www.pilship.com

IMO#	name	flag	year	grt	dwt	loa	bm	kts	type	former names
9351048	CSAV Laja *	Sgp	2008	41,482	50,638	261	32	24	ucc	ex PST Valour-08
9351050	CSAV Lauca *	Sgp	2008	39,906	50,600	261	32	24	ucc	ex PST Victory-08
9605891	Kota Bakti	Sgp	2012	18,567	24,000	161	27	16	ggc	
9638616	Kota Bintang	Sgp	2012	20,633	27,000	180	27	15	ggc	
9638628	Kota Buana	Sgp	2012	20,633	27,000	180	27	15	ggc	
9638630	Kota Budi	Sgp	2013	20,886	27,000	180	27	15	ggc	l/a Rui Cheng
9638604	Kota Bunga	Sgp	2012	20,886	27,000	180	27	15	ggc	
9494589	Kota Cahaya	Sgp	2012	76,097	83,963	298	40	25	ucc	6,600 teu
9494591	Kota Cantik	Sgp	2012	76,097	83,964	298	40	25	ucc	6,600 teu
9494577	Kota Carum	Sgp	2011	76,097	83,963	298	40	25	ucc	6,600 teu
9259393	Kota Ganteng	Hkg	2002	28,676	37,087	227	32	22	ucc	2,475 teu
9616802	Kota Gaya	Sgp	2012	29,015	39,500	222	30	24	ucc	2,824 teu
9252357	Kota Gemar	Hkg	2002	28,676	37,115	227	32	22	ucc	2,475 teu
9252369	Kota Gembira	Hkg	2002	28,676	37,114	227	32	22	ucc	2,475 teu
9259408	Kota Gunawan	Hkg	2003	28,676	37,100	227	32	22	yru	2,475 teu
9130169	Kota Jelita	Sgp	1997	16,252	22,420	179	25	19	ucc	1,684 teu: ex Nordriver-11, Cala Pilar-07, City of Stuttgart-02, Safmarine Inyathi-01, Nordriver-01, Pacific Eagle-01, Nordriver-00, Bogata-99, Nordriver-98

Overseas Shipholding Group : OVERSEAS SANTORINI : *Nico Kemps*

IMO#	name	flag	year	grt	dwt	loa	bm	kts	type	former names
9307413	Kota Kamil	Sgp	2006	31,070	39,782	233	32	23	ucc	3,081 teu
9307425	Kota Karim	Sgp	2006	31,070	39,763	233	32	23	ucc	3,081 teu
9307396	Kota Kasturi	Sgp	2005	31,070	39,916	233	32	23	ucc	3,081 teu: ex Kota Kado-11
9307401	Kota Kaya *	Sgp	2006	31,070	39,932	233	32	23	ucc	3,081 teu
9322308	Kota Lagu	Sgp	2006	39,906	50,689	261	32	24	ucc	4,253 teu
9322310	Kota Lahir	Sgp	2006	39,906	52,525	261	32	24	ucc	4,253 teu
9345702	Kota Laju	Sgp	2007	39,906	52,525	261	32	24	ucc	4,253 teu
9351024	Kota Lambai	Sgp	2008	39,906	50,596	261	32	24	ucc	4,253 teu
9351036	Kota Lambang	Sgp	2008	39,906	50,596	261	32	24	ucc	4,253 teu
9439735	Kota Langsar	Sgp	2010	39,906	50,595	261	32	24	ucc	4,253 teu
9340764	Kota Latif	Sgp	2007	39,906	52,629	261	32	24	ucc	4,253 teu
9439709	Kota Lawa	Sgp	2008	39,906	50,638	261	32	24	ucc	4,253 teu
9438759	Kota Layang	Sgp	2009	39,906	50,595	261	32	24	ucc	4,253 teu
9439711	Kota Layar	Sgp	2009	39,906	50,595	261	32	24	ucc	4,253 teu
9439747	Kota Lukis	Sgp	2010	39,906	50,595	261	32	24	ucc	4,253 teu
9494541	Kota Lumayan	Sgp	2010	39,906	50,604	261	32	24	ucc	4,253 teu
9439761	Kota Lumba	Sgp	2010	39,906	50,604	261	32	24	ucc	4,253 teu
9356830	Kota Nabil	Sgp	2008	20,902	26,000	180	28	20	ucc	1,800 teu
9362293	Kota Naga	Sgp	2008	20,902	25,985	180	28	20	ucc	1,800 teu
9362308	Kota Naluri	Sgp	2008	20,902	25,985	180	28	20	ucc	1,800 teu
9461635	Kota Nanhai	Sgp	2008	20,902	25,985	180	28	20	ucc	1,800 teu
9262310	Kota Nazar	Sgp	2009	20,902	25,985	180	28	20	ucc	1,800 teu
9390240	Kota Nazim	Sgp	2008	20,902	25,985	180	28	20	ucc	1,800 teu
9390252	Kota Nekad	Sgp	2009	20,902	25,985	180	28	20	ucc	1,800 teu
9464761	Kota Nilam	Sgp	2009	20,902	25,985	180	28	20	ucc	1,800 teu
9494620	Kota Nasrat	Sgp	2008	20,902	25,985	180	28	20	ucc	1,800 teu
9494632	Kota Nebula	Sgp	2010	20,902	25,985	180	28	20	ucc	1,800 teu
9535307	Kota Nelayan	Sgp	2010	20,902	25,985	180	28	20	ucc	1,800 teu
9593696	Kota Nipah	Sgp	2011	20,902	25,985	180	28	20	ucc	1,800 teu
9342695	Kota Permata	Hkg	2008	28,340	39,446	222	30	24	ucc	2,824 teu
9603910	Pacific Capella	Sgp	2012	94,710	180,346	295	46		bbu	
9603908	Pacific Canopus	Sgp	2012	94,710	180,330	295	46		bbu	
9595591	Shagang Hongfa	Sgp	2011	93,228	179,461	292	45		bbu	
9595606	Shagang Hongchang	Sgp	2011	93,228	179,469	292	45		bbu	

newbuildings: two 76,000 grt container ships
* owned by subsidiary PST Management Pte Ltd, Singapore (founded 2006 - www.pacificshippingtrust.com)
See chartered ships with 'Kota' prefix in index. Only larger vessels are listed, combined fleet is 85 mainly Far East container feeder ships.

Papachristidis Ltd. U.K.

Funnel: *Blue with broad above narrow blue bands, interrupted by blue 'ФВП' within blue ring on white disc.* **Hull:** *White with red boot-topping.* **History:** *Founded 1981 as Papachristidis (UK) Ltd to 1988.* **Web:** *www.hellespont.com*

9351414	Hellespont Pride	Mhl	2006	42,010	73,727	229	32	14	tco	
9351426	Hellespont									
	Progress **	Mhl	2006	42,010	73,727	229	32	14	tco	
9351438	Hellespont Promise	Mhl	2006	42,010	73,669	229	32	14	tco	

Pacific International Lines (Pte.) Ltd. : KOTA LUMBA : *J. Kakebeeke*

IMO#	name	flag	year	grt	dwt	loa	bm	kts	type	former names
9351440	Hellespont Prosperity **	Mhl	2006	42,010	73,715	229	32	14	tco	
9351452	Hellespont Protector	Mhl	2006	42,010	73,821	229	32	14	tco	
9351464	Hellespont Providence **	Mhl	2006	42,010	73,784	229	32	14	tco	
9187760	Hellespont Tatina *	Mhl	1999	56,324	105,535	239	42	14	tcr	ex Minerva Anna-04, Pine Venture-02

*operated by Hellespont Hammonia GmbH & Co KG, Germany, * managed for Salamon AG, Germany, **managed by Sanko Steamship Co.*

Reederei Stefan Patjens GmbH & Co. KG   Germany

Funnel: *Charterers colours.* **Hull:** *Various.* **History:** Founded 2000 as *Reederei Stefan Patjens until 2006.*
Web: *www.reederei-patjens.de*

IMO#	name	flag	year	grt	dwt	loa	bm	kts	type	former names
9225407	Alexandra P	Lbr	2000	32,322	39,128	211	32	22	ucc	2,732 teu: ex Kota Perabu-11, Alexandra P-10, OOCL Keelung-09, Alexandra P-07, Maersk Plymouth-06, Alexandra-00
9225419	Heike P	Lbr	2000	32,322	39,128	211	32	22	ucc	2,732 teu: ex Kota Perwira-11, Heike P-10, OOCL Bangkok-09, Heike-07, Maersk Pelepas-06, Safmarine Ibhayi-05, Maersk Pelepas-03, Heike-00
9232759	Liwia P	Lbr	2001	32,322	39,128	211	32	22	ucc	2,732 teu: ex OOCL Mumbai-09, Liwia-07, Safmarine Ikapa-06, MSC Canada-03, Liwia-02
9317913	Maersk Drummond	Lbr	2006	53,453	54,058	294	32	23	ucc	5,040 teu: I/a Serena P.
9317937	Maersk Drury	Lbr	2006	53,481	53,911	294	32	23	ucc	5,040 teu: I/a Kathe P.
9317925	Maersk Dryden	Lbr	2006	53,481	53,880	294	32	23	ucc	5,040 teu: I/a Herma P.
9320685	Maersk Dubrovnik	Lbr	2006	53,481	53,900	294	32	23	ucc	5,040 teu: I/a Allise P.
9232747	Meta	Lbr	2001	32,322	39,128	211	32	22	ucc	2,732 teu: ex Maersk Perth-06, I/a Meta
9126986	Rothorn *	Atg	1996	12,029	14,587	157	24	18	ucc	1,122 teu: ex MOL Amazonas-02, Guatamala-01, Rothorn-98
9126974	Weisshorn *	Atg	1996	12,029	14,643	157	24	19	ucc	1,122 teu: ex MSC Ghana-04, Weisshorn-02, DAL East London-01, Weisshorn-00, P&O Nedlloyd Mauritius-99, Weisshorn-98

newbuildings:

Dr. Peters GmbH & Co. KG   Germany

Funnel: *Charterers colours.* **Hull:** *Various former owners or charterers colours.* **History:** *KG investment fund founded in 1960 as Dr Peters GmbH to 1999.* **Web:** *www. drpeters.com and www.ds-schiffahrt.de*

IMO#	name	flag	year	grt	dwt	loa	bm	kts	type	former names
9108154	Alfa Glory **	Mhl	1997	159,422	309,636	333	58	14	tcr	ex Apollo Glory-11, C. Bright-07
9148635	Ashna	Mhl	1999	156,417	301,438	330	58	15	tcr	ex Nordbay-04
9315642	Artemis Glory **	Pan	2006	157,844	306,507	332	58	15	tcr	
9081382	Cape Banks *	Deu	1997	21,162	33,540	179	25	14	tco	ex Chembulk Hong Kong-02, Cape Banks-97
9147253	Cape Bear *	Deu	1997	21,165	33,540	179	25	14	tco	ex Chembulk Vancouver-02, Cape Bear-97
9106508	Cape Sorrell *	Lbr	1997	10,925	13,741	151	24	18	ucc	1,158 teu: ex TS Osaka-09, Cape Sorrell-03, Independent Concept-99, Cape Sorrell-97

Papachristidis Ltd. : HELLESPONT TATINA : *Roy Fenton*

IMO#	name	flag	year	grt	dwt	loa	bm	kts	type	former names
9106493	Cape Spencer *	Lbr	1996	10,925	13,623	151	24	18	ucc	1,158 teu: ex Emirates Karan-08, Cape Spencer-07, TS Hongkong-07, Cape Spencer-03, Fanal Merchant-00, Grafton-99, Cape Spencer-99
9215828	CSAV Papudo *	Lbr	2001	74,373	80,551	304	40	26	ucc	6,479 teu: ex Hyundai Kingdom-11
9215830	CSAV Petorca *	Lbr	2001	74,373	80,596	304	40	26	ucc	6,479 teu: ex Hyundai Republic-11
9215842	CSAV Pirque *	Lbr	2001	74,373	80,494	304	40	26	ucc	6,479 teu: ex Hyundai National-11
9215854	CSAV Porvenir *	Lbr	2001	74,373	80,550	304	40	26	ucc	6,479 teu: ex Hyundai Dominion-11
9215866	CSAV Puyehue *	Lbr	2001	74,373	80,551	304	40	26	ucc	6,479 teu: ex Hyundai Patriot-11
9106479	Cape Sable *	Lbr	1996	10,917	13,700	151	24	18	ucc	1,158 teu: ex Deja Bhum-09, Cape Sable-05
9546904	DS Charme *	Lbr	2011	92,050	176,000	292	45	14	bbu	
9268904	DS Progress	Lbr	2003	39,272	70,427	229	32	15	tcr	ex Sunlight Venture-12
9252187	DS Promoter	Lbr	2002	39,272	70,392	229	32	15	tcr	ex Venture-12, Sanko Venture-12, Stena Venture-07, l/a Sanko Venture
9522178	DS Vision *	Lbr	2011	157,039	297,345	330	60		tcr	
9522180	DS Venture *	Lbr	2011	157,039	297,345	330	60		tcr	
9241683	Elisewin *	Lbr	2002	78,845	149,991	274	48		tcr	ex Eliomar-07
9169691	Front Chief †	Bhs	1999	157,863	311,224	334	58	15	tcr	
9174397	DS Commander †	Bhs	1999	157,863	311,168	334	58	15	tcr	ex Front Commander-12
9176993	Front Commodore †	Lbr	2000	159,397	298,620	333	60	15	tcr	ex Stena Commodore-01
9179646	Front Crown †	Bhs	1999	157,863	311,176	334	58	15	tcr	ex Front President-99
9249312	Front Melody †	Lbr	2001	79,525	150,500	272	46	14	tcr	
9249324	Front Symphony †	Lbr	2001	79,525	149,995	272	46	14	tcr	
9172868	Front Tina †	Lbr	2000	159,463	298,824	333	60	16	tcr	
9169689	Front Warrior	Bhs	1998	79,669	153,181	269	46	14	tcr	
9171826	Kiowa Spirit ††	Bhs	1999	62,619	113,334	253	44	14	tcr	ex Bona Valiant-99
9171838	Koa Spirit ††	Bhs	1999	62,619	113,334	253	44	14	tcr	ex Bona Verity-99
9233789	Leo Glory **	Pan	2003	160,100	309,233	333	58	15	tcr	ex Crude Sun-06, Violando-05
9203289	Mercury Glory **	Pan	2001	157,831	298,990	332	58	15	tcr	
9165346	Neptune Glory **	Pan	1998	156,716	299,127	332	58	15	tcr	
9203277	Pluto Glory **	Pan	2001	157,831	298,911	332	58	15	tcr	
9165932	Saturn Glory **	Pan	1998	156,397	298,982	332	58	15	tcr	
9293741	Sea Fortune 1	Sgp	2003	159,730	299,097	333	60	15	tcr	ex Sea Fortune-06
9205079	Titan Glory **	Pan	2000	159,187	308,491	333	58	14	tcr	ex Millenium Maersk-04
9289477	Younara Glory **	Pan	2004	161,235	320,051	333	60	14	tcr	

newbuildings:
*owned by subsidiary DS-Rendite-Fonds GmbH & Co (formed 2003) or managed by * DS Schiffahrt GmbH & Co KG (formed 2001) with vessels operated by previous owners/operators including ** Gulf Marine Management (Deutschland) GmbH, † Front Line †† Teekay Shipping (USA) Inc.*
also see managed vessels under Reederei F Laeisz GmbH and Oskar Wehr KG (GmbH & Co)

Polish Steamship Co. (Polska Żegluga Morska p.p.)   Poland

Funnel: *Black with red band between two narrow white or yellow bands, interrupted by shield with white letters 'PZM' and trident.*
Hull: *Black, blue or yellow (tch), some with white 'POLSTEAM', red boot-topping.* **History:** *State owned company, founded 1951.*
Web: *www.polsteam.com.pl*

IMO#	name	flag	year	grt	dwt	loa	bm	kts	type	former names
8813946	Armia Krajowa	Vut	1991	41,266	73,505	229	32	14	bbu	
8502535	Armia Ludowa *	Lbr	1987	21,458	33,640	195	25	15	bbu	
9187497	Aurora	Mhl	2000	16,454	24,558	170	28	14	tch	
8502573	Bataliony Chlopskie	Lbr	1988	21,460	33,618	195	25	14	bbu	
9065912	Daria	Cyp	1995	25,190	41,260	186	30	14	bbu	ex Taria-95
9133771	Delia	Cyp	1997	25,206	41,185	186	30	14	bbu	
9133769	Diana	Cyp	1997	25,206	41,425	186	30	14	bbu	
9133783	Dorine	Cyp	1998	25,065	41,488	186	30	14	bbu	
9393450	Drawsko	Bhs	2010	20,603	29,978	190	24	14	bbu	
9594248	Gdynia	Bhs	2012	24,145	37,933	190	29	14	bbu	
9452593	Giewont	Bhs	2010	42,868	79,649	229	32	14	bbu	
9521875	Ina	Lbr	2012	13,579	16,622	150	24	14	bbu	
9180396	Irma	Cyp	2000	21,387	34,948	200	24	15	bbu	
9180384	Iryda	Cyp	1999	21,387	34,939	200	24	14	bbu	
9180358	Isa	Cyp	1999	21,387	34,939	200	24	14	bbu	
9180372	Isadora	Cyp	1999	21,387	34,948	200	24	14	bbu	
9180360	Isolda	Cyp	1999	21,959	34,949	200	24	14	bbu	
9465608	Jawor	Bhs	2010	43,506	79,692	229	32	14	bbu	
9422378	Juno	Bhs	2011	20,603	29,707	190	24	14	bbu	
8908856	Kaliope	Bhs	1995	11,542	16,888	149	23	14	tch	ex Fjordnes-97 (conv bbu-97)
9582506	Karpaty	Lbr	2013	43,025	82,138	229	32	14	bbu	
9436847	Kaszuby	Bhs	2008	24,109	37,965	190	28	14	bbu	
9285029	Kujawy	Bhs	2005	24,109	37,965	190	29	14	bbu	
9423798	Kociewie	Bhs	2009	24,109	38,056	190	29	14	bbu	
9594236	Koszalin	Bhs	2012	23,145	37,884	190	29	14	bbu	
9423786	Kurpie	Bhs	2009	24,109	38,056	190	29	14	bbu	
8919611	Legiony Polskie	Vut	1991	41,237	73,505	229	32	14	bbu	

IMO#	name	flag	year	grt	dwt	loa	bm	kts	type	former names
9441984	Lubie	Bhs	2011	20,603	29,694	190	24	14	bbu	
8219322	Maciej Rataj	Mlt	1985	21,531	33,750	199	25	15	bbu	
9496264	Mamry	Bhs	2012	20,603	30,000	190	24	14	bbu	
9386914	Mazowsze	Bhs	2009	24,109	37,695	190	29	14	bbu	
9285122	Mazury	Bhs	2005	24,109	38,056	190	29	14	bbu	
9393448	Miedwie	Bhs	2010	20,603	29,984	190	24	14	bbu	
9154294	Mitrope	Mlt	1999	11,530	15,718	149	23	13	tch	
9521813	Narew	Bhs	2012	13,579	16,573	150	24	14	bbu	
9154268	Nogat	Cyp	1999	11,848	17,064	149	23	13	bbu	
8502547	Oksywie	Lbr	1987	21,460	33,580	195	25	14	bbu	ex Wladyslaw Gomulka-91
9521837	Olza	Lbr	2012	13,579	16,900	150	24	14	bbu	
9386926	Orawa	Bhs	2009	24,109	38,065	190	29	14	bbu	
9154270	Orla	Mlt	1999	11,848	17,064	149	23	14	bbu	
8813960	Orleta Lwowskie	Vut	1991	41,238	73,505	229	32	14	bbu	
9452610	Ornak	Bhs	2011	43,506	79,677	229	32	14	bbu	
9154282	Pilica	Mlt	1999	11,540	17,064	149	23	14	bbu	
9285134	Podhale	Bhs	2005	24,109	38,056	190	29	14	bbu	
9346811	Podlasie	Bhs	2008	24,109	38,071	190	29	14	bbu	
9488097	Polesie	Bhs	2010	24,055	38,056	190	29	14	bbu	
9011923	Polska Walczaca	Vut	1992	41,220	73,505	229	32	13	bbu	
9346823	Pomorze	Bhs	2008	24,109	38,056	190	29	14	bbu	
9521849	Prosna	Lbr	2012	13,579	16,642	150	24	14	bbu	
9594250	Puck	Bhs	2012	24,245	37,894	190	29	14	bbu	
9521825	Raba	Lbr	2012	13,579	16,900	150	24	14	bbu	
9521758	Regalica	Lbr	2011	13,579	16,006	150	24	14	bbu	
9393462	Resko	Bhs	2010	20,603	29,984	190	24	14	bbu	
8219334	Rodlo	Mlt	1985	21,531	33,742	199	25	15	bbu	
9346835	Roztocze	Bhs	2008	24,109	37,965	191	29	14	bbu	
9452622	Rysy	Bhs	2011	43,506	79,602	229	32	14	bbu	
9521851	San	Lbr	2012	13,579	16,620	150	24	14	bbu	
9521863	Skawa	Lbr	2012	13,579	16,600	150	24	14	bbu	
8813934	Solidarnosc	Vut	1991	41,252	73,470	229	32	14	bbu	
9496252	Solina	Bhs	2012	20,603	29,691	190	24	14	bbu	
8502559	Stanislaw Kulczynski	Mlt	1988	21,456	33,627	195	25	14	bbu	
9582518	Sudety	Lbr	2013	43,025	82,000	229	32	14	bbu	
8813958	Szare Szeregi	Vut	1991	41,191	73,505	229	32	14	bbu	
9594224	Szczecin	Bhs	2012	24,145	37,930	190	28	14	bbu	
9488102	Wadowice II	Bhs	2010	24,055	38,061	190	28	14	bbu	
9285146	Warmia	Bhs	2005	24,109	38,056	190	29	14	bbu	
9393474	Wicko	Bhs	2010	20,603	29,903	190	24	14	bbu	
8901585	Wisla	Vut	1992	9,815	13,770	143	21	13	bbu	ex Wislanes-99
8418758	Ziemia Cieszynska	Lbr	1992	17,464	26,264	180	23	14	bbu	ex Lake Carling-03, Ziemia Cieszynska-93
8418734	Ziemia Gornoslaska	Lbr	1990	17,427	26,209	180	23	14	bbu	ex Lake Charles-03, Ziemia Gornoslaska-91
8418746	Ziemia Lodzka	Lbr	1992	17,458	26,264	180	23	14	bbu	ex Lake Champlain-03, Ziemia Lodzka-92

newbuildings:.
* owned by StarLib Ltd. (formed 1993)

Polish Steamship Co. : JAWOR : *J. Kakebeeke*

PowerGen plc   U.K.

Funnel: *Red with white 'e-on', black top.* **Hull:** *Black with red boot-topping.* **History:** *Formed 1990.* **Web:** *www.eon-uk.com*

| 8402864 | Lord Hinton | Gbr | 1986 | 14,201 | 22,447 | 155 | 25 | 12 | bbu | |

owned by subsidiary E.On UK plc (formed 2004) and managed by Meridian Marine Management Ltd.

KG Projex-Schiffahrts GmbH & Co.   Germany

Funnel: *White lower half and dark blue upper part with white 'PX' between narrow pale blue wavy bands or charterers colours.*
Hull: *Blue with pale blue wavy bands on bows, red boot-topping.* **History:** *Formed 1981.* **Web:** *www.kg-projex.de*

9228526	Bella *	Atg	2001	30,024	35,980	208	32	22	ucc	2,672 teu: ex CSCL Jakarta-09, I/a Bella
9228514	Bonny *	Atg	2001	30,024	36,019	208	32	22	ucc	2,672 teu: ex CSCL Barcelona-09, I/a Bonny
9228540	Bosun *	Atg	2001	30,024	35,977	208	32	22	ucc	2,672 teu: ex CSCL Fos-10, I/a Bosun
9222091	Bravo *	Atg	2001	30,026	36,189	208	32	22	ucc	2,672 teu: ex CSCL Genoa-09, I/a Bravo
9228538	Chief *	Atg	2001	30,024	36,003	208	32	22	ucc	2,672 teu: ex CSCL Kelang-08, I/a Chief
9124378	Glory *	Atg	1996	23,897	30,447	188	30	20	ucc	2,080 teu: ex Clan Amazonas-09, Glory-05, Cap Vincent-01, Glory-00, Crowley Americas-99, Glory-99, Pacifico-98
9350317	Hermes	Atg	2006	27,061	34,365	212	30	22	ucc	2.496 teu
9134608	Master *	Gbr	1997	23,897	30,416	188	30	21	ucc	2,080 teu: ex Maruba Imperator-09, Master I-08, P&O Nedlloyd Brunel-06, Master I-03, Master-02, CMA CGM Paris-02, Lykes Kestrel-01, MOL Europe-00, Maersk Miami-99, I/a Master
9236042	Mentor *	Atg	2002	30,024	35,971	208	32	22	ucc	2,672 teu: ex CSCL Napoli-11, I/a Mentor
9415296	Penelope	Atg	2008	32,269	38,636	211	32	22	ucc	2,672 teu: ex CSAV Totoral-12, I/a Penelope
9124380	Primus *	Atg	1997	23,897	30,502	188	30	20	ucc	2,080 teu: ex Hanjin Palermo-11, Genoa Senator-09, Safmarine Letaba-05, Primus-02, CSAV Guayas-99, Primus-99, Sea Parana-99, Primus-97
9364203	Ulysses	Atg	2006	27,061	34,393	212	30	22	ucc	2,496 teu: ex Maruba Pampero-10, Ulysses-06

* managed for Hansa Treuhand Schiffsbeteiligungs GmbH & Co KG

Pronav Ship Management GmbH & Co. KG   Germany

Funnel: *Operators colours.* **Hull:** *Maroon or black.* **History:** *Founded Hamburg 1995.* **Web:** *www.pronav.com*

9337987	Al Ghariya [df]	Bhs	2008	137,535	121,730	315	50	19	lng	210,110 m³
9337951	Al Ruwais [df]	Bhs	2007	137,535	121,823	315	50	19	lng	210,110 m³
9337963	Al Safliya [df]	Bhs	2007	137,535	121,963	315	50	19	lng	210,110 m³
9337975	Duhail [df]	Bhs	2008	137,535	121,639	315	50	19	lng	210,110 m³
7390143	LNG Gemini [st]	Mhl	1978	95,084	72,472	285	44	20	lng	126,340 m³
7390155	LNG Leo [st]	Mhl	1978	95,084	72,555	285	44	20	lng	126,449 m³
7390179	LNG Virgo [st]	Mhl	1979	95,084	72,629	285	44	20	lng	126,451 m³
9321732	Milaha Qatar [st]	Mlt	2006	96,508	77,803	279	43	20	lng	145,602 m³ ex Maersk Qatar-12
9255854	Milaha Ras Laffan [st]	Mlt	2004	93,226	73,705	279	43	20	lng	138,273 m³ ex Maersk Ras Laffan -12

Ray Car Carriers   Israel

Funnel: *Green with large yellow 'R', narrow black top or charterers colours.* **Hull:** *Blue with dark green upperworks, red boot-topping.*
History: *Founded 1992.* **Web:** *www.raycarcarriers.com or www.stamco.gr*

9446881	Adria Ace	Bhs	2009	41,009	12,300	176	31	20	mve	4,900 ceu
9277826	Amber Arrow	Bhs	2004	57,718	21,120	200	32	20	mve	6,700 ceu
9318486	Coral Leader	Bhs	2006	40,986	12,164	176	31	19	mve	4,900 ceu
9391581	CSCC Asia	Bhs	2009	57,692	21,037	200	32	20	mve	6,700 ceu
9391593	CSCC Europe	Bhs	2009	57,692	21,300	200	32	20	mve	6,700 ceu
9361823	CSCC Shanghai	Bhs	2008	41,009	12,300	176	31	19	mve	4,900 ceu
9361835	CSCC Tianjin ‡	Iom	2008	41,009	12,300	176	31	19	mve	4,900 ceu
9210440	Crystal Ray *	Bhs	2000	57,772	21,400	200	32	20	mve	6,700 ceu
9316309	Danube Highway	Bhs	2006	23,498	7,788	148	25	18	mve	2,130 ceu
9441506	Dignity Ace	Bhs	2010	58,767	20,589	200	32	19	mve	6,700 ceu
9316282	Elbe Highway	Bhs	2005	23,498	7,750	148	25	18	mve	2,130 ceu
9361811	Emerald Leader	Bhs	2008	40,986	12,300	176	31	19	mve	4,900 ceu
9237307	Galaxy Leader	Bhs	2002	48,710	17,127	189	32	20	mve	5,100 ceu
9357327	Garnet Leader	Bhs	2008	57,692	21,020	200	32	20	mve	6,700 ceu
9391567	Gentle Leader	Bhs	2008	57,692	21,122	200	32	20	mve	6,700 ceu
9237319	Global Leader	Bhs	2002	48,710	17,125	199	32	20	mve	5,100 ceu
9357298	Glorious Leader	Bhs	2007	57,692	20,999	200	32	20	mve	6,700 ceu
9441594	Glovis Caravel ‡	Bhs	2012	58,767	20,434	200	32	20	mve	6,700 ceu
9441582	Glovis Clipper ‡	Bhs	2012	58,767	20,434	200	32	20	mve	6,700 ceu

IMO#	name	flag	year	grt	dwt	loa	bm	kts	type	former names
9453107	Glovis Passion ‡	Bhs	2011	36,834	11,196	168	28	20	mve	4,000 ceu
9455715	Glovis Prestige ‡	Bhs	2011	36,834	11,196	168	28	20	mve	4,000 ceu
9357315	Goliath Leader	Bhs	2008	57,692	20,958	200	32	20	mve	6,700 ceu
9357303	Graceful Leader	Bhs	2007	57,692	20,986	200	32	20	mve	6,700 ceu
9388716	Guardian Leader	Bhs	2008	57,692	21,182	200	32	20	mve	6,700 ceu
9441568	Harmony Leader	Bhs	2011	58,767	20,434	200	32	19	mve	6,700 ceu
9441556	Heritage Leader	Bhs	2011	58,767	20,434	200	32	19	mve	6,700 ceu
9441570	Heroic Leader	Bhs	2011	58,767	20,434	200	32	19	mve	6,700 ceu
9277814	Höegh Africa **	Bhs	2004	57,718	21,214	200	32	20	mve	6,700 ceu: ex Hual Africa-09
9277802	Höegh America **	Bhs	2003	57,718	21,182	200	32	20	mve	6,700 ceu: ex Hual America-08
9441520	Horizon Leader	Bhs	2010	58,767	20,434	200	32	19	mve	6,700 ceu
9318503	Istra Ace	Bhs	2007	41,000	12,200	176	31	19	mve	4,900 ceu
9277838	Ivory Arrow	Bhs	2004	57,718	21,300	200	32	20	mve	6,700 ceu
9267912	Jasper Arrow	Bhs	2005	57,692	21,040	200	32	20	mve	6,700 ceu
9361809	Lapis Arrow	Bhs	2006	40,500	12,105	176	31	19	mve	4,900 ceu
9285615	Morning Calm *	Bhs	2004	57,962	21,005	200	32	20	mve	6,700 ceu: l/a Opal Ray
9285627	Morning Champion *	Bhs	2005	57,692	21,106	200	32	20	mve	6,700 ceu
9441609	Morning Classic *	Bhs	2013	58,767	21,000	200	32	19	mve	6,700 ceu
9285639	Morning Courier *	Bhs	2005	57,692	21,053	200	32	20	mve	6,700 ceu
9285641	Morning Crown *	Bhs	2005	57,692	21,052	200	32	20	mve	6,700 ceu
9386225	Nordic Ace	Bhs	2007	23,498	7,378	148	25	18	mve	2,130 ceu
9267924	Onyx Arrow	Bhs	2005	57,692	21,087	200	32	20	mve	6,700 ceu
9210438	Platinium Ray *	Bhs	2000	57,772	21,000	200	32	20	mve	6,700 ceu

Ray Car Carriers : DANUBE HIGHWAY : *ARO*

Ray Car Carriers : HORIZON LEADER : *ARO*

IMO#	name	flag	year	grt	dwt	loa	bm	kts	type	former names
9316311	Seine Highway	Bhs	2007	23,498	8,100	148	25	18	mve	2,130 ceu
9391579	Serenity Ace	Bhs	2008	57,692	21,300	200	32	20	mve	6,700 ceu
9311836	Taipan *	Bhs	2006	57,692	21,021	200	32	20	mve	6,700 ceu: I/a Morning Countess
9311854	Talia **	Bhs	2006	57,700	21,021	200	32	20	mve	6,700 ceu
9327748	Tarifa *	Bhs	2007	57,692	21,120	200	32	20	mve	6,700 ceu: I/a Morning Charisma
9316294	Thames Highway	Bhs	2007	23,498	7,750	148	25	18	mve	2,130 ceu
9395628	Victory Leader	Bhs	2010	49,675	13,363	189	32	19	mve	5,000 ceu
9395630	Violet Ace	Bhs	2011	49,708	13,363	189	32	19	mve	5,000 ceu

newbuilding:
managed by Stamco Ship Management Co. Ltd, Greece (formed 1993).
*Vessels chartered-out to * Eukor Car Carriers Inc (see under Wallenius-Wilhelmsen), ** Wallenius-Wilhelmsen, *** Höegh, ‡ Hyundai Glovis, Kawasaki, NYK, and other operators.*

Carsten Rehder Schiffsmakler und Reederei GmbH   Germany
Funnel: *Black with white 'CR' on black diamond between narrow red bands on braod white band or charterers colours.* **Hull:** *Black or green with red boot-topping.* **History:** *Founded 1903 as Carsten Rehder to 1982.* **Web:** *www.carstenrehder.de*

IMO#	name	flag	year	grt	dwt	loa	bm	kts	type	former names
9363144	Baltic Strait	Lbr	2008	18,102	23,840	182	25	20	ucc	1,698 teu
9363156	Barents Strait	Lbr	2008	18,102	23,844	183	25	20	ucc	1,698 teu
9139634	Clou Ocean	Mhl	1998	10,384	12,184	149	23	19	ucc	1,138 teu: ex Besire Kalkavan-06
9236597	Dover Strait	Mhl	2002	14,241	18,402	159	24	18	ucc	1,118 teu: ex Cape Serrat-04, MOL Sahara-02, Cape Serrat-02
9488580	Eagle Strait	Lbr	2010	33,033	56,800	190	32	14	bbu	
9488592	Emerald Strait	Lbr	2010	33,033	56,830	190	32	14	bbu	
9488578	Endeavour Strait	Lbr	2010	33,033	56,806	190	32	14	bbu	
9488566	Essex Strait	Lbr	2010	33,033	56,872	190	32	14	bbu	
9362736	Melbourne Strait	Atg	2008	21,018	25,849	180	28	20	ucc	1,794 teu
9362724	Macao Strait	Lbr	2008	21,028	25,826	180	28	20	ucc	1,794 teu: ex NileDutch Qingdao-11, Macao Strait-08
9351218	Ocean Emerald	Lbr	2008	18,123	22,314	175	28	20	ucc	1,713 teu: I/a Tasman Strait
9357523	Ocean Mermaid	Lbr	2008	18,123	22,314	175	28	20	ucc	1,713 teu: I/a Torres Strait
9670834	Osaka Strait	Lbr	2013	43,015	51,100	228	37	-	ucc	3,820 teu
9526564	Pacific Trust	Lbr	2010	22,636	34,000	181	30	14	bbu	I/a Labrador Strait
9454242	Sonderborg Strait	Atg	2012	12,297	14,222	158	23	19	ucc	1,085 teu
9454230	Svendborg Strait	Atg	2011	12,514	14,220	158	23	19	ucc	1,085 teu
9670822	Vil Dardanelles	Lbr	2013	43,015	51,100	228	37	-	ucc	3,820 teu
9516777	Wellington Strait	Lbr	2012	18,358	23,368	175	27	20	ucc	1,696 teu
9436068	William Strait	Lbr	2009	18,485	23,707	177	27	20	ucc	1,732 teu: ex Viking Hawk-09
9516789	Winchester Strait	Lbr	2012	18,358	23,295	175	27	20	ucc	1,696 teu

also operates a number of container feeder vessels
newbuildings:

Schiffahrtskontor Rendsburg GmbH   Germany
Funnel: *Blue or charterers colours.* **Hull:** *Black or green with red boot-topping.* **History:** *Founded 1971 as Schiffahrtskontor Rendsburg, Peterson, Schluter & Werner.* **Web:** *www.westerships.com*

IMO#	name	flag	year	grt	dwt	loa	bm	kts	type	former names
9064190	Charlotta	Lbr	1993	14,961	20,140	167	25	17	ucc	1,388 teu: ex Westermuhlen-10, Cala Pinar del Rio-04, Norasia Chicago-01, CSAV New York-00, Westermuhlen-00, Nedlloyd Singapore-96, Westermuhlen-93
9222106	NileDutch Springbok	Lbr	2001	30,047	35,653	208	32	22	ucc	2,764 teu: ex Westermoor-12
9297527	Westerbrook	Lbr	2005	54,592	64,660	294	32	23	ucc	5,042 teu: ex Maersk Dartmouth-10
9137674	Westerburg	Lbr	1997	23,896	30,291	188	30	21	ucc	2,064 teu: ex CMA CGM Accra-07, Westerburg-07, Tuscany Bridge-07, Westerburg-03, Lykes Achiever-01, Westerburg-98, Maersk La Plata-98, Westerburg-97
9316361	Westerdiek	Lbr	2007	32,060	39,000	211	32	21	ucc	2,732 teu: ex MSC Mendosa-09, Westerdiek-07
9127540	Westerems	Lbr	1997	23,896	30,600	188	30	21	ucc	2,064 teu: ex Maersk Novazzano-10, P&O Nedlloyd Horizon-05, Westerems-05, ANL Addax-03, Westerems-02, Lykes Voyager-01, Westerems-98, Maersk Cordoba-98, Westerems-97
9137698	Westerhamm	Deu	1998	23,986	30,259	188	30	21	ucc	2,064 teu: ex Cala Paradiso-08, DAL Karoo-04, Westerhamm-02, Actor-01, Westerhamm-99
9240328	Westerland	Cyp	2002	30,047	35,768	208	32	22	ucc	2,764 teu: ex CSAV Mexico-11, Westerland-05, Alianca Hamburgo-03
9316347	Westertal	Lbr	2006	32,060	38,700	211	32	21	ucc	2,732 teu: ex CMA CGM Melbourne-08, Westertal-06

managed by Hans Peterson & Söhne GmbH & Co KG, Germany (formed 1984).

IMO#	name	flag	year	grt	dwt	loa	bm	kts	type	former names

Rickmers Reederei GmbH & Cie. KG   Germany

Funnel: *Black with houseflag (white 'R' on red over green) on broad white band, or charterers colours.* **Hull:** *Green or black with white 'RICKMERS', red boot-topping or charterer's colours.* **History:** *Founded 1889 as Rickmers Reismuhlen Rhederei & Schiffbau AG, became Reederei Bertram Rickmers GmbH to 1992. Rickmers Linie sold to Hapag Lloyd in 1988 and re-acquired 2000. Acquired CCNI (Deutschland) GmbH (formed 1999) from Compania Chilena de Navegacion Interoceanica in 2004.* **Web:** *www.rickmers.com or www.rickmers-linie.de*

IMO#	name	flag	year	grt	dwt	loa	bm	kts	type	former names
9152753	Aenne Rickmers	Lbr	1998	26,131	30,781	196	30	19	ucc	2,226 teu: ex CP Rome-06, Contship Rome-05, I/a Aenne Rickmers
9152739	Alexandra Rickmers	Lbr	1997	26,131	30,781	195	30	20	ucc	2,226 teu: ex CP London-06, Contship London-05, Alexandra Rickmers-97
9152765	Alice Rickmers †	Lbr	1998	26,131	30,726	196	30	20	ucc	2,226 teu: ex Kota Maju-12, Alice Rickmers-10, Direct Kea-04, CMA CGM Cezanne-01, CGM Cezanne-99, I/a Alice Rickmers
9131254	Anakena ‡	Deu	1996	28,148	44,575	185	32	15	bcb	1,830 teu: ex CCNI Anakena-08, CSAV Valencia-05, CCNI Anakena-04, I/a Valdemosa
9152789	Andre Rickmers	Deu	1998	26,131	30,725	196	30	19	ucc	2,226 teu: ex Marfret Provence-08, CGM Matisse-98, Andre Rickmers-98
9152777	Andreas	Lbr	1998	26,131	30,723	196	30	20	ucc	2,226 teu: ex CGM Renoir-01, I/a Andreas Rickmers
9131204	Anna Rickmers ‡	Lbr	1997	28,148	44,572	185	32	15	bcb	1,830 teu: ex CCNI Chagres-07, Anna Rickmers-98
9334167	ANL Wangaratta	Gbr	2008	39,906	50,596	260	32	24	ucc	4,250 teu: I/d Sui An Rickmers
9324863	ANL Warrain **	Sgp	2007	39,906	50,629	260	32	24	ucc	4,250 teu: ex CMA CGM Purple-08
9324837	ANL Warringa *	Mhl	2007	39,906	50,629	260	32	24	ucc	4,250 teu: ex Vicki Rickmers-07
9324849	ANL Windarra *	Mhl	2007	39,906	50,769	260	32	24	ucc	4,250 teu: ex Maja Rickmers-07
9334155	ANL Wyong **	Gbr	2008	39,906	52,000	261	32	24	ucc	4,250 teu: I/d Olympia Rickmers
9270828	Arut Rickmers §	Deu	2004	21,932	24,219	196	28	22	ucc	1,858 teu: ex Aruni Rickmers-13, Satha Bhum-07, Moni Rickmers-04
9212046	Asta Rickmers §	Mhl	2001	14,278	15,315	159	26	21	ucc	1,216 teu: ex Hub Racer-01, I/d Asta Rickmers
9131266	Atalanta ‡	Lbr	1999	28,148	44,593	185	32	15	bcb	1,830 teu: ex CCNI Arauco-04
9131230	Austin Angol ‡	Mhl	1998	28,148	46,376	185	32	15	bcb	1,830 teu: ex CCNI Angol-08, I/a Valdivia
9105982	Camilla Rickmers	Mhl	1996	16,801	23,045	184	25	19	ucc	1,730 teu: ex MOL Unifier-11, NileDutch President-08, Camilla Rickmers-07, CSAV Livorno-00, Camilla Rickmers-00, CCNI Anakena-98, I/a Camilla Rickmers
9212022	Carla Rickmers §‡	Mhl	2000	14,278	15,299	159	26	21	ucc	1,216 teu: ex OOCL Achievement-09, Carla Rickmers-04
9448140	Cary Rickmers +	Mhl	2010	47,090	12,300	183	32	20	mve	4,900 ceu
9236523	Cathrine Rickmers §	Lbr	2002	51,364	58,341	286	32	25	ucc	4,444 teu: ex Norasia Valparaiso-09, Cathrine Rickmers-02

Schiffahrtskontor Rendsburg : WESTERLAND : *Chris Brooks*

IMO#	name	flag	year	grt	dwt	loa	bm	kts	type	former names
9287900	Charlotte C. Rickmers §	Lbr	2004	54,214	68,187	294	32	24	ucc	5,060 teu: ex Maersk Douala-10
9105968	Christa Rickmers	Atg	1996	16,800	23,064	184	25	19	ucc	1,730 teu: ex Pacific Independence-11, Christa Rickmers-10, CSAV Manzanillo-09, Pacific Challenger-01, Christa Rickmers-99, CCNI Arauco-98, Christa Rickmers-96
9221798	Clipper Emperor §	Mhl	2000	38,878	74,381	225	32	14	bbu	ex Pacemperor-03
9231030	Clipper Monarch §‡	Mhl	2000	38,878	74,381	225	32	14	bbu	ex Pacmonarch-04
9300166	CMA CGM Anapurna	Mhl	2006	21,971	24,069	196	28	23	ucc	1,858 teu: I/a Jacob Rickmers
9324851	CMA CGM Azure ††	Mhl	2007	39,906	50,629	260	32	24	ucc	3,853 teu
9160396	CMA CGM Buenos Aires	Deu	1998	26,131	30,781	196	30	19	ucc	2,226 teu: ex Patricia Rickmers-06, Contship Auckland-05, I/a Patricia Rickmers
9324875	CMA CGM Jade *	Mhl	2007	39,906	50,769	267	32	24	ucc	3,853 teu: I/a Sabine Rickmers
9334143	CMA CGM Onyx *	Sgp	2007	39,906	50,770	267	32	24	ucc	3,853 teu: I/a Erwin Rickmers
9126871	CMA CGM Samba	Mhl	1997	10,743	14,191	163	23	17	ucc	1,162 teu: ex Mabel Rickmers-05, Kribi-98, I/a Mabel Rickmers
9152911	CMA CGM St. Martin §	Mhl	1998	10,752	14,040	163	22	16	ucc	1,162 teu: ex CGM Basse-Terre-01, Lilly Rickmers-98
9105970	CSAV Maresias	Mhl	1996	16,801	23,028	185	25	19	ucc	1,730 teu: ex Delmas Cartier-04, Etha Rickmers-02, CSAV Tokyo-02, Zim Vancouver-01, Etha Rickmers-99, CCNI Antarctico-99, Panamerican-97, CCNI Antartico-96, Etha Rickmers-96
9105994	Deike Rickmers	Mhl	1996	16,801	23,027	184	25	19	ucc	1,728 teu: ex Libra Rio Grande-05, Deike Rickmers-04, P&O Nedlloyd Kowie-03, Deike Rickmers-01, CSAV Genova-00, Deike Rickmers-00, Scorpio Challenger-99, Deike Rickmers-97, Panatlantic-97, I/a Deike Rickmers
9144160	Dorothea Rickmers †	Lbr	1998	16,801	23,027	184	25	19	ucc	1,730 teu: ex Delmas Joliba-11, Dorothea Rickmers-07, WAL Ulanga-03, Dorothea Rickmers-01
9212034	Ernst Rickmers §‡	Mhl	2002	14,278	15,313	159	26	21	ucc	1,216 teu: ex Turkon America-03, Ernst Rickmers-02
9128027	Felicitas Rickmers ‡	Mhl	1997	24,053	28,366	205	27	20	ucc	2,109 teu: ex Maruba Tango-09, Felicitas Rickmers-05, Sea Jaguar-02, Conti Jacksonville-97
9149885	Fiona Rickmers §	Lbr	1998	16,801	23,028	185	25	19	ucc	1,730 teu: ex CCNI Elbe-11, CMA CGM Licorne-10, Fiona Rickmers-04, Libra Barcelona-03, Fiona Rickmers-02, La Hispaniola-02, Zim Soa Paulo I-01, Paranagua-99, I/a Fiona Rickmers
9431692	Hanjin Duesseldorf	Mhl	2009	40,542	50,591	261	32	24	ucc	4,250 teu: I/a Tanja Rickmers
9431680	Hanjin Milano	Mhl	2009	40,542	50,506	261	32	24	ucc	4,250 teu
9431707	Hanjin Montevideo	Mhl	2010	40,542	50,497	261	32	24	ucc	4,250 teu
9404194	Hanjin Newport	Mhl	2009	40,542	50,574	261	32	24	ucc	4,250 teu: I/a India Rickmers
9144158	Helene Rickmers †	Mhl	1998	16,801	23,106	184	25	19	ucc	1,730 teu: ex Lykes Crusader-02, Helene Rickmers-01, CCNI Arica-01, Helene Rickmers-98
9469912	Hyundai Antwerp	Mhl	2011	23,265	30,175	193	28	19	ghl	cr: 2(320),1(100): I/a Rickmers Busan
9469900	Hyundai Dubai	Mhl	2011	23,265	30,104	193	28	19	ghl	cr: 2(320),1(100): I/a Rickmers Inchon
9469883	Hyundai Masan	Mhl	2010	23,265	30,135	193	28	19	ghl	cr: 2(320),1(100): I/a Rickmers Masan
9469895	Hyundai Ulsan	Mhl	2011	23,265	30,162	193	28	19	ghl	cr: 2(320),1(100): I/a Rickmers Pohang
9308003	Ital Fastosa **	Mhl	2006	36,483	42,822	239	32	23	ucc	3,450 teu
9308015	Ital Festosa **	Sgp	2006	36,483	42,822	239	32	23	ucc	3,450 teu
9308027	Ital Fiducia	Mhl	2007	36,483	42,822	239	32	23	ucc	3,450 teu: I/a Moni Rickmers
9270804	Jacky Rickmers §	Mhl	2004	21,932	24,235	196	28	22	ucc	1,858 teu: ex Rithi Bhum-07, I/a Jacky Rickmers
9287895	Jennifer Rickmers §	Lbr	2004	54,214	68,187	294	32	24	ucc	5,060 teu: ex Maersk Durban-10, I/dn Jennifer Rickmers
9216365	Jock Rickmers §‡	Mhl	2001	14,278	15,273	159	26	21	ucc	1,216 teu: ex Vento di Scirroco-12, Jock Rickmers-11, OOCL Advance-09, Jock Rickmers-04, APL Magnolia-01, I/a Jock Rickmers
9128099	Johan Rickmers §‡	Mhl	1997	24,053	28,352	205	27	20	ucc	2,045 teu: ex Delmas Baudin-09, CSAV Itajai-04, Johan Rickmers-03, APL Chile-02, Sea Cougar-99, I/a Conti Oakland
9300154	John Rickmers	Mhl	2006	21,971	24,084	196	28	23	ucc	1,850 teu: ex CMA CGM Everest-11, I/a John Rickmers

IMO#	name	flag	year	grt	dwt	loa	bm	kts	type	former names
9287912	Kaethe C. Rickmers **	Lbr	2004	54,214	68,282	294	32	24	ucc	5,060 teu: Maersk Djibouti-10,l/a Kaethe C.Rickmers
9064774	Lady Elizabeth	Lbr	1993	14,953	20,140	167	25	18	ucc	1,384 teu: ex CMA CGM Tunis-09, Estetrader-08, CMA CGM Venezuela-08, Estetrader-07, City of Oxford-03, Kent Courier-01, Seaboard Toronto-00, Keta-00, Wieland-98, Exporter-97, Red Sea Exporter-95, Wieland-94
9152909	Laurita Rickmers §	Mhl	1998	10,752	14,086	163	22	16	ucc	1,162 teu: ex CMA CGM St. Laurent-11, Laurita-02, Melbridge Pearl-99, Laurita Rickmers-98

Rickmers Reederei : FIONA RICKMERS : *Chris Brooks*

Rickmers Reederei : MAERSK EDMONTON : *J. Kakebeeke*

IMO#	name	flag	year	grt	dwt	loa	bm	kts	type	former names
9134550	Madeleine Rickmers	Mhl	1997	16,801	23,062	184	25	19	ucc	1,730 teu: ex Pacific Freedon-11, Madeleine Rickmers-10, CMA CGM Paulista-10, Madeleine Rickmers-05, Sagittarius Challenger-01, Madeleine Rickmers-97
9289972	Maersk Daesan	Lbr	2005	54,214	68,017	294	32	24	ucc	5,060 teu
9289960	Maersk Davao	Lbr	2005	54,214	68,187	294	32	24	ucc	5,060 teu
9456757	Maersk Edinburgh	Mhl	2010	141,716	142,105	366	48	24	ucc	13,092 teu: l/d Pearl Rickmers
9458030	Maersk Edmonton	Mhl	2011	141,716	142,105	366	48	24	ucc	13,092 teu
9456771	Maersk Eindhoven	Mhl	2010	141,716	142,105	366	48	24	ucc	13,092 teu: l/d Aqua Rickmers
9458078	Maersk Elba	Mhl	2011	141,716	142,105	366	48	24	ucc	13,092 teu
9456769	Maersk Emden	Mhl	2010	141,716	142,105	366	48	24	ucc	13,092 teu :l/d Ruby Rickmers
9456783	Maersk Essen	Mhl	2010	141,716	142,105	366	48	24	ucc	13,092 teu: l/d Cocanee Rickmers
9458092	Maersk Essex	Mhl	2011	141,716	142,105	366	48	24	ucc	13,092 teu
9458080	Maersk Evora	Mhl	2011	141,716	142,105	366	48	24	ucc	13,092 teu
9287924	Margrit Rickmers	Lbr	2005	54,214	68,187	294	32	24	ucc	5,060 teu: ex Maersk Dhaka-10, l/a Margrit Rickmers
9145061	Marie §	Lbr	1999	22,817	35,230	171	31	17	gpc	ex Marie Rickmers-10, CCNI Amadeo-07, CCNI Austral-05, CSAV Genova-03, Lykes Challenger-00, l/a Marie Rickmers
9151917	Marine Rickmers	Deu	1998	11,925	14,381	150	23	18	ucc	1,104 teu: ex P&O Nedlloyd Mahe-05, Marine Rickmers-02, Fanal Mariner-01, Marine Rickmers-99
9352391	MOL Dedication **	Mhl	2008	39,906	50,629	260	32	24	ucc	3,853 teu
9352406	MOL Delight *	Mhl	2008	39,906	50,600	260	32	24	ucc	4,853 teu: l/a Pingel Rickmers
9352418	MOL Destiny **	Lbr	2008	39,906	50,638	260	32	24	ucc	3,853 teu: Ebba Rickmers-09
9352420	MOL Devotion **	Mhl	2009	39,906	50,596	260	32	24	ucc	3,853 teu: ex Clan Rickmers-09
9478494	MOL Dominance **	Mhl	2008	39,906	50,629	260	32	24	ucc	3,853 teu: l/a Sui An Rickmers
9236547	MSC Florida	Mhl	2005	51,364	58,287	286	32	25	ucc	4,425 teu: l/a Maya Rickmers
9270830	Nina Rickmers §	Mhl	2004	21,932	24,279	196	28	23	ucc	1,858 teu: ex CMA CGM Rio Grande-08, APL Kobe-07, Nina Rickmers-04
9236444	Ninghai §‡	Mhl	2003	16,801	23,063	185	25	19	ucc	1,730 teu: ex Tasman Campaigner-12, Robert Rickmers-08, E.R. Stettin-03
9134658	Ningpo	Deu	1997	16,801	22,900	184	25	19	ucc	1,730 teu: ex Pacific Resolution-12, Denderah Rickmers-10, Norasia Bavaria-05, CSAV Busan-03, Zim Seattle-01, Pictor Challenger-99, Denderah Rickmers-97
9082805	Rickmer Rickmers	Atg	1995	16,800	22,900	185	25	19	ucc	1,728 teu: ex Norasia Sindh-04, Rickmer Rickmers-03, Columbus Hong Kong-02, Sassandra Challenger-01, Rickmer Rickmers-00, CSAV Rosario-98, Rickmer Rickmers-95
9253143	Rickmers Antwerp †	Mhl	2003	23,119	29,912	193	28	19	ghl	cr: 2(320),1(100) ex Cape Dart-02
9292022	Rickmers Dalian	Lbr	2004	23,119	29,827	193	28	19	ghl	cr: 2(320),1(120),1(100) ex Rickmers Genoa-05
9238818	Rickmers Hamburg §†	Mhl	2002	23,119	29,980	193	28	19	ghl	cr: 2(320),1(100)
9292010	Rickmers Jakarta †	Mhl	2004	23,119	29,750	193	28	19	ghl	cr: 2(320),1(100) : l/d Genoa

Rickmers Reederei : MAERSK EMDEN : *Hans Kraijenbosch*

IMO#	name	flag	year	grt	dwt	loa	bm	kts	type	former names
9253155	Rickmers New Orleans	Mhl	2003	23,119	29,878	193	28	19	ghl	cr: 2(320),1(100)
9244556	Rickmers Seoul	Mhl	2003	23,119	30,151	193	28	19	ghl	cr: 2(320),1(100)
9238820	Rickmers Singapore	Mhl	2002	23,119	30,018	193	28	19	ghl	cr: 2(320),1(100)
9244544	Rickmers Shanghai †	Mhl	2003	23,119	30,095	193	28	19	ghl	cr: 2(320),1(100)
9235995	Rickmers Tokyo †	Mhl	2002	23,119	29,827	193	28	19	ghl	cr: 2(320),1(100) ex Cape Delgardo-02
9270816	Sally Rickmers	Mhl	2003	21,932	24,277	196	28	23	ucc	1,858 teu: ex Saylemoon Rickmers-13, CMA CGM Oman-08, Saylemoon Rickmers-07, APL Mumbai-07, Saylemoon Rickmers-04
9220079	Sandy Rickmers §	Mhl	2002	14,290	14,901	159	26	22	ucc	1,216 teu: ex OOCL Moscow-09, Sandy Rickmers-07, I/a Mirko Rickmers
9080998	Santiago	Mhl	1996	24,046	32,482	174	31	19	ucc	2,000 teu: ex CCNI Vancouver-07, Togo Star-04, Santiago-02, CCNI Chiloe-00, Maersk Curitiba-98, CCNI Chiloe-96
9197349	Sean Rickmers §†	Mhl	1999	16,986	21,184	168	27	20	ucc	1,620 teu: ex Delmas Zambia-09, Sean Rickmers-08, Kindia-04, Indamex Kindia-03, Kindia-02
9131278	Sophie §‡	Lbr	1999	22,817	35,466	171	31	16	bcb	1,644 teu: ex Sophie Rickmers-10, CCNI Aviles-08, CCNI Antofagasta-05, CSAV Barcelona-03, CCNI Antofagasta-02, CSAV Barcelona-02, CCNI Antofagasta-01, Contship Mexico-01, CCNI Antofagasta-99
9212010	Tete Rickmers §‡	Mhl	2000	14,278	15,317	158	26	21	ucc	1,216 teu
9134672	Ursula Rickmers	Mhl	1997	16,801	22,900	185	25	19	ucc	1,728 teu: ex Zim Sao Paulo II-12, Ursula Rickmers-01
9131216	Valbella ‡	Deu	1998	28,148	44,593	185	32	15	bcb	1,830 teu; ex CCNI Atacama-08, Valbella-98
9448138	Vany Rickmers +	Mhl	2010	47,090	12,300	183	32	20	mve	4,900 ceu
9160413	Willi Rickmers §‡	Mhl	1998	26,125	30,738	196	30	19	ucc	2,226 teu: ex Sea Puma-06, Crowley Lion-01, CSAV Boston-99, I/a Willi Rickmers

newbuildings:

* owned or managed by Rickmers Shipmanagement (Singapore) Pte Ltd (formed 2006), ** owned by associated Rickmers Maritime, Singapore (formed 2007 – www.rickmers-maritime.com) or § for associated Atlantic Ges. Zur Vermittlung Internationaler Investitionen mbH & Co KG (founded1998 – www.atlantic-fonds.com). † managed by Columbus Shipmanagement GmbH, Germany, †† by Bernhard Schulte Shipmanagement (China) Co Ltd, ‡ by Uniteam Marine Shipping GmbH (formed 1974 as subsidiary of KG Reederei Roth GmbH & Co - www.uniteammarine.com), + time chartered to Hyundai Glovis
Also see Nordcapital Holding GmbH (ER Schiffahrt GmbH & Cie KG) and MPC Munchmeyer Petersen & Co GmbH

Rigel Schiffahrts GmbH & Co. KG   Germany
Funnel: *Blue with black 'R' on six-pointed white star on red disc on broad white band.* **Hull:** *Blue with red boot-topping.*
History: *Formed 1990.* **Web:** www.rigel-hb.com

9053220	Alsterstern *	Can	1994	11,426	17,080	161	23	15	tco	
9053218	Havelstern *	Can	1994	11,423	17,080	161	23	14	tco	
9105140	Isarstern	Iom	1995	11,426	17,078	161	23	14	tco	
9411135	Mekong Star	Iom	2009	23,312	37,836	184	25	14	tco	
9411989	Orinoco Star	Iom	2009	23,312	37,872	184	25	14	tco	
9183831	Rhonestern	iom	2000	14,400	21,871	162	27	15	tco	
9183843	Themsestern	Iom	2000	14,400	21,871	162	27	15	tco	
9053206	Travestern	Iom	1993	11,423	17,080	161	23	15	tco	
9183829	Weichselstern	Iom	1999	14,331	21,950	162	27	15	tco	
9183817	Wolgastern	Iom	1999	14,331	21,950	162	27	15	tco	
9411991	Yukon Star	Iom	2009	23,312	37,873	184	25	14	tco	
9412000	Zambezi Star	Iom	2010	23,312	37,874	184	25	14	tco	

also operate smaller tankers
* vessels owned by Coastal Shipping Ltd.,Canada

Ernst Russ GmbH & Co. KG   Germany
Funnel: *Black with red 'ER' and 5-pointed star between narrow red bands on broad white band or charterers colours.* **Hull:** *Black with red boot-topping.* **History:** *Formed 1893, trading as Ernst Russ to 1992.* **Web:** www.ernst-russ.de

9122057	Helene Russ	Lbr	1996	16,801	23,043	184	25	19	ucc	1,730 teu: ex CSAV San Antonio-09, Helene Russ-05, WAL Urundi-04, Helene Russ-01, CMA Rotterdam-00, Helene Russ-99, CSAV Rio de Janeiro-98, I/a Helene Russ
9477359	Jamila	Lbr	2010	16,137	17,152	161	25	19	ucc	1,350 teu
9477335	Jan	Lbr	2009	16,137	17,121	161	25	19	ucc	1,350 teu
9477347	Jost	Lbr	2010	16,137	17,157	161	25	19	ucc	1,350 teu
9477294	Juliana	Lbr	2009	16,137	17,197	161	25	19	ucc	1,350 teu
9470882	Paul Russ	Atg	2010	16,137	17,230	161	25	19	ucc	1,338 teu
9470894	Tillie Russ	Atg	2010	16,137	17,142	161	25	19	ucc	1,350 teu: ex MCC Davao-13, Tillie Russ-10

Also operates ro-ro vessels in European coastal trades.

Saga Forest Carriers International AS   Norway

Funnel: *Black with white outlined dark blue and turquoise 'S' on dark blue above turquoise bands.* **Hull:** *Orange or grey with black 'SAGA', red boot-topping.* **History:** *Pool formed 1991 by NYK with Aaby and Borgestad, who sold to Hesnes Group in 1995. Leif Höegh joined in 2002 but left in 2009 whilst Attic Forest joined the pool in 2009.* **Web:** *www.sagafc.com*

IMO#	name	flag	year	grt	dwt	loa	bm	kts	type	former names
9317406	Saga Adventure	Hkg	2005	29,758	46,627	199	31	15	boh	
9197002	Saga Andorinha **	Gbr	1998	29,729	47,027	199	31	15	boh	ex Andorinha-01
9160798	Saga Beija-Flor	Hkg	1997	29,729	47,029	199	31	14	boh	ex Beija-Flor-03
9014066	Saga Crest ‡	Hkg	1994	29,381	47,069	199	31	15	boh	
9317418	Saga Discovery	Hkg	2006	29,758	46,618	199	31	15	boh	
9343481	Saga Enterprise ‡	Hkg	2006	29,758	46,550	199	31	15	boh	
9343493	Saga Explorer †	Hkg	2006	29,758	46,589	199	31	15	boh	
9613848	Saga Falcon	Hkg	2012	37,499	55,596	200	32	15	boh	
9613862	Saga Fjord	Hkg	2013	38,000	56,000		32	15	boh	
9644524	Saga Fortune	Hkg	2012	37,441	56,023	200	32	15	boh	
9613874	Saga Fram	Hkg	2013	38,000	56,000		32	15	boh	
9613850	Saga Frigg	Hkg	2013	38,000	56,000		32	15	boh	
9343510	Saga Frontier	Hkg	2007	29,758	46,500	199	31	15	boh	
9613836	Saga Future	Hkg	2012	37,499	55,596	200	32	15	boh	
9121297	Saga Horizon	Hkg	1995	29,381	47,016	199	31	15	boh	
9200421	Saga Jandaia	Hkg	1998	29,729	47,016	199	31	15	boh	ex Jandaia-01
9363637	Saga Journey	Hkg	2007	29,758	46,652	199	31	15	boh	
9117739	Saga Monal *	Bhs	1996	36,463	49,755	200	32	16	boh	ex Höegh Monal-04, Saga Challenger-02
9117741	Saga Morus *	Bhs	1997	36,463	56,801	200	32	16	boh	ex Höegh Morus-04
9371062	Saga Navigator	Hkg	2007	29,758	46,673	199	31	15	boh	
9401788	Saga Odyssey	Hkg	2008	29,758	46,500	199	31	15	boh	
9380764	Saga Pioneer	Hkg	2008	29,758	46,627	199	31	15	boh	
9144354	Saga Sky	Hkg	1996	29,381	47,053	199	31	15	boh	
9014078	Saga Spray ‡	Hkg	1994	29,381	47,029	199	31	15	boh	
8918277	Saga Tide	Hkg	1991	29,235	57,471	199	31	15	boh	
9160803	Saga Tucano	Hkg	1998	29,729	47,032	199	31	14	boh	ex Tucano-01
9233466	Saga Viking ‡	Hkg	2002	29,867	46,500	199	31	14	boh	
9233454	Saga Voyager †	Hkg	2001	29,872	46,882	199	31	14	boh	
8918289	Saga Wave	Hkg	1991	29,235	47,062	199	31	15	boh	
9074078	Saga Wind	Hkg	1994	29,381	47,053	199	31	15	boh	

newbuildings: open-hatch bulk carriers, 2 x 52,000dwt (Oshima yd # 10631/2 (2012)], 2 x 56,000dwt [Daewoo(2013)]
*owned by Saga Shipholding (Norway) AS, † owned by Navire Shg. Co. * owned by Attic Forest AS, Norway (formed 2006) ** by Denholm Line Steamers Ltd, UK (formed 1909, parent J&J Denholm Ltd founded 1866). † owned by Navire Shipping, ‡ owned by NYK companies, vessels managed by Anglo-Eastern Ship Management Ltd, Hong Kong (China)*

Samskip HF   Iceland

Ost-West-Handel und Schiffahrt GmbH, Germany

Funnel: *cream with blue globe device split with letters OWH .* **Hull**: *blue with white 'Baltic Reefers', red boot-topping.*
History: *Founded 1946 as Samband Islenzkra Samvinnufelaga until 1991 and Samband Line to 1994. Ost-West founded 1996 as Ost-West-Handel Bruno Bishoff GmbH until 2000.* **Web**: *www.owhbb.de*

IMO#	name	flag	year	grt	dwt	loa	bm	kts	type	former names
9189902	Baltic Hollyhock	Lbr	1999	9,649	11,788	145	22		grf	ex Atlantic Hollyhock-12

Rigel Schiffahrts : YUKON STAR : *ARO*

IMO#	name	flag	year	grt	dwt	loa	bm	kts	type	former names
7710903	Baltic Mariner	Lbr	1979	10,424	9,852	151	22	22	grf	ex Swan Stream-03, Pocantico-93, Isla Pongal-86, Pocantico-84
8616312	Baltic Mercury	Vct	1987	10,298	11,067	146	23	18	grf	ex Teno-12, Lincoln Spirit-00, Lincoln Universal-98, Hornwind-93, Lincoln Universal-92
8520213	Baltic Moon	Vct	1987	10,298	11,022	146	23	18	grf	ex Amer Annapurna-08, Arctic Spirit-99, Arctic Universal-97
8304531	Baltic Navigator	Lbr	1985	11,335	10,572	155	23	21	grf	ex Peggy Dow-07
7800605	Baltic Night	Vct	1980	11,392	10,598	155	23	20	grf	ex Solita Reefer-11, Sun Blossom-09, King-05, Chiquita King-95, Christina-90
8304529	Baltic Novator	Lbr	1984	11,335	10,510	155	23	21	grf	ex Tineke-07
7800588	Baltic Novel	Vct	1980	11,392	10,598	155	23	20	grf	ex Karina-11, Rona Reefer-11, Sun Spirit-09, Queen-05, Chiquita Queen-95, Inanna-90, Lanai-88
8819213	Baltic Pride	Lbr	1989	10,368	10,695	150	23		grf	ex Ivory Tirupati-08
8921470	Baltic Prime	Vct	1990	10,405	10,742	150	23	20	grf	ex Condor Bay-12, Ivory Nina-03, ivory Cape-01
7632278	Baltic Sky	Vct	1978	11,233	12,299	144	24	21	grf	ex Asian Reefer-02
7726706	Baltic Star	Vct	1979	11,243	12,570	144	24	21	grf	ex Stemar Prime-10, Baltic Snow-10, Canadian Star-01, Canadian Reefer-01
8002963	Baltic Strait	Vct	1981	12,167	12,545	146	25	20	grf	ex Salerno-07, Skater-02, Tundra Skater-91, Hilco Skater-88
7726718	Baltic Stream	Mlt	1980	11,243	12,570	144	24	21	grf	ex Ecuadorian Reefer-01
7632280	Baltic Sun	Vct	1978	11,233	12,259	144	24	21	grf	ex Balkan Reefer-02
8404238	Electra	Mlt	1985	9,096	11,464	149	22	17	grf	ex Elektra-01, Astra-96, Astraia-94, Colombian Reefer-93, Cacilia B-86
8224432	Europa	Vct	1984	9,092	11,797	149	22	17	grf	ex Crystal Peony-10, Tampico Bay-05, Pearl Reefer-01, Chilean Reefer-96, Elisabeth S-86
8700228	Zenit	Lbr	1987	13,312	12,848	152	25	18	grf	ex Amer Choapa-08, Choapa-96

The Sanko Steamship Co. Ltd.   Japan

Funnel: Light green with two red rings around red disc on broad white band. **Hull:** Light green with white 'SANKO LINE', red boot-topping. **History:** Formed 1934, filed for bankruptcy in 1985 after massive ordering of newbuildings and financially restructured 1989. In April 2012 the company operated a fleet of 185 owned and chartered vessels but by July 2012 had filed for bankruptcy for the second time. It is attempting a restructuring by cancelling most charters. As of December 2012 only 2 vessels remain owned although some charters are continuing through a proposed restructuring. **Web:** www.sankoline.co.jp

IMO#	name	flag	year	grt	dwt	loa	bm	kts	type
9401922	Sanko Marble	Lbr	2010	30,488	50,779	190	32	14	boh
9401934	Sanko Mercury	Lbr	2010	30,488	50,779	190	32	14	boh
9401910	Sanko Mermaid	Lbr	2009	30,488	50,779	190	32	14	boh
9355513	Sanko Mineral *	Lbr	2008	30,360	50,757	190	32	14	boh
9512939	Sanko Power *	Lbr	2010	93,369	181,196	292	45	14	bbu
9189926	Sanko Sincere	Jpn	1998	29,688	50,655	195	32	15	boh

* owned by Sanko Steamship Co Ltd., other vessels chartered

Saudi National Shipping Co.   Saudi Arabia

Vela International Marine Ltd., UAE

Funnel: Blue with white square outline containing irregular 10-pointed white star on blue/green background or blue with white 'VELA' below two narrow white bands (top of 'V' merged with lower band). **Hull:** Light grey or dark blue with white 'Vela', red boot-topping. **History:** Founded 1933 as California Arabian Standard Oil Co to 1944, then Arabian American Oil Co Ltd to 1988. Government owned since 1980. Vela International subsidiary formed 1990, sold to Saudi National Shg. Co. 2012. Memorandum of Understanding signed June 2012 regarding merger with Bahri. **Web:** www.vela.ae

IMO#	name	flag	year	grt	dwt	loa	bm	kts	type
9378541	Albutain Star	Lbr	2008	162,252	319,430	333	60	-	tcr
9251274	Aldebaran Star	Lbr	2003	60,387	115,999	248	43	-	tco
9384215	Almizan Star	Lbr	2008	162,252	319.423	333	60	-	tcr
9292838	Alnasl Star	Lbr	2005	32,083	49,000	200	32	14	tco
9292826	Altair Star	Lbr	2004	32,083	46,000	200	32	14	tco
9323596	Altarf Star	Lbr	2006	32,083	49,000	200	32	14	tco
9383215	Almizan Star	Lbr	2008	162,252	319,423	333	60	-	tcr
9484716	Antares Star	Lbr	2010	162,863	319,285	333	60		tcr
9237785	Aries Star	Lbr	2003	164,292	316,478	333	60	15	tcr
9237797	Capricorn Star	Lbr	2003	164,292	316,507	333	60	15	tcr
9484742	Homam Star	Lbr	2010	162,863	319,302	333	60		tcr
9384227	Janah Star	Lbr	2008	162,252	318,000	333	60	-	tcr
9237761	Leo Star	Lbr	2002	164,292	316,501	333	60	15	tcr
9484730	Matar Star	Lbr	2010	162,863	319,287	333	60		tcr
9237773	Pisces Star	Lbr	2002	164,292	316,808	333	60	15	tcr
9384239	Saiph Star	Lbr	2009	162,252	319,410	333	60		tcr
9384198	Sirius Star	Lbr	2008	162,252	319,430	333	60	-	tcr
9384203	Vega Star	Lbr	2008	162,252	318,000	333	60	-	tcr

IMO#	name	flag	year	grt	dwt	loa	bm	kts	type	former names
9484728	Virgo Star	Lbr	2010	162,863	319,141	333	60		tcr	
9324497	Zaurak Star	Lbr	2006	32,083	49,000	200	32	14	tco	

newbuildings:
NB Alphard Star is being used as a floating storage unit

Reederei H. Schepers Bereederungs GmbH & Co. KG Germany

Funnel: *Black with black 'S' on red diamond on white band, black top.* **Hull:** *Dark blue with red boot-topping.* **History:** *Formed 1997, formerly trading as Reederei Heinrich und Rudolf Schepers until 1962, late Tim Schepers und Söhne until 1987.* **Web:** *www.hschepers.de*

IMO#	name	flag	year	grt	dwt	loa	bm	kts	type	former names
9429314	Ada S	Atg	2009	26,435	34,333	209	30	22	ucc	2,500 teu
9456238	Christoph S	Atg	2011	32,987	56,770	190	32	14	bbu	
9325441	Constantin S	Atg	2006	27,191	33,216	200	32	22	ucc	2,483 teu
9374117	Ellen S	Atg	2007	9,957	13,766	148	23	19	ucc	1,100 teu : ex Emirates Gondwana-
9232400	Harald S	Atg	2002	25,370	33,742	207	30	22	ucc	2,478 teu: ex Libra Salvador-09, Montemar Salvador-04, NYK Pasion-04, Montemar Salvador-03, I/a Harald S
9349368	Helene S	Atg	2006	27,213	32,878	200	32	22	ucc	2,483 teu
9259381	Jandavid S	Atg	2003	27,227	33,232	200	32	22	ucc	2,483 teu: ex CSAV Shenzhen-06, Jandavid S-03
9390472	Jasper S	Atg	2007	9,965	13,796	148	23	19	ucc	1,100 teu
9299484	Jula S	Deu	2005	25,414	33,796	207	30	21	ucc	2,478 teu: ex CSAV Tianjin-10, I/a Jula S
9327580	Karin S	Atg	2006	9,957	13,734	150	23	18	ucc	1,118 teu: ex Safmarine Pantanal-12, I/a Karin S
9153393	Kerstin S	Deu	1997	25,361	33,936	207	30	21	ucc	2,478 teu: ex Valparaiso Express-08, P&O Nedlloyd Pantanal-05, Kerstin S-97
9456173	Kilian S	Atg	2011	32,987	56,793	190	32	14	bbu	
9306251	Maren S	Atg	2005	9,957	13,839	148	23	19	ucc	1,100 teu
9429326	Maria Katharina S	Atg	2010	26,435	34,333	209	30	22	ucc	2,500 teu
9517434	Mell Seringat	Atg	2011	16,137	17,159	161	25	18	ucc	1,350 teu: Arian-11
9517422	Mell Springwood	Atg	2011	16,137	17,192	161	25	19	ucc	1,350 teu: Tammo-11
9158513	NileDutch Cape Town	Deu	1998	25,624	33,914	207	30	20	ucc	2,478 teu: ex CCNI Cartagena-11, Heinrich S-06, Zim Singapore I-02, I/a Heinrich S

Reederei Rudolf Schepers GmbH & Co. KG   Germany

Funnel: *Black with black 'S' on red diamond on white band, black top.* **Hull:** *Dark blue with red boot-topping.* **History:** *Formed 1994, formerly trading as Reederei Heinrich und Rudolf Schepers until 1962, late Tim Schepers und Söhne until 1987.* **Web:** *www.reederei-schepers.com*

IMO#	name	flag	year	grt	dwt	loa	bm	kts	type	former names
9303766	Adelheid-S	Atg	2006	35,581	44,053	223	32	22	ucc	3,398 teu: ex Emirates Wasl-12, TS Dammam-09, Emirates Wasl-08, Adelheid S-06, Hanjin Pusan-03
9431757	APL Indonesia	Atg	2010	40,542	50,246	261	32	24	ucc	4,256 teu
9431769	APL Sri Lanka	Atg	2010	40,541	50,264	261	32	24	ucc	4,256 teu
9359260	Christopher	Atg	2008	16,023	20,073	170	25	19	ucc	1,440 teu
9418652	CSAV Lanalhue	Atg	2009	40,541	50,269	261	32	24	ucc	4,256 teu
9456123	Hermann S	Atg	2009	32,987	56,721	190	32	14	bbu	
9294018	Julius S	Deu	2004	25,630	33,390	207	30	21	ucc	2,478 teu: ex CMA CGM Brasilia-10, I/a Julius S
9219343	Katharina S	Atg	2001	35,645	42,211	220	32	22	ucc	3,108 teu: ex CSAV Paranagua-09, Norasia Everest-06, APL Venezuela-04, I/a Carolina, I/dn Camilla
9106625	Katrin S	Atg	1995	11,964	14,454	150	23	18	tcc	1,104 teu: ex CSAV Dominicana-08, CCNI Altamira-08, Katrin S-07, Lykes Commodore-06, MSC Panama-04, Katrin S-03, Santa Paula-97, Katrin S-95
9219381	Louis S	Atg	2003	35,881	41,850	220	32	22	ucc	3,091 teu: ex Libra Santos-12, Patricia-04, Amasia-03, I/a Cyrill
9456147	Mia-S	Alt	2010	32,987	56,835	190	32	14	bbu	
9153381	Michaela S	Atg	1997	25,361	33,976	207	30	21	ucc	2,478 teu: ex MSC Cristobal-09, Maersk Nantes-07, Michaela S-04, Contship Spirit-03, Michaela S-97
9088524	NileDutch Congo	Atg	1996	18,166	26,337	179	28	19	ucc	1,906 teu: ex CMA CGM Maya-11, Calaparana-06, Jan S-04, Helene Delmas-01, SCL Zaandam-00, P&O Nedlloyd Zaandam-99, CMBT Africa-97, Morecombe Bay-97, CMBT Africa-96, I/a Jan S
9232412	NileDutch Shanghai	Atg	2002	25,630	33,500	207	30	22	ucc	2,478 teu: ex Thea S-10, CSAV Rio Petrohue-09, Safmarine Kei-04, Thea S-02
9431719	Rudolf Schepers	Atg	2009	40,541	50,300	261	32	24	ucc	4,256 teu

IMO#	name	flag	year	grt	dwt	loa	bm	kts	type	former names
9303742	Tim S	Atg	2005	35,581	44,135	223	32	22	ucc	3,398 teu: ex Emirates Excellence-11, CMA CGM Excellence-09, I/dn Tim S
9383223	TS Jakarta	Atg	2008	26,435	34,362	209	30	22	ucc	2,546 teu: ex Emirates Norika-09, I/a Anne S
9376141	TS Pusan	Atg	2008	26,435	34,331	209	30	22	ucc	2,546 teu: I/a Johannes S

newbuildings: 2 x 92,000dwt bulkers [Yangzijiang (2012)], 2 x 2,546teu container ships

Reederei Karl Schlüter GmbH & Co. KG   Germany

Funnel: Blue with blue 'N' on broad white band, plain black or charterers colours. **Hull:** Various charterers colours.
History: Formed 1986. **Web:** www.rks-rd.de

IMO#	name	flag	year	grt	dwt	loa	bm	kts	type	former names
9345984	APL Dallas †	Lbr	2008	36,007	42,019	231	32	23	ucc	3,400 teu: ex MOL Wave-08, APL Dallas-07
9431812	APL Melbourne †	Lbr	2010	40,541	50,278	261	32	24	ucc	4,250 teu: I/a Jack London
9345996	APL Minneapolis †	Lbr	2008	36,007	41,964	231	32	23	ucc	3,534 teu: ex MOL Wind -13, APL Minneapolis-11, MOL Wind-09, APL Minneapolis-08, I/a Northern Dexterity
9431824	APL Shanghai †	Lbr	2010	40,541	50,201	261	32	24	ucc	4,250 teu: I/a Jonathan Swift
9431800	CSAV Llanquihue †	Lbr	2010	40,541	50,249	261	32	24	ucc	4,250 teu: I/a Joseph Conrad?
9404209	CSAV Lluta †	Lbr	2010	40,541	50,367	261	32	24	ucc	4,250 teu: I/a Jules Verne
9357872	Fritz Reuter	Lbr	2006	18,480	23,700	177	27	20	ucc	1,732 teu: ex Maruba Zonda-08, I/a Fritz Reuter
9323493	Hermann Hesse	Lbr	2007	18,480	23,716	177	27	20	ucc	1,732 teu
9329631	Kota Sabas	Lbr	2007	35,975	42,131	231	32	23	ucc	3,554 teu
9295165	Maersk Danbury *	Lbr	2005	54,271	66,762	294	32	23	ucc	4,992 teu: ex Charles Dickens-05
9295177	Maersk Davenport *	Lbr	2005	54,271	66,762	294	32	23	ucc	4,992 teu: ex Ernest Hemingway-05
9303754	Mark Twain	Lbr	2006	35,581	44,053	231	32	23	ucc	3,398 teu: ex Emirates Eminence-09, CMA CGM Respect-09, I/a Mark Twain
9122409	MSC Uruguay †	Atg	1996	29,115	40,087	196	32	22	ucc	2,908 teu: ex Northern Virtue-01, Hyundai Majesty-99, Northern Virtue-96
9391787	Northern Democrat	Lbr	2009	36,007	41,986	231	32	22	ucc	3,534 teu
9122411	Northern Valour	Atg	1996	29,115	40,114	196	32	22	ucc	2,908 teu: MSC China-09, Ming Fidelity-00, Hyundai Fidelity-98, Northern Valour-96
9155092	Northern Victory	Atg	1997	29,115	40,080	196	32	22	ucc	2,908 teu; ex MSC Salvador-06, Safmarine Everest-02, CMBT Everest-01, I/a Northern Victory
9334844	RHL Astrum *	Lbr	2006	18,480	23,640	177	27	20	ucc	1,740 teu: ex Heinrich Heine-11
9334832	RHL Aurora *	Lbr	2006	18,480	23,685	177	27	20	ucc	1,740 teu: ex Matthias Claudius-11
9248679	Theodor Storm	Lbr	2004	28,270	33,282	213	32	23	ucc	2,586 teu: ex TS Nagoya-13, Theodor Storm-10
9248667	Thomas Mann	Lbr	2003	28,270	33,282	213	32	23	ucc	2,586 teu: ex TS Tokyo-13, Thomas Mann-10
9303778	William Shakespeare	Lbr	2007	35,581	44,023	231	32	23	ucc	3,400 teu: ex Emirates Kanako-12, William Shakespeare-07

* managed for Hansa Hamburg Shipping International GmbH & Co. KG.   ** chartered to Fednav q.v.
† managed by Norddeutsche Reederei H.Schulte

Reederei Rudolf Schepers : CHRISTOPHER : *ARO*

Schoeller Holdings Ltd.   **Cyprus**

Columbia Shipmanagement Ltd., Cyprus

Funnel: *Buff or white with blue 'CSM' on broad red band edged with narrow blue bands, *** black with 'S' symbol on broad white band or charterers colours.* **Hull:** *Green, red or *** black with red boot-topping, AAL vessels, green with 'Austral Asia Line' in white*
History: *Formed 1978.* **Web:** *www.schoeller-holdings.com*

IMO#	name	flag	year	grt	dwt	loa	bm	kts	type	former names
9521564	AAL Bangkok **	Sgp	2012	14,053	18,603	149	23	14	ghl	cr: 2(350)
9498341	AAL Brisbane	Mhl	2010	23,930	32,311	194	28	16	ghl	cr 2(350), 1(100) 2,029 teu
9521540	AAL Dampier **	Sgp	2011	14,053	18,707	149	23	14	ghl	cr: 2(350)
9521095	AAL Fremantle **	Sgp	2011	14,053	18,763	149	23	14	ghl	cr: 2(350): l/a AAL Bali
9498353	AAL Kembla	Mhl	2011	23,930	31,000	194	28	16	ghl	cr: 2(350), 1(100)
9498365	AAL Singapore	Mhl	2011	23,930	32,134	194	28	16	ghl	cr: 2(350), 1(100)
9498377	AAL Shanghai	Mhl	2012	23,930	32,106	194	28	16	ghl	cr: 2(350), 1(100)
9498389	AAL Pusan	Mhl	2012	23,930	32,279	194	28	16	ghl	cr: 2(350), 1(100)
9521552	AAL Nanjing **	Sgp	2012	14,053	19,000	149	23	14	ghl	cr: 2(350)
9498468	*AAL Hong Kong*	Mhl	2013	25,000	31,000	194	28	16	ghl	cr: 2(350), 1(100)
9498470	*AAL Dalian*		2013		31,000					
9498482	*AAL Newcastle*		2014		31,000					
9275103	Anita L.	Cyp	2004	14,308	16,439	155	25	18	ucc	1,221 teu: ex Cape Fresco-11, CNC Hongkong-08, Cape Fresco-04
9253909	Astra ***	Mhl	2002	79,525	149,995	272	46	15	tcr	
9226994	Brunhilde Salamon ***	Mhl	2001	39,126	75,940	225	32	14	bbu	ex Lake Camellia-04
9248954	Calypso †	Mhl	2003	14,308	16,584	155	25	18	ucc	1,221 teu: ex Cape Ferro-11, YM Subic-09, Cape Ferro-05
9324734	Camberley	Lbr	2006	23,003	26,427	174	28	16	lpg	
9187239	Cape Balder ‡	Mhl	2000	81,093	159,998	274	48	15	tcr	ex Hudson-06, Front Sun-03
9187227	Cape Bantry ‡	Mhl	2000	81,093	159,999	274	48	15	tcr	ex Potomac-06, Front Sky-03
9293117	Cape Bari ‡	Mhl	2005	81,076	159,186	274	48	15	tcr	
9293129	Cape Bastia ‡	Mhl	2005	81,076	159,156	274	48	15	tcr	
9228655	Cape Bata ‡	Mhl	2003	81,310	160,289	274	48	15	tcr	
9293131	Cape Bonny ‡	Mhl	2005	81,085	159,152	274	48	15	tcr	
9233777	Cape Bowen ‡	Mhl	2003	81,310	159,988	274	48	15	tcr	
9293143	Cape Brindisi ‡	Mhl	2006	81,076	159,195	274	48	15	tcr	
9231092	Cape Darby	Mhl	2001	23,132	30,537	193	28	19	gpc	cr: 2(100): 1,680 teu: ex Red Cedar-12, Rickmers Houston-09, Golden Isle-08, Cape Derby-07, Golden Isle-06, Cape Darby-04
9231119	Cape Denison ‡	Mhl	2002	23,132	30,396	193	28	19	ghl	cr : 2(100) ex Bright Horizon-11, Pacific Destiny-10, Tasman Explorer-08, Cape Denison-06, CCNI Hong Kong-06, Cape Denison-04
9248928	Cape Falcon †	Mhl	2003	14,308	16,421	155	25	18	ucc	1,221 teu
9347712	Cape Faro	Mhl	2006	15,995	20,316	170	25	19	ucc	1,440 teu
9379363	Cape Fawley	Mhl	2008	15,995	20,358	170	25	19	ucc	1,440 teu
9379375	Cape Felton	Mhl	2008	15,995	20,351	170	25	19	ucc	1,440 teu
9359325	Cape Ferrol	Mhl	2008	15,995	20,346	170	25	19	ucc	1,400 teu
9324162	Cape Flores	Mhl	2005	14,308	16,393	155	25	18	ucc	1,221 teu: ex TS Ningbo-08, MOL Assurance-07, Cape Flores-05

Reederei Karl Schlüter : CSAV LLANQUIHUE : *J. Kakebeeke*

IMO#	name	flag	year	grt	dwt	loa	bm	kts	type	former names
9356842	Cape Forby	Mhl	2006	15,995	20,308	170	25	19	ucc	1,440 teu
9359301	Cape Franklin	Mhl	2006	15,995	20,300	170	25	19	ucc	1,400 teu
9324174	Cape Fraser	Mhl	2005	14,308	16,403	155	25	18	ucc	1,221 teu: ex USL Kea-08, Cape Fraser-06
9248930	Cape Frio ‡‡	Mhl	2003	14,308	16,442	155	25	18	ucc	1,221 teu: ex TS Taichung-10, Cape Frio-05
9359313	Cape Fulmar	Mhl	2007	15,995	20,308	170	25	19	ucc	1,440 teu
9571296	Cape Maas	Mhl	2011	35,708	41,411	212	32	22	ucc	2,758 teu
9571301	Cape Madrid	Mhl	2011	35,708	41,636	212	32	22	ucc	2,758 teu
9348900	Cape Magnus	Mhl	2008	28,007	37,570	222	30	22	ucc	2,742 teu: ex Salah Al Deen-09, Cape Magnus-08, I/a King Adam
9348857	Cape Mahon ‡	Cyp	2007	28,007	37,570	222	30	22	ucc	2,742 teu: ex CSAV Teno-09, Cape Mahon-07, I/a King Aaron
9440150	Cape Male	Mhl	2009	35,878	41,411	212	32	22	ucc	2,758 teu: ex POS Sydney-11, Cape Male-10
9571313	Cape Manila	Mhl	2011	35,708	41,411	212	32	22	ucc	2,758 teu
9360257	Cape Manuel ‡	Cyp	2007	28,007	37,905	222	30	22	ucc	2,742 teu
9571325	Cape Marin	Mhl	2012	35,878	41,463	212	32	22	ucc	2,758 teu
9360271	Cape Mayor	Mhl	2007	28,007	37,909	222	30	22	ucc	2,742 teu: ex CSAV Tubal-09, Cape Mayor-07, I/a King Andrew
9445916	Cape Moss	Mhl	2011	35,878	41,411	212	32	22	ucc	2,758 teu
9436185	Cape Nabil **	Sgp	2010	18,257	23,550	175	27	20	ucc	1,740 teu
9401697	Cape Nassau **	Sgp	2010	18,326	23,328	175	27	20	ucc	1,740 teu
9401685	Cape Nati **	Sgp	2009	18,326	23,263	175	27	20	ucc	1,740 teu
0436173	Cape Nemo **	Sgp	2010	18,257	23,517	175	27	20	ucc	1,740 teu
9360245	CCNI Aquiles ‡	Cyp	2007	28,007	37,867	222	30	22	ucc	2,742 teu: ex Cape Martin-11, King Arthur-07
9259317	Fedor ***	Mhl	2003	41,397	70,156	228	32	14	tco	ex Nidia-04
9231107	Golden Isle ‡	Mhl	2002	23,132	30,537	193	28	19	ggc	cr: 2(100) ex Pacific Dream-09, Tasman Voyager-08, CCNI Shanghai-06, Cape Don-04, Steamers Progress-02
9626572	Grand Breaker	Mhl	2011	33,032	57,000	190	32	14	bbu	
9626584	Grand Pioneer	Mhl	2011	33,032	57,000	190	32	14	bbu	
9498456	Hyundai Incheon	Mhl	2013	23,930	32,128	194	28	16	ghl	cr: 2(350), 1(100); I/a AAL Melbourne
9498444	Hyundai Seoul	Mhl	2012	23,930	32,043	194	28	16	ghl`	cr: 2(350), 1(100); I/a AAL Kobe
9299771	Kanpur	Lbr	2005	57,243	106,094	244	42	14	tcr	ex Alhasbar-06
9360269	King Alfred	Cyp	2007	28,007	37,938	222	30	22	ucc	2,742 teu: ex ANL Birrong-12, King Alfred-10, CMA CGM Kepler-08, King Alfred-07
9108374	King Justus ‡	Mhl	1995	14,241	18,395	159	24	18	ucc	1,129 teu: Condor I-12, ex Condor-09, TMM Chiapas-01, Condor-99, Recife-97, Condor-95
9421843	King Robert	Mhl	2008	89,510	169,676	291	45	14	bbu	ex Golden Sentosa-08
9116412	Meridian Lion ***	Mhl	1997	156,880	300,349	330	58	15	tcr	ex Overseas Meridian-11, Meridian Lion-06
9509126	Noble Regor	Cyp	2012	35,887	41,139	212	32	22	ucc	2,758 teu
9632818	Oriental Trader	Mhl	2012	33,032	57,000	190	32	14	bbu	
9225794	Sag Westfalen	Mhl	2003	26,061	30,453	196	30	22	ucc	2,226 teu: ex CMA CGM Esmeraldas-11, Kaedi-06, Irma Delmas-03
9248942	St. John Glory ‡‡	Mhl	2003	14,308	16,435	155	25	18	ucc	1,221 teu: ex Tiger RMB-10, Cape Fox-08, YM Da Nang-08, TS Yokohama-04, Cape Fox-03

Schoeller Holdings (United Product Tankers Pool) : CAPE BEIRA : F. de Vries

IMO#	name	flag	year	grt	dwt	loa	bm	kts	type	former names
9334480	Vereina	Mhl	2008	16,418	27,112	166	27	14	bbu	ex Casanna-08
9253894	Voyager ***	Mhl	2002	79,525	149,991	272	46	15	tcr	

newbuildings:

*managed by subsidiaries Columbia Shipmanagement Ltd., Cyprus (www.columbia.com.cy) or * by Columbia Shipmanagement (Deutschland) GmbH or ** Columbia Shipmanagement (Singapore) Pte Ltd. ‡ for 40% owned Konig & Cie KG, ‡‡ for Konig subsidiary Marenave Schiffahrts AG (founded 2006 – www.marenave.com), *** for Salamon AG, Germany, † for First Ship Lease Pte Ltd, Bermuda,*
Also see Kristian Gerhard Jebsens Skipsrederei AS, Knutsen OAS Shipping AS and Rickmers Reederei GmbH & Cie KG.

Hanse Bereederung GmbH, Germany

History: *Associate company formed 1976 as Hanse Bereederungs GmbH & Co KG to 2005.* **Web:** *www.hanse-bereederung.de*

IMO#	name	flag	year	grt	dwt	loa	bm	kts	type	former names
9275115	Cape Falster *	Mhl	2005	14,308	16,397	156	25	18	ucc	1,221 teu: ex Vento di Tramontana-12, Cape Falster-11
9347724	Cape Flint	Mhl	2006	15,995	20,312	170	25	19	ucc	1,440 teu
9182019	Cape Negro **	Sgp	1998	17,609	23,752	183	28	19	ucc	1,510 teu: ex Tiger Cape-09, Cape Negro-09, YM Dammam-07, Cape Negro-04, Norasia Malabar-04, Cape Negro-03, Ace Container-03
9182021	Cape Norviega **	Sgp	1998	17,609	24,116	183	28	18	ucc	1,510 teu: ex Justice Container-03
9236585	Cape Santiago *	Mhl	2002	14,241	18,402	159	24	18	ucc	1,129 teu: ex MSC Yaounde-03, Cape Santiago-02
9232773	Euro Max †	Lbr	2002	32,284	39,350	211	32	22	ucc	2,732 teu: CMA CGM Charcot-11, CSAV Rio Loa-07, Euro Max-04, P&O Nedlloyd Dubai-03, l/a Euro Max
9316335	Passat Breeze †	Lbr	2005	32,214	39,008	211	32	22	ucc	2,732 teu: ex CSAV Morumbi-10, Passat Breeze-05
9316359	Passat Spring †	Lbr	2006	32,214	39,063	211	32	22	ucc	2,732 teu:
9071210	Tiger Pearl **	Sgp	1994	17,125	24,136	183	28	20	ucc	1,510 teu: ex CebuTrader-12, Tiger Pearl-11, Prosperity Container-03

*managed by Columbia Shipmanagement Ltd., Cyprus or * by Columbia Shipmanagement (Deutschland) GmbH or*
*** Columbia Shipmanagement (Singapore) Pte. † managed for Passat Schiffahrtsges.*

United Product Tanker (UPT) pool

Funnel: *Owners colours.* **Hull:** *Red with white 'UPT'.* **Web:** *www.uptankers.com*

IMO#	name	flag	year	grt	dwt	loa	bm	kts	type	former names
9540819	Andes ††	Cyp	2011	29,429	49,995	183	32	14	tco	
9260005	Baltic Adonia I **	Cyp	2003	23,235	37,197	183	27	14	tco	ex Arctic Point-09, l/a Baltic Adonia
9208100	Baltic Captain I	Cyp	2000	23,235	37,389	183	27	14	tco	ex Baltic Captain-02, l/a Androcles
9208124	Baltic Chief I	Cyp	2000	23,235	37,389	183	27	14	tco	ex Baltic Chief-01, Baltic Carrier-01, l/a Armodius
9261396	Baltic Sea I **	Cyp	2003	23,235	37,389	183	27	15	tco	ex Glacier Point-09, Baltic Sea-03
9264283	Cape Bacton	Mhl	2004	25,108	35,156	176	31	14	tco	ex Celebes Wind-05, Chabua Amiredjibi-05
9288928	Cape Beale	Mhl	2005	25,108	40,327	176	31	14	tco	
9196119	Cape Beira	Mhl	2005	25,400	40,946	176	31	14	tco	ex Sable-05
9147265	Cape Benat	Lbr	1998	21,165	33,540	179	25	14	tco	
9260263	Cape Bille	Mhl	2003	25,108	35,089	176	31	14	tco	
9260067	Cape Bird	Mhl	2003	25,108	35,070	176	31	14	tco	
9179127	Cape Blanc	Lbr	1998	21,165	33,540	179	25	14	tco	
9260055	Cape Bon	Mhl	2003	25,108	35,089	176	31	14	tco	
9264271	Cape Bradley	Mhl	2004	25,108	35,159	176	31	14	tco	ex J. Shartava-05
9302671	Cape Brasilia	Mhl	2006	25,108	40,227	176	32	14	tco	
9260275	Cape Bruny	Mhl	2004	25,108	35,096	176	31	14	tco	
9401221	Cape Taft	Mhl	2008	42,010	73,711	229	32	14	tco	
9569994	Cape Talara	Mhl	2010	42,010	73,371	229	32	14	tco	
9441154	Cape Tallin	Mhl	2008	42,010	73,711	229	32	14	bbu	
9441166	Cape Tampa	Mhl	2009	42,010	73,719	229	32	14	tco	
9441180	Cape Tees	Mhl	2009	42,010	73,614	229	32	14	tco	
9441192	Cape Texel	Mhl	2009	42,010	73,766	229	32	14	tco	
9570008	Cape Troy	Mhl	2011	42,053	73,180	229	32	14	tco	
9391361	Conti Agulhas ***	Lbr	2008	23,403	37,606	184	27	14	tco	
9391373	Conti Benguela ***	Lbr	2008	23,403	37,606	184	27	14	tco	
9391385	Conti Equator *	Lbr	2008	22,403	37,527	184	27	14	tco	
9391397	Conti Greenland ***	Lbr	2008	22,403	37,606	184	27	14	tco	
9391402	Conti Guinea ***	Lbr	2008	22,403	37,554	184	27	14	tco	
9391414	Conti Humboldt ***	Lbr	2008	22,403	37,602	184	27	14	tco	
9311713	FSL Hamburg *	Sgp	2005	28,068	47,496	183	32	14	tco	ex Nika I-10, l/a Victoria I
9311725	FSL Singapore	Sgp	2006	28,068	47,470	183	32	14	tco	ex Verona I
9118056	Hambisa ‡	Mhl	1997	28,027	44,549	183	32	14	tco	
9540807	Himalaya ††	Cyp	2011	29,429	49,995	183	32	14	tco	
9263203	Mount Adamello ††	Cyp	2004	22,521	40,002	182	27	14	tco	
9470985	Mount Everest ††	Lbr	2010	23,313	37,817	184	27	14	tco	
9360441	Mount Green ††	Cyp	2007	22,521	40,003	182	27	14	tco	

IMO#	name	flag	year	grt	dwt	loa	bm	kts	type	former names
9360415	Mount Hope	Cyp	2007	22,521	40,009	182	27	14	tco	
9360427	Mount Karava ††	Cyp	2007	22,521	40,020	182	27	14	tco	
9470997	Mount Kibo ††	Lbr	2010	23,313	37,843	184	27	14	tco	
9360415	Mount Hope ††	Cyp	2007	22,521	40,009	182	27	14	tco	
9263174	Mount McKinney	Cyp	2004	22,518	39,997	182	27	14	tco	
9263186	Mount Rainier ††	Cyp	2004	22,518	40,012	182	27	14	tco	
9263198	Mount Robson ††	Cyp	2004	22,518	40,014	182	27	14	tco	
9360439	Mount Victoria ††	Cyp	2007	22,521	40,055	182	27	14	tco	
9306677	Sloman Themis	Mhl	2006	22,184	34,628	171	27	14	tco	ex Handytankers Unity-11
9306653	Sloman Thetis	Mhl	2006	22,184	34,662	171	27	14	tco	ex Handytankers Liberty-11
9550709	Summit Africa ††	Cyo	2009	42,010	73,427	229	32	14	tco	
9336505	Summit America ††	Cyp	2006	41,021	74,996	229	32	14	tco	
9336490	Summit Europe ††	Cyp	2006	41,021	74,997	229	32	14	tco	

Pool operated by Schoeller Holdings Ltd. Vessels owned/managed by Schoeller Holdings (managed by Columbia Shipmanagement (Deutschland) GmbH) * managed by Columbia Shipmanagement (Singapore), ** Columbia Shipmanagement Ltd., Cyprus or ‡ for 40% owned Konig & Cie KG, *** managed by NSB Niederelbe Schiffahrts GmbH & Co KG for associated Conti Reedere (Conti Holding GmbH & Co KG – www.conti-gruppe.de), † for Sloman Neptun or †† associated Donnelly Tanker Management Ltd, Cyprus (formed 1995 - www.donnellytanker.com.cy).

The Schulte Group

Germany

Funnel: *Green with white 'S' on red disc and black top or charterer's colours.* **Hull:** *Dark grey with red boot-topping.*
History: *Formed 1937.* **Web:** *www.beschulte.de or www.bs-shipmanagement.com*

IMO#	name	flag	year	grt	dwt	loa	bm	kts	type	former names
9280586	Abram Schulte §	Lbr	2004	41,503	72,663	228	32	14	tco	l/a Penyu Pulan
9380506	Alpine Mathilde *	Hkg	2008	29,266	47,128	183	32	14	tco	
9296822	Angelica Schulte	Lbr	2005	56,163	106,433	243	42	14	tcr	
9215878	Anna Schulte †	Hkg	2001	26,626	34,717	210	30	22	ucc	2,556 teu: ex P&O Nedlloyd Andes-05, P&O Nedlloyd Rose-01, l/a Anna Schulte
9247948	APL Amman	Lbr	2002	35,589	40,995	232	32	22	ucc	3,277 teu: ex MOL World-08, APL Amman-08, ANL Emblem-07, CMA CGM Gauguin-03, Arnold Schulte-02
9328481	APL Bangkok †	Hkg	2006	35,991	42,083	231	32	23	ucc	3,554 teu: l/a Gerhard Schulte
9398254	APL Colorado †	Sgp	2009	75,582	85,836	304	40	25	ucc	6,966 teu
9398230	APL Illinois †	Sgp	2009	75,582	85,824	304	40	25	ucc	6,966 teu: l/a Astrid Schulte
9247950	APL Sharjah	Lbr	2002	35,589	40,995	232	32	22	ucc	3,277 teu: ex CMA CGM Chardin-07, Friedrich Schulte-02, CMA CGM Gauguin-02, l/a Friedrich Schulte
9328493	APL Sydney †	Cyp	2006	35,697	42,102	231	32	23	ucc	3,554 teu: ex Philippa Schulte-06
9398242	APL Tennessee †	Mlt	2009	75,582	85,735	304	40	25	ucc	6,966 teu
9398228	APL Texas	Sgp	2009	75,582	85,713	304	40	25	ucc	6,966 teu
9398216	APL Washington	Sgp	2009	75,582	85,760	304	40	25	ucc	6,966 teu
9231169	Auguste Schulte §	Lbr	2002	27,093	34,662	210	30	22	ucc	2,520 teu: ex CMA CGM Claudel-07, Claudel-02, l/a Alexandria, l/dn Auguste Schulte
9083263	Bahama Spirit ***	Vut	1995	26,792	46,606	188	32	14	bsd	ex Freeport Miner-00, San Pietro-99 (conv bbu-00)
9034717	Baltic Gas *	Sgp	1994	18,360	23,267	160	26	16	lpg	20,910 m³ ex Canaima-09, Henning Maersk-06

The Schulte Group : ABRAM SCHULTE : *Hans Kraijenbosch*

IMO#	name	flag	year	grt	dwt	loa	bm	kts	type	former names
9111462	Caecilia Schulte	Deu	1995	10,749	14,148	163	22	17	ucc	1,162 teu: ex Ridge-11, Caecilia Schulte-07, CGM Cayenne-02, Caecilia Schulte-99, Atika Delmas-98, CMBT Antarctica-98, Caecilia Schulte-96
9436422	Cap Mondego	Lbr	2008	35,991	42,057	231	32	23	ucc	3,554 teu: ex Georg Schulte-08
9360257	Cap Manuel	Cyp	2008	35,991	42,201	231	32	23	ucc	3,554 teu: l/a Guenther Schulte
9408774	Cap Moreton	Lbr	2007	35,991	42,074	231	32	23	ucc	3,554 teu: ex Maruba Cristina-09, Cap Moreton-07, l/a Gabriel Schulte
9231470	Caroline Schulte	Lbr	2001	26,582	34,662	210	30	21	ucc	2,556 teu: ex Cap Bisti-11, Libra Houston-06, Caroline Schulte-02, Thekla Schulte-01
9302956	Catharina Schulte ‡‡	Cyp	2006	26.671	34,629	210	30	21	ucc	2,556 teu: ex Cap Bon-12, l/a Catharina Schulte
9188623	Eilhard Schulte	Lbr	1999	28,078	48,913	190	32	14	bbu	ex Imme Oldendorff-09, Royal Chance-03
9439840	Elisabeth Schulte	Iom	2011	11,246	16,371	145	23	14	tco	
9439876	Elisalex Schulte	Sgp	2011	11,246	16,427	145	23	14	tco	
9209295	Elise Schulte	Hkg	1999	56,239	106,122	241	42	14	tcr	ex Ammon-04
9394519	Emmy Schulte	Gbr	2009	11,233	16,669	145	23	14	tco	
9439864	Erika Schulte	Gbr	2011	11,246	16,427	145	23	14	tco	
9439814	Erin Schulte	Gbr	2009	11,233	16,716	145	23	14	tco	
9222118	Esther Schulte ‡‡	Cyp	2001	26,582	33,871	210	30	22	ucc	2,556 teu: ex P&O Nedlloyd Altiplano-05, Esther Schulte-02, l/a Marianne Schulte
9439826	Eva Schulte	Sgp	2011	11,233	16,621	145	23	14	tco	
9439838	Everhard Schulte	Sgp	2010	11,233	16,658	145	23	14	tco	
9439852	Edzard Schulte	Iom	2011	11,246	16,371	145	23	14	tco	
9309162	Green Ace ≠≠	Cyp	2005	18,344	23,579	176	27	20	ucc	1,740 teu: ex Sea Beta-08, Boomerang 1-06, Sea Beta-06
9436458	Gustav Schulte	Lbr	2009	35,991	42,035	210	30	21	ucc	3,554 teu
9130171	Henrietta Schulte	Lbr	1997	16,281	22,352	179	25	19	ucc	1,684 teu: ex Cap Rojo-08, Henriette Schulte-05, P&O Nedlloyd Lome-04, Fesco Voyager-02, Henriette Schulte-00, CSAV Brasilia-98, Henriette Schulte-97
9366275	High Mars *	Hkg	2008	29,733	51,542	183	32	14	tco	
9366263	High Saturn *	Hkg	2008	29,733	51,527	183	32	14	tco	
9409314	Immanuel Schulte +	Iom	2009	18,311	23,361	160	26	14	lpg	20,600 m³
9155341	Johann Schulte +	Iom	1998	15,180	17,914	155	23	16	lpg	16,500 m³
9161481	Joost Schulte	Lbr	1997	26,040	45,874	188	31	14	bbu	ex May Oldendorff-09, Houyu-03
9146003	Juergen Schulte	Lbr	1997	26,586	48,224	189	31	14	bbu	ex Frederike Oldendorff-09, Mercury Trader-03
9220433	Karin Schulte	Lbr	2000	20,569	25,648	180	28	20	ucc	1,702 teu: ex Rui Yun He-10, Karin Schulte -00
9273442	Kaspar Schulte	Lbr	2004	41,503	72,718	225	32	14	tco	l/a Penyu Hijau
9292125	Konrad Schulte §	Cyp	2005	18,334	23,679	175	27	20	ucc	1,740 teu: ex Cap Maleas-09, Konrad Schulte-05, l/a Lambert Schulte
9435674	Louisa Schulte †	Sgp	2008	18.321	23,252	176	27	20	ucc	1,740 teu
9435686	Ludwig Schulte	Sgp	2008	18,321	23,175	175	27	20	ucc	1,740 teu
9301938	Maersk Needham §	Sgp	2006	26,671	34,704	210	30	22	ucc	2,602 teu; ex Hannah Schulte-08
9301926	Maersk Norwich §	Sgp	2006	26,671	34,396	210	30	22	ucc	2,602 teu: l/a Lucie Schulte

The Schulte Group : LUDWIG SCHULTE : *F. de Vries*

IMO#	name	flag	year	grt	dwt	loa	bm	kts	type	former names
9302944	Margarete Schulte **	Mlt	2006	26,671	34,457	210	30	21	ucc	2,602 teu; ex Cap Bizerta-11, Margarete Schulte-06
9215907	Marianne Schulte †	Lbr	2001	26,718	34,643	210	30	21	ucc	2,556 teu; ex P&O Nedlloyd Acapulco-05, l/a Marianne Schulte
9214525	Mary Schulte	Lbr	2000	20,624	25,850	180	28	20	ucc	1,702 teu: ex Hua Yun He-10
9167148	Max Schulte	Iom	1999	22,181	34,999	171	27	14	tco	ex Maersk Rhone-10, Rita Maersk-03
9123532	MCC Melaka	Lbr	1997	16,281	22,361	192	25	19	ucc	1,684 teu: ex Helen Schulte-10, Libra Ecuador-09, Helen Schulte-03, Direct Kiwi-03, Helen Schulte-99, Libra Houston-98, Helen Schulte-97
9535163	MOL Glide	Hkg	2011	59,307	71,339	275	40	23	ucc	5,605 teu
9531909	MOL Globe	Hkg	2011	59,307	71,000	275	40	23	ucc	5,605 teu
9535149	MOL Grandeur	Hkg	2011	59,307	71,000	275	40	23	ucc	5,605 teu: l/a Hedwig Schulte
9535187	MOL Gratitude	Hkg	2012	59,307	70,590	275	40	23	ucc	5,605 teu
9535204	MOL Growth	Hkg	2012	59,176	71,339	275	40	23	ucc	5,605 teu
9222120	MOL Inca	Lbr	2001	26,582	33,871	210	30	22	ucc	2,556 teu: ex Cap Breton-12, Christiane Schulte-07, Elisabeth Schulte-01
9321017	MOL Pace †	Pan	2006	71,902	72,968	293	40	25	ucc	6,350 teu
9403619	MOL Proficiency †	Mhl	2007	71,777	72,912	293	40	25	ucc	6,350 teu
9101601	MOL Wisdom †	Pan	1995	41,114	39,814	245	32	23	ucc	2,542 teu: ex Alligator Wisdom-01
9605243	MSC Arbatax		2013	92,882	111,000			22	ucc	8,948 teu: l/a Johanna Schulte
9605231	MSC Algeciras		2013	92,882	111,000			22	ucc	8,948 teu: l/a Joseph Schulte
9605255	MSC Antalya		2013	92,882	111,000			22	ucc	8,948 teu: l/a Judith Schulte
9619464	MSC Agadir		2012	108,000	112,150	299	48	22	ucc	8,762 teu: l/a Joel Schulte
9619476	MSC Antigua		2012	108,000	112,150	299	48	22	ucc	8,762 teu: l/a Julius Schulte
9619452	MSC Arica	Hkg	2012	108,000	112,150	299	48	22	ucc	8,762 teu: l/a Jacob Schulte
9232632	SFL Europa *	Mhl	2003	16,803	22,900	185	25	20	ucc	1,728 teu: ex Montemar Europa-09
9394208	Nashwan ##	Sgp	2008	17,852	16,922	154	26	16	lpg	22,594 m³
9364966	Njinsky ##	Sgp	2008	16,804	16,968	154	26	16	lpg	22,598 m³
9034729	Nordic Gas *	Sgp	1994	18,360	23,267	160	26	16	lpg	20,682 m³ ex Henriette Maersk-07
9146728	NSS Bonanza ‡‡	Pan	1996	85,902	170,907	289	47	14	bbu	
9262730	NSS Fortune ‡‡	Pan	2003	93,199	184,872	290	47	14	bbu	
9273088	Omega King ‡	Mhl	2004	42,432	74,999	225	32	14	tcr	ex Everhard Schulte-06
9283679	Omega Queen ‡	Hkg	2004	42,432	74,999	225	32	14	tcr	ex Rudolf Schulte-06
9030967	Ore Fazendao ‡‡	Lbr	1994	164,325	291,435	333	58	14	bor	ex Al Bali Star-10 (conv tcr-10)
9060314	Ore Parati ‡‡	Lbr	1994	158,680	301,542	332	58	14	bor	ex Mirfak Star-10 (conv tcr-10)
9060338	Ore Santos ‡‡	Lbr	1994	158,680	301,591	332	58	14	bor	ex Shaula Star-10 (conv tcr-10)
8323238	Ore Tubarao ‡‡	Lbr	1985	101,222	198,906	300	50	13	bor	ex Ocean Champion-09, Onga Maru-01
9030943	Ore Urucum ‡‡	Lbr	1993	164,325	291,435	333	58	14	bor	ex Libra Star-10 (conv tcr-10)
8802923	Ore Vitoria ‡‡	Lbr	1990	116,427	233,016	315	54	14	bor	ex Rhine Ore-09, Once Maru-01
9203461	Otto Schulte	Lbr	1999	20,624	25,685	180	28	20	ucc	ex Ibn Al Roomi-09
9370707	Pacific Horizon II *	Pan	2007	25,180	37,981	182	28	14	tco	
9043720	Pacific Ruby ‡‡	Hkg	1993	147,902	254,095	324	56	15	bor	ex Atlantic Ruby-03 (conv tcr-08)
9576753	Rebecca Schulte	Sgp	2011	19,793	25,620	186	32	14	tco	
9576789	Reinhold Schulte	Sgp	2012	19,793	25,583	178	27	14	tco	

The Schulte Group : MAERSK NEEDHAM : *Chris Brooks*

IMO#	name	flag	year	grt	dwt	loa	bm	kts	type	former names
9159426	Robert Schulte	Lbr	1997	26,586	48,225	189	31	14	bbu	ex Max Oldendorff-09, Million Trader-03
9576765	Rudolf Schulte	Sgp	2011	19,793	25,583	186	32	14	tco	
9278624	Sabrewing *	Pan	2004	29,647	49,323	186	32	14	tco	
9302554	SCT Chile †	Mhl	2006	54,214	68,080	294	32	24	ucc	5,060 teu: MSC Debra-11
9302566	SCT Santiago †	Mhl	2006	54,214	68,126	294	32	24	ucc	5,060 teu: MSC Benedetta-11
9302580	SCT Zurich †	Mhl	2006	54,214	68,135	294	32	24	ucc	5,060 teu: MSC Olga-11
9057159	Selma †	Atg	1994	14,619	20,275	167	25	17	ucc	1,012 teu: ex Cala Pinar del Rio-09, Nordpol-05, Indamex Taj-02, Abidjan Star II-00, Nordpol-99, TNX Mercury-98, Nordpol-98, San Marino-97, Nordpol-94
9116137	Shark Island #	Atg	1996	18,070	28,587	175	26	14	bbu	ex Christine O-09, Abbot Point-07, Forest Venture-04
9132868	Simon Schulte	Lbr	1996	25,074	46,489	190	31	14	bbu	ex Alfred Oldendorff-09, Diamond Halo-04
9265756	Sophie Schulte §	Hkg	2005	61,991	115,583	241	44	14	tcr	
9215880	Susanne Schulte ‡‡	Sgp	2001	26,626	34,717	210	30	22	ucc	2,556 teu; ex P&O Nedlloyd Aconcagua-05, I/a Susanne Schulte
9215919	Thekla Schulte §	Lbr	2001	26,718	34,677	210	30	22	ucc	2,556 teu; ex P&O Nedlloyd Antisana-05, Thekla Schulte-01, I/a Caroline Schulte
9186687	Weser Stahl ‡‡	Cyp	1999	28,564	47,257	192	32	12	bsd	
9155626	Wilhelm Schulte	Iom	1997	15,180	17,900	155	23	16	lpg	16,500 m³

newbuildings: 6 x 9800 teu container ships (Hyundai Samho S596, shared with XT Holdings)
5 x 5,100 teu container ships (Hanjin – 2013/4) + 5 options, 4 x 2,300teu container ships (Zhejiang Yangfan – 2014/15) + 4 options
owned or managed by subsidiaries Bernhard Schulte Shipmanagement (Deutschland) GmbH & Co KG (formed 2000 as Reimarus Schiffahrtskantor GmbH to 2006, Hanseatic Shipping (Deutschland) GmbH and Vorsetzen Schiffs GmbH (formed 2000) to 2008),
* by Bernhard Schulte Shipmanagement (Singapore) Pte. Ltd., (Eurasia Marine Services to 2001, Eurasia International (Singapore) Pte Ltd to 2008),
** by Bernhard Schulte Shipmanagement (Bermuda) Ltd Partnership (formed 1978 as Atlantic Marine Ltd to 2007, Dorchester Atlantic Marine Ltd to 2008),
† by Bernhard Schulte Shipmanagement (China) Co Ltd (Eurasia Ship Management (Shanghai) Co Ltd to 2008),
†† by Bernhard Schulte Shipmanagement Cyprus) Ltd (formed 1972 as Hanseatic Shipping Co to 2008),
‡ by Bernhard Schulte Shipmanagement (Hong Kong) Ltd (formed 1981 and became wholly owned subsidiary in 1988)
‡‡ by Bernhard Schulte Shipmanagement (India) Pvt. Ltd.
§ by Bernhard Schulte Shipmanagement (Greece)
+ by Bernhard Schulte Shipmanagement (Poland) Sp.z.o.o., ++ Bernhard Schulte Shipmnagement (UK) Ltd.
managed for *** Algoma Central Corp,Canada, §§ for Commerz Real Fonds, Germany, # for Opielok Reederei GmbH, Germany, ~~ Petredec Ltd., ≠ for MC Shipping Inc, Monaco or ≠≠ for Ship Finance International Ltd, Bermuda.
Also see Allocean Ltd, Cido Shipping (HK) Co Ltd, ER Schiffahrt GmbH (Nordcapital Holding GmbH), Kristian Gerhard Jebsen Skipsrederi AS, MPC Munchmeyer Petersen & Co GmbH, The National Shipping Company of Saudi Arabia, NileDutch Africa Line and D Oltmann GmbH & Co

Reederei Thomas Schulte GmbH & Co. KG Germany

Funnel: Black with white 'TS' on red diamond on broad green band. **Hull**: Dark green with red boot-topping. **History**: Founded 1987 by Thomas Schulte having previously worked for family company, Bernhard Schulte since 1968. **Web**: www.schulteship.de

IMO#	name	flag	year	grt	dwt	loa	bm	kts	type	former names
9240873	Annabelle Schulte *	Cyp	2002	27,093	34,638	210	30	22	ucc	2,520 teu: ex P&O Nedlloyd Barossa Valley-05, P&O Nedlloyd Barossa-02, I/a Kynouria
9330537	Annina Schulte ‡	Lbr	2007	28,616	39,462	222	30	21	ucc	2,824 teu: ex Cap Beatrice-12, Annina Schulte-07

The Schulte Group : NSS BONANZA : *ARO*

IMO#	name	flag	year	grt	dwt	loa	bm	kts	type	former names
9306471	Antonia Schulte	Cyp	2005	25,406	33,900	207	30	22	ucc	2,478 tru: ex Maersk Navia-09, P&O Nedlloyd Mariana-05, I/a Antonia Schulte
9309289	APL Shenzhen	Cyp	2006	35,697	42,141	231	32	23	ucc	3,554 teu: ex Maria Schulte-06
9329629	APL Sokhna	Cyp	2006	35,975	42,164	231	32	23	ucc	3,554 teu: ex MOL Wonder-08, APL Sokhna-08, I/a Philippa Shulte
9477610	Balthasar Schulte	Lbr	2012	40,542	49,857	261	32	24	ucc	4,249 teu
9453365	Bella Schulte	Lbr	2011	40,542	49,892	261	32	24	ucc	4,249 teu
9537628	Betis	Lbr	2010	43,506	79,700	229	32	24	bbu	ex Diana Schulte-12
9361623	Bodo Schulte	Lbr	2011	40,542	49,836	261	32	24	ucc	4,249 teu
9477787	Bruno Schulte	Lbr	2012	40,542	49,842	261	32	24	ucc	4,249 teu
9315886	CMA CGM Rose *	Lbr	2005	28,927	39,200	222	30	23	ucc	2,824 teu: ex E.R. Marseille-05
9539494	Hedda Schulte		2013	42,000		227	32	23	ucc	3,421 teu
9263320	Helena Schulte ‡	Cyp	2006	35,697	42,106	231	32	23	ucc	3,554 teu: ex CSAV Itaim-12 I/a Helena Schulte
9531454	Daniela Schulte	Lbr	2010	51,239	93,062	229	38	14	bbu	
9537898	Daphne Schulte	Lbr	2010	51,239	93,077	229	38	14	bbu	
9537903	David Schulte	Lbr	2010	51,239	93,039	229	38	14	bbu	
9537628	Diana Schulte	Lbr	2010	43,506	79,700	229	32	14	bbu	
9537630	Dora Schulte	Lbr	2010	43,506	79,607	229	32	14	bbu	
9537915	Dorian Schulte	Lbr	2010	51,239	93,099	229	38	14	bbu	
9540869	Emma Schulte	Lbr	2012	64,769	115,156	254	43	14	bbu	
9540871	Evelyn Schulte	Lbr	2012	64,110	115,150	254	43	14	bbu	
9162370	Francisca Schulte	Cyp	1998	15,929	22,020	169	27	21	ucc	1,618 teu: ex Safmarine Pakistan-06, Francisca Schulte-03, Maersk San Jose-99, I/a Francisca Schulte
9202479	Frida Schulte	Cyp	2000	17,167	21,152	169	27	18	ucc	1,600 teu: ex Maruba Confidence-09, Maersk Vienna-07, Direct Eagle-04, Spica-00
9448827	Hugo Schulte	Lbr	2010	38,364	47,028	240	32	23	ucc	3,635 teu
9504592	Jacob Schulte	Lbr	2013	39,941	50,488	261	32	24	ucc	4,253 teu
9306483	Julia Schulte	Cyp	2005	25,406	33,900	207	30	22	ucc	2,478 teu: ex Maersk Nanhai-09, P&O Nedlloyd Savannah-05, I/a Julia Schulte
9504607	Julius Schulte		2013		34,000	261	32	24	ucc	2,546 teu
9315836	Kota Pekarang	Lbr	2005	28,927	39,275	222	30	23	ucc	2,824 teu: ex E.R. Manchester-05
9289063	Laura Schulte	Lbr	2004	18,334	23,579	175	27	20	ucc	1,740 teu: ex Maersk Varna-08, Laura Schulte-04, I/a Maximilian Schulte, I/dn Konrad Schulte
9449106	Lilly Schulte	Lbr	2012	38,364	46,956	240	32	23	ucc	3,635 teu
9309277	Lisa Schulte	Cyp	2006	35,697	42,102	231	32	23	ucc	3,534 teu: ex CSAV Panamby-11, I/a Lisa Schulte
9102497	Lissy Schulte	Lbr	1995	16,800	23,001	185	25	20	ucc	1,728 teu: ex P&O Nedlloyd Takoradi-04, Lissy Schulte-01, CSAV Rubens-98, Lissy Schulte-95
9539509	Lucia Schulte		2013		42,000	227	32	23	ucc	3,421 teu
9305879	Maersk Neustadt †	Lbr	2005	25,674	33,594	207	30	22	ucc	2,474 teu: ex Isabelle Schulte-05
9230775	Marie Schulte †	Atg	2001	16,803	22,900	185	25	20	ucc	1,728 teu
9449118	Martha Schulte	Lbr	2012	38,364	46,925	240	32	23	ucc	3,635 teu
9292137	Maximilian Schulte	Cyp	2005	18,334	23,351	176	28	19	ucc	1,696 teu: ex CSAV Rotterdam-11, I/a Maximilian Schulte, I/dn Laura Schulte
9305881	Natalie Schulte †	Cyp	2005	25,674	33,651	207	30	22	ucc	2,474 teu: ex Maersk Neuchatel-09, Natalie Schulte-05
	Noble Matar		2013		42,000	227	32	21	ucc	3,421 teu
9509126	Noble Regor *	Cyp	2012	35,887	41,139	213	32	21	ucc	2,782 teu: I/d OS Izmir
9509138	Noble Rigel *	Cyp	2012	35,887	41,130	213	32	21	ucc	2,782 teu: I/d OS Antalya
9312418	NYK Floresta *	Cyp	2005	25,406	33,900	208	30	22	ucc	2,474 teu: ex Victoria Schulte-05
9294185	Patricia Schulte *	Cyp	2006	28,592	39,418	222	30	22	ucc	2,824 teu
9449120	Paula Schulte	Lbr	2012	38,364	46,500	240	32	23	ucc	3,635 teu
9294159	Sarah Schulte	Cyp	2005	28,592	39,383	222	30	22	ucc	2,824 teu: ex Ariake-10, I/a Sarah Schulte
9337274	Sofia Schulte	Lbr	2007	28,616	39,339	222	30	21	ucc	2,824 teu: ex Cap Cleveland-12, Sofia Schulte-08
9294173	Tatiana Schulte	Cyp	2005	27,779	39,400	222	30	22	ucc	2,824 teu
9397585	UASC Doha *	Lbr	2009	40,030	50,700	260	32	24	ucc	4,526 teu: ex Beatrice Schulte-09
9401063	UASC Jubail	Lbr	2009	40,030	50,570	260	32	24	ucc	4,526 teu: ex Benedict Schulte-09
9401075	UASC Samarra	Lbr	2009	40:030	50,716	260	32	24	ucc	4,526 teu: ex Benita Schulte-09
9315874	Valerie Schulte *	Lbr	2005	28,927	39,200	222	30	23	ucc	2,824 teu: ex Kota Pemimpin-10, I/a E.R. Malta

newbuildings :included in list
* managed by Ocean Shipmanagement GmbH, † for Atlanti zur Vermittlung Internationaler Investitionen GmbH & Co or ‡ for Lloyd Fonds AG

Seaspan Corp.   Canada

Funnel: *Charterers colours.* **Hull:** *Black.* **History:** *Seaspan Ship Mgmt. incorporated 04:2000 (Seaspan International Ltd., Canadian subsidiary of Washington Corp. USA).* **Web:** *www.seaspancorp.com*

IMO#	name	flag	year	grt	dwt	loa	bm	kts	type	former names
9448815	Alianca Itapoa	Hkg	2011	91,051	102,875	334	43	24	ucc	8,208 teu
9492713	Berlin Bridge	Hkg	2011	46,444	58,200	270	35	24	ucc	4,526 teu
9492701	Bilbao Bridge	Hkg	2011	46,444	58,200	270	35	24	ucc	4,526 teu
9492696	Brevik Bridge	Hkg	2011	46,444	58,200	270	35	24	ucc	4,526 teu
9486116	Brotonne Bridge	Hkg	2010	46,444	58,200	270	35	24	ucc	4,526 teu
9494280	Budapest Bridge	Hkg	2011	46,444	58,200	270	35	24	ucc	4,526 teu
9435038	Calicanto Bridge	Hkg	2010	26,404	34,195	210	30	24	ucc	4,526 teu
9472139	Cosco Development	Hkg	2012	141,823	140,609	366	48	25	ucc	13,092 teu
9472189	Cosco Excellence	Hkg	2012	141,823	140,146	366	48	25	ucc	13,092 teu
9472141	Cosco Faith	Hkg	2012	141,823	140,609	366	48	25	ucc	13,092 teu
9472127	Cosco Fortune	Hkg	2012	141,823	140,637	366	48	25	ucc	13,092 teu
9403009	Cosco Fuzhou	Hkg	2007	35,988	42,201	231	32	22	ucc	3,534 teu
9466245	Cosco Glory	Hkg	2011	141,823	140,637	366	48	25	ucc	13,092 teu
9472177	Cosco Harmony	Hkg	2012	141,823	140,453	366	48	25	ucc	13,092 teu
9472165	Cosco Hope	Hkg	2012	141,823	140,241	366	48	25	ucc	13,092 teu
9448786	Cosco Indonesia	Hkg	2010	91,051	101,200	334	43	24	ucc	8,208 teu
9448748	Cosco Japan	Hkg	2010	91,051	102,834	334	43	24	ucc	8,208 teu
9448750	Cosco Korea	Hkg	2010	91,051	102,710	334	43	24	ucc	8,208 teu
9448774	Cosco Malaysia	Hkg	2010	91,051	102,834	334	43	24	ucc	8,208 teu
9448762	Cosco Philippines	Hkg	2010	91,051	101,200	334	43	24	ucc	8,208 teu
9472153	Cosco Pride	Hkg	2011	141,823	140,609	366	48	25	ucc	13,092 teu
9448803	Cosco Prince Ruoert	Hkg	2011	91,051	102,742	334	43	24	ucc	8,208 teu
9448798	Cosco Thailand	Hkg	2010	91,051	101,200	334	43	24	ucc	8,208 teu
9403011	Cosco Yingkou	Hkg	2007	35,988	41,500	231	32	22	ucc	3,534 teu
9443463	CSAV Lebu	Hkg	2010	40,541	50,276	261	32	24	ucc	4,253 teu
9443475	CSAV Lingue	Hkg	2010	40,541	50,435	261	32	24	ucc	4,253 teu
9286011	CSCL Africa	Hkg	2005	90,645	101,612	334	43	25	ucc	8,468 teu: ex-CMA CGM Africa-08, CSCL Africa-08
9290139	CSCL Brisbane	Hkg	2005	39,941	50,748	260	32	24	ucc	4,250 teu
9402627	CSCL Callao	Hkg	2009	26,404	34,194	209	30	22	ucc	2,504 teu
9224312	CSCL Chiwan	Hkg	2001	39,941	50,488	260	32	24	ucc	4,051 teu
9386005	CSCL Lima	Hkg	2008	26,404	34,200	209	30	22	ucc	2,504 teu
9314258	CSCL Long Beach	Hkg	2007	108,069	111,889	337	46	25	ucc	9,580 teu
9402639	CSCL Manzanillo	Hkg	2009	26,404	34,194	209	30	22	ucc	2,504 teu
9290127	CSCL Melbourne	Hkg	2005	39,941	50,796	263	32	24	ucc	4,250 teu
9385984	CSCL Montevideo	Hkg	2008	26,404	34,194	209	30	22	ucc	2,546 teu
9290115	CSCL New York	Hkg	2005	39,941	50,500	263	32	24	ucc	4,250 teu
9385972	CSCL Panama	Hkg	2008	26,404	34,194	209	30	22	ucc	4,051 teu
9402615	CSCL San Jose	Hkg	2008	26,404	33,726	209	30	22	ucc	2,504 teu
9386017	CSCL Santiago	Hkg	2008	26,404	33,725	209	30	22	ucc	2,546 teu
9402615	CSCL San Jose	Hkg	2008	26,404	33,726	209	30	22	ucc	2,546 teu
9385996	CSCL Sao Paulo	Hkg	2008	26,404	34,194	209	30	22	ucc	2,546 teu
9290103	CSCL Sydney	Hkg	2005	39,941	50,869	260	32	24	ucc	4,250 teu
9290098	CSCL Vancouver	Hkg	2005	39,941	50,869	263	32	24	ucc	4,250 teu
9314234	CSCL Zeebrugge	Hkg	2007	108,069	111,889	337	46	25	ucc	9,580 teu
9286009	CSCL Oceania	Cyp	2004	90,645	101,810	334	43	25	ucc	8,468 teu: ex MSC Belgium-09, CSCL Oceania-07

Seaspan Corp. : COSCO GLORY : *Hans Kraijenbosch*

IMO#	name	flag	year	grt	dwt	loa	bm	kts	type	former names
9301782	Dubai Express ‡	Hkg	2006	39,941	50,748	260	32	24	ucc	4,253 teu: ex CP Corbett-06, l/a CP Guerrero, l/dn TMM Guerrero
9402641	Guayaquil Bridge	Hkg	2010	25,320	34,194	209	30	22	ucc	2,546 teu
9301794	Jakarta Express ‡	Hkg	2006	39,600	50,869	260	32	24	ucc	4,253 teu: ex CP Dartmoor-06, CP Banyan-06, l/dn Contship Banyan
9301811	Lahore Express ‡	Hkg	2006	39,941	50,869	260	32	24	ucc	4,253 teu: ex CP Morelos-06
9301859	Manila Express ‡	Hkg	2007	39,941	50,813	261	32	23	ucc	4,253 teu
9407134	MOL Emerald	Hkg	2009	54,940	67,518	294	33	25	ucc	5,087 teu
9407146	MOL Eminence	Hkg	2010	54,940	67,386	294	33	25	ucc	5,087 teu
9407158	MOL Emissary	Hkg	2010	54,940	67,400	294	33	25	ucc	5,087 teu
9407160	MOL Empire	Hkg	2020	54,940	67,400	294	33	25	ucc	5,087 teu
8618308	MSC Carole	Pan	1989	52,191	60,640	294	32	23	ucc	4,814 teu: ex Maersk Moncton-11, MSC Ancona-10, Maersk Moncton-08, Mathilde Maersk-06
8618310	MSC Leanne	Pan	1989	52,191	60,639	184	25	18	ucc	4,814 teu: ex York-11, Cape York-11, Maersk Marystown-08, Maren Maersk-06
8613322	MSC Manu	Pan	1989	52,191	60,639	294	27	23	ucc	4,814 teu: ex Victor-11, Cap Victor-11, Maersk Matane-09, Margrethe Maersk-06
8618293	MSC Veronique	Pan	1989	52,191	60,900	222	32	23	ucc	4,814 teu: ex Maersk Merritt-11, MSC Sweden-10, Maersk Merritt-07, Mette Maersk-06
9301770	New Delhi Express	Hkg	2005	39,941	50,813	260	32	24	ucc	4,253 teu: ex CP Kanha-06, l/a CP Charger, l/dn Lykes Charger
9301847	Rio de Janeiro Express	Hkg	2007	39,941	50,500	260	32	24	ucc	4,253 teu: ex CP Nuevo Leon-07, TMM Nuevo Leon-05
9301823	Rio Grande Express	Hkg	2006	39,941	50,500	260	32	24	ucc	4,253 teu: ex CP Margosa-06
9301809	Saigon Express	Hkg	2006	39,941	50,869	260	32	24	ucc	4,253 teu; ex CP Jasper-06, CP Trader-06, l/dn Lykes Trader
9301835	Santos Express	Hkg	2006	39,941	50,869	260	32	24	ucc	4,253 teu: ex CP Victor-06, l/dn Lykes Victor
9227027	Seaspan Dalian	Hkg	2002	39,941	50,871	260	32	24	ucc	4,051 teu: ex CSCL Dalian-12
9227039	Seaspan Felixstowe	Hkg	2002	39,941	50,789	260	32	24	ucc	4,051 teu: ex CSCL Felixstowe-12
9224300	Seaspan Hamburg	Hkg	2001	39,941	50,790	260	32	24	ucc	4,051 teu: CSAV Licanten-13, CSCL Hamburg-10
9227015	Seaspan Ningbo	Hkg	2002	39,941	50,789	260	32	24	ucc	4,250 teu: ex CSCL Ningbo-12

newbuildings: seven 10,000 teu container ships + 18 options [Yangzijiang SY]

Seatrade Groningen B.V.   Netherlands

Funnel: *Blue with white 'S' and blue 'G' symbol on orange square.* **Hull:** *White with blue 'Seatrade' or charterers name, red boot-topping.* **History:** *Established in 1951 by five captain-owners as NV Scheepvaarts Groningen to 1973. Acquired Dammers & Van der Heide's Shipping & Trading Co BV (formed 1947) in 1989, Triton Schiffahrts GmbH (formed 1994) in 2000 and United Reefers Chartering Ltd (formed 1994 as Global Reefer Trading Ltd to 2002) in 2005. Acquired reefer fleet of Amer Shipping in 2008.* **Web:** *www.seatrade.com or www.reedereitriton.de*

IMO#	name	flag	year	grt	dwt	loa	bm	kts	type	former names
9019652	Aconcagua Bay	Pan	1992	9,074	11,581	149	21	19	grf	ex United Ice-06, Aconcagua-02
9179397	Aracena Carrier #	Pan	1998	7,637	9,011	139	21	20	grf	ex Humboldt Rex-12

Seaspan Corp : CSAV LINGUE : *Hans Kraijenbosch*

IMO#	name	flag	year	grt	dwt	loa	bm	kts	type	former names
8318659	Atlantic Hope ++	Pan	1984	7,777	8,494	142	20	18	grf	ex Magellan Rex-96
9454761	Atlantic Klipper	Nld	2011	14,091	15,692	165	25	23	grf	
9179256	Atlantic Reefer	Ant	1998	13,055	17,322	175	23	21	grf	(len-12)
9454759	Baltic Klipper	Lbr	2010	14,091	15,609	165	25	23	grf	
9158549	Benguela Stream ‡	Nld	1998	9,298	11,016	150	22	20	grf	
9164770	Cala Palma +	Ita	2000	14,868	16,024	190	24	20	grf	
9164782	Cala Pedra +	Ita	2000	14,868	16,024	190	24	20	grf	
9164756	Cala Pino +	Ita	1999	14,868	16,024	190	24	20	grf	
9164768	Cala Pula +	Ita	1999	14,868	16,024	190	24	20	grf	
8801814	Changuinola Bay	Bhs	1988	8,487	9,727	141	21	21	grf	ex Sun Rosie-06, Cap Changuinola-00
9051791	Cold Stream	Ant	1994	8,414	10,066	140	22	19	grf	l/a Prince of Streams
9085479	Cool Expreso	Nld	1994	5,471	7,480	126	16	18	grf	ex Cool Express-12
9143740	Discovery Bay	Bhs	1997	8,924	10,100	142	22	21	grf	
8911073	Everest Bay	Lbr	1989	8,739	9,692	141	21	21	grf	ex United Cold-06, E.W. Everest-02
9081679	Frio Hellenic §	Pan	1998	9,997	11,070	148	22	21	grf	
8920141	Fuji Bay	Lbr	1990	9,070	11,540	149	21	17	grf	ex Amer Fuji-08
8802088	Hansa Bremen ††	Lbr	1989	10,842	12,942	157	23	21	grf	
8909068	Hansa Lübeck ††	Lbr	1990	10,842	12,942	157	23	21	grf	
8909070	Hansa Stockholm ††	Lbr	1991	10,842	12,942	157	23	21	grf	
8802090	Hansa Visby †	Lbr	1989	10,842	12,942	157	23	21	grf	
8908193	Himalaya Bay ++	Lbr	1990	9,070	11,595	149	21	17	grf	ex Amer Himalaya-08
8907888	Humboldt Bay	Lbr	1990	9,070	11,633	149	21	20	grf	ex Amer Whitney-08, Californian Reefer-98, Humboldt Rex-94
8813594	Ivory Ace ++	Bhs	1990	10,394	10,713	150	23	20	grf	
8213603	Kashima Bay †	Cym	1984	9,273	10,647	150	21	19	grf	ex UB Gemini-02, Gemini-96, Kashima Reefer-95
9167796	Klipper Stream *‡	Nld	1998	9,305	10,936	150	22	21	grf	
8312643	Koala Bay †	Lbr	1984	9,057	9,340	149	21	19	grf	ex Mulungisi-07, Koala-95
9179402	Lucena Carrier #	Pan	2000	7,627	9,011	139	21	20	grf	ex Season Trader-12
9072824	Marine Phoenix †	Lbr	1994	7,313	7,957	134	21	19	grf	ex Amber Lily-97
9127928	Pacific	Nld	1996	5,918	8,500	134	16	16	grf	
9179268	Pacific Reefer	Ant	1999	13,055	17,322	175	23	21	grf	(leng-12)
9172959	Royal Klipper *	Nld	2000	11,382	12,906	155	24	21	grf	ex Equator Stream-00
9019640	Runaway Bay	Bhs	1992	9,070	11,579	149	21	17	grf	ex Sun Maria-05, Diamond Reefer-98, Hudson Rex-95
9213777	Santa Catharina	Bhs	2000	8,597	9,259	143	22	19	grf	
9045156	Sea Phoenix †	Lbr	1992	7,303	8,056	134	21	19	grf	ex Amber Cherry-96
8517346	Tama Hope	Bhs	1986	6,579	7,690	146	19	18	grf	ex Lamitan-93, Tama Hope-92
8517358	Tama Star	Bhs	1987	6,579	7,685	146	19	18	grf	ex Bulan-93, Tama Star-92
8911085	Whitney Bay	Lbr	1990	8.739	9,692	141	21	21	grf	ex United Cool-06, E.W. Whitney-03
8807662	Wind Frost	Lbr	1989	9,072	11,622	149	21	19	grf	ex Amer Everest-08, Hokkaido Rex-95

newbuildings:
In addition to the above, the company also operates numerous smaller reefer vessels.
*owned by: * Jaczon bv (www.jaczon.nl): † Roswell Navigation Corp, Greece, †† Leonhardt & Blumberg, § Laskaridis Shipping Co Ltd., # by Norbulk Shipping, UK, + Cosiarma SpA, Genoa, or ++ other various owners. ‡ operated by Geest Line*

Seatrade Groningen B.V. : BALTIC KLIPPER : *ARO*

IMO#	name	flag	year	grt	dwt	loa	bm	kts	type	former names

Triton Schiffahrts GmbH, Germany

Funnel: *as Seatrade or operators colours.* **Hull:** *White with blue 'Seatrade' or charterers name, red boot-topping.* **History:** *company established in Leer,1994, acquired by Seatrade 2000* **web:** www.reedereitriton.de

IMO#	name	flag	year	grt	dwt	loa	bm	kts	type	former names
9158537	Agulhas Stream †	Ant	1998	9,298	11,048	150	22	20	grf	
9045936	Atlantic Mermaid	Lbr	1992	9,829	10,464	142	23	19	grf	
9047271	Bay Phoenix	Gbr	1993	7,326	8,041	134	21	19	grf	ex Summer Phoenix-12, Spring Phoenix-01, Windward Phoenix-99
9016662	Buzzard Bay	Lbr	1992	10,381	10,621	150	23	20	grf	ex French Bay-04, Royal Star-99, Chiquita Honshu-94, Royal Star-92
9064229	Caribbean Mermaid	Lbr	1993	9,829	10,464	142	23	19	grf	ex Northern Mermaid-04, Caribbean Mermaid-02
9167801	Comoros Stream *	Nld	2000	11,382	12,906	155	24	21	grf	
9045948	Coral Mermaid	Lbr	1992	9,829	10,461	142	23	19	grf	ex Arctic Mermaid-06, Maud-04, Coral Mermaid-01
9038488	Eagle Bay	Ant	1992	10,402	10,621	150	23	20	grf	ex Ivory Eagle-03
9143752	Eastern Bay	Lbr	1997	8,917	9,662	143	22	19	grf	ex Eastern Express-05, l/a Frost Express
9175901	Elsebeth *	Lbr	1998	10,519	10,327	152	23	21	grf	
9201869	Elvira *	Lbr	2000	10,532	10,309	152	23	21	grf	
9202857	Emerald *	Lbr	2000	10,532	10,346	152	23	21	grf	
9181170	Esmeralda *	Lbr	1999	10,532	10,358	152	23	21	grf	
9070137	Falcon Bay	Ant	1993	10,374	10,532	150	23	20	grf	ex Ivory Falcon-02
9067128	Fortuna Bay	Ant	1993	10,203	11,585	145	22	19	grf	ex Fortune Bay-03, Uruguayan Reefer-99
9016674	Hawk Bay	Ant	1992	10,381	10,603	150	23	20	grf	ex Roman Bay-04, Roman Star-99, Chiquita Sulu-94
9135169	Hope Bay	Ant	1996	8,396	9,639	143	22	20	grf	
9047245	Lagoon Phoenix	Lbr	1993	7,313	8,044	134	21	19	grf	ex River Phoenix-12, Clover Moon-99, Dover Phoenix-97
9204958	Lombok Strait *	Lbr	2002	14,413	13,512	167	25	22	grf	ex Leopard Max-02
9204960	Luzon Strait *	Lbr	2002	14,413	14,413	167	25	22	grf	ex Tiger Max-02
9064839	Mexican Bay	Lbr	1994	10,203	11,575	145	22	20	grf	ex Mexican Reefer-06
9045924	Pacific Mermaid	Pan	1992	9,820	10,466	142	23	19	grf	
9189873	Polarlight *	Lbr	1998	11,417	10,447	154	24	21	grf	ex Polarlicht-04
9189885	Polarsteam *	Lbr	1999	11,417	10,449	154	24	21	grf	ex Polarstern-03
9014444	Prince of Seas	Lbr	1993	6,363	7,387	120	19	17	grf	
9061198	Prince of Tides	Bhs	1993	7,329	5,360	134	21	19	grf	
9066485	Prince of Waves	Bhs	1993	7,329	8,039	134	21	19	grf	
9194921	Santa Lucia *	Lbr	1999	8,507	9,566	143	22	20	grf	l/a Santa Lucia II
9194957	Santa Maria *	Ant	1999	8,507	9,566	143	22	20	grf	l/a Santa Maria III
9152181	Southern Bay *	Lbr	1997	8,879	9,609	143	22	19	grf	ex Southern Express-05

Seatrade Groningen B.V. (Triton Schiffahrts) : LAGOON PHOENIX : *Chris Brooks*

IMO#	name	flag	year	grt	dwt	loa	bm	kts	type	former names
9045950	Tasman Mermaid	Lbr	1993	9,829	10,457	142	23	19	grf	ex Antarctic Mermaid-06, Skausund-04, Tasman Mermaid-01
9172947	Timor Stream †	Pan	1998	9,307	11,013	150	22	20	grf	ex Stream Express-05
9045168	Water Phoenix	Lbr	1992	7,303	8,075	134	21	19	grf	ex Lake Phoenix-12, Amber Rose-96

* managed by Triton for MPC Munchmeyer Petersen & Co GmbH qv. † operated by Geest Line (www.geestline.co.uk)

Shell Trading & Shipping Ltd. (STASCO)   U.K.

Funnel: Yellow with narrow black top. **Hull:** Red, black or grey with red or blue boot-topping. **History:** Royal Dutch Shell Gp. formed 1907 on 60:40 basis by Royal Dutch Petroleum Co (founded 1890) and Shell Transport & Trading Co Ltd (founded 1897). Took control of Mexican Eagle Petroleum Co in 1919 and formed Shell-Mex Ltd in 1921, which in 1932 merged with BP to form Shell-Mex & BP Ltd until separated in 1975. STASCO responsible for trading and shipping activities of the group. **Web:** www.shell.com

IMO#	name	flag	year	grt	dwt	loa	bm	kts	type	former names
9443401	Aamira (df) +	Mhl	2010	163,922	130,026	345	54	19	lng	266,000 m³
9210828	Abadi (st)	Brn	2002	117,461	72,758	290	46	19	lng	135,000 m³
9431147	Al Bahiya (df) +	Mhl	2010	136,980	121,957	315	50	19	lng	216,000 m³
9443683	Al Dafna (df) +	Mhl	2009	163,922	130,157	345	54	19	lng	266,000 m³
9397286	Al Ghashamiya (df) +	Mhl	2010	135,423	108,988	315	50	19	lng	216,000 m³
9372742	Al Ghuwairiya (df)	Mhl	2008	168,189	154,950	345	55	19	lng	261,700 m³
9431123	Al Karaana (df) +	Mhl	2009	136,980	122,052	315	50	19	lng	210,100 m³
9397327	Al Kharaitiyat (df) +	Mhl	2009	136,168	107,153	315	50	19	lng	216,200 m³
9431111	Al Khattiya (df) +	Mhl	2009	136,980	121,946	315	50	19	lng	210,100 m³
9397315	Al Mafyar (df) +	Mhl	2009	163,922	130,441	345	54	19	lng	266,000 m³
9397298	Al Mayeda (df) +	Mhl	2009	163,922	130,298	345	54	19	lng	266,000 m³
9431135	Al Nuaman (df) +	Mhl	2009	136,980	121,910	315	50	19	lng	210,100 m³
9397339	Al Rekayyat (df) +	Mhl	2009	136,168	107,165	315	50	19	lng	216,200 m³
9397341	Al Sadd (df) +	Mhl	2009	136,980	121,913	315	50	19	lng	210,100 m³
9388821	Al Samriya (df) +	Mhl	2009	168,189	154,900	345	55	19	lng	261,700 m³
9360831	Al Sheehaniya (df) +	Mhl	2009	136,980	122,006	315	50	19	lng	210,000 m³
9496317	Amali (df)	Brn	2011	98,490	72,800	284	43	19	lng	147,228 m³
9496305	Arkat (df)	Brn	2011	98,490	72,800	284	43	19	lng	147,228 m³
7121633	Bebatik (st) *	Brn	1972	48,612	51,579	257	35	18	lng	75,100 m³: ex Gadinia-86
7347768	Belanak (st) *	Brn	1975	48,612	51,579	257	35	18	lng	75,000 m³: ex Gouldia-86
7347732	Bilis (st) *	Brn	1975	52,708	41,370	248	35	18	lng	77,731 m³: ex Geomitra-86
9388833	Bu Samra (df) +	Mhl	2008	163,922	130,442	345	65	19	lng	266,000 m³
7359785	Bubuk (st) *	Brn	1975	52,708	41,370	248	35	18	lng	77,670 m³: ex Genota-86
9387956	Bursa	Hkg	2008	29,733	51,463	183	32	15	tco	
8009129	Estrella Atlantica §	Arg	1982	17,707	28,750	183	29	15	tco	ex Humberto Beghin-95 laid up
8301400	Estrella Austral §	Arg	1984	28,259	45,718	197	32	14	tcr	ex Feosa Ambassador 2-88
9216913	Elka Angelique	Iom	2001	27,539	44,881	183	32	16	tco	ex Ficus-09, I/a Elka Angelique
9216925	Elka Eleftheria	Iom	2001	27,539	44,787	183	32	16	tco	ex Fulgur-09, I/a Elka Eleftheria
9216901	Elka Nikolas	Iom	2001	27,542	44,788	183	32	16	tco	ex Fusus-09, Elka Nikolas-01
9236614	Galea (st)	Sgp	2002	111,459	72,781	290	46	19	lng	134,425 m³
9236626	Gallina (st)	Sgp	2002	111,459	72,781	290	46	19	lng	134,425 m³
9253222	Gemmata (st)	Sgp	2004	111,459	72,727	290	46	19	lng	137,104 m³
9134713	Hippo ‡	Aus	1997	28,810	46,092	183	32	14	tco	ex Araluen Spirit-11, Helix-11
9388819	Lijmiliya +	Mhl	2009	168,189	155,159	335	55	19	lng	261,700 m³

Shell Trading & Shipping Ltd. (STASCO) : AL SAMRIYA : *Hans Kraijenbosch*

IMO#	name	flag	year	grt	dwt	loa	bm	kts	type	former names
7619575	LNG Abuja #	Bmu	1980	93,619	72,571	285	44	19	lng	126,500 m³: ex Louisana-99
9262211	LNG Adamawa (st) #	Bmu	2005	115,993	79,586	289	48	19	lng	141,000 m³
9262209	LNG Akwa Ibom (st) #	Bmu	2004	115,993	79,633	289	48	19	lng	141,000 m³
9241267	LNG Bayelsa (st) #	Bmu	2005	114,354	79,822	289	48	19	lng	141,000 m³
7708938	LNG Bonny (st) #	Bmu	1981	85,616	89,654	287	42	20	lng	133,000 m³: ex LNG 559-90, Rhrnania-86
9262223	LNG Cross River (st) #	Bmu	2005	115,993	79,591	289	48	19	lng	141,000 m³
7619587	LNG Edo (st) #	Bmu	1980	93,619	72,561	285	44	19	lng	126,750 cm: ex Lake Charles-99
7702401	LNG Finima (st) #	Bmu	1984	85,616	71,472	287	42	20	lng	133,000 m³: ex LNG 564-90
7360124	LNG Lagos (st) #	Bmu	1976	81,472	68,206	275	42	18	lng	122,000 m³: ex Gastor-91
7360136	LNG Port Harcourt (st) #	Bmu	1977	81,472	68,122	275	42	19	lng	122,000 m³: ex Nestor-91
9262235	LNG River Niger (st) #	Bmu	2006	115,993	79,541	289	48	19	lng	141,000 m³
9216298	LNG Rivers (st) #	Bmu	2002	114,354	79,866	289	48	19	lng	141,000 m³
9216303	LNG Sokoto (st) #	Bmu	2002	114,354	79,822	289	48	19	lng	141,000 m³
9397303	Mekaines (df) +	Mhl	2009	163,922	130,171	345	54	19	lng	266,000 m³
9337729	Mesaimeer (df) +	Mhl	2009	136,138	107,160	315	50	19	lng	216,200 m³
9337755	Mozah (df) +	Mhl	2009	163,922	128,900	345	54	19	lng	266,000 m³
9406013	Naticina ≠	Mhl	2010	83,805	156,720	274	48	15	tcr	
9399480	Northia ≠	Mhl	2010	83,805	156,719	274	48	15	tcr	
8608872	Northwest Sanderling (st) †	Aus	1989	105,010	66,810	272	47	18	lng	127,000 m³
8913150	Northwest Sandpiper (st) †	Aus	1993	105,010	66,695	272	47	18	lng	127,000 m³
8913174	Northwest Seaeagle (st) †	Bmu	1992	106,283	67,003	272	47	18	lng	127,000 m³
8608705	Northwest Shearwater (st) ††	Bmu	1991	106,283	66,802	272	47	18	lng	127,500 m³
8608884	Northwest Snipe (st) †	Aus	1990	105,010	66,695	272	47	18	lng	127,000 m³
9045132	Northwest Stormpetrel (st) †	Aus	1994	105,010	66,695	272	47	18	lng	127,000 m³
9397353	Onaiza +	Mhl	2009	136,980	121,939	315	50	19	lng	210,150 m³
9248485	Ondina ≠	Iom	2002	156,916	299,157	330	60	16	tcr	ex Front Stratus-06
9480837	Orthis ≠	Mhl	2011	162,203	320,105	333	60	15	tcr	ex Andromeda Glory-12
9196644	Otina ≠	Iom	2002	159,383	298,465	333	60	15	tcr	ex Hakata-04
9372731	Umm Slal (df) +	Mhl	2008	163,922	130,059	345	54	19	lng	266,000 m³
9443413	Rasheeda (df) +	Mhl	2010	163,922	130,208	345	54	19	lng	266,000 m³
9418365	Shagra (df) +	Mhl	2009	163,922	130,102	345	54	19	lng	266,000 m³
9431214	Zarga (df) +	Mhl	2010	163,922	130,211	345	54	19	lng	266,000 m³

newbuildings:
vessels managed by subsidiary STASCO (Shell Trading & Shipping Co., UK) (formerly Shell International Shipping Ltd to 1995)
for + Qatar Gas Transport,Nakilat * Brunei Shell Tankers Sendirian Berhad (formed 1986 jointly with Government of The State of Brunei,
Diamond Gas Carriers BV acquiring 25% in 2002), ** for AP Moller Singapore Pte Ltd, Singapore, # for Bonny Gas Transport, subsidiary of Nigeria
LNG Ltd (formed 1989 as a joint-venture between Nigerian National Petroleum Corp. (49%), Shell Gas b.v. (25.6%), Total LNG Nigeria (15%) and
Eni Int. (10.4%) or ≠ for Frontline Ltd qv.
† operated by Australian LNG Ship Operating Co Pty Ltd (formed 1989 jointly by Shell Co of Australia Ltd and BHP Petroleum Pty Ltd –

Shell Trading & Shipping Ltd. (STASCO) : LNG ADAMAWA : *Chris Brooks*

www.alsoc.com.au) and †† owned by International Gas Transportation Co Ltd (formed jointly with Chevron, BHP, BP and other companies) and managed by BP Shipping Ltd, Bermuda.
‡ owned by Shell Co. of Australia Ltd (founded 1905 as British Imperial Oil Co Ltd to 1937 – www.shell.com.au)
§ owned by Shell Compania Argentina de Petroleo SA (founded 1922 as Diadema Argentina SA de Petroleo to 1960)
Also see vessels under Frontline, Golar LNG Ltd (Frontline) and Viken Shipping AS.

Solvang ASA   Norway

Funnel: *Brown with blue 'CS' on broad white band.* **Hull:** *Brown with red boot-topping.* **History:** *Amalgamation of Skibs Solvang (founded 1936) and Clipper Shipping A/S in 1992.* **Web:** *www.solvangship.no*

IMO#	name	flag	year	grt	dwt	loa	bm	kts	type	former names
9173068	Clipper Harald	Nis	1999	10,692	13,779	146	21	17	lpg	12,423 m³
9358670	Clipper Hebe	Nis	2007	13,893	18,110	155	23	17	lpg	17,128 m³
9358682	Clipper Helen	Nis	2007	13,893	18,110	155	23	17	lpg	16,789 m³
9378163	Clipper Hermod	Nis	2008	13,893	18,110	155	23	17	lpg	17,128 m³
9378151	Clipper Hermes	Nis	2008	13,893	18,880	156	23	17	lpg	17,128 m³
9377078	Clipper Mars	Nis	2008	36,459	43,544	205	32	16	lpg	60,256 m³
9253820	Clipper Moon	Nis	2003	35,012	44,872	205	32	16	lpg	58,201 m³
9372432	Clipper Neptun	Nis	2008	36,459	43,508	205	32	16	lpg	59,058 m³
9372420	Clipper Orion	Nis	2008	36,459	43,475	205	32	16	lpg	60,000 m³
9379404	Clipper Sirius	Nis	2008	42,897	54,048	227	32	16	lpg	75,000 m³
8813063	Clipper Skagen	Nis	1989	11,822	16,137	158	21	15	lpg	14,793 m³ : ex Havkatt-97, Gaz Horizon-94, Sigulda-93
9277943	Clipper Sky	Nis	2004	35,158	44,617	205	32	16	lpg	58,176 m³
9247807	Clipper Star	Nis	2003	34,970	44,807	205	32	16	lpg	58,154 m³
9347516	Clipper Sun	Bhs	2008	47,173	58,677	225	37	16	lpg	82,000 m³
9379399	Clipper Victory	Nis	2009	42,897	54,005	227	32	16	lpg	75,000 m³
9173056	Clipper Viking	Nis	1998	10,692	13,777	146	21	17	lpg	12,409 m³

newbuildings 2 x 84,000 m³ lpg tankers [Hyundai HI 2516/7 (2013)]

OAO 'Sovcomflot'   Russia

Funnel: *Blue with white 'SCF', black top.* **Hull:** *black with white 'SCF' or blue with white 'SCF LPG' or red with red boot-topping.* **History:** *Formed 1988 and first former Soviet shipping enterprise with independent capital, but wholly owned within Russian Federation. Merged with Novoship in 2007.* **Web:** *www.sovcomflot.com*

IMO#	name	flag	year	grt	dwt	loa	bm	kts	type	former names
9316127	Aleksey Kosygin	Lbr	2007	87,146	163,545	281	50	15	tcr	
9451707	Alpine Monique	Sgp	2010	29,130	46,087	183	32		tco	
9610808	*Anatoly Kolodkin*	Lbr	2013		118,105	250	46	14	tco	
9256901	Anichkov Bridge	Lbr	2003	27,829	47,843	183	32	14	tco	
9149237	Azov Sea	Lbr	1998	27,526	47,363	182	32	15	tco	
9149213	Barents Sea	Lbr	1997	27,526	47,431	182	32	15	tco	
9149225	Bering Sea	Lbr	1998	27,526	47,431	182	32	15	tco	
9301392	Captain Kostichev	Cyp	2005	60,434	100,927	247	42	14	tcs	
9310707	Challenge Passage +	Pan	2008	28,823	48,658	180	32	15	tco	
9160530	East Siberian Sea	Lbr	1998	27,526	47,358	182	32	15	tco	
9610793	Georgy Maslov	Lbr	2012	66,818	122,018	250	46	14	tcr	
9249130	Governor Farkhutdinov	Cyp	2004	58,918	108,078	247	42	15	tcs	
9338955	Grand Aniva (st) †	Cyp	2008	122,239	74,044	288	49	19	lng	145,000 m³
9332054	Grand Elena (st) †	Cyp	2007	122,239	74,127	288	49	20	lng	145,000 m³
9256913	Hermitage Bridge	Lbr	2003	28,000	47,842	183	32	14	tco	
9372559	Kapitan Gotskiy	Rus	2008	49,597	71,228	257	34	16	tci	
9149251	Kara Sea	Lbr	1998	27,526	47,343	182	32	15	tco	
9333682	Kirill Lavrov	Cyp	2010	49,866	70,053	257	34	16	tci	
9149263	Laptev Sea	Lbr	1998	27,526	47,314	182	32	15	tco	
9256066	Ligovsky Prospect	Lbr	2003	62,586	114,639	250	44	15	tcr	
9256078	Liteyny Prospect	Lbr	2003	62,586	104,707	250	44	15	tcr	ex Stena Contender-07, Liteyny Prospect-04
9333670	Mikhail Ulyanov	Cyp	2010	49,866	69,830	257	34	16	tci	
9149249	Moscow Sea	Lbr	1998	27,526	47,363	182	32	15	tco	
9511521	Moskovsky Prospect	Lbr	2010	62,504	114,100	250	44	14	tcr	
9256925	Narodny Bridge	Lbr	2003	27,829	47,791	183	32	14	tco	
9256054	Nevskiy Prospect	Lbr	2003	62,586	114,598	250	44	15	tcr	
9610781	Nikolay Zuyev	Lbr	2012	66,818	122,039	250	46	14	tcr	
9155767	Okhotsk Sea	Lbr	1999	27,526	47,363	182	32	15	tco	
9256937	Okhta Bridge	Lbr	2004	27,829	47,000	182	32	14	tco	
9511387	Olympiysky Prospect	Lbr	2010	62,504	113,905	250	44	14	tcr	
9301380	Pavel Chernysh	Cyp	2005	60,434	103,778	247	42	14	tcr	
9186596	Petrodvorets	Lbr	1999	59,731	105,692	248	43	15	tcr	ex Astro Saturn-01
9174672	Petrokrepost	Lbr	1999	59,731	98,039	248	43	15	tcr	ex Astro Maria-01
9223344	Petropavlovsk	Lbr	2002	57,683	106,532	241	42	15	tcr	
9254915	Petrovsk	Lbr	2004	57,683	105,900	241	42	15	tcr	
9254903	Petrozavodsk	Lbr	2003	57,683	106,449	241	42	15	tcr	
	Pskov	Cyp	2014	116,000		300	46	19	lng	170,200 m³

IMO#	name	flag	year	grt	dwt	loa	bm	kts	type	former names
9511533	Primorskiy Prospect	Lbr	2010	62,504	113,860	250	44	14	tcr	
9384435	RN Archangelsk **	Cyp	2008	19,986	30,720	176	30	-	tco	ex Archangelsk-08
9384447	RN Murmansk **	Cyp	2009	19,994	30,720	176	30	-	tco	
9384459	RN Privodino **	Cyp	2009	19,994	30,720	176	30	-	tco	
9249128	Sakhalin Island	Cyp	2004	58,918	108,078	247	42	15	tcs	
9290385	SCF Aldan	Lbr	2005	81,076	159,200	274	48	15	tcr	
9224439	SCF Altai	Lbr	2001	81,085	159,169	274	48	15	tcr	
9577056	SCF Alpine	Lbr	2010	42,208	74,602	228	32	15	tco	
9333436	SCF Amur	Lbr	2007	29,844	47,095	183	32	14	tco	
6910702	SCF Arctic (st)	Lbr	1969	48,454	40,585	243	34	18	lng	71,500 m³: ex Methane Arctic-06, Arctic Tokyo-93
9422457	SCF Baikal	Lbr	2010	81,339	158,097	274	48	15	tcr	l/a SCF Vankor
9305568	SCF Baltica	Lbr	2005	65,293	117,153	250	44	15	tcr	
9290397	SCF Byrranga	Lbr	2005	81,076	159,062	274	48	15	tcr	
9224441	SCF Caucasus *	Lbr	2002	81,085	159,173	274	48	15	tcr	
9224453	SCF Khibiny	Lbr	2002	81,085	159,156	274	48	15	tcr	
	SCF Melampus	Lbr	2014	116,000		300	46	19	lng	170,200 m³
	SCF Mitre	Lbr	2015	116,000		300	46	19	lng	170,200 m³
9333400	SCF Neva	Lbr	2006	29,644	47,125	183	32	14	tco	
9577068	SCF Pacifica	Lbr	2011	42,208	74,534	228	32	15	tco	
9577109	SCF Pearl	Lbr	2011	42,208	74,552	228	32	15	tco	
9333424	SCF Pechora	Lbr	2007	29,844	47,218	183	32	14	tco	
9577070	SCF Pioneer	Lbr	2011	42,208	74,552	228	32	15	tco	
9456927	SCF Plymouth	Lbr	2011	42,208	74,606	228	32	15	tco	
6901892	SCF Polar (st)	Lbr	1969	48,454	40,586	243	34	18	lng	71,500 m³: ex Methane Polar-06, Polar Alaska-94
9577082	SCF Prime	Lbr	2011	42,208	74,581	228	32	15	tco	
9421960	SCF Primorye	Lbr	2009	84,029	158,070	274	48	16	tcr	
9577111	SCF Progress	Lbr	2012	42,208	74,588	228	32	15	tco	
9577094	SCF Provider	Lbr	2011	42,208	74,548	228	32	15	tco	
9577123	SCF Prudencia	Lbr	2012	42,208	74,565	228	32	15	tco	
9421972	SCT Samotlor	Lbr	2010	84,029	158,070	274	48	16	tcr	
9224465	SCF Sayan	Lbr	2002	81,085	159,184	274	48	15	tcr	
9120322	SCF Suek	Lbr	1998	40,538	69,100	225	32	13	bbu	ex Gianni D-09, St. Nicholas-02, l/a Kiev
9422445	SCF Surgut	Lbr	2009	81,339	158,097	274	48	15	tcr	
9324746	SCF Tobolsk	Lbr	2006	23,003	26,424	174	28	15	lpg	35,000 m³
9326598	SCF Tomsk	Lbr	2007	23,003	26,424	174	28	15	lpg	35,000 m³
9231509	SCF Ural	Lbr	2002	81,085	159,169	274	48	15	tcr	
9232864	SCF Valdai	Lbr	2003	81,085	159,313	274	48	15	tcr	
9333412	SCF Yenisei	Lbr	2007	29,844	47,187	183	32	14	tco	
	Sibur Tobol	Lbr	2013	18,300		159	26	16	lpg	20,550 m³
	Sibur Voronezh	Lbr	2013	18,300		159	26	16	lpg	20,550 m³
9522324	Suvorovsky Prospect	Lbr	2011	62,504	113,905	250	44	14	tcr	
9292060	Tavrichesky Bridge	Lbr	2006	27,725	46,697	183	32	14	tco	
9292058	Teatralny Bridge	Lbr	2006	27,725	46,697	183	32	14	tco	
9372561	Timofey Guzhenko	Rus	2009	49,597	72,722	256	34	16	tci	
9292046	Torgovy Bridge	Lbr	2005	27,725	47,363	183	32	14	tco	

OAO 'Sovcomflot' : SCF ARCTIC : *Chris Brooks*

IMO#	name	flag	year	grt	dwt	loa	bm	kts	type	former names
9292034	Tower Bridge	Lbr	2004	27,725	47,363	183	32	14	tco	
9382798	Transsib Bridge *	Lbr	2008	27,725	46,564	183	32	14	tco	
9258167	Troitskiy Bridge	Lbr	2003	27,725	41,158	183	32	14	tco	
9258179	Tuchkov Bridge	Lbr	2004	27,725	47,199	183	32	14	tco	
9344033	Tverskoy Bridge	Lbr	2007	27,725	46,564	183	32	14	tco	
9372547	Vasily Dinkov	Rus	2008	49,597	71,254	257	34	16	tci	
	Velikiy Novgorod	Cyp	2013	116,000		300	46	19	lng	170,200 m³
9301421	Victor Konetsky	Cyp	2005	60,434	101,018	247	42	15	tcs	
9610810	Viktor Bakaev	Lbr	2013	63,000	118,105	250	46		tco	
9301407	Viktor Titov	Cyp	2005	60,434	100,899	247	42	15	tcs	
9311622	Vladimir Tikhonov	Lbr	2006	87,146	162,397	281	50	15	tcr	
9301419	Yuri Senkevich	Cyp	2005	60,434	100,971	247	42	15	tcs	
9418494	Zaliv Aniva	Cyp	2009	60,325	102,946	247	42	15	tcs	

newbuildings:
Managed by Unicom Management Services (Cyprus) Ltd (originally formed in 1991 with Acomarit (30%) whose interest was acquired in 1994 - www.unicom-cy.com), by Unicom Management Services (St. Peterburg) Ltd or ** by Rosneft Joint Stock Co. † jointly owned with NYK.*
+ managed for NYK Bulkship

OAO 'Sovcomflot' : SCF URAL : *Chris Brooks*

OAO 'Sovcomflot' : TIMOFEY GUZHENKO : *ARO*

SCF Novoship J/S Co. (Novorossiysk Shipping Co), Russia

Funnel: *Blue with red and black intertwined ropes between narrow diagonal blue bands on broad diagonal white band.* **Hull:** *Black, brown or red with red boot-topping.* **History:** *Formed 1932 and controlled by the Government of The Russian Federation until privatised in 1993. Merged with Sovcomflot in 2007, but operates as a separate company.* **Web:** www.novoship.ru

IMO#	name	flag	year	grt	dwt	loa	bm	kts	type	former names
9292204	Adygeya	Lbr	2005	57,177	105,926	244	42	14	tcr	I/a Four Stream
9276030	Elbrus	Mlt	2004	29,327	46,655	183	32	14	tco	
9257993	Kaluga *	Lbr	2003	62,395	114,800	250	44	14	tcr	
9258002	Kazan **	Lbr	2003	62,395	115,727	250	44	14	tcr	
9270517	Krasnodar *	Lbr	2003	62,395	115,605	250	44	14	tcr	
9270529	Krymsk *	Lbr	2003	62,395	115,605	250	44	14	tcr	
9180279	Kuban	Lbr	2000	56,076	106,562	243	42	14	tcr	I/a Moscow Glory
9412347	Leonid Loza	Lbr	2011	83,747	156,572	274	48	15	tcr	
9165530	Moscow	Lbr	1998	56,076	106,553	243	42	15	tcr	
9166390	Moscow Kremlin	Lbr	1998	56,076	106,521	243	42	15	tcr	
9165542	Moscow River	Lbr	1999	56,075	106,552	243	42	15	tcr	
9180267	Moscow Stars	Lbr	1999	56,076	106,450	243	42	14	tcr	
9166417	Moscow University	Lbr	1999	56,076	106,521	243	42	15	tcr	
9413573	NS Africa	Lbr	2009	62,372	111,682	250	44	15	tco	
9413547	NS Arctic	Lbr	2009	62,372	111,107	250	44	15	tcr	
9413559	NS Antarctic	Lbr	2009	62,372	111,107	250	44	15	tcr	
9413561	NS Asia	Lbr	2009	62,372	111,682	250	44	15	tco	
9412335	NS Bora	Lbr	2010	83,747	156,838	274	48	15	tcr	
9412359	NS Bravo	Lbr	2010	83,747	156,694	274	48	15	tcr	
9411020	NS Burgas	Lbr	2009	83,747	156,572	274	48	15	tcr	
9341067	NS Captain *	Lbr	2006	57,248	105,926	244	42	14	tcr	
9306782	NS Century	Lbr	2006	57,248	105,926	244	42	14	tcr	
9299680	NS Challenger	Lbr	2005	57,248	105,926	244	42	14	tcr	
9299719	NS Champion	Lbr	2005	57,248	105,926	244	42	14	tcr	
9341081	NS Clipper	Lbr	2006	57,248	105,926	244	42	14	tcr	
9312884	NS Columbus	Lbr	2007	57,248	105,788	244	42	14	tcr	
9306794	NS Commander *	Lbr	2006	57,248	105,926	244	42	14	tcr	
9299707	NS Concept	Lbr	2005	57,248	105,926	244	42	14	tcr	
9299692	NS Concord	Lbr	2005	57,248	105,926	244	42	14	tcr	
9341093	NS Consul	Lbr	2006	57,248	105,926	244	42	14	tcr	
9341079	NS Corona	Lbr	2006	57,248	105,926	244	42	14	tcr	
9312896	NS Creation	Lbr	2007	57,248	105,802	244	42	14	tcr	
9609732	*NS Energy*	Lbr	2013	41,000	74,120	225	32	14	bbu	
9339325	NS Laguna	Lbr	2007	61,449	115,831	250	44	15	tcr	
9339301	NS Leader	Lbr	2007	61,449	115,857	250	44	15	tcr	
9339313	NS Lion *	Lbr	2007	61,449	115,831	250	44	15	tcr	
9339337	NS Lotus *	Lbr	2008	61,449	115,849	250	44	15	tcr	
9329667	NS Parade *	Lbr	2008	25,467	40,119	176	31	15	tco	
9328955	NS Point	Lbr	2008	25,467	40,149	176	31	15	tco	
9322968	NS Power	Lbr	2006	25,467	40,161	176	31	15	tco	
9322956	NS Pride	Lbr	2006	25,467	40,042	176	31	15	tco	
9309576	NS Silver	Lbr	2005	27,357	47,197	176	31	14	tco	
9318553	NS Spirit	Lbr	2006	27,357	46,941	176	31	14	tco	

OAO 'Sovcomflot' (SCF Novoship J/S Co.) : NS LION : *Hans Kraijenbosch*

IMO#	name	flag	year	grt	dwt	loa	bm	kts	type	former names
9309588	NS Stella	Lbr	2005	27,357	47,197	176	31	14	tco	
9318541	NS Stream	Lbr	2006	27,357	46,941	176	31	14	tco	
9609744	NS Yakutia	Lbr	2013	41,000	74,120	225	32	14	bbu	
9276028	Pamir *	Mlt	2004	29,327	46,654	183	32	14	tco	
9625956	SCF Shanghai	Lbr	2013	167,700	320,000	332	60	14	tcr	
9625968	Svet	Lbr	2013	167,700	320,000	332	60	14	tcr	
9105073	Tikhoretsk	Lbr	1996	26,218	40,791	181	32	14	tco	
9112131	Tomsk	Lbr	1997	26,218	40,703	181	32	15	tco	
9112129	Tver	Lbr	1996	26,218	40,743	181	32	15	tco	

newbuildings:
* managed by subsidiary Novoship (UK) Ltd, UK (formed 1992 - www.novoship.co.uk) ** for Bluewater Engineering BV, Netherlands.

Spar Shipping AS   Norway

Funnel: *White with white 'S' on blue spade, narrow black top.* **Hull:** *Black with red boot-topping.* **History:** *Established 1990 and commenced ship-owning in 1994.* **Web:** *www.sparshipping.com*

IMO#	name	flag	year	grt	dwt	loa	bm	kts	type	former names
9299290	Spar Canis	Nis	2006	32,474	53,565	190	32	14	bbu	
9490844	Spar Capella *	Nis	2011	32,839	58,000	190	32	14	bbu	
9497830	Spar Corona	Nis	2011	32,839	58,000	190	32	14	bbu	
9490791	Spar Corvus	Nis	2011	32,839	58,000	190	32	14	bbu	
9154608	Spar Cetus	Nis	1998	25,982	45,725	186	30	15	bbu	ex Golden Protea-02
9299305	Spar Draco *	Nis	2006	32,474	53,565	190	32	14	bbu	
9307580	Spar Gemini *	Nis	2007	32,474	53,565	190	32	14	bbu	
9490806	Spar Hydra	Nis	2011	32,839	58,000	190	32	14	bbu	
9328534	Spar Libra	Nis	2006	32,474	53,565	190	32	14	bbu	ex Bulk Navigator-11, Arya Payk-09, Bulk Navigator-06
8805169	Spar Leo *	Nis	1989	36,074	65,850	226	32	13	bbu	ex Alianthos-04, CS Elegant-99, Rubin Elegant-94, Young Senator-92
9154610	Spar Lupus	Nis	1998	25,982	45,146	186	30	15	bbu	ex Golden Aloe-02
9289025	Spar Lynx *	Nis	2005	32,474	53,565	190	32	14	bbu	
9289013	Spar Lyra *	Nis	2005	32,474	53,565	190	32	14	bbu	
9490727	Spar Mira	Nis	2010	32,839	58,000	190	32	14	bbu	
9077238	Spar Neptun	Nis	1994	36,559	70,101	225	32	15	bbu	ex Apollon-04, Gran Trader-99
9114622	Spar Orion	Nis	1996	26,449	47,639	190	31	14	bbu	ex Western Orion-01
9557111	Spar Rigel	Nis	2010	32,837	58,000	190	32	14	bbu	
9307578	Spar Scorpio *	Nis	2006	32,474	53,565	190	32	14	bbu	
9104615	Spar Sirius	Nis	1996	25,968	45,402	186	30	14	bbu	ex Western Transporter-01
9328522	Spar Spica	Nis	2005	32,474	53,565	190	32	14	bbu	ex Bulk Voyager-11, Arya Payam-09, Bulk Voyager-05, Paracan-05
9299288	Spar Taurus *	Nis	2005	32,474	53,565	190	32	14	bbu	
9490856	Spar Ursa	Nis	2011	32,838	58,000	190	32	14	bbu	
9490870	Spar Vega *	Nis	2011	32,839	58,000	190	32	14	bbu	
9299276	Spar Virgo *	Nis	2005	32,474	53,565	190	32	14	bbu	

* operate in the Supra8 Pool, formed June 2011 (www.navig8bulk.com)

Spliethoff's Bevrachtingskantoor B.V.   Netherlands

Funnel: *Orange with black 'S' on diagonally quartered white/red/orange/blue flag.* **Hull:** *Brown with white 'spliethoff', green above red boot-topping.* **History:** *Formed 1921.* **Web:** *www.spliethoff.nl*

IMO#	name	flag	year	grt	dwt	loa	bm	kts	type	former names
9420784	Damgracht	Nld	2009	13,558	18,143	157	23	17	ggc	cr: 3(120)
9420796	Danzigergracht	Nld	2009	13,558	18,143	157	23	17	ggc	cr: 3(120)
9420801	Deltagracht	Nld	2009	13,558	18,143	157	23	17	ggc	cr: 3(120)
9420813	Diamantgracht	Nld	2009	13,706	17,966	157	23	17	ggc	cr: 3(120)
9420772	Dijksgracht	Nld	2008	13,558	17,381	157	23	17	ggc	cr: 3(120)
9420825	Dolfijngracht	Nld	2009	13,706	17,967	157	23	17	ggc	cr: 3(120)
9420837	Donaugracht	Nld	2009	13,706	17,967	157	23	17	ggc	cr: 3(120)
9420849	Dynamogracht	Nld	2008	13,706	17,967	157	23	17	ggc	cr: 3(120)
9571492	Maasgracht	Nld	2011	9,524	11,749	142	19	15	ggc	
9571507	Marsgracht	Nld	2011	9,524	11,759	142	19	15	ggc	
9571519	Merwedegracht	Nld	2011	9,524	11,759	142	19	15	ggc	
9571521	Minervagracht	Nld	2011	9,524	11,759	142	19	15	ggc	
9571533	Molengracht	Nld	2012	9,524	11,744	142	19	15	ggc	
9571345	Muntgracht	Nld	2012	9,524	11,744	142	19	15	ggc	
9288069	Saimaagracht	Nld	2004	18,321	23,660	185	26	19	ggc	
9288071	Sampogracht	Nld	2005	18,321	23,688	185	26	19	ggc	
9202510	Scheldegracht	Nld	2000	16,639	21,250	168	25	19	ggc	
9197363	Schippersgracht	Ant	2000	16,641	21,402	168	25	19	ggc	
9197375	Singelgracht	Nld	2000	16,641	21,402	168	25	19	ggc	
9197947	Slotergracht	Nld	2000	16,641	21,402	168	25	19	ggc	
9202522	Sluisgracht	Nld	2001	16,639	21,250	172	25	19	ggc	
9202546	Snoekgracht	Nld	2000	16,641	21,400	168	25	19	ggc	
9202558	Spaarnegracht	Nld	2000	16,641	21,402	168	25	19	ggc	

IMO#	name	flag	year	grt	dwt	loa	bm	kts	type	former names
9197911	Spiegelgracht	Nld	2000	16,641	21,400	168	25	19	ggc	
9202534	Spuigracht	Nld	2001	16,639	21,349	172	25	19	ggc	
9202508	Stadiongracht	Nld	2000	16,639	21,250	172	25	19	ggc	
9288045	Statengracht	Nld	2004	16,676	21,250	173	26	19	ggc	
9288057	Suomigracht	Nld	2004	18,321	23,660	185	26	19	ggc	

also owns Ro-Ro's and smaller vessels operating in coastal trades.

BigLift Shipping B.V., Netherlands

Funnel: *Yellow with black 'BigLift'.* **Hull:** *Yellow with blue 'BigLift', red or black boot-topping.* **History:** *Formed 1973 by Nedlloyd Groep NV as Mammoet Shipping BV, joint venture as Mammoet-Hansa AG from 1989, Spliethoff's gained control in 1995, renamed 2000.* **Web:** *www.bigliftshipping.com*

IMO#	name	flag	year	grt	dwt	loa	bm	kts	type	former names
9153898	Da Fu **	Pan	1998	14,021	16,957	153	23	15	ghl	
9153886	Da Hua **	Pan	1998	14,021	16,957	153	23	15	ghl	
9153903	Da Qiang **	Pan	1998	14,021	16,957	153	23	15	ghl	
9153874	Da Zhong **	Pan	1998	14,021	16,957	153	23	15	ghl	
9148116	Han Yi *	Sgp	1998	10,990	16,069	138	23	15	ghl	ex Enchanter-11, Sailer Jupiter-98
8300389	Happy Buccaneer (2)	Nld	1984	16,341	13,740	146	28	15	ghl	cr: 2(700)
9551935	Happy Delta	Nld	2011	14,784	18,276	157	26	16	ghl	cr: 1(120),2(400)
9551947	Happy Diamond	Nld	2011	14,784	18,148	157	26	16	ghl	cr: 1(120),2(400)

Spliethoffs Bevrachtingskantoor B.V. : DANZIGERGRACHT : *Hans Kraijenbosch*

Spliethoffs Bevrachtingskantoor B.V. : SAMPOGRACHT : *ARO*

IMO#	name	flag	year	grt	dwt	loa	bm	kts	type	former names
9551959	Happy Dover	Nld	2011	14,784	18,074	157	26	16	ghl	cr: 1(120),2(400)
9551961	Happy Dragon	Nld	2011	14,784	18,103	157	26	16	ghl	cr: 1(120),2(400)
9551973	Happy Dynamic	Nld	2011	14,784	18,043	157	26	16	ghl	cr: 1(120),2(400)
9139311	Happy Ranger	Nld	1997	10,990	12,950	138	23	16	ghl	cr: 2(400)
9139294	Happy River	Nld	1997	10,990	12,950	138	23	16	ghl	cr: 2(400)
9139309	Happy Rover	Nld	1997	10,950	12,950	138	23	16	ghl	cr: 2(400)
9457220	*Happy Sky*	Nld	2013	15,000	18,680	155	27	16	ghl	cr: 2(900)
9457232	*Happy Star*	Nld	2013	15,000	16,860	155	27	16	ghl	cr: 2(900)

* owned by Pool member Mitsui OSK Lines Ltd (managed by New Asian Shipping Co. Ltd, Hong Kong) qv or ** by Guangzhou Ocean Shipping (COSCO), China.

Siem Industries Inc.   Norway

Star Reefers Shipowning

Funnel: *White with red Siem logo beneath blue top, or operators colours.* **Hull:** *Lilac grey, white or blue with blue waterline over red boot-topping.* **History:** *Founded 1909 as Vestey Brothers, renamed Blue Star Line Ltd in 1911. Blue Star Ship Management Ltd. formed 1974. Vestey Group sold container business and Austasia Line subsidiary to P&O in 1998 (later to become Blue Star Holdings) and the reefers in 2001 to Swan Reefer ASA, which was a 1998 amalgamation of Irgens Larsen (formerly Rederiet Helge R Myhre to 1992 and Kvaerner Shipping AS (formed 1955) to 1995) and Swan Shipping A/S (formed 1989) before being renamed in 2001 and acquired by Siem Industries in 2002.* **Web:** *www.star-reefers.com*

IMO#	name	flag	year	grt	dwt	loa	bm	kts	type	former names
8713562	Afric Star	Lbr	1990	11,590	12,683	159	24	18	grf	ex Tundra Consumer-04, Del Monte Consumer-00
8816156	Almeda Star	Bhs	1990	11,658	12,714	159	24	20	grf	ex Tundra King-05, Del Monte Pride-91
8816170	Andalucia Star	Bhs	1991	11,658	12,714	159	24	20	grf	ex Tundra Princess-05, Del Monte Spirit-91
8816168	Avelona Star	Bhs	1991	11,658	12,714	159	24	20	grf	ex Tundra Queen-05, Del Monte Quality-91
8713550	Avila Star	Lbr	1990	11,590	12,519	159	24	18	grf	ex Tundra Trader-04, Del Monte Trader-99
9019119	Cape Town Star *	Bhs	1993	10,614	10,629	150	23	21	grf	ex Caribbean Reef-03, Hornbreeze-98, Geestcrest-95, Hornbreeze-95, Caribbean Universal-94
9150810	Caribbean Star *	Lbr	1997	11,435	10,362	154	24	20	grf	ex Hornsea-00, Caribbean Star-98
9017276	Chile Star	Lbr	1993	10,629	10,620	150	23	21	grf	ex Polar Chile-05, Trajan-96
9172480	Colombian Star	Pan	1998	11,733	10,371	154	24	21	grf	
9150822	Costa Rican Star *	Lbr	1998	11,435	10,350	154	24	21	grf	ex Hornwind-02, Costa Rican Star-98
9172458	Cote d'Ivoirian Star	Pan	1998	11,733	10,350	154	24	21	grf	
9038945	Dunedin Star *	Bmu	1994	8,665	11,793	151	20	22	grf	ex Chiquita Joy-06, Joy-00, Chiquita Joy-97
9019121	Durban Star *	Bhs	1993	10,614	10,629	150	23	20	grf	ex Coral Reef-03, Horncloud-98, Geesttide-95, Horncloud-94, Coral Universal-94
8814299	Ecuador Star	Lbr	1992	10,629	10,452	150	23	21	grf	ex Polar Ecuador-05, Justinian-96
8906975	Honduras Star	Lbr	1992	10,629	10,593	150	23	21	grf	ex Polar Colombia-05, Appian-95
9053658	Regal Star *	Bhs	1993	10,375	10,520	150	23	20	grf	ex Tauu-96, Hornstrait-95, Chiquita Tauu-94
9206061	Solent Star	Lbr	2001	10,804	9,709	150	23	21	grf	
9206059	Southampton Star	Lbr	1999	10,804	9,709	150	23	21	grf	
9350989	Star Best †	Sgp	2007	14,030	13,191	163	26	22	grf	
9517903	Star Care †	Sgp	2009	14,022	13,300	163	26	22	grf	
9517927	Star Endeavour I †	Sgp	2010	14,022	12,967	163	26	22	grf	ex Star Endeavour-11
9330056	Star First †	Sgp	2006	14,030	13,202	163	26	22	grf	

Siem Industries Inc. (Star Reefers) : COLOMBIAN STAR : *ARO*

IMO#	name	flag	year	grt	dwt	loa	bm	kts	type	former names
9517939	Star Leader †	Sgp	2010	14,022	12,944	163	26	22	grf	
9517915	Star Pride †	Sgp	2009	14,022	12,955	163	26	22	grf	
9338747	Star Prima †	Sgp	2006	14,030	13,189	163	26	22	grf	
9438494	Star Quality †	Sgp	2009	14,030	13,193	163	26	22	grf	
9438482	Star Service I †	Spg	2008	14,030	13,207	163	26	22	grf	ex Star Service-11
9438509	Star Standard †	Sgp	2009	14,030	13,201	163	26	22	grf	
9350991	Star Stratos †	Sgp	2007	14,030	13,186	163	26	22	grf	
9438511	Star Trust †	Sgp	2009	14,030	13,189	162	26	22	grf	
8917596	Timaru Star	Bmu	1993	8,665	11,793	151	20	20	grf	ex Chiquita Brenda-05, Brenda-00, Chiquita Brenda-97, Chiquita Joy-93
9017264	Uruguay Star	Lbr	1993	10,629	10,593	150	23	21	grf	ex Polar Uruguay-05, Hadrian-96
8917584	Wellington Star	Bhs	1992	7,944	11,103	141	20	21	grf	ex Bothnian Reefer-03

*vessels managed by Star Reefers Poland Sp z.oo, Poland or * Star Reefers UK Ltd.*
   † chartered from Grace Ocean Pte. Ltd., Hong Kong

Siem Thoen Car Carriers AS
Funnel: *White with red Siem logo, narrow blue band beneath red top.* **Hull**: *grey or blue with blue waterline over red boot topping.*
History: *Founded.* **Web**: *Siemshipping.com*

IMO#	name	flag	year	grt	dwt	loa	bm	kts	type	
9427940	CSAV Rio Blanco	Lbr	2010	47,057	11,760	182	32	20	mve	5,013 ceu
9177040	Dresden	Pan	2000	37,237	12,743	178	31	20	mve	3,919 ceu
9431836	Höegh Beijing	Nis	2010	47,232	12,250	181	32	20	mve	4,910 ceu
9460899	Ocean Challenger	Sgp	2010	60,213	18,671	200	32	20	mve	6,330 ceu
9190858	Verona	Pan	2000	37,237	12,778	178	31	20	mve	3,919 ceu

Starship Constellation Group   Monaco

International Andromeda Shipping SAM
Funnel: *Grey with 5-pointed star (of colour to match name) superimposed on white 'A'.* **Hull**: *Black with red boot-topping.*
History: *Founded 1992.* **Web**: *www.andromeda-shipping.com*

IMO#	name	flag	year	grt	dwt	loa	bm	kts	type	former names
9290830	Emerald Stars	Nis	2005	23,298	37,270	183	27	14	tco	ex Emerald Star-10, Emerald-05
9217448	Green Stars	Nis	2001	23,682	35,858	183	27	14	tco	ex Green Star- British Enterprise-06, I/a Indigo Star
9433597	Orange Stars	Mhl	2011	61,314	115,756	249	44	14	tcr	
9433585	Pink Stars	Mhl	2010	61,314	115,592	249	44	14	tcr	
9290828	Scarlet Star	Nis	2005	23,298	37,252	183	27	14	tco	

Stena AB   Sweden

Funnel: *White 'S' on wide red band separated from narrow blue top and black base by narrow white bands.* **Hull**: *Black or dark blue. with red boot-topping (Stena C series (†) with Stena Weco' in white, Stena P series with 'Stena Bulk' in white and P max in red/white or (Shuttle tankers) red with 'Stena Teekay' in black, red boot-topping: LNG tankers - light blue with 'Stena Bulk LNG' in white and Dragon's head).* **History**: *Founded 1939 as Sten A Olsson Handels A/B to 1963, then Stena Line A/B to 1977. Concordia Maritime AB (formed 1984), jointly owned with Neste, took over Universe Tankships (Delaware) LLC in 1996.* **Web**: *www.stena.com*

IMO#	name	flag	year	grt	dwt	loa	bm	kts	type	former names
9152507	Stena Alexita (2) ‡	Nor	1998	76,836	127,466	263	46	15	tcs	
9322827	Stena Antarctica **	Cym	2006	61,371	114,849	250	44	15	tcr	ex Four Antarctica-06
9322839	Stena Atlantica **	Cym	2006	61,371	114,896	250	44	15	tcr	ex Four Atlantica-06

Siem Industries Inc. (Star Reefers) : STAR PRIDE : *Hans Kraijenbosch*

IMO#	name	flag	year	grt	dwt	loa	bm	kts	type	former names
9315393	Stena Blue Sky [st]	Pan	2006	97,754	84,363	285	43	20	lng	145,700 m³; ex Bluesky-11
9282625	Stena Chiron	Bhs	2005	40,690	72,825	229	32	14	tcr	ex Daedalos-08
9283617	Stena Chronos	Bhs	2004	40,690	72,829	229	32	14	tcr	ex Ikaros-09
9283629	Stena Callas	Bhs	2004	40,690	72,854	229	32	14	tcr	ex Aspropyrgos-09
9272204	Stena Concept †	Bmu	2005	27,357	47,171	183	32	14	tco	
9258595	Stena Concert †	Bmu	2004	27,463	47,288	183	32	14	tco	ex Stena Italica-08
9252425	Stena Conqueror †	Bmu	2003	27,335	47,323	183	32	14	tco	l/a Hellenica
9252436	Stena Conquest †	Ita	2003	27,335	47,136	183	32	14	tco	ex Hispanica-03
9272199	Stena Contest †	Bmu	2005	27,357	47,171	183	32	15	tco	
9413327	Stena Clear Sky [df]	Bmu	2011	109,949	96,811	298	46	20	lng	173,593 m³: l/a Crystal Sky
9383900	Stena Crystal Sky [df]	Bmu	2011	109,949	96,889	298	46	20	lng	173,611 m³: l/a Clear Sky
9379131	FR8 Fortitude	Mhl	2007	29,597	46,763	183	32	14	tco	ex Stena FR8 2-12, FR8 Fortitude-07
9206671	Stena Natalita (2) ‡	Bhs	2001	62,393	108,073	250	43	14	tcs	
9299123	Stena Paris *	Bmu	2005	36,064	65,125	290	40	14	tco	
9391476	Stena Penguin *	Bmu	2010	36,168	64,834	290	40	14	tco	
9299159	Stena Performance *	Bmu	2006	36,064	65,125	290	40	14	tco	
9312456	Stena Perros *	Bmu	2007	36,168	65,086	290	40	14	tco	
9390032	Stena Polaris *	Bmu	2010	36,168	64,917	290	40	14	tco	
9413523	Stena Premium *	Bmu	2011	36,168	67,055	290	40	14	tco	
9312444	Stena President *	Bmu	2007	36,168	65,112	290	40	14	tco	
9299147	Stena Primorsk *	Lbr	2006	36,064	65,125	290	40	14	tco	
9390020	Stena Progress *	Bmu	2009	36,064	65,125	290	40	14	tco	

Starship Constellation Gp., (International Andromeda Shg.) : EMERALD STARS : *Tom Walker*

Stena AB (Stena Bulk AB) : STENA CHIRON : *M. Lennon*

IMO#	name	flag	year	grt	dwt	loa	bm	kts	type	former names
9299135	Stena Provence *	Bmu	2006	36,168	65,125	290	40	14	tco	
9188099	Stena Sirita (2) ‡	Nor	1999	77,410	127,466	263	46	15	tcs	
9579042	Stena Suede	Bmu	2011	81,187	159,158	274	48	14	tcr	
9592214	Stena Sunrise	Bmu	2013	81,187	159,034	274	48	14	tcr	
9579030	Stena Superior	Bmu	2011	81,187	159,236	274	48	14	tcr	
9585895	Stena Supreme	Bmu	2012	81,187	159,031	274	48	14	tcr	

newbuildings:
* operated by affiliate Concordia Maritime AB and managed by Northern Marine Management Ltd, UK (www.nmm-stena.com)
** on charter from Premuda SpA, Italy and managed by Northern Marine Management Ltd or † operated by Stena Weco (established as j/v with Weco, subsidiary of Dannebrog). ‡ jointly owned with Ugland Marine Services AS and managed by Standard Marine Tonsberg AS, Norway. Also see Neste Oil Corporation

Stolt-Nielsen Transportation Group Ltd. U.S.A.

Funnel: White with large white 'S' on red square, narrow black top. **Hull:** Yellow with black 'STOLT TANKERS', red or pink boot-topping. **History:** Founded 1886 as subsidiary of Stolt-Nielsen SA, Luxembourg (founded 1891), B Stolt-Nielsen & Co to 1931, B Stolt-Nielsen & Sonner A/S to 1961, Jacob Stolt-Nielsen A/S to 1970, Stolt-Nielsen Rederi A/S to 1999, when Stolt Tankers BV was relocated from Norway to Netherlands and Stolt-Nielsen Transportation Group BV to 2007. **Web:** www.stolt-nielsen.com

IMO#	name	flag	year	grt	dwt	loa	bm	kts	type	former names
9351543	Basuto ‡	Sgp	2006	16,442	25,196	159	26	15	tco	ex Stolt Basuto-10
9311012	Glory	Lbr	2005	20,059	33,302	174	28	15	tco	ex Stolt Glory-10
9124469	Stolt Achievement (me)	Cym	1999	25,427	37,000	177	31	16	tco	
9360934	Stolt Ami #	Pan	2006	11,708	19,963	144	24		tco	
8309529	Stolt Aquamarine	Cym	1986	23,964	38,746	177	32	15	tco	
9511167	Stolt Bobcat	Lbr	2009	13,517	23,432	155	25	15	tco	ex Golden Legend-11
9414084	Stolt Breland	Nld	2010	25,841	43,475	183	32	-	tco	
9102124	Stolt Capability (me) *	Lbr	1998	24,625	37,042	177	31	16	tco	
9168647	Stolt Commitment	Cym	2000	23,206	37,438	183	32	16	tco	ex Bow Century-11
9178197	Stolt Concept (me)	Cym	1999	24,495	37,236	177	31	16	tco	
9102071	Stolt Confidence (me)	Cym	1996	24,625	37,015	177	31	16	tco	
9296731	Stolt Courage	Lbr	2004	20,058	32,329	174	28	15	tco	
9102095	Stolt Creativity (me)	Cym	1997	24,625	37,271	177	31	16	tco	
9102112	Stolt Efficiency (me)	Cym	1998	24,625	37,271	177	31	16	tco	
9178202	Stolt Effort (me)	Cym	1999	24,495	37,155	177	31	16	tco	
8909543	Stolt Emerald	Cym	1986	23,964	38,719	177	32	15	tco	
9284697	Stolt Endurance	Lbr	2004	20,058	32,306	174	28	15	tco	
9359363	Stolt Facto +	Cym	2008	26,328	46,011	183	32	-	tco	
9214305	Stolt Focus	Cym	2001	23,190	37,467	183	32	16	tco	ex Bow Favour-11
9414072	Stolt Groenland	Cym	2009	25,881	43,478	183	32		tco	
9359399	Stolt Gulf Mirdif +	Cym	2010	26,329	46,011	183	32		tco	
9359387	Stolt Gulf Mishref +	Cym	2010	26,329	46.089	183	32	-	tco	ex Stolt Pluto-10
8906925	Stolt Helluland	Cym	1990	18,994	31,454	175	30	15	tco	
8819093	Stolt Hill	Cym	1992	22,620	40,159	176	32	14	tco	ex Montana Star-06, Star Sapphire-02
9102069	Stolt Innovation (me)	Cym	1996	24,625	36,896	177	31	16	tco	
9102083	Stolt Inspiration (me)	Cym	1997	24,625	37,205	177	31	16	tco	
9102100	Stolt Invention (me) *	Lbr	1998	24,625	37,271	177	31	16	tco	
9414058	Stolt Island	Cym	2008	25,834	43,593	183	32	-	tco	
8320119	Stolt Jade	Cym	1986	23,964	38,746	177	32	15	tco	

Stena AB (Stena Bulk AB) : STENA PROVENCE : *ARO*

IMO#	name	flag	year	grt	dwt	loa	bm	kts	type	former names
8906937	Stolt Markland	Cym	1991	18,994	31,433	175	30	15	tco	
9425980	Stolt Megami #	Mhl	2008	12,099	19,997	148	24		tco	
9005390	Stolt Mountain	Cym	1994	22,620	40,024	176	32	14	tco	ex Montana Sun-06, Sun Sapphire-02
9414060	Stolt Norland	Cym	2009	25,841	37,141	183	32	-	tco	
9124471	Stolt Perseverance (me)	Cym	2000	25,196	37,059	177	31	16	tco	
9374521	Stolt Pondo ‡	Pan	2007	19,380	33,232	170	27	14	tco	ex Pondo-12, Stolt Pondo-10
9352200	Stolt Sagaland	Cym	2008	25,841	44,044	183	32	-	tco	
8309531	Stolt Sapphire *	Lbr	1986	23,964	38,746	177	32	15	tco	
9149495	Stolt Sea (me)	Cym	1999	14,742	22,198	163	24	15	tco	
9359375	Stolt Sisto +	Cym	2010	26,329	46,011	183	32	-	tco	
9352212	Stolt Sneland	Cym	2008	25,841	44,080	183	32	-	tco	
9149524	Stolt Span (me) *	Lbr	1998	14,775	22,273	163	24	15	tco	
9168611	Stolt Spray (me)	Cym	2000	14,180	22,460	163	24	15	tco	
9169940	Stolt Stream (me)	Cym	2000	14,180	22,199	163	24	15	tco	
9149512	Stolt Sun (me)	Cym	2000	14,900	22,210	163	24	15	tco	
9168623	Stolt Surf (me)	Cym	2000	14,900	22,198	163	24	15	tco	
9358644	Stolt Swazi ‡	Pan	2007	11,676	19,996	144	24	15	tco	
8309555	Stolt Topaz	Cym	1986	23,964	38,818	177	32	15	tco	
9274305	Stolt Vanguard #	Lbr	2004	15,711	25,261	159	26	15	tco	
8911669	Stolt Vestland	Cym	1992	19,034	31,494	175	30	15	tco	
9196711	Stolt Viking (me)	Cym	2001	16,754	26,707	166	27	15	tco	ex Isola Blu-05, l/a Isola Verde
8911657	Stolt Vinland	Cym	1992	19,034	31,434	175	30	15	tco	
9274317	Stolt Virtue #	Sgp	2004	15,715	25,230	159	26	15	tco	
9274329	Stolt Vision #	Sgp	2005	15,976	25,147	159	26	15	tco	
9351531	Stolt Zulu ‡	Sgp	2006	16,442	25,197	159	26	15	tco	
9311024	Strength	Lbr	2005	20,059	33,209	174	28	15	tco	ex Stolt Strength-10

newbuildings: five x 38,000dwt product tankers [Hudong Zhonghua (2015)]
*managed by Stolt Tankers BV, Netherlands. * owned by NYK Stolt Tankers SA (formed jointly in 2000 with NYK, Japan)*
+ Gulf Stolt Tankers, # time chartered by Stolt-Nielsen ‡ time chartered to Unicorn Tankers

Avance Gas Holding Ltd., Norway

History: *Stolt-Nielsen Gas formed 2007, established Avance Gas as it's operating company in 2009. SNG merged its assets with Sungas Holdings Ltd. in 2010 and then with Transpetrol in 2012*

IMO#	name	flag	year	grt	dwt	loa	bm	kts	type	former names
9364382	Iris Glory	Pan	2008	48,425	54,707	226	37	17	lpg	83,700 m³
9387750	Progress	Cym	2009	47,266	58,560	225	37	17	lpg	80,793 m³
9354935	Promise	Mlt	2009	47,276	54,984	226	37	17	lpg	83,800 m³; ex Maran Gas Knossos-12, l/d Knossos Gas
9387762	Prospect	Cym	2009	47,266	58,551	225	37	17	lpg	80,797 m³
9350599	Providence	Mlt	2008	47,276	54,784	226	37	17	lpg	83,800 m³; ex Maran Gas Vergina-12, l/a Vergina Gas
9364394	Thetis Glory	Pan	2008	48,425	54,707	226	37	17	lpg	83,700 m³
9238284	Stolt Avance	Cym	2003	46,393	53,677	227	36	17	lpg	82,500 m³. ex Althea Gas-10
9393682	Venus Glory	Pan	2008	48,654	54,474	226	37	17	lpg	83,700 m³

Stolt-Nielsen Transportation Group : GLORY : *Hans Kraijenbosch*

Suisse-Atlantique Soc. de Navigation Maritime S.A. Switzerland

Funnel: *Black with red diagonal cross and two stars on yellow houseflag interrupting two yellow bands.* **Hull:** *Black or grey with red boot-topping.* **History:** *Founded 1941 as Société de Navigation Maritime Suisse-Atlantique to 1956, then Soc d'Armement Maritime Suisse-Atlantique to 1986.* **Web:** *www.suisat.com*

IMO#	name	flag	year	grt	dwt	loa	bm	kts	type	former names
9176759	Celerina	Che	1999	39,161	73,035	225	32	14	bbu	
9583706	Charmey	Che	2011	22,697	34,275	181	30	14	bbu	
9176747	Corviglia	Che	1999	39,161	73,035	225	32	14	bbu	
9177648	General Guisan	Che	1999	39,161	73,035	225	32	14	bbu	
9542817	Lavaux	Che	2010	22,697	34,000	181	30	14	bbu	
9294161	Maersk Juan	Che	2005	28,592	39,384	221	30	23	ucc	2,824 teu: ex Jaun-05
8311737	Maersk Jenaz	Che	2005	28,911	39,384	221	30	23	ucc	2,824 teu: ex Jenaz-05
9542831	Moleson	Che	2010	22,697	34,266	181	30	14	bbu	
9177650	Nyon	Che	1999	39,161	73,035	225	32	14	bbu	
9542829	Romandie	Che	2010	22,697	34,348	181	30	14	bbu	
9253002	Sils	Che	2003	27,779	40,878	221	30	22	ucc	2,824 teu: ex Norasia Sils-06, Sils-03
9276743	Silvaplana	Che	2003	17,951	29,721	171	27	14	bbu	ex F.D. Clara d'Amato-07, Benedetta d'Amato-06
9276779	Silvretta	Che	2003	17,951	29,721	171	27	14	bbu	ex F.D. Umberto d'Amato-07, Umberto d'Amato-07
9583691	Vully	Che	2011	22,697	34,000	181	30	14	bbu	

John Swire & Sons Ltd. U.K.

The China Navigation Co. Ltd., Hong Kong (China)

Funnel: *Black with diagonally quartered houseflag (white top/bottom, red sides, central vertical blue line).* **Hull:** *Black some with white 'INDOTRANS', red, grey or pink boot-topping.* **History:** *Parent founded 1816 and China Navigation formed 1872. The Bank Line services acquired 2003 (see under Andrew Weir).* **Web:** *www.swire.com or www.cnco.com.hk*

IMO#	name	flag	year	grt	dwt	loa	bm	kts	type	former names
8100997	Erawan	Iom	1982	35,716	64,643	225	32	13	btv	ex Camarina-99, Starfest-95, Yamashiro Maru-90
9003847	Changsha *	Hkg	1991	18,391	23,737	185	28	18	ggc	ex Pacific Mariner-11, Pacific Adventurer-09, Changsha-05, Pacific Challenger-99
9003835	Chekiang *	Hkg	1991	18,391	23,271	185	28	18	ggc	ex Pacific Voyager-11, Chekiang-05, Atlantic Challenger-99
9007374	Chenan	Hkg	1992	18,391	25,554	185	28	18	ggc	ex Pacific Discoverer-12, Tasman Chief-07, Chenan-05, Andes Challenger-99
9007362	Chengtu	Hkg	1991	18,391	25,661	185	28	18	ggc	ex Pacific Explorer-11, Chengtu-05, Asian Challenger-99
9595967	Emerald	Hkg	2012	24,195	37,200	190	28	14	bbu	
9103116	Kwangsi	Hkg	1995	18,468	23,783	185	28	19	ggc	ex Tasman Mariner-11, PacificPathfinder-09, Tasman Mariner-09, Delmas Blosseville-04, Tropical Challenger-03, Delmas Blosseville-02, Tropical Challenger-99
9070709	Kwangtung	Hkg	1994	18,451	23,683	185	28	19	ggc	ex Tasman Provider-11, Meridian Challenger-03, Delmas Forbin-02, Meridian Challenger-00
9103104	Kweilin	Hkg	1995	18,468	23,586	185	28	19	ggc	ex Tasman Commander-11, Oceanic Challenger-04, Delmas Joinville-02, Oceanic Challenger-01,
9070694	Kweichow	Hkg	1994	18,451	23,000	185	28	19	ggc	ex Tasman Endeavour-11, Caribbean Challenger-03
9614476	Shansi	Sgp	2013	25,483	31,000	200	28	15	gmp	2,028 teu

newbuildings: further 7 x 31,000dwt multipurpose cargo ships (2013), Shantung, Shaoshing, Shengking, Shuntian, Siagtan, Soochow, Szcechuan.

8 x 39,500dwt geared bulkers [CSSC Chengxi Shipyard] (late 2013-2014), Wanlui, Wantung, Wanyi, Wanyuan, Wuchang, Wuchow, Wuhu, Wulin.

* owned by Swire Navigation Co Ltd, Hong Kong.

Technomar Shipping Inc. Greece

Funnel: *Light blue with two yellow parallel horizontal lines and capital 'T' or charterer's colours.* **Hull:** *Black with red boot-topping or charterer's colours.* **History:**

IMO#	name	flag	year	grt	dwt	loa	bm	kts	type	former names
9349605	Agios Dimitrios	Grc	2011	74,175	85,701	299	40	25	ucc	6,572 teu: l/a Fourth Ocean
9635676	Alexandra	Mhl	2013	71,021	27,042	270	42		ucc	6,900 teu
9275361	Athena	Pan	2003	34,610	43,093	235	32	22	ucc	2,762 teu: ex OOCL Xiamen-11
9318125	CMA CGM Dolphin	Pan	2007	54,309	65,980	294	33	25	ucc	5,040 teu
9318113	CMA CGM Orca	Pan	2006	54,309	65,890	294	33	25	ucc	5,040 teu
9280641	CMA CGM Strauss	Lbr	2004	65,247	73,235	277	40	24	ucc	5,770 teu
9280653	CMA CGM Verdi	Lbr	2004	65,247	73,235	277	40	24	ucc	5,770 teu

IMO#	name	flag	year	grt	dwt	loa	bm	kts	type	former names
9121247	Dimitris Y	Lbr	1996	31,131	38,650	210	32	22	ucc	2,682 teu: ex Pommern-12, Kota Pusaka-12, Pommern-10, Kota Pusaka-09 Pommern-02, P&O Nedlloyd Unity-01, Pommern-97, Sea Excellence-97, Pommern-96
9129823	Eleni I	Lbr	1996	16,165	22,250	168	27	21	ucc	1,608 teu: ex Warnow Trader-12, MOL Agility-09, Warnow Trader-06, CMA CGM Springbok-06, Warnow Trader-03, Libra Valencia-99, Warnow Trader-96
9102306	Japan	Hkg	1996	66,046	67,752	276	40	24	ucc	5,344 teu; ex OOCL Japan-11
8905543	Maersk Tangier	Mlt	1990	17,700	21,238	161	28	18	ucc	1,316 teu: ex Torben Maersk-07
8820212	Maersk Tarragona	Lbr	1990	17,700	21,229	161	28	18	ucc	1,316 teu: ex Tobias Maersk-07, TRSL Antares-96, Tobias Maersk-95
8820200	Maersk Torino	Lbr	1990	17,700	21,229	161	28	18	ucc	1,316 teu: ex Trein Maersk-07, TRSL Arcturus-97, Trein Maersk-95
8820224	Maersk Trapani	Lbr	1990	17,700	21,238	161	28	18	ucc	1,316 teu: ex Thorkil Maersk-07, CMA CGM Hispaniola-06, Marienborg-04, Thorkil Maersk-00
9203502	Maira	Pan	2000	25,294	32,308	207	30	22	ucc	2,506 teu: ex Santa Annabella-10, P&O Nedlloyd Agulhas-05, MOL Paraguay-02, P&O Nedlloyd Agulhas-01, Santa Annabella-00
9121259	Mamitsa	Lbr	1996	31,131	38,650	210	32	22	ucc	2,682 teu: ex Potsdam -12, Kota Pelangi-11, Potsdam-10, Kota Pelangi-09, Potsdam-02, Ipex Emperor-99, Sea Elegance-97, Potsdam-96
9635664	Mary	Mhl	2013	71,021	80,274	270	42		ucc	6,900 teu
9122605	Melina	Pan	1995	58,923	61,489	300	37	23	ucc	4,706 teu: ex Swan-10, MOL Mosel-09, APL Qingdao-08, MOL Mosel-02, Mosel-00
9209104	Newyorker	Pan	2001	25,294	32,299	207	30	22	ucc	2,506 teu: ex Santa Alina-10, P&O Nedlloyd Apapa-05, MOL Santos-02, P&O Nedlloyd Apapa-01, I/a Santa Alina
9203526	Nikolas	Lbr	2000	25,294	32,391	207	30	22	ucc	2,506 teu: ex Santa Alexandra-09, CMA CGM Okume-09, Santa Alexandra-08, P&O Nedlloyd Abidjan-05, MOL San Paulo-02, P&O Nedlloyd Abidjan-01, Santa Alexandra-00
9102318	OOCL Britain	Hkg	1996	66,046	67,958	276	40	24	ucc	5,344 teu
9143075	OOCL Netherlands	Hkg	1997	66,086	67,473	276	40	24	ucc	5,344 teu
9122203	Pisti	Pan	1996	31,207	38,400	210	32	22	ucc	2,890 teu: Tara-10, Nautic-10, Norasia Telamon-07, Telamon-04, Contship Ambition-03, Telamon-02
9143063	Singapore	Hkg	1997	66,086	67,473	276	41	24	ucc	5,390 teu: ex OOCL Singapore-11
9155389	YM Dalian	Pan	2000	18,335	23,577	176	27	20	ucc	1,740 teu: ex Anthea-12, YM Dalian-12, Anthea-11, Hansa Sonderburg-10, CP Kestrel-06, Direct Kestrel-05, Hansa Sonderburg-01

newbuildings: 2 x 6,900 teu container ships (Hyundai Samho, 2013)

Teekay Corporation   Bahamas

Funnel: *White with blue edged red 'TK' symbol, narrow black top.* **Hull:** *Black with red boot-topping.* **History:** *Founded 1973 by Torben Karlshoej, as Teekay Shipping Co Inc, Canada to 1990, then Western Marine Agencies to 1991. Formed Teekay Shipping (Australia) Pty Ltd in 1998 on acquisition of Caltex Petroleum's Australian Tankships Pty Ltd (formed by 1996 merger of Ampol Ltd (founded 1936 as Australian Motorists Petrol Co Ltd to 1949, formerly Ampol Petroleum Ltd to 1982) and Caltex Tanker Co (Australia) Pty Ltd (formed 1972 as Botany Bay Tanker Co (Australia) Pty Ltd to 1985). Teekay Marine Services GmbH, Germany formed 2003. Acquired Naviera F Tapias SA in 2004, which had been a Spanish subsidiary of AP Moller to 1991 (formed 1988). In 2007 acquired 50% of OMI (founded 1962 as Ogden Marine Inc and spun-off from Ogden Corp. in 1984 as OMI Corp, subsidiary being formed in 1998).* **Web:** www.teekay.com

IMO#	name	flag	year	grt	dwt	loa	bm	kts	type	former names
9250737	African Spirit	Bhs	2003	79,668	151,736	269	46	-	tcr	
9325697	Al Areesh (st)	Bhs	2007	99,106	90,617	288	43	20	lng	151,700 m³
9325702	Al Daayen (st)	Bhs	2007	99,106	90,617	288	43	20	lng	151,700 m³
9360879	Al Huwaila (st)	Bhs	2008	135,848	109,503	315	50	20	lng	217,000 m³
9360881	Al Kharsaah (st)	Bhs	2008	135,848	109,484	315	50	20	lng	217,000 m³
9360908	Al Khuwair (st)	Bhs	2008	135,848	109,555	315	50	20	lng	217,000 m³
9325685	Al Marrouna (st)	Bhs	2007	99,106	90,617	288	43	20	lng	151,700 m³
9360893	Al Shamal (st)	Bhs	2008	135,848	107,500	315	50	20	lng	217,000 m³
9326524	Alexander Spirit †	Bhs	2007	25,382	40,083	175	31	14	tco	ex Miss Marina-09
9207027	Algeciras Spirit +	Cni	2000	83,724	160,240	274	48	15	tcr	ex Nuria Tapias-04
9247443	Americas Spirit	Bhs	2003	63,213	111,920	256	45	-	tcr	I/dn Limerick Spirit
9001784	Arctic Spirit (st)	Bhs	1993	55,174	48,857	239	40	18	lng	89,880 m³: ex Arctic Sun-07
9247431	Asian Spirit	Bhs	2004	79,668	151,693	269	46	15	tcr	
9239484	Ashkini Spirit *	Bhs	2003	84,789	165,010	274	50	15	tcr	ex Ingeborg-07, Aegean Lady-04

IMO#	name	flag	year	grt	dwt	loa	bm	kts	type	former names
9247455	Australian Spirit	Bhs	2004	63,213	111,942	256	45	15	tcr	
9282041	Axel Spirit	Bhs	2004	62,929	115,392	250	44	15	tcr	
9186651	Bahamas Spirit	Bhs	1996	57,947	107,261	247	42	17	tcr	ex Sanko Trader-01
9411226	Bermuda Spirit *	Bhs	2009	81,384	158,769	274	48		tcr	
9236420	Catalunya Spirit (st)	Cni	2003	90,835	72,204	284	43	19	lng	138,000 m³: ex Inigo Tapias-04
9191333	Constitution Spirit *	Mhl	1999	58,288	104,623	243	42		tcr	ex Constitution-08
9390628	Dilong Spirit *	Bhs	2009	85,037	159,021	275	45		tcr	
9312846	Donegal Spirit *	Bhs	2006	57,325	105,611	244	42	-	tco	
9292515	Erik Spirit *	Bhs	2005	63,500	114,780	250	44	15	tcr	
9282053	Esther Spirit *	Bhs	2004	62,929	115,444	250	44	15	tcr	
9247429	European Spirit	Bhs	2003	79,668	151,848	269	46	-	tcr	ex Cork Spirit-03
9281009	Everest Spirit *	Bhs	2004	62,845	115,048	250	44	14	tcr	
9247364	Galicia Spirit (st)	Cni	2004	94,822	79,166	280	43	19	lng	138,000 m³: ex Elvira Tapias-04
9312858	Galway Spirit *	Bhs	2006	57,325	105,594	244	42	-	tco	
9230517	Ganges Spirit *	Bhs	2002	81,270	159,452	274	48	15	tcr	ex Delaware-07
9286229	Godavari Spirit *	Mlt	2004	81,074	159,106	274	48	15	tcr	ex Angelica-07, Athenian Glory-04
9146730	Goonyella Trader †	Lbr	1996	85,437	170,873	289	45	14	bbu	
9411238	Hamilton Spirit *	Bhs	2009	81,384	158,769	274	48		tcr	
9292503	Helga Spirit *	Bhs	2005	62,929	115,444	250	44	15	tcr	
9230048	Hispania Spirit	Cni	2004	94,822	79,363	280	43	19	lng	138,000 m³: ex Fernando Tapias-04
9212759	Huelva Spirit +	Cni	2001	83,724	160,383	274	48	15	tcr	ex Iria Tapias-04
9283784	Hugli Spirit †	Bhs	2005	29,242	46,889	183	32	14	tco	ex Brazos-07, I/a Athenian Splendour
9379208	Jiaolong Spirit *	Bhs	2009	85,030	159,021	271	47		tcr	
9236353	Iskmati Spirit *	Mhl	2003	84,789	165,000	274	50	15	tcr	ex Arlene-07
9192337	Kanata Spirit	Bhs	1999	62,685	113,021	249	44	14	tcr	
9192349	Kareela Spirit *	Bhs	1999	62,685	113,021	249	44	14	tcr	
9286281	Kaveri Spirit *	Bhs	2004	81,074	159,100	274	48	-	tcr	ex Janet-07, Athenian Olympics-04
9171826	Kiowa Spirit	Bhs	1999	62,619	113,269	253	44		tcr	I/a Bona Valiant
9171840	Kyeema Spirit	Bhs	1999	62,619	113,357	253	44	14	tcr	I/a Bona Vigour
9312860	Limerick Spirit *	Bhs	2007	57,325	105,547	244	42	-	tcr	
9259276	Madrid Spirit (st)	Cni	2004	90,835	77,213	284	43	19	lng	138,000 m³: ex Ivan Tapias-04
9221683	Mahanadi Spirit *	Bhs	2000	28,539	47,037	183	32	14	tco	ex Guadalupe-07, Alam Bakti-00
9291262	Matterhorn Spirit	Bhs	2005	63,694	114,834	254	44	14	tcr	
9269075	Narmada Spirit *	Bhs	2003	81,074	159,199	274	48	-	tcr	ex Adair-07, Athenian Victory-04
9181534	Nassau Spirit *	Bhs	1998	57,925	107,181	236	42	14	tcr	ex Avalon Spirit-06, Nassau Spirit-02
9197715	Navion Bergen ††	Nis	1999	56,207	105,641	239	42	14	tcs	ex Bergitta-07, (conv tcr-07)
9145188	Navion Britannia ** (2)	Nor	1998	72,110	124,821	265	43	15	tcs	
9045974	Navion Clipper ** ††	Bhs	1993	42,159	78,228	221	38	14	tcs	ex Polyclipper-98
9063079	Navion Europa ** (me2)	Nor	1995	73,637	130,596	265	43	15	tcs	ex Jorunn Knutsen-98
9308077	Navion Gothenburg ††	Bhs	2006	82,647	152,244	274	48	-	tcs	ex Roviken-07, (conv tcr-07)
9063067	Navion Norvegia **	Nor	1995	73,637	130,865	265	43	15	tcs	ex Hanne Knutsen-98
9168934	Navion Scandia ** (2)	Nor	1998	72,132	126,749	265	43	14	tcs	
9274525	Nordic Rio ††	Bhs	2004	83,120	151,294	277	48	14	tcs	(conv tcr-05)
9189158	Pacific Triangle †	Lbr	2000	100,330	184,744	300	50	14	bbu	

Teekay Corporation (Teekay Navion Offshore Loading) : NANSEN SPIRIT : *Chris Dornom*

IMO#	name	flag	year	grt	dwt	loa	bm	kts	type	former names
9385192	Pinnacle Spirit *	Bhs	2008	81,732	160,391	274	48	-	tcr	
9001772	Polar Spirit (st)	Bhs	1993	66,174	48,817	239	40	18	lng	89,880 m³: ex Polar Eagle-08
9215048	SC Laura	Bhs	2001	61,764	109,325	243	42		tco	ex Maersk Pointer-07
9191345	Sentinal Spirit *	Mhl	1999	58,288	104,601	244	42		tcr	ex Sentinel-08
9313486	SPT Explorer	Bhs	2008	57,657	105,804	241	42	15	tcr	
9313498	SPT Navigator	Bhs	2008	57,657	105,773	241	42	15	tcr	
9208033	Stena Spirit ††	Bhs	2001	83,120	152,244	274	48	15	tcs	ex Erviken-01 (conc tcr-02)
9404833	Summit Spirit *	Bhs	2008	81,732	160,400	274	48		tcr	
9396725	Tandara Spirit †	Mhl	2008	30,040	50,760	183	32	14	tco	ex Helcion-11, l/a Mexico
9333632	Tangguh Hiri (df)	Bhs	2008	101,957	84,467	282	44	-	lng	155,000 m³
9361990	Tangguh Sago (df)	Bhs	2009	101,957	84,484	282	44	-	lng	155,000 m³
9283722	Teesta Spirit *	Bhs	2004	29,242	46,921	183	32	14	tco	ex Jeanette-07, l/a Athenian Harmony
9283241	Teide Spirit §	Mlt	2004	83,594	159,426	274	48	15	tcr	
9203784	Tenerife Spirit +	Cni	2000	83,724	160,373	274	48	15	tcr	ex Bosco Tapias-04
9378369	Tianlong Spirit *	Bhs	2009	85,037	159,021	273	47		tcr	
9288899	Toledo Spirit §	Esp	2005	83,724	159,342	274	48	-	tcr	
9230505	Yamuna Spirit *	Bhs	2002	81,270	159,435	274	48	15	tcr	ex Dakota-07
9404845	Zenith Spirit *	Bhs	2009	81,732	160,510	272	48		tcr	

newbuildings: 4 x 154,000dwt shuttle tankers 2013 [Samsung 2037-2040]
*vessels owned/managed by Teekay Shipping Glasgow Ltd, UK, * owned/managed by Teekay Marine Singapore Pte.*
*** owned by Navion Offshore Loading AS, Norway*
† owned/managed by Teekay Australia
†† managed by Petroleo Brasileiro SA, Brazil (www2.petrobras.com.br)
§ owned by Compania Espanola de Petroleos SA (CEPSA), Spain
+ owned by Canarias Petroleos
In addition, the companies also operate numerous FPSO (floating production and storage offshore) and FSO (floating storage offshore) vessels.
Also see Chevron Corp, Conoco Phillips Inc, USA and DS-Rendite-Fonds GmbH & Co, Germany (under Dr Peters GmbH)

Teekay Navion Offshore Loading, Singapore
Funnel: *White with blue edged red 'TK' symbol, narrow black top.* **Hull:** *Black with red boot-topping*

IMO#	name	flag	year	grt	dwt	loa	bm	kts	type	former names
9438858	Amundsen Spirit	Bhs	2010	66,563	109,290	249	44		tcs	
9002386	Basker Spirit	Bhs	1992	56,020	97,069	241	41	14	tcs	ex Navion Basker-05, Nordic Yukon-05, Wilma Yukon-01, Wilomi Yukon-96
9268112	Fuji Spirit	Bhs	2003	57,664	106,360	241	42	14	tcr	
9077331	Gotland Spirit	Bhs	1995	52,875	95,370	244	42	14	tcr	ex Bona Rider-99, Venessa-96
9281011	Kilimanjaro Spirit	Bhs	2004	62,845	115,048	250	44	14	tcr	
9017082	Luzon Spirit	Bhs	1992	57,448	98,629	245	41	14	tcr	
9438860	Nansen Spirit	Bhs	2010	66,563	109,239	249	44		tcs	
9204752	Navion Anglia * (2)	Nor	1999	72,449	126,749	265	43	15	tcs	
9168922	Navion Hispania (2)	Nor	1999	72,132	126,749	265	43	14	tcs	
9200926	Navion Marita †	Cym	1999	58,117	103,894	246	42	14	tcs	ex Nordic Marita-07
9168946	Navion Oceania * (2)	Nor	1999	72,132	126,749	265	43	14	tcs	
9209130	Navion Oslo	Bhs	2001	55,796	100,257	238	42	14	tcs	ex Bertora-08
9248435	Navion Stavanger †	Bhs	2003	80,691	148,729	277	46	14	tcs	ex Nordic Stavanger-04, Nordic Liberita-03
9127411	Navion Svenita †	Bhs	1997	58,269	106,506	250	42	14	tcs	ex Nordic Svenita-06, Svenner-98
9012305	Navion Torinita	Bhs	1992	58,959	108,683	244	42	14	tcs	ex Nordic Torinita-05, Torinita-96

Teekay Corporation (Teekay Navion Offshore Loading) : PETRONORDIC : *ARO*

IMO#	name	flag	year	grt	dwt	loa	bm	kts	type	former names
9274513	Nordic Brasilia †	Bhs	2004	83,119	150,939	275	48	14	tcs	l/a Roviken (conv tcr-09)
9208045	Nordic Spirit †	Bhs	2001	83,120	152,292	274	48	15	tcs	ex Storviken-02 (conc tcr-02)
9466130	Peary Spirit	Bhs	2010	66,563	109,325	249	44		tcs	
9233818	Petroatlantic	Bhs	2003	54,865	92,968	235	42	14	tcs	
9233806	Petronordic	Bhs	2002	54,885	92,995	234	42	14	tcs	
9041758	Poul Spirit	Bhs	1995	57,463	105,351	245	41	14	tcr	
9466142	Scott Spirit	Bhs	2010	66,563	109,334	249	44		tcs	

*vessels owned/managed by Teekay Navion Offshore Loading, * owned by Navion Offshore Loading AS, Norway,*
† managed by Petroleo Brasileiro SA, Brazil (www2.petrobras.com.br)

MALT LNG Transport ApS, Norway

Funnel: Hull: **History:** *Joint venture between Teekay LNG Operating LLC and Marubeni Corporation, Japan incorporated 2009 Acquired all shares of Maersk LNG A/S in late 2011*

IMO#	name	flag	year	grt	dwt	loa	bm	kts	type	former names
9339260	Arwa Spirit	Mhl	2008	104.169	82,187	286	43	19	lng	165,500 m³ ex Maersk Arwa-12
9342487	Magellan Spirit	Dnk	2009	104,169	82,265	286	43	19	lng	165,500 m³ ex Maersk Magellan-12
9336737	Methane Spirit	Sgp	2008	104,169	82,115	286	43	19	lng	163,195 m³ ex Maersk Methane-12
9336749	Marib Spirit	Mhl	2008	104,169	82,114	285	43	19	lng	165,500 m³ ex Maersk Marib-12
9369904	Meridian Spirit	Dnk	2010	104,169	81,929	285	43	19	lng	165,772 m³ ex Maersk Meridian-12
9369899	Woodside Donaldson	Sgp	2009	104,169	82,085	285	43	19	lng	165,936 m³

vessels managed by TeeKay Shipping Glasgow Ltd.
all dual fuel diesel electric propulsion (df)

Thien & Heyenga GmbH   Germany

Funnel: *Buff with houseflag comprising black over red with white 'T&H' over blue bands or charterers colours.* **Hull:** *Black, grey, red or blue with red boot-topping.* **History:** *Formed 1977.* **Web:** *www.tuh.de*

IMO#	name	flag	year	grt	dwt	loa	bm	kts	type	former names
9450911	Amsterdam Bridge	Pan	2009	42,112	54,405	260	32	24	ucc	4,380 teu: l/a Stadt Marburg
9395123	Arsos †	Cyp	2007	15,375	18.480	166	25	19	ucc	1,284 teu
9395082	Fouma †	Cyp	2007	15,375	18,480	166	25	19	ucc	1,284 teu: ex Maersk Recife-10
9056430	Seaboxer	Mlt	1994	16,749	24,046	183	28	19	ucc	1,552 teu: ex Nantai Venus-99
9333060	Stadt Aachen	Atg	2007	35,573	44,146	223	32	22	ucc	3,400 teu
9445904	Stadt Cadiz	Atg	2010	35,878	41,234	197	32	22	ucc	2,758 teu
9450923	Stadt Coburg	Atg	2009	42,112	54,327	260	32	24	ucc	4,380 teu
9320049	Stadt Dresden	Atg	2006	27,971	37,938	222	30	21	ucc	2,700 teu: ex SCI Kiran-09, l/dn Stadt Dresden
9459278	Stadt Freiburg	Atg	2010	42,112	54,325	260	32	24	ucc	4,380 teu
9395094	Stadt Gera	Cyp	2007	15,375	18,236	166	25	19	ucc	1,284 teu: ex Maersk Rades-09
9395135	Stadt Gotha	Atg	2008	15,375	18,299	166	25	19	ucc	1,284 teu: l/dn Stadt Dresden
9395056	Stadt Jena	Atg	2007	15,375	18,279	166	25	19	ucc	1,284 teu: ex TS Xiamen-08, Stadt Jena-07
9333058	Stadt Köln **	Atg	2007	35,375	44,234	223	32	22	ucc	3,400 teu: ex Emirates Indus-11, Stadt Köln-11
9320037	Stadt Rostock **	Atg	2006	27,971	37,929	222	30	21	ucc	2,700 teu: ex SCI Jyoti-09, l/dn Stadt Rostock
9440306	Stadt Sevilla	Atg	2010	35,878	41,253	197	32	22	ucc	2,758 teu
9211157	Stadt Schwerin	Atg	1999	14,241	18,440	159	24	18	ucc	1,129 teu: ex Melfi Halifax-08, MSC Ireland-04, Jork Venture-02, l/a Armin, l/dn Stadt Schwerin
9320051	Stadt Weimar	Atg	2006	27,971	37,934	222	30	21	ucc	2,700 teu
9320025	Stadt Wismar **	Atg	2006	27,971	37,786	222	30	21	ucc	2,700 teu
9395044	Varamo †	Cyp	2007	15,375	18,480	166	25	19	ucc	1,284 teu

newbuildings:
*** managed for Konig & Cie GmbH & Co KG † managed by Marlow Navigation Co.Ltd, Cyprus*

A/S Dampskibsselskabet Torm   Denmark

Funnel: *Black with blue 'T' on white band between two red bands.* **Hull:** *Black or grey with red boot-topping.* **History:** *Formed 1889 and 30% owned by Beltest Shipping Co. Ltd., Cyprus. Owns 32% of Dampskibsselskabet 'Norden' A/S, Denmark q.v.. In 2007 acquired 50% of OMI (founded 1962 as Ogden Marine Inc and spun-off from Ogden Corp in 1984 as OMI Corp). In 2008 acquired 50% of FR8, Singapore (formed 2003).* **Web:** *www.torm.com*

IMO#	name	flag	year	grt	dwt	loa	bm	kts	type	former names
9465992	Torm Agnes **	Sgp	2011	30,241	50,274	183	32		tco	
9466013	Torm Agnete **	Dis	2010	30,241	50,247	183	32		tco	
9466001	Torm Alexandra **	Dis	2010	30,241	50,216	183	32		tco	
9465966	Torm Alice **	Nis	2010	30,241	50,216	183	32		tco	
9465980	Torm Almena **	Sgp	2010	30,241	50,247	183	32		tco	
9466025	Torm Amalie *	Sgp	2012	30,241	50,273	183	32		tco	
9251028	Torm Amazon	Pan	2002	28,539	47,275	183	32	14	tco	ex Amazon-07
9543550	Torm Anabel *	Sgp	2012	30,470	49,999	183	32	14	tco	
9300556	Torm Anholt *	Sgp	2004	39,035	74,195	225	32	14	bbu	
9180982	Torm Anne *	Sgp	1999	28,932	45,507	180	32	14	tco	
9543548	Torm Arawa *	Sgp	2012	30,241	49,999	183	32	14	tco	

IMO#	name	flag	year	grt	dwt	loa	bm	kts	type	former names
9465978	Torm Aslaug **	Dis	2010	30,241	50,263	183	32	14	tco	
9442495	Torm Atlantic +	Pan	2011	44,366	83,456	229	32	14	bbu	
9287132	Torm Bornholm *	Sgp	2004	40,030	75,912	225	32	14	bbu	
9263693	Torm Camilla	Dis	2003	30,024	44,990	183	32	14	tco	ex Gron Falk-05
9263708	Torm Carina **	Dis	2003	30,024	46,219	183	32	14	tco	
9262091	Torm Caroline	Dis	2002	28,381	46,414	183	32	14	tco	ex Vit Falk-05, High Vit Falk-03
9215103	Torm Cecilie	Dis	2001	28,381	46,414	183	32	14	tco	ex Rod Falk-05, High Rod Falk-03
9230854	Torm Charente **	Dis	2001	23,740	35,751	183	27	14	tco	ex Charente-08
9215098	Torm Clara	Dis	2000	28,381	45,999	183	32	14	tco	ex Svart Falk-05, High Svart Falk-03
9277785	Torm Emilie	Dis	2004	42,493	74,999	228	32	16	tco	
9364588	Torm Esbjerg +	Hkg	2008	29,733	51,505	183	32	15	tco	
9277723	Torm Estrid	Dis	2004	42,432	74,999	225	32	14	tco	
9302114	Torm Fox **	Dis	2004	23,246	37,025	183	27	14	tco	ex Fox-08
9250490	Torm Freya	Dis	2003	30,058	46,342	183	32	14	tco	
9288930	Torm Garonne	Dis	2004	23,346	37,178	183	27	14	tco	ex Garonne-08
9240897	Torm Gerd	Dis	2002	30,058	46,300	183	32	14	tco	
9240885	Torm Gertrud	Dis	2002	30,058	46,362	183	32	14	tco	
9199127	Torm Gudrun **	Nis	2000	57,031	99,965	244	42	14	tco	
9172193	Torm Gunhild	Dis	1999	28,909	45,457	181	32	14	tco	
9425502	Torm Gyda **	Dis	2009	23,332	36,207	184	27	14	tco	
9143532	Torm Helene **	Dis	1997	57,031	99,999	244	42	14	tco	
9363479	Torm Hellerup +	Phl	2008	28,056	45,990	180	32	-	tco	
9288021	Torm Helvig	Dis	2005	30,018	46,187	183	32	14	tco	
9283710	Torm Horizon	Dis	2004	29,242	46,955	183	32	14	tco	ex Horizon-08, Athenian Horizon-04
9243320	Torm Ingeborg **	Nis	2003	57,095	99,900	244	42	14	tco	
9461130	Torm Island +	Pan	2010	43,012	82,194	229	32	14	bbu	
9277797	Torm Ismini	Dis	2004	42,432	74,999	228	32	15	tco	
9290646	Torm Kansas	Dis	2006	29,242	46,922	184	32	14	tco	ex Kansas-08
9169512	Torm Kristina **	Nis	1999	57,080	105,002	244	42	14	tco	
9375616	Torm Laura	Dis	2008	29,283	53,160	183	32	14	tco	
9390769	Torm Lene	Dis	2008	29,283	53,160	183	32	14	tco	
9392470	Torm Lilly	Dis	2009	29,283	53,160	183	32	14	tco	
9282986	Torm Loire **	Dis	2004	23,246	37,106	183	27	14	tco	ex Loire-08
9392468	Torm Lotte	Dis	2009	29,293	53,160	183	32		tco	
9392482	Torm Louise	Dis	2009	29,283	53,160	183	32		tco	
9212383	Torm Madison	Dis	2000	23,842	35,833	183	27	14	tco	ex Madison-08, Nina-01
9358400	Torm Maren	Dis	2008	61,724	109,672	245	42	15	tco	
9306627	Torm Margit *	Sgp	2007	61,724	109,672	245	42	15	tcr	
9299343	Torm Margrethe *	Sgp	2006	61,724	109,637	245	42	15	tcr	
9299355	Torm Marie *	Sgp	2006	61,724	109,637	245	42	15	tcr	
9319698	Torm Marina §	Nis	2007	61,724	109,672	245	42	15	tcr	
9246798	Torm Mary	Dis	2002	30,058	46,634	183	32	14	tco	
9358412	Torm Mathilde	Dis	2008	61,724	109,672	245	42	14	tco	
9254240	Torm Moselle	Dis	2003	28,567	47,038	183	32	14	tco	ex Moselle-08
9221671	Torm Neches *	Sgp	2000	28,539	47,052	183	32	14	tco	ex Neches-08, Alam Bayu-00
9234678	Torm Ohio **	Dis	2001	23,235	37,278	183	27	14	tco	ex Ohio-08, I/a Borak
9443009	Torm Orient	Pan	2008	39,737	76,636	225	32	-	bbu	

A/S Dampskibsselskabet Torm : TORM LOTTE : *Hans Kraijenbosch*

IMO#	name	flag	year	grt	dwt	loa	bm	kts	type	former names
9317456	Torm Pacific +	Pan	2009	40,017	77,171	225	32	14	bbu	
9290660	Torm Platte	Dis	2006	29,242	46,955	183	32	14	tco	ex Platte-07
9290579	Torm Ragnhild	Dis	2005	30,018	46,187	183	32	14	tco	
9473834	Torm Regina +	Pan	2011	31,572	55,886	190	32		bbu	
9290658	Torm Republican	Dis	2006	29,242	46,955	183	32	14	tco	ex Republican-08
9215086	Torm Rhone **	Dis	2000	23,740	35,769	183	27	-	tco	ex Rhone-08, Prospero-01
9254070	Torm Rosetta	Dis	2003	28,567	47,038	183	32	14	tco	ex Rosetta-08
9381524	Torm Saltholm +	Pan	2008	44,146	83,685	229	32	14	bbu	
9247778	Torm San Jacinto	Mhl	2002	28,539	47,038	183	32	15	tco	ex San Jacinto-08
9295323	Torm Saone **	Dis	2004	23,246	36,986	183	27	14	tco	ex Saone-07
9273260	Torm Sara *	Sgp	2003	41,690	72,718	228	32	15	tco	ex Penyu Agar-05
9290957	Torm Signe *	Sgp	2005	41,503	72,718	228	32	15	tco	ex Penyu Siski-05
9295086	Torm Sofia *	Sgp	2005	41,503	72,650	228	32	15	tco	ex Penyu Daun-05
9302126	Torm Tevere **	Dis	2005	23,246	36,990	183	28	14	tco	ex Tevere-08, Tiber-05
9318333	Torm Thames	Dis	2005	29,214	47,036	184	32	14	tco	ex Thames-08
9250488	Torm Thyra	Dis	2003	30,058	46,308	183	32	14	tco	
9461142	Torm Trader +	Pan	2010	43,012	82,181	229	32	14	bbu	
9212395	Torm Trinity	Dis	2000	23,842	35,833	183	27	14	tco	ex Trinity-08, Snipe-01
9243318	Torm Valborg **	Dis	2003	57,095	99,999	244	42	14	tcr	
9307798	Torm Venture	Nis	2007	42,048	73,701	229	32	-	tco	
9246803	Torm Vita	Dis	2002	30,058	46,308	183	32	14	tco	

newbuildings:
*owned by: * Torm Singapore (Pte.) Ltd (formed 1979), § owned jointly with TorghattenTrafikkselskap ASA*
*managed by: ** by Torm Shipping India Pvt. Ltd.*
+ chartered from various Japanese, Singapore or Philippine owners
company operates about 115 vessels in the Torm LR1, Torm LR2, Torm MR and Torm Handy product tanker pools.

Rederi AB Transatlantic Sweden

Funnel: *Yellow with blue 'TA' symbol within blue ring, narrow blue base and top.* **Hull:** *Grey or white with red boot-topping.*
History: *Transatlantic (originally founded 1904) was acquired by Bilspedition AB in 1988, which also acquired Cool Carriers (1987), Gorthon (1988), Incotrans (1988), Atlantic Container Line (1988-90) and Swedish Orient (1991). All were later sold, Gorthon Lines AB (formed 1915) to B&N Bylock & Nordsjofrakt AB in 1990, before being spun-off in 1997, acquiring the associated Sea Partner AB management company in 2000, which was renamed Gorthon Fleet Services AB. In 2004 a Gorthon-B&N Transatlantic joint venture was formed and in 2005 B&N Nordsjofrakt merged with Gorthon Lines as Transatlantic.* **Web:** *www.rabt.se*

IMO#	name	flag	year	grt	dwt	loa	bm	kts	type	former names
9216626	Transfighter	Swe	2001	20,851	18,972	179	26	17	urr	ex Finnfighter-09, (len-06)
9213088	Transeagle	Nld	2002	13,340	16,612	142	22	15	ggc	ex Nordon-09
9248552	Transhawk	Gib	2004	13,340	16,558	142	22	15	ggc	ex Sandon-08
9213090	Transosprey	Gib	2003	16,037	20,396	174	22	16	ggc	ex Prinsenborg-10 (len-08)
9216638	Transpine	Swe	2002	20,851	18,855	179	26	17	urr	ex Finnpine-08 (len-06)
9232785	Transwood	Swe	2002	20,851	18,855	179	26	17	urr	ex Finnwood-08 (len-06)
8515893	Transreel	Swe	1987	18,773	10,917	166	23	20	urr	ex Viola Gorthon-09

managed by Transatlantic Fleet Services AB (formed 1992). Also operates Ro-Ro vessels on Baltic routes.

Transeste Schiffahrt GmbH Germany

Funnel: *Mainly in charterers colours.* **Hull:** *Black, dark grey, blue or red with red boot-topping.* **History:** *Formed 1956.*
Web: *www.transeste.de*

A/S Dampskibsselskabet Torm : TORM MARY : *Chris Brooks*

IMO#	name	flag	year	grt	dwt	loa	bm	kts	type	former names
9179816	Estebroker *	Atg	1999	25,705	33,843	208	30	22	ucc	2,468 teu: ex CSAV Trinidad-08, Hanjin Dubai-07, Trade Bravery-05, TPL Merchant-02, Lykes Crusader-01
9568562	Harm	Lbr	2011	51,225	93,183	229	38	14	bbu	
9333371	Helle Ritscher *	Lbr	2006	17,360	22,254	179	28	21	ucc	1,719 teu: ex DAL East London-09, Helle Ritscher-06
9179828	Jan Ritscher *	Atg	1999	25,705	33,843	208	30	22	ucc	2,468 teu: ex MOL Satisfaction-12, Trade Zale-05, TPL Eagle-02, TMM San Antonio-01, Jan Ritscher-99
9333383	Jonni Ritscher *	Lbr	2006	17,189	22,243	179	28	21	ucc	1,719 teu: ex CMA CGM Caribbean-08, Jonni Ritscher-06
9568574	Piet	Lbr	2011	51,225	93,200	229	38	14	bbu	
9226413	Ulf Ritscher *	Deu	2001	25,705	33,795	208	30	22	ucc	2,524 teu: ex NYK Espirito-09, Sea Tiger-04, I/a Ulf Ritscher
9456240	Widar *	Lbr	2011	32,987	56,859	190	32	14	bbu	
9252735	Widukind *	Lbr	2006	35,881	42,200	221	32	22	ucc	3,104 teu: ex SCI Diya-08, Widukind-07, Hera-06
9226425	Wotan	Deu	2001	25,703	33,795	208	30	22	ucc	2,524 teu: ex CCNI Rimac-11, Wotan-06, MSC Venezuela-03, I/a Wotan

*managed for owning partner companies Reederei Gerd Ritscher KG (founded 1956 www.ritschership.com) or * Reederei Dietrich Tamke KG (founded 1970), both Germany*

TransPetrol Ltd.   Bermuda

Funnel: Black with white 'tp' above white wavy lines. Hull: Black or brown with red or grey boot-topping. History: Formed 1979 as TransPetrol Maritime Services NV until 2005. Web: www.transpetrol.com

IMO#	name	flag	year	grt	dwt	loa	bm	kts	type
9289788	Advance II *	Sgp	2006	30,032	46,101	183	32	14	tco
9289776	Affinity	Sgp	2005	42,661	73,741	228	32	15	tco
9389978	Alpine Confidence	Sgp	2010	60,205	107,600	244	42	14	tcr
9430272	Alpine Eternity	Sgp	2009	29,130	46,105	183	32	14	tco
9430284	Alpine Loyalty	Sgp	2010	29,130	46,151	183	32	14	tco
9430296	Alpine Venture	Sgp	2010	29,130	46,046	183	32	14	tco
9273650	Endeavour	Sgp	2004	30,032	46,101	183	32	14	tco
9479840	Luctor	Pan	2011	29,419	50,383	183	32	14	tco
9289752	Perseverence	Sgp	2005	42,661	73,788	228	32	15	tco
9289764	Reliance II *	Sgp	2006	30,032	46,101	183	32	14	tco
9273246	Resolve	Sgp	2004	30,032	46,048	183	32	14	tco
9479838	Turmoil	Pan	2011	29,419	50,358	183	32	14	tco

newbuildings:
*operated by subsidiary TransPetrol Maritime Services Ltd, Belgium and * owned by TransPetrol TMAS, Norway.*
Also see Stolt-Nielsen/Avance Gas

Tsakos Shipping & Trading S.A.   Greece

*Funnel: Yellow with red 'T' on broad white band edged with narrow blue bands, narrow black top. Hull: Black * with white 'TEN', red boot-topping. History: Founded in Piraeus, 1970. Web: www.tsakos.net or www.tenn.gr*

IMO#	name	flag	year	grt	dwt	loa	bm	kts	type	former names
9315800	Aegeas *	Grc	2007	23,325	39,378	183	27	14	tco	
9292620	Afrodite *	Bhs	2005	30,053	52,700	186	32	14	tco	ex Western Antarctic-06
9289518	Ajax *	Bhs	2005	30,053	52,700	186	32	14	tco	ex Western Baltic-06
9302607	Alaska *	Grc	2006	85,421	163,250	274	50	15	tcr	
9314882	Amphitrite *	Grc	2006	23,325	36,660	183	27	14	tco	ex Antares-09
9265366	Andes *	Grc	2003	39,085	68,439	229	32	14	tco	
9315795	Andromeda *	Grc	2007	23,325	39,378	183	27	14	tco	
9315185	Antarctic *	Lbr	2007	85,421	163,216	274	50	14	tcr	
9289532	Apollon *	Bhs	2005	30,053	53,148	186	32	14	tco	ex Western Pacific-06
9302592	Archangel *	Grc	2006	85,421	163,216	274	50	15	tcr	
9315173	Arctic *	Grc	2007	85,431	163,152	274	50	15	tcr	
9292967	Ariadne *	Bhs	2005	30,053	52,700	186	32	14	tco	ex Western Icelandic-06
9314894	Arion *	Grc	2006	23,325	39,478	183	27	14	tco	
9289520	Aris *	Bhs	2005	30,053	53,106	186	32	14	tco	ex Western Atlantic-06
9291640	Artemis *	Bhs	2005	30,053	53,039	186	32	14	tco	ex Western Arctic-06
9411197	Asahi Princess *	Lbr	2009	55,909	105,361	229	42	14	tcr	
9442744	Beijing 2008	Lbr	2007	43,158	82,561	229	32	14	bbu	
9315903	Bosporos *	Grc	2007	23,310	39,589	183	27	14	tco	
9623879	Brazil	Grc	2014	82,700	156,000	264	48	14	tcs	
9315898	Byzantion *	Grc	2007	23,310	39,589	183	27	14	tco	
9227273	Cap Talbot	Lbr	2001	40,085	51,060	257	32	23	ucc	3,739 teu: ex Cap San Antonio-12
9215660	Cap Trafalgar	Lbr	2001	40,085	51,101	257	32	22	ucc	3,739 teu: ex Cap San Nicolas-12
9382982	Chantal *	Lbr	2009	41,676	74,329	228	32	14	tco	
9283796	Delphi *	Grc	2004	25,124	37,432	176	31	15	tco	
9288772	Didimon *	Grc	2004	25,124	37,432	176	31	15	tco	ex Dodoni-05

IMO#	name	flag	year	grt	dwt	loa	bm	kts	type	former names
9565950	Dimitris P. *	Lbr	2011	81,314	157,740	274	48	14	tcr	
9567702	Euro	Bhs	2012	81,314	157,539	274	48	14	tcr	
9299666	Eurochampion 2004 *	Grc	2005	85,431	164,808	274	50	15	tcr	
9299678	Euronike *	Grc	2005	85,431	164,565	274	50	15	tcr	ex Euroniki-05
9567697	Eurovision	Bhs	2013	81,314	157,500	274	48	14	tcr	
9015539	Hanjin Elizabeth	Pan	1992	50,792	62,723	290	32	24	ucc	4,024 teu: ex Hanjin Barcelona-05
9021693	Hanjin Irene	Pan	1994	50,792	62,742	290	32	24	ucc	4,024 teu: ex Hanjin Tokyo-05
9434773	Ian M.	Grc	2010	93,916	179,700	292	45	15	bbu	
9256028	Inca *	Grc	2003	39,085	68,439	229	32	14	tco	
9123922	Irenes Logos	Pan	1995	18,716	24,370	194	28	20	ucc	1,611 teu: ex CCNI Mejillones-10, CMA CGM Limon-08, Irenes Logos-06, Ise-02
9303780	Irenes Rainbow	Grc	2006	28,592	39,382	222	30	23	ucc	2,824 teu: ex Kota Segar-10, l/a Irenes Rainbow
9315862	Irenes Reliance	Grc	2005	28,592	39,396	222	30	23	ucc	2,824 teu
9315850	Irenes Remedy	Grc	2005	28,592	39,382	222	30	23	ucc	2,824 teu
9411185	Ise Princess *	Lbr	2009	55,909	105,361	229	42	14	tcr	
9330472	Izumo Princess *	Grc	2007	55,909	105,374	229	42	14	tcr	
9002609	La Esperanza ‡	Pan	1993	158,475	299,700	344	56	14	tcr	ex EHM Maersk-03, British Valour-02, Elisabeth Maersk-97
9002623	La Madrina *	Grc	1993	158,475	299,700	344	56	14	tcr	ex Maersk Estelle-04, Estelle Maersk-98

Tsakos Shipping & Trading : APOLLON : *F. de Vries*

Tsakos Shipping & Trading : SELINI : *ARO*

IMO#	name	flag	year	grt	dwt	loa	bm	kts	type	former names
9031650	La Paz ‡	Pan	1995	158,475	299,700	344	56	14	tcr	ex Evelyn Maersk-03
9002693	La Prudencia *	Grc	1992	158,475	298,900	344	56	14	tcr	ex Maersk Eleo-04, Eleo Maersk-98
9442756	London 2012	Lbr	2007	43,158	82,562	229	32	14	bbu	
9394753	Manousos P	Lbr	2008	43,158	82,549	229	32	14	bbu	
9380661	Maria Princess *	Lbr	2008	55,909	105,346	229	42	14	tcr	
9256016	Maya *	Grc	2003	39,085	68,439	229	32	14	tco	
9158903	Millennium ‡	Pan	1998	156,692	301,171	331	58	15	tcr	
9324277	Neo Energy (st) ‡	Lbr	2007	100,253	85,602	288	44	19	lng	149,700 m³
9380673	Nippon Princess *	Grc	2008	55,909	105,392	229	42		tcr	
9305611	Promitheas *	Grc	2006	66,919	117,055	250	44	15	tco	
9305623	Propontis *	Grc	2006	66,919	116,610	250	44	15	tco	
9305609	Proteas *	Grc	2006	66,919	117,055	250	44	15	tco	
9623867	Rio	Grc	2016	82,700	156,000	264	48	14	tcs	
9358541	Sakura Princess *	Grc	2007	55,909	105,385	229	42	-	tcr	
9382968	Salamina *	Lbr	2009	41,676	74,251	228	32		tco	
9439199	Sapporo Princess *	Grc	2010	55,909	105,354	229	42		tcr	
9382956	Selini *	Lbr	2009	41,676	74,296	228	32		tco	
9390692	Socrates *	Lbr	2008	41,676	74,327	228	32		tco	
9565948	Spyros K. *	Lbr	2011	81,314	157,647	274	48		tcr	
9388297	Selecao *	Lbr	2008	41,676	74,296	228	32	15	tco	
9229374	Silia T *	Lbr	2002	84,586	164,286	274	50	15	tcr	
9390692	Socrates *	Lbr	2008	41,676	74,327	228	32	14	tco	
9434785	Stella	Lbr	2009	93,916	179,700	292	45		bbu	
9233222	Triathlon *	Grc	2002	84,586	164,445	274	50	14	tcr	
9439204	Uraga Princess *	Grc	2010	55,909	105,344	229	42		tcr	
9382970	World Harmony *	Lbr	2009	41,676	74,471	228	32		tco	
9394765	Yiannis B.	Lbr	2008	43,158	82,591	229	32	14	bbu	

newbuildings
Managed by Tsakos Colombia Shipmanagement (TCM) SA, (formed 2010 as j/v with Schoeller Holdings) **Web:** www.tcsm.gr: vessels operated by * Tsakos Energy Navigation Ltd (TEN) (formed 1993 as Maritime Investment Fund Ltd to 1996) or ‡ by Hyundai Merchant Marine Co Ltd.

A/S Uglands Rederi Norway

Funnel: Yellow with white 'U' on broad red band below black top. **Hull:** Grey, blue or orange with black or white 'UGLAND', green or red boot-topping. **History:** Formed 1930. **Web:** www.jjuc.no

IMO#	name	flag	year	grt	dwt	loa	bm	kts	type	former names
9494060	Bonita	Nis	2010	32,315	58,105	190	32	14	bbu	
9403176	Carmencita	Nis	2009	32,379	58,773	190	32	14	bbu	
9298519	Favorita	Nis	2005	30,078	52,292	190	32	14	bbu	
9223992	Fermita	Nis	2001	30,053	52,380	190	32	14	bbu	
9493975	Isabelita	Nis	2010	32,297	58,470	190	32	14	bbu	
9520936	Kristinita	Nis	2011	32,315	58,105	190	32	14	bbu	
9146558	Livanita	Nis	1997	26,044	45,426	186	30	15	bbu	
9131888	Mattea * (2)	Can	1997	76,216	126,380	272	46	15	tcs	
9281724	Rosita	Nis	2004	30,076	52,292	190	32	14	bbu	
9384540	Senorita	Nor	2008	32,379	58,300	190	32	14	bbu	
9583134	Star Norita	Nis	2012	32,371	58,470	190	32	14	bbu	
9223980	Tamarita	Nis	2001	30,053	52,292	190	32	14	bbu	
9216389	Vinland * (2)	Nis	2000	76,567	125,827	272	46	14	tcs	

newbuildings:
owned or managed by subsidiaries Ugland Marine Services AS (formed 1996) and Ugland Shipping A/S (formed 1964)
managed * by Canship Ugland Ltd (formed jointly with Canship Ltd). Also see Stena AB and Teekay Corp.

United Arab Shipping Co. (SAG) Kuwait

Funnel: Black, broad white band with red/purple bands above and black/green bands below black 6-spoked wheel containing black crossed anchors on blue centre disc. **Hull:** Light grey with black 'UASC', green band over red boot-topping. **History:** Founded 1976 as Kuwait Shipping Co (SAK) to 1977. Formed jointly by The Governments of the United Arab Emirates, the States of Bahrain, Kuwait and Qatar, the Kingdom of Saudi Arabia and the Republic of Iraq. **Web:** www.uasc.net

IMO#	name	flag	year	grt	dwt	loa	bm	kts	type	former names
9152258	Abu Dhabi	Are	1998	48,154	49,844	277	32	24	ucc	3,802 teu
9525869	Ain Snan	Mlt	2012	141,077	145,274	366	48	26	ucc	13,26 teu
9349514	Al Bahia	Are	2008	75,579	85,517	306	40	25	ucc	6,921 teu
9349552	Al Hilal	Pan	2008	75,579	79,030	306	40	25	ucc	6,921 teu
9349538	Al Manamah	Pan	2008	75,579	85,517	306	40	25	ucc	6,921 teu
9149770	Al Noof	Qat	1998	48,154	49,993	277	32	24	ucc	3,802 teu
9525924	Al Qibla	Mlt	2012	141,077	145,237	366	48	26	ucc	13,296 teu
9349540	Al Rawdah	Pan	2008	75,579	85,226	306	40	25	ucc	6,435 teu
9525912	Al Riffa	Mlt	2012	141,077	145,534	366	48	26	ucc	13,296 teu
9349497	Al Safat	Kwt	2008	75,579	85,437	306	40	25	ucc	6,435 teu
9525883	Al Ula	Mlt	2012	141,077	145,528	366	48	26	ucc	13,296 teu
9154543	Al-Abdali	Kwt	1998	48,154	49,844	277	32	24	ucc	3,802 teu
9149756	Al-Farahidi	Bhr	1998	48,154	50,004	277	32	24	ucc	3,802 teu
9152272	Al-Mutanabbi	Bhr	1998	48,154	49,844	277	32	24	ucc	3,802 teu

IMO#	name	flag	year	grt	dwt	loa	bm	kts	type	former names
9154529	Al-Sabahia	Kwt	1998	48,154	49,848	277	32	24	ucc	3,802 teu
9154531	Asir	Sau	1998	48,154	49,856	277	32	24	ucc	3,802 teu
9149768	Deira	Are	1998	48,154	49,993	277	32	24	ucc	3,802 teu
9152260	Fowairet	Qat	1998	48,154	49,993	277	32	24	ucc	3,802 teu
9349502	Hatta	Are	2008	75,579	85,614	306	40	25	ucc	6,435 teu
9349540	Jazan	Pan	2008	75,579	85,463	306	40	25	ucc	6,435 teu
9525936	Jebel Ali	Mlt	2012	141,077	145,149	366	48	26	ucc	13,296 teu
9525900	Malik al Ashtar	Mlt	2012	141,077	145,527	366	48	26	ucc	13,296 teu
9349526	Mayssan	Bhr	2008	75,579	85,517	306	40	25	ucc	6,919 teu
9149744	Najran	Sau	1998	48,154	49,993	277	32	24	ucc	3,802 teu
9525857	Umm Salal	Mlt	2011	141,077	145,327	366	48	26	ucc	13,296 teu
9525871	Unayzah	Mlt	2012	141,077	145,520	366	48	26	ucc	13,296 teu
9525895	Tayma	Mlt	2012	141,077	145,451	366	48	26	ucc	13,295 teu

United Arab Chemical Carriers LLC, Dubai

Funnel: *Black, broad white band with UACC and blue & green logo .* **Hull:** *Black, some with 'U.A.C.C.' in white, red boot topping*
History: *Formed 2007, largest shareholder is UASC with Arabian Chemical Carriers of Saudia Arabia. Vessels managed by UASC*
Web: uacc.ae

9254927	UACC Ibn Al Atheer	Pan	2003	28,059	45,994	180	32	14	tco	ex Pacific Sunshine-08
9485631	UACC									
	Ibn Al Haitham	Mlt	2009	42,010	73,338	229	32	14	tco	

A/S Uglands Rederi : SENORITA : *Nico Kemps*

United Arab Shipping Co. : MAILK AL ASHTAR : *ARO*

IMO#	name	flag	year	grt	dwt	loa	bm	kts	type	former names
9254939	UACC Al Medina	Pan	2003	28,059	45,987	180	32	14	tco	ex Nord Sea-08
9296585	UACC Consensus	Pan	2005	28,059	45,896	180	32	14	tco	ex High Consensus-09
9550694	UACC Eagle	Mhl	2009	42,010	73,410	229	32	14	tco	ex Summit Asia-11
9550682	UACC Falcon	Mhl	2009	42,010	73,427	229	32	14	tco	ex Summit Australia-11
9288289	UACC Harmony	Pan	2005	28,059	45,913	180	32	14	tco	ex High Harmony-09
9485629	UACC Ibn Sina	Mlt	2008	42,010	73,338	229	32	14	tco	
9489065	UACC Masafi	Mhl	2012	29,274	45,352	183	32	15	tco	
9489077	UACC Messila	Mhl	2012	29,168	45,352	183	32	15	tco	
9489089	UACC Mansouria	Mhl	2013	28,300	45,000	183	32	15	tco	L - 22:03:2012
9489091	UACC Marah		2013		45,000	183	32	15	tco	L - 01:06:2012
	UACC Marwan		2013		45,000	183	32	15	tco	
	UACC Muharraq		2013		45,000	183	32	15	tco	
9428360	UACC Shams	Lbr	2009	30,006	50,138	183	32	14	tco	ex Tyrrhenian Wave-11, Indiana-09
9428358	UACC Sila	Lbr	2009	30,006	50,105	183	32	14	tco	ex Ionian Wave-11, I/a Banksy
9272400	UACC Strait	Pan	2004	28,059	45,934	180	32	14	tco	ex Nord Strait-09
9272395	UACC Sound	Pan	2003	28,059	45,975	180	32	14	tco	ex Nord Sound-09

newbuildings: in list

Vale S.A. Brasil/Singapore

Funnel: Green with green and yellow 'V' on broad white band beneath black top. **Hull:** Black with red boot-topping.
History: Shipping arm of Brazilian mining company Cia. Vale do Rio Doce, formed 2009. **Web:** www.vale.com

IMO#	name	flag	year	grt	dwt	loa	bm	kts	type	former names
8906688	Ore Mutuca	Mlt	1990	77,096	149,495	270	43	13	bbu	ex Juneau-09, Amazon-07, Bulk Atlanta-05, Cape Asia-00
8802923	Ore Vitoria	Lbr	1988	116,427	233,016	315	54	14	bor	ex Rhine Ore-10, Onie Maru-01
9575448	Vale Beijing *	Mhl	2011	199,959	404,389	361	66	15	bor	
9488918	Vale Brasil	Sgp	2011	198,980	402,347	362	65	15	bor	I/a Ore China
9593919	Vale Carajas	Sgp	2012	198,980	402,285	362	65	15	bor	
9522972	Vale China	Sgp	2011	201,384	400,606	360	65	15	bor	
9532525	Vale Dalian	Sgp	2012	201,384	400,398	360	65	15	bor	
9532513	Vale Dongjiakou	Sgp	2012	201,384	400,606	360	65	15	bor	
9575462	Vale Espirito Santo *	Mhl	2012	200,000	403.627	360	65	15	bor	
9532537	Vale Hebei	Sgp	2012	201,384	400,535	360	65	15	bor	
9575474	Vale Indonesia	Sgp	2012	199,959	404,389	360	65	15	bor	
9572331	Vale Italia	Sgp	2011	198,980	400,000	362	65	15	bor	ex Vale Sao Luis-11, I/a Ore Shanghai VB
9532551	*Vale Jiangsu*	Sgp	2013	201,000	400,000				bor	L - 26:07:2012
9566514	Vale Liwa **	Mhl	2012	201,528	400,000				bor	
9572343	Vale Malaysia	Sgp	2012	198,980	402,285	362	65	15	bor	ex Ore Brasil-12
9593957	Vale Minas Gerais	Sgp	2012	198,980	400,000	362	65	15	bor	
9575450	Vale Qingdao *	Mhl	2012	199,959	403,919	361	66	15	bor	
9572329	Vale Rio de Janiero	Sgp	2011	198,900	402,303	362	65	15	bor	I/a Ore Beijing
9566526	Vale Saham **	Mhl	2012	201,528	400,000				bor	L - 13:09:2012
9532549	Vale Shandong	Sgp	2012	201,000	400,000				bor	
9566538	Vale Shinas **	Mhl	2012	201,528	400,000				bor	L - 28:08:2012
9565065	Vale Sohar **	Mhl	2012	201,384	400,000	360	65	15	bor	

*newbuildings: total 19 for Vale fron Jiangsu Rongsheng and Daewoo and 16 from Chinese & Korean yards for charter to Vale vessels
owned/managed by Vale Shipping Enterprises S.A., chartered from * STX, ** Oman Shipping*

United Arab Shipping Co. (United Arab Chemical Carriers) : UACC IBN SINA : *Hans Kraijenbosch*

IMO#	name	flag	year	grt	dwt	loa	bm	kts	type	former names

Viken Shipping AS   Norway

Funnel: *Cream with narrow blue band on white band on broad red band beneath black top.* **Hull:** *dark green with white 'Viken' with red boot-topping.* **History:** *Formed 1993 and de-merged from joint venture with Mowinckel in 2002. Acquired Wallem Group jointly with Clearwater Investments in 2006.* **Web:** *www.vikenshipping.com*

IMO#	name	flag	year	grt	dwt	loa	bm	kts	type	former names
9492000	Angra Dos Reis	Bhs	2012	62,753	105,185	248	42	14	tcs	
9587192	Dolviken	Nis	2012	81,453	159,058	274	48	14	tcr	
9274812	Erviken	Nis	2004	82,647	152,146	275	48	14	tcr	
8321931	Federal Fuji *	Bhs	1986	17,814	29,536	183	23	14	bbu	
8321929	Federal Polaris *	Bhs	1985	17,815	29,536	183	23	14	bbu	
9321677	Kronviken	Nis	2006	61,653	113,450	249	44	14	tcr	
9492050	Madre de Deus	Bhs	2012	62,221	109,250	248	42	14	tcs	
9492062	Rio Grande	Bhs	2012	62,753	105,190	248	42	14	tcs	
9492139	Sao Luiz	Bhs	2013	62,753	105,213	248	42	14	tcs	
9492127	Sao Sebastiao	Bhs	2013	62,753	105,190	248	42	14	tcs	
9321689	Solviken	Nis	2007	61,653	114,523	249	44	14	tcr	
9308065	Storviken	Nis	2006	82,647	152,013	274	48	14	tcr	
9285835	Telleviken	Iom	2005	62,806	115,340	250	44	15	tco	ex Tanea-11, Ganstar-05
9285847	Tofteviken	Iom	2005	62,806	115,340	250	44	15	tco	ex Torinia-11, Gansky-05
9285859	Troviken	Iom	2006	62,806	115,345	250	44	15	tco	ex Trochus-11, I/a Gansea
8212099	Utviken *	Bhs	1987	17,191	30,052	189	23	16	bbu	ex C. Bianco-95, Bijelo Polije-92

managed by subsidiary Wallem Shipmanagement Norway AS (renamed from Viken Ship Management AS in 2006).
*on long-term charter to * Fednav Ltd., Canada (Federal xx in Fednav colours)*

F. A. Vinnen & Co. (GmbH & Co.)   Germany

Funnel: *Black with black 'M' on broad white band, white with blue 'V' or charterers colours.* **Hull:** *Black with red boot-topping.* **History:** *Formed 1918 as E. C. Schramm & Co to 1920.* **Web:** *www.vinnen.com*

IMO#	name	flag	year	grt	dwt	loa	bm	kts	type	former names
9456991	CCNI Arauco	Lbr	2012	50,885	61,983	249	37	24	ucc	4,532 teu: I/a Merkur Harbour
9301469	CMA CGM L'Etoile	Lbr	2005	26,626	34,500	210	30	21	ucc	2,556 teu: ex E.R. Camargue-05
9236511	Merkur Bay	Deu	2002	30,047	35,770	208	32	22	ucc	2,764 teu
9122033	Merkur Beach *	Lbr	1996	16,800	22,900	185	26	19	ucc	1,728 teu: ex CMA CGM Cartagena-11, Merkur Beach-06, Delmas Charcot-03, Merkur Beach-02, MSC Quito-02, Merkur Beach-99, CSAV Rahue-98, I/a Merkur Beach
8912766	Merkur Bridge *	Lbr	1993	9,597	12,575	150	22	17	ucc	1,012 teu: ex UASC Umm Qasar-11, H&H Tide-09, Merkur Bridge-08, Sinar Banda-02, Kota Seri-01, Merkur Bridge-99, New Orient-99, Merkur Bridge-98, Ratana Ganya-97, TSL Bravo-96, Merkur Bridge-93

Vale S.A. : VALE RIO DE JANIERO : *Hans Kraijenbosch*

IMO#	name	flag	year	grt	dwt	loa	bm	kts	type	former names
9135925	Merkur Cloud	Lbr	1996	15,929	22,026	168	27	21	ucc	1,608 teu: ex Kota Molek-07, Merkur Cloud-04, Calapalos-02, I/a Merkur Cloud
9620607	*Merkur Fjord*	Lbr	2013	42,789	51,500	228	37	20	ucc	3,800 teu
9620619	*Merkur Ocean*	Lbr	2013	42,789	51,500	228	37	20	ucc	3,800 teu
9102734	Merkur Star	Lbr	1996	29,181	39,528	203	31	19	ucc	2,604 teu: ex MSC Natal-12, Merkur Star-06, MSC Oman-03, Merkur Star-02, CMA CGM Seurat-02, Merkur Star-00, Houston Express-98, Merkur Star-96, I/a John Lykes
9162368	Merkur Tide	Lbr	1998	15,929	22,026	168	27	21	ucc	1,708 teu: ex MOL Heritage-11, Merkur Tide-08, YM Dubai-07, Merkur Tide-04, Calaparana-03, Merkur Tide-01, Atlantico-01, I/a Merkur Tide
9456989	Zim Istanbul	Lbr	2009	41,331	51,602	262	32	24	ucc	4,255 teu: ex Merkur Horizon

newbuildings:
* managed for Hansa Treuhand Schiffs GmbH & Co KG, Germany qv

H. Vogemann GmbH Germany

Funnel: *Red with white 'V', black top.* **Hull:** *Black with red boot-topping.* **History:** *Founded 1886.* **Web:** *www.vogemann.de*

IMO#	name	flag	year	grt	dwt	loa	bm	kts	type	former names
9081784	Bel East	Lbr	1995	36,074	68,519	224	32	14	bbu	ex Belem -12, Xin Xing Hai-97, Northern Venture-01
9490454	Voge Challenger **	Lbr	2010	43,692	79,648	229	32	15	bbu	I/a King Harvey
9420851	Voge Dignity	Lbr	2009	24,066	38,334	183	27	14	tco	
9541318	Voge Enterprise **	Lbr	2011	43,692	79,409	229	32	15	bbu	
9123702	Voge Eva *	Lbr	1997	14,762	23,407	154	26	14	bbu	ex Clipper Beaufort-07, Sea Amelita-03
9143714	Voge Felix *	Lbr	1997	14,599	24,279	157	26	15	bbu	ex Andros-06, Sea Wisdom-03
9339181	Voge Master **	Deu	2006	88,930	174,093	289	45	14	bbu	ex Avore-07
9154866	Voge Paul **	Lbr	1998	14,762	23,494	156	26	15	bbu	ex Clipper Bounteous-07, Joint Spirit-03, Sea Harvest-98
9110523	Voge Prestige **	Lbr	1995	39,283	75,100	225	32	14	bbu	ex National Prestige-07
9154854	Voge Renate *	Lbr	1997	14,762	23,407	154	26	15	bbu	ex Clipper Breeze-07, Joint Bright-03, Sea Splendor-98
9420863	Voge Trust	Lbr	2009	24,066	38,349	183	27	14	tco	
9177109	Voge West **	Lbr	1995	38,236	70,728	225	32	14	bbu	ex Xinshi Hai-08, Brazilian Venture-01
9174658	Vogebulker **	Lbr	1999	86,191	169,168	289	45	14	bbu	ex Heng Shan-04
9122095	Vogecarrier *	Lbr	1996	85,706	164,303	289	43	15	bbu	ex Eurotrader-04, Cherokee-00
9475301	Vogerunner	Deu	2009	89,603	176,838	289	45	16	bbu	
9122100	Vogesailor *	Lbr	1996	86,706	164,188	289	43	15	bbu	ex Eurosailor-05, Comanche-00
9108257	Vogevoyager	Lbr	1996	37,663	72,105	224	32	15	bbu	ex Far Eastern Auspice-02

newbuildings:
* managed by Wallem GmbH & Co KG (joint venture as Vogemann-Wallem Ltd.) or ** by KG Reederei Roth GmbH & Co (founded 1972 as Josef Roth Reederei until 1988 - www.reederei-roth.de)

Vroon B.V. Netherlands

Funnel: *White with three wavy blue lines at base of blue 'V', narrow blue or black top, * white with blue 'V' tick symbol inside red square outline, blue top or † white with blue 'LE', blue top.* **Hull:** *White, grey, black, blue or red withlarge white 'V', red boot-topping.* **History:** *Formed 1890.* **Web:** *www.vroon.nl or www.iverships.com*

IMO#	name	flag	year	grt	dwt	loa	bm	kts	type	former names
9298715	Acadian *	Can	2005	23,356	37,515	183	27	14	tco	
9138161	Aegean Express **	Pan	1997	15,095	18,581	169	27	18	ucc	1,439 teu: ex YM Bangkok-02, Kuo Ting-01
9148532	Arabian Express **	Pan	1997	15,095	18,300	169	27	18	ucc	1,439 teu: ex Kuo Yang-03
9203588	Asian Dynasty +	Phl	1999	55,719	21,224	200	32	20	mve	6,480 ceu
9426324	Bahamian Express	Gib	2010	21,018	25,937	180	28	20	ucc	1,795 teu
9501772	Belgian Express	Gib	2010	21,018	25,774	180	28	20	ucc	1,795 teu
9298739	Great Eastern *	Mhl	2005	23,356	37,515	183	27	14	tco	
9451721	Imola Express	Gib	2010	36,711	11,215	168	28	19	mve	3,700 ceu
9474383	Istrian Express	Gib	2011	12,514	14,233	158	25	19	ucc	1,084 teu
9474395	Italian Express	Gib	2012	12,514	14,213	158	25	19	ucc	1,084 teu
9207982	Iver Exact *	Nld	2007	29,456	46,575	183	32	14	tco	
9307994	Iver Example *	Nld	2007	29,456	46,784	183	32	14	tco	
9126003	Iver Excel *	Nld	1997	29,289	45,750	183	32	14	tco	
9207716	Iver Experience *	Nld	2000	29,289	45,650	183	32	15	tco	
9126015	Iver Expert *	Nld	1997	29,289	45,809	183	32	14	tco	
9207728	Iver Exporter *	Mhl	2000	29,289	45,683	183	32	15	tco	
9314208	Iver Express *	Nld	2007	29,456	46,825	183	32	14	tco	
9350642	Iver Progress *	Mhl	2007	23,421	37,412	184	27	14	tco	
9351921	Iver Prosperity *	Mhl	2007	23,421	37,456	184	27	14	tco	
9442122	Le Mans Express	Gib	2010	36,711	11,215	168	28	19	mve	3,700 ceu
9174490	Libra Leader ‡	Pan	1998	57,674	22,734	200	32	19	mve	5,980 ceu
9440148	Magny Cours Express	Gib	2009	36,711	11,174	168	28	19	mve	3.700 ceu

IMO#	name	flag	year	grt	dwt	loa	bm	kts	type	former names
9451719	Monza Express	Gib	2009	36,711	11,174	168	28	19	mve	3,700 ceu
9298727	New England *	Mhl	2005	23,356	37,515	183	27	14	tco	
9298703	Nor'easter *	Mhl	2005	23,356	37,515	183	27	14	tco	
9553218	Peruvian Express	Mhl	2012	43,692	79,252	229	32	14	bbu	
9487873	Scandinavian Express	Gib	2010	51,209	93,038	230	38	14	bbu	
9487885	Scotian Express	Gib	2011	51,209	93,019	230	38	14	bbu	
9434321	Sebring Express	Phl	2009	43,810	15,154	180	30	19	mve	3,930 ceu
9448061	Sepang Express	Phl	2009	43,810	15,154	180	30	19	mve	3,930 ceu
9498717	Siberian Express	Gib	2012	51,209	93,000	230	38	14	bbu	
9498729	Sicilian Express	Gib	2012	51,209	93,000	230	38	14	bbu	
9434319	Silverstone Express	Phl	2009	43,810	15,154	180	30	19	mve	3,930 ceu

Vroon B.V. : SCANDINAVIAN EXPRESS : *Nico Kemps*

Vroon B.V. : SEBRING EXPRESS : *Nico Kemps*

IMO#	name	flag	year	grt	dwt	loa	bm	kts	type	former names
9448073	Suzuka Express	Phl	2010	43,810	15,154	180	30	19	mve	3,930 ceu

newbuildings:
*tankers operated by wholly owned subsidiary * Iver Ships BV*
*+ time chartered to Eukor   ** managed by Fleet Management Ltd., Hong Kong (www.fleetship.com), ‡ by Hachiuma Steamship Co. Ltd.*
NB: in addition to the vessels listed above, the company also operates 9 livestock carriers with 4 new vessels scheduled for 2013 delivery.

Wagenborg Shipping B.V.   Netherlands

Funnel: *Black with two narrow white bands.* **Hull:** *Light grey with broad red band interrupted by two diagonal white stripes and white 'WAGENBORG', black boot-topping.* **History:** *Founded 1898 as E. Wagenborg's Scheepvaart Expeditiebedrijf NV to 1972 and Wagenborg Scheepvaart BV to 1987.* **Web:** *www.wagenborg.com*

IMO#	name	flag	year	grt	dwt	loa	bm	kts	type	former names
9546497	Adriaticborg	Nld	2011	11,885	17,294	143	22	17	ggc	ex CCNI Topocalma-12, Adriaticborg-11
9365661	Africaborg	Nld	2008	11,894	17,356	143	22	17	ggc	ex CCNI Topocalma-11, Tianshan-09, Africaborg-08
9466348	Alamosborg	Nld	2011	11,885	17,294	143	22	17	ggc	
9466374	Alaskaborg	Nld	2012	11,894	17,350	143	22	17	ggc	
9466300	Albanyborg	Nld	2010	11,885	17,294	143	22	17	ggc	ex CCNI Tolten-12, Albanyborg-11
9333541	Amazoneborg	Nld	2007	11,894	17,355	143	22	17	ggc	
9365659	Americaborg	Nld	2007	11,894	17,356	143	22	17	ggc	
9333527	Amstelborg *	Nld	2006	11,894	17,356	143	22	17	ggc	
9466336	Amurborg	Nld	2011	11,885	17,294	143	22	17	ggc	
9466324	Andesborg	Nld	2011	11,885	17,284	143	22	17	ggc	
9466312	Aragonborg	Nld	2010	11,885	17,294	143	22	17	ggc	
9333539	Arneborg *	Nld	2006	11,894	17,356	143	22	17	ggc	
9466295	Arubaborg	Nld	2010	11,864	17,407	143	22	17	ggc	
9333553	Asiaborg	Nld	2007	11,894	17,300	143	22	17	ggc	
9466350	Atlanticborg	Nld	2012	11,885	17,294	143	22	17	ggc	
9397171	Australiaborg	Nld	2007	11,894	17,356	143	22	17	ggc	
9466362	Avonborg	Nld	2012	11,864	17,300	143	22	17	ggc	
9466051	Azoresborg	Nld	2010	11,864	17,407	143	22	17	ggc	
9248564	Nassauborg	Nld	2005	16,037	16,615	143	22	16	ggc	
9232797	Oranjeborg	Nld	2004	18,289	15,126	159	26	17	urr	l/a Finnbirch
9592563	Reestborg	Nld	2013	19,000	23,000	170	20	13	ggc	
9592575	Reggeborg	Nld	2014	19,000	23,000	170	20	13	ggc	
9355812	Rijnborg	Nld	2007	16,523	18,450	176	24	21	ucc	1,712 teu: ex Katharina-08, Rijnborg-07
9546461	Taagborg	Nld	2013	11,864	21,359	172	22		ggc	
9546459	Thamesborg	Nld	2013	11,864	21,359	172	22		ggc	
9546473	Tiberborg	Nld	2013	11,864	21,359	172	22		ggc	
9546485	Trinityborg	Nld	2013	11,864	21,359	172	22		ggc	

* managed for Allocean Maritime Ltd, UK.
The company also operates ro-ro vessels on northern European routes and numerous smaller vessels.

Wagenborg Shipping B.V. : NASSAUBORG : Hans Kraijenborg

Wallenius Wilhelmsen Logistics   Norway/Sweden

Wallenius Lines AB, Sweden

Funnel: *Yellow with yellow 'OW' on broad green band* **Hull:** *Green with green 'WALLENIUS WILHELMSEN' on white upperworks, green or red boot-topping* **History:** *founded 1934 as Rederi AB Soya. Wallenius Wilhelmsen merged operations in 1999.*
Web: *www.walleniuslines.com, www.walleniusmarine.com*

IMO#	name	flag	year	grt	dwt	loa	bm	kts	type	former names
8202367	Aegean Breeze **	Sgp	1983	29,874	12,527	164	28	18	mve	3,100 ceu: (rbt-10)
9316139	Aida	Swe	2006	60,942	22,564	199	32	19	mve	6,700 ceu
9377494	Aniara	Swe	2008	71,673	30,089	232	32	-	mve	7,600 ceu
8202355	Arabian Breeze **	Sgp	1983	29,874	12,577	164	28	18	mve	3,100 ceu: (rbt-10)
8202381	Asian Breeze **	Sgp	1983	29,874	12,562	164	28	18	mve	3,100 ceu: (rbt-10)
8312590	Baltic Breeze **	Sgp	1983	29,979	12,466	164	28	18	mve	3,100 ceu: (rbt-10)
9531715	Bess †	Pan	2010	58,750	18,013	200	32	20	mve	6,284 ceu
9176565	Boheme ††	Sgp	1999	67,264	28,360	228	32	20	mve	7,194 ceu: (len-05)
9505027	Carmen	Swe	2011	74,258	30,140	232	32	19	mve	7,600 ceu
9122655	Don Carlos	Swe	1997	67,141	28,142	228	32	20	mve	7,200 ceu: (len-06)
9182934	Don Juan	Sgp	1995	55,598	22,514	199	32	20	mve	5,846 ceu
9138513	Don Pasquale	Swe	1997	67,141	28,142	228	32	20	mve	7,200 ceu: (len-07)
9138525	Don Quijote	Sgp	1998	67,141	28,142	228	32	20	mve	7,200 ceu: (len-06)
9176577	Elektra	Sgp	1999	67,264	22,588	228	32	20	mve	7,194 ceu: (len-05)
8320767	Falstaff	Swe	1985	51,858	28,529	200	32	20	mve	5,406 ceu
9332925	Faust	Swe	2007	71,583	30,383	228	32	-	mve	7,500 ceu
9332949	Fedora	Swe	2008	71,583	30,386	228	32	-	mve	7,500 ceu
9332937	Fidelio	Swe	2008	71,583	30,137	228	32	-	mve	7,500 ceu
9505041	Figaro	Swe	2011	74,258	30,140	232	32		mve	7,934 ceu
8321325	Isolde	Swe	1985	51,071	28,396	200	32	19	mve	5,293 ceu
7917551	Madame Butterfly	Sgp	1981	50,681	28,689	200	32	19	mve	5,234 ceu
9179725	Manon	Swe	1999	67,264	14,863	228	32	20	mve	7,194 ceu: (len-05)
8016550	Medea	Sgp	1982	50,681	28,566	200	32	19	mve	5,234 ceu
9189251	Mignon	Swe	1999	67,264	28,127	228	32	20	mve	7,194 ceu: (len-05)
9312834	Morning Chorus +	Sgp	2007	57,536	21,500	200	32	20	mve	6,500 ceu
9377509	Oberon	Swe	2008	71,673	24,600	232	32	-	mve	7,620 ceu
9316141	Otello	Swe	2006	60,942	30,134	199	32	19	mve	6,700 ceu
9515395	Parsifal	Sgp	2011	75,251	43,878	265	32		urr	5,990 ceu
9409338	Porgy †	Pan	2009	58,752	18,009	200	32		mve	6,284 ceu
9515412	Salome	Sgp	2012	75,251	43,878	265	32		urr	5,990 ceu
9665798	Tosca	Sgp	2013	61,106	22,585	200	32	20	mve	6,459 teu
8321333	Tristan	Swe	1985	51,071	28,536	200	32	19	mve	5.293 ceu
9070450	Turandot	Sgp	1995	55,598	22,815	199	32	20	mve	5,846 ceu
9240160	Undine	Swe	2003	67,264	22,616	228	32	20	mve	7,194 ceu: (len-06)

newbuildings:
*vessels owned by subsidiaries of Wallenius Marine AB, ** operated by United European Car Carriers*
vessels chartered in from: † Sedona Car Lines, Panama or †† SSC Shipmanagement : + chartered to Eukor Car Carriers

Wallenius Wilhelmsen Logistics (Wallenius Lines AB) : FAUST : *Chris Dornom*

IMO#	name	flag	year	grt	dwt	loa	bm	kts	type	former names

Wilhelmsen Ship Management, Norway

Funnel: *Black with two narrow light blue bands.* **Hull:** *Red with white 'WALLENIUS WILHELMSEN', red boot-topping.* **History:** *Wilhelmsen founded 1861 as Wilh. Wilhelmsen Enterprises A/S to 1985. Wallenius Wilhelmsen merged operations in 1999.* **Web:** *www.walleniuslines.com, www.walleniusmarine.com, www.wilh-wilhelmsen.com, www.ww-group.com or www.2wglobal.com*

IMO#	name	flag	year	grt	dwt	loa	bm	kts	type	former names
9312822	Morning Concert +	Gbr	2006	57,415	21,500	200	32	20	mve	5,400 ceu
9460887	Queen Sapphire †	Sgp	2009	60,213	18,638	200	32	20	mve	6,340 ceu
8309579	Tagus *	Nis	1985	48,357	21,900	195	32	19	mve	5,409 ceu: ex Nosac Express-96
8513560	Tai Shan +	Nis	1986	48,676	15,577	190	32	18	mve	4,635 ceu: ex Nosac Tai Shan-96
8204975	Taiko	Nis	1984	66,635	43,986	262	32	21	mve	6,350 ceu: ex Barber Hector-88 (conv urc-03)
8506749	Takara +	Nis	1986	48,547	15,546	190	32	18	mve	4,635 ceu: ex Nosac Takara-96
9191319	Talisman	Nis	2000	67,140	38,500	241	32	20	mve	5,496 ceu
9218648	Tamerlane *	Nis	2001	67,140	38,500	241	32	20	mve	5,496 ceu
9191307	Tamesis *	Nis	2000	67,140	39,516	241	32	20	mve	5,496 ceu
8204951	Tampa	Nis	1984	66,635	44,013	262	32	21	mve	4,474 ceu: ex Barber Tampa-89 (conv urc-03)
8605167	Tancred +	Nis	1987	48,676	15,577	190	32	18	mve	4,635 ceu: ex Nosac Sea-96, Nosac Tancred-89
9191321	Tarago *	Nis	2000	67,140	39,516	241	32	20	mve	7,400 ceu
8309581	Tasco *	Nis	1985	48,393	22,067	195	32	19	mve	5,409 ceu: ex Nosac Explorer-96, Nosac Tasco-89
8018168	Terrier +	Nis	1982	47,947	17,863	194	32	19	mve	4,500 ceu: ex Nosac Rover-96, Nosac Barbro-89, Nopal Barbro-84
8204963	Texas	Nis	1984	66,635	44,080	262	32	21	mve	6,350 ceu: ex Barber Texas-89 (conv urc-05)
9505039	Tiger	Mlt	2011	74,255	30,140	228	32		mve	7,945 ceu
9377511	Tijuca	Nis	2008	71,673	30,089	232	32	-	mve	7,620 ceu
9377523	Tirranna	Nis	2009	71,673	29,936	232	32	-	mve	7,620 ceu
9505053	Titania	Mlt	2011	74,255	30,907	228	32		mve	7,934 ceu
9293624	Toledo *	Gbr	2005	61,321	19,628	200	32	20	mve	6,354 ceu
9375264	Tomar *	Nis	2006	61,328	22,144	200	32	20	mve	6,354 ceu
9319753	Tombarra *	Gbr	2006	61,321	19,628	200	32	20	mve	6,354 ceu
9605786	Tongala	Mlt	2012	61,106	22,585	200	32	20	mve	6,459 ceu
9515383	Tønsberg	Mlt	2011	74,622	41,820	265	32		urr	5,990 ceu
9310109	Topeka *	Gbr	2006	61,321	19,600	200	32	20	mve	6,354 ceu
9398321	Torino	Gbr	2009	61,328	22,160	200	32	20	mve	6,354 ceu
9302205	Toronto *	Gbr	2005	61,321	19,628	200	32	20	mve	6,354 ceu
9293612	Torrens *	Gbr	2004	61,321	14,512	200	32	20	mve	6,354 ceu
9319765	Tortugas *	Gbr	2006	61,321	14,512	200	32	20	mve	6,354 veu
9398333	Toscana	Gbr	2009	61,328	22,250	200	32	20	mve	6.354 ceu
8520680	Trianon **	Nis	1987	49,792	15,536	190	32	18	mve	5,828 ceu: ex Nosac Star-96
8602579	Trinidad **	Nis	1987	49,750	15,528	190	32	18	mve	5,929 ceu: ex Nosac Sky-96
9505065	Tugela	Mlt	2011	72,295	28,837	230	32		mve	8,000 ceu
9505089	Tulane	Mlt	2012	72,295	28,818	230	32		mve	7,880 ceu
9515400	Tysla	Mlt	2012	75,251	43,878	265	33		urr	5,990 ceu

newbuildings: 9605798 Mitsubishi yd 2285 6,500 ceu, HHI yd 2263 8,000 ceu

Wallenius Wilhelmsen Logistics (Wilhelmsen Ship Management) : TALISMAN : *Chris Brooks*

IMO#	name	flag	year	grt	dwt	loa	bm	kts	type	former names

* managed by Wilhelmsen Ship Management AS, (www.wilhelmsen.com), ** by Wilhelmsen Lines Car Carrier Ltd, UK (for Caiano Shipping AS, Norway or Icon Capital Corp, USA) † chartered from MMS Co., Japan, See also Paal Wilson & Co. and Dockwise NV
+ chartered to Eukor Car Carriers

American Roll-on Roll-off Carrier Inc., USA

Funnel: *White with USA national flag and 'ARC' houseflag either side of black anchor, narrow black top..* **Hull:** *Blue with blue 'ARC' on white superstructure* **History:** *Founded 1990, an ASL Group company* **Web:** *www.arrcnet.com*

IMO#	name	flag	year	grt	dwt	loa	bm	kts	type	former names
8919922	Courage	Usa	1991	52,288	29,213	203	32	19	mve	ex Aida-05
9121273	Endurance	Nis	1996	72,708	48,988	265	32	20	mve	4,923 ceu: ex Taronga-10 (conv urc-06)
9129706	Freedom	Usa	1997	49,821	19,884	190	32	19	mve	ex Takamine-03
9126297	Honor	Usa	1996	49,821	19,844	190	32	19	mve	ex Takasago-05
9070448	Independence II	Usa	1994	55,598	22,862	199	32	20	mve	ex Titus-08
8919934	Integrity	Usa	1992	52,479	29,152	203	32	20	mve	ex Otello-05
8320779	Liberty	Mhl	1985	51,858	28,509	200	32	20	mve	5,432 ceu: ex Faust-03
9080297	Resolve	Usa	1994	49,443	20,082	190	32	19	mve	4,635 ceu: ex Tanabata-03, Nosac Tanabata-96

Eukor Car Carriers Inc., South Korea

Funnel: *Cream with white curved cross on blue globe or owners colours.* **Hull:** *Light blue, most with 'EUKOR' on cream superstructure, or owners colours.* **History:** *Founded 2002 by Walleniusrederierna AB (40%), Wilhelmsen ASA (40%), Hyundai Motor Group (10%) and Kia Motor Corp. (10%).* **Web:** *www.eukor.com*

IMO#	name	flag	year	grt	dwt	loa	bm	kts	type	former names
9158616	Asian Captain	Pan	1998	71,383	25,765	229	32	20	mve	7,916 ceu: (len-06)
9176606	Asian Empire	Pan	1998	71,383	25,765	229	32	20	mve	7,916 ceu: (len-06)
9203576	Asian Majesty	Kor	1999	71,383	25,818	229	32	20	mve	7,916 ceu: (len-06)
9122954	Asian Parade	Sgp	1996	67,010	21,407	229	32	20	mve	8,086 ceu: (len-07)
9203590	Asian Trust	Sgp	2000	55,729	21,321	200	32	20	mve	6,677 ceu
9122966	Asian Vision	Sgp	1997	55,680	21,421	200	32	20	mve	6,246 ceu
9477919	Morning Camilla *	Pan	2009	60,876	22,692	200	32	20	mve	6,502 ceu
9574092	Morning Cara *	Pan	2011	59,454	18,907	200	32	19	mve	6,502 ceu
9338709	Morning Carina *	Pan	2007	60,876	22,755	200	32	19	mve	6,502 ceu
9336086	Morning Carol	Pan	2008	57,542	21,044	200	32	20	mve	6,645 ceu
9338723	Morning Caroline *	Pan	2008	60,876	22,717	200	32	19	mve	6,502 ceu
9338711	Morning Catherine *	Pan	2008	60,876	22,678	200	32	19	mve	6,502 ceu
9477830	Morning Cecilie *	Pan	2008	60,876	22,699	200	32	20	mve	6,502 ceu
8016548	Morning Cedar	Sgp	1982	50,681	28,100	200	32	19	mve	5,340 ceu: ex Carmen-10
9336062	Morning Celesta	Pan	2008	57,542	20,500	200	32	20	mve	6,645 ceu
9519133	Morning Celine *	Pan	2009	60,799	22,641	200	32	20	mve	6,502 ceu
9329461	Morning Cello *	Sgp	2007	57,542	21,059	200	32	20	mve	6,645 ceu
9338694	Morning Charlotte *	Pan	2007	60,876	22,578	200	32	20	mve	6,502 ceu
9574054	Morning Christina *	Pan	2010	59,454	18,922	200	32	20	mve	6,502 ceu
9620683	Morning Claire *	Pan	2012	60,825	16,722	200	32	20	mve	6,502 ceu
9336074	Morning Composer	Pan	2008	57,542	21,052	200	32	20	mve	6,645 ceu
9336050	Morning Conductor	Pan	2008	57,542	20,500	200	32	20	mve	6,645 ceu
9519145	Morning Cornelia *	Pan	2010	60,876	22,746	200	32	20	mve	6,502 ceu
9329473	Morning Cornet *	Sgp	2007	57,542	20,500	200	32	20	mve	6,645 ceu
9574080	Morning Crystal *	Pan	2011	59,524	18,918	200	32	20	mve	6,502 ceu

Wallenius Wilhelmsen Logistics (American Roll-on Roll-off Carrier Inc.) : COURAGE : *ARO*

IMO#	name	flag	year	grt	dwt	loa	bm	kts	type	former names
9445980	Morning Lady	Pan	2010	70,687	27,343	232	32	19	mve	8,011 ceu
9445992	Morning Laura	Pan	2010	70,687	27,297	232	32	19	mve	8,011 ceu
9446001	Morning Lena	Pan	2010	70,687	27,297	232	32	19	mve	8,011 ceu
9446013	Morning Lily	Pan	2011	70,687	27,283	232	32	19	mve	8,011 ceu
9383106	Morning Linda	Pan	2008	68,701	28,061	232	32	20	mve	8,011 ceu
9383417	Morning Lisa	Pan	2008	68,701	28,084	232	32	20	mve	8,011 ceu
9383431	Morning Lucy	Pan	2009	68,701	28,000	232	32	20	mve	8,011 ceu
9383429	Morning Lynn	Pan	2009	68,701	28,000	232	32	20	mve	8,011 ceu
9367580	Morning Margareta *	Sgp	2008	51,917	17,386	180	32	19	mve	5,340 ceu
8602775	Morning Marvel	Kor	1987	47,219	15,680	190	32	18	mve	ex Patriot-12, Fidelio-03, Skaukar-94, Nosac Skaukar-92
8708907	Morning Melody *	Pan	1988	47,068	13,162	180	32	19	mve	5,150 ceu: ex Phoenix Diamond-04
9318515	Morning Menad *	Bhs	2007	41,192	12,300	180	32	19	mve	4,750 ceu
9367592	Morning Ninni *	Sgp	2008	51,917	17,372	180	32	19	mve	5,340 ceu
7917563	Morning Spruce	Sgp	1981	50,681	28,210	198	32		mve	5,340 ceu: ex Figaro-10

managed mainly by Eukor Car Carriers Inc, South Korea, Eukor Shipowning Singapore Pte Ltd, or by Wilhelmsen Shipmanagement Singapore Pte Ltd or Wilhelmsen Ship Management (Korea) Ltd
* chartered from various owners.
also see chartered vessels under Cido Shipping, Ray Shipping, Vroon and Zodiac (Ofer Bros).

Wallenius Wilhelmsen Logistics (Eukor Car Carriers) : ASIAN VISION : *Chris Brooks*

Wallenius Wilhelmsen Logistics (Eukor Car Carriers) : MORNING CECILIE : *Hans Kraijenbosch*

IMO#	name	flag	year	grt	dwt	loa	bm	kts	type	former names

Wan Hai Lines Ltd.   Taiwan

Funnel: Blue with large white 'W'. **Hull:** Light grey with white outlined 'WAN HAI LINES' in blue and red (A's) lettering, red boot-topping.
History: Founded 1992. **Web:** www.wanhai.com.tw

IMO#	name	flag	year	grt	dwt	loa	bm	kts	type	former names
9294886	Brazil Express	Sgp	2005	42,894	52,146	269	32	23	ucc	4,252 teu: ex Wan Hai 506-11
9455296	CCNI Antuco	Sgp	2012	46,904	57,830	259	38	24	ucc	4,532 teu: ex Wan Hai 511-12
9294862	India Express	Sgp	2005	42,579	51,300	269	32	23	ucc	4,252 teu: ex Wan Hai 503-11
9305001	King Adrian	Lbr	2004	27,915	37,978	215	30	21	ucc	2,702 teu: ex Cosco Sydney-09, l/a Frisia Leipzig
9326419	MOL Dawn	Sgp	2007	42,894	52,146	269	32	23	ucc	4,252 teu: ex Wan Hai 508-12
9326421	MOL Daylight	Sgp	2007	42,894	52,146	269	32	23	ucc	4,252 teu: ex Wan Hai 509-12, Prosperity Bridge-10, Wan Hai 509-09
9238155	Wan Hai 301	Sgp	2001	26,681	30,250	200	32	24	ucc	2,495 teu
9238167	Wan Hai 302	Sgp	2002	26,681	30,234	200	32	24	ucc	2,495 teu
9238179	Wan Hai 303	Sgp	2002	26,681	30,500	200	32	24	ucc	2,495 teu
9238181	Wan Hai 305	Sgp	2002	26,681	30,246	200	32	24	ucc	2,495 teu
9237084	Wan Hai 306	Sgp	2002	25,836	34,026	197	30	21	ucc	2,226 teu
9237096	Wan Hai 307	Sgp	2002	25,836	34,026	197	30	21	ucc	2,226 teu
9248641	Wan Hai 311	Sgp	2005	27,800	32,937	213	32	22	ucc	2,646 teu
9248693	Wan Hai 312	Sgp	2006	27,800	33,055	213	32	22	ucc	2,646 teu
9248708	Wan Hai 313	Sgp	2006	27,800	32.937	213	32	22	ucc	2,646 teu
9302695	Wan Hai 315	Sgp	2006	27,800	32,937	213	32	22	ucc	2,646 teu
9342700	Wan Hai 316	Sgp	2007	27,800	32.937	213	32	22	ucc	2,646 teu
9342712	Wan Hai 317	Sgp	2008	27,800	33,055	213	32	22	ucc	2,646 teu
9294848	Wan Hai 501	Sgp	2005	42,579	52,249	269	32	23	ucc	4,252 teu
9294850	Wan Hai 502	Sgp	2005	42,579	52,146	269	32	23	ucc	4,252 teu: ex Dong Hai Bridge-09, Wan Hai 502-06
9326407	Wan Hai 507	Sgp	2007	42,894	52,146	269	32	23	ucc	4,252 teu: ex Kota Salam-08, l/a Wan Hai 507
9326433	Wan Hai 510	Sgp	2008	42,894	52,146	269	32	23	ucc	4,252 teu: ex America Express-12, Wan Hai 510-11
9457622	Wan Hai 512	Sgp	2012	47,309	57,830	259	37	24	ucc	4,120 teu
9457634	Wan Hai 513	Sgp	2012	46,904	57,830	259	37	24	ucc	4,120 teu
9457646	Wan Hai 515	Sgp	2013	47,300	57,830	259	37	24	ucc	4,120 teu
9457658	*Wan Hai 516*	Sgp	2013	47,300	57,800	259	37	24	ucc	4,120 teu
9457660	*Wan Hai 517*	Sgp	2013	47,300	57,800	259	37	24	ucc	4,120 teu
9327786	Wan Hai 601	Sgp	2007	66,199	67,797	276	40	26	ucc	6,039 teu: ex Hyundai Lyon-12, Wan Hai 601-10
9327798	Wan Hai 602	Sgp	2007	66,199	67,797	276	40	26	ucc	6.039 teu
9327803	Wan Hai 603	Sgp	2007	66,199	67,797	276	40	26	ucc	6,039 teu
9331165	Wan Hai 605	Sgp	2008	66,199	67,797	276	40	26	ucc	6,039 teu

owned/managed by subsidiary Wan Hai Lines (Singapore) Pte Ltd, Singapore (formed 1997).
also owns 29 other 12-19,000 grt container ships operating mainly in the Far East.

Warwick & Esplen Ltd.   U.K.

The Hadley Shipping Co. Ltd.

Funnel: Yellow with black 'HSC' inside white diamond, black top. **Hull:** Black with red boot-topping. **History:** Formed 1926.
Web: www.angloeasterngroup.com

IMO#	name	flag	year	grt	dwt	loa	bm	kts	type	former names
9305087	Cerafina	Gbr	2005	40,524	74,759	225	32	13	bbu	ex Clare -12, Golden Gunn-07
9307657	Clymene	Gbr	2006	40,244	73,600	225	32	14	bbu	ex Ming Mei-06
9223198	Cymbeline	Iom	2001	38,299	73,060	225	32	14	bbu	

managed by Anglo-Eastern (UK) Ltd., UK.

Oskar Wehr KG (GmbH & Co.)   Germany

Funnel: Black with blue 'W' in blue ring over two blue bands in centre and towards top of broad yellow band or charterers colours. **Hull:** Blue or grey with diagonal yellow stripe and blue or red boot-topping. **History:** Formed 1945. **Web:** www.wehrship.de

IMO#	name	flag	year	grt	dwt	loa	bm	kts	type	former names
9397860	Anni Selmer	Mhl	2009	31,222	56,000	190	32	14	bbu	
9435064	Charlotte Selmer	Mhl	2011	92,079	176,000	292	45	14	bbu	
9149897	Elqui ‡	Mhl	1999	16,177	23,026	184	26	19	ucc	1,730 teu: l/a Wehr Schulau
9434711	Frederike Selmer	Mhl	2009	32,957	56,847	190	32	14	bbu	
9290866	Frieda Selmer	Mhl	2004	31,218	55,718	190	32	14	bbu	
9435076	Greta Selmer	Mhl	2011	92,079	175,181	292	45	14	bbu	
9290878	Helene Selmer	Mhl	2005	31,218	55,741	190	32	14	bbu	
9434448	Hugo Selmer	Mhl	2010	92,079	175,401	292	45	14	bbu	
9500584	Ingwar Selmer	Mhl	2011	31,784	55,733	190	32	14	bbu	
9476642	Klara Selmer	Mhl	2012	92,079	175,247	292	45	14	bbu	
9435052	Lene Selmer	Mhl	2010	92,079	175,401	292	45	14	bbu	
9301330	Maersk Dellys	Mhl	2006	54,193	67,470	294	32	24	ucc	5,089 teu: ex Wehr Singapore-06

IMO#	name	flag	year	grt	dwt	loa	bm	kts	type	former names
9301328	Maersk Derince	Deu	2005	54,193	67,470	294	32	24	ucc	5,089 teu: ex Wehr Hongkong-06
9324083	Mimi Selmer	Mhl	2005	31,500	55,711	190	32	14	bbu	
9232644	Nienstedten ‡	Mhl	2001	16,802	23,000	185	25	19	ucc	1,730 teu; ex Wehr Nienstedten-12, African Cheetah-11, Wehr Nienstedten-09, Libra Chile-09, I/a Wehr Nienstedten
9331866	Therese Selmer	Mhl	2006	31,500	56,000	190	32	14	bbu	
9476630	Tom Selmer	Mhl	2011	92,079	175,154	292	45	14	bbu	
9232383	Wehr Alster	Mhl	2002	25,630	33,767	207	30	21	ucc	2,546 teu: ex CSAV Rio Baker-09, CCNI Arica-04, Wehr Alster-02
9134622	Wehr Altona *	Mhl	1997	16,801	23,021	184	25	19	ucc	1,728 teu: ex African Ubuntu-11,Wehr Altona-10, CCNI Hamburgo-09, Wehr Altona-08, Lykes Pathfinder-02, Norasia Yantian-01, CSAV Ningpo-00, Kota Sejarah-00, CSAV Rio de la Plata-99, I/a Wehr Altona
9232395	Wehr Bille	Mhl	2002	25,624	33,739	208	30	21	ucc	2,474 teu: ex NileDutch Singapore-12, Wehr Bille-10, NYK Estrela-09, CSAV Rio Cochamo-05, Wehr Bille-04, CCNI Antartico-03, Wehr Bille-02
9149902	Wehr Blankensee ‡	Mhl	1999	16,177	23,021	184	26	19	ucc	1,730 teu: ex CSAV Montreal-07, Norasia Montreal-01, Illapel-00, I/a Wehr Blankensee
9236688	Wehr Elbe ‡	Mhl	2001	25,703	33,795	203	30	22	ucc	2,524 teu: ex CSAV Callao-08, I/a Wehr Elbe
9204477	Wehr Flottbek **	Deu	1999	16,802	22,878	184	25	19	ucc	1,730 teu: ex CCNI Fortuna-09, Wehr Flottbek-08, Alianca Bahia-01, Wehr Flottbek-00
9252981	Wehr Havel	Mhl	2002	25,703	33,795	208	30	21	ucc	2,524 teu: ex CCNI Andes-11, Wehr Havel-10, CSAV Rio Tolten-09, Wehr Havel-04
9144134	Wehr Koblenz ‡	Mhl	1997	16,801	23,051	184	25	20	ucc	1,726 teu: ex CCNI Bilboa-09, Wehr Koblenz-08, MOL Springbok-06, P&O Nedlloyd Portbury-06, P&O Nedlloyd Calypso-05, Costa Rica-02, Wehr Koblenz-01, Panamerican-01, CSAV Rio Amazonas-99, I/a Wehr Koblenz
9144146	Wehr Müden *	Mhl	1998	16,801	22,983	184	25	19	ucc	1,730 teu: ex DAL Mauritius-10, Wehr Müden-10, CMA CGM Azteca-10, Wehr Müden-06, CSAV Hong Kong-06, Wehr Müden-03, TMM Quetzal-01, Wehr Müden-01, CSAV Valencia-00, Crowley Express-00, CSAV Rimac-99, I/a Wehr Müden
9252993	Wehr Oste	Mhl	2002	25,703	33,670	208	30	21	ucc	2,524 teu: ex CCNI Concepcion-11, Wehr Oste-10, Callao Express-10, P&O Nedlloyd Yarra Valley-06, Wehr Oste-03

Oskar Wehr KG : WEHR ELBE : *Nico Kemps*

IMO#	name	flag	year	grt	dwt	loa	bm	kts	type	former names
9134634	Wehr Ottensen †	Mhl	1997	16,801	23,051	184	25	20	ucc	1,728 teu: ex CMA CGM Parati-10, Delmas Suffren-08, Bremen Senator-06, Wehr Ottensen-04, Indamex Nhava Sheva-02, Wehr Ottensen-01, CSAV Rio Grande-99, Wehr Ottensen-98
9204489	Wehr Rissen **	Deu	1999	16,802	23,028	185	25	19	ucc	1,730 teu: ex MOL Utility-09, Wehr Rissen-08, Delmas Mascareignes-07, CMA CGM Bourgainville-04, Wehr Rissen-99
9243239	Wehr Trave	Mhl	2002	25,705	33,795	207	30	21	ucc	2,524 teu: ex CSAV Valparaiso-11, Wehr Trave-10 CSAV Rio Puelo-09, CCNI Aysen-04, I/a Wehr Trave
9243241	Wehr Warnow	Mhl	2002	25,705	33,793	208	30	21	ucc	2,524 teu: ex CCNI Constitucion-11, Wehr Warnow-10, CSAV Rio Maule-09, Columbus China-04, Wehr Warnow-02
9236690	Wehr Weser ‡	Mhl	2001	25,703	33,795	203	30	22	ucc	2,524 teu: ex Libra New York-09, I/a Wehr Weser

*managed for Dr Peters GmbH & Co KG, ** for Hansa Treuhand Schiffs AG, † for Konig & Cie GmbH or ‡ for Lloyd Fonds AG, all Germany.*

Westfal-Larsen & Co. AS   Norway

Funnel: *Yellow with two narrow black bands, narrow black top.* **Hull:** *Dark blue with 'WESTFAL-LARSEN' in white, red boot topping.*
History: *Formed 1905.* **Web:** *www.wlco.no*

IMO#	name	flag	year	grt	dwt	loa	bm	kts	type	former names
9387671	Berganger	Nis	2009	29,644	46,195	183	32	14	tco	
9387683	Brimanger	Nis	2009	29,644	46,265	183	32	14	tco	
9387695	Falkanger	Nis	2009	29,644	46,239	183	32	14	tco	
9387700	Fauskanger	Nis	2009	29,644	46,195	183	32	14	tco	
9387712	Finnanger	Nis	2009	29,644	46,251	183	32	14	tco	
9387724	Fjellanger	Nis	2010	29,644	46,287	183	32	14	tco	
9112222	Mauranger	Nis	1995	25,707	41,109	180	31	14	tco	ex Bow Tribute-01
9112234	Moldanger	Nis	1997	25,707	40,845	180	31	14	tco	ex Bow Triton-01
9212371	Ravnanger	Nis	2000	28,246	46,541	183	32	14	tco	ex Minerva Joanna-07
9212369	Risanger	Nis	2000	28,246	46,270	183	32	14	tco	ex Minerva Julie-07
9524762	Taranger	Nis	2011	29,712	45,870	183	32	14	tco	
9524774	Torvanger	Nis	2012	29,712	45,318	183	32	14	tco	

managed by Westfal-Larsen Management AS (formed 1996)

Oskar Wehr KG : FRIEDA SELMER : *ARO*

IMO#	name	flag	year	grt	dwt	loa	bm	kts	type	former names

Masterbulk Pte. Ltd., Singapore
Funnel / Hull: *As above.* **History:** *fomed July 1995 as spin-off from Westfal-Larsen.* **Web:** *www.masterbulk.com.sg*

IMO#	name	flag	year	grt	dwt	loa	bm	kts	type	former names
8221765	Austanger	Iom	1985	20,915	30,173	169	27	15	boh	ex Star Austanger-09, Anthony Rainbow-92
8507200	Geiranger	Sgp	1986	27,972	43,131	200	29	15	boh	ex Star Geiranger-09
8507212	Grindanger	Sgp	1986	27,972	43,131	201	29	15	boh	ex Star Grindanger-09
9079119	Hardanger	Sgp	1995	34,364	44,251	199	31	16	boh	ex Star Hardanger-09
9079121	Heranger	Sgp	1995	37,150	44,251	199	31	16	boh	ex Star Heranger-08
9081801	Hosanger	Sgp	1995	37,150	44,251	199	31	16	boh	ex Star Hosanger-08
9100073	Hoyanger	Sgp	1995	34,363	44,251	199	31	16	boh	ex Star Hoyanger-09
9186209	Ikebana	Sgp	1999	30,840	39,751	185	31	16	boh	ex Star Ikebana-09
9186211	Indiana	Sgp	2000	30,745	39,760	185	31	16	boh	ex Star Indiana-09
9186223	Inventana	Sgp	2000	30,745	39,789	185	31	16	boh	ex Star Inventana-09
9186235	Isoldana	Sgp	2000	30,745	39,465	185	31	16	boh	ex Star Isoldana-09
9189938	Mariana	Iom	1998	29,688	50,655	195	32	14	bbu	ex Sanko Spring-11
9189940	Mobilana	Iom	1998	29,688	50,655	195	32	14	bbu	ex Sanko Stream-11
9253868	Okiana	Sgp	2003	36,324	48,661	199	32	16	boh	ex Star Okiana-09
9253856	Optimana	Sgp	2003	36,324	48,661	199	32	16	boh	ex Star Optimana-09
9253870	Osakana	Sgp	2004	36,324	48,661	199	32	16	boh	ex Star Osakana-09
9249295	Oshimana	Sgp	2003	36,324	48,661	199	32	16	boh	ex Star Oshimana-07
9401805	Panamana	Sgp	2010	39,258	54,694	213	32	15	boh	
9401790	Pelicana	Sgp	2009	39,258	54,694	213	32	15	boh	
9371086	Posidana	Sgp	2008	39,258	54,500	213	32	15	boh	
9380788	Providana	Sgp	2007	39,258	54,694	213	32	15	boh	
9000314	Siranger	Sgp	1991	11,878	17,012	149	23	14	boh	ex Star Siranger-09, T.S.Adventure-93

managed by Westfal-Larsen Management AS (formed 1996):

Anders Wilhelmsen & Co. AS   Norway
Funnel: *Black with white 'W' on red over black divided diamond between two narrow red bands on broad white band.* **Hull:** *Grey or red with red boot-topping.* **History:** *Formed 1939 as A Wilhelmsen to 1964 and sometime 47% owner of Euronav. OHT formed 2005.* **Web:** *www.wilhelmsen.com or www.oht.no*

IMO#	name	flag	year	grt	dwt	loa	bm	kts	type	former names
8616168	Osprey **	Nis	1989	38,722	53,000	223	45	15	ohl	ex Heavylift Ancora-09, Ancora-08, Songa Ancora-08, Ancora-05, Leon Spirit-04, Borja Tapias-04 (conv tcr/sht-08)
7931454	Eagle *	Nis	1981	31,021	31,809	199	42	14	ohl	ex Heavylift Eagle-09, Willift Eagle-08, Willift Lady-06, Lucky Lady-06, Albe-94, World Cliff-90, Cliff-84, World Cliff-83 (conv tcr/sht-06)
7915278	Falcon *	Nis	1981	31,027	31,908	199	42	14	ohl	ex Heavylift Falcon-09, Willift Falcon-08, Nilos-08, Nile-95, World Zeal-90 (conv tcr/sht-07)

Westfal-Larsen & Co. AS Masterbulk Pte : AUSTANGER : *Hans Kraijenbosch*

IMO#	name	flag	year	grt	dwt	loa	bm	kts	type	former names
8616556	Hawk *	Nis	1989	38,722	54,000	223	45	15	ohl	ex Heavylift Hawk-09, Hawk-08, Hawker-08, Front Transporter-07, Genmar Transporter-04, Crude Transporter-03, Nord-Jahre Transporter-00, Jahre Transporter-93 (conv tcr/sht-08)
9123075	Wilana	Nis	1997	79,494	149,706	270	45	15	tcr	
9151840	Wilmina	Mlt	1997	79,494	149,775	270	45	15	tcr	
9416422	Wilsky	Mlt	2009	84,735	164,787	274	50	15	tcr	ex Crude Gamma-09

*managed by Wilhelmsen Marine Services AS and * operated by Offshore Heavy Transport AS, Norway (** managed by Songa Ship Mgmt.)*

Westfal-Larsen & Co. AS : MARIANA : *ARO*

Westfal-Larsen & Co. AS : OSAKANA : *ARO*

Reederei Gebruder Winter GmbH & Co. KG — Germany

Funnel: *Mainly charterers colours.* **Hull:** *Grey, blue or red with red boot-topping.* **History:** *Founded in 1900 and shipowners since 1970 as Schiffahrtskontor Reederei Gebruder Winter to 1999.* **Web:** *www.winter-ship.de*

IMO#	name	flag	year	grt	dwt	loa	bm	kts	type	former names
9445887	Calandra	Atg	2010	35,878	41,411	213	32	22	ucc	2,758 teu: ex Pos Melbourne-11, Calandra-10
9445899	Calidris	Mhl	2012	35,878	41,108	213	32	22	ucc	2,758 teu
9143245	Classica	Deu	1998	23,297	30,241	188	30	21	ucc	2,048 teu: ex Adelaide Express-09, Classica-06, Safmarine Mtata-05, Maersk Dakar-04, Classica-02, Libra Buenos Aires-02, Classica-01, CMA Djakarta-00, Jolly Ocra-99, Classica-98
9354674	Clipper	Atg	2008	18,199	23,831	182	25	21	ucc	1,700 teu
9143233	Columba	Deu	1998	23,897	30,258	188	30	21	ucc	2,048 teu: ex Cap Serrat-09, Columba-08, Safmarine Gonubie-08, Libra Houston-02, TMM Veracruz-01, APL Atlantic-00, Columba-99, Maersk Genoa-98, l/a Columba
9241918	Commander	Atg	2004	30,051	35,770	208	32	22	ucc	2,677 teu: ex Maersk Pecem-09, Commander-04
9354662	Convent	Atg	2008	18,263	23,978	182	25	21	ucc	1,700 teu: ex Cassandra B-10, Convent-08
9430870	Corvette	Atg	2010	18,327	23,295	175	27	19	ucc	1,740 teu
9228552	Kota Perkasa	Atg	2001	30,047	35,770	208	32	22	ucc	2,672 teu: ex Commodore-10, MSC Andes-02, Commodore-01
9430868	Mell Solomon	Atg	2009	18,326	23,294	175	27	19	ucc	1,740 teu: ex Catena-09

* also operates smaller feeder container ships

Reederei Hermann Wulff — Germany

Funnel: *Yellow with green 'W' on white diamond, black top or charterers colours.* **Hull:** *Black or green with red boot-topping.* **History:** *Formed 1960 by fifth generation of seafaring family.* **Web:** *www.reederei-wulff.de*

IMO#	name	flag	year	grt	dwt	loa	bm	kts	type	former names
9232761	Antje Wulff	Lbr	2002	32,284	39,216	211	32	22	ucc	2,732 teu: ex Ibn Abdoun-10, CMA CGM Seagull-05, P&O Nedlloyd Dammam-03, Antje-Helen Wulff-02
9185401	Elbwolf	Lbr	1999	32,221	39,340	211	32	21	ucc	2,732 teu: ex Ibn Khaldoun-10, Aramac-05, Elbwolf-02, Ipex Equality-01, Elbwolf-99
9537381	H-G Buelow	Lbr	2011	32,987	56,892	190	32	14	bbu	
9316373	Hermann Wulff *	Deu	2006	32,322	39,340	211	32	22	ucc	2,732 eu: ex Ibn Khallikan-12, OOCL Energy-08, Hermann Wulff-06
9185413	Ibn Asakir	Lbr	1999	32,322	39,128	211	32	22	ucc	2,673 teu: ex CSAV Rio Maipo-07, NYK Prosperity-04, Weserwolf-03, Columbia Bridge-01, Weserwolf-00
9401271	Ilse Wulff	Lbr	2009	75,604	85,622	304	40	27	ucc	6,500 teu: ex Al Khor-12, l/a Ilse Wulff
9498896	Johannes Wulff	Lbr	2010	50,697	93,272	229	38	14	bbu	
9498901	John Wulff	Lbr	2010	50,729	93,282	229	38	14	bbu	
9056284	Kollmar	Lbr	1993	16,233	21,540	182	25	20	ucc	1,667 teu: ex Ilse Wulff-06, Nigeria Star-03, Ilse Wulff-01, Direct Kookaburra-01, Isle Wulff-99, Maersk Pretoria-99, Maersk Pireaus-98, TSL Unity-98, Ilse Wulff-95, Contship Rotterdam-94, Ilse-93
9056272	Manuela	Lbr	1993	16,233	21,540	182	25	20	ucc	1,667 teu: ex Inaba-06, Hermann-04, P&O Nedlloyd Cotonou-03, Hermann-02, Direct Kea-01, MSC Cali-99, Hermann-99, Maersk Aarhus-98, Hermann-98, Sea Harmony-97, Hermann-96, CCNI Angol-96, Hermann-95, Contship New York-95, Hermann-93, Deppe Europe-93, Hermann-93
9252101	MSC Firenze	Lbr	2006	51,350	58,260	292	32	24	ucc	4,546 teu: ex Maersk Duesseldorf-08, Hijaz-08, Maersk Diadem-06, Viktoria Wulff-06
9537379	Suse	Lbr	2011	32,987	56,925	190	32	14	bbu	

* managed for Ship Invest Emissionshaus AG, Germany.

XT Management Ltd. — Israel

Funnel: *Blue or charterers colours.* **Hull:** *Various colours.* **History:** *Founded 1957 as Mediterranean Seaways Ltd to 1967 and Mediterranean Lines Ltd to 1970. Formerly Ofer Brothers Holdings Ltd., restyled XT Management, 2010* **Web:** *www.oferg.com*

IMO#	name	flag	year	grt	dwt	loa	bm	kts	type	former names
9330654	Blue Diamond *	Lbr	2006	32,572	53,538	190	32	14	bbu	
8704183	Cap Roca	Lbr	1990	35,303	42,221	234	32	21	ucc	2,640 teu: ex New York Express-96, Berlin Express-93, POL Jos-92, Berlin Express-91
9119139	Cape Carmel	Bmu	1996	92,194	179,869	290	46	14	bbu	ex Pytchley-05, SGC Capital-98
9189249	Cape Tavor	Lbr	1999	87,363	172,515	289	45	15	bbu	ex Cape Lowlands-06, La Selva-04
9051820	Car Star	Lbr	1993	41,931	17,189	196	29	18	mve	4,513 ceu: ex Bujin-10,

IMO#	name	flag	year	grt	dwt	loa	bm	kts	type	former names
8913459	Caribbean Sea	Lbr	1992	37,071	46,975	237	32	21	ucc	3,005 teu: ex Zim Florida-05, St. Petersburg Mariner-03, St. Petersburg Senator-02
9267546	Cala Pira	Bmu	2004	18,931	15,052	186	25	20	grf	ex Carmel Bio-Top-11, l/a Rio Yarkon
9167534	Cala Paradiso	Bmu	2003	18,931	15,052	186	25	20	grf	ex Carmel Eco-Fresh-11, l/a Rio Alexandre
9198927	Finisterre *	Lbr	1991	29,841	32,675	200	32	18	ucc	2,022 teu: ex Cap Finisterre-12
9311763	Lorraine	Lbr	2006	27,786	37,800	222	30	22	ucc	2,742 teu: ex Cape Mayor-06
9626558	Kestrel	Lbr	2013	16,800	21,500	172	27		ucc	
9619438	MSC Albany	Lbr	2012	94,000	112,516	299	48	22	ucc	8,800 teu
9619426	MSC Altamira	Lbr	2012	94,017	112,516	299	48	22	ucc	8,800 teu
9619440	NAS Anchorage	Lbr	2013	94,017	112,516	299	48	22	ucc	8,,800 teu
8913435	North Sea *	Lbr	1992	37,071	46,975	237	32	21	ucc	2,668 teu: ex Zim Singapore-04, Korea Star-03, Moscow Mariner-02, Moscow Senator-02, Choyang Moscow-98
9331713	Red Diamond	Lbr	2011	32,637	53,500	190	32	14	bbu	
9330666	White Diamond	Lbr	2008	32,578	53,538	190	32	14	bbu	
9231793	Zim California	Isr	2002	53,453	62,740	294	32	24	ucc	4,839 teu
9471202	Zim Constanza	Isl	2010	40,542	50,107	261	32	24	ucc	4,253 teu
9318187	Zim Genova	Lbr	2007	39,906	50,532	261	32	24	ucc	4,253 teu
9318175	Zim Livorno	Lbr	2006	39,906	50,689	261	32	24	ucc	4,253 teu
9231779	Zim Mediterranean	Lbr	2002	53,453	62,686	294	32	24	ucc	4,839 teu
9322322	Zim Shekou	Lbr	2007	39,906	50,629	260	32	24	ucc	4,253 teu
9471214	Zim Tarragona	Isl	2010	40,542	50,088	261	32	24	ucc	4,253 teu
9322334	Zim Vancouver	Lbr	2007	39,906	50,532	261	32	24	ucc	4,253 teu: ex Pearl River I-12, Zim Vancouver-07

newbuildings:

*vessels owned by Ofer (Ships Holdings) Ltd., * owned by subsidiary Kotani Shipmanagement Ltd, Cyprus (founded jointly with Zodiac Maritime Agencies Ltd in 1999)*

Zodiac Maritime Agencies Ltd., U.K.

Funnel: *Blue with blue 'Z' on white disc with globe outline.some with black top or charterers colours.* **Hull:** *Black, grey, red or white with red boot-topping.* **History:** *Formed 1976, acquired 50% P&O share of Associated Bulk Carriers in 2000 and balance in 2003.* **Web:** *www.zodiac-maritime.com*

IMO#	name	flag	year	grt	dwt	loa	bm	kts	type	former names
9332846	APL London	Gbr	2008	71,786	72,982	293	40	25	ucc	6,350 teu
9332872	APL Toyko	Gbr	2009	71,786	72,982	293	40	25	ucc	6,350 teu
9070462	Asian Beauty ++	Gbr	1994	44,481	13,308	185	31	18	mve	4,363 ceu
9070474	Asian Glory ++	Gbr	1994	44,818	13,363	184	31	18	mve	4,363 ceu
9255983	Battersea Park	Lbr	2002	11,590	19,949	146	24	14	tco	ex Chemstar Moon-11
9238753	Bavaria	Gbr	2003	39,941	50,811	260	32	24	ucc	4,253 teu: ex Bavaria Express-12, CP Indigo-06, Contship Indigo-05, APL Panama-04
9640102	Beihai Park	Lbr	2012	11,600	19,800	146	24	14	tco	
9276250	Belsize Park	Gbr	2003	11,590	19,937	146	24	14	tco	
9367827	Blackpool Tower	Gbr	2009	26,638	34,252	213	29	22	ucc	2,578 teu
9162497	Botswana	Lbr	1998	75,637	81,819	300	40	24	ucc	6,214 teu: ex MSC Botswana-12, NYK Andromeda-10
9538945	Bridgegate	Gbr	2010	29,977	53,477	190	32	23	bbu	
9143489	Brother Glory	Gbr	1998	27,105	46,211	190	31	13	bbu	
9040508	Buccleuch *	Bmu	1993	90,820	182,675	284	47	13	bbu	
9337107	Cape Albatross †	Pan	2007	101,963	203,185	300	50	14	bbu	
9446623	Cape Buzzard	Lbr	2011	92,746	181,399	292	45	14	bbu	
9296212	Cape Condor †	Pan	2004	90,091	180,181	289	45	14	bbu	
9035589	Cape Eagle	Gbr	1993	81,589	161,475	280	45	14	bbu	
9035591	Cape Falcon	Gbr	1993	81,589	149,480	280	45	14	bbu	
9344289	Cape Flamingo	Gbr	2005	90,092	180,201	290	45	14	bbu	
9300594	Cape Harrier †	Pan	2005	89,651	177,005	289	45	14	bbu	
9077379	Cape Hawk	Gbr	1995	81,589	161,425	280	45	14	bbu	
9304540	Cape Heron †	Pan	2005	88,494	177,656	290	45	14	bbu	
9036014	Cape Kestrel	Gbr	1993	81,589	161,475	280	45	14	bbu	
9056818	Cape Merlin	Gbr	1994	77,503	150,966	273	43	13	bbu	ex Universal Spirit-01
9077367	Cape Osprey	Gbr	1996	81,589	161,448	280	45	14	bbu	ex Sanko Oriole-03
9493755	Cape Seagull	Lbr	2012	91,792	180,000	292	45	14	bbu	
9136577	Cape Stork	Gbr	1996	83,658	171,039	278	45	14	bbu	ex Lowlands Rose-04
9432880	Carrera	Gbr	2008	46,800	12,296	183	32	20	mve	4,902 ceu
9460318	Castlegate	Gbr	2008	29,923	53,503	190	32	15	bbu	
9463059	CMA CGM Effingham	Gbr	2011	141,649	140,700	366	48	25	ucc	13,092 teu: ex Maersk Effingham-12
9463047	CMA CGM Enfield	Gbr	2011	141,649	141,406	366	48	25	ucc	13,092 teu: ex Maersk Enfield-12
9463023	CMA CGM Erving	Gbr	2011	141,649	141,377	366	48	25	ucc	13,092 teu: Maersk Erving-12
9005508	Cornwall	Lbr	1992	11,361	16,225	145	22		lpg	16,664 m³ ex Richmond Bridge-11, Garrison Savannah-09, Maralunga-07, Fezzano-02, Maralunga-94
9493200	Crystalgate	Gbr	2010	17,025	28,183	169	27	14	bbu	
9325178	CSAV Rio Aysen	Gbr	2007	46,800	12,322	183	32	20	mve	4,902 ceu

280

IMO#	name	flag	year	grt	dwt	loa	bm	kts	type	former names
9308807	CSAV Rio Grande	Gbr	2007	46,800	12,315	183	32	20	mve	4,902 ceu
9494905	CSAV Rio Grey	Lbr	2009	60,387	17,245	200	32	20	mve	6,295 ceu
9308792	CSAV Rio Imperial	Gbr	2006	46,800	12,322	183	32	20	mve	4,902 ceu
9325180	CSAV Rio Nevado	Gbr	2007	46,800	12,322	183	32	20	mve	4,902 ceu
8807650	Cumbria	Lbr	1990	13,455	13,453	146	23	14	lpg	17,957 m³ ex Victoire-04, Kelvin-96
9103702	Darwin	Gbr	1996	51,938	60,348	294	32	23	ucc	4,507 teu: ex MSC Darwin-09, Maersk Darwin-08, ANL Indonesia-03, Indonesia-02, APL Indonesia-01
9479929	Derby	Gbr	2011	45,812	53,028	226	37		lpg	80,156 m³
9454010	Devon	Gbr	2010	45,812	53,010	226	37		lpg	80,199 m³
9470088	Dorset	Gbr	2011	45,812	53,076	226	37		lpg	80,204 m³
9403877	Essex	Lbr	2009	22,914	26,533	174	28		lpg	35,556 m³
8902395	Eurus Lima	Lbr	1990	19,595	15,672	203	28	21	grf	506 teu: ex Edyth L.-07
8902400	Eurus Lisbon	Lbr	1991	19,595	15,646	203	28	21	grf	506 teu: ex Frances L.-07
9015321	Eurus London	Lbr	1992	19,595	15,844	203	28	21	grf	506 teu: ex Courtney L,-07, Martha L.-xx
9105633	Fernie *	Bmu	1996	63,153	122,292	266	41	14	bbu	
9615042	Friendly Islands	Lbr	2012	17,033	28,387	169	27	14	bbu	
9082312	Handan Steel	Lbr	1994	147,580	264,932	333	60	15	bor	ex Golden Jewel-09, Han-Ei-07 (conv tcr-08)
9105645	Grafton *	Bmu	1996	63,153	122,301	266	41	14	bbu	
9276262	Green Park	Gbr	2003	11,590	19,940	146	24	14	tco	
9505998	Greenwich Park	Lbr	2011	11,987	19,991	146	24	14	tco	ex Sanko Neptune-11
9053579	Guofeng Enterprise	Lbr	1993	149,323	260,995	330	59	15	bor	ex Silver Jewel-10, Grand Mountain-08, Mitsumine-04, (conv tcr-10)
9115690	Guofeng First	Bmu	1996	108,083	211,320	312	50	14	bbu	ex Kildare-09, SGC Express-98
9082312	Handan Steel	Lbr	1994	149,282	264,971	333	60	14	bor	ex Golden Jewel-09, Han-Ei- (conv tcr-08)
8902656	Hangang Elite	Lbr	1991	88,946	155,150	275	50	15	bor	ex Skyway-09, Genmar Spartiate-06, Bruce Smart-00 (conv tcr-10)
9113305	Heythrop	Bmu	1996	85,364	165,729	288	44	13	bbu	
9505986	Highbury Park	Lbr	2011	11,987	19,991	146	24	14	tco	ex Sanko Noble-12
9233856	Holsatia	Gbr	2003	39,941	50,913	260	32	24	ucc	4,253 teu: ex Holsatia Express-12, CP Provider-06, Lykes Provider-05
9305659	Hyundai Busan	Gbr	2006	74,651	80,102	304	40	27	ucc	6,763 teu
9110391	Hyundai Discovery	Gbr	1996	64,054	51,120	275	40	25	ucc	5,711 teu: ex MSC Discovery-11, Hyundai Discovery-09 in casualty/repair ACX Hibiscis
9393022	Hyundai Global	Gbr	2009	94,511	99,086	340	46	27	ucc	8,562 teu
9305661	Hyundai Hongkong	Gbr	2006	74,651	80,120	304	40	27	ucc	6,763 teu
9110377	Hyundai Independence	Gbr	1996	64,054	68,537	275	40	25	ucc	5,711 teu
9110389	Hyundai Liberty	Gbr	1996	64,054	68,539	275	40	25	ucc	5,711 teu: ex MOL Infinity-12, APL Liberty-11, Hyundai Liberty-07
9332884	Hyundai Long Beach	Gbr	2009	71,786	72,982	293	40	26	ucc	6,350 teu
9393319	Hyundai Loyalty	Gbr	2009	94,511	95,810	340	46	27	ucc	8,562 teu
9393307	Hyundai Mercury	Gbr	2009	94,511	95,810	340	46	27	ucc	8,562 teu
9385025	Hyundai New York	Gbr	2009	71,786	72,982	293	40	26	ucc	6,350 teu
8608157	Hyundai No.106 ++	Lbr	1987	42,469	12,848	184	31	18	mve	4,795 ceu
8608169	Hyundai No.107 ++	Lbr	1987	42,469	12,989	184	31	18	mve	4,795 ceu
8608145	Hyundai No.109 ++	Lbr	1987	31,355	9,694	174	28	19	mve	3,510 ceu: ex Toronto-99, Hyundai No.109-97
9385013	Hyundai Oakland	Gbr	2009	71,786	72,982	293	40	26	ucc	6,350 teu
9305647	Hyundai Shanghai	Gbr	2006	74,651	80,262	304	40	26	ucc	6,763 teu
9305685	Hyundai Singapore	Gbr	2006	74,651	85,250	304	40	26	ucc	6,763 teu
9393321	Hyundai Splendor	Gbr	2009	94,511	98,968	340	46	26	ucc	8,562 teu
9385001	Hyundai Tacoma	Gbr	2009	71,786	72,982	293	40	26	ucc	6,350 teu
9305673	Hyundai Tokyo	Gbr	2006	74,651	80,059	304	40	26	ucc	6,763 teu
9463085	Hyundai Vancouver	Gbr	2010	71,821	71,987	293	40	26	ucc	6,350 teu
9113317	Irfon *	Bmu	1996	85,364	165,729	288	44	13	bbu	
9367815	Jakarta Tower	Gbr	2008	26,638	34,325	213	29	22	ucc	2,578 teu: ex Thirsk-08
9343118	Kent †	Lbr	2007	22,914	26,438	174	28	-	lpg	35,205 m³
9384887	Kyoto Tower	Gbr	2007	17,229	21,975	172	28	19	ucc	1,708 teu
8808068	Laiwu Steel Harmonious	Lbr	1989	150,454	270,857	337	58	16	bor	ex Eastern Jewel-08, T.S. Asclepius-02 (conv tcr-09)
9172485	Lesotho	Lbr	1997	75,637	81,819	300	40	24	ucc	6,214 teu: ex MSC Lesotho-12, NYK Antares-10
9640097	Lincoln Park	Gbr	2012	11,733	19,801	146	24	14	tco	
9640114	Lumphini Park	Gbr	2013	11,600	19,800	146	24	14	tco	
9640126	Kitanihon 562	Gbr	2013	11,600	19,800	146	24	14	tco	
9640138	Kitanihon 565	Gbr	2013	11,600	19,800	146	24	14	tco	
9463011	Maersk Edison	Gbr	2011	141,649	141,448	366	48	25	ucc	13,092 teu
9463035	Maersk Eubank	Gbr	2011	141.649	141.398	366	48	25	ucc	13,092 teu
9112088	Meynell	Bmu	1997	93,629	185,767	292	48	15	bbu	ex SG Universe-98
9363857	Millennium Park	Gbr	2008	11,590	19,998	146	24	14	tco	
9532197	Morning Cloud	Lbr	2011	40,325	74,962	225	32	14	bbu	ex Sanko Frontier-12

IMO#	name	flag	year	grt	dwt	loa	bm	kts	type	former names
9289910	Morning Midas +	Gbr	2006	46,800	12,672	183	32	20	mve	4,902 ceu
9289908	Morning Miracle +	Gbr	2006	46,800	12,600	183	32	20	mve	4,902 ceu
9152297	Mozambique	Lbr	1998	76,847	82,275	299	40	24	ucc	6,208 teu: ex MSC Mozambique-12, NYK Canopus-10
9073995	MSC Catania	Gbr	1994	60,117	63,163	300	37	23	ucc	4,963 teu: ex Sandra Azul-07, NYK Altair-01
9103685	MSC Colombia	Gbr	1996	51,931	60,348	294	32	23	ucc	4,507 teu: ex Maersk Doha-07, P&O Nedlloyd Caribbean-03, Germany-02, APL Germany-02, OOCL Germany-98
9074042	MSC Messina	Gbr	1995	60,117	63,014	300	37	23	ucc	4,963 teu: ex Sandra Blanca-07, NYK Vega-01
9103697	MSC Venezuela	Gbr	1996	51,931	60,348	294	32	23	ucc	4,507 teu: ex Maersk Dundee-07, France-03, APL France-01, OOCL France-98
9233844	Nagoya Tower	Gbr	2003	39,941	50,841	260	32	24	ucc	4,253 teu: ex Saxonia Express-11, CP Monterrey-06, TMM Monterrey-05
9114206	Newforest	Bmu	1996	93,629	185,688	292	48	15	bbu	ex SGC Foundation-98
9493365	Noble Ace	Gbr	2011	59,515	18,946	200	32	19	mve	6,203 ceu
9232096	Norasia Bellatrix	Lbr	2002	50,242	58,814	282	32	24	ucc	4,369 teu: ex Hanjin Pennsylvania-04
8813075	Northumberland	Gbr	1990	11,822	16,137	158	21	15	lpg	15,094 m³ ex Nelly Maersk-03, Reinanger-98, Anne-Laure-97, Sloka-93
9030735	NYK Kai	Pan	1993	50,606	59,658	288	32	24	ucc	3,618 teu: ex Kai-95
8408387	Ormond	Bmu	1986	96,794	187,025	300	47	13	bbu	
9432919	Osaka Car	Gbr	2009	46,800	12,321	183	32	19	mve	4,902 ceu

XT Management (Zodiac Maritime) : JAKARTA TOWER : *ARO*

XT Management (Zodiac Maritime) : MAERSK EDISON : *Hans Kraijenbosch*

IMO#	name	flag	year	grt	dwt	loa	bm	kts	type	former names
9238777	Osaka Tower	Gbr	2003	39,941	50,759	260	32	24	ucc	4,253 teu: ex Hammonia Express-11, CP Aguascalientes-06, TMM Aguascalientes-05
9233832	Qingdao Express	Gbr	2003	39,941	50,886	260	32	24	ucc	4,253 teu: ex Westfalia Express-10, CP Deliverer-06, Lykes Deliverer-05
9119141	Quorn	Bmu	1996	92,194	179,869	290	46	14	bbu	ex SG China-98
9339351	Princes Park	Lbr	2005	11,690	19,727	144	24	14	tco	ex Bow Europe-12
9112301	Rutland	Bmu	1997	85,848	170,013	292	46	14	bbu	ex SG Fortune-98
9017020	Santa Monica	Lbr	1991	43,213	39,376	253	32	23	ucc	3,054 teu: ex NYK Seabreeze-99
9367839	Seoul Tower	Gbr	2009	26,688	34,325	212	30	22	ucc	2,578 teu
9002738	Shagang Giant	Lbr	1993	155,359	308,902	332	60	14	bor	ex Starlight Jewel-08, Front Tartar-01, Tartar-00 (conv. tcr-08)
9519573	Shagang Volition	Lbr	2012	152,306	298,004	327	55	14	bor	
9521980	Shagag Faith	Lbr	2013	152,306	298,085	327	55	14	bor	
9112313	Snowdon	Bmu	1998	85,848	170,079	292	46	14	bbu	l/a SG Creation
9363845	Stanley Park	Gbr	2008	11,590	19,994	146	24	14	tco	
9493212	Stargate	Gbr	2011	17,025	28,221	169	27	14	bbu	
9152284	Swaziland	Lbr	1998	76,848	82,275	300	40	24	ucc	6,148 teu: ex MSC Swaziland-12, NYK Castor-10
8500525	Taunton	Bmu	1986	95,835	186,324	300	47	13	bbu	ex Marine Crusader-89
9238765	Thuringia Express	Gbr	2003	39,941	50,785	260	32	24	ucc	4,253 teu: ex CP Tamarind-06, Contship Tamarind-05, APL Honduras-04, Lykes Adventurer-03
9432907	Tokyo Car	Gbr	2008	46,800	12,352	183	32	20	mve	4,902 ceu
9384875	Tokyo Tower †	Gbr	2007	17,229	21,975	172	28	19	ucc	1,708 teu
9432892	Triumph	Gbr	2008	46,800	12,300	183	32	20	mve	4,902 ceu
8806498	Vine	Bmu	1990	63,106	114,975	266	42	14	bbu	
8810114	Waterford	Bmu	1990	77,113	149,513	270	43	12	bbu	
9493224	Westgate	Gbr	2011	17,025	28,202	169	27	14	bbu	
9493236	Woodgate	Gbr	2011	17,025	28,219	169	27	14	bbu	
9008691	Wugang Asia	Lbr	1992	150,203	264,484	322	58	15	bor	ex Asian Jewel-08, Helios Breeze-04 (conv tcr-09)
9085352	Wugang Atlantic	Lbr	1995	156,281	281,226	328	57	14	bor	ex Atlantic Jewel-08, C. Trust-07, C. Achiever-03, Yukong Achiever-97 (conv tcr-09)
9510486	Wugang Caifu	Lbr	2012	153,604	299,382	327	55	14	bor	
9510474	Wugang Haoyun	Gbr	2011	153,604	297,980	327	55	14	bor	
9002685	Wugang Orient	Lbr	1991	146,548	267,710	326	57	14	bor	ex Orient Jewel-08, Nichiyo-03, Boho-94, l/a Sea Duchess (conv tcr-08)
9157648	YM Hamburg	Gbr	1997	40,268	49,238	259	32	23	ucc	3,961 teu: ex Ville de Virgo-04
9143166	YM Kaohsiung	Gbr	1998	40,068	50,059	259	32	23	ucc	4,031 teu: ex Ville de Tanya-05
9157650	YM Shanghai	Gbr	1997	40,268	49,225	259	32	23	ucc	4,113 teu: ex Ville d'Antares-04
9168324	Zambia	Lbr	1998	76,847	82,171	300	40	24	ucc	6,148 teu: ex MSC Zambia-12, NYK Sirius-10
9384932	Zenith Leader	Gbr	2007	62,080	22,602	200	32	20	mve	6,501 ceu
9322358	Zim India	Gbr	2007	39.912	50,607	261	32	24	ucc	4,253 teu
9231781	Zim Panama	Gbr	2002	53,453	66,686	294	32	24	ucc	4,992 teu
9280861	Zim Pusan	Gbr	2004	53,453	62,740	294	32	24	ucc	4,992 teu
9280859	Zim Shenzhen	Gbr	2004	53,453	62,740	294	32	24	ucc	4,992 teu
9318151	Zim Xiamen	Gbr	2006	39,906	50,689	261	32	24	ucc	4,253 teu

newbuildings: order for six 16,000 teu boxboats 399 x 54m [STX], and ten 5,000 teu boxboats [STX], 2 chemical tankers, 141 x 24m [Kitanihon 531, 533 (2013)]: 2 x 180,000dwt bbu 9521409 STX 1461, 9531294 STX1449
† manged for various Japanese owners or * for Unique Shipping (HK) Ltd, Hong Kong (China)
+ chartered to EUKOR Car Carriers ++ chartered to Hyundai Glovis

Tanker Pacific Management (Singapore) Pte. Ltd., Singapore
Funnel: Light blue with broad yellow band. Hull: Black with red boot-topping. History: Subsidiary founded 1989.
Web: www.tanker.com.sg

IMO#	name	flag	year	grt	dwt	loa	bm	kts	type	former names
9192260	Arafura Sea	Sgp	2000	57,680	105,856	244	43	15	tcr	
9161314	Aral Sea	Sgp	1999	58,129	104,884	244	42	14	tcr	ex Bali Sea-04
9271585	Archway	Lbr	2004	78,896	150,581	274	38	14	tcr	ex Monte Granada-12
9192258	Barents Sea	Sgp	2000	57,680	105,588	248	43	15	tcr	
9085429	Bering Sea	Sgp	1996	53,639	96,124	243	42	14	tcr	
9180217	Black Sea	Sgp	1999	58,129	104,943	244	42	14	tcr	
9588146	Brightway	Sgp	2012	83,824	160,396	274	48	14	tcr	
9588158	Broadway	Sgp	2012	83,824	160,142	274	48	14	tcr	
9253325	Ceram Sea	Sgp	2004	57,680	105,666	248	43	15	tcr	
9242156	Ceylon	Sgp	2002	28,029	46,001	180	32	15	tco	ex Akebono-04
9253313	Coral Sea	Sgp	2003	57,680	105,665	244	43	15	tcr	
9133850	Cosmic Jewel	Lbr	1997	163,720	300,955	340	56	15	tcr	ex Tantramar-07, Irving Primrose-02
9590307	Crossway	Sgp	2012	83,824	160,024	274	48	14	tcr	
9594872	Emerald Splendor	Sgp	2012	42,411	74,986	228	32	14	tco	
9594884	Emerald Success	Lbr	2013	42,400	74,435	228	32		tco	
9594896	Emerald Summit	Sgp	2013	42,400	74,435	228	32		tco	

IMO#	name	flag	year	grt	dwt	loa	bm	kts	type	former names
9594901	Emerald Supreme	Lbr	2013	42,400	74,435	228	32		tco	
9590319	Fairway	Sgp	2013	83,824	160,000	274	48	14	tcr	
9402328	Kara Sea	Sgp	2010	59,180	115,191	244	42	14	tcr	
9184392	Maritime Jewel	Lbr	2000	157,833	299,364	332	58	15	tcr	ex Limburg-03
9120918	Nara	Sgp	1996	28,433	47,172	183	32	15	tcr	ex Eagle Vela-04, NOL Vela-00
9384564	North Sea	Sgp	2008	59,177	115,325	244	42	14	tcr	
9402782	Pacific Beryl	Sgp	2010	26,916	47,377	180	32	14	tco	ex Sanko Lynx-11
9402770	Pacific Citrine	Sgp	2010	26,916	47,378	180	32	14	tco	ex Sanko Libra-11
9573660	Pacific Diamond	Lbr	2010	28,778	49,917	180	32	14	tco	
9573672	Pacific Garnet	Lbr	2011	28,778	47,879	180	32	14	tco	
9539585	Pacific Lapis	Lbr	2013	28,426	50,007	183	32		tco	
9539597	Pacific Onyx	Lbr	2013	28,426	50,000	183	32		tco	
9573696	Pacific Quartz	Lbr	2011	28,778	47,941	180	32	14	tco	
9573701	Pacific Sapphire	Lbr	2011	28,778	47,906	180	32	14	tco	
9539561	Pacific Topaz	Lbr	2012	28,426	50,013	183	32	14	tco	
9539573	Pacific Zircon	Lbr	2013	28,426	50,000	183	32	14	tco	
9457593	Ross Sea	Sgp	2011	59,180	114,542	244	42	14	tcr	
9121194	Savannah	Sgp	1996	28,433	47,172	183	32	15	tcr	ex Eagle Sagitta-04, NOL Sagitta-00
9457608	Sunda Sea	Sgp	2011	59,180	114,531	244	42	14	tcr	

newbuildings: 4 x 49,610dwt tco (2014/5)
* managed by Zodiac Maritime Agencies Ltd.

Zim Integrated Shipping Services Ltd., Israel

Funnel: White with blue 'ZIM' below seven gold stars (four above three). **Hull:** White or grey with green boot-topping, or black with white 'ZIM' and red boot-topping. **History:** Founded 1945 as Zim Israel Navigation Co Ltd with 48% government share and 49% owned by Israel Corp (57.3% owned by Ofer Bros). Government share acquired in 2004 and company renamed. **Web:** www.zim.com

IMO#	name	flag	year	grt	dwt	loa	bm	kts	type	former names
9046241	Asia Star	Mlt	1994	16,043	20,194	177	28	19	ucc	1,512 teu: ex Delmas Charcot-04, Indamex New York-03, San Antonio-00, Jolly Avorio-00, San Antonio-99
9473626	GSL Africa	Lbr	2010	27,213	32,906	200	32	22	ucc	2,553 teu: l/a Seared
9203473	Novorossiysk Star	Mlt	1999	20,624	25,572	180	28	20	ucc	1,702 teu: ex Australia Star-06, Kota Sejati-06, Bai Yun He-04
9223746	Odessa Star *	Mlt	2000	20,569	25,638	180	28	20	ucc	1,702 teu; ex Hongkong Star-06, Xiang Yun He-06
9398462	Tianjin	Lbr	2010	114,044	116,440	349	46	25	ucc	10,070 teu: ex Zim Tianjin-11
9398448	Zim Antwerp	Lbr	2009	114,044	116,294	349	46	25	ucc	10,070 teu
9113654	Zim Asia	Lbr	1996	41,507	45,850	254	32	21	ucc	3,429 teu
9113678	Zim Atlantic	Lbr	1996	41,507	45,850	254	32	21	ucc	3,429 teu
9280835	Zim Barcelona	Isr	2004	53,450	54,740	294	32	24	ucc	4,814 teu
9398424	Zim Chicago	Lbr	2010	91,158	108,574	334	43	25	ucc	8,208 teu
9139921	Zim China	Lbr	1997	41,507	45,850	254	32	21	ucc	3,429 teu
9398436	Zim Djibouti	Lbr	2009	114,044	116,440	349	46	25	ucc	10,070 teu
9113692	Zim Europa	Lbr	1997	41,507	45,850	254	32	21	ucc	3,429 teu
9288904	Zim Haifa	Isr	2004	54,626	66,938	254	32	24	ucc	5,040 teu
9139919	Zim Iberia	Lbr	1998	41,507	46,350	254	32	21	ucc	3,429 teu
9113680	Zim Jamaica	Lbr	1997	41,507	45,850	254	32	21	ucc	3,429 teu
9398395	Zim Los Angeles	Lbr	2009	91,158	108,574	349	46	25	ucc	8,200 teu
9401776	Zim Moskva	Lbr	2009	40,741	52,316	259	32	24	ucc	4,308 teu
9398400	Zim Ningbo	Lbr	2009	91,158	108,427	349	46	25	ucc	8,208 teu
9113666	Zim Pacific	Lbr	1996	41,507	45,850	254	32	21	ucc	3,429 teu
9318163	Zim Qingdao	Lbr	2006	39,906	50,689	261	32	24	ucc	4,250 teu
9398450	Zim Rotterdam	Lbr	2010	114,044	116,499	349	46	25	ucc	10,070 teu
9398412	Zim San Diego	Lbr	2010	91,158	108,464	334	43	25	ucc	8,208 teu
9139907	Zim U.S.A.	Isr	1997	41,200	46,250	254	32	21	ucc	3,429 teu
9403396	Zim Ukrayina	Lbr	2009	40,741	52,316	259	32	24	ucc	4,308 teu
9231808	Zim Virginia	Isr	2002	53,453	62,740	294	32	24	ucc	4,839 teu
9322346	Zim Yokohama	Lbr	2007	39,906	50.532	261	32	24	ucc	4,253 teu: ex Yokohama-12, Zim Yokohama-09

newbuildings:
* owned by subsidiary Therica Shipping Corp, Hong Kong (China)

Yangming Marine Transport Corp.   Taiwan

Funnel: Black with yellow band on broad red band interupted by white square containing blue 'Y' on white 'M' symbol within red outline. **Hull:** Black with white 'YANG MING', red boot-topping. **History:** Government controlled and formed 1973. **Web:** www.yml.com.tw

IMO#	name	flag	year	grt	dwt	loa	bm	kts	type	former names
9287778	Giuseppe Rizzo +	Lbr	2004	41,205	77,684	225	32	14	bbu	
9461099	KM Hongkong +	Lbr	2010	42,942	82,131	229	32	14	bbu	
9544401	KM Imabari +	Pan	2009	39,737	76,619	225	32	14	bbu	
9461087	KM Keelung +	Lbr	2010	42,942	82,072	229	32	14	bbu	
9359545	KM Mt. Jade +	Lbr	2008	42,707	81,487	225	32	14	bbu	
9454278	KM Sydney +	Twn	2010	42,707	80,638	225	32	14	bbu	
9286889	Medi Taipei +	Lbr	2003	39,727	76,633	225	32	14	bbu	

IMO#	name	flag	year	grt	dwt	loa	bm	kts	type	former names
9200653	Taipower Prosperity I +	Twn	2000	49,565	88,005	236	38	14	bbu	
8807739	YM America	Lbr	1992	46,728	46,785	276	32	21	ucc	3,604 teu: ex Ming America-04
9443580	YM Antwerp	Hkg	2008	40,030	50,500	260	32	24	ucc	4,526 teu
9203629	YM Bamboo	Lbr	2001	64,005	68,615	275	40	26	ucc	5,551 teu: ex Bamboo Bridge-06, Jupiter Bridge-05, Ming Bamboo-02
9450571	YM Busan **	Hkg	2009	40,030	50,500	260	32	24	ucc	4,526 teu
9198288	YM Cosmos	Pan	2001	64,254	68,413	275	40	25	ucc	5,551 teu: ex Ming Cosmos-05
9159189	YM Cultivation +	Twn	1996	35,905	69,163	225	32	14	bbu	ex Ming Cultivation-04, Bel Best-02
9224489	YM Cypress	Lbr	2001	64,254	68,303	275	40	25	ucc	5,551 teu: ex Cypress Bridge-06, Mercury Bridge-05, Ming Cypress-02
9062087	YM East	Twn	1995	46,697	45,995	276	32	21	ucc	3,725 teu: ex Ming East-05, Maersk Long Beach-96, Ming East-95
9353280	YM Efficiency	Lbr	2009	42,741	52,773	269	32	24	ucc	4,250 teu
9353266	YM Elixir	Lbr	2008	42,741	51,870	269	32	24	ucc	4,250 teu
9353278	YM Enhancer	Lbr	2008	42,741	52,773	269	32	24	ucc	4,250 teu
9353254	YM Eminence	Lbr	2009	42,741	52,773	269	32	24	ucc	4,250 teu
9353292	YM Eternity	Lbr	2009	42,741	51,870	269	32	24	ucc	4,250 teu
9278090	YM Fountain	Lbr	2004	64,254	68,615	275	40	26	ucc	5,551 teu
9267156	YM Great	Pan	2004	66,332	67,270	279	40	26	ucc	5,570 teu
9224491	YM Green	Lbr	2001	64,254	68,413	275	40	26	ucc	5,571 teu: ex Ming Green-05
9298997	YM March **	Pan	2004	66,332	67,270	279	40	25	ucc	5,570 teu: I/a Ming March
9485007	YM Masculinity	Lbr	2012	76,787	81,145	306	40	25	ucc	6,600 teu
9484998	YM Milestone	Lbr	2011	76,787	81,145	306	40	25	ucc	6,600 teu
9457737	YM Mobility	Lbr	2011	76,787	81,145	306	40	25	ucc	6,600 teu
9455870	YM Mutuality	Lbr	2011	76,787	81,145	306	40	25	ucc	6,600 teu
9387097	YM New Jersey **	Pan	2006	54,828	65,123	294	32	23	ucc	6,600 teu
9001215	YM North	Lbr	1995	46,697	45,995	276	32	21	ucc	3,725 teu: ex Ming North-05
9198276	YM Orchid	Pan	2000	64,254	68,303	275	40	26	ucc	5,551 teu: ex Ming Orchid-05
9203631	YM Pine	Lbr	2001	64,005	68,615	275	40	26	ucc	5,551 teu: ex Pine Bridge-06, Venus Bridge-05, Ming Pine-02
9198264	YM Plum	Pan	2000	64,254	68,413	275	40	26	ucc	5,551 teu: ex Ming Plum-05
9287780	YM Rightness +	Lbr	2004	41,205	77,684	225	32	14	bbu	
9001227	YM South	Twn	1995	46,697	45,995	276	32	21	ucc	3,725 teu; ex Ming South-05
9294800	YM Success	Lbr	2004	64,254	68,615	275	40	25	ucc	5,551 teu
9337444	YM Uberty	Lbr	2008	90,507	103,614	333	43	25	ucc	8,236 teu
9462706	YM Ubiquity **	Twn	2012	90,532	103,600	333	43	25	ucc	8,236 teu
9302645	YM Ultimate	Lbr	2007	90,389	101,411	336	43	25	ucc	8,200 teu
9462718	YM Unanimity **	Lbr	2012	90,532	103,600	333	43	25	ucc	8,236 teu
9462732	YM Unicorn	Lbr	2013	90,500	103,600	333	43	25	ucc	8,236 teu
9302633	YM Unison	Lbr	2006	90,389	101,030	336	43	25	ucc	8,200 teu
9337482	YM Uniform	Lbr	2009	90,507	103,614	333	43	25	ucc	8,236 teu
9462691	YM Uniformity **	Twn	2012	90,532	103,235	333	43	25	ucc	8,236 teu
9302619	YM Unity	Lbr	2006	90,389	101,411	336	43	25	ucc	8,200 teu
9462720	YM Upsurgence **	Lbr	2012	90,500	103,600	333	43	25	ucc	8,236 teu
9337468	YM Upward	Lbr	2008	90,507	103,607	333	43	25	ucc	8,236 teu
9337470	YM Utility	Lbr	2009	90,507	103,614	333	43	25	ucc	8,236 teu

Yangming Marine Transportation Corp : YM UNISON : *ARO*

IMO#	name	flag	year	grt	dwt	loa	bm	kts	type	former names
9302621	YM Utmost	Lbr	2006	90,389	101,411	336	43	25	ucc	8,200 teu
9337456	YM Utopia	Lbr	2008	90,507	103,614	333	43	25	ucc	8,236 teu
9267601	YM Virtue +	Lbr	2003	39,749	73,840	225	32	14	bbu	ex Ming Virtue-05
9278088	YM Wealth	Lbr	2004	64,254	68,615	275	40	26	ucc	5,551 teu
9001239	YM West	Twn	1995	46,697	45,995	276	32	21	ucc	3,725 teu: ex Ming West-05, Maersk Singapore-96, Ming West-95
9118317	YM Zenith	Twn	1996	46,697	45,995	276	32	21	ucc	3,725 teu; ex Ming Zenith-04

newbuildings: further 90,000 grt container ships

* owned by YML Shipping Enterprise Corp Ltd, Taiwan (formed 1999) or ** chartered from various owners. + operated by subsidiary Kwang Ming Line. Also owns 15 feeder container ships (15-16,500 grt) operating mainly in the Far East and manages five tankers owned by associated Government controlled Chinese Petroleum Corp (formed 1959 - wwwcpc.com.tw). Also see other chartered ships with 'YM' prefix in index.

Reederei Horst Zeppenfeld GmbH & Co. KG Germany

Funnel: Cream with black top. **Hull:** Black with red boot-topping. **History:** Founded 1971. **Web:** www.zeppenfeld.com

IMO#	name	flag	year	grt	dwt	loa	bm	kts	type	former names
9301990	Aldebaran	Lbr	2008	32,903	37,274	207	32	22	ucc	2,785 teu: ex MSC Andes-10, Cala Pigafetta-09
9339612	Algol *	Sgp	2008	16,162	17,350	161	25	19	ucc	1,345 teu: ex USL Condor-09, Algol-06
9339600	Alioth *	Sgp	2006	16,162	17,219	161	25	19	ucc	1,345 teu
9295505	Mizar	Lbr	2005	16,162	17,350	161	25	19	ucc	1,347 teu

* owned by associated Reederei Navylloyd AG, Switzerland (founded 1981)

Index

Teekay Corporation (Teekay Navion Offshore Loading) : NAVION OSLO : *John Davidson*

IMO	Page	IMO	Page	IMO	Page	IMO	Page	IMO	Page
5124162	17	7725166	85	8209729	151	8406298	118	8515532	177
5255777	18	7726706	226	8211514	124	8406406	55	8515893	260
5260679	31	7726718	226	8212099	101	8406705	142	8517279	186
5282483	17	7800588	226	8212099	266	8406729	142	8517346	239
5282627	17	7800605	226	8213603	239	8407735	29	8517358	239
5383304	17	7812115	40	8214152	109	8407931	40	8517891	146
5424562	18	7822457	25	8214164	109	8408387	282	8517944	124
6409351	9	7825411	80	8214176	109	8408844	107	8519019	123
6417097	17	7827213	18	8215481	109	8408868	92	8519186	145
6419057	17	7902295	19	8215534	110	8408818	148	8520213	226
6602898	19	7903093	121	8215778	176	8408882	92	8520680	271
6611863	30	7904621	40	8217881	13	8408832	145	8521220	15
6821080	18	7915278	48	8218706	142	8408894	92	8521232	15
6901892	244	7915278	49	8219322	216	8410940	150	8521218	109
6905745	18	7915278	277	8219334	216	8410952	146	8521397	146
6910544	10	7917551	270	8221777	108	8413033	146	8521402	145
6910702	244	7917563	273	8221765	277	8413851	133	8600179	70
7032997	30	7925493	148	8223000	199	8413875	148	8600208	158
7046936	18	7925508	148	8223012	199	8413887	149	8602263	132
7108514	8	7926148	133	8224432	226	8414178	99	8602476	204
7108930	21	7927984	18	8300365	184	8414740	148	8602579	271
7111078	29	7931454	48	8300377	184	8414752	145	8602828	130
7118404	31	7931454	277	8300389	248	8417754	177	8602775	273
7121633	241	8000214	24	8301400	241	8417766	177	8603509	9
7211074	29	8000977	87	8304529	226	8417948	80	8604292	131
7214715	25	8001000	86	8304531	226	8418734	216	8605167	271
7217395	21	8002597	29	8308147	126	8418746	216	8607749	182
7225910	29	8002963	226	8308159	127	8418758	216	8608078	121
7229447	63	8005109	108	8309397	126	8419702	150	8608080	121
7304314	21	8007808	205	8309402	127	8419714	146	8608200	149
7320344	122	8009129	241	8309529	252	8419726	148	8608145	281
7325629	28	8011330	108	8309531	253	8420804	55	8608157	281
7328243	62	8013613	121	8309555	253	8420878	9	8608169	281
7328445	156	8016548	272	8309713	127	8420787	108	8608585	83
7342469	126	8016550	270	8309579	271	8420799	108	8608705	242
7347536	17	8018168	271	8309581	271	8420892	146	8608872	242
7347732	241	8019356	30	8309828	108	8420907	148	8608884	242
7347768	241	8019368	18	8309830	108	8434254	18	8609589	145
7357452	100	8024014	29	8309842	108	8500525	283	8610277	95
7358561	17	8024026	24	8311737	254	8501426	116	8610526	159
7358573	30	8025331	86	8312590	270	8501452	117	8610887	142
7359785	241	8025343	86	8312643	239	8502468	181	8611398	15
7360124	242	8026074	67	8313685	127	8502535	215	8612134	27
7360136	242	8026799	124	8313697	127	8502547	216	8612251	129
7361934	103	8027298	29	8313702	127	8502559	216	8612316	130
7382720	103	8100882	176	8314134	13	8502573	215	8613188	184
7382732	103	8100997	254	8314122	27	8502717	148	8613308	80
7390143	217	8106056	124	8314471	55	8502834	108	8613310	80
7390155	217	8106068	124	8314483	55	8505836	148	8613322	238
7390179	217	8112914	197	8315205	75	8506294	21	8614194	194
7391214	122	8113554	86	8316522	100	8506373	27	8616168	277
7391422	28	8113566	87	8316699	127	8506749	271	8616283	180
7408081	100	8119376	145	8316704	127	8507200	277	8616295	179
7408093	100	8121757	175	8316730	127	8507212	277	8616300	180
7413232	122	8121769	175	8318025	66	8507509	177	8616312	226
7422881	37	8121771	175	8318051	65	8507652	121	8616556	48
7428433	156	8122828	95	8318083	66	8507664	121	8616520	150
7428469	156	8130019	149	8318659	239	8508280	108	8616556	278
7428471	156	8130681	126	8319689	69	8508369	85	8616958	130
7433610	78	8130875	86	8319718	130	8509181	30	8616922	180
7500401	142	8130899	86	8320119	252	8509375	146	8616934	180
7507265	108	8130966	121	8320386	37	8509387	150	8617938	87
7507293	108	8131104	57	8320767	270	8510934	177	8617940	87
7517507	100	8131881	142	8320779	272	8511316	146	8618190	58
7619575	242	8131893	142	8321325	270	8511328	152	8618293	238
7619587	242	8131934	142	8321333	270	8512281	24	8618308	238
7625811	30	8201480	21	8321711	65	8512279	87	8618310	238
7632278	226	8201624	148	8321723	66	8512891	146	8619429	135
7632280	226	8201636	149	8321905	124	8512906	145	8619431	135
7702401	242	8201648	146	8321929	100	8512944	127	8619443	135
7704590	75	8201674	149	8321931	100	8512956	127	8619455	135
7704605	75	8201686	148	8321929	266	8512968	127	8619467	135
7708938	242	8202355	270	8321931	266	8512970	127	8619479	135
7710903	226	8202367	270	8323238	234	8512982	126	8700280	12
7721225	142	8202381	270	8324373	126	8513467	92	8700230	184
7721237	142	8203438	30	8325901	177	8513479	92	8700228	226
7721249	142	8203440	30	8400634	126	8513510	181	8700474	19
7721251	142	8203359	177	8402864	217	8513716	68	8700773	9
7721263	142	8204951	271	8404238	226	8513728	68	8700785	9
7724306	75	8204963	271	8406262	117	8513730	68	8703397	79
7725142	85	8204975	271	8406274	118	8513560	271	8704183	279
7725154	85	8207329	127	8406286	116	8514590	66	8705266	27

8705230	66	8814768	57	8908715	187	9000699	21	9015187	85
8705278	27	8816156	249	8908856	215	9000730	199	9015199	85
8705242	66	8816168	249	8909082	97	9000742	199	9015204	85
8705486	84	8816170	249	8909068	239	9000986	36	9015216	85
8705618	61	8817631	19	8909070	239	9000998	55	9015321	281
8707226	58	8818740	65	8909543	252	9001033	84	9015541	111
8707343	15	8818843	99	8910108	91	9001045	83	9015498	178
8708244	161	8819093	252	8910081	140	9001253	47	9015539	262
8708672	30	8819213	226	8910093	140	9001318	47	9015656	177
8709133	41	8819500	23	8911102	185	9001215	285	9015785	108
8708907	273	8819512	23	8911073	239	9001227	285	9016662	240
8709119	124	8819940	84	8911085	239	9001239	286	9016674	240
8709169	148	8819952	84	8911657	253	9001772	257	9016868	135
8709145	192	8819964	84	8911669	253	9001784	255	9017020	283
8709157	192	8819926	185	8912120	107	9002386	257	9017082	257
8709298	197	8819938	185	8912132	107	9002611	123	9017318	126
8709573	8	8819976	167	8912182	57	9002635	123	9017264	250
8709640	150	8819988	167	8912144	107	9002776	58	9017276	249
8710857	27	8819990	167	8912156	107	9002609	262	9018008	154
8711344	9	8820004	167	8912297	37	9002623	262	9018464	102
8711356	10	8820016	162	8912302	37	9002693	263	9018555	123
8711368	116	8820195	169	8912663	49	9002685	283	9018658	200
8711370	117	8820200	255	8912613	208	9002908	100	9019119	249
8712178	27	8820212	255	8912754	74	9002738	283	9019121	249
8712324	161	8820224	255	8912766	266	9003304	107	9019729	112
8712324	184	8820822	113	8913162	21	9003835	254	9019640	239
8713550	249	8821046	12	8913150	242	9003847	254	9019652	238
8713562	249	8821591	123	8913174	242	9004176	177	9021332	182
8714190	150	8821620	111	8913411	152	9004786	36	9021461	123
8714229	117	8821632	123	8913461	107	9004803	135	9021423	182
8714205	152	8821644	112	8913423	152	9005053	135	9021679	111
8714994	133	8821656	123	8913447	146	9005065	135	9021681	135
8715546	134	8821668	111	8913514	182	9005261	135	9021693	262
8715857	152	8821925	68	8913435	280	9005534	46	9030137	85
8715869	146	8821929	68	8913459	280	9005546	47	9030149	85
8715871	151	8821931	68	8913679	84	9005558	47	9030723	80
8716502	10	8821943	68	8913667	111	9005560	47	9030802	156
8716899	24	8822583	108	8913954	208	9005390	253	9030852	108
8718110	83	8822595	108	8913966	208	9005508	280	9030814	156
8718122	84	8837928	142	8915433	27	9005780	133	9030864	109
8800274	58	8843446	26	8915445	27	9006502	202	9030826	156
8800286	55	8900323	92	8915665	47	9006617	210	9030838	156
8800511	61	8900335	92	8915677	47	9006851	59	9030840	156
8801814	239	8900517	205	8915689	47	9007207	133	9030735	282
8802068	28	8900529	205	8915691	47	9007491	31	9031064	107
8802002	120	8901391	96	8915796	47	9007362	254	9030943	234
8802014	120	8901585	216	8915794	142	9007374	254	9030967	234
8802210	97	8901884	97	8916267	182	9007532	127	9031650	263
8802088	239	8902371	57	8917546	184	9007544	127	9031959	93
8802090	239	8902424	55	8917560	185	9007489	185	9031961	94
8802882	29	8902539	117	8917572	185	9007817	80	9032496	134
8802894	29	8902541	118	8917584	250	9007829	80	9034717	232
8802923	234	8902553	116	8917596	250	9007831	80	9034729	234
8802923	265	8902395	281	8917778	146	9007958	178	9035010	64
8803410	146	8902400	281	8918136	24	9008419	27	9035060	64
8804725	99	8902565	117	8918057	148	9008421	27	9035137	93
8805169	247	8902577	116	8918241	96	9008598	15	9035266	41
8806096	65	8902802	107	8918215	127	9008574	152	9035589	280
8806101	65	8902656	281	8918227	127	9008603	145	9035591	280
8806204	21	8902955	87	8918239	127	9008706	125	9035981	83
8806747	26	8902967	87	8918277	225	9008689	160	9035993	83
8806498	283	8903167	185	8918289	225	9008744	156	9036002	152
8806852	101	8903923	26	8918930	87	9008732	185	9036014	280
8806864	100	8903935	26	8918942	86	9008691	283	9036442	55
8807088	24	8904111	86	8919001	96	9009023	57	9036454	55
8807662	239	8904123	86	8918954	150	9009504	109	9036909	117
8807650	281	8905426	182	8918966	149	9010079	92	9037159	125
8807997	15	8905543	255	8918980	148	9011038	107	9037719	113
8807739	285	8905878	152	8918978	152	9011492	108	9037721	113
8808068	281	8905969	117	8919037	198	9011923	216	9037733	113
8808628	86	8906731	79	8919049	198	9012041	120	9037745	110
8808587	194	8906743	80	8919051	198	9012305	257	9038135	143
8810114	283	8906755	79	8919245	12	9012905	37	9038323	184
8812631	42	8906822	61	8919257	12	9013282	143	9038488	240
8812667	36	8906688	265	8919269	12	9013311	135	9038835	184
8812772	61	8906925	252	8919271	210	9013426	53	9038907	118
8812784	61	8906937	253	8919611	215	9014066	225	9038919	118
8813063	243	8906975	249	8919984	70	9014078	225	9039119	18
8813075	282	8907216	31	8919922	272	9014432	100	9038945	249
8813594	239	8907424	27	8919934	272	9014418	210	9039145	110
8813934	216	8907333	210	8920141	239	9014470	210	9039157	110
8813946	215	8907931	80	8921470	226	9014444	240	9039171	113
8813958	216	8907943	97	9000168	28	9014755	85	9039169	123
8813960	216	8907876	185	9000259	15	9014767	85	9039183	113
8814299	249	8907888	239	9000314	277	9014808	159	9039195	113
8814744	29	8908193	239	9000493	146	9014810	160	9039250	149

9039640	35	9053505	182	9070137	240	9081837	93	9102978	22
9039652	36	9053579	281	9070620	23	9081784	267	9102734	267
9039597	173	9053660	210	9070632	23	9081801	277	9102992	12
9039884	133	9053878	9	9070448	272	9082350	35	9103037	47
9040429	18	9053658	249	9070450	270	9082324	131	9102930	189
9040508	280	9054119	180	9070462	280	9082336	180	9102928	197
9041057	133	9054224	111	9070474	280	9082348	180	9103128	108
9041253	9	9055448	97	9070644	144	9082374	195	9103130	108
9041227	65	9055462	98	9070711	95	9082312	281	9103180	158
9041239	65	9055474	98	9070723	94	9082312	281	9103104	254
9041174	142	9055620	42	9070735	94	9082609	94	9103116	254
9041459	106	9055486	184	9070694	254	9082683	94	9103685	282
9041758	258	9056088	194	9070759	195	9082738	95	9103697	282
9042063	37	9056090	194	9070709	254	9082805	223	9103702	281
9042439	157	9056296	124	9070905	133	9082960	135	9103996	15
9042441	157	9056272	279	9070931	192	9083287	62	9104005	15
9042453	157	9056284	279	9071272	92	9083304	105	9104196	42
9043005	65	9056430	258	9071210	231	9083316	105	9104603	42
9043017	66	9056818	280	9071480	91	9083263	232	9104615	247
9043055	108	9057123	40	9071557	108	9083964	55	9104885	102
9043043	210	9057173	206	9071569	108	9084190	58	9104811	177
9043627	66	9057159	235	9071595	95	9084494	34	9104902	118
9043639	65	9057458	42	9071521	194	9085340	59	9105009	92
9043641	66	9057496	41	9072094	75	9085390	211	9105023	127
9043691	124	9057446	205	9072111	75	9085522	80	9105035	127
9043689	132	9059602	93	9072135	66	9085572	42	9105073	247
9043756	146	9059614	93	9072147	66	9085534	92	9105126	202
9043720	234	9059616	93	9072446	24	9085352	283	9105140	224
9044023	42	9059638	93	9072824	239	9085546	92	9105396	42
9043990	96	9059640	93	9073050	36	9085560	80	9105578	136
9044700	177	9059688	53	9073062	152	9085558	92	9105633	281
9045132	242	9059951	133	9073438	70	9085429	283	9105645	281
9045156	239	9059963	141	9073701	184	9085479	239	9105906	143
9045168	241	9060182	65	9074004	107	9086071	133	9105920	140
9045560	36	9060285	140	9074119	34	9086966	71	9105932	169
9045780	107	9060314	234	9074133	136	9087025	175	9105968	221
9045792	107	9060338	234	9073995	282	9087013	197	9105970	221
9045807	100	9060637	150	9074078	225	9087283	59	9105982	220
9045924	240	9060649	150	9074042	282	9087295	122	9105994	221
9045936	240	9060601	208	9074389	178	9087972	102	9106297	27
9046112	65	9061112	98	9074391	179	9087946	160	9106302	27
9045948	240	9061124	98	9074511	72	9088110	98	9106170	169
9046124	65	9061136	98	9074511	94	9088122	98	9106182	169
9045950	241	9061198	240	9074585	93	9088237	121	9106194	169
9045974	256	9061928	112	9074535	179	9088251	112	9106209	169
9046328	92	9062087	285	9074547	180	9088249	121	9106481	165
9046227	202	9062984	118	9075345	79	9088524	227	9106479	215
9046241	284	9062960	149	9075333	123	9088689	208	9106493	215
9046502	92	9062996	117	9075723	70	9100073	277	9106508	214
9046514	92	9062972	187	9075709	121	9100396	50	9106704	42
9046526	92	9063067	256	9075711	121	9101493	97	9106625	227
9047245	240	9063079	256	9077070	127	9101508	85	9107306	127
9047271	240	9063653	95	9077082	127	9101510	85	9107772	18
9047506	176	9063665	95	9077123	180	9101522	145	9107784	18
9047491	197	9064126	22	9077288	45	9101596	159	9107796	18
9047518	197	9064322	85	9077290	145	9101601	234	9107887	79
9047752	175	9064190	219	9077329	112	9101730	152	9108166	39
9047764	197	9064334	85	9077276	179	9101819	116	9108178	39
9047996	159	9064267	167	9077410	70	9102198	99	9108128	117
9048914	18	9064279	167	9077238	247	9102203	99	9108130	118
9050137	13	9064229	240	9077458	86	9102148	161	9108255	51
9050369	94	9064396	162	9077460	86	9102150	161	9108221	141
9050371	95	9064401	162	9077331	257	9102069	252	9108154	214
9050383	94	9064684	167	9077460	178	9102071	252	9108233	141
9050395	95	9064750	146	9077367	280	9102083	252	9108300	95
9051351	157	9064748	149	9077379	280	9102095	252	9108295	192
9051363	157	9064786	141	9077836	70	9102100	252	9108362	134
9051375	158	9064798	141	9078830	131	9102112	252	9108398	107
9051478	148	9064762	187	9078842	129	9102124	252	9108257	267
9051480	146	9064774	222	9079157	42	9102239	175	9108374	230
9051492	150	9064853	195	9079169	42	9102241	175	9108702	105
9051507	149	9064839	240	9079133	112	9102253	175	9109031	12
9051600	64	9065182	192	9079145	113	9102265	175	9109017	192
9051612	64	9065443	152	9079171	170	9102277	175	9109029	192
9051806	161	9065625	83	9079119	277	9102289	209	9110042	160
9051818	160	9065912	215	9079121	277	9102291	208	9110107	159
9051791	239	9066667	20	9079547	47	9102318	209	9110315	111
9051820	279	9066485	240	9080297	272	9102502	46	9110377	281
9052343	182	9067128	240	9080613	47	9102514	46	9110389	281
9052604	42	9067556	66	9080998	224	9102306	255	9110391	281
9052989	134	9067568	66	9081215	86	9102318	255	9110652	35
9053127	62	9067570	66	9081203	179	9102485	176	9110561	194
9053232	97	9070058	9	9081382	214	9102497	236	9110523	267
9053206	224	9070022	192	9081813	93	9102710	150	9110896	101
9053218	224	9070163	141	9081679	239	9102722	146	9110901	101
9053220	224	9070175	141	9081825	93	9102746	146	9110913	101

ID	Value	ID	Value	ID	Value	ID	Value	ID	Value
9110925	100	9117313	95	9124469	252	9132480	177	9139488	136
9110951	91	9117325	95	9124471	253	9132492	177	9139490	135
9110975	148	9117387	50	9125217	94	9132519	177	9139505	151
9111058	93	9117600	205	9125229	94	9132686	94	9139634	219
9111319	21	9117739	225	9125451	130	9132789	99	9139713	178
9111357	42	9117741	225	9125607	75	9132868	235	9139725	178
9111369	42	9117900	108	9125619	75	9133068	170	9139737	179
9111383	111	9118135	100	9125592	195	9133070	170	9139749	178
9111395	113	9118147	101	9125736	64	9133082	171	9139971	42
9111486	80	9118056	231	9125918	42	9133410	68	9139907	284
9111474	141	9118381	212	9125786	205	9133422	68	9139919	284
9111462	233	9118317	286	9125906	104	9133446	128	9139921	284
9111565	192	9118501	140	9126003	267	9133458	128	9140530	41
9111620	157	9118628	100	9126015	267	9133460	128	9140528	138
9111632	156	9118721	9	9126297	272	9133587	208	9140530	138
9111644	156	9119139	279	9126479	202	9133769	215	9141065	27
9111802	22	9119141	283	9126481	203	9133771	215	9141077	27
9111955	35	9120334	205	9126807	18	9133850	283	9141261	135
9112090	55	9120322	244	9126819	18	9134165	100	9141314	91
9112117	61	9120748	65	9126871	221	9134232	97	9141273	135
9112088	281	9120750	66	9126974	214	9134244	97	9141285	135
9112129	247	9120762	65	9126986	214	9134268	98	9141297	136
9112131	247	9120774	66	9127150	58	9134270	98	9141302	135
9112272	107	9120786	65	9127502	39	9134282	98	9141326	113
9112260	123	9120798	65	9127514	40	9134490	106	9141338	112
9112284	123	9120877	10	9127526	39	9134581	40	9141405	133
9112296	117	9120932	36	9127538	40	9134593	40	9141807	17
9112222	276	9120944	36	9127411	257	9134517	139	9141778	203
9112234	276	9120841	167	9127667	61	9134505	205	9141780	202
9112301	283	9120853	167	9127540	219	9134646	74	9141792	202
9112313	283	9120865	166	9127784	40	9134550	223	9142150	99
9112571	139	9120918	284	9127796	40	9134608	217	9142162	97
9112789	10	9121003	211	9127801	40	9134658	223	9142174	98
9112806	188	9121194	284	9127813	40	9134684	206	9142186	98
9112973	196	9121247	255	9128025	96	9134672	224	9142198	98
9113147	61	9121259	255	9127928	239	9134622	275	9142473	113
9113379	100	9121297	225	9128037	184	9134634	276	9142485	113
9113446	92	9121273	272	9128049	184	9134713	241	9142980	38
9113305	281	9121730	105	9128051	185	9135169	240	9142942	80
9113317	281	9121742	105	9128128	112	9135652	59	9143051	72
9113458	143	9122045	80	9128130	111	9135638	82	9143001	169
9113642	41	9122057	224	9128027	221	9135664	59	9143013	169
9113616	202	9122033	266	9128063	185	9135901	173	9143025	169
9113654	284	9122095	267	9128142	111	9135913	173	9143037	169
9113666	284	9122100	267	9128166	123	9135925	267	9143099	185
9113678	284	9122203	255	9128099	221	9136046	157	9143063	255
9113680	284	9122394	91	9128283	77	9136577	280	9143075	255
9113692	284	9122435	85	9128180	192	9136931	177	9143207	197
9113915	129	9122447	85	9128192	193	9137428	176	9143219	197
9114189	86	9122552	12	9128207	195	9137430	176	9143166	283
9114191	86	9122409	228	9128532	27	9137648	77	9143233	279
9114165	123	9122411	228	9128477	140	9137674	219	9143321	197
9114177	123	9122590	55	9129811	54	9137698	219	9143245	279
9114232	197	9122605	255	9129706	272	9137894	124	9143518	91
9114244	197	9122655	270	9129873	145	9138123	143	9143544	117
9114206	282	9122916	36	9129885	151	9138109	205	9143556	116
9114610	42	9122930	123	9129823	255	9138276	53	9143568	117
9114593	139	9122928	128	9129940	211	9138290	53	9143697	61
9114622	247	9122942	123	9130121	54	9138329	28	9143489	280
9115705	55	9122954	272	9130169	212	9138305	54	9143532	259
9115731	111	9122966	272	9130171	233	9138238	128	9143702	108
9115743	111	9123221	46	9130614	161	9138240	128	9143879	81
9115717	195	9123154	149	9130937	108	9138317	53	9143740	239
9115729	195	9123099	205	9130949	110	9138161	267	9143714	267
9115690	281	9123166	145	9130951	108	9138381	109	9143752	240
9116137	235	9123192	157	9131058	112	9138288	208	9144031	89
9116357	44	9123075	278	9131072	113	9138393	109	9144043	89
9116369	43	9123374	34	9131084	113	9138458	50	9144055	90
9116400	210	9123398	135	9131113	156	9138410	109	9144196	9
9116412	230	9123507	177	9131125	156	9138422	109	9144067	206
9116553	123	9123532	234	9131216	90	9138513	270	9144158	221
9116577	99	9123659	155	9131137	189	9138525	270	9144160	221
9116589	99	9123661	155	9131149	189	9138628	205	9144134	275
9116591	99	9123740	95	9131151	189	9138850	10	9144146	275
9116606	99	9123772	65	9131242	173	9139000	65	9144392	126
9116618	99	9123702	267	9131204	220	9139012	65	9144316	205
9116747	95	9123922	262	9131216	224	9139024	65	9144328	205
9116864	23	9124146	42	9131230	220	9139036	65	9144407	127
9116876	23	9124354	44	9131266	196	9139048	66	9144354	225
9116890	169	9124366	44	9131254	220	9139050	66	9144756	178
9116905	170	9124392	96	9131266	220	9139062	65	9144768	178
9116955	128	9124378	217	9131357	133	9139282	136	9145061	223
9116917	170	9124380	217	9131278	224	9139294	249	9145229	177
9116967	128	9124512	114	9131840	72	9139309	249	9145231	177
9116970	143	9124524	114	9131876	64	9139311	249	9145188	256
9117181	80	9124500	194	9131888	263			9146015	34

ID	Value	ID	Value	ID	Value	ID	Value	ID	Value
9146003	233	9152297	282	9158575	83	9164653	95	9169691	215
9146302	96	9152583	140	9158587	83	9164847	64	9169940	253
9146314	96	9152595	140	9158551	143	9164835	102	9170286	42
9146455	166	9152600	140	9158604	123	9164756	239	9170298	42
9146467	167	9152507	250	9158513	227	9164768	239	9170652	96
9146479	166	9152856	44	9158537	240	9164770	239	9171292	26
9146584	161	9152739	220	9158549	239	9164782	239	9171278	95
9146558	263	9152753	220	9158616	272	9165011	103	9171280	121
9146807	42	9152765	220	9158874	61	9165358	117	9171448	36
9146728	234	9152959	29	9158886	61	9165360	118	9171436	78
9146730	256	9152777	220	9158898	123	9165293	211	9171498	162
9147071	136	9152789	220	9158965	136	9165346	215	9171503	162
9147083	136	9152909	222	9158949	156	9165516	183	9171826	215
9147095	187	9152911	221	9158903	263	9165530	246	9171838	215
9147100	187	9153381	227	9159103	185	9165542	246	9171826	256
9147112	187	9153513	102	9159115	185	9165932	215	9171840	256
9147253	214	9153408	208	9159189	285	9166390	246	9172208	78
9147435	36	9153393	227	9159426	235	9166417	246	9172234	155
9147265	231	9153549	160	9159567	95	9166675	102	9172248	155
9147447	206	9153563	158	9159660	125	9166687	102	9172258	156
9147617	205	9153551	186	9159658	156	9166649	145	9172260	156
9147758	138	9153612	140	9159830	21	9166651	144	9172272	156
9148025	82	9153783	121	9159672	189	9166704	121	9172193	259
9148116	248	9153850	167	9159684	189	9166742	102	9172648	10
9148532	267	9153862	164	9160011	30	9166778	167	9172458	249
9148659	140	9153874	248	9160229	77	9166780	167	9172480	249
9148635	214	9153886	248	9160205	189	9166792	166	9172485	281
9148808	155	9153898	248	9160425	44	9166895	180	9172674	102
9149304	90	9153903	248	9160437	44	9167136	62	9172650	128
9149316	90	9154232	143	9160396	221	9167162	41	9172662	128
9149328	91	9154191	193	9160413	224	9167174	62	9172777	13
9149213	243	9154206	193	9160619	133	9167186	62	9172844	102
9149225	243	9154218	195	9160530	243	9167227	22	9172856	102
9149237	243	9154220	194	9160798	225	9167150	168	9172870	133
9149380	105	9154268	216	9160803	225	9167148	234	9172868	215
9149249	243	9154270	216	9160932	162	9167198	189	9172947	241
9149251	243	9154282	216	9161168	52	9167534	280	9173082	115
9149392	104	9154294	216	9161182	52	9167796	239	9172959	239
9149263	243	9154529	264	9161170	144	9167801	240	9173094	115
9149653	50	9154531	264	9161273	128	9168180	172	9173109	115
9149665	50	9154543	263	9161285	128	9168154	205	9173111	115
9149495	253	9154608	247	9161259	157	9168192	172	9173056	243
9149512	253	9154610	247	9161297	151	9168207	172	9173135	204
9149524	253	9154848	122	9161508	55	9168219	172	9173721	62
9149689	205	9154854	267	9161314	283	9168221	172	9173733	61
9149823	83	9154866	267	9161481	233	9168324	183	9173745	105
9149835	83	9155028	112	9161716	23	9168324	283	9173757	105
9149794	135	9155078	112	9161728	22	9168635	197	9174218	64
9149847	83	9155107	150	9161766	112	9168611	253	9174220	64
9149859	83	9155145	123	9161778	112	9168623	253	9174282	182
9149861	83	9155157	122	9162215	167	9168647	252	9174397	215
9149873	82	9155119	169	9162227	168	9168831	99	9174608	81
9149744	264	9155121	169	9162253	204	9168843	99	9174610	82
9149756	263	9155133	169	9162265	204	9168855	99	9174660	36
9149768	264	9155092	228	9162277	202	9168867	99	9174490	267
9149770	263	9155303	127	9162370	236	9168879	99	9174672	243
9149885	221	9155365	140	9162368	267	9169029	146	9174658	267
9149897	274	9155377	140	9162485	182	9168922	257	9175066	77
9149902	275	9155391	139	9162497	182	9169031	150	9175078	125
9150303	68	9155341	233	9162605	141	9169043	146	9175080	141
9150183	192	9155389	255	9162617	141	9168934	256	9175781	167
9150195	192	9155626	235	9162631	145	9169055	145	9175793	167
9150200	192	9155808	102	9162497	280	9168946	257	9175808	167
9150212	192	9155767	243	9162643	149	9169067	150	9175975	91
9150339	158	9156462	27	9162875	135	9169122	116	9175925	186
9150341	160	9156474	21	9162887	135	9169134	116	9176008	112
9150315	198	9156515	12	9163192	40	9169158	99	9176010	113
9150614	162	9156527	12	9163207	40	9169160	99	9175901	240
9150913	15	9157478	178	9163269	125	9169249	95	9176022	156
9150834	102	9157478	178	9164017	92	9169316	69	9176034	156
9150810	249	9157698	79	9164029	92	9169328	69	9176395	121
9150822	249	9157703	79	9164184	55	9169380	39	9176644	35
9151527	91	9157662	156	9164201	125	9169421	102	9176632	124
9151814	127	9157674	156	9164213	125	9169524	13	9176711	103
9151826	127	9157715	189	9164225	163	9169495	44	9176682	145
9151864	140	9157727	189	9164237	162	9169500	44	9176565	270
9151905	143	9157648	283	9164245	167	9169550	13	9176577	270
9151840	278	9157650	283	9164249	167	9169419	208	9176761	93
9151917	223	9157777	181	9164251	169	9169603	34	9176773	93
9152181	240	9158147	77	9164263	169	9169615	133	9176606	272
9152284	183	9158159	177	9164275	167	9169627	133	9176747	254
9152296	183	9158264	102	9164536	38	9169512	259	9176759	254
9152258	263	9158288	124	9164586	123	9169691	102	9176929	133
9152260	264	9158276	181	9164627	94	9169706	156	9176993	102
9152272	263	9158496	53	9164639	94	9169718	156	9176993	215
9152284	283	9158563	83	9164641	95	9169689	215	9177052	160

9177026	192	9182631	38	9189093	34	9194476	184	9200823	79
9177038	192	9182643	38	9189108	34	9194866	44	9200718	194
9177040	250	9182655	62	9189160	74	9194878	44	9200653	285
9177143	161	9182667	62	9189134	125	9194983	139	9200938	21
9177155	184	9182629	129	9189122	156	9194995	139	9200940	24
9177109	267	9182710	72	9189158	256	9194969	182	9200847	171
9177428	124	9182746	105	9189419	24	9194921	240	9200926	257
9177430	183	9182954	108	9189421	24	9195157	27	9201695	129
9177545	178	9182966	108	9189342	168	9195169	27	9201736	160
9177557	178	9182928	156	9189251	270	9194957	240	9202041	52
9177569	178	9182930	156	9189354	168	9195195	23	9201869	240
9177571	178	9182978	108	9189249	279	9195200	22	9202053	144
9177583	178	9182942	156	9189366	168	9196119	231	9202481	88
9177624	205	9182934	270	9189495	168	9196606	102	9202479	236
9177686	184	9183257	62	9189500	168	9196644	102	9202508	248
9177648	254	9183269	123	9189782	60	9196618	211	9202510	247
9177650	254	9183324	100	9189768	82	9196632	212	9202522	247
9177806	99	9183506	12	9189873	240	9196644	242	9202534	248
9177820	210	9183348	184	9189885	240	9196838	80	9202546	247
9177985	50	9183350	184	9189902	225	9196840	80	9202649	146
9177947	210	9183517	30	9189926	226	9196852	80	9202651	151
9178276	37	9183374	184	9189938	277	9196864	80	9202558	247
9178288	38	9183609	139	9190092	124	9196711	253	9202663	148
9178290	38	9183708	48	9189940	277	9196955	99	9202857	240
9178317	61	9183855	27	9190119	100	9196967	99	9203291	124
9178329	114	9183776	204	9190505	134	9196890	186	9203277	215
9178197	252	9183817	224	9190638	133	9196979	99	9203289	215
9178202	252	9183829	224	9190731	163	9196981	99	9203514	97
9178331	156	9183831	224	9190743	163	9196905	186	9203538	97
9178343	156	9183843	224	9190755	163	9196993	99	9203461	234
9178537	97	9184392	284	9190767	163	9196917	186	9203473	284
9178678	162	9184835	39	9190779	163	9197002	225	9203502	255
9178757	100	9184859	121	9190781	163	9197351	78	9203526	255
9179218	97	9184940	69	9190858	250	9197284	197	9203576	272
9179127	231	9184914	105	9191034	105	9197296	197	9203588	267
9179256	239	9185047	186	9191395	62	9197349	224	9203590	272
9179268	239	9185281	92	9191400	161	9197363	247	9203629	285
9179593	34	9185293	92	9191412	161	9197375	247	9203631	285
9179397	238	9185487	63	9191307	271	9197545	80	9203904	128
9179402	239	9185499	63	9191424	161	9197739	141	9203784	257
9179581	122	9185504	62	9191333	256	9197715	256	9203942	145
9179622	125	9185451	121	9191319	271	9197832	161	9203965	152
9179646	102	9185516	62	9191321	271	9197844	162	9204477	275
9179701	56	9185463	121	9191345	257	9197935	105	9204489	276
9179646	215	9185528	105	9191474	186	9197909	141	9204764	106
9179725	270	9185530	105	9191498	185	9197894	211	9204776	106
9180011	42	9185401	279	9191876	121	9197911	248	9204752	257
9179816	261	9185413	279	9192167	26	9197947	247	9204972	38
9179828	261	9185774	34	9192179	26	9198123	110	9204984	38
9180138	62	9186326	86	9192228	102	9198082	157	9205081	106
9180152	51	9186302	121	9192351	15	9198135	110	9204958	240
9180164	51	9186338	86	9192363	15	9198094	153	9205093	106
9180281	56	9186209	277	9192387	24	9198109	209	9204960	240
9180217	283	9186211	277	9192399	24	9198111	209	9205079	215
9180267	246	9186223	277	9192428	74	9198355	9	9205811	34
9180279	246	9186235	277	9192430	75	9198367	9	9205847	39
9180358	215	9186596	243	9192258	283	9198264	285	9205885	100
9180360	215	9186754	144	9192260	283	9198276	285	9205897	101
9180372	215	9186651	256	9192337	256	9198288	285	9205902	100
9180384	215	9186687	235	9192349	256	9198575	162	9205916	101
9180396	215	9187045	70	9192442	165	9198587	162	9205938	100
9180786	60	9187033	92	9192454	166	9198563	198	9205964	131
9180920	171	9186950	182	9192466	166	9198927	280	9205976	129
9180968	152	9187289	160	9192478	166	9199127	259	9205988	131
9180982	258	9187227	229	9192741	189	9199268	209	9206011	130
9181132	185	9187239	229	9192753	189	9199270	209	9205990	161
9181144	185	9187489	10	9192765	189	9199783	75	9206023	131
9181168	186	9187497	215	9192777	189	9199795	74	9206035	130
9181170	240	9187796	10	9193226	116	9199830	105	9206059	249
9181376	124	9187887	15	9193238	116	9199842	104	9206061	249
9181493	50	9187899	15	9193288	116	9200330	100	9206396	182
9181479	69	9187760	214	9193290	118	9200366	104	9206614	79
9181560	124	9187863	145	9193240	169	9200378	104	9206671	251
9181649	56	9187875	145	9193252	169	9200380	103	9207120	158
9181546	182	9188037	12	9193305	118	9200392	105	9207027	255
9181558	182	9188154	99	9193264	169	9200407	105	9207388	160
9181534	256	9188099	252	9193317	118	9200419	100	9207730	97
9181651	148	9188219	202	9193276	167	9200445	100	9207754	184
9181663	150	9188647	10	9193551	79	9200562	60	9207716	267
9181675	152	9188790	49	9193563	79	9200421	225	9207728	267
9182019	231	9188623	233	9193680	40	9200677	194	9208021	43
9182021	231	9188818	49	9193719	40	9200689	194	9207982	267
9182277	181	9188805	70	9193721	57	9200691	194	9208198	70
9182289	183	9188829	70	9193733	57	9200809	80	9208203	70
9182356	158	9188788	125	9194127	36	9200811	80	9208227	57
9182368	158	9189081	34	9194139	143	9200706	194	9208033	257

ID	Value	ID	Value	ID	Value	ID	Value	ID	Value
9208239	57	9214898	162	9219795	162	9224300	238	9228356	23
9208112	189	9214903	162	9219800	162	9224312	237	9228368	22
9208045	258	9215048	135	9220079	224	9224506	130	9228370	40
9208100	231	9215050	171	9220316	207	9224518	130	9228564	85
9208124	231	9215048	257	9220328	207	9224520	130	9228576	85
9208356	38	9215115	190	9220433	233	9224532	129	9228514	217
9208485	189	9215165	163	9220615	109	9224544	130	9228526	217
9208638	38	9215177	163	9220627	109	9224439	244	9228538	217
9208833	61	9215086	260	9220847	75	9224441	244	9228540	217
9209221	27	9215189	163	9220859	75	9224453	244	9228552	279
9209104	255	9215191	163	9220861	75	9224465	244	9228655	229
9209130	257	9215098	259	9220990	34	9224726	10	9228837	134
9209271	158	9215103	259	9221009	34	9224489	285	9228849	134
9209295	233	9215256	197	9220885	165	9224491	285	9228801	190
9209506	161	9215268	197	9220897	166	9224738	77	9228813	190
9209518	159	9215270	197	9220952	175	9224740	76	9228992	42
9209934	49	9215347	127	9221073	65	9224685	205	9229295	77
9210139	21	9215311	164	9220964	175	9224697	206	9229300	183
9210141	20	9215282	197	9221085	65	9224702	206	9229302	183
9210153	20	9215323	168	9221097	65	9224714	206	9229324	183
9210050	152	9215295	197	9221102	65	9224946	74	9229336	183
9210062	152	9215490	15	9221059	139	9224958	74	9229348	183
9210074	152	9215309	197	9221061	139	9225079	115	9229386	189
9210220	13	9215543	46	9221279	12	9225005	205	9229374	263
9210086	152	9215672	86	9221281	12	9225249	81	9229659	15
9210218	24	9215634	194	9221205	95	9225251	81	9229647	156
9210098	152	9215646	194	9221217	95	9225328	81	9229829	116
9210438	218	9215660	261	9221360	71	9225330	81	9229831	118
9210440	217	9215892	141	9221554	10	9225421	39	9229843	118
9210892	170	9215828	215	9221566	10	9225433	40	9229855	116
9210828	241	9215830	215	9221633	39	9225342	182	9229972	101
9210907	170	9215842	215	9221657	136	9225407	214	9229984	100
9211169	44	9215854	215	9221853	34	9225419	214	9229996	100
9211157	258	9215866	215	9221865	34	9225615	195	9230000	100
9211482	167	9215878	232	9221839	75	9225665	149	9230062	58
9211597	60	9215880	235	9221889	34	9225677	149	9230115	12
9211494	167	9215907	234	9221671	259	9225641	195	9230050	99
9211872	156	9215919	235	9221683	256	9225770	75	9230098	153
9212058	34	9216092	80	9221906	54	9225653	194	9230074	187
9212010	224	9216224	62	9221918	56	9225782	75	9230086	187
9212022	220	9216248	61	9221815	192	9225794	230	9230048	256
9212034	221	9216391	60	9221798	221	9226396	152	9230402	15
9212046	220	9216406	60	9221827	192	9226530	34	9230309	132
9212400	124	9216298	242	9221970	114	9226504	145	9230311	132
9212383	259	9216303	242	9222132	141	9226516	145	9230426	189
9212589	53	9216365	221	9222091	217	9226413	261	9230488	150
9212369	276	9216389	263	9222106	219	9226425	261	9230490	149
9212371	276	9216547	134	9222118	233	9226891	12	9230505	257
9212395	260	9216559	134	9222120	234	9226906	13	9230517	256
9212694	205	9216705	37	9222168	189	9226815	140	9230787	93
9212709	206	9216729	38	9222297	72	9226918	150	9230907	78
9212759	256	9216717	64	9222302	72	9226920	150	9230775	236
9212864	208	9216626	260	9222170	211	9226932	146	9230878	158
9213105	53	9216638	260	9222273	192	9227003	78	9230969	77
9213117	54	9217022	114	9222285	192	9226994	229	9230892	189
9213169	161	9216901	241	9222467	44	9227015	238	9230880	211
9213088	260	9217034	114	9222455	162	9227027	238	9230971	135
9213090	260	9216913	241	9222443	184	9227039	238	9230854	259
9213272	116	9216987	173	9222974	46	9227285	86	9230995	200
9213284	116	9216925	241	9222986	45	9227297	204	9231107	143
9213375	34	9216999	173	9223318	105	9227302	204	9231030	221
9213296	211	9217553	87	9223198	274	9227479	37	9231236	42
9213301	211	9217565	87	9223497	60	9227314	204	9231248	42
9213313	211	9217448	250	9223344	243	9227326	200	9231250	44
9213325	211	9218131	27	9223590	54	9227508	23	9231157	144
9213416	156	9218404	101	9223590	129	9227510	23	9231262	44
9213454	160	9218416	101	9223758	66	9227273	261	9231121	197
9213571	45	9218650	178	9223760	65	9227338	204	9231092	229
9213583	45	9218662	180	9223825	42	9227481	62	9231133	197
9213806	184	9218789	62	9223954	10	9227340	204	9231107	230
9213818	184	9218674	178	9223899	119	9227778	65	9231145	196
9213777	239	9218777	78	9223904	119	9227948	56	9231119	229
9214123	60	9218686	178	9223746	284	9227912	109	9231298	60
9214202	45	9218648	271	9223887	175	9227924	109	9231169	232
9214214	43	9218832	130	9224049	116	9227998	141	9231482	97
9214135	133	9219056	211	9224051	118	9228045	133	9231494	97
9214226	45	9219331	30	9223980	263	9228071	108	9231511	141
9214147	133	9219264	162	9223992	263	9228057	132	9231614	81
9214317	197	9219276	162	9224272	78	9228057	133	9231470	233
9214305	252	9219355	90	9224271	105	9228186	15	9231509	244
9214513	66	9219367	87	9224295	94	9228069	141	9231688	70
9214551	92	9219379	92	9224324	66	9228198	15	9231626	210
9214563	91	9219393	91	9224324	78	9228174	60	9231810	80
9214525	234	9219418	91	9224336	66	9228144	108	9231822	80
9214745	62	9219343	227	9224348	66	9228344	23	9231755	194
9214757	166	9219381	227	9224283	189	9228306	69	9231951	18

9231779	280	9235062	198	9238519	130	9243590	114	9248150	194
9231781	283	9235141	127	9238521	131	9243617	96	9248162	194
9231793	280	9235268	Europe	9238571	130	9243605	114	9248473	102
9231808	284	9235244	36	9238686	128	9243564	205	9248526	60
9232072	135	9235098	194	9238698	128	9243825	61	9248485	102
9232084	135	9235103	194	9238789	44	9243837	129	9248497	102
9232101	135	9235256	78	9238791	44	9243849	129	9248423	189
9232113	135	9235359	196	9238806	44	9244022	80	9248538	101
9232058	205	9235361	197	9238739	200	9244063	79	9248540	101
9232060	205	9235401	187	9238741	200	9244219	39	9248502	156
9232096	282	9235531	169	9238856	102	9244257	100	9248435	257
9232462	70	9235543	167	9238753	280	9244544	224	9248485	242
9232448	93	9235555	164	9238818	223	9244556	224	9248552	260
9232450	93	9235565	167	9238820	224	9244623	184	9248564	269
9232503	58	9235579	164	9238765	283	9244635	184	9248667	228
9232515	57	9235713	36	9238777	283	9244659	210	9248679	228
9232400	227	9235725	36	9238868	208	9244661	210	9248641	274
9232412	227	9235696	81	9239616	99	9244673	210	9248813	127
9232383	275	9235907	73	9239484	255	9244934	80	9248825	127
9232395	275	9235816	192	9239783	12	9244946	79	9248693	274
9232565	117	9235828	192	9239795	12	9244881	204	9248708	274
9232577	116	9235957	96	9239628	211	9245005	159	9248916	129
9232589	117	9235880	180	9239630	211	9245017	160	9248928	229
9232591	211	9235969	96	9239850	75	9245031	156	9248930	230
9232606	211	9235892	180	9239886	43	9245029	160	9248942	230
9232618	211	9236004	77	9239862	75	9245598	109	9248954	229
9232620	211	9236016	78	9239898	44	9245744	162	9249025	205
9232632	234	9235983	196	9239903	44	9245756	162	9249178	64
9232644	275	9235995	224	9239874	75	9245768	162	9249180	64
9232802	126	9236171	60	9239848	139	9245770	162	9249207	98
9232814	127	9236195	60	9239977	63	9246102	20	9249219	98
9232747	214	9236042	217	9240160	270	9246310	44	9249221	98
9232759	214	9236212	140	9240328	219	9246346	44	9249233	98
9232773	231	9236250	105	9240512	36	9246396	65	9249245	98
9232761	279	9236224	140	9240433	127	9246401	65	9249271	82
9232785	260	9236236	140	9240445	127	9246308	205	9249128	244
9232929	127	9236389	10	9240809	204	9246580	109	9249130	243
9232931	127	9236248	155	9240873	235	9246592	109	9249257	141
9232797	269	9236432	133	9240885	259	9246578	133	9249312	102
9232890	206	9236353	256	9240897	259	9246607	108	9249324	102
9232864	244	9236535	90	9241190	38	9246621	99	9249312	215
9233258	18	9236470	160	9241205	38	9246683	92	9249324	215
9233272	77	9236482	160	9241102	206	9246695	92	9249295	277
9233234	154	9236444	223	9241114	206	9246712	88	9250191	51
9233313	105	9236420	256	9241281	98	9246633	212	9250220	131
9233222	263	9236638	86	9241293	98	9246700	207	9250232	129
9233404	133	9236523	220	9241308	98	9246798	259	9250464	20
9233416	133	9236547	223	9241310	98	9246803	260	9250531	93
9233454	225	9236511	266	9241322	98	9247144	22	9250543	93
9233466	225	9236652	145	9241267	242	9247168	134	9250660	79
9233492	205	9236585	231	9241449	140	9247182	175	9250488	260
9233703	34	9236597	219	9241451	206	9247285	141	9250490	259
9233741	125	9236614	241	9241475	205	9247388	54	9250622	161
9233765	189	9236626	241	9241487	205	9247405	70	9250725	64
9233791	208	9236688	275	9241657	129	9247493	63	9250696	138
9233789	215	9236690	276	9241669	129	9247508	63	9250701	138
9233777	229	9237072	36	9241798	63	9247364	256	9250751	197
9233806	258	9236975	169	9241802	81	9247572	69	9250737	255
9233818	258	9236987	164	9241695	190	9247584	69	9250892	157
9233923	189	9236999	166	9241815	81	9247546	129	9250907	157
9233832	283	9237008	166	9241683	215	9247429	256	9250971	160
9233844	282	9237151	146	9241918	279	9247431	255	9250983	160
9233856	281	9237345	12	9242091	137	9247558	130	9250995	160
9234068	101	9237084	274	9242118	114	9247443	255	9251078	138
9234070	101	9237357	10	9242120	114	9247455	256	9251028	258
9234082	101	9237096	274	9242089	200	9247728	18	9251286	190
9234094	101	9237395	71	9242302	128	9247792	51	9251274	226
9234109	178	9237307	217	9242156	283	9247819	57	9251365	159
9234111	179	9237319	217	9242314	128	9247730	183	9251377	159
9234123	179	9237486	89	9243148	58	9247742	183	9251389	159
9234135	178	9237503	133	9243150	56	9247754	183	9251391	159
9234214	104	9237527	182	9243162	116	9247786	183	9251406	166
9234256	98	9237747	99	9243174	118	9247924	109	9251561	51
9234331	66	9237761	226	9243198	118	9247778	260	9251573	51
9234343	67	9237773	226	9243203	118	9247936	109	9251640	106
9234355	67	9237785	226	9243306	80	9247807	243	9251652	106
9234367	67	9237797	226	9243286	118	9247974	105	9251597	162
9234616	54	9238038	52	9243239	276	9247986	105	9251602	162
9234628	54	9238040	51	9243241	276	9247948	232	9251614	166
9234654	157	9238052	143	9243318	260	9247950	232	9251626	166
9234666	211	9238313	49	9243320	259	9248112	73	9251638	166
9234678	259	9238155	274	9243461	129	9248083	115	9251690	149
9235000	157	9238167	274	9243394	209	9248124	75	9251688	152
9235074	116	9238179	274	9243473	130	9248095	115	9251705	146
9235050	145	9238181	274	9243409	209	9248136	194	9251717	150
9235086	116	9238284	253	9243667	20	9248148	194	9251822	52

9251846	144	9255945	105	9261401	190	9268112	257	9274317	253
9252058	71	9255854	217	9261396	231	9268916	69	9274329	253
9252096	39	9255983	280	9261657	84	9268930	69	9274616	94
9251999	209	9256016	263	9261712	159	9268942	69	9274513	258
9252008	209	9256028	262	9261724	159	9268930	110	9274525	256
9252230	115	9256212	84	9261736	159	9268992	60	9274628	164
9252204	158	9256054	243	9261748	159	9268904	215	9274630	164
9252254	114	9256224	84	9261889	73	9269063	72	9274642	170
9252333	36	9256066	243	9261891	73	9269245	55	9274654	170
9252216	159	9256078	243	9261906	73	9269257	56	9274678	170
9252101	279	9256315	52	9261908	73	9269075	256	9274800	94
9252266	114	9256327	52	9261815	174	9269960	58	9274725	210
9252228	161	9256298	171	9261827	174	9270440	67	9275024	47
9252187	215	9256365	144	9262118	66	9270452	67	9274812	266
9252357	212	9256377	140	9262120	67	9270464	67	9275036	47
9252369	212	9256389	140	9262132	67	9270476	67	9275048	47
9252539	99	9256391	140	9262144	67	9270488	62	9275050	47
9252436	251	9256468	64	9262156	130	9270490	62	9275062	47
9252448	251	9256406	140	9262168	130	9270567	160	9275103	229
9252541	187	9256418	139	9262091	259	9270517	246	9275115	231
9252553	186	9256597	56	9262209	242	9270529	246	9275361	254
9252565	188	9256470	209	9262211	242	9270737	70	9275646	39
9252577	186	9256482	209	9262223	242	9270749	70	9275634	80
9253014	38	9256535	195	9262235	242	9270804	221	9275658	95
9253026	38	9256755	80	9262310	213	9270816	224	9275660	95
9253038	38	9256767	103	9262522	119	9270907	136	9275737	210
9253117	56	9256793	103	9262534	119	9270828	220	9275749	211
9253105	103	9256755	150	9262572	143	9270830	223	9275957	60
9253064	157	9257046	71	9262704	183	9270919	137	9275969	141
9253076	157	9257060	60	9262716	183	9271248	122	9275971	150
9252981	275	9257058	71	9262728	183	9271391	129	9276004	134
9253002	254	9257010	124	9262754	161	9271341	208	9276016	155
9252993	275	9256901	243	9262766	162	9271406	153	9276028	247
9253208	109	9257084	60	9262730	234	9271353	208	9276030	246
9253210	108	9256913	243	9263174	232	9271511	100	9276406	70
9253143	223	9256925	243	9263186	232	9271432	210	9276250	280
9253181	189	9257137	36	9263198	232	9271614	78	9276262	281
9253234	136	9256937	243	9263203	231	9271561	158	9276561	154
9253155	224	9257149	36	9263332	146	9271591	189	9276573	154
9253193	189	9257498	125	9263344	145	9271597	184	9276585	154
9253246	136	9257503	125	9263320	236	9271626	189	9276597	154
9253258	136	9257802	157	9263643	171	9271585	283	9276743	254
9253222	241	9257993	246	9263693	259	9271925	68	9276779	254
9253296	187	9258002	246	9263708	259	9271834	210	9277400	93
9253301	187	9258167	245	9264271	231	9272216	68	9277486	81
9253313	283	9258179	245	9264283	231	9272228	68	9277668	137
9253325	283	9258466	38	9264790	76	9272230	68	9277858	51
9253715	103	9258519	56	9264893	184	9272345	60	9277747	206
9253727	118	9258521	56	9265407	166	9272199	251	9277759	206
9253741	117	9258624	54	9265366	261	9272204	251	9277761	206
9253818	57	9258600	105	9265548	99	9272383	76	9277773	206
9253739	209	9258612	105	9265756	235	9272391	81	9277773	259
9253820	243	9258595	251	9265861	210	9272395	265	9277802	218
9253894	231	9258868	51	9265873	210	9272400	265	9277814	218
9253856	277	9258870	51	9265885	210	9272668	198	9277826	217
9253909	229	9258882	51	9266231	198	9272773	204	9277785	259
9253868	277	9258894	51	9266243	198	9272929	82	9277797	259
9253870	277	9259329	95	9266267	198	9272888	130	9277838	218
9254082	106	9259379	96	9266841	50	9272890	132	9278052	95
9254070	260	9259331	161	9266853	51	9273076	30	9278064	95
9254422	53	9259343	162	9266865	51	9273064	133	9277943	243
9254240	259	9259276	256	9266877	52	9273210	46	9278105	83
9254458	141	9259317	230	9266944	95	9273088	234	9278181	10
9254642	108	9259393	212	9266982	58	9273375	95	9278117	83
9254654	108	9259381	227	9266956	95	9273337	156	9278143	146
9254692	130	9259408	212	9266994	58	9273246	261	9278155	150
9254836	41	9259886	62	9267003	58	9273260	260	9278088	286
9254850	93	9259991	190	9267015	58	9273442	233	9278090	285
9254862	93	9260122	60	9267027	134	9273557	133	9278519	139
9254903	243	9260017	190	9267209	101	9273624	210	9278492	169
9254915	243	9260029	190	9267156	285	9273636	210	9278739	42
9254927	264	9260005	231	9267417	76	9273791	91	9278636	158
9254939	265	9260055	231	9267429	119	9273806	91	9278624	235
9255189	71	9260067	231	9267663	69	9273818	82	9278791	100
9255074	205	9260263	231	9267651	130	9273650	261	9278985	122
9255244	169	9260275	231	9267637	183	9273894	184	9279329	69
9255268	180	9260419	162	9267546	280	9273909	181	9279331	68
9255270	180	9260421	162	9267649	183	9273985	130	9279513	60
9255282	180	9260433	162	9267675	159	9273923	199	9279549	82
9255294	180	9260445	162	9267687	161	9273947	199	9279757	161
9255488	106	9260457	162	9267699	161	9274094	56	9279812	192
9255490	106	9260469	162	9267601	286	9273959	199	9279965	146
9255684	155	9260902	60	9267936	123	9273961	199	9279977	151
9255696	154	9260914	178	9267912	218	9274434	77	9279989	152
9255880	143	9261205	156	9267924	218	9274446	77	9280386	154
9255933	105	9261360	60	9268083	205	9274305	253	9280598	72

ID	No.	ID	No.	ID	No.	ID	No.	ID	No.
9280603	73	9284752	182	9288837	51	9290830	250	9293909	123
9280615	74	9284697	252	9288849	52	9290866	274	9293894	158
9280627	75	9284926	62	9288875	64	9290878	274	9293911	158
9280637	75	9285005	208	9288851	114	9290957	260	9293947	190
9280641	75	9285029	215	9288772	261	9291119	141	9294109	60
9280653	75	9285122	216	9288887	189	9291236	61	9294020	207
9280665	90	9285134	216	9288899	257	9291248	62	9294018	227
9280586	232	9285146	216	9288928	231	9291133	181	9294159	236
9280641	254	9285354	120	9289051	133	9291389	70	9294240	161
9280811	85	9285407	71	9288904	284	9291391	70	9294173	236
9280653	254	9285419	71	9288930	259	9291262	256	9294252	161
9280873	36	9285495	121	9289104	149	9291640	261	9294161	254
9280885	36	9285483	169	9289013	247	9292101	58	9294185	236
9280847	80	9285500	169	9289116	152	9292113	58	9294290	161
9280809	206	9285471	209	9289025	247	9292010	223	9294305	161
9280835	284	9285653	43	9289128	149	9292022	223	9294343	132
9280859	283	9285665	43	9289087	201	9292149	114	9294355	132
9280861	283	9285677	43	9289063	236	9292151	114	9294329	162
9281151	36	9285689	43	9289099	201	9292163	102	9294331	161
9281009	256	9285691	43	9289180	172	9292034	245	9294367	130
9281011	257	9285706	51	9289192	172	9292046	244	9294408	96
9281267	150	9285718	51	9289207	172	9292058	244	9294379	163
9281279	149	9285720	51	9289491	64	9292060	244	9294381	167
9281437	62	9285732	52	9289544	46	9292175	132	9294472	78
9281853	93	9285744	51	9289477	215	9292216	136	9294513	38
9281724	263	9285756	51	9289556	196	9292125	233	9294484	70
9281920	95	9285615	218	9289568	197	9292230	132	9294525	38
9281932	95	9285627	218	9289681	84	9292137	236	9294393	173
9281906	129	9285639	218	9289518	261	9292242	132	9294537	206
9281918	130	9285641	218	9289520	261	9292254	132	9294563	184
9281944	137	9285796	66	9289532	261	9292266	132	9294549	205
9282041	256	9285823	94	9289738	82	9292357	82	9294666	141
9282053	256	9285861	154	9289740	81	9292204	246	9294678	141
9282259	146	9285988	83	9289922	47	9292565	77	9294812	89
9282261	145	9285990	82	9289934	47	9292486	157	9294824	88
9282479	51	9285835	266	9289946	47	9292498	157	9294836	88
9282481	51	9285847	266	9289958	47	9292577	123	9295012	35
9282493	50	9285859	266	9289752	261	9292606	95	9295000	64
9282508	51	9286047	190	9289764	261	9292503	256	9294800	285
9282510	82	9286009	237	9289776	261	9292515	256	9295036	56
9282522	82	9286011	237	9289788	261	9292632	156	9294848	274
9282558	82	9286059	190	9290086	78	9292761	100	9294850	274
9282780	69	9286267	75	9289960	223	9292620	261	9294862	274
9282730	127	9286231	193	9289908	282	9292628	226	9294886	274
9282625	251	9286243	195	9289910	282	9292838	226	9294989	188
9282792	153	9286255	195	9289972	223	9292979	156	9294991	187
9282950	44	9286229	256	9290165	90	9292967	261	9295206	85
9282962	44	9286281	256	9290177	90	9293155	122	9295086	260
9282974	46	9286774	47	9290098	237	9293117	229	9295244	116
9282986	259	9286798	35	9290103	237	9293129	229	9295256	117
9283306	61	9286786	48	9290115	237	9293131	229	9295268	116
9283186	199	9286803	36	9290127	237	9293167	201	9295165	228
9283198	199	9286889	284	9290139	237	9293143	229	9295177	228
9283203	199	9287168	82	9290347	77	9293179	201	9295218	194
9283215	199	9287132	259	9290282	151	9293272	109	9295220	194
9283227	199	9287340	120	9290294	162	9293272	110	9295270	176
9283239	199	9287417	108	9290309	161	9293399	15	9295282	176
9283289	171	9287429	104	9290440	85	9293430	136	9295335	134
9283291	171	9287778	284	9290452	85	9293442	132	9295347	124
9283241	257	9287780	285	9290402	203	9293454	132	9295385	150
9283643	63	9287895	221	9290414	204	9293466	132	9295397	146
9283693	48	9287900	221	9290490	134	9293519	159	9295361	201
9283681	77	9287912	222	9290385	244	9293531	159	9295373	201
9283617	251	9287924	223	9290426	203	9293583	123	9295323	260
9283629	251	9288021	259	9290397	244	9293571	158	9295579	71
9283837	70	9288045	248	9290464	194	9293595	158	9295567	138
9283679	234	9288083	210	9290476	194	9293636	161	9295593	184
9283710	259	9288057	248	9290488	194	9293648	160	9295505	286
9283722	257	9288095	210	9290531	151	9293650	159	9295830	122
9283784	256	9288069	247	9290543	152	9293662	158	9295842	121
9283796	261	9288071	247	9290555	201	9293739	130	9295945	87
9283875	184	9288265	95	9290567	201	9293612	271	9295971	72
9283887	184	9288291	101	9290579	260	9293624	271	9295969	75
9284192	122	9288273	175	9290779	89	9293753	194	9295957	88
9284269	82	9288356	95	9290787	89	9293741	215	9296195	154
9284362	71	9288426	70	9290804	88	9293765	194	9296212	280
9284489	42	9288461	70	9290816	88	9293777	194	9296585	265
9284570	60	9288473	70	9290646	259	9293789	194	9296731	252
9284491	188	9288411	138	9290658	260	9293791	194	9296822	232
9284582	156	9288289	265	9290660	260	9293832	156	9297345	51
9284594	156	9288394	178	9290775	158	9293806	194	9297369	51
9284702	100	9288409	180	9290945	89	9293844	156	9297371	51
9284764	69	9288540	138	9290919	141	9293870	137	9297321	154
9284776	69	9288760	50	9290921	141	9293818	194	9297333	153
9284740	181	9288813	51	9290933	139	9293820	194	9297503	95
9284738	184	9288825	51	9290828	250	9293923	100	9297541	61

9297515	95	9300386	99	9302619	285	9305087	274	9307748	50
9297553	61	9300398	99	9302621	286	9305300	169	9307750	50
9297474	204	9300403	99	9302633	285	9305312	169	9307762	50
9297527	219	9300415	99	9302645	285	9305465	42	9307578	247
9297840	207	9300427	99	9302695	274	9305477	42	9307580	247
9297852	207	9300439	99	9302877	163	9305489	43	9307786	56
9297864	203	9300441	99	9302889	163	9305491	42	9307657	274
9297876	203	9300453	99	9302891	163	9305506	42	9307827	155
9297987	158	9300465	98	9302982	105	9305570	79	9307815	189
9298193	106	9300477	99	9302994	105	9305582	79	9307798	260
9298313	62	9300570	130	9302968	156	9305532	134	9308039	99
9298325	62	9300582	183	9302944	234	9305594	79	9308003	221
9298351	115	9300556	258	9302956	233	9305556	180	9308015	221
9298363	115	9300752	120	9303156	69	9305568	244	9308027	221
9298375	115	9300594	280	9303168	69	9305635	207	9307994	267
9298387	115	9300790	208	9303170	69	9305702	149	9308182	115
9298507	153	9300805	209	9303106	141	9305714	148	9308223	82
9298636	88	9300996	82	9303182	69	9305609	263	9308194	114
9298648	88	9300972	115	9303194	69	9305611	263	9308065	266
9298519	263	9301005	82	9303118	159	9305623	263	9308077	256
9298650	153	9300984	114	9303209	69	9305647	281	9308247	101
9298686	169	9301043	82	9303211	69	9305659	281	9308431	37
9298698	169	9301067	69	9303223	69	9305661	281	9308390	144
9298818	63	9301079	69	9303302	52	9305673	281	9308405	144
9298703	268	9301122	52	9303314	52	9305685	281	9308493	56
9298715	267	9301146	39	9303247	139	9305855	154	9308417	144
9298820	166	9301134	52	9303364	71	9305867	154	9308429	144
9298727	268	9301433	44	9303376	138	9305879	236	9308508	79
9298739	267	9301445	44	9303429	138	9305881	236	9308510	79
9299020	119	9301457	44	9303522	47	9306067	88	9308546	53
9299032	119	9301471	91	9303534	47	9306079	87	9308558	53
9299044	119	9301483	91	9303528	95	9306029	152	9308637	47
9298997	285	9301495	92	9303560	103	9306158	89	9308649	47
9299123	251	9301328	275	9303546	169	9306160	89	9308728	133
9299135	252	9301330	274	9303558	169	9306172	89	9308821	61
9299147	251	9301380	243	9303651	197	9306184	89	9308857	61
9299159	251	9301392	243	9303728	191	9306196	89	9308869	60
9299276	247	9301524	127	9303730	190	9306201	87	9308883	181
9299288	247	9301407	245	9303845	78	9306213	88	9308792	281
9299290	247	9301536	127	9303742	228	9306225	87	9308895	182
9299305	247	9301419	245	9303754	228	9306237	88	9308807	281
9299460	100	9301421	245	9303766	227	9306287	89	9309021	76
9299460	100	9301469	266	9303924	70	9306251	227	9308948	171
9299472	100	9301720	105	9303778	228	9306550	47	9308950	171
9299472	100	9301770	238	9303780	262	9306548	58	9309162	233
9299422	170	9301782	238	9304033	22	9306562	93	9309409	38
9299434	163	9301794	238	9304045	27	9306574	93	9309411	38
9299343	259	9301809	238	9304057	27	9306641	41	9309277	236
9299355	259	9301811	238	9304125	69	9306665	41	9309289	236
9299446	170	9301823	238	9304095	100	9306471	236	9309423	154
9299458	163	9301835	238	9304067	133	9306483	236	9309435	153
9299604	60	9301847	238	9304186	78	9306639	171	9309447	151
9299563	125	9301988	97	9304239	78	9306653	232	9309459	152
9299549	149	9301964	124	9304241	95	9306627	259	9309461	152
9299628	74	9301859	238	9304289	78	9306677	232	9309473	148
9299551	152	9301976	124	9304306	197	9306809	176	9309629	68
9299630	74	9301940	211	9304411	146	9306811	176	9309667	101
9299484	227	9301926	233	9304423	150	9306782	246	9309576	246
9299642	73	9301952	212	9304435	148	9306794	246	9309588	247
9299525	201	9301938	233	9304447	201	9306938	166	9309930	67
9299654	75	9302073	130	9304459	201	9306940	166	9309942	67
9299537	201	9302085	130	9304605	154	9306990	117	9309954	67
9299800	74	9302097	130	9304617	154	9307023	116	9309966	66
9299812	74	9302102	130	9304629	174	9307035	160	9310032	67
9299680	246	9302138	130	9304540	280	9307047	160	9310044	67
9299666	262	9302140	130	9304772	66	9307009	209	9310056	67
9299692	246	9301990	286	9304655	184	9307011	208	9309978	191
9299678	262	9302152	130	9304667	184	9307059	160	9309980	190
9299707	246	9302164	130	9304784	67	9307217	67	9310109	271
9299719	246	9302176	130	9304796	67	9307188	103	9310238	209
9299927	47	9302114	259	9304801	67	9307190	103	9310240	209
9299939	47	9302126	260	9304813	66	9307231	67	9310408	60
9299771	230	9302205	271	9304693	188	9307205	103	9310513	108
9299874	176	9302499	37	9304708	188	9307229	83	9310642	82
9299862	189	9302437	119	9304734	174	9307243	83	9310537	189
9299886	176	9302449	119	9304746	174	9307176	161	9310599	136
9300192	71	9302578	150	9304758	196	9307346	41	9310604	138
9300221	82	9302554	235	9304760	196	9307267	207	9310769	138
9300178	138	9302566	139	9305099	39	9307279	207	9310707	243
9300207	138	9302657	235	9305104	39	9307396	213	9311036	139
9300219	137	9302580	235	9304966	188	9307401	213	9311012	252
9300300	65	9302592	261	9304978	188	9307413	213	9311024	253
9300154	221	9302774	82	9305051	141	9307425	213	9311177	138
9300312	65	9302669	190	9305001	274	9307633	123	9311139	182
9300166	221	9302607	261	9305178	119	9307645	123	9311191	138
9300324	65	9302671	231	9305180	119	9307736	57	9311270	184

ID	Value	ID	Value	ID	Value	ID	Value	ID	Value
9311567	58	9314246	66	9316828	130	9320752	172	9323821	127
9311579	58	9314210	172	9316927	108	9320764	172	9323819	166
9311581	58	9314234	237	9317523	69	9320831	184	9323936	171
9311593	142	9314208	267	9317406	225	9320843	184	9323948	171
9311608	142	9314258	237	9317559	78	9321017	234	9324150	101
9311622	245	9314806	124	9317418	225	9321237	159	9324100	161
9311696	172	9314832	124	9317547	100	9321213	184	9324289	55
9311701	172	9314844	136	9317456	260	9321249	159	9324291	55
9311713	231	9314856	136	9317767	71	9321251	159	9324083	275
9311830	119	9314923	74	9317690	205	9321263	159	9324306	56
9311725	231	9314961	42	9317705	205	9321299	184	9324318	56
9311828	129	9314868	136	9317963	72	9321304	184	9324320	56
9311842	119	9314870	136	9317987	56	9321471	145	9324162	229
9311880	88	9314818	190	9317975	75	9321483	162	9324174	230
9311775	199	9314820	190	9317860	197	9321495	162	9324435	37
9311787	199	9314935	75	9318046	42	9321500	162	9324277	263
9311799	199	9314973	42	9318058	44	9321512	162	9324497	227
9311763	280	9314947	72	9317951	154	9321524	162	9324710	104
9311836	219	9314985	44	9318060	46	9321536	162	9324734	229
9311854	219	9314911	171	9317913	214	9321548	162	9324746	244
9312078	119	9315070	55	9317925	214	9321550	162	9324837	220
9312080	119	9315082	56	9318101	43	9321691	77	9324849	220
9312092	109	9314882	261	9317937	214	9321706	77	9324851	221
9312092	110	9314894	261	9318010	155	9321718	77	9324863	220
9312432	145	9315056	171	9318034	189	9321720	77	9325025	60
9312470	121	9315056	172	9318113	254	9321653	156	9324875	221
9312482	121	9315197	172	9318125	254	9321665	156	9325063	62
9312559	66	9315202	172	9318321	99	9321744	103	9325221	69
9312561	67	9315214	172	9318151	283	9321756	103	9325233	69
9312573	67	9315226	172	9318163	284	9321768	103	9325324	82
9312585	67	9315238	172	9318175	280	9321770	103	9325178	280
9312418	236	9315240	172	9318187	280	9321677	266	9325180	281
9312597	67	9315252	172	9318319	172	9321732	217	9325439	132
9312494	171	9315173	261	9318462	121	9321689	266	9325441	227
9312509	171	9315185	261	9318333	260	9321897	205	9325609	191
9312511	171	9315343	114	9318474	121	9321902	206	9325611	191
9312444	251	9315367	94	9318527	108	9322023	130	9325788	69
9312456	251	9315355	114	9318486	181	9322267	62	9325790	69
9312652	114	9315446	171	9318498	183	9322255	99	9325764	130
9312755	113	9315458	171	9318486	217	9322279	105	9325776	132
9312767	113	9315537	100	9318503	218	9322281	105	9325685	255
9312779	111	9315537	100	9318515	273	9322293	171	9325697	255
9312781	183	9315393	251	9318541	247	9322310	189	9325702	255
9312913	51	9315549	100	9318553	246	9322308	213	9325908	143
9312793	183	9315769	51	9319404	132	9322310	213	9326055	139
9312925	51	9315812	38	9319545	93	9322322	280	9326067	139
9312808	183	9315642	214	9319480	197	9322334	280	9326407	274
9312810	183	9315824	38	9319674	171	9322346	284	9326419	274
9312937	111	9315848	44	9319686	172	9322358	283	9326421	274
9312949	112	9315915	99	9319703	171	9322463	180	9326433	274
9312822	271	9315953	99	9319698	259	9322475	180	9326603	133
9312846	256	9315795	261	9319753	271	9322487	180	9326524	255
9312834	270	9315800	261	9319765	271	9322499	180	9326598	244
9312858	256	9315965	99	9319870	206	9322504	196	9326770	74
9312860	256	9315836	236	9320087	20	9322516	196	9326718	127
9312884	246	9315874	236	9320099	20	9322695	162	9326720	127
9312896	246	9315850	262	9320001	119	9322700	162	9326706	145
9312975	183	9315886	236	9320013	120	9322736	138	9326823	91
9312987	183	9315862	262	9320025	258	9322712	166	9326835	91
9312999	183	9315898	261	9320142	145	9322827	250	9326744	194
9313008	181	9315903	261	9320037	258	9322839	250	9326756	195
9313008	183	9316098	141	9320049	258	9323015	114	9326768	193
9313096	162	9316139	108	9320051	258	9323027	114	9326782	201
9313101	162	9316115	134	9320295	71	9322956	246	9326794	201
9313137	132	9316153	105	9320300	70	9322968	246	9326902	93
9313113	162	9316165	105	9320312	70	9323039	205	9326914	93
9313149	132	9316220	105	9320233	162	9323041	205	9326926	93
9313125	162	9316232	115	9320245	162	9323326	136	9326938	93
9313199	110	9316244	115	9320348	70	9323338	136	9327097	54
9313204	110	9316127	243	9320257	162	9323340	136	9327102	54
9313216	110	9316139	270	9320374	103	9323352	136	9327114	156
9313228	110	9316141	270	9320465	67	9323364	136	9327138	155
9313242	144	9316323	90	9320477	67	9323376	136	9327140	155
9313527	133	9316282	217	9320477	67	9323388	136	9327360	124
9313486	257	9316294	219	9320403	149	9323390	136	9327384	124
9313498	257	9316309	217	9320556	12	9323405	136	9327372	190
9313905	166	9316311	219	9320439	149	9323481	140	9327396	190
9313917	166	9316335	231	9320398	195	9323560	62	9327401	190
9313929	162	9316347	219	9320453	152	9323508	122	9327554	156
9313931	167	9316361	219	9320427	195	9323510	122	9327669	89
9313943	166	9316359	231	9320441	194	9323522	123	9327671	88
9313955	166	9316373	279	9320697	118	9323493	228	9327683	88
9313967	166	9316593	85	9320702	118	9323584	162	9327580	227
9314064	76	9316672	62	9320685	214	9323596	226	9327736	130
9314090	188	9316608	190	9320738	172	9323780	130	9327748	219
9314222	67	9316701	161	9320740	172			9327786	274

ID	Value	ID	Value	ID	Value	ID	Value	ID	Value
9327798	274	9332810	70	9335173	65	9338937	97	9344033	245
9327803	274	9332822	70	9335068	176	9338876	161	9344435	53
9328168	135	9332951	36	9335185	65	9338888	184	9344423	119
9328170	135	9332834	182	9335197	72	9338955	243	9344289	280
9328596	67	9332846	280	9335202	72	9339272	151	9344552	173
9328601	67	9332975	171	9335874	68	9339284	146	9344564	173
9328481	232	9332872	280	9335886	69	9339296	145	9344710	90
9328493	232	9333149	9	9335874	137	9339181	267	9344722	90
9328522	247	9332987	172	9335983	91	9339260	258	9344631	200
9328534	247	9332884	281	9335953	181	9339301	246	9344643	200
9328728	158	9333151	15	9335965	184	9339351	197	9344655	200
9328955	246	9332999	168	9336048	152	9339313	246	9344667	200
9329459	35	9333163	10	9336165	91	9339480	82	9344679	200
9329447	210	9333008	168	9336177	91	9339325	246	9344681	201
9329461	272	9333010	168	9336189	92	9339337	246	9344693	201
9329526	209	9333175	13	9336191	91	9339545	74	9344708	186
9329473	272	9333022	168	9336050	272	9339351	283	9345366	77
9329538	209	9332925	270	9336062	272	9339595	90	9345403	65
9329540	209	9333034	172	9336074	272	9339612	159	9345415	65
9329552	209	9332937	270	9336086	272	9339806	69	9345427	65
9329693	135	9332949	270	9336402	41	9339600	286	9345439	65
9329643	187	9333046	196	9336414	41	9339612	286	9345611	78
9329679	156	9333072	196	9336426	41	9339844	69	9345764	36
9329708	135	9333058	258	9336490	232	9339818	124	9345623	181
9329710	135	9333060	258	9336505	232	9339820	130	9345702	213
9329722	135	9333228	155	9336763	136	9339832	131	9345818	104
9329631	228	9333369	88	9336787	138	9339868	173	9345958	115
9329629	236	9333395	90	9336866	101	9339959	101	9345960	115
9329667	246	9333371	261	9336737	258	9339947	126	9345972	115
9329784	135	9333383	261	9336749	258	9340439	38	9346029	87
9329863	161	9333400	244	9336945	77	9340415	93	9346005	188
9330032	23	9333412	244	9336971	105	9340477	38	9346017	187
9330068	201	9333606	51	9336983	105	9340489	38	9345984	228
9330070	201	9333424	244	9337028	174	9340491	82	9345996	228
9330056	249	9333618	51	9337133	156	9340544	69	9346160	141
9330343	63	9333620	51	9337250	120	9340556	69	9346304	122
9330355	63	9333436	244	9337262	120	9340570	69	9346380	55
9330496	99	9333527	269	9337107	280	9340582	162	9346433	124
9330563	36	9333539	269	9337212	210	9340594	170	9346445	190
9330501	99	9333541	269	9337397	41	9340623	166	9346457	190
9330599	64	9333553	269	9337274	236	9340635	210	9346756	60
9330604	64	9333785	70	9337511	68	9340764	213	9346768	59
9330549	135	9333632	257	9337523	68	9341110	202	9346811	216
9330513	202	9333670	243	9337597	114	9341067	246	9346823	216
9330525	202	9333682	243	9337444	285	9341122	202	9346835	216
9330678	50	9333797	129	9337456	286	9341079	246	9347035	52
9330472	262	9333826	159	9337468	285	9341081	246	9347047	52
9330616	121	9333838	159	9337470	285	9341093	246	9347059	52
9330537	235	9333840	159	9337482	285	9341512	81	9347061	52
9330707	123	9333852	159	9337614	183	9341433	162	9347176	35
9330719	123	9334234	69	9337652	183	9341445	171	9347255	202
9330721	123	9334246	69	9337664	183	9341940	56	9347267	202
9330698	175	9334143	221	9337676	183	9342217	56	9347279	201
9330745	131	9334155	220	9337688	183	9342281	27	9347281	202
9330812	105	9334167	220	9337705	210	9342176	172	9347293	201
9330654	279	9334351	96	9337717	210	9342205	169	9347308	200
9330666	280	9334375	88	9337731	212	9342580	40	9347425	112
9330874	77	9334349	196	9337743	210	9342499	171	9347437	112
9330989	39	9334351	196	9337729	242	9342504	171	9347449	111
9330991	39	9334387	180	9337913	67	9342516	171	9347542	122
9331000	75	9334519	135	9337925	67	9342528	171	9347554	122
9331048	37	9334521	136	9337755	242	9342487	258	9347566	123
9331012	75	9334480	231	9337937	67	9342695	213	9347578	122
9331165	274	9334571	206	9337949	66	9342700	274	9347580	123
9331555	105	9334715	101	9337951	217	9342712	274	9347592	123
9331634	156	9334662	172	9338058	120	9342891	130	9347607	123
9331749	50	9334674	172	9337963	217	9342906	182	9347619	123
9331646	156	9334686	172	9337975	217	9343132	12	9347516	243
9331658	156	9334856	10	9337987	217	9343156	108	9347724	229
9331660	156	9334698	180	9338084	202	9343168	109	9347724	231
9331672	156	9334868	10	9338589	138	9343170	108	9347877	105
9331713	280	9334703	180	9338632	132	9343194	93	9347856	134
9331866	275	9334882	58	9338620	161	9343118	281	9348053	199
9332054	243	9334832	110	9338797	133	9343266	133	9348065	199
9332157	154	9334844	110	9338694	272	9343340	70	9348077	199
9332212	105	9334818	140	9338709	272	9343388	184	9348089	199
9332303	68	9334923	65	9338711	272	9343390	184	9348091	199
9332315	68	9334935	67	9338826	161	9343495	184	9348106	199
9332195	210	9334894	131	9338802	190	9343613	71	9348156	168
9332200	208	9334832	228	9338723	272	9343481	225	9348168	168
9332523	35	9334920	140	9338747	250	9343493	225	9348170	167
9332550	115	9334844	228	9338838	161	9343510	225	9348302	53
9332511	172	9335032	176	9338840	161	9343716	117	9348297	119
9332535	175	9335044	176	9338814	190	9343728	116	9348493	90
9332547	169	9335056	176	9338852	161	9343730	117	9348431	186
9332690	167			9338864	161	9343986	139	9348447	173

ID	Value	ID	Value	ID	Value	ID	Value	ID	Value	ID	Value
9348443	186	9352391	223	9357092	194	9361623	236	9368895	121		
9348455	186	9352406	223	9357107	195	9361811	182	9368900	121		
9348467	186	9352418	223	9357119	193	9361809	218	9368912	121		
9348704	73	9352420	223	9357121	194	9361811	217	9369758	146		
9348649	171	9352561	153	9357298	217	9361823	217	9369734	206		
9348651	172	9352559	162	9357303	218	9361835	217	9370018	18		
9348663	196	9352860	103	9357315	218	9361990	257	9369899	258		
9348675	196	9353084	201	9357327	217	9362322	74	9369904	258		
9348687	196	9353096	200	9357523	219	9362267	131	9370202	158		
9348699	196	9353242	57	9357781	134	9362334	144	9370214	161		
9348857	230	9353101	200	9357793	134	9362293	213	9370329	138		
9348900	230	9353113	200	9357808	134	9362437	75	9370408	81		
9349174	46	9353125	201	9357810	134	9362308	213	9370537	57		
9349368	227	9353137	200	9357846	110	9362542	10	9370707	234		
9349681	23	9353149	200	9357858	140	9362530	24	9370800	158		
9349617	99	9353228	187	9357860	140	9362396	199	9370812	158		
9349629	99	9353230	187	9357901	182	9362401	199	9371062	225		
9349497	263	9353254	285	9357913	182	9362413	199	9371086	277		
9349502	264	9353266	285	9357872	228	9362449	173	9371402	46		
9349514	263	9353278	285	9357925	182	9362712	38	9371579	129		
9349526	264	9353280	285	9357949	199	9362724	219	9371581	129		
9349538	263	9353292	285	9357951	199	9362736	219	9372456	24		
9349540	264	9353620	59	9357963	199	9362877	162	9372315	186		
9349552	263	9353527	211	9357975	199	9363015	59	9372327	186		
9349564	263	9353530	211	9358290	171	9363027	60	9372470	149		
9349605	254	9353541	211	9358292	171	9363035	59	9372482	150		
9349813	146	9353553	212	9358436	38	9363039	60	9372494	152		
9349825	150	9353565	210	9358400	259	9363041	59	9372420	243		
9349796	195	9353577	211	9358412	259	9363053	60	9372432	243		
9349801	195	9353589	211	9358632	93	9363168	50	9372547	245		
9349875	136	9353591	210	9358541	263	9363118	158	9372559	243		
9349887	136	9353606	212	9358644	253	9363144	219	9372561	244		
9350070	101	9353797	102	9358760	243	9363156	219	9372731	242		
9350018	179	9353802	102	9358761	159	9363364	84	9372742	241		
9350094	104	9354167	183	9358862	243	9363376	84	9372682	144		
9350020	179	9354662	279	9358890	46	9363481	197	9372872	144		
9350032	178	9354674	279	9358905	46	9363493	197	9372999	122		
9350288	57	9354791	177	9358888	197	9363479	259	9373486	110		
9350290	57	9354923	193	9359002	165	9363819	38	9373462	140		
9350343	82	9354935	253	9359014	165	9363821	38	9373498	110		
9350381	72	9355161	59	9359026	165	9363637	225	9373474	139		
9350393	73	9355238	69	9359038	165	9363699	182	9373622	119		
9350422	57	9355240	69	9359040	165	9363948	159	9373644	119		
9350317	217	9355252	69	9359052	165	9363950	158	9374040	77		
9350604	57	9355185	160	9359260	227	9363845	283	9374088	59		
9350599	253	9355197	161	9359301	230	9363857	281	9374038	129		
9350642	267	9355202	181	9359313	230	9364203	230	9374052	130		
9350800	129	9355214	184	9359325	229	9364382	253	9374117	227		
9350850	189	9355226	182	9359363	252	9364394	253	9374301	122		
9350862	189	9355288	171	9359375	253	9364588	259	9374372	68		
9350927	132	9355331	171	9359387	252	9364813	101	9374571	145		
9351127	74	9355343	171	9359399	252	9365001	55	9374583	145		
9351139	75	9355355	173	9359791	20	9364992	200	9374595	144		
9351141	74	9355367	167	9359806	20	9364966	234	9374521	253		
9351024	213	9355408	183	9359545	284	9365477	119	9374844	134		
9350989	249	9355410	183	9360142	74	9365489	119	9375305	112		
9350991	250	9355551	65	9360154	72	9365817	82	9375264	271		
9351036	213	9355563	65	9360245	230	9365659	269	9375496	112		
9351048	212	9355575	65	9360257	230	9365661	269	9375501	112		
9351050	212	9355604	103	9360257	233	9365788	201	9375513	111		
9351062	211	9355513	226	9360269	230	9365790	200	9375616	259		
9351159	130	9355733	27	9360271	230	9365805	200	9375953	70		
9351218	219	9355757	209	9360453	157	9366263	233	9376012	91		
9351414	213	9355769	209	9360465	157	9366275	233	9376141	228		
9351426	213	9355812	269	9360568	69	9367188	118	9376816	190		
9351438	213	9356074	172	9360415	232	9367205	118	9376828	191		
9351440	214	9356086	167	9360415	232	9367170	209	9376878	161		
9351452	214	9356098	167	9360427	232	9367176	209	9376945	189		
9351464	214	9356103	167	9360439	232	9367578	182	9377224	58		
9351581	149	9356115	167	9360441	231	9367607	181	9377236	58		
9351593	145	9356127	164	9360697	90	9367683	139	9377248	58		
9351531	253	9356139	168	9360764	174	9367580	273	9377078	243		
9351543	252	9356141	172	9360752	199	9367671	190	9377133	192		
9351737	71	9356153	172	9360910	84	9367592	273	9377145	192		
9352004	164	9356165	172	9360831	241	9367748	191	9377406	59		
9352016	164	9356294	75	9360879	255	9367815	281	9377470	109		
9351921	267	9356309	74	9360881	255	9367827	280	9377482	108		
9352028	164	9356311	74	9360893	255	9367839	283	9377420	171		
9352030	172	9356610	53	9360908	255	9368302	58	9377559	53		
9352042	172	9356696	183	9361079	99	9368314	58	9377561	54		
9352195	190	9356701	183	9360934	252	9368326	70	9377573	54		
9352298	106	9356713	183	9361249	103	9368338	70	9377494	270		
9352303	106	9356816	115	9361251	104	9368730	115	9377688	82		
9352315	106	9356830	213	9361445	99	9368742	114	9377509	270		
9352200	253	9356842	230	9361512	210	9368838	39	9377511	271		
9352212	253	9357080	194	9361524	210	9368871	104	9377523	271		

ID	Val	ID	Val	ID	Val	ID	Val	ID	Val	ID	Val
9377781	57	9384021	211	9388821	241	9394753	263	9398424	284		
9377779	61	9384100	134	9388833	241	9394765	263	9398436	284		
9377652	190	9384033	211	9389071	61	9394870	171	9398448	284		
9378321	49	9384198	226	9389083	61	9394882	167	9398450	284		
9378151	243	9384203	226	9389095	61	9394894	167	9398462	284		
9378163	243	9384215	226	9389100	61	9395020	53	9398682	94		
9378448	12	9384227	226	9389253	36	9395032	54	9398694	94		
9378450	12	9384239	226	9389265	36	9395068	54	9398709	94		
9378462	15	9384370	152	9389215	126	9395070	54	9398711	95		
9378474	9	9384435	244	9389382	111	9394935	211	9398735	95		
9378486	10	9384447	244	9389394	110	9394947	212	9398747	95		
9378498	12	9384590	102	9389409	111	9395109	54	9398759	95		
9378319	210	9384459	244	9389411	112	9395111	54	9398888	10		
9378369	257	9384605	102	9389497	155	9394959	212	9398905	12		
9378618	70	9384540	263	9389502	155	9395147	130	9398876	49		
9378620	70	9384564	284	9389514	155	9395161	130	9398917	12		
9378632	70	9384954	76	9389526	155	9395044	258	9399002	146		
9378541	226	9385037	56	9389643	99	9395056	258	9399014	146		
9378814	67	9384875	283	9389693	84	9395214	120	9399026	149		
9379131	251	9384887	281	9389708	84	9395094	258	9399038	146		
9379208	256	9384932	283	9389679	210	9395082	258	9399040	148		
9379363	229	9385087	138	9389825	173	9395226	258	9399052	146		
9379375	229	9385001	281	9389978	261	9395238	120	9399193	74		
9379399	243	9385013	281	9390020	251	9395240	120	9399208	74		
9379404	243	9385025	281	9390022	251	9395305	61	9399210	75		
9379612	61	9385192	257	9390185	122	9395252	120	9399222	75		
9379624	61	9385477	126	9390240	213	9395317	61	9399260	176		
9379662	138	9385611	86	9390252	213	9395123	258	9399272	176		
9379674	138	9385673	122	9390616	66	9395264	120	9399349	155		
9379894	197	9385843	56	9390472	227	9395329	61	9399351	155		
9379909	197	9385879	142	9390680	122	9395331	61	9399363	155		
9379911	197	9385972	237	9390628	256	9395135	258	9399478	61		
9380398	153	9385984	237	9390692	263	9395290	171	9399507	37		
9380477	106	9385996	237	9390692	263	9395525	88	9399492	61		
9380489	106	9386005	237	9390769	259	9395496	171	9399480	242		
9380506	232	9386017	237	9391268	84	9395628	219	9399739	196		
9380570	190	9386299	58	9391361	193	9395630	219	9399741	196		
9380582	191	9386304	59	9391373	193	9396000	93	9399753	196		
9380594	191	9386225	218	9391385	194	9396012	93	9399765	196		
9380738	77	9386471	86	9391397	194	9396024	93	9399777	196		
9380740	77	9386483	86	9391361	231	9395927	196	9399789	196		
9380829	81	9386512	60	9391402	194	9395939	196	9399791	196		
9380661	263	9386495	86	9391373	231	9395941	196	9399868	123		
9380805	120	9386976	52	9391414	194	9395953	196	9399870	123		
9380673	263	9386988	52	9391385	231	9396141	108	9399806	196		
9380831	154	9387073	20	9391397	231	9396153	108	9400069	39		
9380764	225	9387085	20	9391402	231	9396373	191	9400071	88		
9380788	277	9386938	175	9391414	231	9396385	191	9400095	88		
9381134	99	9386940	175	9391476	251	9396725	257	9400186	91		
9381172	62	9386952	175	9391646	95	9397236	70	9400203	91		
9381237	184	9386914	216	9391567	217	9397157	161	9400215	87		
9381392	114	9386964	175	9391579	219	9397248	70	9400112	195		
9381524	260	9386926	216	9391581	217	9397357	51	9400136	195		
9381665	131	9387009	175	9391593	217	9397171	269	9400289	80		
9381677	160	9387138	122	9391660	199	9397286	241	9400174	208		
9381861	177	9387279	95	9391672	199	9397298	241	9400198	207		
9381873	177	9387281	95	9391751	131	9397303	242	9400514	66		
9382097	197	9387097	285	9391763	131	9397315	241	9400473	119		
9382396	121	9387334	105	9391775	131	9397327	241	9400526	66		
9382700	139	9387346	105	9391787	187	9397339	241	9400485	119		
9382750	154	9387358	105	9391799	187	9397341	241	9400538	66		
9382762	154	9387360	105	9391787	228	9397353	242	9400540	66		
9382798	245	9387542	78	9392341	184	9397602	86	9400552	66		
9382956	263	9387554	77	9392353	182	9397614	86	9400564	66		
9382968	263	9387671	276	9392559	114	9397585	236	9400576	66		
9382970	263	9387683	276	9392561	114	9397913	90	9400681	102		
9382982	261	9387695	276	9392468	259	9397860	274	9400679	210		
9383235	92	9387700	276	9392470	259	9398096	58	9401051	92		
9383247	91	9387712	276	9392482	259	9397999	158	9401099	82		
9383259	91	9387724	276	9392925	171	9398101	123	9401166	86		
9383261	91	9387750	253	9393084	56	9398175	56	9401104	152		
9383106	273	9387762	253	9393096	56	9398084	56	9401116	146		
9383215	226	9387970	95	9393101	56	9398058	56	9401178	86		
9383223	228	9388003	95	9393022	281	9398060	210	9401130	146		
9383508	138	9388015	95	9393307	281	9398216	232	9401141	148		
9383417	273	9388027	95	9393319	281	9398228	232	9401063	236		
9383429	273	9387956	241	9393321	281	9398230	232	9401075	236		
9383431	273	9388302	197	9393448	216	9398242	232	9401295	133		
9383869	61	9388340	159	9393450	215	9398254	232	9401233	211		
9383936	23	9388314	197	9393462	216	9398311	148	9401221	231		
9383948	22	9388352	159	9393474	216	9398383	149	9401283	207		
9383974	110	9388297	263	9393682	253	9398321	271	9401271	279		
9384069	61	9388704	93	9394040	191	9398333	271	9401661	82		
9383900	251	9388716	218	9394208	234	9398395	284	9401673	82		
9384095	134	9389019	36	9394519	233	9398400	284	9401685	230		
9384019	211	9388819	241	9394832	39	9398412	284	9401697	230		

9401776	197	9406099	70	9411381	172	9419723	139	9427639	61
9401879	127	9406104	71	9411733	93	9419723	139	9427641	61
9401788	225	9406116	70	9411939	154	9419735	139	9427926	135
9401776	284	9406128	71	9411941	155	9419773	197	9427938	135
9401790	277	9406013	242	9412098	37	9419785	196	9427940	135
9401805	277	9406269	93	9412103	37	9419797	196	9427952	135
9401910	226	9406180	207	9412062	93	9420045	121	9427964	135
9401922	226	9406544	55	9412074	94	9420057	121	9427940	250
9401934	226	9406465	159	9412086	94	9420772	247	9428463	34
9402029	171	9406611	82	9412036	158	9420784	247	9428358	265
9402328	284	9406623	82	9411989	224	9420796	247	9428360	265
9402586	119	9406635	82	9411991	224	9420801	247	9428499	142
9402598	119	9406659	62	9412000	224	9420813	247	9428970	127
9402562	194	9406647	82	9412335	246	9420825	247	9428982	127
9402574	194	9406738	113	9412347	246	9421061	12	9428994	127
9402615	237	9407122	58	9412359	246	9420837	247	9429003	127
9402615	237	9407043	197	9412581	189	9420849	247	9429314	227
9402627	237	9407079	197	9412816	111	9420851	267	9429326	227
9402639	237	9407134	238	9412828	111	9420863	267	9430038	104
9402641	238	9407146	238	9412880	103	9421831	60	9430272	261
9402706	181	9407158	238	9412995	157	9421843	134	9430284	261
9402718	181	9407263	134	9413004	157	9421843	230	9430296	261
9402756	182	9407160	238	9413327	251	9422067	104	9430363	199
9402902	37	9407275	134	9413418	173	9422079	104	9430375	199
9402914	37	9407287	134	9413690	60	9422081	104	9430387	199
9402926	37	9407328	178	9413523	251	9421960	244	9430399	199
9402809	191	9407330	178	9413547	246	9421972	244	9430519	192
9402770	284	9407665	49	9413717	77	9422196	157	9430765	207
9402782	284	9407677	49	9413559	246	9422201	157	9430935	38
9403059	71	9407689	49	9413561	246	9422378	215	9430777	207
9403009	237	9407885	53	9413573	246	9422445	244	9430789	207
9403164	82	9408073	61	9413779	70	9422457	244	9430868	279
9403011	237	9408205	102	9413834	37	9423035	38	9430870	279
9403114	188	9408841	112	9413779	123	9423255	138	9431111	241
9403229	84	9408853	111	9414022	36	9423449	106	9431123	241
9403176	263	9408865	111	9414034	37	9423516	173	9431135	241
9403281	158	9408877	113	9414058	252	9423578	138	9431147	241
9403279	182	9408774	233	9414060	253	9423580	138	9431276	163
9403413	97	9408956	172	9414072	252	9423592	138	9431214	242
9403396	197	9409027	129	9414084	252	9423566	197	9431288	171
9403504	95	9409039	129	9414292	139	9423762	34	9431290	171
9403516	95	9409041	129	9414278	191	9423774	34	9431305	171
9403530	95	9409053	129	9414632	133	9423712	163	9431317	171
9403396	284	9409077	138	9414876	124	9423918	34	9431360	144
9403621	179	9409182	59	9415296	217	9423920	34	9431434	85
9403619	234	9409194	74	9415727	160	9423786	215	9431460	85
9403762	177	9409144	129	9415844	207	9423798	215	9431503	94
9403774	178	9409209	74	9416020	93	9424089	138	9431680	221
9403877	281	9409170	192	9416109	49	9424120	138	9431692	221
9404194	112	9409261	133	9416422	278	9424132	137	9431707	221
9404314	24	9409273	133	9416692	77	9424546	114	9431719	227
9404194	221	9409340	129	9416733	78	9424558	114	9431836	121
9404209	228	9409326	186	9416848	77	9424560	114	9431848	121
9404429	177	9409352	171	9417086	15	9424572	113	9431850	121
9404431	177	9409314	233	9417098	15	9424649	81	9431862	121
9404649	146	9409338	270	9416965	183	9424651	82	9431757	227
9404651	146	9409481	161	9417000	157	9424883	13	9431769	227
9404663	152	9410301	70	9416977	183	9424900	160	9431800	228
9404675	150	9410387	161	9417012	157	9424912	160	9431812	228
9404780	177	9410569	27	9416989	183	9424924	160	9431824	228
9404792	178	9410727	72	9416991	183	9424936	160	9431836	250
9404807	178	9410741	72	9417024	157	9425277	103	9432115	68
9404819	178	9410753	72	9417251	134	9425382	199	9432139	68
9404857	209	9410765	72	9417244	209	9425526	139	9432141	68
9404869	209	9410648	192	9417256	209	9425552	189	9432147	68
9404871	209	9410650	192	9417268	209	9425502	259	9432153	68
9404833	257	9410777	72	9417270	209	9425875	76	9432165	68
9404883	209	9410789	73	9417892	157	9425980	253	9432206	152
9405019	76	9410791	73	9418119	189	9426207	95	9432218	210
9404845	257	9410806	74	9418377	39	9426322	43	9432828	119
9405033	187	9410882	124	9418365	242	9426283	139	9432880	280
9405033	188	9410894	125	9418494	245	9426312	127	9432892	283
9405227	161	9410909	155	9418640	196	9426350	182	9432907	283
9405423	62	9410959	105	9418652	227	9426362	182	9432919	282
9405538	93	9410997	102	9418930	68	9426386	159	9433585	250
9405540	93	9411032	106	9418975	114	9426374	184	9433597	250
9405552	93	9411020	246	9418987	114	9426324	267	9433793	82
9405564	93	9411135	224	9418999	113	9426790	110	9433834	190
9406024	70	9411185	262	9419008	113	9426805	110	9433846	190
9406049	50	9411197	261	9419230	196	9426817	110	9434369	35
9406001	102	9411226	256	9419242	197	9426881	120	9434371	36
9406037	70	9411317	176	9419254	196	9427380	50	9434383	35
9406063	50	9411238	256	9419474	153	9427392	50	9434395	36
9406051	70	9411329	176	9419541	176	9427550	70	9434412	35
9406075	70	9411367	172	9419644	183	9427562	70	9434319	268
9406087	71	9411379	172	9419668	183	9427627	61	9434321	268

9434553	62	9439735	213	9444730	199	9450430	116	9455648	207
9434565	62	9439747	213	9444742	199	9450363	187	9455650	207
9434539	127	9439761	213	9444845	199	9450442	117	9455820	82
9434448	274	9439814	233	9445590	18	9450375	204	9455715	218
9434620	210	9439826	233	9445502	209	9450387	204	9455961	137
9434632	210	9439838	233	9445514	209	9450600	73	9455973	153
9434711	274	9439840	233	9445526	209	9450612	74	9455870	285
9434773	262	9439852	233	9445538	209	9450624	73	9456123	227
9434785	263	9439864	233	9445576	204	9450636	75	9456147	227
9435038	237	9439876	233	9445588	204	9450648	72	9456173	227
9435052	274	9440045	209	9445631	210	9450703	105	9456238	227
9435064	274	9440320	35	9445916	230	9450715	103	9456367	107
9435076	274	9440332	36	9445904	258	9450727	105	9456379	107
9435246	140	9440150	230	9445887	279	9450739	105	9456240	261
9435258	140	9440148	267	9445899	279	9450741	105	9456678	77
9435753	113	9440306	258	9445980	273	9450571	285	9456757	223
9435765	114	9440772	200	9445992	273	9450753	103	9456769	223
9435674	233	9440784	200	9446001	273	9450765	104	9456771	223
9435856	52	9440796	200	9446013	273	9450777	105	9456783	223
9435686	233	9440801	200	9446532	112	9451094	24	9457012	34
9435868	52	9440813	200	9446570	137	9450911	258	9456977	129
9435894	211	9440825	204	9446594	129	9450923	258	9456953	174
9435909	211	9440837	204	9446623	280	9451484	129	9457000	128
9436068	219	9441001	150	9447017	62	9451707	243	9456965	174
9436329	52	9441154	231	9446881	217	9451905	72	9456927	244
9436331	52	9441166	231	9447536	55	9451719	268	9456989	267
9436173	230	9441180	231	9447548	54	9451721	267	9456991	266
9436185	230	9441207	211	9447550	55	9451927	72	9457220	249
9436355	82	9441192	231	9447562	55	9451939	72	9457232	249
9436367	82	9441295	137	9447732	170	9451965	72	9457593	284
9436379	82	9441300	137	9447847	89	9452490	94	9457608	284
9436460	124	9441312	138	9447861	89	9452505	94	9457622	274
9436472	114	9441324	138	9447873	79	9452517	94	9457634	274
9436484	114	9441398	138	9447885	89	9452634	41	9457646	274
9436422	233	9441403	138	9447897	79	9452646	41	9457658	274
9436458	233	9441415	138	9447902	89	9452658	41	9457660	274
9436678	191	9441427	138	9447914	79	9452660	41	9457737	285
9436847	215	9441506	217	9448011	55	9452593	215	9458030	223
9437048	53	9441520	218	9448023	188	9452610	216	9458078	223
9437050	53	9441556	218	9448035	188	9452622	216	9458080	223
9437062	53	9441568	218	9448047	189	9452854	188	9458092	223
9437115	54	9441570	218	9448059	189	9453212	38	9458377	112
9437127	54	9441582	217	9448061	268	9453224	38	9458389	111
9437139	54	9441594	217	9448073	269	9453236	38	9458590	35
9437141	54	9441609	218	9448140	220	9453248	38	9458494	141
9437189	54	9441855	190	9448138	224	9453250	38	9458688	36
9437191	54	9441984	216	9448308	114	9453262	38	9458614	210
9437270	129	9442172	86	9448346	114	9453107	218	9458822	155
9437282	129	9442249	133	9448358	113	9453298	146	9458834	155
9437531	66	9442122	267	9448360	113	9453365	236	9458858	155
9437555	66	9442378	153	9448372	114	9453559	73	9458999	129
9437543	66	9442536	111	9448384	113	9453781	85	9459008	176
9437567	66	9442641	38	9448310	190	9453793	85	9459010	176
9437866	26	9442495	259	9448322	191	9453963	95	9459022	176
9437907	109	9442861	130	9448334	190	9453975	95	9459034	176
9437919	109	9442744	261	9448712	190	9453987	95	9459137	138
9437921	108	9442885	129	9448724	190	9453999	95	9459149	138
9437933	109	9442756	263	9448748	237	9454010	281	9459151	137
9437945	109	9443011	83	9448750	237	9454230	219	9459278	258
9438066	21	9443023	83	9448762	237	9454242	219	9459412	140
9438078	21	9443035	83	9448774	237	9454395	72	9459527	122
9438016	106	9443047	83	9448786	237	9454400	73	9459632	156
9438030	94	9443059	83	9448798	237	9454412	74	9460459	49
9438028	106	9443073	129	9448803	237	9454424	74	9460461	49
9438042	95	9443009	259	9448815	237	9454436	74	9460356	201
9438054	95	9443425	190	9448827	236	9454448	72	9460318	280
9438523	84	9443401	241	9449106	236	9454450	74	9460899	250
9438535	84	9443413	242	9449118	236	9454278	284	9460887	271
9438482	250	9443463	237	9449120	236	9454515	111	9461051	117
9438494	250	9443475	237	9449780	50	9454527	112	9461087	284
9438509	250	9443669	114	9449792	50	9454486	184	9461099	284
9438511	250	9443580	285	9449821	54	9454498	184	9461130	259
9438759	213	9443683	241	9449819	72	9454711	66	9461142	260
9439060	36	9443865	157	9449845	54	9454723	66	9461374	145
9439072	35	9444027	112	9449869	54	9454711	123	9461398	152
9438858	257	9444039	111	9450296	188	9454759	239	9461415	146
9438860	257	9444261	160	9450301	188	9454761	239	9461465	111
9439113	55	9444285	178	9450313	186	9455040	34	9461386	201
9439058	184	9444417	86	9450325	188	9455052	68	9461477	112
9439199	263	9444455	49	9450399	118	9455296	274	9461439	152
9439204	263	9444467	49	9450404	118	9455545	36	9461398	201
9439539	102	9444479	49	9450337	187	9455557	36	9461489	112
9439541	102	9444649	99	9450416	118	9455569	35	9461491	111
9439498	200	9444716	199	9450349	187	9455703	82	9461403	201
9439709	213	9444819	104	9450351	186	9455686	155	9461415	201
9439711	213	9444728	199	9450428	117			9461505	112

ID	Value	ID	Value	ID	Value	ID	Value	ID	Value
9461427	201	9465992	258	9472139	237	9479369	58	9486116	237
9461441	201	9466001	258	9472141	237	9479852	12	9487172	210
9461659	139	9466013	258	9472153	237	9479864	12	9487184	210
9461661	139	9466025	258	9472165	237	9479838	261	9487653	41
9461673	139	9466051	269	9472177	237	9479840	261	9488035	85
9461685	139	9466130	258	9472189	237	9479929	281	9488047	85
9461697	139	9466142	258	9472529	133	9480150	176	9487873	268
9461794	49	9466245	237	9473028	82	9480162	176	9488059	85
9461635	213	9466295	269	9473224	70	9480174	201	9488061	85
9461764	105	9466300	269	9473236	70	9480186	201	9488061	85
9461776	105	9466312	269	9473274	41	9480198	201	9487885	268
9461831	127	9466324	269	9473248	70	9480203	201	9488097	216
9461843	127	9466336	269	9473250	70	9480215	201	9488102	216
9461855	127	9466348	269	9473315	41	9480227	201	9488566	219
9461790	209	9466350	269	9473327	41	9480526	59	9488578	219
9461867	178	9466362	269	9473341	41	9480538	59	9488580	219
9461879	178	9466374	269	9473731	83	9480837	242	9488592	219
9461881	179	9466867	66	9473626	284	9481049	49	9488803	134
9461893	179	9466996	113	9473913	49	9481051	49	9488918	265
9462017	180	9467005	113	9473925	49	9481075	49	9489065	265
9462029	179	9467017	114	9473937	49	9481532	92	9489077	265
9462031	180	9466960	187	9473834	260	9481520	136	9489089	265
9462043	178	9466972	187	9474137	76	9482299	64	9489091	265
9462366	120	9466984	186	9474199	76	9482304	64	9489845	76
9462512	138	9467043	188	9474228	76	9482249	130	9490040	10
9462811	34	9467055	187	9474230	76	9482524	130	9490052	10
9462691	285	9467251	66	9474242	76	9482550	136	9489974	144
9462706	285	9467263	66	9474254	76	9482562	136	9489986	143
9462718	285	9467265	66	9474266	76	9482653	49	9490105	152
9462720	285	9467287	66	9474278	76	9482665	49	9490442	134
9462732	285	9467299	66	9474280	76	9482574	178	9490466	134
9463011	281	9467304	66	9474383	267	9482586	178	9490648	41
9463023	280	9467316	66	9474618	41	9482847	125	9490454	267
9463035	281	9467407	149	9474620	41	9482859	125	9490624	103
9463047	280	9467419	149	9474395	267	9482861	125	9490636	103
9463059	280	9467421	150	9474632	41	9482873	125	9490612	130
9463085	281	9467392	180	9474644	41	9483126	15	9490703	41
9463205	180	9467433	146	9474785	104	9483188	43	9490662	103
9463267	129	9467445	149	9475258	201	9483190	43	9490686	104
9463281	129	9467457	149	9475301	267	9483205	43	9490698	104
9463293	129	9467548	125	9475600	64	9483217	43	9490818	41
9463308	129	9467550	125	9475674	83	9483229	43	9490832	105
9463310	129	9467562	125	9475686	83	9483231	43	9490727	247
9463322	129	9467574	125	9475698	83	9483243	43	9490882	112
9463334	129	9467586	125	9475624	160	9483255	43	9490894	111
9463346	129	9467598	125	9475703	83	9483267	43	9490909	123
9463633	120	9467603	125	9475636	160	9483279	43	9490911	123
9463645	120	9467627	124	9475648	160	9483451	50	9490791	247
9463657	120	9468293	182	9475650	160	9483516	133	9490806	247
9463671	120	9468308	182	9475525	41	9483712	26	9490844	247
9464214	86	9469259	105	9476537	41	9484003	65	9490856	247
9464247	86	9469560	152	9476721	124	9484261	65	9490870	247
9464417	78	9469560	201	9476630	275	9484273	65	9491238	39
9464388	129	9469572	200	9476642	274	9484285	65	9491252	39
9464376	190	9469778	169	9476733	184	9484297	65	9491874	136
9464546	42	9469780	169	9476757	161	9484302	65	9491886	136
9464560	68	9469869	155	9476745	182	9484340	65	9491898	136
9464522	112	9469871	155	9476812	139	9484388	65	9492000	266
9464455	181	9469883	221	9476836	137	9484493	62	9492050	266
9464572	124	9469895	221	9476848	137	9484429	146	9492062	266
9464584	124	9469900	221	9476977	101	9484443	145	9492127	266
9464596	124	9469912	221	9477294	88	9484467	152	9492139	266
9464663	125	9470088	281	9477309	90	9484481	146	9492335	105
9464669	120	9470258	211	9477311	90	9484431	201	9492696	237
9464675	125	9470260	210	9477335	88	9484455	201	9492701	237
9464761	213	9470272	211	9477347	88	9484479	201	9492713	237
9465095	187	9470284	211	9477359	88	9484560	199	9492907	76
9465241	45	9470765	112	9477438	12	9484572	199	9493016	59
9465253	45	9470820	136	9477385	91	9484704	197	9493028	59
9465265	46	9470923	35	9477294	224	9484716	226	9493054	113
9465277	45	9470961	119	9477335	224	9484728	227	9493066	111
9465306	46	9470973	119	9477347	224	9484730	226	9493200	280
9465318	42	9470882	224	9477359	224	9484742	226	9493212	283
9465289	146	9470894	224	9477593	133	9484924	83	9493224	283
9465291	151	9471018	119	9477610	236	9484807	205	9493236	283
9465370	109	9471032	119	9477787	236	9484936	83	9493365	282
9465394	85	9470985	231	9477878	208	9484948	83	9493652	95
9465382	109	9470997	232	9477880	209	9484998	285	9493664	95
9465708	59	9471123	119	9477892	209	9485007	285	9493676	95
9465710	60	9471202	280	9477830	272	9485629	265	9493688	95
9465608	215	9471214	280	9477921	182	9485631	264	9493690	95
9465796	39	9471408	200	9477919	272	9485887	38	9493755	280
9465801	60	9472086	107	9478494	223	9485899	38	9493975	263
9465966	258	9472098	106	9478638	211	9485899	38	9494060	263
9465978	259	9472103	106	9479163	58	9485904	38	9494280	237
9465980	258	9472127	237	9479046	188	9485930	38	9494486	70

No.	Pg	No.	Pg	No.	Pg	No.	Pg	No.	Pg
9494541	213	9505065	271	9516739	139	9525479	167	9535151	88
9494577	212	9505089	271	9516741	140	9525481	167	9535175	89
9494589	212	9505833	43	9516753	141	9525493	163	9535199	88
9494591	212	9505900	186	9516765	140	9525857	264	9535216	88
9494620	213	9506069	56	9516777	219	9525869	263	9535149	234
9494632	213	9505936	198	9516789	219	9525871	264	9535163	234
9494905	281	9505986	281	9516959	61	9525883	263	9535187	234
9495038	180	9505998	281	9517422	227	9525895	264	9535204	234
9495040	179	9506459	24	9517434	227	9525900	264	9535307	213
9495402	207	9506382	174	9517903	249	9525912	263	9535864	69
9495414	207	9506394	174	9517915	250	9525924	263	9535876	69
9495765	110	9506710	129	9517927	249	9525936	264	9536155	174
9495777	110	9506734	128	9517939	250	9526564	219	9536363	177
9496135	108	9506746	128	9518892	157	9526875	164	9536375	178
9496147	138	9506758	128	9518907	157	9526887	164	9536818	182
9496329	124	9507519	43	9519066	43	9526899	164	9536820	191
9496331	124	9507520	43	9519078	43	9526904	164	9536973	111
9496252	216	9507532	43	9519107	129	9526916	164	9536959	130
9496264	216	9507544	44	9519195	42	9526930	164	9536961	130
9496305	241	9507788	43	9519119	129	9526928	167	9536909	184
9496317	241	9507790	44	9519092	161	9526942	164	9536985	111
9496434	124	9507881	43	9519121	161	9526954	172	9537264	52
9496678	63	9507893	43	9519286	41	9526966	172	9537276	52
9496680	63	9507908	43	9519298	41	9526978	164	9537379	279
9497165	138	9508304	52	9519303	41	9526978	167	9537381	279
9497177	137	9508316	52	9519315	41	9527025	167	9537551	112
9497323	93	9508380	52	9519339	41	9527037	167	9537563	111
9497335	93	9508392	76	9519341	41	9527049	167	9537628	236
9497414	38	9509126	230	9519133	272	9527051	167	9537628	236
9497880	108	9509126	236	9519145	272	9527063	167	9537630	236
9497830	247	9509138	236	9519717	112	9527180	137	9537745	171
9498248	177	9509401	186	9519767	77	9527192	137	9537757	171
9498250	177	9509607	54	9519573	283	9527910	137	9537769	171
9498262	177	9509621	54	9519779	77	9527922	137	9537848	174
9498274	177	9509633	54	9520376	103	9528031	61	9537898	236
9498341	229	9509645	54	9520998	42	9528043	61	9537903	236
9498353	229	9509671	54	9520936	263	9527996	138	9537915	236
9498365	229	9509683	53	9521095	229	9528005	138	9538749	129
9498377	229	9509700	54	9521435	206	9528017	138	9538892	119
9498389	229	9509774	54	9521447	206	9528029	138	9538880	173
9498444	230	9509970	119	9521540	229	9528196	76	9538945	280
9498456	230	9510187	139	9521552	229	9528201	76	9539183	160
9498468	229	9510199	139	9521564	229	9528861	138	9539169	181
9498470	229	9510474	283	9521758	216	9529293	61	9539171	181
9498482	229	9510486	283	9521813	216	9529280	127	9539212	160
9498597	184	9511167	252	9521825	216	9529475	61	9539224	158
9498602	182	9511387	243	9521837	216	9529487	61	9539236	158
9498723	95	9511521	243	9521849	216	9529499	61	9539365	173
9498717	268	9511533	244	9521851	216	9529592	126	9539389	173
9498729	268	9511820	104	9521863	216	9529645	155	9539482	180
9498810	197	9511832	105	9521875	215	9529956	171	9539494	236
9498937	76	9512747	82	9522128	61	9529968	171	9539509	236
9498822	197	9512939	226	9521980	283	9530228	211	9539664	110
9498834	197	9513402	161	9522087	200	9530890	78	9539688	110
9498846	197	9513438	139	9522099	201	9530905	77	9539729	112
9498896	279	9513440	139	9522178	215	9531466	178	9539731	111
9498901	279	9513749	112	9522180	215	9531478	178	9539561	284
9499450	108	9513751	162	9522324	244	9531507	178	9539573	284
9499486	155	9514030	112	9522635	200	9531454	236	9539585	284
9499876	133	9514171	70	9522647	200	9531519	178	9539597	284
9499888	133	9514987	49	9522881	124	9531636	127	9540821	191
9500584	274	9514999	49	9522893	124	9531648	127	9540807	231
9501239	88	9515008	49	9523005	67	9531739	181	9540819	231
9501332	118	9515204	182	9523017	67	9531741	181	9540869	236
9501344	116	9515216	182	9523029	67	9531753	182	9540871	236
9501356	117	9515474	159	9523031	67	9531882	55	9541380	77
9501368	118	9515383	271	9522972	265	9531715	270	9541318	267
9501370	117	9515395	270	9524205	143	9531909	234	9541813	139
9501772	267	9515400	271	9524762	276	9532276	111	9541825	139
9502506	21	9515412	270	9524774	276	9532288	111	9542130	155
9502518	21	9515682	42	9525285	171	9532197	281	9542166	155
9502568	159	9515723	70	9525297	171	9532513	265	9542178	155
9502867	88	9515747	91	9525302	171	9532525	265	9542283	158
9502908	88	9515759	91	9525314	171	9532537	265	9542520	71
9502910	88	9516105	77	9525326	171	9532549	265	9542532	71
9502946	88	9516117	77	9525338	171	9532551	265	9542544	71
9502958	88	9516129	103	9525340	171	9532757	62	9542817	254
9502972	88	9516404	65	9525352	171	9532771	180	9542829	254
9503275	41	9516416	65	9525364	167	9532783	179	9542831	254
9503287	41	9516428	65	9525376	167	9534779	135	9543251	188
9504592	236	9516430	65	9525388	167	9534781	135	9543603	123
9504607	236	9516442	65	9525390	171	9534793	135	9543548	258
9505027	270	9516442	65	9525405	171	9534808	135	9543550	258
9505039	271	9516454	65	9525455	167	9535058	161	9544138	138
9505041	270	9516466	65	9525467	167	9535137	88	9544140	138
9505053	271	9516478	65	9525479	163	9535096	140	9544152	136

9544164	137	9567441	134	9583706	254	9595498	98	9612313	189
9544401	284	9567453	134	9584059	160	9595503	98	9612325	189
9544736	189	9567661	156	9584499	61	9595515	98	9612870	79
9544748	188	9567659	161	9584504	60	9595591	213	9612882	79
9544750	188	9567697	262	9584624	15	9595606	213	9612997	116
9544762	189	9567702	262	9584712	15	9595888	100	9613006	116
9544918	158	9568031	190	9585106	77	9595890	101	9613018	117
9544920	158	9568043	190	9585285	20	9595905	101	9613020	117
9546459	269	9568562	261	9585651	81	9595917	101	9613666	110
9546461	269	9568574	261	9585663	81	9595967	254	9613678	112
9546473	269	9568809	184	9585895	252	9596026	205	9613836	225
9546485	269	9569932	71	9587166	205	9596038	205	9613848	225
9546497	269	9569944	71	9587192	266	9597111	112	9613850	225
9546904	215	9569970	79	9587453	106	9597185	58	9613862	225
9547506	190	9569841	211	9588079	130	9597197	58	9613874	225
9549281	142	9569994	231	9588081	130	9597240	157	9614476	254
9550709	232	9570008	231	9588003	130	9597252	157	9614842	119
9550682	265	9570838	85	9588299	64	9597472	180	9614892	76
9550694	265	9570840	85	9588146	283	9597484	179	9614854	119
9551674	41	9570852	85	9588158	283	9597795	110	9614921	69
9551686	41	9571375	52	9588419	76	9597800	113	9615042	281
9551698	41	9571387	52	9588392	171	9597812	113	9615195	131
9551703	41	9571399	52	9588445	189	9597977	76	9616230	28
9551923	142	9571296	230	9588469	189	9597989	76	9616302	111
9551935	248	9571301	230	9588615	63	9597991	76	9616802	212
9551947	248	9571313	230	9588603	95	9598012	158	9618305	80
9551959	249	9571325	230	9588768	210	9598256	157	9618317	80
9551961	249	9571345	247	9589085	39	9598268	157	9618783	86
9551973	249	9571492	247	9589097	39	9598995	189	9618812	112
9552379	132	9571507	247	9589140	95	9599004	188	9618824	112
9552410	129	9571519	247	9589164	72	9599016	188	9619452	234
9552886	126	9571521	247	9589152	95	9599779	71	9619464	234
9552898	127	9571533	247	9589970	123	9599901	138	9619426	280
9553103	184	9572329	265	9590307	283	9599913	138	9619555	153
9553115	184	9572331	265	9590319	284	9600528	103	9619476	234
9553218	268	9572343	265	9590589	123	9601132	10	9619438	280
9554200	160	9573757	129	9590591	123	9601314	178	9619440	280
9555307	139	9573763	130	9590606	123	9602174	138	9619892	138
9555292	190	9573660	284	9590826	78	9602186	138	9619921	165
9555723	9	9573672	284	9590929	138	9603362	129	9619933	165
9557123	103	9573696	284	9591052	159	9603386	130	9619945	163
9557111	247	9573701	284	9591739	123	9603398	130	9619945	164
9558220	130	9574042	50	9592214	252	9603506	90	9619957	164
9558799	210	9574066	129	9592422	210	9603520	90	9619969	165
9559690	76	9574078	129	9592434	210	9603562	90	9619971	165
9559705	76	9574107	130	9592563	269	9603908	213	9619983	165
9560352	131	9574054	272	9592575	269	9603910	213	9619995	165
9560364	131	9574080	272	9592680	198	9604093	98	9620295	186
9560376	131	9574092	272	9592692	198	9604110	98	9620607	267
9561253	161	9574612	160	9593402	95	9604134	98	9620619	267
9561265	158	9574729	89	9593696	213	9604732	138	9620683	272
9561277	159	9575448	265	9593854	108	9604768	111	9620944	175
9561289	159	9575450	265	9593866	108	9604744	138	9620956	175
9561368	190	9575462	265	9593878	108	9604938	130	9620968	175
9561370	190	9575474	265	9593880	108	9604938	130	9620970	175
9561382	190	9575668	76	9593892	108	9604940	184	9622588	208
9561485	171	9576296	112	9593907	108	9605023	138	9622590	209
9561497	171	9576727	124	9593919	265	9605231	234	9622605	209
9562673	161	9576739	124	9594121	90	9605243	234	9622628	209
9562685	161	9576741	124	9593957	265	9605255	234	9622631	208
9562697	161	9576753	234	9594224	216	9605724	123	9622916	197
9563237	211	9576765	235	9594224	216	9605853	95	9623661	206
9564097	137	9576789	234	9594236	215	9605865	95	9623673	206
9564138	177	9577056	244	9594248	215	9605786	271	9623829	132
9564384	40	9577068	244	9594250	216	9605891	212	9623867	263
9565140	177	9577070	244	9594470	54	9606479	158	9623879	261
9565065	265	9577082	244	9594494	54	9606546	138	9624029	192
9565338	115	9577094	244	9594822	157	9606821	101	9624328	42
9565546	130	9577109	244	9594834	157	9606833	101	9624237	158
9565558	130	9577111	244	9594846	157	9606912	27	9625528	123
9565560	130	9577123	244	9594858	157	9606924	27	9625530	123
9565948	263	9577410	106	9595008	135	9607875	161	9625542	123
9565950	262	9577422	106	9595010	135	9608697	42	9625554	123
9566382	130	9577898	188	9594872	283	9608702	42	9625970	145
9566605	127	9579030	252	9594884	283	9609732	246	9625956	247
9566564	189	9579042	252	9594896	283	9609744	247	9625968	247
9566514	265	9579864	85	9594901	284	9610391	161	9626314	111
9566526	265	9581203	64	9595149	81	9610406	161	9626522	175
9566538	265	9581239	34	9595321	20	9610418	159	9626534	175
9566629	182	9581241	34	9595254	188	9610420	161	9626572	230
9567025	76	9581681	34	9595436	98	9610781	243	9626584	230
9567063	55	9581708	36	9595448	98	9610793	243	9626558	280
9567403	134	9582506	215	9595450	98	9610808	243	9627978	208
9567415	134	9582518	216	9595462	98	9610810	245	9627980	208
9567427	134	9583134	263	9595474	98	9612143	71	9629031	98
9567439	134	9583691	254	9595486	98	9612284	189	9629043	98

Ships by name

Name	Page
Andre Rickmers	220
Andreas	220
Andromeda	261
Andromeda Leader	181
Andromeda Spirit	186
Andromeda Voyager	64
Andromeda	153
Anemona	158
Angeles	196
Angelica Schulte	232
Angistri	93
Anglia	37
Angol	196
Angra Dos Reis	266
Anguila	87
Anhui	196
Aniara	270
Anichkov Bridge	243
Anita L.	229
Anja Kirk	139
Anke	87
Anking	96
ANL Benalla	135
ANL Binburra	144
ANL Wangaratta	220
ANL Warrain	220
ANL Warringa	220
ANL Windarra	220
ANL Wyong	220
Anna Maersk	162
Anna Oldendorff	204
Anna Rickmers	220
Anna Schulte	232
Annaba	87
Annabella	62
Annabelle Schulte	235
Anne Mette Bulker	136
Anneleen Knutsen	133
Anni Selmer	274
Annina Schulte	235
Annoula	34
Antarctic	261
Antarctica	77
Antares J	128
Antares Leader	181
Antares Star	226
Antares Voyager	64
Anthea	196
Antikeros	93
Antje Wulff	279
Antonia Schulte	236
Antonia	49
Antonio	196
Antonis Angelicoussis	34
Antonis I. Angelicoussis	64
Antonis	94
Antwerp Max	94
Antwerpen	99
Antwerpen Express	116
Anvil Point	101
Apatura	54
Aphrodite Leader	181
APL Accolade	178
APL Accolade	178
APL Achiever	178
APL Advance	178
APL Advisor	178
APL Agate	178
APL Agile	178
APL Almandine	178
APL Amazonite	178
APL Ambassador	178
APL Ambition	178
APL Amman	232
APL Arabia	186
APL Ascent	178
APL Aspire	178
APL Atlanta	115
APL Austria	178
APL Bahrain	196
APL Bangkok	232
APL Barcelona	178
APL Belgium	178
APL Brisbane	196
APL Cairo	178
APL Canada	42
APL Chicago	196
APL China	178
APL Chongxing	178
APL Colorado	232
APL Coral	178
APL Cyprine	178
APL Dalian	178
APL Dallas	228
APL Denver	115
APL Doha	196
APL Dublin	178
APL Egypt	186
APL England	178
APL Florida	178
APL Garnet	178
APL Garnet	86
APL Germany	178
APL Guangzhou	196
APL Gwangyang	178
APL Holland	178
APL Hong Kong	178
APL Illinois	232
APL India	42
APL Indonesia	227
APL Iolite	178
APL Ireland	178
APL Iris	178
APL Jade	179
APL Japan	179
APL Jeddah	179
APL Kennedy	179
APL Korea	179
APL Le Havre	179
APL London	280
APL Los Angeles	115
APL Malaysia	186
APL Managua	53
APL Melbourne	228
APL Minneapolis	228
APL Minnesota	179
APL New Jersey	179
APL New York	179
APL Ningbo	179
APL Norway	179
APL Oakland	115
APL Oregon	179
APL Pearl	179
APL Peru	115
APL Philippines	179
APL Pusan	179
APL Qingdao	179
APL Riyadh	196
APL Salalah	179
APL Sardonyx	86
APL Scotland	180
APL Seattle	196
APL Seoul	196
APL Shanghai	228
APL Sharjah	232
APL Shenzhen	236
APL Singapore	180
APL Sokhna	236
APL Southampton	180
APL Spain	180
APL Spinel	86
APL Sri Lanka	227
APL Sydney	232
APL Temasek	180
APL Tennessee	232
APL Texas	232
APL Thailand	180
APL Tourmaline	180
APL Toyko	280
APL Turkey	180
APL Turquoise	180
APL Vancouver	180
APL Washington	232
APL Yangshan	180
APL Zeebrugge	180
Apollo	54
Apollo Bulker	137
Apollon	261
Apollon Leader	181
Apolytares	153
Apulia	90
Aquamarine Ace	158
Aquarius Ace	158
Aquarius Leader	181
Aquarius Voyager	64
Aquitania	38
Arabian Breeze	270
Arabian Express	267
Arabiyah	135
Aracari Arrow	125
Aracena Carrier	238
Arafura Sea	283
Aragonborg	269
Aral Sea	283
Arcadia Highway	129
Arcadia	13
Archangel	261
Archway	283
Arctic	261
Arctic Bay	189
Arctic Blizzard	189
Arctic Breeze	189
Arctic Bridge	189
Arctic ID	42
Arctic Lady	122
Arctic Princess	122
Arctic Spirit	255
Arctic	100
Arcturus Voyager	64
Ardennes Venture	77
Ardmore Seamaster	189
Arelia	88
Ariadne	261
Ariana	88
Arica Bridge	129
Aries Star	226
Aries Voyager	64
Aries	39
Arion	261
Arion	17
Aris	261
Aristides N.P.	96
Arkat	241
Armia Krajowa	215
Armia Ludowa	215
Arminia	92
Arneborg	269
Arnold Maersk	162
Arsos	258
Artania	21
Artemis	261
Artemis Glory	214
Artemis Leader	181
Arthur Maersk	162
Artois	77
Arubaborg	269
Arundel Castle	176
Arut Rickmers	220
Arwa Spirit	258
AS Alicantia	38
AS Andalusia	38
AS Asturia	38
AS Carelia	38
AS Caria	38
AS Carinthia	38
AS Castor	39
AS Catalania	38
AS Cypria	38
AS Elbia	38
AS Elenia	38
AS Elysia	38
AS Jutlandia	38
AS Mars	39
AS Oceania	38
AS Octavia	38
AS Olivia	38
AS Omaria	38
AS Ophelia	38
AS Orelia	38
AS Pegasus	40
AS Poseidon	40
AS Savonia	38
AS Saxonia	38
AS Scandia	38
AS Scotia	38
AS Valdivia	38
AS Valentia	38
AS Valeria	38
AS Varesia	38
AS Venetia	38
AS Venus	40
AS Victoria	38
AS Vincentia	38
AS Virginia	38
Asahi Bulker	137
Asahi Princess	261
Ashkini Spirit	255
Ashley Sea	115
Ashna	214
Asia Star	284
Asiaborg	269
Asian Beauty	280
Asian Breeze	270
Asian Captain	272
Asian Chorus	123
Asian Dynasty	267
Asian Emperor	124
Asian Empire	272
Asian Glory	280
Asian Grace	123
Asian Jade	122
Asian King	124
Asian Legend	123
Asian Majesty	272
Asian Parade	272
Asian Progress II	161
Asian Progress III	161
Asian Progress IV	161
Asian Spirit	158
Asian Spirit	255
Asian Sun	123
Asian Trust	272
Asian Venture	123
Asian Vision	272
Asiatic	139
Asir	264
Assos Striker	94
Asta Rickmers	220
Asteria Leader	181
Astor	27
Astoria Bridge	129
Astra	229
Astral Ace	158
Astrea	62
Astro Antares	36
Astro Arcturus	36
Astro Challenge	36
Astro Chloe	36
Astro Chorus	36
Astro Perseus	36
Astro Phoenix	36
Astro Polaris	36
Astro Saturn	36
Astro Sculptor	36
Astro Sirius	36
Asuka II	21
Atacama	143
Atalandi	153
Atalanta	220
Atalanta	196
Athena	17
Athena	254
Athens Bridge	129
Athens Highway	129
Athens Star	62
Athens Trader	141
Athinea	62
Atlanta Express	116
Atlantic Canyon	110
Atlantic Cartier	109
Atlantic Companion	109
Atlantic Compass	109
Atlantic Concert	109
Atlantic Conveyor	110
Atlantic Erica	184
Atlantic Frontier	68
Atlantic Gemini	68
Atlantic Grace	68
Atlantic Hawk	141
Atlantic Hero	141
Atlantic Highway	129
Atlantic Hope	239
Atlantic Hope	68
Atlantic Horizon	141
Atlantic Klipper	239
Atlantic Latvia	189
Atlantic Levantia	189
Atlantic Liguria	189
Atlantic Livadia	189
Atlantic Lobelia	189
Atlantic Lombardia	189
Atlantic Lutetia	189
Atlantic Mermaid	240
Atlantic Mirage	122
Atlantic Muse	122
Atlantic Reefer	239
Atlantic Sirius	68
Atlantic Star	24
Atlantic Star	68
Atlantic Symphony	68
Atlanticborg	269
Atlas Highway	129
Atlas Leader	181
Auguste Schulte	232
Auk Arrow	126
Aurelia	54
Auriga J	128
Auriga Leader	181
Aurora Bulker	137
Aurora	13
Aurora	215
Aurora	54
Austanger	277
Austin Angol	220
Australia Express	205
Australiaborg	269
Australian Spirit	256
Australis	62
Austria	92
Austria	90
Authentic	139
Autumn E	205
Autumn Wave	184
Autumn Wind	184
Ava D.	87
Avalon	54
Avelona Star	249
Avila Star	249
Avonborg	269
Avra	55
Axel Maersk	162
Axel Spirit	256
Axel	189
Axios	141
Azalea Ace	158
Azamara Journey	24
Azamara Quest	24
Azoresborg	269
Azov Sea	243
Azul Cielo	158
Azul Fortuna	158
Azumasan	161
Azura	13
Azure Bulker	137
Baco-Liner 1	40
Baco-Liner 2	40
Bahama Spirit	232
Bahamas Spirit	256
Bahamian Express	267
Bahia Blanca	199
Bahia Castillo	199
Bahia Grande	199
Bahia Laura	199
Bahia Negra	199
Bahia	199
Bahra	135
Bahri Abha	175
Bahri Hofuf	175
Bahri Jazan	175
Bahri Jeddah	175
Bahri Tobuk	175
Bahri Yanbu	175
Bai Chay Bridge	129
Bakkedal	133
Balao	133
Balchen	133
Balder	133
Baldock	133
Baleares	133
Balgarka	177

Name	Page
Bali Sea	124
Balkan	46
Ballerita	133
Balmoral	21
Balsa	133
Balthasar Schulte	236
Baltic Adonia I	231
Baltic Advance	189
Baltic Ambition	124
Baltic Bear	105
Baltic Breeze	270
Baltic Breeze	105
Baltic Captain I	231
Baltic Champion	190
Baltic Chief I	231
Baltic Commander I	189
Baltic Commodore	190
Baltic Cougar	105
Baltic Cove	105
Baltic Faith	124
Baltic Favour	190
Baltic Force	124
Baltic Freedom	190
Baltic Frost	190
Baltic Gas	232
Baltic Highway	129
Baltic Hollyhock	225
Baltic ID	42
Baltic Jaguar	105
Baltic Klipper	239
Baltic Leopard	105
Baltic Mariner	190
Baltic Mariner	226
Baltic Marshall	124
Baltic Merchant	124
Baltic Mercury	226
Baltic Monarch	190
Baltic Moon	226
Baltic Navigator	226
Baltic Night	226
Baltic Novator	226
Baltic Novel	226
Baltic Panther	105
Baltic Pride	226
Baltic Prime	226
Baltic Sapphire	190
Baltic Sea I	231
Baltic Sky I	190
Baltic Sky	226
Baltic Soul	190
Baltic Star	177
Baltic Star	226
Baltic Strait	219
Baltic Strait	226
Baltic Stream	226
Baltic Sun II	190
Baltic Sun	226
Baltic Swift	190
Baltic Wave	190
Baltic Wind	190
Baltic Wind	105
Baltic Wolf	105
Baltic	205
Baltimore Bridge	129
Balto	133
Baltrum Trader	53
Banasol	133
Banastar	133
Banda Sea	124
Bandaisan	161
Bangkok Express	186
Bangkok Highway	129
Bangor	133
Baniyas	133
Bantry	133
Baogang Spirit	129
Barbet Arrow	126
Barcelona Express	116
Barcelona Knutsen	133
Barents Sea	243
Barents Sea	283
Barents Strait	219
Bargara	60
Barkald	133
Barmbek	110
Barrington Island	93
Barry	133
Baru	133
Basker Spirit	257
Basle Express	116
Bastogne	99
Basuto	252
Bataliony Chlopskie	215
Battersea Park	280
Bavaria	92
Bavaria	280
Bay Bridge	129
Bay Phoenix	240
Bay Ranger	94
BBC Amazon	52
BBC Congo	52
BBC Danube	52
BBC Elbe	52
BBC Ems	52
BBC Ganges	52
BBC Hudson	52
BBC Mississippi	52
BBC Neptune	52
BBC Nile	52
BBC Oder	52
BBC Ostfriesland	52
BBC Parana	52
BBC Pluto	52
BBC Rheiderland	52
BBC Seattle	52
BBC Seine	52
BBC Volga	52
BBC Weser	52
Beachy Head	101
Bear Mountain Bridge	129
Beate Oldendorff	204
Bebatik	241
Beihai Park	280
Beijing 2008	261
Beijing Express	116
Bel East	267
Belaia	139
Belanak	241
Belasitza	177
Belgian Express	267
Belgian Reefer	184
Belgica	90
Bella	217
Bella Schulte	236
Bellavia	85
Belmar	61
Belnor	41
Belocean	41
Belsize Park	280
Belstar	41
Beltnes	152
Benguela Stream	239
Bentonville	162
Bergamot Ace	158
Berganger	276
Berge Aconcagua	54
Berge Aoraki	54
Berge Arctic	54
Berge Arzew	56
Berge Atlantic	55
Berge Atlas	55
Berge Blanc	55
Berge Bonde	55
Berge Bureya	55
Berge Denali	55
Berge Elbrus	55
Berge Enterprise	55
Berge Everest	55
Berge Fjord	55
Berge Fuji	55
Berge Jaya	55
Berge Kibo	55
Berge Lhotse	55
Berge Lyngor	55
Berge Nantong	56
Berge Neblina	55
Berge Ningbo	56
Berge Odel	55
Berge Phoenix	55
Berge Prosperity	55
Berge Stahl	55
Berge Summit	57
Berge Townsend	55
Berge Vik	55
Berge Vinson	55
Berge Yotei	55
Bergen Max	94
Bering ID	42
Bering Sea	243
Bering Sea	283
Berlian Ekuator	99
Berlin Bridge	237
Berlin Express	116
Berlin Trader	53
Bermuda Spirit	256
Bernhard Oldendorff	205
Bess	270
Betis	236
Betty Knutsen	133
BG Freight Iberia	144
Bianco Bulker	42
Bianco Dan	42
Bianco ID	42
Bianco Olivia Bulker	42
Bianco Venture	42
Bianco Victoria Bulker	42
Bilbao Bridge	237
Bilbao Knutsen	133
Bilis	241
Billesborg	85
Bing He	65
Bing N	58
Birgit Knutsen	133
Bishu Highway	129
Black Marlin	86
Black Sea	283
Black Watch	21
Blackpool Tower	280
Blue Diamond	279
Blue Marlin	86
Blue Marlin	190
Blue Matterhorn	110
Bneider	135
Bodil Knutsen	133
Bodo Schulte	236
Bogdan	177
Boheme	270
Bonavia	85
Bonita	263
Bonita	61
Bonn Express	116
Bonny	217
Bordeira	61
Borkum Trader	53
Bosporos	261
Bosporus Highway	129
Bosun	217
Botafogo	61
Botswana	280
Boudicca	21
Bow Americas	197
Bow Architect	197
Bow Atlantic	197
Bow Cape	197
Bow Cardinal	197
Bow Cecil	197
Bow Cedar	197
Bow Chain	197
Bow Cheetah	197
Bow Clipper	197
Bow Eagle	197
Bow Elm	197
Bow Engineer	197
Bow Europe	197
Bow Fagus	197
Bow Faith	197
Bow Firda	197
Bow Flora	197
Bow Flower	197
Bow Fortune	197
Bow Harmony	197
Bow Hector	197
Bow Heron	197
Bow Jubail	175
Bow Kiso	197
Bow Lima	197
Bow Lind	197
Bow Mekka	175
Bow Oceanic	197
Bow Rio	68
Bow Riyad	176
Bow Saga	197
Bow Sagami	197
Bow Santos	197
Bow Sea	197
Bow Sirius	197
Bow Sky	197
Bow Spring	197
Bow Star	197
Bow Summer	197
Bow Sun	197
Box Trader	38
Box Voyager	39
Braemar	21
Brasilia Highway	129
Brattingsborg	85
Brave Sailor	34
Braverus	94
Bravery Ace	158
Bravo	217
Brazil	261
Brazil Express	274
Brazilian Reefer	184
Braztrans I	78
Bregen	41
Bremen	27
Bremen Bridge	129
Bremen Express	116
Bremen Max	94
Brevik Bridge	237
Bridgegate	280
Bright Fortune	190
Brightway	283
Brigit Maersk	162
Brilliance of the Seas	22
Brilliant Ace	158
Brimanger	276
Britanis	62
British Beech	50
British Chivalry	50
British Commerce	50
British Cormorant	50
British Councillor	50
British Courage	50
British Courtesy	51
British Curlew	50
British Cygnet	51
British Diamond	51
British Eagle	51
British Emerald	51
British Emissary	51
British Ensign	51
British Envoy	51
British Esteem	51
British Explorer	51
British Falcon	51
British Fidelity	51
British Gannet	51
British Harmony	51
British Hazel	51
British Holly	51
British Innovator	51
British Integrity	51
British Kestrel	51
British Liberty	51
British Loyalty	51
British Mallard	51
British Merchant	51
British Merlin	51
British Oak	51
British Osprey	51
British Pride	51
British Progress	51
British Purpose	51
British Robin	51
British Ruby	51
British Sapphire	51
British Security	51
British Serenity	51
British Swift	51
British Tenacity	51
British Trader	52
British Tranquility	52
British Unity	52
British Vine	52
British Willow	52
Britta Maersk	162
Bro Agnes	53
Bro Alma	53
Bro Anna	53
Bro Anton	162
Bro Atland	162
Bro Axel	53
Bro Deliverer	162
Bro Designer	162
Bro Developer	162
Bro Distributor	162
Bro Nakskov	162
Bro Nibe	162
Bro Nyborg	162
Bro Sincero	53
Broadway	283
Brooklyn Bridge	129
Brother Glory	280
Brotonne Bridge	237
Brugge Max	94
Brugge Venture	99
Brunhilde Salamon	229
Bruno Schulte	236
Brussels Bridge	129
Brussels	99
Bu Samra	241
Bubuk	241
Buccleuch	280
Budapest Bridge	237
Budapest Express	116
Buenos Aires Express	173
Bulgaria	177
Bulk Asia	205
Bulk Avenir	41
Bulk Europe	205
Bulk Jupiter	126
Bulk Leo	126
Bulknes	152
Bumbi	137
Bunga Akasia	155
Bunga Alamanda	155
Bunga Allium	155
Bunga Angelica	155
Bunga Angsana	155
Bunga Aster	155
Bunga Azalea	155
Bunga Bakawali	155
Bunga Balsam	155
Bunga Banyan	155
Bunga Begonia	155
Bunga Kantan Dua	155
Bunga Kantan Satu	155
Bunga Kantan Tiga	155
Bunga Kasturi	156
Bunga Kasturi Dua	156
Bunga Kasturi Empat	156
Bunga Kasturi Enam	156
Bunga Kasturi Lima	156
Bunga Kasturi Tiga	156
Bunga Kelana 3	156
Bunga Kelana 4	156
Bunga Kelana 5	156
Bunga Kelana 6	156
Bunga Kelana 7	156
Bunga Kelana 8	156
Bunga Kelana 9	156
Bunga Kelana Dua	156
Bunga Kelana Satu	156
Bunga Kenanga	156
Bunga Laurel	155
Bunga Lavender	155
Bunga Lilac	155
Bunga Lily	155
Bunga Lotus	155
Bunga Melati 3	155
Bunga Melati 4	155
Bunga Melati 5	156
Bunga Melati 6	156
Bunga Melati 7	156
Bunga Melati Dua	155
Bunga Melati Satu	155
Bunga Raya Tiga	156
Bunga Teratai 3	156
Bunga Teratai 4	156

Name	Page
Bunga Teratai Dua	156
Bunga Teratai	156
Burgia	93
Bursa	241
Busan Express	186
Butterfly	200
Buxcliff	192
Buxcoast	192
Buxcontac	192
Buxfavourite	192
Buxhansa	192
Buxharmony	192
Buxhill	192
Buxlagoon	192
Buxlink	192
Buxmelody	192
Buxmoon	192
Buxsailor	192
Buxstar	192
Buxtaurus	192
Buyi He	65
Buzzard Bay	240
BW Amazon	55
BW Austria	57
BW Bauhinia	55
BW Borg	57
BW Boss	57
BW Broker	57
BW Columbia	55
BW Confidence	57
BW Danube	55
BW Danuta	57
BW Denise	57
BW Edelweiss	56
BW Energy	57
BW GDF Suez Brussels	58
BW GDF Suez Paris	58
BW Havfrost	57
BW Havis	57
BW Helios	57
BW Hermes	57
BW Hudson	56
BW Kronborg	56
BW Lake	56
BW Lena	56
BW Liberty	57
BW Lion	56
BW Lord	57
BW Lotus	56
BW Loyalty	57
BW Luck	56
BW Luna	56
BW Nantes	57
BW Nice	57
BW Nysa	56
BW Orinoco	56
BW Peony	56
BW Prince	57
BW Princess	57
BW Rhine	56
BW Seine	56
BW Shinano	56
BW Suez Boston	58
BW Suez Everett	58
BW Thames	56
BW Trader	58
BW Ubud	56
BW Ulan	56
BW Utah	56
BW Utik	56
BW Vision	58
BW Yangtze	56
BW Zambeze	56
Byron	60
Byzantion	261
C. Prosperity	205
Cabo Hellas	210
Cabo Sounion	210
Cadiz Knutsen	133
Caecilia Schulte	233
Caesar	36
Cala Palma	239
Cala Paradiso	280
Cala Pedra	239
Cala Pino	239
Cala Pira	280
Cala Pula	239
Calandra	279
Calicanto Bridge	237
Calida	61
Calidris	279
California Highway	129
Calisto	88
Callisto	50
Calm Seas	39
Calypso	229
Camberley	229
Camellia	72
Camellia Ace	158
Camilla Bulker	137
Camilla Maersk	162
Camilla Rickmers	220
Canada Express	116
Canadian Highway	129
Canberra Express	116
Canelo Arrow	126
Canopus Leader	181
Cap Blanche	199
Cap Castillo	144
Cap Charles	77
Cap Diamant	77
Cap Domingo	86
Cap Doukato	86
Cap Egmont	96
Cap Felix	77
Cap Ferrato	206
Cap Frio	206
Cap Gabriel	186
Cap George	186
Cap Georges	77
Cap Gilbert	186
Cap Graham	186
Cap Gregory	186
Cap Guillaume	77
Cap Hamilton	200
Cap Harald	200
Cap Harriett	200
Cap Harrisson	200
Cap Harvey	200
Cap Henri	200
Cap Irene	186
Cap Jackson	199
Cap Jean	77
Cap Jervis	199
Cap Lara	77
Cap Laurent	77
Cap Leon	77
Cap Manuel	233
Cap Melville	199
Cap Mondego	233
Cap Moreton	233
Cap Norte	196
Cap Palliser	200
Cap Palmas	199
Cap Palmerston	200
Cap Pasado	199
Cap Pasley	200
Cap Patton	200
Cap Philippe	77
Cap Pierre	77
Cap Portland	200
Cap Roberta	200
Cap Roca	279
Cap Romuald	77
Cap Talbot	261
Cap Theodora	77
Cap Trafalgar	261
Cap Verde	200
Cap Victor	77
Cap Vilano	199
Cape Acacia	129
Cape Albatross	280
Cape Alliance	129
Cape Althea	129
Cape Amanda	129
Cape Apricot	129
Cape Aster	129
Cape Awoba	129
Cape Bacton	231
Cape Balder	229
Cape Banks	214
Cape Bantry	229
Cape Bari	229
Cape Bastia	229
Cape Bata	229
Cape Beale	231
Cape Bear	214
Cape Beira	231
Cape Benat	231
Cape Bille	231
Cape Bird	231
Cape Blanc	231
Cape Bon	231
Cape Bonny	229
Cape Bowen	229
Cape Bradley	231
Cape Brasilia	231
Cape Brindisi	229
Cape Bruny	231
Cape Buzzard	280
Cape Camellia	129
Cape Carmel	279
Cape Celtic	129
Cape Condor	280
Cape Darby	229
Cape Denison	229
Cape Dover	129
Cape Dream	129
Cape Eagle	280
Cape Enterprise	129
Cape Eternity	129
Cape Falcon	229
Cape Falcon	280
Cape Falster	231
Cape Faro	229
Cape Fawley	229
Cape Felton	229
Cape Ferrol	229
Cape Flamingo	280
Cape Flint	231
Cape Flora	129
Cape Flores	229
Cape Forby	230
Cape Franklin	230
Cape Fraser	230
Cape Frio	230
Cape Fulmar	230
Cape Future	129
Cape Glory	129
Cape Harrier	280
Cape Hawk	280
Cape Heron	280
Cape Infinity	129
Cape Jacaranda	129
Cape Kestrel	280
Cape Keystone	129
Cape Liberty	129
Cape Lotus	129
Cape Maas	230
Cape Madrid	230
Cape Magnolia	129
Cape Magnus	230
Cape Mahon	230
Cape Male	230
Cape Manila	230
Cape Manuel	230
Cape Maple	130
Cape Marin	230
Cape Mayor	230
Cape Med	130
Cape Melville	144
Cape Merlin	280
Cape Mollini	144
Cape Mondego	144
Cape Moreton	144
Cape Moss	230
Cape Nabil	230
Cape Nassau	230
Cape Nati	230
Cape Negro	231
Cape Nemo	230
Cape Norviega	231
Cape Olive	130
Cape Orchid	130
Cape Osprey	280
Cape Provence	130
Cape Rainbow	130
Cape Riviera	130
Cape Rosa	130
Cape Sable	215
Cape Sakura	130
Cape Salvia	130
Cape Sampagita	130
Cape Santiago	231
Cape Seagull	280
Cape Sentosa	130
Cape Sophia	130
Cape Sorrell	214
Cape Spencer	215
Cape Stork	280
Cape Taft	231
Cape Talara	231
Cape Tallin	231
Cape Tampa	231
Cape Tavor	279
Cape Tees	231
Cape Texel	231
Cape Town Highway	130
Cape Town Star	249
Cape Triumph	130
Cape Troy	231
Cape Tsubaki	130
Cape Universe	130
Cape Vanguard	130
Cape Victory	130
Capitola	60
Capri	60
Capricorn Star	226
Capricorn Voyager	64
Capricornus Leader	181
Captain Costas	96
Captain Kostichev	243
Captain Michael	77
Car Star	279
Cardonia	38
Cargo	190
Caribbean Emerald	68
Caribbean Highway	130
Caribbean ID	42
Caribbean Mermaid	240
Caribbean Princess	15
Caribbean Sea	280
Caribbean Sea	192
Caribbean Star	249
Caribe	162
Carl Oldendorff	205
Carla Maersk	162
Carla Rickmers	220
Carlos Fischer	200
Carlotta Star	152
Carmel	61
Carmen	270
Carmencita	263
Carnation Ace	158
Carnival Conquest	9
Carnival Destiny	9
Carnival Dream	9
Carnival Ecstasy	9
Carnival Elation	9
Carnival Fantasy	9
Carnival Fascination	9
Carnival Freedom	9
Carnival Glory	9
Carnival Imagination	9
Carnival Inspiration	10
Carnival Legend	10
Carnival Liberty	10
Carnival Magic	10
Carnival Miracle	10
Carnival Paradise	10
Carnival Pride	10
Carnival Sensation	10
Carnival Spirit	10
Carnival Splendor	10
Carnival Triumph	10
Carnival Valor	10
Carnival Victory	10
Carola E.	187
Carolina Star	152
Caroline Maersk	162
Caroline Oldendorff	205
Caroline Schulte	233
Carpathia	38
Carrera	280
Carry	190
Carsten Maersk	162
Carvival Breeze	9
Cary Rickmers	220
Cassiopeia Bulker	137
Cassiopeia Leader	181
Castlegate	280
Castor Voyager	64
Catalina	60
Catalina Star	152
Catalunya Spirit	256
Catamarca	196
Catharina Bulker	137
Catharina Schulte	233
Catherine Knutsen	133
Cathrin Oldendorff	205
Cathrine Rickmers	220
Cattleya Ace	158
CCNI Ancud	173
CCNI Andes	110
CCNI Andino	68
CCNI Angamos	200
CCNI Antuco	274
CCNI Aquiles	230
CCNI Arauco	266
CCNI Aysen	110
Cecilie Maersk	162
Cedar	198
Cedar Arrow	126
Celebrity Century	24
Celebrity Constellation	24
Celebrity Eclipse	24
Celebrity Equinox	24
Celebrity Infinity	24
Celebrity Millennium	24
Celebrity Reflection	24
Celebrity Silhouette	24
Celebrity Solstice	24
Celebrity Summit	24
Celerina	254
Celestial Wing	158
Celina Star	152
Centaurus Leader	181
Centaurus	86
Century Highway No. 2	130
Century Leader No.3	181
Century Leader No.5	181
Cepheus Leader	181
Cerafina	274
Ceram Sea	283
Certoux	72
Cervia	85
Cetus Leader	181
Ceylon	283
Chacabuco	88
Chaconia	99
Chaiten	184
Challenge Passage	243
Chambesy	72
Champel	72
Champion Cornelia	61
Champion Express	61
Champion Pioneer	61
Champion Pleasure	181
Champion Pride	181
Champion Spirit	61
Champion Star	61
Champion Tide	61
Champion Trader	61
Changsha	254
Changuinola Bay	239
Channel Ranger	94
Chantal	261
Chao He	65
Charles Island	93
Charleston Express	116
Charlotta	219
Charlotte Bulker	137
Charlotte Bulker	68
Charlotte C. Rickmers	221
Charlotte Maersk	162
Charlotte Selmer	274
Charmey	254
Chastine Maersk	162
Chekiang	254
Chemtrans Jacobi	62

Name	Pg	Name	Pg	Name	Pg	Name	Pg	Name	Pg
Cosco Hong Kong	65	Crown Topaz	185	CSCL Manzanillo	237	Diamantgracht	247	Dynamic Striker	95
Cosco Hope	237	Crux J	128	CSCL Mars	66	Diamantis P.	96	Dynamogracht	247
Cosco Houston	65	Crystal Ace	158	CSCL Melbourne	237	Diamond Jasmine	161	E. Oldendorff	205
Cosco Indonesia	237	Crystal Bay	196	CSCL Mercury	66	Diamond Princess	15	E.R. Albany	43
Cosco Istanbul	65	Crystal Pioneer	158	CSCL Montevideo	237	Diamond Seas	39	E.R. Barcelona	43
Cosco Italy	65	Crystal Ray	217	CSCL Neptune	66	Diana	215	E.R. Basel	43
Cosco Japan	237	Crystal Serenity	20	CSCL New York	237	Diana Bolten	50	E.R. Bavaria	43
Cosco Kaohsiung	65	Crystal Symphony	20	CSCL Oceania	237	Diana Schulte	236	E.R. Bayern	43
Cosco Korea	237	Crystalgate	280	CSCL Panama	237	Didimon	261	E.R. Bayonne	43
Cosco Long Beach	43	CS Calla	71	CSCL Pusan	83	Dignity Ace	217	E.R. Beilun	43
Cosco Malaysia	237	CS Calvina	71	CSCL Qingdao	66	Dijksgracht	247	E.R. Bergamo	43
Cosco Napoli	43	CS Candy	71	CSCL Rotterdam	66	Dilong Spirit	256	E.R. Berlin	43
Cosco Netherlands	65	CS Caprice	71	CSCL San Jose	237	Dimitris P.	262	E.R. Bern	43
Cosco New York	65	CS Caroline	71	CSCL San Jose	237	Dimitris Y	255	E.R. Bilbao	43
Cosco Ningbo	79	CS Chara	71	CSCL Santiago	237	Dimitrovsky Komsomol	177	E.R. Bogense	43
Cosco Oceania	65	CS Crystal	71	CSCL Sao Paulo	237	Dionysus Leader	182	E.R. Bologna	43
Cosco Pacific	65	CS Discovery	90	CSCL Saturn	66	Discovery Bay	239	E.R. Bordeaux	43
Cosco Philippines	237	CS Manatee	71	CSCL Star	66	Discovery	8	E.R. Borneo	43
Cosco Portugal	65	CS Sacha	71	CSCL Sydney	237	Disney Dream	18	E.R. Bornholm	43
Cosco Pride	237	CS Salina	71	CSCL Uranus	66	Disney Fantasy	18	E.R. Boston	43
Cosco Prince Ruoert	237	CS Savannah	71	CSCL Vancouver	237	Disney Magic	18	E.R. Bourgogne	43
Cosco Qingdao	65	CS Solaris	71	CSCL Venus	66	Disney Wonder	18	E.R. Brandenburg	43
Cosco Rotterdam	65	CS Sonoma	71	CSCL Zeebrugge	237	Ditlev Reefer	185	E.R. Brazil	43
Cosco Seattle	43	CS Soraya	71	Cumbria	281	Divinus	95	E.R. Bremen	43
Cosco Shanghai	65	CS Vanguard	71	Cygnus Voyager	64	Dockwise Vanguard	86	E.R. Bremerhaven	43
Cosco Shengshi	123	CSAV Brasilia	53	Cymbeline	274	Dole Africa	92	E.R. Brest	43
Cosco Shengshi	66	CSAV Cantabrian	187	Cypress Trail	49	Dole America	92	E.R. Brighton	43
Cosco Shenzen	43	CSAV Houston	43	D. Skalkeas	106	Dole Asia	92	E.R. Brisbane	44
Cosco Singapore	65	CSAV Itajai	88	Da Fu	248	Dole California	92	E.R. Bristol	44
Cosco Spain	65	CSAV La Ligua	90	Da He	65	Dole Chile	92	E.R. Buenos Aires	44
Cosco Taicang	65	CSAV Laja	212	Da Hua	248	Dole Colombia	92	E.R. Caen	44
Cosco Tengfei	66	CSAV Lanalhue	227	Da Qiang	248	Dole Costa Rica	92	E.R. Calais	44
Cosco Thailand	237	CSAV Lanco	66	Da Zhong	248	Dole Ecuador	92	E.R. Canberra	44
Cosco Tianjin	65	CSAV Lanco	78	Daedalus Leader	182	Dole Europa	92	E.R. Cannes	44
Cosco Vancouver	43	CSAV Laraquete	90	Daio Southern Cross	182	Dole Honduras	92	E.R. Copenhagen	44
Cosco Xiamen	65	CSAV Lauca	212	DAL Kalahari	96	Dolfijngracht	247	E.R. Cuxhaven	44
Cosco Yantian	79	CSAV Lebu	237	Dalia	158	Dolviken	266	E.R. Dallas	44
Cosco Yingkou	237	CSAV Lingue	237	Dalian Express	116	Don Carlos	270	E.R. Darwin	44
Cosco Yokohama	43	CSAV Lirquen	206	Dalian Highway	130	Don Juan	270	E.R. Denmark	44
Cosmic Jewel	283	CSAV Llanquihue	228	Dallas Express	116	Don Pascuale	43	E.R. Elsfleth	44
Cosmic	139	CSAV Lluta	228	Damgracht	247	Don Pasquale	270	E.R. Fremantle	44
Cosmos Ace	158	CSAV Lonquimay	173	Dan Cisne	139	Don Quijote	270	E.R. Hamburg	44
Costa Atlantica	10	CSAV Maresias	221	Dan Eagle	139	Donau Trader	53	E.R. Helgoland	44
Costa Classica	10	CSAV Papudo	215	Dan Sabia	139	Donau	99	E.R. Kingston	44
Costa Deliziosa	12	CSAV Paris	91	Daniel N	58	Donaugracht	247	E.R. Lübeck	44
Costa Fascinosa	12	CSAV Petorca	215	Daniela Bolten	50	Donegal Spirit	256	E.R. Malmo	44
Costa Favolosa	12	CSAV Pirque	215	Daniela Schulte	236	Dong He	65	E.R. Martinique	44
Costa Fortuna	12	CSAV Porvenir	215	Danship Bulker	42	Dora Schulte	236	E.R. Melbourne	44
Costa Luminosa	12	CSAV Puyehue	215	Danube Highway	217	Dorado Leader	182	E.R. New York	44
Costa Magica	12	CSAV Ranco	187	Danubia	38	Dorian Schulte	236	E.R. Pusan	44
Costa Mediterranea	12	CSAV Rauten	187	Danzigergracht	247	Dorikos	86	E.R. Santiago	44
Costa neoRomantica	12	CSAV Recife	53	Daphne Schulte	236	Dorine	215	E.R. Stralsund	44
Costa Pacifica	12	CSAV Renaico	187	Daphne	88	Dorothea Rickmers	221	E.R. Sweden	44
Costa Rican Star	249	CSAV Rio Aysen	280	Dar Salwa	135	Dorra	175	E.R. Sydney	44
Costa Serena	12	CSAV Rio Blanco	250	Daria	215	Dorset	281	E.R. Wilhelmshaven	44
Costa Victoria	12	CSAV Rio Bueno	135	Darwin	281	Dover Highway	130	E.R. Yantian	44
Costa Voyager	12	CSAV Rio de Janeiro	53	Davakis G	94	Dover Strait	219	Eagle	48
Cote d'Ivoirian Star	249	CSAV Rio Geike	124	David Schulte	236	Drawsko	215	Eagle	277
Cotinga Arrow	126	CSAV Rio Grande	281	Dawn Princess	15	Dream Angel	69	Eagle Albany	156
Cougar Ace	158	CSAV Rio Grey	281	Daytona	61	Dream Beauty	69	Eagle Anaheim	156
Courage	272	CSAV Rio Illapel	135	Deep Seas	39	Dream Diamond	69	Eagle Arrow	126
Courageous Ace	158	CSAV Rio Imperial	281	Deike Rickmers	221	Dream Diva	69	Eagle Atlanta	156
Courcheville	99	CSAV Rio Itata	135	Deira	264	Dream Jasmine	69	Eagle Augusta	156
CPO America	200	CSAV Rio Nevado	281	Delhi Highway	130	Dream Orchid	69	Eagle Auriga	156
CPO Asia	200	CSAV Rio Serrano	121	Delia	215	Dream Seas	39	Eagle Austin	156
CPO England	200	CSAV Romeral	144	Delmas Keta	75	Dresden Express	116	Eagle Baltimore	156
CPO Europe	200	CSAV Rungue	144	Delmas Swala	75	Dresden	250	Eagle Bay	240
CPO Finland	200	CSAV Rupanco	187	Delos Ranger	95	DS Charme	215	Eagle Beaumont	156
CPO France	200	CSAV Suape	53	Delphi	261	DS Commander	215	Eagle Birmingham	157
CPO Germany	200	CSAV Taltal	187	Delphi Ranger	95	DS Crown	102	Eagle Boston	157
CPO Italy	200	CSAV Valencia	91	Delphin	17	DS Progress	215	Eagle Carina	157
CPO Norway	200	CSCC Asia	217	Delphinus Leader	182	DS Promoter	215	Eagle Centaurus	157
CPO Oceana	201	CSCC Europe	217	Delta Ranger	95	DS Venture	215	Eagle Columbus	157
CPO Russia	201	CSCC Shanghai	217	Deltagracht	247	DS Vision	215	Eagle Corona	157
CPO Sweden	201	CSCC Tianjin	217	Demeter	88	Dubai Express	238	Eagle Kangar	157
Crane Arrow	126	CSCL Africa	237	Demeter Leader	182	Dublin Express	116	Eagle Kinabalu	157
Cristina Star	152	CSCL America	82	Derby D.	83	Duhail	217	Eagle Kinarut	157
Cronus Leader	181	CSCL Asia	66	Derby	281	Duka	83	Eagle Klang	157
Crossway	283	CSCL Brisbane	237	Desimi	61	Dukhan	190	Eagle Kuantan	157
Crown Emerald	184	CSCL Callao	237	Despina P.	96	Duncan Island	93	Eagle Kuching	157
Crown Garnet	184	CSCL Chiwan	237	Deutschland	17	Dunedin Star	249	Eagle Louisiana	157
Crown Jade	185	CSCL Europe	83	Deva	83	Duqm	161	Eagle Miri	157
Crown Opal	185	CSCL Jupiter	66	Devon	77	Durban Bulker	137	Eagle Otome	157
Crown Princess	15	CSCL Le Havre	83	Devon	281	Durban Highway	130	Eagle Paraiba	157
Crown Ruby	185	CSCL Lima	237	DHL Forester	137	Durban Star	249	Eagle Parana	157
Crown Sapphire	185	CSCL Long Beach	237	Dhonoussa	93	Düsseldorf Express	116	Eagle Phoenix	157

Eagle San Antonio	157	EM Psara	97	Eternus	95	Ever Smart	99	Federal Rhine	100
Eagle San Diego	157	EM Spetses	97	Etoile	38	Ever Smile	99	Federal Rideau	100
Eagle San Juan	157	Emden	130	Eugen Maersk	162	Ever Steady	99	Federal Sable	100
Eagle San Pedro	157	Emerald	240	Eugenie	77	Ever Strong	99	Federal Saguenay	101
Eagle Seville	157	Emerald Ace	158	Eupen	99	Ever Summit	99	Federal Sakura	101
Eagle Stavanger	157	Emerald Leader	182	Euphony Ace	158	Ever Superb	99	Federal Schelde	101
Eagle Stealth	157	Emerald Leader	217	Euphrates Highway	130	Ever Uberty	99	Federal Seto	101
Eagle Strait	219	Emerald Princess	15	Eurasian Highway	130	Ever Ultra	99	Federal Severn	101
Eagle Subaru	157	Emerald Splendor	283	Euro Max	231	Ever Ulysses	99	Federal Shimanto	101
Eagle Sydney	157	Emerald Stars	250	Euro Spirit	186	Ever Unicorn	99	Federal Skeena	101
Eagle Tacoma	157	Emerald Strait	219	Euro	262	Ever Unific	99	Federal Skye	101
Eagle Tampa	157	*Emerald Success*	283	Eurochampion 2004	262	Ever Union	99	Federal St. Laurent	101
Eagle Texas	157	*Emerald Summit*	283	Eurodam	12	Ever Unique	99	Federal Sutton	101
Eagle Toledo	157	*Emerald Supreme*	284	Euronike	262	Ever Unison	99	Federal Swift	101
Eagle Torrance	157	Emerald	254	Europa 2	28	Ever United	99	Federal Venture	101
Eagle Trenton	157	Emilie Bulker	137	Europa	226	Ever Unity	99	Federal Welland	101
Eagle Tucson	157	Eminent Ace	158	Europa	27	Ever Uranus	99	Federal Weser	101
Eagle Turin	157	Emirates Dar es Salaam	88	European Emerald	69	Ever Urban	99	Federal Yoshino	101
Eagle Valencia	157	Emirates Ganges	91	European Highway	130	Ever Ursula	99	Federal Yukina	101
Eagle Vancouver	157	Emirates Kabir	91	European Spirit	256	Ever Useful	99	Federal Yukon	101
Eagle Varna	157	Emirates Nile	91	Eurovision	262	Ever Utile	99	Fedor	230
Eagle Venice	157	Emirates Zambezi	91	Eurus Lima	281	Everest Bay	239	Fedora	270
Eagle Vermont	157	Emma Bulker	137	Eurus Lisbon	281	Everest Spirit	256	FEG Success	122
Eagle Vienna	158	Emma Maersk	162	Eurus London	281	Everhard Schulte	233	Fei He	65
Eagle Virginia	158	Emma Schulte	236	Eva Bulker	137	Evinco	53	Fei Yun He	65
East Castle	176	Emmy Schulte	233	Eva N	58	Evros	141	Felicitas Rickmers	221
East Siberian Sea	243	Empress	110	Eva Schulte	233	Excalibur	99	Felicity Ace	158
Eastern Bay	240	Empress Dragon	65	Evelyn Maersk	162	Excel	99	Felicity	77
Eastern Highway	130	Empress Heaven	65	Evelyn Schulte	236	Excelerate	99	Fermita	263
Ebba Maersk	162	Empress Phoenix	65	Ever Champion	194	Excellence	99	Fernandina	59
Ecola	60	Empress Sea	65	Ever Charming	194	Excello	53	Fernando	196
Ecuador Star	249	Empress	24	Ever Chivalry	194	Excelsior	99	Fernie	281
Eddystone	101	Ems Trader	53	Ever Conquest	194	Exemplar	99	Fesco Amalthea	196
Edith Kirk	139	Ems	205	Ever Dainty	97	Expedient	99	Fidelio	270
Edith Maersk	162	Emu Arrow	126	Ever Decent	97	Expedition	29	Fides	108
Edward N	58	Enchantment of the Seas	22	Ever Delight	97	Explorer	30	Fiesta	205
Edzard Schulte	233	Endeavour	261	Ever Deluxe	98	Explorer	99	Figaro	270
Eeklo	99	Endeavour Strait	219	Ever Develop	98	Explorer of the Seas	22	Filikon	77
Egret Bulker	137	Endurance	272	Ever Devote	98	Express	99	Finch Arrow	127
EGS Crest	124	Energy Centaur	95	Ever Diadem	98	Exquisite	99	Finesse	78
EGS Tide	124	Energy Centurion	95	Ever Diamond	98	Eyrene	144	Finisterre	280
EGS Wave	124	Energy Century	95	Ever Divine	98	Fairpartner	129	Finnanger	276
Eilbek	110	Energy Challenger	95	Ever Dynamic	98	Fairplayer	129	Finnmarken	18
Eilhard Schulte	233	Energy Champion	95	Ever Eagle	98	*Fairway*	284	Fiona Rickmers	221
Eishun	49	Energy Chancellor	95	Ever Elite	98	Fakarava	60	Firmament Ace	158
EIT Palmina	119	Energy Commander	95	Ever Envoy	98	Falcon	277	Fiskardo	153
Elbe Highway	217	Energy Conqueror	95	Ever Ethic	98	Falcon Arrow	127	Fitnes	152
Elbe Max	95	Energy Enterprise	124	Ever Excel	98	Falcon Bay	240	Fjellanger	276
Elbe	205	Energy Panther	95	Ever Laden	98	Falcon	48	Flamengo	199
Elbe	83	Energy Patriot	95	Ever Lambent	98	Falkanger	276	Flanders Harmony	100
Elbrus	246	Energy Pioneer	95	Ever Lasting	98	Falstaff	270	Flanders Tenacity	100
Elbwolf	279	Energy Power	95	Ever Laurel	98	Famenne	77	Flandre	78
Electra	226	Energy Pride	95	Ever Lawful	98	Fauskanger	276	Flecha	60
Elegant Ace	158	Energy Progress	95	Ever Leader	98	Faust	270	Flora Delmas	75
Elektra	270	Energy Protector	95	Ever Leading	98	Faust	44	Florida Highway	130
Eleni D.	106	Energy Puma	95	Ever Legacy	98	Favorita	263	Flottbek	110
Eleni I	255	Energy R.	206	Ever Legend	98	Federal Agno	100	FMG Grace	76
Eleni P.	96	Energy Ranger	95	Ever Legion	98	Federal Asahi	100	FMG Matilda	76
Eleonora Maersk	162	Energy Skier	95	Ever Libra	98	Federal Baffin	100	Force Ranger	95
Eli Knutsen	133	Energy Sprinter	95	Ever Lifting	98	Federal Danube	100	Fortaleza Knutsen	133
Elisa Delmas	75	Epic	139	Ever Linking	98	Federal Elbe	100	Fortuna Bay	240
Elisabeth Knutsen	133	Equuleus Leader	182	Ever Lissome	98	Federal Ems	100	Fortune	56
Elisabeth Schulte	233	Erato	106	Ever Lively	98	Federal Franklin	100	Fortune Amaryllis	69
Elisalex Schulte	233	Erawan	254	Ever Living	98	Federal Fuji	100	Fortune Apricot	69
Elise Schulte	233	Eridanus Leader	182	Ever Loading	98	Federal Fuji	266	Fortune Clover	69
Elisewin	215	Erik Spirit	256	Ever Lovely	98	Federal Hudson	100	Fortune Iris	69
Elizabeth I. A.	36	Erika Schulte	233	Ever Lucent	98	Federal Hunter	100	Fortune Miracle	69
Elka Angelique	241	Erikoussa	93	Ever Lucid	98	Federal Katsura	100	Fortune Plum	69
Elka Eleftheria	241	Erin Schulte	233	Ever Lunar	98	Federal Kivalina	100	Fortune Sunny	69
Elka Nikolas	241	Ermis	137	Ever Lyric	98	Federal Kumano	100	Fortune Violet	69
Ellen S	227	Ernest N	58	Ever Peace	98	Federal Kushiro	100	Forward Bright	182
Ellinis	62	Ernst Oldendorff	205	Ever Pearl	98	Federal Leda	100	Fouma	258
Elly Maersk	162	Ernst Rickmers	221	Ever Power	98	Federal Maas	100	Fourni	93
Elqui	274	Erviken	266	Ever Pride	98	Federal Mackinac	100	Fowairet	264
Elsborg	85	Esmeralda	240	Ever Prima	98	Federal Mackinac	100	FPMC 25	190
Elsebeth	240	Essen Express	117	Ever Racer	98	Federal Margaree	100	FPMC 26	190
Elversele	99	*Essen Express*	117	Ever Radiant	98	Federal Margaree	100	FR8 Fortitude	251
Elvia	85	Essex Strait	219	Ever Reach	98	Federal Mattawa	100	Fram	18
Elvira	240	Essex	281	Ever Refine	98	Federal Mattawa	100	Francisca Schulte	236
Elvira Bulker	137	Estebroker	261	Ever Respect	98	Federal Miramichi	100	Frankfurt Express	117
EM Andros	96	Estelle Maersk	162	Ever Result	98	Federal Nakagawa	100	Franziska Bolten	50
EM Astoria	96	Esther Schulte	233	Ever Reward	98	Federal Oshima	100	Fraternity	78
EM Athens	97	Esther Spirit	256	Ever Safety	98	Federal Polaris	100	Fredensborg	85
EM Chios	97	Estrella Atlantica	241	Ever Salute	99	Federal Polaris	266	Frederike Selmer	274
EM Hydra	97	Estrella Austral	241	Ever Shine	99	Federal Power	100	Freedom	272
EM Ithaki	97	Eternal Ace	158	Ever Sigma	99	Federal Progress	100	Freedom Ace	158

Name	No.
Freedom of the Seas	22
Freja Andromeda	139
Freja Atlantic	139
Freja Baltic	139
Freja Crux	139
Freja Fionia	139
Freja Hafnia	139
Freja Lupus	139
Freja Maersk	162
Freja Nordica	139
Freja Pegasus	139
Freja Polaris	190
Freja Taurus	139
Fremantle Express	117
Frida Maersk	162
Frida Schulte	236
Frieda Selmer	274
Friendly Islands	281
Friendly Seas	39
Frio Hellenic	239
Frisia Bonn	119
Frisia Helsinki	119
Frisia Kiel	119
Frisia Lissabon	119
Frisia Loga	119
Frisia Lübeck	119
Frisia Nürnberg	119
Frisia Rostock	119
Frisia Rotterdam	119
Frisia Wismar	119
Fritz Reuter	228
Fritzi N	58
Front Ardenne	102
Front Ariake	102
Front Brabant	102
Front Cecilie	102
Front Century	102
Front Champion	102
Front Chief	102
Front Chief	215
Front Circassia	102
Front Comanche	102
Front Commerce	102
Front Commodore	102
Front Commodore	215
Front Crown	215
Front Eminence	102
Front Endurance	102
Front Energy	102
Front Falcon	102
Front Force	102
Front Glory	102
Front Hakata	102
Front Kathrine	102
Front Melody	102
Front Melody	215
Front Njord	102
Front Odin	102
Front Opalia	102
Front Page	102
Front Pride	102
Front Queen	102
Front Scilla	102
Front Serenade	102
Front Signe	102
Front Splendour	102
Front Stratus	102
Front Symphony	102
Front Symphony	215
Front Tina	215
Front Vanguard	102
Front Warrior	215
Frontier	110
Frontier Ace	158
Frontier	194
FSL Hamburg	231
FSL Singapore	231
FSO Asia	78
Fuji Bay	239
Fuji Maru	19
Fuji Spirit	257
Fujikawa	130
Fulvia	85
Funchal	17
Furious	95
Futura	180
Future	34
Gaia Leader	182
Galaxy Ace	158
Galaxy Leader	217
Galea	241
Galicia Spirit	256
Gallia	144
Gallina	241
Galveston	60
Galway Spirit	256
Gandhi	62
Gandria	103
Ganges Spirit	256
Gannet Bulker	137
Gan-Trophy	170
Gao He	65
Garnet Leader	217
Gas Al Kuwait II	135
Gas Al Mutlaa	135
Gas Al Negeh	135
Gas Al-Gurain	135
Gas Diana	182
Gas Taurus	182
Gaschem Adriatic	119
Gaschem Antarctic	119
Gaschem Bremen	119
Gaschem Hamburg	119
Gaschem Nordsee	194
Gaschem Pacific	194
Gaschem Stade	119
GasLog Savannah	103
GasLog Shanghai	103
GasLog Singapore	103
Gassan	161
GDF Suez Cape Ann	122
GDF Suez Neptune	122
Gdynia	215
Geiranger	277
Gemini Voyager	64
Gemini	145
Gemmata	241
Genciana	159
Genco Acheron	103
Genco Aquitaine	103
Genco Ardennes	103
Genco Augustus	103
Genco Auvegne	103
Genco Avra	103
Genco Bay	103
Genco Beauty	103
Genco Bourgogne	103
Genco Brittany	104
Genco Carrier	104
Genco Cavalier	104
Genco Challenger	104
Genco Champion	104
Genco Charger	104
Genco Claudius	104
Genco Commodus	104
Genco Constantine	104
Genco Explorer	104
Genco Hadrian	104
Genco Hunter	104
Genco Knight	104
Genco Languedoc	104
Genco Leader	104
Genco Loire	104
Genco London	104
Genco Lorraine	104
Genco Mare	104
Genco Marine	104
Genco Maximus	104
Genco Muse	104
Genco Normandy	105
Genco Ocean	105
Genco Picardy	105
Genco Pioneer	105
Genco Predator	105
Genco Progress	105
Genco Prosperity	105
Genco Provence	105
Genco Pyrenees	105
Genco Raptor	105
Genco Reliance	105
Genco Rhone	105
Genco Spirit	105
Genco Success	105
Genco Sugar	105
Genco Surprise	105
Genco Thunder	105
Genco Tiberius	105
Genco Titus	105
Genco Vigour	105
Genco Warrior	105
Genco Wisdom	105
General Guisan	254
Generous	95
Genius	95
GenMar Agamemnon	105
GenMar Ajax	105
GenMar Argus	105
GenMar Atlas	105
GenMar Companion	105
GenMar Compatriot	105
GenMar Concord	105
GenMar Consul	105
Genmar Daphne	105
GenMar Defiance	105
Genmar Elektra	105
GenMar George T.	105
GenMar Harriet G.	105
GenMar Hercules	105
GenMar Hope	105
GenMar Horn	105
GenMar Kara G.	105
GenMar Maniate	105
GenMar Minotaur	105
GenMar Orion	105
GenMar Phoenix	105
GenMar Poseidon	105
GenMar Spartiate	105
GenMar Spyridon	105
GenMar St. Nikolas	105
GenMar Strength	105
GenMar Ulysses	106
GenMar Victory	106
GenMar Vision	106
GenMar Zeus	106
Genoa Bridge	130
Genoa Express	117
Gentle Leader	217
Genuine Ace	159
Georg Jacob	125
Georg Maersk	162
George N.	58
George Washington Bridge	130
Georgi Grigorov	177
Georgia Highway	130
Georgy Maslov	243
Geraldine Manx	138
Gerd Knutsen	133
Gerd Maersk	162
Ghawar	175
Ghazal	175
Ghent Max	95
Giannutri	190
Giewont	215
Gijon Knutsen	133
Gimi	103
Giuseppe Rizzo	284
Gjertrud Maersk	162
Gladiator	95
Glasgow Express	117
Glen Canyon Bridge	130
Global Leader	217
Global Spirit	186
Global Victory	59
Gloria	93
Gloric	139
Glorious Ace	159
Glorious Hibiscus	182
Glorious Jasmine	182
Glorious Leader	217
Glorious Lotus	182
Glorious Maple	182
Glorious Peony	182
Glorious Plumeria	182
Glorious Sakura	182
Glorius	95
Glory	217
Glory	252
Glovis Advance	123
Glovis Caravel	217
Glovis Century	123
Glovis Challenge	123
Glovis Clipper	217
Glovis Composer	123
Glovis Conductor	123
Glovis Master	123
Glovis Mermaid	123
Glovis Passion	218
Glovis Prestige	218
GMT Polaris	124
GMT Venus	124
Godavari Spirit	256
Golar Arctic	103
Golar Grand	103
Golar Maria	103
Golar Mazo	103
Golar Viking	103
Golden Gate Bridge	130
Golden Iris	30
Golden Isle	143
Golden Isle	230
Golden Princess	15
Golden Seas	39
Golden Trader	106
Goliath Leader	218
Good Hope Max	95
Goodwill	110
Goonyella Trader	256
Gotland Spirit	257
Governor Farkhutdinov	243
Goya	173
Graceful Leader	218
Grafton	281
Graig Cardiff	138
Graig Rotterdam	138
Gran Bretagna	108
Grand Aniva	243
Grand Benelux	108
Grand Breaker	230
Grand Celebration	13
Grand Champion	69
Grand Choice	69
Grand Cosmo	69
Grand Dahlia	69
Grand Diamond	69
Grand Duke	69
Grand Elena	243
Grand Hero	69
Grand Holiday	13
Grand Legacy	69
Grand Mark	69
Grand Mercury	69
Grand Mistral	13
Grand Neptune	69
Grand Orion	69
Grand Pace	69
Grand Pavo	69
Grand Pearl	69
Grand Phoenix	69
Grand Pioneer	230
Grand Pioneer	69
Grand Princess	15
Grand Quest	69
Grand Race	69
Grand Ruby	69
Grand Sapphire	69
Grand Sea	161
Grand Vega	69
Grand Venus	69
Grand Victory	69
Grande Africa	110
Grande Amburgo	108
Grande America	108
Grande Angola	108
Grande Anversa	108
Grande Argentina	110
Grande Atlantico	108
Grande Benin	108
Grande Brasile	110
Grande Buenos Aires	108
Grande Cameroon	108
Grande Colonia	108
Grande Congo	108
Grande Costa d'Avorio	109
Grande Detroit	110
Grande Detroit	109
Grande Ellade	109
Grande Europa	109
Grande Francia	109
Grande Gabon	109
Grande Ghana	109
Grande Guinea	109
Grande Italia	109
Grande Marocco	109
Grande Mediterraneo	109
Grande Napoli	109
Grande Nigeria	109
Grande Portogallo	109
Grande Progresso	130
Grande Roma	109
Grande San Paolo	109
Grande Scandinavia	109
Grande Senegal	109
Grande Sicilia	110
Grande Sicilia	109
Grande Sierra Leone	109
Grande Spagna	109
Grande Togo	109
Grandeur of the Seas	22
Grasmere Maersk	167
Great Challenger	69
Great Dream	69
Great Eastern	267
Great Morning	69
Great Navigator	69
Great River	110
Great River	69
Great Summit	69
Grebe Arrow	127
Grebe Bulker	138
Green Ace	233
Green Bay	124
Green Brazil	107
Green Chile	107
Green Concordia	107
Green Costa Rica	107
Green Cove	124
Green Dale	124
Green Guatemala	107
Green Honduras	107
Green Italia	107
Green Lake	124
Green Magic	108
Green Maveric	108
Green Music	108
Green Park	281
Green Point	124
Green Point	62
Green Ridge	124
Green Stars	250
Green Toledo	108
Green Wave	124
Greenwich Bridge	130
Greenwich Park	281
Grena	173
Greta Selmer	274
Grete Maersk	163
Grey Fox	143
Grindanger	277
Grouse Arrow	127
Grumant	142
Gry Bulker	138
GSL Africa	284
Guang Dong Bridge	130
Guangzhou Highway	130
Guardian Leader	218
Guayaquil Bridge	238
Gudrun Maersk	163
Gunhild Kirk	139
Gunvor Maersk	163
Guofeng Enterprise	281
Guofeng First	281
Gustav Schulte	233
H Fyn	139
Habari	175
Hadiyah	135
Hainan Baosha 001	95
Hainan Baosha 011	95
Hainan Baosha 012	95

Name	Pg	Name	Pg	Name	Pg	Name	Pg	Name	Pg
Hakkaisan	161	Hanjin Gothenburg	194	Hanjin Sur	113	Harefield	127	HHL Tokyo	114
Hakusan	161	Hanjin Greece	83	Hanjin Tacoma	113	Harm	261	HHL Valparaiso	114
HAL Patriot	119	Hanjin Haiphong	135	Hanjin Taipei	194	Harmen Oldendorff	205	HHL Venice	114
HAL Pendant	119	Hanjin Hamburg	111	Hanjin Tianjin	113	Harmony Ace	159	HHL Volga	114
Halifax Express	79	*Hanjin Harmony*	88	Hanjin Tubarao	113	Harmony Leader	218	Hibernia	96
Hambisa	231	Hanjin Haypoint	111	Hanjin United Kingdom	113	Harriette N	58	High Challenge	81
Hamburg	28	Hanjin Hinase	111	Hanjin Valencia	113	Hartland Point	101	High Courage	81
Hamburg Bridge	130	Hanjin Hirose	111	Hanjin Vancouver	113	Hastings Castle	176	High Efficiency	81
Hamburg Express	117	Hanjin Irene	262	Hanjin Versailles	83	Hatsu Courage	194	High Endeavour	81
Hamburg Max	95	Hanjin Isabel	111	Hanjin Vienna	194	Hatsu Crystal	194	High Endurance	82
Hamburg Star	62	Hanjin Italy	83	Hanjin Washington	113	Hatta	264	High Energy	82
Hamburg Trader	141	Hanjin Jebel Ali	111	Hanjin Wilmington	113	Havelstern	224	High Light	82
Hamilton Spirit	256	Hanjin Kaohsiung	111	Hanjin Xiamen	113	Hawk	278	High Mars	233
Hammersmith Bridge	130	Hanjin Kingston	111	Hanjin Yantian	194	Hawk	48	High Pearl	82
Hammonia Adriaticum	91	Hanjin Korea	111	Hanne Knutsen	133	Hawk Arrow	127	High Performance	82
Hammonia Africum	91	Hanjin Lima	194	Hannover Bridge	130	Hawk Bay	240	High Power	82
Hammonia Balticum	91	Hanjin Lisbon	194	Hanoi Bridge	130	Hawtah	175	High Presence	82
Hammonia Bavaria	91	Hanjin Liverpool	111	Hanover Express	117	Heather Knutsen	133	High Priority	82
Hammonia Berolina	91	Hanjin London	111	Hans Scholl	63	Hebridean Princess	9	High Progress	82
Hammonia Caspium	91	Hanjin Long Beach	111	Hansa Aalesund	139	Hedda Schulte	236	High Prosperity	82
Hammonia Galicia	91	Hanjin Los Angeles	111	Hansa Africa	139	Hedvig Bulker	138	High Saturn	233
Hammonia Gallicum	91	Hanjin Madrid	194	Hansa Altenburg	139	Heidelberg Express	117	High Seas	82
Hammonia Husum	91	Hanjin Malta	111	Hansa Arendal	139	Heijin	182	High Spirit	82
Hammonia Internum	91	Hanjin Manila	111	Hansa Atlantic	139	Heike P	214	High Strength	82
Hammonia Ionium	91	Hanjin Manzanillo	111	Hansa Augsburg	139	Helen Bolten	50	High Tide	82
Hammonia Korsika	91	Hanjin Marseilles	111	Hansa Augustenburg	139	Helen N	58	High Valor	82
Hammonia Malta	91	Hanjin Marugame	112	Hansa Bergen	140	Helena Schulte	236	High Venture	82
Hammonia Massilia	91	Hanjin Matsue	112	Hansa Berlin	140	Helene J	128	Highbury Park	281
Hammonia Pacificum	91	Hanjin Matsuyama	112	Hansa Brandenburg	140	Helene Knutsen	133	Hildegaard	143
Hammonia Pomerenia	91	Hanjin Miami	194	Hansa Bremen	239	Helene Rickmers	221	Hilli	103
Hammonia Roma	91	Hanjin Milano	221	Hansa Caledonia	140	Helene Russ	224	Himalaya	231
Hammonia Teutonica	91	Hanjin Monaco	112	Hansa Calypso	140	Helene S	227	Himalaya Bay	239
Hammonia Thracium	91	Hanjin Montevideo	221	Hansa Castella	140	Helene Selmer	274	Hippo	241
Hammonia Toscana	91	Hanjin Mumbai	112	Hansa Centaur	140	Helga Spirit	256	Hispania Spirit	256
Hammonia Venetia	91	Hanjin Mundra	135	Hansa Centurion	140	Helios Leader	182	Hispania	145
Han Yi	248	Hanjin Muscat	112	Hansa Century	114	Helle Ritscher	261	HMS Laurence	145
Handan Steel	281	Hanjin Nagoya	112	Hansa Cloppenburg	140	Hellespont Pride	213	Hoechst Express	117
Handan Steel	281	Hanjin Netherlands	112	Hansa Coburg	140	Hellespont Progress	213	Höegh Africa	218
Hangang Elite	281	Hanjin New Orleans	112	Hansa Constitution	114	Hellespont Promise	213	Höegh America	218
Hani He	65	Hanjin New York	112	Hansa Duburg	140	Hellespont Prosperity	214	Höegh Asia	121
Hanjin Africa	88	Hanjin Newcastle	112	Hansa Europe	140	Hellespont Protector	214	Höegh Bangkok	121
Hanjin Albany	110	Hanjin Newport	112	Hansa Flensburg	140	Hellespont Providence	214	Höegh Beijing	121
Hanjin Algeciras	83	Hanjin Newport	221	Hansa Freyburg	140	Hellespont Tatina	214	Höegh Beijing	250
Hanjin America	88	Hanjin Nhava Sheva	112	Hansa Greifswald	140	Helsinki	194	Höegh Berlin	121
Hanjin Amsterdam	194	Hanjin Norfolk	112	Hansa Kirkenes	140	Helsinki Bridge	130	Höegh Brasilia	121
Hanjin Asia	88	Hanjin Odessa	112	Hansa Kristiansand	140	Heluan	46	Hoegh Caribia	49
Hanjin Athens	194	Hanjin Oslo	112	Hansa Langeland	140	Helvetia One	95	Höegh Chennai	121
Hanjin Atlanta	110	Hanjin Ottawa	194	Hansa Liberty	114	Helvetia	91	Höegh Copenhagen	121
Hanjin Balikpapan	111	Hanjin Palermo	194	Hansa Limburg	140	Hemus	177	Höegh Delhi	121
Hanjin Baltimore	194	Hanjin Paris	112	Hansa Lübeck	239	Henna	27	Höegh Detroit	121
Hanjin Basel	194	Hanjin Philadephia	135	Hansa Ludswigsburg	140	Henrietta Schulte	233	Höegh Dubai	69
Hanjin Beijing	111	Hanjin Phoenix	135	Hansa Magdeburg	140	Henry Hudson Bridge	130	Höegh Inchon	121
Hanjin Belewan	111	Hanjin Piraeus	112	Hansa Marburg	140	Henry Oldendorff	205	Höegh Kobe	121
Hanjin Berlin	111	Hanjin Pittsburg	112	Hansa Meersburg	140	Heranger	277	Höegh Kunsan	121
Hanjin Blue Ocean	88	Hanjin Port Headland	112	Hansa Narvik	140	Hercules Highway	130	Höegh Manila	121
Hanjin Bombay	111	Hanjin Port Kelang	112	Hansa Nordburg	140	Hercules Leader	182	Höegh Maputo	121
Hanjin Boston	194	Hanjin Port Kembla	112	Hansa Offenburg	140	Heritage Leader	218	Höegh Masan	121
Hanjin Brazil	111	Hanjin Port Walcott	112	Hansa Oldenburg	140	Hermann Hesse	228	Höegh Oceania	69
Hanjin Bremerhaven	111	Hanjin Portland	135	Hansa Pacific	140	Hermann S	227	Höegh Osaka	121
Hanjin Brisbane	111	Hanjin Praha	135	Hansa Papenburg	140	Hermann Wulff	279	Höegh Oslo	121
Hanjin Brussels	194	Hanjin Pretoria	135	Hansa Ravensburg	140	Hermes	217	Höegh Seoul	121
Hanjin Buchanan	111	Hanjin Punta Arenas	194	Hansa Reggensburg	140	Hermitage Bridge	243	Höegh Shanghai	121
Hanjin Budapest	111	Hanjin Pyeong Taek	112	Hansa Rendsburg	140	Heroic Ace	159	Höegh Singapore	121
Hanjin Buenos Aires	83	Hanjin Ras Laffan	112	Hansa Riga	140	Heroic Leader	218	Höegh St. Petersburg	121
Hanjin Cape Lambert	111	Hanjin Ras Tanura	112	Hansa Ronneburg	140	Heroic Striker	95	Höegh Sydney	121
Hanjin Capetown	111	Hanjin Richards Bay	112	Hansa Rostock	140	Heroic	139	Höegh Trader	121
Hanjin Chennai	111	Hanjin Rio de Janiero	112	Hansa Salzburg	141	Hestia Leader	182	Höegh Transit	121
Hanjin Chicago	194	Hanjin Rizhao	112	Hansa Stockholm	239	Heythrop	281	Höegh Transporter	121
Hanjin China	111	Hanjin Roberts Bank	112	Hansa Victory	114	H-G Buelow	279	Höegh Trapeze	121
Hanjin Chongqing	111	Hanjin Rome	112	Hansa Visby	239	HHL Amazon	113	Höegh Treasure	121
Hanjin Colombo	135	Hanjin Rostock	112	Hanseatic	28	HHL Amur	113	Höegh Trident	121
Hanjin Constantza	83	Hanjin Rotterdam	112	Happy Buccaneer	248	HHL Bilbao	113	Höegh Triton	121
Hanjin Copenhagen	194	Hanjin Saijo	112	Happy Delta	248	HHL Congo	113	Höegh Trooper	121
Hanjin Dalian	111	Hanjin Saldanha Bay	112	Happy Diamond	248	HHL Fremantle	113	Höegh Tropicana	121
Hanjin Dallas	194	Hanjin Samarinda	112	Happy Dover	249	HHL Hamburg	113	Höegh Trove	121
Hanjin Dalrymple Bay	111	Hanjin San Diego	135	Happy Dragon	249	HHL Hong Kong	113	Höegh Xiamen	121
Hanjin Dangjin	111	Hanjin San Francisco	112	Happy Dynamic	249	HHL Kobe	113	Hojin	182
Hanjin Duesseldorf	221	Hanjin Santana	112	Happy Ranger	249	HHL Lagos	113	Holsatia	281
Hanjin Durban	111	Hanjin Santos	83	Happy River	249	HHL Lisbon	114	Homam Star	226
Hanjin Elizabeth	262	Hanjin Seattle	112	Happy Rover	249	HHL Macao	114	Honduras Star	249
Hanjin Europe	88	Hanjin Shanghai	112	*Happy Sky*	249	HHL Mississippi	114	Hong Kong Bridge	130
Hanjin Fos	111	Hanjin Shenzhen	112	*Happy Star*	249	HHL New York	114	*Hong Kong Express*	117
Hanjin Gdynia	111	Hanjin Shikoku	112	Harad	175	HHL Nile	114	Hong Xing	68
Hanjin Geneva	194	Hanjin Sines	112	Harald S	227	HHL Rhine	114	Honolulu Bridge	130
Hanjin Germany	83	Hanjin Sooho	88	Harbour Bridge	130	HHL Richards Bay	114	Honor	272
Hanjin Gladstone	111	Hanjin Spain	113	Hardanger	277	HHL Rio di Janiero	114	Hood Island	93

Name	Page
Hooge	52
Hope Bay	240
Hope	83
Horaisan	161
Horizon Leader	218
Horizon	24
Hornbay	120
Horncap	120
Horncliff	120
Hosanger	277
Houston Bridge	130
Houston Express	187
Hoyanger	277
HR Constellation	91
HR Constitution	91
HR indication	91
HR Intonation	92
HR Margaretha	92
HR Maria	92
HR Marion	92
HS Alcina	114
HS Bach	114
HS Beethoven	114
HS Berlioz	114
HS Bizet	114
HS Bruckner	114
HS Carmen	114
HS Challenger	114
HS Chopin	114
HS Debussy	114
HS Discoverer	114
HS Elektra	114
HS Haydn	114
HS Humboldt	114
HS Liszt	114
HS Livingstone	114
HS Medea	114
HS Mozart	114
HS Schubert	114
HS Scott	114
HS Smetana	114
HS Tosca	114
HS Wagner	114
Hudson Leader	182
Huelva Spirit	256
Hugli Spirit	256
Hugo N	58
Hugo Schulte	236
Hugo Selmer	274
Humber Bridge	130
Humboldt Bay	239
Humen Bridge	130
Hurst Point	101
Hyperion Leader	182
Hyundai 2527	94
Hyundai 2528	94
Hyundai 2529	94
Hyundai 2539	94
Hyundai Advance	83
Hyundai Ambition	83
Hyundai Antwerp	221
Hyundai Aquapia	122
Hyundai Atlas	122
Hyundai Bangkok	122
Hyundai Brave	122
Hyundai Bridge	83
Hyundai Busan	281
Hyundai Colombo	122
Hyundai Commodore	83
Hyundai Concord	122
Hyundai Confidence	122
Hyundai Cosmopia	122
Hyundai Courage	122
Hyundai Discovery	281
Hyundai Dubai	221
Hyundai Dynasty	122
Hyundai Ecopia	122
Hyundai Faith	122
Hyundai Federal	83
Hyundai Force	123
Hyundai Forward	123
Hyundai Freedom	123
Hyundai Future	83
Hyundai General	123
Hyundai Global	281
Hyundai Glory	123
Hyundai Goodwill	123
Hyundai Grace	123
Hyundai Greenpia	123
Hyundai Harmony	70
Hyundai Highness	123
Hyundai Highway	83
Hyundai Hongkong	281
Hyundai Incheon	230
Hyundai Independence	281
Hyundai Integral	123
Hyundai Jakarta	123
Hyundai Liberty	281
Hyundai Long Beach	281
Hyundai Loyalty	281
Hyundai Masan	221
Hyundai Mercury	281
Hyundai New York	281
Hyundai No.103	124
Hyundai No.106	281
Hyundai No.107	281
Hyundai No.109	281
Hyundai Oakland	281
Hyundai Oceanpia	123
Hyundai Olympia	123
Hyundai Paramount	123
Hyundai Pioneer	123
Hyundai Platinum	123
Hyundai Power	123
Hyundai Premium	123
Hyundai Prestige	123
Hyundai Privilege	123
Hyundai Progress	83
Hyundai Prosperity	123
Hyundai Seoul	230
Hyundai Shanghai	281
Hyundai Singapore	281
Hyundai Smart	83
Hyundai Speed	83
Hyundai Spirit	123
Hyundai Splendor	281
Hyundai Sprinter	83
Hyundai Stride	83
Hyundai Success	123
Hyundai Sun	123
Hyundai Supreme	123
Hyundai Tacoma	281
Hyundai Talent	123
Hyundai Technopia	123
Hyundai Tenacity	83
Hyundai Tianjin	194
Hyundai Together	83
Hyundai Tokyo	281
Hyundai Trust	123
Hyundai Ulsan	221
Hyundai Unity	123
Hyundai Universal	123
Hyundai Utopia	123
Hyundai Vancouver	281
Hyundai Vision	123
Hyundai Vladivostok	83
Hyundai Voyager	123
Ian M.	262
Iberica Knutsen	133
Ibis Arrow	127
Ibis Bulker	138
Ibn Asakir	279
Ibn Sina	194
Ibukisan	161
Ice Base	124
Ice Beam	190
Ice Blade	190
ID Black Sea	42
ID Bulker	42
ID Copenhagen	42
ID Harbour	42
ID Mermaid	42
ID North Sea	42
ID Red Sea	42
ID Tide	42
Idas Bulker	42
Ideal Bulker	42
Idship Bulker	42
Ikebana	277
Ikomasan	161
Ilse Wulff	279
Immanuel Schulte	233
Imola Express	267
Imperius	95
Ina	215
Inca	262
Independence II	272
Independence of the Seas	23
Independence	83
Independent Accord	88
Independent Concept	88
Independent Pursuit	92
Independent Venture	187
Independent Voyager	92
India Express	274
Indiana	277
Indiana Highway	130
Industrial Faith	128
Industrial Fighter	128
Industrial Force	128
Ingwar Selmer	274
Innovator	113
Integrity	272
Inventana	277
Ioanna D.	106
Ioannis Zafirakis	141
Irene SL	94
Irenes Logos	262
Irenes Rainbow	262
Irenes Reliance	262
Irenes Remedy	262
Irfon	281
Irini	97
Iris Ace	159
Iris Glory	253
Irma	215
Iron Baron	95
Iron King	95
Iron Queen	95
Iryda	215
Isa	215
Isabelita	263
Isabella	63
Isadora	215
Isarstern	224
Ise Princess	262
Iskmati Spirit	256
Island Escape	29
Island Princess	15
Island Ranger	95
Island Sky	29
Isodora	145
Isolda	215
Isoldana	277
Isolde	145
Isolde	270
Istra Ace	218
Istrian Express	267
Isuzugawa	130
Itajai Express	120
Ital Contessa	194
Ital Fastosa	221
Ital Festosa	221
Ital Fiducia	221
Ital Florida	99
Ital Fortuna	99
Ital Fulgida	99
Ital Laguna	180
Ital Libera	180
Ital Lirica	180
Ital Lunare	180
Ital Massima	99
Ital Mattina	99
Ital Melodia	99
Ital Milione	99
Ital Moderna	99
Ital Oceano	114
Ital Onesta	115
Ital Onore	115
Ital Ordine	120
Ital Oriente	120
Ital Ottima	120
Ital Unica	99
Ital Universo	99
Ital Usodimare	99
Italian Express	267
Italy Express	117
Ithaki	50
Ivan Papanin	142
Ivar Reefer	185
Iver Exact	267
Iver Example	267
Iver Excel	267
Iver Experience	267
Iver Expert	267
Iver Exporter	267
Iver Express	267
Iver Progress	267
Iver Prosperity	267
Ivory Ace	239
Ivory Arrow	218
Ivory Dawn	185
Ivory Girl	185
IVS Beachwood	138
IVS Ibis	138
IVS Kanda	138
IVS Kawana	138
IVS Kestrel	138
IVS Kingbird	138
IVS Kinglet	138
IVS Kite	138
IVS Kittiwake	138
IVS Knot	138
IVS Kwaito	138
IVS Kwela	138
IVS Magpie	138
IVS Nightjar	138
IVS Orchard	138
IVS Sentosa	138
IVS Shikra	138
Izumo Princess	262
Jacamar Arrow	127
Jacky Rickmers	221
Jacob Schulte	236
Jacques Jacob	125
Jade Arrow	124
Jaeger Arrow	127
Jaguar Max	95
Jakarta Express	238
Jakarta Tower	281
James River Bridge	130
Jamila	224
Jamila	88
Jan Ritscher	261
Jan	224
Jan	88
Jana	175
Janah Star	226
Jandavid S	227
Janice N	58
Janus	145
Japan	255
Jasmine Knutsen	133
Jasper Arrow	218
Jasper S	227
Jawor	215
Jazan	264
Jean LD	142
Jebel Ali	264
Jennifer Rickmers	221
Jenny N	58
Jens Maersk	163
Jepperson Maersk	163
Jervis Bay	46
Jewel of the Seas	23
Jia Xing	68
Jiaolong Spirit	256
Jill Jacob	125
Jin He	65
Jingpo He	65
Jingu	182
Jinsei Maru	182
Jo Acer	198
Jo Betula	198
Jo Ilex	198
Jo Kashi	198
Jo Kiri	198
Jo Pinari	198
Jo Provol	198
Jock Rickmers	221
Johan Rickmers	221
Johann Jacob	125
Johann Schulte	233
Johanna Oldendorff	205
Johannes Maersk	163
Johannes Wulff	279
John Oldendorff	205
John Rickmers	221
John Wulff	279
Jolly	97
Jonni Ritscher	261
Joost Schulte	233
Jorgen Reefer	185
Josephine Maersk	163
Jost	224
Jost	88
JPO Aires	207
JPO Aquarius	207
JPO Cancer	207
JPO Capricornus	207
JPO Delphinus	207
JPO Dorado	207
JPO Gemini	207
JPO Leo	207
JPO Sagittarius	207
JPO Scorpius	207
JPO Tucana	207
JPO Vela	207
JPO Virgo	207
JPO Volans	207
JPO Vulpecula	207
Juergen Schulte	233
Juist Trader	53
Jula S	227
Julia N	58
Julia Schulte	236
Julian	46
Juliana	224
Juliana	88
Julie Delmas	75
Julius S	227
Julius Schulte	236
Jumbo Javelin	129
Jumbo Jubilee	129
Jümme Trader	53
Juno	215
Jupiter	145
Jupiter Leader	182
Jupiter Spirit	186
Jurkalne	136
Jurmo	180
Kaethe C. Rickmers	222
Kahla	175
Kaijin	182
Kaimon II	161
Kalamata	84
Kaliope	215
Kaltene	136
Kaluga	246
Kamari	61
Kaminesan	161
Kanata Spirit	256
Kandava	136
Kandilousa	93
Kanpur	230
Kapitan Danilkin	142
Kapitan Gotskiy	243
Kapitan Sviridov	142
Kara Sea	243
Kara Sea	284
Kareela Spirit	256
Karekare	61
Karen Knutsen	133
Karen Maersk	163
Karin S	227
Karin Schulte	233
Karine Bulker	138
Karmen	79
Karoline N	58
Karpaty	215
Kasagisan	161
Kashima Bay	239
Kashimasan	161
Kaspar Schulte	233
Kassel	182
Kastos	93
Kaszuby	215
Kate Maersk	163
Katharina S	227

Name	Pg	Name	Pg	Name	Pg	Name	Pg	Name	Pg
Maersk Drummond	214	Maersk Kure	80	Maersk Semarang	201	Maran Penelope	37	Mark C	61
Maersk Drury	214	Maersk Kushiro	172	Maersk Sembawang	172	Maran Plato	37	Mark Twain	228
Maersk Dryden	214	Maersk Kwangyang	172	Maersk Senang	172	Maran Poseidon	37	Marselisborg	85
Maersk Dubrovnik	214	Maersk Kyrenia	167	Maersk Sentosa	172	Maran Pythia	37	Marsgracht	247
Maersk Dunbar	207	Maersk La Paz	164	Maersk Seoul	47	Maran Sagitta	37	Marstal Maersk	165
Maersk Duncan	207	Maersk Laberinto	164	Maersk Serangoon	172	Maran Taurus	37	Martha Schulte	236
Maersk Dunedin	201	Maersk Laberinto	167	Maersk Seville	47	Marathonas	84	Martorell	159
Maersk Edgar	164	Maersk Labrea	167	Maersk Sheerness	47	Marbella	60	Marvellous	34
Maersk Edinburgh	223	Maersk Laguna	164	Maersk Simone	171	MarCajama	143	Marvelous Ace	159
Maersk Edison	281	Maersk Lamanai	167	Maersk Singapore	47	MarCarolina	143	Mary Maersk	165
Maersk Edmonton	223	Maersk Lanco	167	Maersk Sofia	47	Marchen Maersk	165	Mary Schulte	234
Maersk Edward	170	Maersk Lavras	167	Maersk Stepnica	164	MarCherokee	144	Mary	255
Maersk Eindhoven	223	Maersk Lebu	164	Maersk Stockholm	172	MarChicora	144	Master	217
Maersk Elba	223	Maersk Leon	172	Maersk Stralsund	47	Marco Polo	17	Mastera	180
Maersk Eli	171	Maersk Leticia	164	Maersk Surabaya	201	MarColorado	144	Matala	61
Maersk Elizabeth	170	Maersk Lima	164	Maersk Sydney	47	MarComanche	144	Mataquito	88
Maersk Ellen	170	Maersk Lins	167	Maersk Taikung	172	Mare Action	134	Matar Star	226
Maersk Elliot	170	Maersk Lirquen	164	Maersk Tangier	255	Mare Ambassador	134	Mathilde Maersk	165
Maersk Emden	223	Maersk Londrina	167	Maersk Tanjong	172	Mare Arcticum	116	Mattea	263
Maersk Erin	164	Maersk Lota	172	Maersk Tarragona	255	Mare Atlantic	134	Matterhorn Spirit	256
Maersk Essen	223	Maersk Luz	164	Maersk Taurus	172	Mare Atlanticum	116	Matthew	122
Maersk Essex	223	Maersk Madrid	86	Maersk Texas	169	Mare Baltic	134	Matz Maersk	165
Maersk Etienne	170	Maersk Malacca	86	Maersk Torino	255	Mare Britannicum	116	Maule	39
Maersk Eubank	281	Maersk Marmara	171	Maersk Trapani	255	Mare Caribbean	134	Maullin	88
Maersk Evora	223	Maersk Marmara	172	Maersk Tukang	172	Mare Caribicum	116	Mauranger	276
Maersk Gairloch	167	Maersk Mc-Minlay Moller	164	Maersk Utah	169	Mare Doricum	116	Max Jacob	125
Maersk Garonne	164	Maersk Mediterranean	171	Maersk Vallvik	172	Mare Lycium	116	Max Schulte	234
Maersk Gateshead	167	Maersk Merlion	86	Maersk Value	172	Mare Pacific	134	Maximilian Schulte	236
Maersk Georgia	169	Maersk Miami	47	Maersk Varna	172	Mare Phoenicium	116	Maximus	95
Maersk Gironde	164	Maersk Michigan	169	Maersk Venture	172	Mare Superum	116	Maya	263
Maersk Global	178	Maersk Missouri	169	Maersk Vilnius	172	Mare Tracer	134	Mayssan	264
Maersk Glory	178	Maersk Montana	169	Maersk Virginia	169	Mare Trader	134	Mayview Maersk	165
Maersk Grace	178	Maersk Nairobi	97	Maersk Virtue	172	Mare Transporter	134	Mazowsze	216
Maersk Hakone	171	Maersk Nautica	171	Maersk Visby	172	Mare Traveller	134	Mazury	216
Maersk Harmony	178	Maersk Nautilus	171	Maersk Visual	172	Maren Bulker	138	MCC Benoa	54
Maersk Hayama	171	Maersk Navarin	171	Maersk Wave	121	Maren Maersk	165	MCC Maura	54
Maersk Heiwa	171	Maersk Nectar	171	Maersk Wisconsin	169	Maren S	227	MCC Melaka	234
Maersk Heritage	178	Maersk Needham	233	Maersk Wolgast	70	Marfret Guyane	144	MCC Shanghai	174
Maersk Hirado	171	Maersk Neptune	171	Maersk Wyoming	169	Marfret Marajo	144	MCT Alioth	115
Maersk Honour	178	Maersk Neustadt	236	Maganari	60	Marfret Sormiou	144	MCT Almak	115
Maersk Humber	178	Maersk Newport	119	Magelby Maersk	164	Margarete Schulte	234	MCT Altair	115
Maersk Humber	178	Maersk Newport	164	Magellan Spirit	258	Margot N	58	MCT Arcturus	115
Maersk Idaho	169	Maersk Newton	171	Magic Striker	95	Margrethe Maersk	165	MCT Breithorn	115
Maersk Illinois	169	Maersk Noble	171	Magnavia	85	Margrit Rickmers	223	MCT Matterhorn	115
Maersk Ilma	171	Maersk Nordenham	119	Magny Cours Express	267	Marguerite Ace	159	MCT Monte Rosa	115
Maersk Ingrid	171	Maersk Norfolk	168	Mahanadi Spirit	256	Maria A. Angelicoussi	34	MCT Rhine	115
Maersk Innoshima	167	Maersk Norwich	233	Main Trader	54	Maria A. Angelicoussis	37	MCT Stockhorn	115
Maersk Inverness	168	Maersk Nottingham	47	Maira	255	Maria Katharina S	227	Meandros	141
Maersk Iowa	169	Maersk Noumea	97	Majestic	139	Maria Oldendorff	205	Med	205
Maersk Isabella	171	Maersk Nucleus	171	Majesty of the Seas	23	Maria Princess	263	Medcoral	54
Maersk Izmir	168	Maersk Ohio	169	Majorca	60	Maria	106	Medea	270
Maersk Jakobstad	196	Maersk Palermo	172	Makronissos	93	Maria	78	Medfrisia	54
Maersk Jambi	196	Maersk Patras	172	Maliakos	86	Mariana	277	Medi Baltimore	82
Maersk Jefferson	196	Maersk Pearl	171	Malik al Ashtar	264	Marianne Kirk	139	Medi Bangkok	82
Maersk Jena	196	Maersk Peary	169	Malindi	59	Marianne Schulte	234	Medi Cagliari	82
Maersk Jenaz	254	Maersk Pelican	172	Malleco	88	Marib Spirit	258	Medi Chennai	82
Maersk Jennings	196	Maersk Pembroke	172	Malyovitza	177	Maribella	62	Medi Hong Kong	82
Maersk Juan	254	Maersk Penang	172	Mamitsa	255	Maribo Maersk	165	Medi Lausanne	82
Maersk Kalamata	79	Maersk Penguin	171	Mamry	216	Marichristina	62	Medi Lisbon	82
Maersk Kalea	171	Maersk Petrel	171	Manasota	60	Marie	223	Medi Nagasaki	82
Maersk Kalmar	164	Maersk Phoenix	171	Mandarin Arrow	127	Marie Delmas	75	Medi Segesta	82
Maersk Kampala	164	Maersk Phuket	172	Manhattan	196	Marie Schulte	236	Medi Sentosa	82
Maersk Karachi	167	Maersk Piper	171	Manhattan Bridge	131	Marielle Bolten	50	Medi Shanghai	82
Maersk Karlskrona	92	Maersk Prime	171	Manila Express	238	Marie-Paule	106	Medi Taipei	284
Maersk Katalin	171	Maersk Princess	171	Manolis P.	97	Marietta	50	Medi Tokyo	82
Maersk Katarina	171	Maersk Privilege	171	Manon	270	Marietta	62	Medi Valencia	82
Maersk Kawasaki	79	Maersk Producer	171	Manousos	263	Marijeannie	62	Medi Venezia	82
Maersk Kaya	171	Maersk Progress	171	Manuela	279	Mariloula	62	Medi Vitoria	82
Maersk Kelso	168	Maersk Promise	171	Maple Ace II	159	Marin Maersk	165	Mediterranean Highway	131
Maersk Kendal	168	Maersk Prosper	171	Maple Grove	101	Marina	80	Mediterranean ID	42
Maersk Kensington	168	Maersk Rapier	168	Maple Hill	101	Marina Ace	159	Medontario	54
Maersk Kentucky	169	Maersk Rhode Island	169	Mapocho	78	Marina	21	Medpearl	54
Maersk Kiel	167	Maersk Ronneby	167	Maran Altair	36	Marine Bulker	42	Megalonissos	93
Maersk Kiera	171	Maersk Rosyth	164	Maran Atlas	36	Marine Phoenix	239	MegaStar Aries	27
Maersk Kimi	168	Maersk Saigon	47	Maran Callisto	36	Marine Reliance	70	MegaStar Taurus	27
Maersk Kingston	80	Maersk Salalah	164	Maran Canopus	36	Marine Rickmers	223	Mein Schiff 1	27
Maersk Kinloss	168	Maersk Salina	172	Maran Capella	36	Mariner of the Seas	23	Mein Schiff 2	27
Maersk Kithira	168	Maersk Sana	47	Maran Capricorn	36	Marinicki	62	Mein Schiff 3	27
Maersk Klaipeda	167	Maersk Sandra	171	Maran Carina	36	Marinos	97	Mein Schiff 4	27
Maersk Kleven	92	Maersk Santana	47	Maran Cassiopeia	36	Mariperla	62	Mekaines	242
Maersk Kobe	80	Maersk Sara	171	Maran Castor	36	Marit Maersk	165	Mekong Star	224
Maersk Kokura	80	Maersk Sarnia	47	Maran Centaurus	36	Maritime Fidelity	138	Melbourne Strait	219
Maersk Kolkata	80	Maersk Savannah	164	Maran Corona	36	Maritime Jewel	284	Melina	255
Maersk Kotka	92	Maersk Sebarok	172	Maran Cygnus	37	Marivia	85	Mell Selarang	82
Maersk Kowloon	171	Maersk Seletar	172	Maran Gas Coronis	37	Marivictoria	62	Mell Sentosa	110
Maersk Kuantan	171	Maersk Semakau	172	Maran Lyra	37	Marjan	175	Mell Seringat	227

Name	Pg	Name	Pg	Name	Pg	Name	Pg	Name	Pg
Mell Solomon	279	Mineral Honshu	76	MOL Efficiency	159	Morning Caroline	272	MSC Anna	145
Mell Springwood	227	Mineral Hope	76	MOL Emerald	238	Morning Catherine	272	MSC Annamaria	145
Mell Stamford	115	Mineral Kyoto	76	MOL Eminence	238	Morning Cecilie	272	MSC Annick	145
Melody	19	Mineral Kyushu	77	MOL Emissary	238	Morning Cedar	272	MSC Ans	145
Mendocino	60	Mineral Manila	77	MOL Empire	238	Morning Celesta	272	*MSC Antalya*	234
Mentor	217	Mineral New York	77	MOL Encore	159	Morning Celine	272	MSC Antares	45
Mercosul Manaus	172	Mineral Ningbo	77	MOL Endeavor	159	Morning Cello	272	*MSC Antigua*	234
Mercosul Santos	172	Mineral Nippon	77	MOL Endowment	159	Morning Champion	218	MSC Antonia	145
Mercosul Suape	172	Mineral Noble	77	MOL Endurance	159	Morning Charlotte	272	MSC Antwerp	80
Mercury Ace	159	Mineral Oak	77	MOL Enterprise	159	Morning Chorus	270	*MSC Arbatax*	234
Mercury Glory	215	Mineral Shikoku	77	MOL Excellence	159	Morning Christina	272	MSC Ariane	145
Mercury Leader	182	Mineral Sines	77	MOL Expeditor	159	Morning Claire	272	MSC Arica	234
Merian	46	Mineral Stonehenge	77	MOL Experience	159	Morning Classic	218	MSC Armonia	20
Meridian Ace	159	Mineral Subic	77	MOL Explorer	159	Morning Cloud	281	MSC Asli	145
Meridian Lion	230	Mineral Tianjin	77	MOL Express	159	Morning Composer	272	MSC Astrid	145
Meridian Spirit	258	Mineral Water	77	MOL Garland	88	Morning Concert	271	MSC Asya	145
Merkur Bay	266	Minerva	9	MOL Gateway	88	Morning Conductor	272	MSC Athens	80
Merkur Beach	266	Minerva Alexandra	153	MOL Generosity	88	Morning Cornelia	272	MSC Athos	80
Merkur Bridge	266	Minerva Alice	153	MOL Genesis	88	Morning Cornet	272	MSC Atlantic	146
Merkur Cloud	267	Minerva Anna	153	MOL Glide	234	Morning Courier	218	MSC Augusta	146
Merkur Fjord	267	Minerva Antonia	153	MOL Globe	234	Morning Crown	218	MSC Aurora	146
Merkur O.	206	Minerva Astra	153	MOL Grandeur	234	Morning Crystal	272	MSC Ayala	146
Merkur Ocean	267	Minerva Clara	153	MOL Gratitude	234	Morning Lady	273	MSC Banu	146
Merkur Star	267	Minerva Concert	153	MOL Growth	234	Morning Laura	273	MSC Barbara	146
Merkur Tide	267	Minerva Doxa	154	MOL Guardian	89	Morning Lena	273	MSC Barcelona	201
Merlin Arrow	127	Minerva Eleonora	154	MOL Inca	234	Morning Lily	273	MSC Bari	201
Mermaid Ace	159	Minerva Ellie	154	MOL Integrity	160	Morning Linda	273	MSC Beatrice	146
Merwedegracht	247	Minerva Emma	154	MOL Loire	160	Morning Lisa	273	MSC Beijing	201
Mesaimeer	242	Minerva Georgia	154	MOL Maestro	160	Morning Lucy	273	MSC Benedetta	45
Messini	80	Minerva Gloria	154	MOL Magnificence	160	Morning Lynn	273	MSC Beryl	180
Messologi	84	Minerva Grace	154	MOL Majesty	160	Morning Margareta	273	MSC Bettina	146
Meta	214	Minerva Helen	154	MOL Maneuver	160	Morning Marvel	273	MSC Bilbao	92
Methane Alison Victoria	103	Minerva Iris	154	MOL Marvel	160	Morning Melody	273	MSC Bremen	206
Methane Becki Anne	103	Minerva Joanna	154	MOL Matrix	160	Morning Menad	273	MSC Brianna	146
Methane Heather Sally	103	Minerva Julie	154	MOL Maxim	160	Morning Mercator	121	MSC Brindisi	115
Methane Jane Elizabeth	103	Minerva Libra	154	MOL Mission	160	Morning Midas	282	MSC Bruxelles	201
Methane Julia Louise	103	Minerva Lisa	154	MOL Modern	160	Morning Miracle	282	MSC Busan	201
Methane Kari Elin	103	Minerva Marina	154	MOL Motivator	160	Morning Ninni	273	MSC Cadiz	201
Methane Lydon Volney	103	Minerva Maya	154	MOL Pace	234	Morning Spruce	273	MSC Caitlin	146
Methane Mickie Harper	103	Minerva Nike	154	MOL Paradise	160	Moscow	246	MSC Camille	146
Methane Nile Eagle	103	Minerva Nounou	154	MOL Paramount	160	Moscow Kremlin	246	MSC Canberra	146
Methane Patricia Camila	103	Minerva Rita	154	MOL Partner	160	Moscow River	246	MSC Candice	146
Methane Princess	103	Minerva Roxanne	154	MOL Performance	160	Moscow Sea	243	MSC Capella	146
Methane Rita Andrea	103	Minerva Sophia	154	MOL Precision	160	Moscow Stars	246	MSC Caracas	208
Methane Shirley Elisabeth	103	Minerva Symphony	154	MOL Premium	160	Moscow University	246	MSC Carla	146
Methane Spirit	258	Minerva Vaso	154	MOL Priority	160	Mosel Ace	160	MSC Carmen	146
Methania	100	Minerva Vera	155	MOL Proficiency	234	Mosel Trader	54	MSC Carole	238
Mette Maersk	165	Minerva Virgo	155	MOL Progress	160	Mosel	206	MSC Carolina	146
Mexican Bay	240	Minerva Xanthe	155	MOL Promise	160	Moskovsky Prospect	243	MSC Carouge	194
Meynell	281	Minerva Zen	155	MOL Solution	160	Mount Adamello	231	MSC Catania	282
MG Shipping	182	Minerva Zenia	155	MOL Spring	205	Mount Everest	231	MSC Challenger	80
Mia-S	227	Minerva Zoe	155	MOL Symphony	145	Mount Green	231	MSC Charleston	201
Michaela S	227	Minerva	145	MOL Tyne	160	Mount Hope	232	MSC Chiara	146
Michigan Highway	131	Minervagracht	247	MOL Winter	205	Mount Hope	232	MSC Chicago	201
Michigan Trader	54	Minna	88	MOL Wisdom	234	Mount Karava	232	MSC Claudia	146
Miden Max	95	Miraculous Ace	159	Moldanger	276	Mount Kibo	232	MSC Clementina	146
Midjur	177	Miramarin	59	Molengracht	247	Mount McKinney	232	MSC Clorinda	146
Midnatsol	18	Mire	173	Moleson	254	Mount Rainier	232	MSC Colombia	282
Miedwie	216	Mississauga Express	117	Mona Century	160	Mount Robson	232	MSC Cordoba	195
Mighty Servant 1	86	Mitrope	216	Mona Liberty	160	Mount Victoria	232	MSC Coruna	201
Mighty Servant 3	86	Mizar	286	Mona Linden	160	Mozah	242	MSC Cristiana	146
Mignon	270	Mobilana	277	Monarch of the Seas	23	Mozambique	282	MSC Cristina	45
Mikhail Kutuzov	142	Modern Express	70	Monemvasia	155	Mozu Arrow	127	MSC Daniela	146
Mikhail Strekalovskiy	142	Modern Link	70	Monica P.	97	MS Simon	63	MSC Danit	146
Mikhail Ulyanov	243	Modern Peak	70	Moniuszko	68	MS Sophie	63	MSC Davos	89
Milagro	59	MOL Advantage	159	Monte Aconcagua	199	MSC Accra	107	MSC Deila	146
Milaha Qatar	217	MOL Amazonia	88	Monte Alegre	199	MSC Ada	107	MSC Deila	201
Milaha Ras Laffan	217	MOL Bravery	159	Monte Azul	199	MSC Adele	145	MSC Denisse	146
Milan Express	117	MOL Caledon	201	Monte Cervantes	199	MSC Adriana	145	MSC Didem	146
Milau Bulker	138	MOL Celebration	159	Monte Olivia	199	MSC Adriatic	45	MSC Diego	146
Millennium	263	MOL Charisma	159	Monte Pascoal	199	*MSC Agadir*	234	MSC Divina	20
Millennium Park	281	MOL Comfort	159	Monte Rosa	199	MSC Agata	145	MSC Don Giovanni	146
Milos	106	MOL Competence	159	Monte Sarmiento	199	MSC Alabama	145	MSC Donata	146
Mimi Selmer	275	MOL Continuity	159	Monte Tamaro	199	MSC Albany	280	MSC Edith	146
Min He	65	MOL Cosmos	159	Monte Verde	199	MSC Alessia	194	MSC Ela	146
Mindanao	102	MOL Courage	159	Montecristo	60	MSC Alexa	145	MSC Elena	146
Mindoro	61	MOL Creation	159	Montego	61	MSC Alexandra	145	MSC Eleni	146
Mineral Antwerpen	76	MOL Cullinan	201	Monterey	61	*MSC Algeciras*	234	MSC Eleonora	146
Mineral Beijing	76	MOL Dawn	274	Montevideo Express	45	MSC Alicante	201	MSC Eloise	146
Mineral Belgium	76	MOL Daylight	274	Montreal Express	117	MSC Altair	45	MSC Emanuela	146
Mineral China	76	MOL Dedication	223	Monza Express	268	MSC Altamira	280	MSC Emma	39
Mineral Dalian	76	MOL Delight	223	Morning Calm	218	MSC Alyssa	145	MSC England	206
Mineral Dragon	76	MOL Destiny	223	Morning Camilla	272	MSC America	145	MSC Erminia	146
Mineral Faith	76	MOL Devotion	223	Morning Cara	272	MSC Anafi	107	MSC Esthi	146
Mineral Haiku	76	MOL Dominance	223	Morning Carina	272	MSC Angela	145	MSC Eugenia	146
Mineral Hokkaido	76	MOL Earnest	159	Morning Carol	272	MSC Aniello	145	MSC Eva	146

Name	Pg
Nord Houston	188
Nord Hummock	190
Nord Imagination	190
Nord Independence	190
Nord Innovation	190
Nord Inspiration	190
Nord Integrity	190
Nord Intelligence	190
Nord London	188
Nord Maru	188
Nord Melbourne	188
Nord Mermaid	190
Nord Montreal	189
Nord Mumbai	189
Nord Neptune	189
Nord Nightingale	190
Nord Observer	190
Nord Obtainer	190
Nord Optimiser	190
Nord Organiser	191
Nord Peak	189
Nord Pisces	189
Nord Power	189
Nord Princess	191
Nord Pyxis	189
Nord Rotterdam	189
Nord Sakura	191
Nord Seoul	189
Nord Shanghai	189
Nord Snow Queen	191
Nord Swan	191
Nord Thumbelina	191
Nord Treasure	189
Nord Vancouver	189
Nordamerika	124
Nordbay	206
Nordby Maersk	166
Nord-Energy	188
Norderoog	52
Nordic Ace	218
Nordic Apollo	189
Nordic Aurora	189
Nordic Barents	42
Nordic Bothnia	42
Nordic Brasilia	258
Nordic Breeze	189
Nordic Cosmos	189
Nordic Discovery	189
Nordic Fighter	189
Nordic Freedom	189
Nordic Gas	234
Nordic Grace	189
Nordic Harrier	189
Nordic Hawk	189
Nordic Hunter	189
Nordic Jupiter	189
Nordic Mistral	189
Nordic Moon	189
Nordic Passat	189
Nordic Rio	256
Nordic Saturn	189
Nordic Spirit	258
Nordic Sprite	189
Nordic Vega	189
Nordic Voyager	189
Nordic Zenith	189
Nordkap	189
Nordkapp	18
Nordlake	206
Nordlys	18
Nordmark	206
Nordnorge	18
Nordpol	189
Nordrose	206
Nordstjernen	18
Nordstrength	206
Nordtramp	189
Norfolk Express	118
Norient Saturn	191
Norient Scorpius	191
Norient Solar	191
Norient Star	191
Norman Lady	122
Normannia	38
North Sea	280
North Sea	284
North Star	139
Northern Debonair	187
Northern Delight	195
Northern Democrat	228
Northern Democrat	187
Northern Democrat	187
Northern Diplomat	187
Northern Diversity	187
Northern Divinity	187
Northern Endeavour	187
Northern Endurance	187
Northern Enterprise	187
Northern Happiness	195
Northern Jaguar	187
Northern Jamboree	187
Northern Jasper	187
Northern Javelin	187
Northern Jubilee	187
Northern Pioneer	195
Northern Power	187
Northern Practise	188
Northern Precision	188
Northern Prelude	188
Northern Promotion	188
Northern Spirit	124
Northern Valence	188
Northern Valour	228
Northern Victory	228
Northern Vigour	188
Northern Vivacity	188
Northern Volition	188
Northia	242
Northumberland	282
Northwest Sanderling	242
Northwest Sandpiper	242
Northwest Seaeagle	242
Northwest Shearwater	242
Northwest Snipe	242
Northwest Stormpetrel	242
Northwest Swan	64
Norwegian Breakaway	27
Norwegian Dawn	27
Norwegian Epic	27
Norwegian Gem	27
Norwegian Getaway	27
Norwegian Jade	27
Norwegian Jewel	27
Norwegian Pearl	27
Norwegian Sky	27
Norwegian Spirit	27
Norwegian Star	27
Norwegian Sun	27
Norwid	68
Novaya Zemlya	142
Novia	85
Novorossiysk Star	284
NS Africa	246
NS Antarctic	246
NS Arctic	246
NS Asia	246
NS Bora	246
NS Bravo	246
NS Burgas	246
NS Captain	246
NS Century	246
NS Challenger	246
NS Champion	246
NS Clipper	246
NS Columbus	246
NS Commander	246
NS Concept	246
NS Concord	246
NS Consul	246
NS Corona	246
NS Creation	246
NS Energy	246
NS Lagun	246
NS Leader	246
NS Lion	246
NS Parade	246
NS Point	246
NS Power	246
NS Pride	246
NS Silver	246
NS Spirit	246
NS Stella	247
NS Stream	247
NS Yakutia	247
NS Lotus	246
NSS Bonanza	234
NSS Fortune	234
Ntabeni	95
Nuuk Maersk	166
NYK Adonis	182
NYK Altair	182
NYK Andromeda	182
NYK Antares	182
NYK Aphrodite	183
NYK Apollo	183
NYK Aquarius	183
NYK Argus	183
NYK Artemis	183
NYK Athena	183
NYK Atlas	183
NYK Canopus	183
NYK Castor	183
NYK Clara	183
NYK Cosmos	207
NYK Daedalus	183
NYK Daniella	183
NYK Delphinus	183
NYK Demeter	183
NYK Deneb	183
NYK Diana	183
NYK Floresta	236
NYK Galaxy	195
NYK Helios	208
NYK Hermes	208
NYK Hyperion	208
NYK Kai	282
NYK Leo	183
NYK Libra	183
NYK Loadstar	183
NYK Lynx	183
NYK Lyra	183
NYK Lyttelton	188
NYK Oceanus	183
NYK Olympus	183
NYK Orion	183
NYK Orpheus	183
NYK Pegasus	183
NYK Phoenix	183
NYK Remus	183
NYK Rigel	183
NYK Romulus	183
NYK Rosa	183
NYK Rumina	183
NYK Sirius	183
NYK Terra	183
NYK Themis	183
NYK Theseus	183
NYK Triton	183
NYK Vega	183
NYK Venus	183
NYK Veronica	183
NYK Vesta	183
NYK Virgo	183
Nyon	254
Nysted Maersk	166
Oakland Express	80
Oasis of the Seas	23
Obelix Bulker	42
Oberon	270
Ocean Breeze	101
Ocean Ceres	183
Ocean Challenger	250
Ocean Countess	17
Ocean Crystal	60
Ocean Cygnus	183
Ocean Diamond	28
Ocean Dignity	41
Ocean Emerald	219
Ocean Highway	131
Ocean Hope	205
Ocean Majesty	19
Ocean Mermaid	219
Ocean Preface	141
Ocean Prefect	141
Ocean Prelate	141
Ocean President	141
Ocean Princess	15
Ocean Probe	141
Ocean Producer	141
Ocean Prologue	141
Ocean Promise	141
Ocean Protector	141
Ocean Quest	41
Ocean Spirit	41
Ocean Trader	205
Ocean Trader I	54
Oceana	13
Oceanis	62
Octavia	85
Odessa Star	284
Odin	58
Ogna	173
OIG Giant	119
OIG Giant II	119
Okhotsk Sea	243
Okhta Bridge	243
Okiana	277
Oksywie	216
Oland	93
Olga Maersk	166
Oliver Jacob	125
Olivia Maersk	166
Olivia	145
Olivia	85
Oluf Maersk	166
Olympia	145
Olympia	78
Olympian Highway	131
Olympic Faith	208
Olympic Flag	208
Olympic Flair	208
Olympic Future	208
Olympic Hawk	208
Olympic Legacy	208
Olympic Legend	208
Olympic Liberty	208
Olympic Serenity	208
Olympic Spirit II	208
Olympic Sponsor	208
Olympius	95
Olympiysky Prospect	243
Olza	216
Omaha	59
Omega King	234
Omega Queen	234
Omega Trader	161
Onaiza	242
Ondina	242
Onyx Ace	160
Onyx Arrow	218
OOCL America	208
OOCL Antwerp	208
OOCL Asia	208
OOCL Atlanta	208
OOCL Australia	208
OOCL Bangkok	208
OOCL Beijing	208
OOCL Belgium	208
OOCL Berlin	209
OOCL Brisbane	209
OOCL Britain	209
OOCL Britain	255
OOCL Brussels	209
OOCL Busan	209
OOCL California	209
OOCL Canada	209
OOCL Charleston	209
OOCL Chicago	209
OOCL China	39
OOCL Chongxing	209
OOCL Dalian	209
OOCL Europe	209
OOCL Guangzhou	209
OOCL Hamburg	209
OOCL Hong Kong	39
OOCL Houston	209
OOCL Jakarta	209
OOCL Kaohsiung	209
OOCL Kobe	209
OOCL Kuala Lumpur	209
OOCL Le Havre	209
OOCL London	209
OOCL Long Beach	209
OOCL Luxembourg	209
OOCL Miami	209
OOCL Montreal	209
OOCL Nagoya	209
OOCL Netherlands	255
OOCL New York	209
OOCL New Zealand	209
OOCL Ningbo	209
OOCL Norfolk	209
OOCL Oakland	209
OOCL Panama	209
OOCL Qingdao	209
OOCL Rotterdam	209
OOCL San Francisco	209
OOCL Savannah	209
OOCL Seoul	209
OOCL Shanghai	209
OOCL Shenzhen	209
OOCL Southampton	209
OOCL Texas	209
OOCL Tianjin	209
OOCL Tokyo	209
OOCL Washington	209
OOCL Yokohama	209
OOCL Zhoushan	210
Oosterdam	12
Opal Ace	160
Opal Leader	183
Optimana	277
Orange Blossom	40
Orange Sky	40
Orange Star	40
Orange Stars	250
Orange Sun	40
Orange Wave	40
Oranjeborg	269
Orawa	216
Orchard Bulker	138
Orchid Ace	160
Ore Fazendao	234
Ore Mutuca	265
Ore Parati	234
Ore Santos	234
Ore Sudbury	36
Ore Tubarao	234
Ore Urucum	234
Ore Vitoria	234
Ore Vitoria	265
Oregon	60
Oregon Highway	131
Oriana	13
Orient Accord	124
Orient Adventure	124
Orient Alliance	124
Orient Approach	124
Orient Cavalier	124
Orient Centaur	124
Orient Champion	124
Orient Crusader	124
Orient Defender	124
Orient Delivery	124
Orient Queen	18
Orient Strength	125
Orient Sun	125
Orient Target	125
Orient Tide	125
Orient Tiger	125
Orient Trader	125
Orient Trail	125
Orient Transit	125
Orient Tribune	125
Oriental Angel	70
Oriental Diamond	123
Oriental Gold	123
Oriental Green	61
Oriental Jade	161
Oriental Ruby	123
Oriental Trader	230
Orinoco Star	224
Orion II	30
Orion Leader	183
Orion Pride	113
Orion Voyager	64
Orion	30
Orion	40
Orla	216
Orleta Lwowskie	216
Ormond	282

Ornak 216
Orsula 101
Ortelius 30
Orthis 242
Osaka Car 282
Osaka Express 118
Osaka Strait 219
Osaka Tower 283
Osakana 277
Oshimana 277
Oslo Trader 54
Osogovo 177
Osprey 49
Osprey 277
Osprey Arrow 127
Osprey 100
Ostende Max 95
Otello 270
Otina 242
Otowasan 161
Ottawa Express 118
Otto Schulte 234
Overseas Acadia 210
Overseas Alcesmar 210
Overseas Alcmar 210
Overseas Ambermar 210
Overseas Anacortes 210
Overseas Andromar 210
Overseas Antigmar 210
Overseas Ariadmar 210
Overseas Atalmar 210
Overseas Athens 210
Overseas Beryl 210
Overseas Boston 210
Overseas Chinook 210
Overseas Eliane 210
Overseas Equatorial 210
Overseas Everest 210
Overseas Everglades 211
Overseas Fran 211
Overseas Goldmar 211
Overseas Houston 211
Overseas Jademar 211
Overseas Josefa Camejo 211
Overseas Kilimanjiro 211
Overseas Kimolos 211
Overseas Kythno 211
Overseas Leyte 211
Overseas Limar 211
Overseas Long Beach 211
Overseas Los Angeles 211
Overseas Luxmar 211
Overseas Luzon 211
Overseas Maremar 211
Overseas Martinez 211
Overseas McKinley 211
Overseas Milos 211
Overseas Mindoro 211
Overseas Mulan 211
Overseas Mykonos 211
Overseas Nedimar 211
Overseas New York 211
Overseas Newcastle 211
Overseas Nikiski 211
Overseas Palawan 211
Overseas Pearlmar 211
Overseas Petromar 211
Overseas Portland 211
Overseas Raphael 211
Overseas Reymar 211
Overseas Rosalyn 211
Overseas Rosemar 211
Overseas Rubymar 211
Overseas Sakura 211
Overseas Samar 211
Overseas Santorini 211
Overseas Serifos 211
Overseas Shirley 211
Overseas Sifnos 211
Overseas Silvermar 211
Overseas Skopelos 211
Overseas Sovereign 212
Overseas Tampa 212
Overseas Tanabe 212
Overseas Texas City 212
Overseas Visayas 212
Overseas Yellowstone 212
Overseas Yosemite 212
Pabal 119
Pabur 119
Pacific Ace 123
Pacific Alliance 161
Pacific Apollo 70
Pacific Beauty 70
Pacific Beryl 284
Pacific Brave 70
Pacific Bulker 138
Pacific Canopus 213
Pacific Capella 213
Pacific Champ 59
Pacific Citrine 284
Pacific Condor 70
Pacific Crystal 70
Pacific Dawn 15
Pacific Diamond 284
Pacific Empire 70
Pacific Fantasy 205
Pacific Fighter 205
Pacific Garnet 284
Pacific Garnet 70
Pacific Glory 160
Pacific Highway 131
Pacific Horizon 234
Pacific ID 42
Pacific Jewel 15
Pacific Jewel 70
Pacific Lapis 284
Pacific Link 195
Pacific Mermaid 240
Pacific Oasis 70
Pacific Onyx 284
Pacific Opal 70
Pacific Partner 162
Pacific Pearl 15
Pacific Polaris 70
Pacific Poppy 70
Pacific Princess 15
Pacific Quartz 284
Pacific Reefer 239
Pacific Royal 59
Pacific Ruby 234
Pacific Sapphire 284
Pacific Success 123
Pacific Topaz 284
Pacific Triangle 256
Pacific Trust 219
Pacific Venus 30
Pacific Zircon 284
Pacific 239
Paciific Jewel 123
Paglia 135
Pago 196
Palena 89
Palma Bulker 138
Palmela 160
Palva 180
Pamir 247
Panamana 277
Pangal 89
Panormos 59
Pantelis 94
Pantelis 97
Panther Max 95
Paola 138
Paradise Ace 160
Paradise N 135
Paramount Halifax 95
Paramount Hamilton 95
Paramount Hanover 95
Paramount Hatteras 95
Paramount Helsinki 95
Paramount Hydra 95
Parana 135
Paranagua Express 199
Parandowski 68
Parapola 155
Paris Express 118
Paris JR 107
Paris Trader 54
Paros 50
Paros Seas 39
Parramatta 59
Parsifal 270
Parsifal 46
Partagas 60
Partici 196
Pascale Knutsen 133
Passama 136
Passat Breeze 231
Passat Spring 231
Passero 136
Patagonia 119
Patani 119
Patara 136
Patara 119
Patea 119
Paterna 119
Patnos 119
Patras 119
Patricia 119
Patricia Schulte 236
Patris 62
Patroclus 37
Paul Gauguin 21
Paul Oldendorff 205
Paul Russ 224
Paula Schulte 236
Pavel Chernysh 243
Pavel Vavilov 142
Paxi 50
Pazific 136
Pearl Ace 160
Pearl Seas 39
Peary Spirit 258
Pegasus Ace 160
Pegasus Highway 131
Pegasus 37
Pelagos 93
Pelicana 277
Pelleas 201
Penda Bulker 138
Penelop 143
Penelope 217
Penguin Arrow 127
Perelik 177
Perla Bulker 138
Persenik 177
Perseus Leader 183
Perseus Trader 162
Perseverence 261
Peruvian Express 268
Peruvian Reefer 185
Pescara 196
Petalidi 61
Petani 59
Peterpaul 125
Petersfield 127
Petkum 52
Petrel Bulker 138
Petroatlantic 258
Petrodvorets 243
Petrohue 89
Petrokrepost 243
Petronordic 258
Petropavlovsk 243
Petrovsk 243
Petrozavodsk 243
Phaethon 37
Philadelphia Express 118
Phoenix Leader 184
Phoenix Vanguard 162
Phoenix Vigor 162
Phoenix Voyager 64
Phyllis N 58
Piavia 85
Pierre LD 142
Piet 261
Pilica 216
Piltene 136
Pinchat 72
Pine Arrow 127
Pink Stars 250
Pinnacle Spirit 257
Pioneer Atlantic 42
Pioneer Pacific 42
Pioneer 36
Pipit Arrow 127
Pirin 177
Piro 136
Pisces Star 226
Pisti 107
Pisti 255
Plana 177
Planet Ace 160
Platinium Ray 218
Pleiades Leader 184
Pleiades Spirit 186
Plover Arrow 127
Pluto Glory 215
Pluto 40
Pochard 119
Podhale 216
Podlasie 216
Poetic 139
Pohang 136
Polar 136
Polar 125
Polar Adventure 79
Polar Discovery 79
Polar Endeavour 79
Polar Enterprise 79
Polar Resolution 79
Polar Spirit (st) 257
Polar Star 18
Polaris Ace 160
Polaris J 128
Polarlight 240
Polarlys 18
Polarsteam 240
Polesie 216
Pollux 40
Polonia 92
Polska Walczaca 216
Polyaigos 93
Pomorye 142
Pomorze 216
Pompano 59
Pona 136
Pontresina 136
Poplar Arrow 127
Porgy 270
Portland Express 118
Porto 136
Portugal 136
Pos Achat 41
Pos Alexandrit 41
Pos Almandin 41
Pos Amazonit 41
Pos Ambition 113
Pos Amethyst 41
Pos Ametrin 41
Pos Aquamarin 41
Pos Aragonit 41
Pos Aventurin 41
Pos Azurit 41
Pos Bravery 113
Pos Challenger 113
Pos Courage 70
Pos Dedicator 113
Pos Dignity 70
Pos Eternity 70
Pos Freedom 70
Pos Glory 70
Pos Harmony 70
Pos Harvester 113
Pos Island 70
Pos Tansanit 41
Pos Topas 41
Pos Tuerkis 41
Pos Turmalin 41
Poseidon Leader 184
Posen 136
Posidana 277
Postojna 89
Poul Spirit 258
Pounda 59
Power D 206
Power Ranger 95
Powhatan 136
Prague Express 118
Praia 197
Precious Ace 160
Precious Seas 39
Premium do Brasil 200
Premnitz 136
President Adams 180
President Jackson 180
President Polk 180
President Truman 180
Prestige Ace 160
Prestige New York 122
Pride of America 27
Primorskiy Prospect 244
Primrose Ace 160
Primus 217
Prince of Seas 240
Prince of Tides 240
Prince of Waves 240
Princes Park 283
Princess Danae 17
Princess Daphne 17
Princess VII 124
Prinsendam 12
Priwall 136
Procyon Leader 184
Progress Ace 161
Progress 253
Prometheus Leader 184
Prominent Ace 161
Promise 253
Promitheas 263
Propontis 263
Prosna 216
Prospect 253
Prosper 80
Prospero 53
Prosperous Seas 39
Proteas 263
Providana 277
Providence 253
Pskov 243
Pu He 66
Puck 216
Pucon 89
Puelche 89
Puelo 89
Puffin Arrow 127
Puffin Bulker 138
Puffin 119
Pugwash 136
Puma Max 95
Purha 180
Purple Beach 143
Pusan 136
Puteri Delima 156
Puteri Delima Satu 156
Puteri Firus Satu 156
Puteri Firus 156
Puteri Intan 156
Puteri Intan Satu 156
Puteri Mutiara Satu 156
Puteri Nilam 156
Puteri Nilam Satu 156
Puteri Zamrud 156
Puteri Zamrud Satu 156
Puze 136
Pyotr Velikiy 142
Pyxis Leader 184
Qing Yun He 66
Qingdao Express 283
Queen Ace 161
Queen Ace 184
Queen Elizabeth 12
Queen Mary 2 12
Queen Sapphire 271
Queen Victoria 12
Queen Zenobia 195
Quest for Adventure 24
Quetzal Arrow 127
Quorn 283
Raba 216
Radiance of the Seas 23
Ramlah 175
Randgrid 79
Rapallo 60
Raraka 60
Ras Maersk 166
Rasgas Asclepius 37
Rasheeda 242
Ravnanger 276

325

Name	Pg	Name	Pg	Name	Pg	Name	Pg	Name	Pg
Tugela	271	Universal Queen	123	Vienna Express	118	*Wan Hai 516*	274	Wladyslaw Orkan	68
Tulane	271	Uraga Princess	263	Vietnam Express	118	*Wan Hai 517*	274	Wolgastern	224
Tulip	206	Uranus	40	Vigdis Knutsen	134	Wan Hai 601	274	Woodgate	283
Turama	31	Ursula Rickmers	224	Vigor SW	138	Wan Hai 602	274	Woodside Donaldson	258
Turandot	270	Uruguay Star	250	Viking Amber	49	Wan Hai 603	274	Woolloomooloo	61
Turid Knutsen	133	Usma	136	Viking Chance	49	Wan Hai 605	274	World Harmony	263
Turmoil	261	Ute Oltmann	208	Viking Constanza	49	Wanhe	66	World Spirit	186
Tver	247	Utopia Ace	161	Viking Coral	49	Warmia	216	Wotan	261
Tverskoy Bridge	245	Utviken	101	Viking Diamond	49	Warnow Dolphin	54	Wren Arrow	127
TW Beijing	90	Utviken	266	Viking Drive	49	Warnow Moon	54	Wugang Asia	283
TW Hamburg	90	Uzava	136	Viking Emerald	49	Warnow Orca	54	Wugang Atlantic	283
TW Jiangsu	90	Vadela	61	Viking Ocean	49	Warnow Porpoise	54	Wugang Caifu	283
TW Manila	90	Valbella	90	Viking Odessa	49	Warnow Sun	54	Wugang Haoyun	283
Two Million Ways	206	Valbella	224	Viking Sea	49	Warnow Vaquita	54	Wugang Orient	283
Tysla	271	Valdivia	90	*Viktor Bakaev*	245	Warnow Whale	54	Wybelsum	52
Tzarevetz	177	Vale Beijing	265	Viktor Titov	245	Warrior	95	Xiang He	66
UACC Al Medina	265	Vale Brasil	265	Viktor Tkachyov	142	Washington Express	118	Xibohe	66
UACC Consensus	265	Vale Carajas	265	Vil Dardanelles	219	Washusan	162	Xin Bei Lun	66
UACC Eagle	265	Vale China	265	Vilamoura	61	Watban	175	Xin Beijing	66
UACC Falcon	265	Vale Dalian	265	Ville d'Aquarius	75	Water Phoenix	241	Xin Chang Sha	66
UACC Harmony	265	Vale Dongjiakou	265	Ville d'Orion	75	Waterford	283	Xin Chang Shu	66
UACC Ibn Al Atheer	264	Vale Espirito Santo	265	Vincent Thomas Bridge	132	Weaver Arrow	127	Xin Chi Wan	66
UACC Ibn Al Haitham	264	Vale Hebei	265	Vine	283	Wehr Alster	275	Xin Chong Qing	66
UACC Ibn Sina	265	Vale Indonesia	265	Vinland	263	Wehr Altona	275	Xin Da Lian	66
UACC Mansouria	265	Vale Italia	265	Vinni	192	Wehr Bille	275	Xin Da Yang Zhou	66
UACC Marah	265	*Vale Jiangsu*	265	Violet Ace	219	Wehr Blankensee	275	Xin Dan Dong	67
UACC Marwan	265	Vale Liwa	265	Violetta	90	Wehr Elbe	275	Xin Fang Cheng	67
UACC Masafi	265	Vale Malaysia	265	Vipava	90	Wehr Flottbek	275	Xin Fei Zhou	67
UACC Messila	265	Vale Minas Gerais	265	Virginia	197	Wehr Havel	275	Xin Fu Zhou	67
UACC Muharraq	265	Vale Qingdao	265	Virginia Bridge	132	Wehr Koblenz	275	Xin Hai Kou	67
UACC Shams	265	Vale Rio de Janiero	265	Virgo Leader	184	Wehr Müden	275	Xin Hang Zhou	67
UACC Sila	265	Vale Saham	265	Virgo Star	227	Wehr Oste	275	Xin Hong Kong	67
UACC Sound	265	Vale Shandong	265	Virtuous Striker	95	Wehr Ottensen	276	Xin Huang Pu	67
UACC Strait	265	Vale Shinas	265	Vision of the Seas	23	Wehr Rissen	276	Xin Jin Zhou	67
UAFL Zanzibar	96	Vale Sohar	265	Vitality	86	Wehr Trave	276	Xin Lan Zhou	67
UASC Ajman	208	Valencia Bridge	132	Vitosha	177	Wehr Warnow	276	Xin Lian Yun Gang	67
UASC Doha	236	Valencia Express	118	Vivace	132	Wehr Weser	276	Xin Los Angeles	67
UASC Jeddah	204	Valencia Knutsen	133	Vladimir Tikhonov	245	Weichselstern	224	Xin Mei Zhou	67
UASC Jubail	236	Valentina	90	Vliet Trader	54	Weissshorn	214	Xin Nan Sha	67
UASC Khor Fakkan	204	Valerie Schulte	236	Voge Challenger	267	Welle	206	Xin Nan Tong	67
UASC Ramadi	204	Valiant Ace	161	Voge Dignity	267	Wellington Express	118	Xin Ning Bo	67
UASC Samarra	236	Vancouver Bridge	132	Voge Enterprise	267	Wellington Star	250	Xin Ou Zhou	67
UASC Shuaiba	204	Vancouver Express	204	Voge Eva	267	Wellington Strait	219	Xin Pu Dong	67
UASC Shuwaikh	92	Vany Rickmers	224	Voge Felix	267	Weser Stahl	235	Xin Qin Huang Dao	67
UASC Sitrah	90	Varamo	258	Voge Master	267	Weser	206	Xin Qin Zhou	67
UBC Laguna	120	Varzuga	142	Voge Paul	267	Westerbrook	219	Xin Qing Dao	67
UBC Lemessos	120	Vasily Dinkov	245	Voge Prestige	267	Westerburg	219	Xin Quan Zhou	67
UBC Limas	120	Vasos	107	Voge Renate	267	Westerdam	12	Xin Ri Zhao	67
UBC Livorno	120	Vecchio Bridge	132	Voge Trust	267	Westerdiek	219	Xin Shan Tou	67
UBC Longkou	120	Vecht Trader	54	Voge West	267	Westerems	219	Xin Shanghai	67
UBC Luzon	120	Veendam	12	Vogebulker	267	Westerhamm	219	Xin Su Zhou	67
UBC Odessa	120	Vega Leader	184	Vogecarrier	267	Westerland	219	Xin Tai Cang	67
UBC Ohio	120	Vega Rose	101	Vogerunner	267	Western Highway	132	Xin Tian Jin	67
UBC Olimbus	120	Vega Star	226	Vogesailor	267	Westertal	219	Xin Wei Hai	67
UBC Onsan	120	Vega Trader	162	Vogevoyager	267	Westfield	127	Xin Wu Han	67
UBC Oristano	120	Vega Voyager	64	Vola 1	177	Westgate	283	Xin Xia Men	67
UBC Ottawa	120	Vega	40	Volans Leader	184	Westwood Cascade	204	Xin Ya Zhou	67
UBC Salaverry	120	*Velikiy Novgorod*	245	Volendam	12	Westwood Discovery	204	Xin Yan Tai	67
UBC Santa Marta	120	Velopoula	94	Voula Seas	39	Westwood Pacific	204	Xin Yan Tian	67
UBC Stavanger	120	Venice Bridge	132	Voyager	231	White Diamond	280	Xin Yang Pu	67
UBC Tampico	120	Venice	61	Voyager of the Seas	23	White Sea	195	Xin Yang Shan	67
UBC Tokyo	120	Vento di Grecale	206	Voyager	8	Whitney Bay	239	Xin Yang Zhou	67
Ugale	136	Vento di Maestrale	54	Vulkan	46	Wicko	216	Xin Ying Kou	67
Ulf Ritscher	261	Ventura	13	Vully	254	Widar	261	Xin Zhan Jiang	67
Ulriken	102	Ventura	60	Wadowice II	216	Wieniawski	68	Xin Zhang Zhou	67
Ultra Paguera	119	Venus	29	Wafrah	135	Wilana	278	Xin Zheng Zhou	67
Ulysses	217	Venus Glory	253	Wafrah	175	Wild Cosmos	185	Xiu He	65
Umiak I	101	Venus Leader	184	Wan Hai 301	274	Wild Heather	185	Xpedition	22
Umm Al Aish	135	Venus R.	206	Wan Hai 302	274	Wild Lotus	186	X-Press Makalu	188
Umm Bab	37	Venus Spirit	186	Wan Hai 303	274	Wild Peony	186	Ya He	66
Umm Salal	264	Vera D.	90	Wan Hai 305	274	Wilhelm E.	188	Yacht Express	87
Umm Slal	242	Veracruz Express	118	Wan Hai 306	274	Wilhelm Schulte	235	Yakumosan	162
Unayzah	264	Vereina	231	Wan Hai 307	274	Willi Rickmers	224	Yamatogawa	132
Undine	270	Verila	177	Wan Hai 311	274	William Shakespeare	228	Yamuna Spirit	257
Uni Challenge	138	Verona	250	Wan Hai 312	274	William Strait	219	Yantian Express	118
Unique Developer	191	Verrazano Bridge	132	Wan Hai 313	274	Wilmina	278	Yellow Sea	195
Unique Explorer	139	Vesteralen	18	Wan Hai 315	274	Wilsky	278	Yeoman Bank	37
Unique Guardian	191	Vibeke	192	Wan Hai 316	274	Winchester Strait	219	Yeoman Bontrup	37
United Spirit	186	Vicente	197	Wan Hai 317	274	Wind Frost	239	Yeoman Bridge	37
Unity Pride	113	Victor Konetsky	245	Wan Hai 501	274	Wind Spirit	9	Yiannis B.	263
Universal Brave	61	Victoria	90	Wan Hai 502	274	Wind Star	9	YM America	285
Universal Crown	123	Victoria Bridge	132	Wan Hai 507	274	Wind Surf	9	YM Antwerp	285
Universal Hope	123	Victoria Trader	54	Wan Hai 510	274	Windsor Adventure	101	YM Bamboo	285
Universal Peace	123	Victorious Ace	161	Wan Hai 512	274	Windsor Knutsen	134	YM Busan	285
Universal Pioneer	161	Victorius	95	Wan Hai 513	274	Wisla	216	YM Cosmos	285
Universal Prime	61	Victory Leader	219	Wan Hai 515	274	Wisteria Ace	161	YM Cultivation	285